LIMNOLOGY

McGraw-Hill Publications in the Zoological Sciences

E. J. Boell, Consulting Editor

There are also the related series of McGraw-Hill Publications in the Botanical Sciences, of which Edmund W. Sinnott is Consulting Editor, and in the Agricultural Sciences, of which R. A. Brink is Consulting Editor.

LIMNOLOGY

Paul S. Welch, Ph.D.

Professor of Zoology, University of Michigan

SECOND EDITION

New York   Toronto   London

McGRAW-HILL BOOK COMPANY, INC.

1952

LIMNOLOGY

THE MAPLE PRESS COMPANY, YORK, PA.

PREFACE TO THE SECOND EDITION

Approximately one and a half decades have passed since the first edition of this book was published. During that period such a wealth of new material has appeared that a revision is now necessary. As usual in the preparation of revisions, space limitations must be observed. Little of the original matter has lost its value; therefore little could be eliminated without sacrifice of what appears to be essential to the purposes of this book. Under these conditions it seemed wise to retain the original structural pattern. Additions and revisions were necessary throughout the text and the bibliography has been rebuilt.

The writer acknowledges indebtedness to the many persons who from time to time made suggestions for the improvement of this volume.

PAUL S. WELCH

ANN ARBOR, MICH.
December, 1951

v

PREFACE TO THE FIRST EDITION

This book is an outgrowth of a course in general limnology given by the author at the University of Michigan during the past sixteen years. It has been a pioneering venture accompanied by all the difficulties characteristic of any attempt to compose a book of general scope in a new field. In the older and better developed fields of biology, writers of textbooks profit much from the efforts, judgments, and experiences of previous authors, but the author of this book has been compelled to steer his enterprise largely unaided through the voluminous and widely scattered research literature. So numerous are the gaps and incomplete data in present-day limnological knowledge that many serious difficulties in the choice, treatment, and integration of materials were unavoidable. Therefore the author cannot hope that his selection and treatment of materials will meet the unqualified approval of all limnologists. He does believe, however, that most of the important features of the subject, as it now exists, have been included; also that useful and reasonably well-grounded materials are presented.

In this book, the term "limnology" has been used in its broadest sense, i.e., to include all forms of inland waters, running or standing. More space is given to the standing-water series, but merely because lakes have received much more attention than have the running waters and more mature information is available.

The author has drawn freely from the contributions of the great host of investigators. Many authorities are mentioned specifically in the text, but it was obviously impracticable to cite the authority for all materials used. The bibliography will indicate many of the sources of information. Original data resulting from the researches of the author, his graduate students, and his associates have been woven into most sections of the book.

The desirability of an approach to the subject matter of limnology through introductory consideration of the principal physical and chemical factors operative in natural, unmodified waters has been demonstrated in the teaching experience of the author. Certain facts of physics and chemistry, particularly those pertinent to limnology, must be clearly in mind before the biological phenomena which involve them can be studied. These facts need to be reviewed and given a limnological bearing before the student is in a satisfactory position to undertake an examination of the biological superstructure which rests upon them. The

vii

early chapters of this volume have been written to comply with these needs.

This book is constructed on the general assumption that the reader has a background of training in physics, chemistry, botany, and zoology. It is intended, for the most part, to meet the needs of senior and graduate students.

Materials relating to limnological methods and practices have been omitted, since it was felt that they belong more properly in a book of directions for field and laboratory work. The author has such a field and laboratory guide in preparation.

The constant and rapid appearance of new research literature has continually necessitated revisions and alterations in the manuscript. It is a matter of much regret to the author that even if this treatise was up to date when it went to press it could not be so by the time it reached publication. A few outstanding works of very recent date have been taken into account by additions and revisions in the proofs.

The author wishes to express his indebtedness to the following persons, who have read the portions of the manuscript indicated, for their valuable suggestions and criticisms: to Professor Frank E. Eggleton, University of Michigan, Chaps. I to IV inclusive and Chap. XIII; to Professor Chauncey Juday, University of Wisconsin, Chaps. IV to VII inclusive, also a general examination of the whole manuscript; to Professors H. H. Bartlett and J. H. Ehlers, University of Michigan, Chap. XI; to Professor G. E. Nichols, Yale University, Chap. XVI; to Professor F. C. Gates, Kansas State College, Chap. XVI; to Professor Will Scott, University of Indiana, Chap. XVII; to Professor H. W. Emerson, University of Michigan, portion of Chap. X; to Dean E. B. Fred, University of Wisconsin, for suggestions relating to Chap. X; and to Dr. Marie Cimini Susskind for a general reading of certain portions of the manuscript.

For permission to reproduce illustrations acknowledgment is due to Dean R. N. Chapman, University of Hawaii, and to Professor J. G. Needham, Cornell University. Similar acknowledgment is also due to Charles C. Thomas, Publisher, Springfield, Ill.

For permission to quote or otherwise use copyrighted material acknowledgment is due to Professor H. S. Jennings, Johns Hopkins University; Professor Edwin C. Miller, Kansas State College; the late Dr. Einar Naumann, Lunds Universitets Limnologiska Institution, Sweden; and Professors V. E. Shelford and H. B. Ward, University of Illinois. Similar acknowledgment is also due to Edward Arnold & Company, Publishers, London; Cambridge University Press, Cambridge, England; the Chemical Rubber Company, Cleveland, Ohio; Urban & Schwarzenberg, Berlin, Germany; John Wiley & Sons, Inc., New York; and The Williams & Wilkins Company, Baltimore, Md.

For permission to use certain unpublished material, the author is indebted to Dr. W. C. Gorham, formerly of the University of Michigan, and Professor H. B. Baker, University of Pennsylvania.

The author is indebted to many of his colleagues, associates, and former graduate students who have given assistance in various ways during the building of the manuscript; also to Eva Grace Welch for general criticism of the manuscript and for assistance in the construction of the index.

Paul S. Welch

Ann Arbor, Mich.
April, 1935

CONTENTS

PART I
PRELIMINARY CONSIDERATIONS

CHAPTER I

INTRODUCTION

A satisfactory understanding of aquatic life requires a knowledge not only of the organisms themselves but also of those external influences which directly or indirectly affect them. A suitable environment is necessary for any organism, since life depends upon the continuance of a proper exchange of essential substances and energies between the organism and its surroundings. That subdivision of biology which has as its special province the study of interrelations between organisms and their environments is commonly known as *ecology*. Certain other terms, e.g., *natural history, hexiology, biology, bionomics,* and *ethology*, have occasionally been used as names for the same or a roughly similar field. In fact, there is evidence that the term ethology antedates the term ecology, but the latter has almost universal adoption and will doubtless continue to be the accepted designation.

The definition of ecology is expressed in various ways, but one feature is common to all, viz., that the *interrelations existing between organisms and their environments* are the principal concern of the subject. Shelford (1929) proposed that ecology should be defined as *the science of communities*. The effect of such a revision is to appear to exclude from the province of ecology certain biological relations heretofore included, such as those of a single species to its environment (*autecology; individual ecology*). Whether or not this conception becomes the accepted one the future alone will determine. Owing to the great difficulty of making any study of a single organism in relation to its native habitat without involving the organic community of which it is a part, there seem to be grounds for retaining the older definition, at least for the present.

The term *environment* implies space on, below, or above the surface of the earth. The earth is divisible into (1) the *lithosphere*, which comprises the land masses; and (2) the *hydrosphere*, which includes the oceans, lakes, streams, and subterranean waters. Upon the hydrosphere is based the science known as *hydrography*. Hydrography may be subdivided into *oceanography*, which is concerned with the great masses of salt water; and *limnology*, which includes, in its broader usage, the various bodies and systems of inland waters (usually fresh water). While there are several important differences between the fresh and marine waters other than mere extent of surface and mass, oceanography and limnology have

3

many things in common, and advances in either field often figure prominently in the progress of the other.

OCEANOGRAPHY

As an organized, integrated body of knowledge, oceanography is a distinctly modern subject. Its beginnings, traceable into the very remote past, arose as additions to knowledge gained incidentally in connection with various voyages, expeditions, and miscellaneous observations by ancient seagoers. Even after men began to study the seas for their own sake, there was a long period of time during which the activities were little more than occasional and often random explorations actuated by a desire to learn something about the nature of the great, mysterious expanse of unknown waters; rarely were they strictly scientific in character. In the meantime, the various sciences—chemistry, physics, geology, and biology—were passing through a period of great development, ultimately advancing to the place where their methods and results could be effectively used in unfolding complex phenomena of nature. Because of its character, oceanography could not progress very far until other sciences had provided means of investigating the multitude of intricate ocean phenomena. The advent of modern scientific methods and their application to problems of the sea put oceanography on a new and scientific basis. The whole story has been summarized in the following quotation:[1]

Thus, in this brief story of the growth of knowledge of the oceans, we have first the ancient explorers and writers up to the time of Ptolemy (about 150 A.D.), then the great age of geographical discovery at the end of the fifteenth and beginning of the sixteenth century, and finally the modern expeditions beginning with Cook's voyages of 150 years ago and extending up to the present time. . . . Cook and his immediate successors bring us to about the end of the eighteenth century, and we may conveniently group the advances in knowledge of the science of the sea during the nineteenth century in three periods—the period of Edward Forbes, the great Manx naturalist; the period of Wyville Thomson, ending with its climax, the *Challenger* expedition; and the post-*Challenger* period of Sir John Murray and modern oceanography, which brings us practically to the methods and knowledge of today.

LIMNOLOGY

HISTORY

Limnology, as a distinct field of science, has existed less than 60 years. Beginnings of knowledge concerning fresh-water life, like those of marine life, arose in the remote past, possibly before the days of Aristotle (384–

---

[1] From HERDMAN, "Founders of Oceanography and Their Work," Edward Arnold and Co., 1923.

322 B.C.). These early beginnings, often strange mixtures of fact and fancy, have little or no scientific value. As time went on and man's knowledge of his surroundings slowly increased, certain conspicuous fresh-water phenomena were observed and recorded in simple fashion, often with increasing accuracy. The whole story is really that of the rise of biological science in the substance of which the roots of future subdivisions of biology were present but undifferentiated. However, aside from the historical interest involved, no significant contributions of a strictly limnological nature were made for at least nineteen hundred years after the time of Aristotle, although, as pointed out by some writers, certain facts relating to the habits of fishes, emergences of aquatic insects, aquatic plants, and other similar, easily observable phenomena had been described. Additions to knowledge were, however, in the nature of more or less isolated accumulations of unrelated observations, few of which the modern limnologist can utilize in other than historical ways.

Invention of the Microscope. The profound influence of the invention of the microscope on the rise of biology in general is well known. This event was one of the most, if not the most, significant development in the early history of man's knowledge of aquatic life, since it not only opened the door to the whole world of microscopic organisms but also provided a new and effective means of studying the various higher types of life in water. The early story of the microscope is an incomplete one. The identity of the first maker of lenses, the inventor of the first compound microscope—these and other related matters are obscure. It is said that the science of optics began with the writings of Euclid (about 300 B.C.). Ultimately, the relation of light rays to mirrors crept into this science, and, in time, the magnifying quality of a simple lens was discovered. The first magnifying devices were exceedingly crude and ineffective, but they gradually underwent an improvement which was accompanied by increasing interest in the world of minute things. Familiarity with lenses led to the invention of the compound microscope during the last years of the sixteenth century. The stimulating effect of this invention can scarcely be overestimated. Anton van Leeuwenhoek (1632–1723) described for the first time minute organisms in water. The first classification of microscopic organisms of consequence was by a Danish biologist, Otto Friedrich Müller, in 1786, in his great pioneering work "Animalcula Infusoria Fluviatilia et Marina." Then, in 1838, Ehrenberg published his famous treatise on "The Infusion Animalcules as Complete Organisms," a volume which marks the beginning of those great advances in knowledge which occurred during the following century. Further details of this early history must be omitted here.

Influence of Marine Zoology. In the meantime, zoologists had become attracted by the richness and diversity of the marine fauna, and while there was a growing investigation of fresh waters, such work was greatly overshadowed by the progress in marine zoology during most of the nineteenth century.   However, this was not without gain to fresh-water biology, since the development of methods of study and an increase in biological knowledge in general aided indirectly but materially the later advances of limnology.   Oceanography likewise began to take on more definite form, and its gain also contributed indirectly to the progress of limnology at a later time, since marine and fresh-water biotas have many features in common.

Discovery of Plankton.   After the advent of the microscope, the next great stimulus to aquatic investigation was the discovery of *plankton*. While the knowledge that microscopic organisms live in water extends back at least to Leeuwenhoek, that vast, heterogeneous group of sus-pended, drifting, microscopic organisms which inhabits both fresh and salt waters was not found until much later.   It does not seem to be clear who should be credited with the discovery of plankton.   Needham and Lloyd (1930) attribute it to Liljeborg and Sars, who found it

. . . by drawing fine nets through the waters of the Baltic.   They found a whole fauna and flora, mostly microscopic—a well-adjusted society of organisms, with its producing class of synthetic plant forms and its consuming class of animals; and among the animals, all the usual social groups, herbivores and carnivores, parasites and scavengers.

About 1845, Johannes Müller and several of his pupils began the study of plankton in the North Sea near Helgoland, using a very fine net so effectively that such nets came rapidly into use.   Later, another worker, Peter Erasmus Müller, discovered micro-Crustacea in the waters of certain Swiss lakes, thereby dispelling the previously held idea that clear lakes were devoid of microscopic life.   It was not until later, however, that a definite name was given to this mass of drifting microscopic life. In 1887, Hensen proposed the term *plankton* to include all the minute animals, plants, and debris which are suspended in natural waters.   Sub-sequently, Haeckel used it in a broader sense, including as plankton pelagic life of all kinds, large or small.   However, Hensen's use of the term has become practically universal.   As a result of the discovery of plankton, the last part of the nineteenth and the first decade of the twentieth century became a very active period in its study.

Development of Limnology.   While Peter Erasmus Müller is some-times credited with laying the foundation of limnological research by his plankton discoveries in fresh water, and while it appears that Anton Fritsch began lacustrine investigations in the Bohemian Forest as early as 1871, it remained for F. A. Forel (1841–1912), a professor in the University of Lausanne, Switzerland, to recognize the real biological opportunity in lake investigations and, by his work, to become the founder of modern limnology. Since his contributions occupy such a significant place in the history of limnology, some of the principal ones will be mentioned. In 1869 appeared his "Instruction à l'étude de la fauna profonde du Lac Léman"; in 1874–1879, "Matériaux pour servir à l'étude de la fauna profonde du Léman"; in 1892–1904, he published his monumental and epoch-making work "Le Léman. Monographie limnologique," in three volumes, which was not only the first comprehensive limnological treatise but which also opened up a whole new field of biological research. In 1885 appeared his "La fauna profonde des lacs Suisses" for which he was awarded a prize. Then, in 1901, he published the "Handbuch der Seenkunde. Allgemeine Limnologie," a book of 249 pages which is the first general presentation of limnology from the modern standpoint. In fact, it might well be termed the first textbook of limnology. In brief, limnology is indebted to Forel for the first knowledge concerning the profundal fauna of fresh-water lakes, for the first program for *limnological* investigations of such waters, and for the execution of such a program, resulting in "Le Léman" which was long a model for subsequent work. His "Programm für limnologische Untersuchungen" appears in summarized form in the appendix of the "Handbuch" and indicates how comprehensive was his vision of limnology and how complete was his anticipation of the future of this subject. His contributions were numerous. Chumley (1910) listed 116 limnological papers published by Forel during the period 1868–1909.

It has been contended that F. Simony should be regarded as the founder of limnology because he was said to be the first to discover (about 1850) thermal stratification. Important as that discovery was, it is far from being of the same magnitude as the accomplishments of Forel.

Among other things, Forel's work led to the formation, in 1887, as a part of the Swiss Natural History Society, of a Limnological Commission in Switzerland which promoted limnological work in a substantial way. Later (1890), an International Commission was established. The impetus to fresh-water investigation began to be felt in both Europe and and America, quickly manifesting itself in the establishment of fresh-water biological stations. Only brief mention of the principal centers of this movement will be made.

In 1888, Professor Anton Fritsch established in the Bohemian Forest the first fresh-water biological station, a portable laboratory which was moved about to different lakes. Another pioneer station which had a productive history down to the present time was founded in 1891 at Plön, Germany, by O. Zacharias. Then followed soon thereafter the establishment of fresh-water stations in Germany, France, Norway, Sweden, Switzerland, Denmark, Austria, Italy, Scotland, Russia, Finland,

Belgium, and the United States. From these early fresh-water stations and from workers not directly associated with stations came a rapidly increasing number of contributions. For a period of time, much of the work clung to the traditional approaches to fresh-water biology rather than to the avenues opened by Forel; nevertheless, it yielded a mass of information which later added materially to the early groundwork of modern limnology. Adequate discussion of the growth of the subject during the period of about 1890–1910 requires more space than is available here. However, special attention should be called to the following investigations which had their inception during this period: (1) the work of Zschokke and his associates on the alpine lakes of Switzerland; (2) the work of Sir John Murray and his associates which resulted in the publication of the extensive six-volume "Bathymetrical Survey of the Scottish Fresh-water Lochs"; (3) the Plankton Expedition of Victor Hensen to the North Atlantic Ocean in connection with which certain improved plankton methods were used; (4) the work of Apstein on the plankton of the Holstein lakes; (5) the investigations of Wesenberg-Lund and his students on Danish lakes; (6) the investigations of Woltereck and his students, first at the Biological Station at Lunz, Austria, and later in connection with the University of Leipzig; (7) the researches of Reighard and Ward and their coworkers on certain portions of the Great Lakes in North America; and (8) the work of Birge and Juday and coworkers on the inland lakes of Wisconsin.

Progress in the limnological field since about 1910, particularly since 1918, has been rapid and far-reaching; also, during that period, limnology became more completely an integrated, coherent branch of science.

Early Fresh-water Investigations in America. Previous to about 1870, the innumerable American lakes, including the Great Lakes, were little known biologically save for a few general facts and such fragmentary information as resulted from fishing activities, observations of explorers, and the more or less random collections which found their way into the hands of biologists whose interests were, for the most part, taxonomic.

Scattered, pioneer accounts of the biology of the Great Lakes appeared from time to time during the first three-fourths of the nineteenth century, and they, together with less important, primitive records made during the previous century, constitute the remote beginnings of our knowledge. As might be expected, the more substantial of these early efforts were concerned with the fishes. The volume by Louis Agassiz (1850) on "Lake Superior: Its Physical Character, Vegetation, and Animals" contains, among other things, 131 pages dealing with the fishes of that lake. In 1870, Stimson published a short account of the deep-water fauna of Lake Michigan. Smith and Verrill (1871) made deep-water dredgings in Lake Superior and published on the invertebrates collected. Milner

(1874) published an extensive account of the fisheries of the Great Lakes. Nothing more of consequence was attempted until about 1894. In 1886, the Allis Lake Laboratory, a privately supported institution and said to be the first fresh-water biological station in America, was established at Milwaukee, Wisconsin, but its life was brief, and none of its work was concerned with the general biology of the Great Lakes.

In the meantime, interested workers were giving attention to some of the smaller inland lakes. Forbes made a study of certain high lakes of the Rocky Mountains, results of which were published in 1893 and which for a long time constituted the only biological information concerning lakes in western United States. During the decade of 1890–1900, four fresh-water biological stations were founded, viz., by the University of Minnesota at Gull Lake, Minnesota, 1893; by the University of Illinois on the Illinois River, 1894; by the University of Indiana at Turkey Lake, Indiana, 1895; and by the University of Montana on Flathead Lake, Montana, 1899. Early work was also done by Birge and Marsh on Wisconsin lakes, by Whipple in the New England states, by Reighard in Michigan, and by others. In 1893, work was again undertaken on the Great Lakes by a party, maintained by the Michigan Fish Commission, of about one-half dozen men under the direction of Prof. J. E. Reighard. Lake St. Clair was the seat of the work, and a series of reports resulted. The work of the following year was conducted by a similar party directed by Prof. H. B. Ward on Lake Michigan in the region of Charlevoix, Michigan, and a second series of reports was published. Unfortunately, this program, so well begun, was interrupted, and work of a strictly limnological sort on the Great Lakes vanished until 1928 when a cooperative survey of Lake Erie was undertaken under the joint auspices of the U.S. Bureau of Fisheries, the New York State Conservation Department, the Ontario Department of Game and Fisheries, the Health Department of the City of Buffalo, the Buffalo Society of Natural Sciences, and the Ohio Department of Game and Fisheries. Two reports (Fish, 1929) have appeared.

The stimuli of scientific interest and of the necessities of public health brought about the initiation of systematic surveys of water supplies and of water systems in general, the Massachusetts State Board of Health taking the lead in about 1887. Subsequently, similar work was undertaken by various municipal and government departments, all of which contributed, directly and indirectly, to the sum total of limnological information.

The last five decades have witnessed a striking growth of limnological accomplishment in America. The researches of Kofoid on the Illinois River, of Birge and Juday on Wisconsin lakes, of Needham on New York lakes, and of many other investigators who worked during this formative period did much to lay a foundation for American limnology. Phenomenal progress of the general subject of ecology inevitably had a constructive influence on limnology; and, because of its many ramifications, limnology has likewise profited from simultaneous advances of other sciences.

DEFINITION OF LIMNOLOGY

Limnology is now commonly defined as *that branch of science which deals with biological productivity of inland waters and with all the causal influences which determine it.*

Biological productivity, as used in this definition, includes its qualitative and quantitative features and its actual and potential aspects. Under the term *inland waters* are included all kinds or types of water—running or standing; fresh, salt, or other physicochemical composition—which are wholly or almost completely included within the land masses. *Causal influences* involve those various factors—physical, chemical, biological, meteorological, *et al.*—which determine the character and quantity of biological production.

Limnology is essentially a synthetic science composed of elements some of which extend beyond the limits of biology as ordinarily conceived. It is primarily ecological in its bearing. It depends upon the proper application and integration of certain facts, principles, and methods of chemistry, physics, geology, hydrography, meteorology, and others, to the solution of problems which are, in the end, biological in nature. Biological productivity is the central, unifying feature which ties the whole subject into a coherent, orderly, organized field. Necessary stress on the different plant and animal communities is not precluded since they are the direct result of the biological productivity of waters which they occupy. Inland waters differ to a striking degree in the quality and quantity of life which they contain. To understand the natural circumstances responsible for this tremendous difference in such waters and to identify and evaluate the influences which govern a particular form of productivity are the aim and province of modern limnology.

Older Terms and Usages. Historically, the term *limnology* was used as the name for that branch of science which dealt exclusively with *lakes* and the companion term *rheology* was employed for the running-water series. The term rheology should be eliminated from limnological terminology since it is now an established name for an entirely different field, viz., the study of flow or deformity of plastic and very viscous substances such as oils, paints, lacquers and similar materials.

In the past, certain terms were used loosely as more or less equivalent to the term limnology, viz., hydrobiology, fresh-water biology, aquatic biology, aquatic ecology, and limnobiology. Most of them were names under which a wide variety of subject matter was included, only part of which may have been limnological in nature. Such terms, if they are to be retained at all, should be used exclusively for such aquatic floristic-faunistic studies as seem desirable under special circumstances.

Formerly, the term *limnography* had a limited use, sometimes apparently as an equivalent for limnology. It has practically vanished from limnological literature.

CHAPTER II

INLAND WATERS

Extent of Inland Waters. When compared with the total expanse of oceans and seas, the inland waters of the globe seem insignificant. However, such a comparison is misleading when stated in that way because of the magnitude of marine waters, occupying as they do roughly three-fourths of the earth's surface. A more satisfactory appreciation of the expanse of inland waters results from a comparison with the area of land surfaces which surround them. Unfortunately, such a comparison is very difficult to make, owing to the absence of sufficient information as to the areas occupied by inland waters. Definite information on number and areas of the North American lakes is lacking for so many regions of the continent that only a very rough estimate is possible. It appears that the number of lakes in North America must be not less than 40,000 and the combined area must exceed 225,000 sq. miles. This area is approximately 0.02 of the area of the whole continent. For example, the lakes of Michigan, of which there are about 11,000 (ponds included), have an area of 1,137 sq. miles (Brown, 1943), roughly 0.02 of the area of the state, while the vast array of lakes in Minnesota is said to exceed 5,000 sq. miles in total area. In addition, there are the numerous units of the running-water series (brooks, creeks, rivers) whose combined area of exposed water is of no small magnitude but on which dependable data are lacking at the present time. Certain it is that on all continents, particularly North America and Europe, the combined area of the various waters, running and standing, comprises a larger portion of the total area than is usually appreciated.

The amount of water beneath the surface of the land is very great, although the actual quantity is not known. It has been stated that, if the entire amount of underground water were accumulated at the surface of the land, it would form a layer whose depth has been variously estimated at 29 to 914 m. Unfortunately, these estimates differ so widely that they are of slight value. Some underground waters, especially subterranean streams and basins, are normal environments for certain aquatic organisms and must be taken into account in considering the various aquatic habitats of the earth. A general work dealing with underground waters from the limnological standpoint is that of Chappius (1927).

Distribution of Inland Waters. With certain minor exceptions, all land areas have at least a small amount of inland water. Some regions are very generously supplied with lakes and streams, particularly those regions once subjected to ancient glaciation. Canada and northern United States possess an immense supply of lakes, among them the Great Lakes, which constitute the greatest body of fresh water on the globe. Portions of Europe are also noted for their generous supply of lakes and streams. In certain regions, disappearance of inland waters during the dry season forms the basis for special biological phenomena resulting from the intermittent character of the environments.

Lotic Environments (Running-water Series). Under the designation of *lotic environments*, or an older equivalent expression the *running-water series*, are included all forms of inland waters in which the entire body of water moves continuously in a definite direction. Stated genetically, it is the *brook → creek → river* series. Expressed in this way, the sequence of changes is indicated through which, in the past, a river grew out of a mere rivulet on the primitive, undissected land surface by continued erosion.

Lentic Environments (Standing-water Series). The *lentic environments* (*lenitic* or *static* of some authors), sometimes known as the *standing-water series*, include all forms of inland water (lakes, ponds, swamps, and their various intergrades) in which the water motion is not that of a continuous flow in a definite direction. Essentially, the water is standing, although a certain amount of water movement may occur such as wave action, internal currents, or flowage in the vicinity of inlets and outlets. The genetic sequence of these units is as expressed above, viz., *lake → pond → swamp*.

Dynamics of Lotic and Lentic Environments. Certain progressive, predictable changes occur in all units of both the lotic and the lentic series. These are the changes which are inevitable, although the time required may vary greatly in different units of the same series. In the lotic series, the tiny rivulet gradually deepens, widens its bed, and cuts back at its head, thus in time extending its length and increasing its cross section to that size which justifies the designation of brook. This process continues by the same general type of action, ultimately producing a creek and then finally a river, with all of the intergrading conditions produced in such a gradual transformation. However, at the far reaches of the river thus produced are its earlier evolutionary stages—creeks, brooks, and rivulets—in the evolutionary sequence but in a continually changing position, moving upstream until halted by some circumstance, such as the arrival at, or the cutting through, a drainage divide. A *migration of environments* is the direct result of this evolution. Headwater conditions migrate farther and farther inland, followed in succession by environments characteristic of brooks, creeks, and rivers. Faunas occupying each of the different environments must (1) accompany these migrations or (2) become adapted to the gradually altering conditions, or (3) they will become extinct.   Ordinarily, these environmental migrations are very slow, in point of time, and give ample opportunity for the characteristic organisms of particular environments to make the necessary responses.   The ultimate fate of any lotic series, whose constant work is the degradation of the land, is the reduction of its bed to base level.

In the lentic series, natural processes work toward extinction, mainly by the gradual filling of basins.   The order of change is indicated in a series already mentioned, viz., lake → pond → swamp.   In some instances, particularly in small, shallow lakes, a human life span is more than ample for witnessing the passage of a lake through the pond stage into swamp conditions and finally into relatively dry land.   In the larger lakes, the time required is correspondingly greater, and it will be many centuries before some of them pass from one stage to the next one.   Lakes of the magnitude of the Great Lakes are as subject to these natural filling processes as are the diminutive ones, but, for obvious reasons, the actual filling is so slow that great periods of time must elapse before it becomes very apparent.   Filling is due primarily to:

1. Wind-blown materials, such as dust, sand, and debris of various sorts.   In any region, the total amount of such materials transported by wind is very much greater than is ordinarily realized.

2. Sediments brought into a lake by inflowing streams and by incoming, run-off water as it flows down adjacent land slopes.

3. Wave action, cutting away exposed shores and depositing eroded materials in a lake basin.

4. Plants, particularly the higher aquatic plants which grow in shallow water, produce deposits of organic matter.   Marl producers assist in this process, also those plants which secrete silica and other insoluble substances.

5. Accumulating remains of animal life, especially shells.

Not all lakes become extinct by filling alone.   Other processes may contribute to this end.   For example, an outlet may cut down its level at the point of exit from a basin, thus gradually draining the lake.

These stages in the extinction of standing water result in a more or less definite, predictable *evolution of environments* which, in the long run, has a profound influence on the history and fate of lake organisms.   Populations, characteristic of lake environments, must in time be succeeded by populations characteristic of ponds and finally by swamp populations. Since the normal length of life of lake organisms is relatively short, varying from an hour or less to just a few years, a single generation may not be affected by this large, underlying environmental evolution; nevertheless, the future of the race to which any organism belongs is almost certainly determined by this inevitable change in surroundings.

CHAPTER III

LAKES, THEIR ORIGIN AND DIVERSITY

DEFINITION

The terms *lake*, *pond*, and *swamp* are in very common use, and in limnology they serve a useful function not only in describing an evolutionary sequence but also in expressing existing sets of conditions in standing water which differ in certain characteristic ways from each other. Distinctions between a lake and a pond are not only arbitrary but also very diverse. Area, depth, or both area and depth, usually appear as the essential part of attempted definitions, but what area and what depth distinguish a lake from a pond are matters of difference of opinion. Ponds are occasionally dignified by the term lake, and sometimes larger waters, qualifying by some criteria as lakes, are called ponds. Likewise, widened parts of rivers are commonly called lakes, even though some of these expansions may be quite long and narrow and with water flowage which departs from the usual conception of a lake. Unfortunately, the term is sometimes applied to bodies of water along seacoasts which lie at sea level and have direct connections with the sea. Since nature provides almost every conceivable intergrade from one kind of standing water to another and since there is no possibility of a distinction which is not, to some degree, arbitrary, it is highly desirable that in any discussion involving the term lake the meaning be made as clear as possible.

Forel (1892) defined a lake as a body of standing water occupying a basin and lacking continuity with the sea. By this definition, he eliminated those so-called lakes which are merely semi-isolated, small arms of the sea. He also defined a pond as a lake of slight depth, and a swamp was defined as a pond of such small depth that it is occupied by rooted vegetation whose stalks extend into the air. Thus, Forel's definition, in the last analysis, includes all units of the whole standing-water series under the term lake. Muttkowski (1918) formulated a set of criteria which would make a lake include only those bodies of standing water which are of considerable expanse and which are deep enough to *stratify thermally*, thus eliminating all ponds, large and small, and all bodies of water sometimes classed as lakes of the *third order* (page 63). Carpenter (1928) holds that the true difference between a lake and a pond is one of *depth* and not area. According to this conception, a pond should be

15

defined as a quiet body of water in which the littoral zone of floating-leaved vegetation extends to the middle of the basin and in which the biota is very similar to that of the littoral zone of lakes.   Thienemann (1926) and Lenz (1928) apparently accept Forel's definition.

A lake is sometimes defined as a body of standing water completely isolated from the sea and having an area of open, relatively deep water sufficiently large to produce somewhere on its periphery a *barren, wave-swept shore*.   In such a definition, expanse of open water exposed to the action of prevailing winds is of greater significance than depth of water. Protected waters must have a larger area of open water in order to provide any barren, wave-swept shore than is necessary in the exposed ones. The test indicated in this definition usually presents no difficulty on waters having sandy or earthy shore margins where the wave-swept, barren shore, whether it be but a few feet or several miles in extent, is easily recognized.   This definition may be difficult to apply where the shores and bottom of basins are wholly rock and very steep, and where even the protected shore has not developed the characteristic evidences of protection, such as floating and emergent vegetation and muck deposits on the bottom.   Barren, wave-swept shore or shoal is distinguished by (1) complete absence of attached, aquatic plants; (2) absence of accumulations of finely divided organic matter on the bottom; (3) absence of air-breathing invertebrates; and (4) presence of only those invertebrates which maintain their position by some form of burrowing.   Marl lakes, because of the usual paucity of rooted plants on all shores, protected or exposed, and because of the barren, marly bottom on all sides of the basin, also require very close scrutiny in order to determine the true wave-swept shore mentioned in the definition.   In such lakes, other evidences, e.g., marl drifts, indicate a wave-swept shore in the sense in which it is used here.   Large bog waters, completely surrounded by overgrowing margins, are also difficult to classify on this basis, since the partly floating mat is of such a nature as to conceal any effects of wave action.   This definition of a lake is not ideal from another standpoint.   Basins with unusual protection on all sides or basins in a region of reduced wind action would need to be of large expanse in order for any wave-swept shore to be developed—an expanse so great that to designate them as ponds would be absurd.   After all, size must enter into the distinction.   For limnological purposes, it is possible that Forel's definitions are about as satisfactory as any now proposed.   None seems to be wholly ideal.

In this book, the author chooses to employ the term pond for that class of very small, very shallow bodies of standing water in which quiet water and extensive occupancy by higher aquatic plants are common characteristics.   All larger bodies of standing water will be referred to as lakes.

ORIGIN OF LAKES

Lake basins originate in many different ways, the principal ones being as follows:

1. Glacial action. Regions once covered by ancient glaciers are often rich in inland lakes, as, for example, northern United States and much of Canada. Glaciers form lakes (*a*) by digging out basins; (*b*) by the deposition of moraines and debris so as to form a closed basin; (*c*) by actual ice obstruction of the lower end of a mountain valley, forming an ice-barrier basin above the glacier; and (*d*) by the melting of huge masses of ice embedded in the glacial debris.

2. Landslides which obstruct valleys.

3. Solution of underlying rock with subsequent sinking of surface, as, for example, limestone sinks.

4. Crustal movements of the earth, such as upwarping which forms a dam or downwarping which forms a basin.

5. Craters of extinct volcanoes.

6. Various activities of rivers, such as change of channel producing oxbow lakes, obstruction at mouths of tributaries forming lakes just above them, and drift jams which obstruct streams.

SIZE OF LAKES

Lakes differ in area from those barely larger than a pond to those of great size. Lake Superior, the largest body of *fresh* water on the globe, has an area of more than 31,000 sq. miles. The Caspian Sea, with an area of about 170,000 sq. miles, is sometimes considered as having the qualifications of a lake. If so regarded, it would occupy first place in size among lakes. This, however, does not invalidate the statement for Lake Superior, since the waters of the Caspian Sea are saline. It is stated that Lake Chad, Africa, has an area of about 40,000 sq. miles in the wet season but is reduced to about 6,000 sq. miles in the dry season. Each of the continents possesses a few very large lakes. Ten of the large lakes of North America, including the Great Lakes, have a combined area of approximately 127,000 sq. miles. However, the number of lakes whose area exceeds 5,000 sq. miles is utterly insignificant compared with the many thousands of lakes of lesser magnitude. Of the 11,000 or more lakes and ponds in Michigan, the largest (Houghton Lake) has an area of slightly more than 30 sq. miles. In Wisconsin, where the number of lakes is said to be several thousand, the largest (Lake Winnebago) has an area of 215 sq. miles.

DEPTH OF LAKES

Lakes also differ widely in depth. While the greatest lake depths never approach those of the oceans, it is a striking fact that a remarkable

lake in southern Siberia, Lake Baikal, has a maximum depth of about
1,706 m. (5,600 ft.). In North America, Crater Lake in Oregon is
about 608 m. (1,996 ft.) deep; Lake Tahoe, about 487 m. (1,600 ft.);
Lake Chelan, Washington, 457 m. (1,500 ft.); Seneca Lake, New York,
188 m. (618 ft.); Lake Superior, about 393 m. (1,290 ft.); Lake Michigan,
281 m. (924 ft.); Lake Huron, 228 m. (750 ft.); Lake Ontario, 237 m.
(780 ft.); and Lake Erie, 64 m. (210 ft.). Such depths are, however,
relatively rare, since most lakes have a maximum depth of less than 30 m.
"Bottomless" lakes of local fame are pure fiction; many of them have
been found to have bottoms at depths of only 10 to 20 m.

ELEVATION OF LAKES

Even in elevation, lakes present a striking diversity. While, as a rule,
the elevation of the surface is above sea level, exceptions are known in
which the lake surface is far below it. Lakes which conform to the rule
vary from those with slight altitude to high mountain lakes some of which
exceed 3,600 m. (11,810 ft.) elevation.

The elevation of bottoms of lake basins is, also, as a rule, above sea
level, although exceptions occur; for example, Lake Erie has a bottom
which is *above* sea level, while in the other four Great Lakes the bottoms
are *below* to the following extents: Lake Superior, about 210 m. (688 ft.);
Lake Ontario, about 163 m. (535 ft.); Lake Michigan, about 98 m. (324
ft.); and Lake Huron, about 52 m. (170 ft.). This means that if all outlets of the Great Lakes were eroded down to sea level, all other things
remaining the same, Lake Erie would be dry land, but the other four lakes
could still have maximum depths equal to the values mentioned above.

Surface elevations of virtually all lakes are subject to variations from
season to season and from year to year. These seasonal variations are
often detectable by the increasing amount of exposed beach during the
summer or during the dry season, although care should be taken not to
mistake increasing extent of beach due to the *beach building* of wave
action on an exposed sandy shore for drop in level of water surface.
High-water years and low-water years—periods during which the general
water level in lakes of a whole region is either higher or lower than the
ordinary average condition—are well known. These are matters of
some limnological importance, since they involve extensions or reductions
of the shallow-water zones. An increase in the extent of shallow water
is likely to increase the productivity; a low-water condition, however,
may have the opposite effect. Unusual fall in water level sometimes
exposes shoal areas, thus eliminating the principal rooted vegetation
zones and temporarily robbing the lake of its most productive region.
This is particularly true of a lake whose basin is of such a form that the

shallow shoals are terminated at their lakeward margins by an abrupt declivity leading precipitously into deep water.

Considerable change in surface level, annual or periodic, may have various other limnological effects, such as the increase or decrease of (1) outflow of water at outlets, (2) erosion and transportation of shore materials due to wave action, (3) formation of beach pools, (4) water supply of already existing beach pools, (5) contact of water with earthy deposits on shores, (6) inflow of waters from contributing streams and lakes, and (7) available space for shallow-water bottom organisms.

LAKE MARGINS

NATURE OF MARGINS

The line of demarcation between land and water is definite or indefinite depending upon a number of natural circumstances. Lake basins with steep incline of bottom at the shore regions have margins which are less subject to changes than are those whose slope of shoal bottom is so slight that even the smaller alterations in water level either expose or inundate peripheral areas of considerable extent. Hence, the margins may or may not be so definite as maps indicate. In lakes with bordering, low-lying swamp, bog, or marsh areas, the margin not only shifts with changes of lake elevation but it is also more or less intangible at any particular time. Not infrequently, a lake basin is of such a form that one part of its margin is steep and definite while another part has extensive tracts virtually at water level. Amount of marginal slope, after all, determines the degree of definiteness of a lake margin.

HIGH-WATER AND LOW-WATER MARKS

High-water marks can usually be identified by ridges of debris and of certain kinds of bottom materials; also by erosion marks on headlands and elsewhere. Other evidences of high-water effects may be available which are purely matters of local circumstances and need not be catalogued here. Low-water marks are often less easily recognized but may sometimes be inferred from the positions of the more permanent animal and plant zones of shallow waters. The nature of a margin has much to do with determining how clearly high- and low-water marks may be indicated.

SHORE DYNAMICS

Natural waters are notoriously restless. Except at times of complete calm, which may be rare during whole seasons, water is in some form of motion, varying from relatively gentle to violent. Having a density about 775 times that of air and at the same time being the most labile of all liquids, it has a great potential ability to produce changes on the shore against which it beats. In the inland lakes, wave action is the principal form of water movement that produces shore changes.

In many lakes, particularly those of glacial origin, the shore line of today is much more regular and simplified than it was in the initial stages of existence. When the basins were first formed, the shore line manifested all of the irregularities which the geological, formative agents gave it. Not infrequently, these were in the form of sharp peninsulas, deep angular bays, and sinuosities of various kinds, all of which offered resistance to the free sweep of surface water moving under the influence of wind. Since water has a remarkable ability to erode and to transport, obviously the most prominent of these early irregularities were the first to feel the modifying influence of the water.

Modification of the original shore line has been accomplished by two main processes: (1) shore cutting and (2) shore building. Although these two processes are distinct, they may go on simultaneously but in different places.

Shore Cutting. On a shore which faces directly into waves, i.e., the crest of the oncoming wave is more or less parallel to the shore line, the final plunge of a wave lashes against the opposing land, loosening a certain amount of it. The amount of material loosened depends entirely upon its nature and resistance. If the shore is composed of glacial drift or of some other relatively soft materials, it will yield to the continual bombardment of waves. As water from a spent wave retreats down the slope of the beach, it carries and rolls a certain amount of loosened material into the lake whence it may be transported to other locations by gravity, by undertows, or by alongshore currents. Fine silt, remaining in suspension for a considerable time, becomes scattered widely, ultimately settling to the bottom. The remaining materials, if they are of a heterogeneous composition, such as unsorted glacial deposit, will undergo a sorting process, the heaviest boulders remaining nearer the original location and the next smaller sizes being dropped in order, so that ultimately a cross section of the shore and bottom of such a region would show the following succession of sorted materials, beginning at the shore and extending out into the water: boulders, cobblestones, coarse gravel, fine gravel, and sand. On high, abrupt shores which face the water, undercutting takes place, leading to the occasional fall of overhanging masses into the water. These masses also undergo dissolution and sorting by the water.

If a promontory is so situated that the waves produced by prevailing winds run past it, i.e., the waves run across its free end, the ends of the waves cut hard against the projecting point, constantly eroding and carrying away its materials, thus shortening and rounding off the penin-

sula. In this fashion, peninsulas may be completely worn away, an'
an irregular shore line made more and more regular.

In regions of rock outcrop, some shores are so resistant that cutting
takes place very slowly. However, erosion is facilitated by rock fragments picked up by the waves and hurled against the shore.

Shore Building. *Shore building* results from several processes all of
which produce additions to the original lake margins. A very common
example is the familiar beach ridge which occurs along the outer margins
of certain beaches as a result of wave action. Also, on exposed, sandy
beaches, a form of beach building is of common occurrence during the
summer. In this process, waves coming on to the gently sloping shoal
whose water depth is less than the depth of wave influence strike the
inclined bottom, pushing and carrying ahead some of the sand. Each
succeeding wave continues the pushing and carrying, ultimately dropping
sand at the water's edge. Under favorable circumstances, the end result
is a substantially increased breadth of beach (above water level). The
casual observer is likely to attribute increasing expanse of beach to fall
in water level, whereas it may happen that the beach increase is largely
due to beach building. The results of such beach building are often
wholly or in part temporary, since subsequent action of ice and higher
waters may redistribute the accumulated sand.

Barrier beaches are ridges of sand formed in the face of the strongest,
prevailing wave action. In general, they are parallel to the shore and
located in shallow water some distance from the margin. By direct
action of heavy waves, a ridge of sand is pounded up to and above the
level of the water; in fact, it is claimed that under favorable conditions
such a sand ridge can actually be seen to grow during a heavy storm.
Once formed, wind action may aid secondarily in increasing the height
of such a ridge when its initial stage is followed by a fall in lake level.
A certain lack of agreement seems to exist among authorities concerning
the best conditions for the formation of barrier beaches, some claiming
that the best conditions appear to be a fairly constant water level,
together with very shallow shoal water which grows very gradually
deeper and a set of lake conditions of such a nature that storms produce
large waves; while, contrariwise, it is claimed that a lowering of the water
level or an elevation of the land is required. Such ridges, particularly
when first formed, may not be connected to the shore at the ends, but,
in time, such connections are to be expected, and, when formed, a lagoon,
sometimes called a *barrier beach pool*, is produced. Such pools are always
shallow, usually very shallow. Permanent barrier beach pools are much
more likely to occur in very large lakes such as the Great Lakes than in
small ones; in fact, such a pool in permanent form seems to be a rarity
in the inland lakes, although temporary ones are frequent. When

ᵗermanently formed, these pools not only modify the form of the shore, but they constitute, at least for a time, a very favorable habitat for many aquatic organisms. Owing to shallow depth and their occurrence in a region of shifting materials, filling is likely to go on rapidly, making the life of such pools relatively short.

Currents. Important as waves are in shore-building activities, they are secondary to the surface currents which pass alongshore, carrying and dropping materials. In the smaller inland lakes, these currents are largely determined by the prevailing winds. As these currents pass

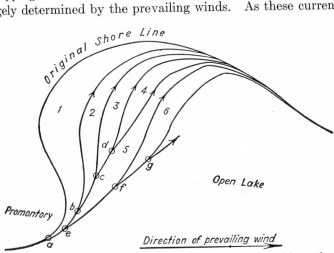

Fig. 1. Diagram showing gradual filling of a small bay by beach-pool formation. Arabic numerals indicate relative age and order of formation of pools, 1 being the first and oldest, and 6 the most recent. The letters a, b, c, d, e, f, g mark the position and chronological sequence of the initial ends of the sand spits. Arrowheads on sand bars indicate the direction of growth of each bar.

projecting headlands, they pick up loose materials and transport them elsewhere. Since shore lines often present a series of sinuosities, along-shore currents tend to pass more directly from one headland to the next instead of following closely the concave shore line. Having encountered a headland and picked up a load of material, the current loses some of its initial velocity when it reaches the other side of the promontory and, as a result, deposits along its path some of the load of suspended material. Eventually, a sand spit begins to grow out from some point on the more protected side of the headland, which, in time, reaches the shore somewhere along the side of the bay, forming a bar which completely cuts off a small portion of the lake and establishes a *sand-spit beach pool* (Fig. 1). Incidentally, a step in the process of smoothing out the concavity in the shore line is completed. Owing to the general tendency of the alongshore current to follow in a slight degree the course of the shore line, the sand spit does not ordinarily pass in a straight course from one headland to the next but instead tends to approximate a sigmoid form (convex part at the initial end and the concave part at the concluding end) and follows roughly the form of the shore line, thus cutting off only a narrow portion of the lake. Before the first sand spit is completed, another may begin forming from the lakeward side of the first, but somewhat farther along, and will repeat the history of the first in a general way. This process continues until the bay is completely obliterated and the shore line extends more or less directly from one original headland to the other. Vegetation begins to invade the growing sand spit: first, certain sedges and small seedlings; then some of the shrublike plants; and finally forest trees. Since the time elapsing between the first growth of trees on the bar and the capture of the pool by vegetation is sufficient to give the trees a long start over the latter, it is often possible to trace out the positions of ancient bars and pools, long after the depressions have disappeared, by the rows of larger trees and stumps separated by forest growths of much younger age. In one of the bays of Douglas Lake, Michigan, there is a series of such beach pools of which at least six can be readily recognized, grading from the outer one—the bar of which was just recently completed—to the ancient, extinct ones behind. Local circumstances may prevent as perfect and definite a sequence as the one just mentioned, but the general process of sand-spit formation is as described. Beach pools so formed are often remarkably fine habitats for aquatic organisms. Such a series as the one described above presents splendid conditions for the study of ecological succession.

General Effect of Shore Building. The cutting down of headlands, the smoothing out of bays and other irregularities, and the general straightening of shore lines all combine to form a lake with reduced shore line. The progressive elimination of marginal irregularities goes on until finally no more bays remain to be cut off in that region of the lake, and, while minor shore adjustments may follow, the climax of the process has essentially been reached. One effect of aging is, therefore, the reduction of shore line, and, since it is a well-known limnological fact that, other things being equal, the greater the length of shore line of a lake the greater its productivity, it thus results that, in this respect, the lake automatically reduces its own productivity. However, other influences of aging may offset this effect.

Ice Action. Lake margins are subject to modifications due to ice action. Ice exerts its influence on the shore in two general ways: (1) by ice expansion and (2) by ice jams.

Expansion Action. Ice, when once formed on a lake surface, expands or contracts with the rise and fall of the temperature. Since air temperatures rise and fall during the winter, sometimes over a considerable range, the ice changes in volume. An appreciable drop of temperature causes the ice to contract and thus produces cracks which refill with more ice. Then, when a rise of temperature produces an expansion of the whole ice mass, action upon shore is exerted. If the shore is of such a nature that the ice cannot shove, the ice may buckle. However, on many sloping shores, the expanding ice overrides them; and if the shore materials are of a yielding sort, an irregular ridge called an *ice rampart* is likely to be formed by shoving a portion of the marginal material to a higher level and leaving it in the form of a ridge. Where conditions favor permanency of ramparts once formed, successive shoves may build up a considerable accumulation of displaced materials, forming an *ice-push terrace*.

Ice Jams. Ice fields, thawed loose from the shores in early spring, may be blown against the shore, exerting great pressures. Also, masses of broken-up ice drift with the wind and produce jams on and against the shore. Ice ramparts similar to those formed by ice expansion frequently result. Since these jams are wind produced and since the spring winds vary in direction, any of the less-protected shores also may be affected. Various other shore distortions may result, such as the change or the actual destruction of sand bars, recession of banks, formation of irregularities in shores having materials of unequal resistance, and shifts in position of boulders. Ice jams are more effective on the larger lakes.

As would be expected, the scouring action of ice on shores may virtually obliterate certain habitats so that the space formerly occupied by one biota may either be restocked with a similar biota or else replaced by another population better adapted to the new conditions.

LAKE BOTTOMS

The term *bottom* is here used to include all parts of the bottom of a lake basin from the water's edge to the deepest region.

DIVERSITY

The greatest diversity prevails in the bottom of different kinds of lakes, as well as in individual lakes of the same type. All lakes of a particular region may have had the same origin, may have begun their history with essentially the same materials composing the basin, and may exist under the same climatic conditions, yet the bottom materials may be, and often are, markedly dissimilar in the different lakes. Every lake accumulates deposits on its bottom. The kinds of bottom deposits and the rate of deposition are largely matters of local circumstances; likewise, the distribution of materials, once they are in the lake, also depends upon local conditions; therefore, two lakes of similar position, size, depth, age, and original basin materials may now differ markedly with respect to their bottom deposits.

The nature of bottom deposits is a preeminently important feature in determining biological productivity. Different kinds of bottom deposits maintain different kinds of organisms, and different amounts of bottom deposits, within limits, aid in an important way in determining differences in quantitative biological productivity.

Sources of Bottom Materials

The principal sources of bottom materials are:

1. Bodies of plankton organisms which die and sink.
2. Plant and animal remains from the littoral zone.
3. Wind-blown materials, both organic and inorganic.
4. Silt, clay, and similar materials introduced by tributaries or washed in directly by run-off water from adjacent slopes. Since these additions to the bottom are usually more extensive at certain times of year, such as spring floods and spring thaws, a definite stratification of the bottom may occur, so that a transverse section of the deposits shows an alternation of a clay layer or other kinds of inwash with another layer of very different character representing an accumulation during other times of year.
5. Marl, largely calcium carbonate produced by plants and animals or precipitated from the water by inorganic processes (page 100).
6. Remains of floating blanket Algae.
7. Eroded materials from the shore zones.

All of these materials may contribute to the bottom of a lake, or local circumstances may determine that certain ones either predominate or are totally absent. Newly deposited, organic materials undergo decomposition, ultimately changing their character. Since there is a continual addition of new bottom-making materials settling through the water, a transverse section of the bottom deposits shows a gradient varying from the topmost, newly deposited materials down to the deeper, more chemically stable substances. Those animals which normally live in bottom deposits inhabit only the upper few inches of depth.

Classification of Bottom Deposits

As previously indicated, a great diversity of bottom deposits exists in lakes. Predominance of certain materials in the mixtures produces different types of deposits. However, a satisfactory classification of deposits is yet to be made. Long-continued, intensive studies of soils have enabled soil physicists and others to establish soil classifications of great value; but in spite of the fact that bottom deposits are soils, in a certain sense, they are still too little known to make possible anything but the roughest classifications. There is great need for critical study of bottom deposits.

Caspari (1910) classified the deposits in the Scottish lochs into three main varieties or types: (1) sand or grit; (2) clay; and (3) brown mud. Three other types occurred sporadically and were listed as rarities: (4) diatom ooze; (5) ochreous mud; and (6) calcareous deposits. The predominating component in each of these types is obvious from the name, except in the following: brown mud in the Scottish lochs has as its chief constituent an impalpable, brown, humus-like substance resulting from the decay of vegetable matter. Ochreous muds are described as characterized by a high content of limonitic iron, which gives them a distinct red color. Since the Scottish lochs have bottom deposits which are said to differ very little from loch to loch, it is obvious that this classification is not broad enough to include all kinds of bottom. It is mentioned here merely as representing one of the early attempts to distinguish types of deposits. Scandinavian limnologists (Lundqvist, 1927, *et al.*) have made extensive studies of the lake-bottom deposits of southern Sweden, and they employ a classification based upon the relative proportion of clay and fossil material in them. This classification is restricted in its applicability and employs a terminology based upon an unfortunate word derivation. Veatch (1931) and Roelofs (1944) presented tentative classifications based upon their studies of Michigan lakes. The following outline modified from Roelofs' work is conservative and deals only with the principal types.

I. Homogeneous: having uniform composition.
  A. Inorganic.
    1. Bed rock or solid rock.
    2. Boulders: rocks more than 12 in. in diameter.
    3. Rubble: rocks 3–12 in. in diameter.
    4. Gravel: ⅛–3 in. in diameter.
    5. Sand: may be divided into coarse and fine.
    6. Clay: very finely divided mineral matter; no gritty feeling; usually gray in color.
    7. Marl: Calcium carbonate; usually gray in color.
  B. Organic.
    1. Detritus: coarse plant materials, fragmented but little decayed.
    2. Fibrous peat: partially decayed plant remains; parts of plants recognizable.
    3. Pulpy peat: very finely divided plant remains; particles unrecognizable; green to brown; consistency variable, often semifluid.
    4. Muck: black; finely divided organic matter; decomposition very advanced.
II. Heterogeneous: composed of two or more kinds of material.
    1. Alluvium: mixed sedimentary material from inflowing streams.
    2. Various combinations of two or more recognizable homogeneous types.

Classifications of bottom deposits are still in the pioneer stage. Intensive work in this field and the adoption of a standard terminology for bottom types is a major need in limnology.

STRATIFICATION OF BOTTOM DEPOSITS

Not infrequently bottom deposits show horizontal stratification. This condition represents a chronology in which alternating or changing conditions in the past brought about differences in deposition. Sometimes this lamination is very distinct. Third Sister Lake, near Ann Arbor, Mich., shows within the profundal zone a total bottom deposit of about 11.6 m. and stratified as follows: (1) Uppermost stratum, 1.2 m. thick; composed of clearly defined layers of soft, black, largely organic detritus, about 0.5 to 1.0 cm. thick, alternating with a much firmer, grayish, clay layer having an average thickness of about 1.0 to 2.0 cm. The clay layer is so firm and sticky that the layers can be separated, thus making it possible to secure almost pure samples of both kinds of material. The clay layer is inwash from the drainage basin during the spring; the blackish ooze layer is deposited largely during the remainder of the year and almost wholly by processes going on within the lake itself. (2) Peat, 5.5 m. thick. (3) Alternating layers of peat and marl, 2.4 m. thick. (4) Fine sand, 2.1 m. thick. (5) Sandy marl, 0.3 m. thick.

Stratification of bottom deposits differs greatly in different lakes and with the different sets of conditions which produce it. A lake may be so situated and so composed that no stratification in its bottom deposits is detectable. Sometimes vertical cores show the total bottom deposit to be divisible only into a few major horizontal strata composed of contrasting materials. Sometimes major strata are themselves composed of *varves*. A *varve* is a form of layering due to the annual procession of the seasons and generally consists of two laminae, one formed during the summer and the other during the winter. Varves occur in some of the deep glacial clay deposits of some lakes, also in some lake deposits now in the process of formation. They are known to vary in thickness from a few millimeters to 30 cm. or more. Wilson[1] (1943) reported 12,223 varves in bottom sediments in Sandusky Bay, Lake Erie.

HISTORICAL SIGNIFICANCE OF BOTTOM DEPOSITS

Bottom deposits, if they remain in place as formed, constitute a historical record of a lake, the oldest deposits being at the bottom of the original basin and the most recent at the top, with intervening materials occurring in the order of their formation in past time. Much information concerning ancient conditions within the lake itself and past conditions on shore has been secured through the study of these bottom materials. Deposits differ greatly in degree of disintegration, varying from those so

[1] The investigations of Wilson (1936, 1938, 1943, 1945), Twenhofel and Broughton (1939), and others have contributed much to the knowledge of lake sediments in the Great Lakes region.

completely reduced that they yield little recognizable materials to those in which the partial preservation of animals and plants provides much evidence of past events.   Pollen, diatom shells, fragments of exoskeletons of plankton Crustacea and of insects, shells of Mollusca, and deposits of marl are among the common witnesses of ancient history.   Many studies have been made of historical significance of various kinds of lamination in bottom deposits in different kinds of lakes, yielding much in unfolding the story of the past.   Varves afford means of measuring the time involved in the deposition of strata and the establishment of chronologies for lakes.

BASIN SEAL

A phenomenon known as *basin seal* occurs in many, possibly most, lakes.   When present the basin is sealed, sides and bottom, against significant outseepage and in some instances apparently against consequential inseepage.   Available evidence seems to indicate that this sealing is produced by the more chemically stable, finely divided elements of the bottom sediments which are deposited upon, and worked into the interstices of, the lake basin.   Sometimes, this sealing seems to be very complete.   It may account for the many instances of dry basins which occur but a few yards inland from a lake in spite of the fact that the bottom of the basin is well below the lake-surface elevation.   Artificial interruption of this seal locally is known to produce, under some conditions, immediate outdrainage.

GENERAL DIVERSITY OF LAKES

Until recent times, all lakes were looked upon, even by many biologists, as being relatively similar.   While such simple things as differences in color, taste, hardness, turbidity, aquatic animals, and aquatic plants were known, lakes were generally thought of as being much the same wherever found.   A partial survival of this idea is still prevalent among laymen at large.   With the advent of limnology and its modern methods of environmental analysis has come the established fact that lakes, as a class, manifest a most amazing physical, chemical, and biological diversity.   In fact, there are reasons for believing that from the standpoint of environments produced, the lakes of North America present a greater diversity than do the lands of the continent.   This statement sounds, at first, startling and exaggerated for the simple reason that since man is a land animal, the inherent diversities of the land areas are a much more intimate part of his life.   As a partial indication of lake diversity, it might be stated that lakes are large, medium, or small; deep or shallow; protected or unprotected; with or without tributaries and outlets; fresh, brackish, or salt; acid, neutral, or alkaline; hard, medium, or soft; turbid or clear;

surrounded by bog, swamp, forest, or open shores; high or low in dissolved content; with or without stagnation zones; with marl, muck, sand, or false bottoms; with or without vegetation beds; with high, medium, and low biological productivity; young, mature, or senescent; and so on. Within each of the various groups of characters mentioned above, as well as within the numerous ones not listed, every imaginable intergrade exists. These many characters occur in multitudinous combinations, thus accounting for the remarkable lake diversity already mentioned.

PART II

NATURE OF INLAND-WATER ENVIRONMENTS

Water, together with its contained substances and energies, constitutes the immediate environment of aquatic organisms. Therefore, an analysis of the fundamental features of natural, uncontaminated waters is the necessary approach to an understanding of interrelationships. Interrelationships cannot be adequately determined until the things interrelated are themselves understood, at least to some extent. An exhaustive analysis of all of the possible factors and influences operative in water cannot be undertaken here. Space and aims of this book dictate that the treatment be brief and consider only the more basic conditions. Most of the following described physical and chemical features have, in one way or another, significant influences on aquatic life. It should be understood in advance that each physical and chemical influence is described not as a purely physical or chemical phenomenon but as a contributor to the sum total of those circumstances which make possible the existence of the various phenomena of biological productivity.

CHAPTER IV

PHYSICAL CONDITIONS AND RELATED PHENOMENA

MORPHOMETRY

That branch of limnology which deals with the measurement of significant morphological features of any basin and its included water mass is known as *morphometry*. Certain fundamental conditions of production arise directly out of size and form interrelations. Therefore it becomes necessary for the limnologist to make various measurements of shore line, area, depth, slope, volume, and other morphological features and to establish from them certain ratios which serve as indices of lake differences. Details of these procedures belong more properly to field and laboratory work (see Welch, 1948) and will not be treated here.

PHYSICAL FEATURES OF WATER

PRESSURE

Water is a heavy substance. Pure water weighs 62.4 lb. per cu. ft. at 4°C. This is a direct result of its density. Since density changes with differences in temperature, compression, substances in solution, and substances in suspension, the weight of a cubic foot of natural water is not always the same. It is roughly about 0.2 lb. per cu. ft. lighter at 27°C. than at 4°C., and it has been estimated that substances in solution and suspension in inland waters usually do not add more than about 0.1 lb. per cu. ft. to the weight. However, for ordinary purposes, calculations of pressure on the basis of 62.4 lb. per cu. ft. are customary. In calculating pressures in the sea, a value of 64 lb. per cu. ft. is commonly used. The pressure at any subsurface position is the weight of the superimposed column of water plus the atmospheric pressure at the surface. For example, if a measure of the pressure at a depth of 100 ft. on a square inch of bottom is desired, it will be necessary to determine the weight of a column of water 1 sq. in. in transverse section and 1,200 in. high plus the atmospheric pressure per square inch at the surface. Pressures may be expressed in any convenient units of weight per unit of area or, as is sometimes done, in the numbers of atmospheres. Pressures in water, as depth increases, rapidly become great, so that ultimately a crushing effect is imposed upon objects submerged to considerable depths. This collapse under pressure is called *implosion*. Apparatus which includes inner spaces to which water has no access must be protected against the crushing effects of pressure in deep water. It has been related that during the famous *Challenger* explorations, the beam of a trawl returned from its first deep submergence with the wood so compressed that the denser knots protruded from the surface. While it is true that depths in lakes, barring exceptions such as Lake Baikal, Siberia, are very small compared to those in oceans, nevertheless pressures at the bottoms of shallow lakes are of considerable magnitude, as, for example, in a lake having a maximum depth of 100 ft. (30 m.), the pressure in the deepest region is about 58 lb. per sq. in., or almost 4 atmospheres.

COMPRESSIBILITY

Water is virtually incompressible. The coefficient of compressibility for each atmosphere of pressure is usually given as 52.5×10^{-6} at 0°C. for pressures of 1 to 25 atmospheres; as 50.0×10^{-6} at 10°C., pressures of 1 to 25 atmospheres; and as 49.1×10^{-6} at 20°C., pressures of 1 to 25 atmospheres. Coefficients change with still greater pressures, but for those usually met in lakes, compressibility (sometimes called *elasticity*) is negligible for ordinary purposes. For the great ocean depths, it becomes a matter of more appreciable proportions where, according to Johnstone (1928), if the sea were suddenly to become absolutely incompressible the volume of the ocean would be increased by 11,000,000 cu. km., and the sea level would rise about 15 fathoms (27.5 m.). Making a similar computation for fresh water, Lake Superior waters, suddenly rendered absolutely incompressible, would rise in level about 9 in. (about 23 cm.), and an ordinary inland lake with a maximum depth of 100 ft. (30 m.), under the same circumstances, would rise about 0.01 in. (0.25 mm.). Since increasing pressure compresses water to such an exceedingly slight degree (thereby increasing its density to the same slight extent), objects sink in water of uniform temperature at essentially the same rate at all levels, contrary to popular impression. This means that if an object will sink at all, it will sink to the bottom unless other influences intervene. The modifying effects of viscosity will be mentioned later (page 36). Herdman (1923) states that a solid mass of iron weighing 1,000 g. shows at 4,000 m. depth only the insignificant difference of 0.3 per cent in weight.

DENSITY

Some of the most remarkable phenomena in limnology are dependent upon density relations in water.

Variations Due to Pressure. Water at the surface, subject to a pressure of only 1 atmosphere, is considered as having a density of unity (1.0); at a pressure of 10 atmospheres, the density is about 1.0005; at 20 atmospheres, the density is about 1.001; and at 30 atmospheres, it is about 1.0015.

Variations Due to Temperature. Pure water forms ice at 0°C., and steam at 100°C., but the main interest here is in the changes of density of the liquid due to temperature. Water possesses that unique quality of having its *maximum density* (Fig. 2) not just before it forms ice but at 4°C. (39.2°F.). Strangely enough, it actually becomes progressively *less dense (lighter)* as it cools from 4°C. to the freezing point.

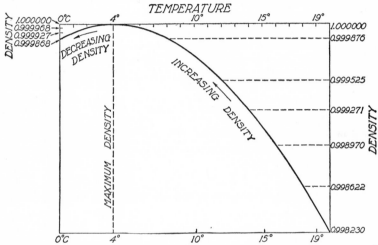

Fig. 2. Graph showing relation between density and temperature in pure water. Curve discontinued at 20°C.

The performance of many, possibly most, inland waters parallels closely that of pure water, as shown in Fig. 2. However, one departure should be mentioned, viz., it is a well-established fact that with increasing hydrostatic pressure the temperature of maximum density in pure water becomes lower than 4°C. although the change is of small magnitude. It seems likely that this fact explains the occurrence of temperatures slightly lower than 4°C. at the bottom of very deep inland lakes in summer (Wright, 1931; Eddy, 1943).

In natural environments, water is ordinarily least dense (lightest) at the maximum summer temperature. As it cools down during autumn and early winter, it gradually *increases* in density until 4°C. is reached. Further cooling *decreases* density until the 0°C. is reached.

According to Coker (1938), sea water becomes heavier as it cools until the freezing point is reached, i.e., the temperature of maximum density is at 0°C. instead of 4°C. as in pure water.

Changes Due to Dissolved Substances. All natural waters contain substances in solution. The concentrations of these substances vary widely, although, as a rule, the total amount in fresh water is less than that in sea water. Such substances usually increase the density of water, the amount of increase depending upon the concentration of dissolved materials and upon their specific gravity. A marked influence of this sort occurs in salt lakes in which the density may exceed that of the oceans. Evaporation increases density by concentrating the dissolved materials; dilution reduces the density.

Changes Due to Substances in Suspension. All waters, as they occur in nature, contain some suspended particulate matter. The quality and quantity of these substances vary greatly in different waters and at different times. Silt and certain other materials are heavier than water and thus increase its weight; others may have a specific gravity similar to that of water and cause no significant change in its weight. *Density currents* and related phenomena may be caused by substances in suspension.

Mobility (Viscosity)

Water is an exceedingly mobile liquid. Nevertheless, it has internal friction (viscosity). This viscosity varies with the temperature. Water

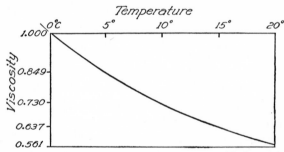

Fig. 3. Graph showing change in viscosity of pure water with change in temperature.

is distinctly more mobile at ordinary summer temperatures than it is just before it freezes (Fig. 3). For the present purposes, the values given in Table 1 indicate the essential features of this variation with temperature.

Table 1. Changes in the Viscosity of Pure Water Due to Temperature Changes

Temperature, °C.	Percentage of Viscosity
0	100
5	84.9
10	73.0
15	63.7
20	56.1
25	49.8
30	44.6

The mixing and stirring of water in nature are largely due to wind action. It is evident from the table given above that the response of water to a wind of fixed velocity would differ with different temperatures of the water. Much more work is required of the wind to produce a certain result when the water is near freezing than when it is near summer temperatures. Pressure does not cause any significant change in viscosity.

BUOYANCY

Buoyancy is a direct outcome of density and varies with the same factors. The law of Archimedes is as follows: A body in water is buoyed up by a force equal to the weight of the water displaced. The greater the density the greater the buoyant force; the denser the water the higher will a floating object ride in the water. Ships passing from fresh water into sea water rise a little higher, and the same ships with the same loads would ride somewhat higher in winter than in summer. Submerged bodies of all sorts are, of course, under the same influences and subject to the same changes of buoyant force.

MOVEMENTS OF WATER

Movements of water have numerous and far-reaching limnological relations. Some understanding is therefore necessary of the major physical features of water movements. The principal forms of movements of water are waves, currents, and seiches.

Waves. Waves are mainly wind produced. They occur on every body of water in forms and magnitudes depending upon various local conditions, such as area of open water; direction, duration, and velocity of winds; shape of shore line; and relative amounts of deep and shallow water. On the Great Lakes, waves may become formidable in size and action; on the smallest of the inland waters, waves, while potentially present, are always minimal, although not without their limnological significance. The greater the expanse of water over which the wind blows the greater the potential wave height, wave length, and wave velocity.

In open water where a wave is free to move without modification, wave motion is essentially as follows: Assuming that a wave is already formed and in action, each particle of water describes a vertical, circular path and theoretically returns to the position from which it started; therefore, the wave moves along, producing a vertical rise and fall at successive positions but no horizontal movement of the water. Such a wave is sometimes called a *wave of oscillation*. Not infrequently, such a wave is modified by circumstances, as, for example, the wind, when its velocity is such that it blows the crest of the wave over, causing it to fall forward and thus produce a *whitecap* in which actual horizontal motion of the water does occur. Likewise, as a wave from the open lake approaches the shallow water, certain changes occur one of which is that the wave height is increased and then the top pitches forward in a sort of forward rolling motion, forming *surf*. This also results in horizontal motion or flow of the water. Surf is often explained as due to the drag of the bottom of the wave when it encounters the shoal, causing the top to outrun the bottom and thus fall over, but there appear to be some serious objections to this explanation.

Stevenson (Cornish, 1934) presents the following formula for computing the maximum height of waves in small bodies of water: $h = \frac{1}{3} \sqrt{F}$ in which h is maximum height in meters and F is the fetch of the wind in kilometers. If F is less than 10 km., a small correction is required. Both wave height and wave length increase as the distance from shore becomes greater. For an extended treatment of waves in large bodies of water, the reader is referred to Sverdrup, Johnson, and Fleming (1942).

Waves in which there is a definite forward movement of the water itself are known as *waves of translation*. These may result from the effect of waves of oscillation coming on to a very gentle sloping shoal and forming breakers, as already mentioned. They may also result from the sudden addition of a considerable volume of water to the lake.

Water thrown up on shore by waves runs back down the slope, forming undertow. Often, the downflowing water is met by the next expiring wave, so that shifting shore materials are alternately swept or rolled back and forth.

Depth of wave action is a matter of considerable limnological importance, but, unfortunately, precise information as to its extent in different conditions is lacking. It has been claimed that in the sea, wave action may exert an influence to a depth of 182 m. (600 ft.). It is sometimes stated that the maximum depth of wave action is equal to the wave length. According to other statements, the disturbance caused by waves extends to a distance below the surface equal only to the height of the wave. There is reason for believing that truth lies somewhere between these two extremes.

Currents. Currents in lakes are mainly of three kinds, viz., *vertical*, *horizontal*, and *returning* (sometimes called undertow currents).

True vertical currents seldom occur in inland lakes but may be present in large waters such as the Great Lakes. When present in inland lakes, they are the result of some unusual thermal, morphological, or hydrostatic circumstance. Upwelling of water from some deep source is an example.

Horizontal currents are common in lakes. They are usually produced by wind and often modified by the shape of shore line and form of the basin. It is claimed that in lakes as large as the Great Lakes, surface velocity is about 5 per cent of that of the wind causing it but is less than 5 per cent in the smaller lakes. The velocity of surface water in oceans at 45°N. lat. is said to be about 2 per cent that of the wind producing it. Stromsten (1927) reported that in Lake Okoboji, Iowa, a wind of 800 ft. per minute produced a current of 25 ft. per min.; also that after thermal stratification was established, only the heaviest winds disturbed the water below 20 m. depth.

The ratio of wind velocity to water movement diminishes as the wind velocity increases. Also, water velocity diminishes with increase in depth. The data presented in Table 2 probably indicate, in a general way, the expectation in the smaller lakes.

TABLE 2.   RELATION OF WATER MOVEMENT TO WIND VELOCITY AND TO DEPTH
Data from Whipple (1927)[1]

Wind velocity, miles per hr.	Rate of surface-water movement, ft. per min.	Percentage
5	13	3
30	26	1

Depth, ft.	Approximate percentage of water velocity at surface
10	60
20	25

[1] Reprinted by permission from "The Microscopy of Drinking Water," 4th ed., John Wiley & Sons, Inc.

Lakes with large inflow or large outflow, or both, have areas of flowage not due to wind action. This is particularly true of those lakes which are expansions of a river system through which surface water drifts as a result of the general current.

Returning currents are formed when water is piled up on an exposed shore as a result of an onshore wind. Such action raises the water level at that position, and, as a result, the excess water may return underneath along the bottom. The magnitude and duration of such currents depend upon the velocity and duration of the wind. Steady, vigorous, onshore winds may set up return currents which extend to the opposite side of the lake. During the summer when a lake is thermally stratified and the upper portion of the water (*epilimnion*) is approximately of the same temperature and hence of the same density, a strong, steady wind of some hours' duration continually drifts the water upon the exposed shore whence, barring special circumstances, the excess water may return

down the slope of the basin to a considerable depth.   Encountering there
the colder, denser water of the *thermocline region* (page 52), this downflowing, returning current is diverted in a horizontal direction and flows
toward the opposite shore, maintaining a level above the thermocline.
In such a circulation, the upper stratum of the epilimnion flows toward
one shore; the lower stratum (the return current) flows toward the
opposite shore; and the stratum between the two, which is known as
the *shearing plane* (Fig. 4), is practically without motion.   Whipple
(1927) found evidence, based upon the use of floats adjusted to different
levels, that such a return current may also occur in part beneath the

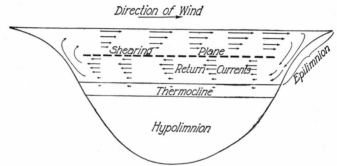

Fig. 4.   Diagram showing character of water circulation in the epilimnion and formation
of a shearing plane.   Differences in length and width of arrows represent differences
in velocity of water movement.   Such a circulation depends upon a wind of sufficient
velocity and duration to produce it.

thermocline.   If this is true, then the *hypolimnion* (the region below the
thermocline) is not so completely devoid of circulation as is sometimes
supposed.   Other workers have found evidences of subthermocline circulation, the nature of which is as yet little understood (page 56).   During
the spring and fall *overturns* (pages 49, 59), when the water is of uniform
density from top to bottom, return currents may extend even to the
bottom of relatively deep inland lakes.   Not all return currents are submerged.   If wave fronts meet the shore line obliquely, the water piled up
on shore may seek to reestablish the water level by flowing off laterally
on the surface and along the shore line.   Various forms of these alongshore, return currents, such as lateral whirls or eddies, may result from
the modifying circumstances of local shore and basin characters.

Tides.   In inland lakes, tides are almost imperceptible, even in the
Great Lakes.   Lake Michigan is said to have a tide of about 5 cm.   This
virtually means that tides in fresh waters are, so far as known, negligible
phenomena in limnology.

Seiches.   In lakes and along the seacoasts, oscillations of the water
level occur. under certain circumstances, which are called *seiches* (pro-

nounced *sâches*). While these phenomena have been known to some extent for at least two centuries, Forel (1895) was the first to make an extensive study of them. A seiche consists of a local, periodic rise and fall of the water level. It is an example of a *standing wave* in which the water particles do not travel in circular orbits but the advance and return of the particle are in the same path. Any influence which produces a *temporary*, local depression or elevation of water level may produce a seiche. Those influences which most commonly produce seiches in lakes are (1) winds, temporarily strong, which pile up water on the exposed margin of the lake; (2) sudden change in barometric pressure over a portion of the lake area; (3) earthquakes; (4) landslides; and (5) sudden, very heavy rainfall at one end of a lake. Of these, the first seems to be far the most common cause, particularly in the smaller inland lakes. A sudden, vigorous, summer storm accompanied by high, steady wind, which subsides as abruptly as it began, piles up water on the exposed shore, thus making the water level high at that point and correspondingly low on the opposite shore. When the "blow" is over, the lake surface begins to swing, with alternating rise and fall on each of the two opposite shores, the swing diminishing rapidly in amplitude and ultimately disappearing completely.

Each lake has its own *period of oscillation* depending upon its essential dimensions. The amplitude, depending upon the dimensions of the lake and the intensity of the initial cause, may vary from a fraction of a centimeter in small lakes to 1 m. or more in large ones. In Lake Geneva, Switzerland, it is reported that the amplitude of a seiche may reach about 2 m. Seiches of considerable magnitude occur on the Great Lakes, becoming most noticeable in the protected coves and bays. Seiches on Lake Erie sometimes expose, for a short time, the shallow-water bottoms along the protected side of the peninsula known as Cedar Point, opposite Sandusky, Ohio. For example, it has been reported that on one occasion in 1922 the water receded 9 m. from shore line. Seiches in the inland lakes, although present, are seldom if ever seen by the casual observer, since their amplitude is so small. Rarely, where local circumstances provide the necessary setting, seiches may cause a current to run in and later run out through narrow straits or narrowly contracted passages, imitating in a slight way the back-and-forth flow of the tide on the seashore through narrow passages between islands or other bodies of land near shore.

Forel (1895) used the following formula for computing the period of oscillation of a seiche in a lake whose basin has definite regularity of bottom:

$$t = \frac{l}{\sqrt{gh}}$$

where t = time of one-half oscillation in seconds.

　l = length of axis of seiche in meters.

　g = acceleration of gravity (9.809 m./sec.²).

　h = depth of water in meters.

More complicated formulas were worked out for lakes having irregular basins.

Whipple (1927) presents the following formula:[1]

$$t = \frac{2l}{3,600 \ \sqrt{dg}}$$

where t = time of oscillation in hours.

　l = length of lake (or length of axis of seiche) in feet.

　d = mean depth in feet along axis of seiche.

　g = acceleration of gravity (32.16 ft./sec.²).

Whipple states that when this formula is applied to seiche conditions in Lake Erie, the calculated period is 14.4 hr., and the interval by direct observation is from 14 to 16 hr.

Forel (1895) showed that seiches are of different forms, as follows:

1. Longitudinal seiche—one whose axis corresponds with the direction of the long axis of the lake.

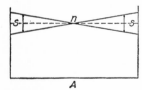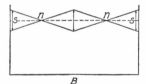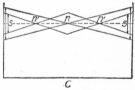

| A | B | C |

Fig. 5.　Diagrams indicating the nature of three different kinds of seiches. *A* represents a uninodal seiche; *B*, a binodal seiche; and *C*, a dicrotic seiche. *n, n′*, nodes; *s*, surface of water when immobile.　Vertical arrows indicate extent of the swing or oscillation at the positions indicated.　(*Modified from Forel*, 1895.)

2. Transverse seiche—one whose axis lies in the direction of one of the shorter axes of the lake.

Both longitudinal and transverse seiches are of three forms:

　a. Uninodal—having one node (Fig. 5*A*).

　b. Binodal—having two nodes (Fig. 5*B*).

　c. Dicrotic seiche—having two beats (show as two peaks on a limnograph) due to interference of uninodal and binodal seiches (Fig. 5*C*).

　d. Plurinodal—having several nodes.

Lesser known forms of water motion are sometimes called seiches, as, for example, the short-period, back-and-forth flow of water through

[1] Reprinted by permission from "The Microscopy of Drinking Water," 4th ed., John Wiley & Sons, Inc.

narrow channels in certain localities in very large lakes; and the *subsurface seiche*, a type which has been postulated as the cause of certain submerged currents in Lake Erie.

Subsurface waves, sometimes produced in large bodies of water, occur where subsurface water is denser than the overlying water. A strong, localized wind starts an impulse (wave) in the underlying layer of water which moves forward in the direction of the wind. As this wave moves along, the warmer lighter water just in front of it passes over the crest of the wave but in the opposite direction, thus producing a surface current

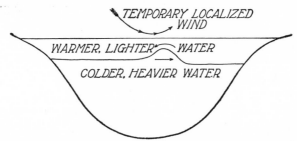

Fig. 6. Diagram showing formation of subsurface wave by the action of a temporary, localized wind. The wave is in the heavier, underlying water, and moves forward in the direction of the wind. Surface water, however, passes over the crest of the submerged wave and a surface current may thus be produced *against* the wind. (*Modified from Sandström*, 1919.)

(Fig. 6) opposite to the direction of the wind. Such surface currents running against the wind have been reported from the oceans, the Great Lakes, and elsewhere.

Subsurface seiches usually arise from a temporary displacement of the thermocline (Fig. 7) by the weight of piled-up surface water on one side of a lake due to strong wind action. Since the superimposed layers of water are of such density that the waters resist mixing, the underlying. cold, heavy water will be depressed under the region of temporarily accumulated surface waters and will rise to a corresponding degree under the opposite shore waters. When calm follows storm, the underlying heavy water begins to restore equilibrium by seeking its level again, swinging to the other side but going past its original level. A swing in the opposite direction ensues, thus setting up a succession of diminishing standing waves. Such seiches have been reported many times from inland lakes, also from Lake Erie.

For an extended account of seiches and other forms of deviation in the horizontal water level produced in lakes by the wind, the reader is referred to Hellström (1941); also to Sverdrup *et al.* (1942) for similar phenomena in oceans.

Molar Agents. Water in motion has a well-known carrying power the magnitude of which depends upon (1) velocity of the water; (2) volume of the water; and (3) nature (shape, size, and specific gravity) of the materials carried. All forms of water movement tend to put into action what are commonly called *molar agents*. A molar agent in water is merely a body either carried in suspension or rolled and pushed about by water movements which may not be of sufficient strength to lift it completely. In lakes, waves are the principal cause of molar-agent action. Their action on the shoals is commonly a combination of the

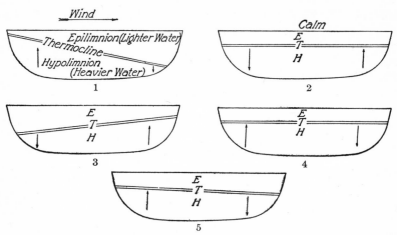

FIG. 7. Diagrams showing origin, by wind, and subsequent action of a subsurface seiche. Arrows indicate the character of the oscillations. Amount of swing of thermocline exaggerated. (*Modified from Sandström, 1919.*)

carrying of smaller particles and the rolling on the bottom of the larger bodies. The rolling coefficient is commonly expressed as the ratio of the *surface* of a body to its weight. Very finely divided particles of rock whose specific gravity is much greater than that of water may, nevertheless, remain in suspension for a time, even after the water has quieted down. Molar action, in its various forms, inflicts severe grinding action on shores and shoals. In this process, the molar agents themselves suffer from the grinding, undergoing constant wear. Substances in suspension will be treated more fully in the discussion of turbidity (page 87).

SURFACE FILM

When water is exposed to air, it acts as if it were encased within an extremely thin, elastic, surface membrane. This boundary is commonly known as the *surface film* and is interpreted as a manifestation of unbalanced molecular action. In the interior of the water, the molecules do not exhibit any such phenomena, since in that position they are attracted to each other in all directions, neutralize the attraction of one another, and are thus balanced. However, at the surface film, a phenomenon called *surface tension* occurs, due to unbalanced attractions between molecules at the surface, since the surface molecules are attracted on one side only, and upward attraction is lacking because there are no water molecules above them. It happens, therefore, that a surface tension is produced which acts inwardly, and the molecules act as if they formed a tightly stretched, elastic membrane over the water. This surface tension diminishes with rise of temperature, and it is also lowered by organic substances in solution, although most salts increase it. In pure water, it is said to be greater than in any other liquid except mercury. Objects which do not wet may be supported on top of this film, even though their specific gravity is several times greater than that of the underlying water. A time-honored demonstration is the supporting of a dry, steel needle on the surface film. The limnologist is accustomed to seeing, at times along sandy lake shores, patches of sand floating on the surface film. The under surface of the surface film also serves as a mechanical support for certain objects in nature. Light rays, impinging from above, penetrate it if the angle of incidence is not too great, but beyond a certain angle the surface film reflects light. Viewed from below, especially at an angle, it appears as an exceedingly smooth, somewhat silvery, opaque film. This film is now known to have many limnological relations, the more important ones of which will be discussed later.

Knowledge of surface tension in inland waters is scanty. The only paper of consequence appears to be that of Hardman (1941). On the basis of 100 measurements made on about 40 Wisconsin lakes, she found that (1) only nine consistently maintained a surface tension equal to that of pure water; (2) considerable variation occurs in some lakes; (3) substances of organic origin exert a greater influence in depressing surface tension than do other chemical factors; (4) no difference was detected between the northern soft-water and the southern hard-water lakes of Wisconsin; (5) variations in pH of 4.5 to 9.5 did not appear to affect commonly the surface tension unless organic acids were presumed to be present; (6) colored bog lakes often manifested reduced surface tension; (7) stagnant water was likely to have reduced surface tension; (8) variations caused by temperature changes are usually slight; (9) depressant films on water may be blown about by a steady wind thus developing local variations in surface tension. Table 3 indicates the amount of reduction found in certain kinds of natural situations.

Masses of foam, sometimes of considerable size, appear occasionally along the shore in inland lakes. Hardman observed reduced surface tension in regions of foam formation and suggested that the piling up of an organic film by a steady, strong, onshore wind operating for several hours might cause such an emulsion.

TABLE 3.   RANGE OF SURFACE-TENSION DEPRESSIONS IN VARIOUS SITUATIONS
From Hardman

Situation	Surface-tension Depression, Dynes per cm.
Oligotrophic lakes.................	0–2
Eutrophic lakes...................	0–20
Bog lakes.......................	0–20
Lakes with foam..................	2–9
Near *Lemna* and lilies..............	5–20
During plankton bloom............	0–20

TEMPERATURE

Temperature is one of the most important factors in an aquatic environment. In fact, it is possible that no other single factor has so many profound influences and so many direct and indirect effects. It, therefore, becomes necessary to give a rather detailed discussion here. Certain inherent thermal properties of water will be treated first.

Specific Heat. Water has the greatest *specific heat* of all substances, except liquid hydrogen and lithium at high temperatures. Since this heat capacity is so great, it is used as the standard in expressing specific heats of other substances. The heat capacity of water is given the value of 1 (i.e., specific heat of water is 1), and the specific heats of other substances are recorded as the ratios of their thermal capacities to that of water. More specifically, the numerical value of the specific heat of any substance is the number of calories of heat necessary to raise the temperature of 1 g. of the substance to the extent of 1°C.

Since the specific heat of water is so great, a lake must absorb vast quantities of heat in order to increase its temperature by 1°C., and this explains the slow rate of warming up of lake water in spring; likewise, its slow cooling in autumn is due to the large amounts of heat which must be given off. Thus, it is seen that the response to the major changes in air temperatures is a very deliberate one. Water temperatures always lag far behind the larger changes of air temperatures.

Latent Heat of Fusion. Another peculiarity is that before water at 0°C. can become ice, it must give off a large amount of heat, and, conversely, when ice has just been formed at the freezing point, it must absorb a large amount of heat before it can transform into the fluid state. Actually, it requires about 80 units of heat to change 1 g. of ice to the liquid state when both are at 0°C. The heat thus involved is called *latent heat of fusion*. From the statement just made, it follows that the amount of heat required merely to convert ice into water with no change of temperature would, after the conversion has occurred, raise the temperature of the same amount of water about 80°C. Latent heat of fusion is thus eighty times greater than the specific heat, although the specific heat of water is greater than that of all other substances save two.

Combined Effect of Specific Heat and Latent Heat of Fusion. In lakes and other natural waters, the cooling of water in autumn with subsequent ice formation in winter and the disappearance of ice followed by warming up of the water in spring involve interchanges with the air of vast quantities of heat. As a consequence, the changes of water temperature are slow. In northern Michigan, for example, where the winter comes early, the larger inland lakes may not freeze over until December or early January; while in spring, the ice may not disappear completely until April.

Evaporation. Water, including ice and snow, evaporates at all environmental temperatures. In evaporation heat is consumed. That quantity of heat necessary to convert 1 g. of water at 100°C. into steam without altering the temperature of the latter is known as *latent heat of evaporation*, sometimes called *heat of vaporization*. Water has the remarkable peculiarity of requiring 536 heat units for this conversion, a quantity of heat much greater than that of many other liquids. When evaporation occurs, the necessary heat required to make the change from water to steam must come from somewhere. It may come from some source of high temperature, such as the sun; it may be withdrawn from the water itself from bodies in or around it, thus lowering their temperature. Rate of evaporation is determined by several factors usually acting simultaneously, viz., temperature, relative amount of free surface of the water, vapor pressure, barometric pressure, and amount of wind action. The manner in which these factors operate is too well known to require description here. Still another factor, viz., quality of the water, sometimes affects evaporation in a significant way. According to Harding (1942), the rate of evaporation of water decreases about 1 per cent for each 1 per cent increase in salt content until such content reaches about 30 per cent. Sea water "would be expected to have a rate of evaporation about 2 to 3 per cent less than that of similarly exposed fresh water." It would thus seem that in various inland saline waters evaporation is significantly slower than in comparable fresh waters. There appears to be little information available as to the extent to which rate of evaporation is affected by substances in solution in the so-called fresh waters; possibly, for limnological purposes, the effect is commonly negligible.

The removal of heat by vaporization of water in nature goes on more or less continuously and plays an important part in the heat cycle of water and the superimposed air.

Thermal Conductivity. The thermal conductivity of water is very low. If the water of a lake were heated only by conduction from the surface, the whole thermal complex would be radically different. Heating of water artificially by conduction alone would alter man's whole economic scheme. The influence of conduction in the transmission and distribution of heat, compared with certain other factors, is distinctly minor. Heat coming to a lake from the sun is partly absorbed and to some extent conducted, but the really effective heat distribution is due to wind action in agitating the water and, to a much more limited extent, to convection currents.

Convection. When water in a beaker is heated by a flame placed below it, those portions of water first heated expand and rise while the upper, colder, denser (and therefore heavier) portions sink. If the heat supply continues for some time, there are thus set up ascending and descending currents, by means of which heat is carried all through the total water mass. This form of heat distribution is known as *convection*. Most forms of artificial heating of water are of this type. It should be noted, however, that the relation of the sun to a lake surface is just the reverse of that of a beaker and flame, since the source of heat is above instead of below; and it might appear at first thought that no convection currents would result, since the water being heated is already at the surface. However, convection does occur under the following conditions: (1) cooling and sinking of surface water, as when the sun sets and under conditions of falling air temperature; (2) entry of colder water from a surface tributary; (3) cooling of surface water with the passing of autumn into winter; (4) alternations of cloudy and clear skies; (5) alternations of winds and calm; (6) entry of cooler subterranean water at a high level in the basin; (7) advent of a cold rain; and (8) cooling of the surface water by evaporation. These and other possible conditions produce a situation in which convection currents are in action most of the time in surface waters at least during the open season.

Thermal Relations of Ice. When water has reached a temperature of 0°C. and has given up the large amount of latent heat of fusion, it changes its physical state and becomes ice. In so doing, certain other significant thermal changes suddenly come into existence. The ice expands (coefficient of expansion = 1.125), and its density becomes less (0.917), thereby becoming lighter than the underlying water, and hence it floats. The specific heat is only about one-half that of the water from which it was formed (0.505 at temperature 0 to -21°C.), but the thermal conductivity becomes twice as great (0.005). Transmission of sun's heat to the water through the ice in winter will be discussed in another place (page 81), but it should be pointed out here that while it might appear that because of its reduced specific heat and its increased conductivity the ice would facilitate passage of heat from the water to the colder air in winter, only a relatively small amount of heat is actually lost in this way. The thermal conductivity of ice, even though twice that of water, is nevertheless relatively ineffective, and the ice cover seriously interferes with the passage of heat from water to the air.

General Effect of Thermal Relations. It is apparent from the previous discussion that, thermally, water is unique in a number of respects. Upon these unique features rests the explanation of many phenomena in aquatic biology. It is interesting to speculate on the nature of that aquatic world which would have existed if specific heat, latent heat of fusion, and latent heat of evaporation were smaller than they are at present or if density and temperature relations of ice were not as they are. Under present circumstances, water in nature is a great storehouse of heat without at the same time becoming a menace to the adjustments of life to temperature as they now exist.

Thermal Stratification. In the deeper lakes, a seasonal, thermal phenomenon occurs which is so profound and so far-reaching in its influence that it forms, directly and indirectly, the substructure upon which the whole biological framework rests, particularly in the temperate zone. Therefore, a clear understanding of the salient features of *thermal stratification* is a necessity. The cycle of events now to be described is the normal expectation in temperate lakes of the *second order* (page 64). The description will begin arbitrarily with the *spring overturn* (Fig. 8).

Spring Overturn. If a vertical series of temperature records is taken at regular intervals of depth from surface to bottom just before the ice cover goes off, it will be found that the temperature of the water just under the ice is very near the freezing point and that at successive depths it is gradually and very slightly warmer. Bottom-water temperatures differ somewhat in different lakes and according to conditions described later (page 61), but they tend to be near the temperature of maximum density (4°C.). This condition is one in which the *colder but lighter* (less dense) water is on top of *warmer but heavier* water at the bottom. With the coming of spring and its gradually rising air temperatures, the ice begins to disappear, and the surface water rises in temperature. When the *surface* water rises to 4°C., or thereabouts, *heavier water is now produced on top of the lighter water* immediately below, and the former tends to sink through the latter, the mixing often being aided by spring winds. In this process, the underlying colder but lighter water tends to rise to the surface where it, in turn, is warmed up to a temperature of 4°C. and then sinks if there still remains any colder but lighter water below. This continues until the whole lake becomes *homothermous* (of the same temperature throughout from surface to bottom) and therefore of the same density. Being now of the same density throughout, the whole lake, under the influence of spring winds, will circulate or mix from surface to bottom, producing the phenomenon known as the *spring overturn*, or the *spring circulation*. Thermal resistance is at a minimum, and relatively light winds may cause complete circulation. Mixing by convection has become essentially nil, except at night when the surface layer cools and tends to sink, the convection currents so produced playing a part in mixing some of the upper water only. Rise of temperature of the lake to 4°C., after the disappearance of ice, may take place in a few days.

Disappearance of the permanent ice cover of winter now exposes surface water to the atmosphere. Surface water then slowly gains heat. The slightly warmed water, reaching a temperature above 4°C., is *lighter* than the underlying water mass and if immobile will remain at the top.

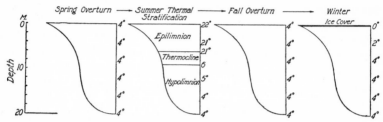

Fɪɢ. 8. Diagrams showing essential temperature relations in a temperate lake of the second order, during the four principal seasons. Numbers to the right of each diagram represent the temperature conditions from surface to bottom expressed in degrees centigrade. Various detailed values used in these diagrams, such as depths, temperature decline in the thermocline, and temperature distribution, differ in different lakes, but the essential features in this seasonal cycle remain the same in temperate lakes of the second order.

However, the difference in density between surface and underlying water is very slight, and resistance to mixing is correspondingly small. This resistance is known as *thermal resistance*. When thermal resistance is small, the amount of work required to mix the lighter, warmer water with the heavier, colder underlying water is minimal. For example, it requires only 0.0067 erg to mix a column of water 1 sq. cm. in transverse area and 1 m. high in which the temperature gradient is uniform and whose upper surface has a temperature of 5°C. and its lower surface a temperature of 4°C. Thus a tiny breeze can stir this lighter water into the heavier water. Heavy winds, common in spring, continue to circulate the whole lake. As the slow heating process at the surface continues and the thermal resistance remains small at all horizontal levels, warmer water may be mixed all the way to the bottom. Consequently, the temperature of bottom water also slowly rises as spring advances. Heat intake at the surface accelerates as spring advances, owing primarily to increasing length of day and increasing verticalness of the sun. Presently, the rate of heat intake by surface water begins to outrun the ability of average winds to continue mixing warmer water into underlying colder waters, thus setting up differences of thermal resistance of increasing magnitude at various horizontal levels. By late spring or early summer these differences in thermal resistance finally become too great to be overcome by existing winds, and mixing of the whole water mass ceases. This marks the end of the spring overturn. During this overturn period the temperature of bottom water may have been built up to a level several degrees above the initial 4°C. For example, in one of the submerged depressions in Douglas Lake, Michigan, bottom temperatures (depth 22 m.) at the end of the spring overturn, period of 1939–1948, were successively as follows: 7.5, 5.4, 6.2, 7.0, 8.3, 6.0, 9.5, 9.7, 7.8, 10.0°C. Thus the initial bottom-water temperature for the subsequent summer stagnation period is determined. On some occasions it may happen in a temperate lake of the second order that, because of unusually vigorous and long protracted wind action, bottom temperature builds up so high that the thermal resistance between top and bottom water is too slight to overcome wind action at the surface. Then circulation of the water mass continues more or less all summer. For example, in Douglas Lake, Michigan, which stratifies thermally in summer with great regularity, peculiar spring meteorological conditions in 1918 built up the bottom temperature to 15°C. in June, thus leaving but a very few degrees difference in temperature between top and bottom, and no stratification occurred during that summer.

Stratification. As stated above, the spring overturn is terminated when accelerating heat intake at the surface leads to the formation of a vertical temperature gradient within which the thermal resistance becomes too great for the existing winds to continue mixing the whole water mass. Then the circulation becomes partial and increasingly confined to the upper water. As the surface-water temperature continues to rise and becomes correspondingly lighter, more and more thermal resistance is offered to a mixing by wind action of surface water with the lower heavier water, until the situation arises when surface-water temperature is much higher than that of underlying water, possibly a difference of 10°C. or more. Then only surface water can be circulated by the wind. Coincident with this situation, or shortly thereafter, a *thermal stratification* comes into existence. A series of vertical temperature records taken at regular and frequent depth intervals from top to bottom, using apparatus suitable for such work, would show (1) the upper layer of the lake, known as the *epilimnion*, in which the water temperature is essentially uniform; (2) a stratum next below, known as the *thermocline* in which there is a phenomenal drop in temperature per unit of depth; and (3) the lowermost region or stratum, known as the *hypolimnion*, in which the temperature from its upper limit to the bottom is nearly uniform.

The transition from spring overturn to thermal stratification is a struggle for supremacy between the two events. It is a direct reflection of events in the atmosphere. Incipient stratification develops only to be dispersed within the next few hours by rising wind. Temporary thermoclines may form, disappear, re-form possibly at some other level, and disappear again. Late in the transition period, two or three thermoclines sometimes form along the same vertical temperature gradient one above the other; these may be broken up by a vigorous storm, or, if weather conditions permit, they may consolidate later to form the permanent thermocline. Occasionally a temporary thermocline may last for several days before it is dispersed.

The dates of beginning and ending of the spring overturn vary from year to year. In Michigan this overturn usually has a duration of about 4 to 6 weeks. In some lakes and under unusual circumstances the overturn may extend much beyond these limits; e.g., the writer has records of spring overturns which lasted 7 to 13 weeks. The long extent of the overturn usually provides ample opportunity for the whole water mass to become thoroughly mixed and circulated.

Occasionally, and under the following special circumstances, an *incomplete* or *partial overturn* may occur: (1) larger inland lakes with unusually great depths, (2) small lakes with depths much greater than ordinary ones, (3) small lakes of ordinary depth under the influence of calm weather and a spring season of rapidly rising air temperatures, and (4) small lakes unusually well sheltered from the wind. In the first instance (1), unusually great depth alone imposes a possible difficulty to a complete mixing at the bottom. The second condition (2) is one in which the area is too small to permit sufficient wind action to produce complete circulation. In the third instance (3), a combination of a calm period with rapidly rising air temperature may cause the surface water to become warm enough, and hence light enough, to make it impossible for subsequent winds to force the upper water very far into the heavier, underlying water. Under the last condition (4), virtual absence of wind action leaves only the mixing due to convection.

EPILIMNION. The epilimnion, being almost homothermous throughout, is the zone of summer circulation. Because of this circulation, any significant changes in air temperatures are followed, to some extent, by the water of the epilimnion, so that there may be periods of thermal rise or fall, within summer limits, of the whole stratum.

THERMOCLINE. The most unique stratum is the *thermocline*. When once formed, the demarcation between epilimnion and thermocline is very distinct. The water of the epilimnion, with its almost uniform temperatures, is rather abruptly succeeded (Fig. 9) by a layer of water in which the fall in temperature throughout its whole thickness is very rapid. This sudden transition from epilimnion to thermocline is often very abrupt. When a series of vertical temperature records taken during conditions of thermal stratification is plotted in the form of a curve, it will be seen that the part of the curve representing the epilimnion rounds off into the part representing the thermocline, so that there is, even in the sharpest of thermocline formations, a small transition stratum. Therefore, any rule to determine the exact position of the upper limit of the thermocline would be arbitrary. However, the need for a standard practice in recording thermocline position led Birge to formulate, about forty-five years ago, the rule which is now widely followed. The essential

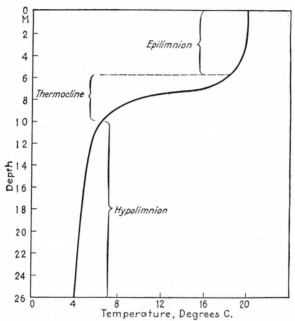

Fig. 9. Curve representing a typical vertical distribution of temperature during the summer stagnation period in a temperate lake of the second order. The form of the curve is characteristic of the usual condition in thermal stratification.

feature of this rule is that where the fall in temperature with increasing depth from the surface is *less than* 1°C. *per m.* (0.548°F. per ft.), that position is still within the epilimnion; but where the temperature decline *becomes* 1°C. *per m. of depth*, that circumstance marks the *upper limit* of the thermocline; and, finally, the *lower limit* of the thermocline is similarly determined but in the reverse order, viz., where the drop in temperature with increasing depth *first becomes less than* 1°C. *per m.* It should be noted that the typical transition from thermocline to hypolimnion is more gradual than that from epilimnion to thermocline, and the demarcation established by the rule described above is to that extent a more arbitrary one.

The fall of temperature within the thermocline varies with different lakes, with different seasons, and with the progress of the summer. Temperature changes as great as 7.8°C. per foot have been recorded, but it is probable that such extreme drops are very rare.   In fact, the author has never met conditions, in many hundreds of temperature records taken on many diverse lakes, in which the temperature fall exceeded about 5.5°C. per foot.   Temperature fall in the thermocline is not uniform but is commonly greater in the upper levels.

The initial date of definite thermal stratification varies with different lakes, with latitude, with altitude, with meteorological differences in the same latitudes, with physiographic characters, with different submerged depressions, and with different seasons.   Seasonal differences in the same lake are often striking, as, for example, in certain northern Michigan lakes, the date of beginning of thermal stratification has varied, during a period of fifteen years, from late May in one season to the last week in July in another.   In the early stages of formation, thermal stratification may appear temporarily, only to disappear again under the influence of increased wind action.   The date of permanent stratification is, to a large extent, determined by the area of the lake, the date usually being earlier in the smaller lakes within the same region.

Ordinarily, the thermocline forms first as a relatively thick stratum, often with its upper limit not very remote from the surface, and the lower limit quite deep.   In Douglas Lake, Michigan, it is not uncommon for the initial thermocline limits to be about 4 to 18 m.   The decline of temperature per unit of depth is less than it will be later in the season, although sufficient to qualify the whole stratum as a thermocline.   Sometimes, the thermocline originates as two or three thermoclines, one above the other, which subsequently fuse to form one thermocline.   Once formed, the thermocline undergoes a gradual seasonal change as the summer progresses.   Its upper limit gradually drops in depth, thus increasing the volume of the epilimnion and reducing the thermocline volume.   Likewise, the lower limit may rise in position for a time, but the amount of rise is usually slight.   In the record mentioned above (initial thermocline position at about 4 to 18 m.), the thermocline position was about 12 to 17 m. by the middle of August, with the concentration still continuing; also the drop in temperature per unit of depth had doubled.   In some instances, this concentration may reduce the thickness of the thermocline to 1 m. or less just before the autumn overturn, and the descent of the upper limit of the thermocline may be such as to increase the epilimnion four or five times its original volume.   Not infrequently, the thermocline manifests, in addition to its concentration, a gradual sinking of its median plane so that the whole thermocline is dropping to a lower and lower depth level, a process which continues until the overturn.   In the subsequent discussion of chemical stratification and its relation to the productivity of the lake (page 125), it will be shown that this sinking of the upper limit of the thermocline has a compensating effect on biological production. It should be noted that there are exceptions to the seasonal history just described, but it represents the ordinary expectation in temperate lakes of the second order.

The general position of the thermocline for the whole summer depends a great deal upon the area over which the wind has full opportunity to exert its influence. In lakes having similar conditions of depth, exposure, altitude, location, and so on, the smaller the surface area the higher the thermocline position. Irregular lakes with long ramifying arms and lakes containing islands of unusual size or number may have a total area of considerable size, but the areas of free wind sweep may be very much reduced and thus actually be less exposed than many smaller lakes; also the thermocline position may be high. In a certain small, ovoid Michigan lake, about 305 × 215 m. and approximately 18 m. in depth, the thermocline position at the end of August, 1926, was 2 to 6 m. In this lake, the epilimnion is of very small volume throughout the season, while the hypolimnion has a relatively large volume.

A *secondary thermocline* is sometimes formed but is never permanent, lasting, ordinarily, but a short time. Such a phenomenon may occur when the primary thermocline is deep and when the epilimnion shows a difference of several degrees of temperature between the surface and its lower limit. Such a thermocline is a thin one, and the drop of temperature per unit of depth is small although sufficient to qualify as thermocline conditions. So far as known, it is always formed above the primary thermocline. As many as three thermocline strata may be present temporarily, when thermal stratification conditions are just taking form.

It must not be assumed that because thermocline formation is found in a certain lake it is an invariable feature. Since meteorological conditions are intimately concerned with thermal stratification, they may actually be of such a nature during the spring and early summer of a particular season as to prevent completely any stratification. There are, of course, all gradations between those lakes which are too shallow to stratify permanently in the summer and those whose depths are such that stratification is certain. Among these intergrades are lakes whose depths are just great enough to establish thermal stratification during a calm spring and summer but which would not stratify during more blustery seasons. Such intermediates would, over an extensive series of years, show about an equal number of stratified and unstratified conditions. However, in lakes whose depth-area relations are such that thermal stratification is the regular expectation, exceptional meteorological conditions may, at more or less rare intervals, prevent stratification completely. In one Michigan lake, whose summer thermal history has been followed carefully, thermal stratification was absent for one out of 37 summers, the exceptional instance being due, apparently, to an unusually regular series of spring and early summer storms, spaced at intervals of about one week and of sufficient vigor to circulate the water and gradually to raise the bottom-water temperature far above the normal condition, so that finally the contrast (thermal resistance) between bottom- and surface-water temperatures was not great enough to prevent summer circulation from affecting the whole lake. The very deep inland lakes are probably never subject to this occasional absence of stratification.

Vertical oscillations of the thermocline are not uncommon. Vertical temperature records taken at regular and frequent intervals sometimes show the upper surface of the thermocline at one level at one time and at another level a short time later. Such oscillations are usually the result of violent summer squalls which pile up surface water on the exposed side of the lake, the increased weight of the water depressing the thermocline locally. When calm follows, the colder, heavier water of the thermocline and hypolimnion returns to its former position as the surface water again seeks its normal level, but in so doing a swing is set up which continues for a time. Thus, the thermocline rises and falls with decreasing amplitude until, with continued calm, it may finally manifest only very minor swings, which may be due to irregular currents in the hypolimnion resulting from the original major movement. These swings of the thermally stratified water constitute a *temperature seiche*.

HYPOLIMNION. One of the principal influences of the thermocline, when once permanently formed, is to isolate the hypolimnion from the epilimnion and its circulation. While it is claimed that under some circumstances a certain amount of water from the epilimnion may be forced down into the hypolimnion and a minor, subthermocline circulation thus set up, the thermocline constitutes an effective barrier against influences or disturbances originating at the surface. Subsurface seiches may swing hypolimnion waters from side to side, and, in those special cases in which subterranean water supplies enter the lake basin below the thermocline, the hypolimnion may show deviations from the usual condition. Alsterberg and others claim that the wind not only causes circulation of the epilimnion but also produces secondary and tertiary horizontal currents in the hypolimnion (Fig. 10). Subthermocline movements are greatly in need of further study.

A small but definite rise of temperature during the summer at the bottom of the hypolimnion has been observed (Welch, 1927) in certain lakes. The increment seems always to be of a gradual nature. The total temperature increase for the season is usually small. In Douglas Lake, Michigan, where it is known to occur, it is not a regular event, but appears to be absent during some summers. No satisfactory explanation of these heat gains is yet available.

Modifications of Thermal Stratification. While the type of thermal stratification just described prevails, so far as is known, for the vast majority of North American temperate lakes of the *first* and *second orders* (page 63), various modifications may occur either temporarily or permanently. Some of them are as follows:

1. Thermocline at the surface. In such an instance, temperature decline of thermocline magnitude begins at the surface, extends to some depth, and gives place to a typical hypolimnion. The epilimnion is thus eliminated. It is sometimes argued that such a condition should not be designated as a thermocline. However, since it is typical in all respects

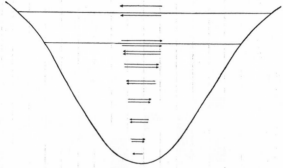

Fig. 10. Diagram representing Alsterberg's conclusions with reference to movements of water in the hypolimnion induced by wind-produced circulation of the epilimnion. (*Redrawn from Alsterberg, 1927.*)

save the presence of its upper limit at the surface, there seems to be some justification in regarding it as a thermocline. The writer has found this phenomenon only as a temporary condition. It is said to appear occasionally as a local and temporary phenomenon in Lake Erie. An extensive calm seems to be a necessary element in the existence of such a situation. Ordinarily, it is of rare occurrence.

2. Diminutive stratification. Under special conditions, very shallow water, sometimes not more than 0.5 m. in depth, may show a typical diminutive thermal stratification. Complete protection from surface disturbance, as, for example, in a small, almost completely inclosed cove, and certain bottom conditions which seemed to function in helping to keep the bottom water cold (large amounts of semisuspended and suspended materials) appear to be important factors in those instances observed by the writer.

3. Partial or complete absence of thermal stratification in lakes having large inflow of cold, heavy, mountain water and large outflow. Certain lakes of northern Italy are said to lack the typical thermal stratification for this reason.

4. Submerged depression individuality. In lake basins which contain, in the general basin, isolated depressions separated completely from each other by relatively shallow water, it may happen that each depression acts as a separate unit or as if it were a separate lake, except that all such depressions in the same lake possess essentially the same epilimnion. Each depression may have its own thermocline which differs in position and thickness in the different depressions, and each depression may have

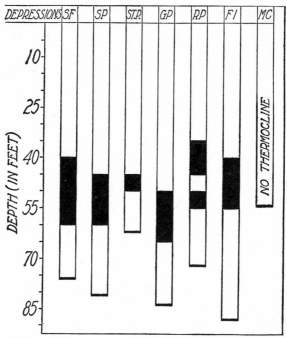

FIG. 11. Diagram showing depression individuality in thermal stratification as exemplified in Douglas Lake, Michigan, Aug. 12, 1922. Each vertical column represents a vertical section through the region of maximum depth of each of the seven, isolated, submerged depressions within the main lake basin. Shaded blocks in each column indicate the positions of the thermocline. Each depression is acting independently. Letters at top of columns are abbreviations for names of the depressions. One depression (*RP*) shows both a primary and a secondary thermocline on this date.

its own individual seasonal history. Furthermore, certain depressions may stratify thermally, while certain ones nearby and of similar depth and exposure may not stratify at all. Douglas Lake, Michigan (Fig. 11), manifests this depression individuality in a striking way in its six, major, submerged depressions, and instances in other lakes are now known. Obviously, temperature records made in one depression of a multiple-depression lake basin would not give a correct picture of conditions in that lake.

Terminology of Thermal Stratification. The terms *epilimnion* and *hypo-*

limnion were first proposed by Birge in 1910 and have had almost universal adoption in work on lakes, but several names are applied to the thermocline. The term *thermocline* was first used by Birge in 1897 as equivalent to the German term *Sprungschicht* employed earlier by Richter. Later, Wedderburn proposed the term *discontinuity layer.* Since then, the terms *transition zone, mesolimnion,* and *metalimnion* have been proposed. It is sometimes referred to in French as the *couche de saut thermique.* However, the term *thermocline* is now so widely used that it will probably continue to be the approved designation.

Since the terms epilimnion and hypolimnion, because of their derivation, are not strictly applicable to the sea where thermal stratification is occasionally found, Atkins (1925) has proposed the term *epithalassa* for the upper stratum and *hypothalassa* for the lowest stratum of the sea but retaining the term *thermocline* for the intermediate stratum.

Summer Stagnation Period. When thermal stratification is permanently established, the lake enters upon what is known as the *summer stagnation period,* so named, probably, because the water of the hypolimnion becomes "stagnated" for the summer and at least part of the autumn. Birge has expressed the condition of the summer stagnation period as follows:

During the summer, then, our typical northern lakes really consist of two lakes, one superimposed on the other: first, the lake above the thermocline, whose temperature is high and whose water is kept in active movement by the wind; and below this, the stagnant mass of water below the thermocline, having a low temperature, denser and more viscous than the upper water, in which the gaseous and other products of decomposition are accumulating and from which they are only slowly and partially discharged.

The chemical and other changes which result from this stagnation will be described later (page 124).

Fall Overturn. With the passing of summer and early autumn, declining air temperatures begin to cause a cooling of the surface waters of the lake. Water thus cooled and rendered heavier sinks, and convection currents are set up so that the temperature throughout the epilimnion is equalized and lowered. This lowering of temperature progresses until the epilimnion comes to have as low temperature as has the upper part of the thermocline; then successively it attains the same temperature as the various deeper levels in the thermocline, and finally it drops to the same temperature level as the hypolimnion, and then the whole lake becomes homothermous and consequently of the same density. Conditions are now such that wind action can circulate the water from top to bottom, with the result that the whole lake takes on a uniform character in all of its various strata.

If the hypolimnion maintains during the summer a temperature higher than 4°C., the overturn will begin when the water of the epilimnion and thermocline falls to that higher temperature, but the circulation will continue while the whole lake cools down to 4°C. by the formation, sinking, and mixing of colder, heavier water at the surface. Essentially, the fall overturn is a repetition of the spring overturn, the only outstanding difference being that the former is terminated by declining air temperatures and not by increasing temperatures. That the total mass of water is stirred thoroughly in a complete, typical overturn is clearly demonstrated by the resulting physical, chemical, and, to a certain extent, biological uniformity of the water during the period of the overturn.

Like the spring overturn, the fall overturn usually continues for a considerable but variable period. In Michigan lakes the period is known to have a variation of 3 to 8 weeks. Its duration depends upon the general rate of decline of air temperatures. Seasons vary greatly with respect to the date of onset of ice cover. Delayed ice cover usually results in prolonged fall overturn. A fall-overturn period of several weeks and the usual autumn winds ensure that again the lake is thoroughly mixed from top to bottom.

Winter Stagnation Period. Declining air temperatures in early winter lower the temperature of the surface water until it falls below 4°C., after which the water becomes *colder* but progressively *lighter*. Being lighter, it no longer sinks but remains at the surface. When compared with the summer stagnation period, the *temperature* conditions are just the reverse—the *warmer* water is at the bottom with the cold water on top—but with respect to *density* the conditions are the same, i.e., the *lighter* water is at the top. Ultimately, the permanent ice cover forms on the surface and blankets off the lake completely from wind disturbances; then the whole lake resembles, in a general way, the hypolimnion of the summer stagnation period.

Coleman (1922) describes the consequences which would result if that peculiar property of water of becoming *lighter instead of heavier* on cooling below 4°C. were absent as follows:

If water followed the usual law when cooled below 39.2° (4°C.), it would sink to the bottom instead of remaining at the surface, and at length the whole body of water would reach the freezing point of 32° (0°C.), when ice would be formed and, being heavier than water, would accumulate at the bottom. During a long winter, the whole lake would be transformed into a solid block of ice . . . Some of the surface ice would thaw in the summer, but in deep lakes the lower parts would be perpetually frozen.

A very thin layer of water just below the ice is near freezing temperature, and, for a relatively short distance below, the rise in temperature is rapid, up to about 3°C. From that point on to the bottom, the rise in temperature may be very slight. This vertical temperature distribution, when plotted in the usual way, gives a graph which in mere form has a certain resemblance to the curve of thermal distribution during the summer stagnation period, except that the curve is reversed and lacks the epilimnion portion. This condition is sometimes spoken of as an *inverse stratification*, but it falls far short of the stratification of the summer period, and it is an open question whether it should be referred to as a true stratification.

The temperature of the bottom waters, during this period, depends upon local circumstances. In the deeper lakes, it tends to be at or near the temperature of maximum density (4.0°C.); in shallow lakes, it is likely to be colder than 4°C., although exceptions may occur. Gain of heat through the ice and exchange of heat with the basin will be discussed later (pages 71, 72). Certain very important, far-reaching chemical and biological changes occur during the winter stagnation period which, in some respects, represent a close parallel to those of the summer stagnation period. These will also be described in a subsequent chapter (page 130).

Thermal Stratification in the Great Lakes and Larger Bodies of Water. That large bodies of water tend to manifest thermal stratification seems evident from what is now known. However, the great mass of water makes possible certain influences not present to any important degree in inland lakes, as, for example, the much greater depths to which wave action may extend, and the existence of vertical currents of considerable magnitude. Such influences, particularly the large vertical currents, interrupt a thermal stratification or prevent it from forming. While the whole subject of thermal stratification in vast bodies of water is still in a formative stage, it appears that in such waters there is no continuous thermocline extending from one shore to the other, as is the case in the inland lakes of the first and second orders, but instead it is formed only in certain regions. A well-defined thermocline was found in the eastern portion of Lake Erie (Parmenter, 1929) and in Lake Michigan (Church 1942, 1945). Eddy (1943) found no thermocline in western Lake Superior. Regional thermoclines may occur at certain times and places, in the Great Lakes. Some idea of temperature conditions in certain of the Great Lakes may be obtained from the fact that summer records from the deeper parts show bottom temperatures at or *very near* 4°C.; also that the surface waters of Lakes Ontario, Erie, Michigan, and Huron usually warm up in summer to about 20°C. (variations in both directions) so that the difference between bottom and surface temperature is ample for the formation of thermal stratification, whenever the disturbing influences of such vast lakes will permit. In Lake Superior, surface temperatures in summer are ordinarily somewhat lower, but even there regional thermal stratification may occur.

It has been found that the temperature of the lowermost water in certain deep lakes is *below* 4°C. Kemmerer, Bovard, and Boorman (1923) reported that in Crater Lake, Oregon, the water temperatures decreased from 3.9° at 100 m. depth to 3.5°C. at 600 m. depth. Similar phenomena have long been known for the very deep waters of certain European lakes, and similar ones have been found in the Great Lakes (Wright, 1931; Eddy, 1943) and in certain Japanese lakes (Yoshimura, 1932). Without doubt, this reduction of temperature below 4°C. is the result of pressure. Physicists have already established the fact that water at maximum density under pressure exhibits temperatures below 4°. However, since the abyssal temperatures are not so low as those which accompany the physical effects of pressure on pure water under experimental conditions, deep-water temperatures may be the outcome of pressure modified by other influences not yet understood.

It is interesting to note here that thermal stratification occurs, at least to a limited extent, in the oceans. It is a well-developed phenomenon in the English Channel where a definite thermocline occurs at times during the summer; also in October or November, the waters become homothermous from top to bottom. Oceanographic literature contains several records of vertical temperature distribution in the open ocean which when plotted in the usual way yield curves whose shape is that of a typical thermal stratification curve. Hentschel reported a thermocline in the Atlantic Ocean at a depth of 100 m.

Thermal Stratification in Tropical Lakes. It has been reported (Ruttner, 1931) that in tropical East India (Java, Sumatra, and elsewhere), smaller lakes with areas of about 0.4 to 0.8 sq. mile have distinct thermoclines but that in larger lakes where the wind action has greater effect, thermal stratification is less marked. It should be noted, however, that while it is claimed that thermal stratification occurs, and while Ruttner's curves are so drawn that they have the characteristic shape of an epilimnion-thermocline-hypolimnion curve, the fall in temperature within the region referred to as the thermocline fails to qualify as a thermocline under Birge's rule (temperature decline of 1°C. or more per meter). During the period over which these lakes were studied by Ruttner, the contrast between bottom and surface temperatures was only about 4.5°C., sometimes less, even in lakes of considerable depths. The thermal resistance is, therefore, small, and this so-called thermal stratification is easily eliminated by wind action. If Ruttner's curves had been so drawn that the space units on both ordinates and abscissas were of equal dimension, as is commonly done, the curves would have little resemblance to those representing a typical thermal stratification. Examinations of tropical African lakes (Worthington and Beadle, 1932) have demonstrated no thermoclines in large ones, such as Lake Rudolph, Lake Victoria Nyanza, and others, although in one large lake (Lake Edward; area, 580 sq. miles;

depth, 117 m.), a definite thermocline at 40 to 66 m. was found. But this is interpreted by the discoverers not as a true thermocline but as due to a heavier layer of more saline water introduced by rivers from surrounding volcanic regions or from underground sources and prevented from mixing by its greater density.

A few limnologists find objections to Birge's definition of the limits of a thermocline. Some of them contend that a stratum of water, irrespective of the amount of fall of temperature within it, be it ever so slight, which contains sufficient density difference (thermal resistance) to establish any kind of thermal stratification should be designated as a thermocline. Such an interpretation provides no specific limits and inevitably leads to uncertainty. An extreme departure from common usage is that of Hutchinson (1941) who, apparently for certain purposes at least, prefers to regard the thermocline as a *plane* chosen at the lower termination of the epilimnion. It seems likely that some of the reported occurrences of thermal stratification in tropical lakes and elsewhere were based upon unusual criteria for identifying thermoclines.

Modified Thermal Stratification. Many departures from typical thermal stratification have been described. They arise from the great array of conditions under which lakes exist. Names have been given to some of these atypical temperature conditions, as, for example: *Dichothermy*— summer stratification with minimum temperature at some intervening level, sometimes in upper part of hypolimnion, instead of the usual minimum at bottom; sometimes called *temperature-inversion phenomenon;* may be either temporary or permanent. *Mesothermy*—maximum temperature at some intervening level; may occur in late summer or early autumn; temporary. *Poikilothermy*—both maximum and minimum temperatures in some intervening layer; said to occur on warm days following a cool period; temporary.

Classification of Lakes. Various classifications of lakes have been proposed, but perhaps the most satisfactory one has grown out of that developed by Forel and later modified by Whipple.[1] It is as follows:

I. Polar lakes.—Surface temperatures never above 4°C.
    Order 1.   Bottom water at 4°C. throughout year; one circulation period possible in summer, usually none.
    Order 2.   Temperature of bottom water varies but not far from 4°C.; one circulation period in summer.
    Order 3.   Temperature of bottom water very similar to that of surface water; circulation more or less continuous except when frozen.
II. Temperate lakes.—Surface temperatures vary above and below 4°C.
    Order 1.   Temperature of bottom water at 4°C. throughout year; two circulation periods possible (one in spring and one in autumn), often none.

[1] From "The Microscopy of Drinking Water," 4th ed., John Wiley & Sons, Inc., 1927.

Order 2. Temperature of bottom water varies but not far from 4°C.; two circulation periods (one in spring and one in autumn).

Order 3. Temperature of bottom water very similar to that of surface water; circulation continuous except when frozen.

III. Tropical lakes.—Surface temperatures always above 4°C.

Order 1. Temperature of bottom water near 4°C. throughout year; one circulation period possible in winter.

Order 2. Temperature of bottom water varies but not far from 4°C.; one circulation period in winter.

Order 3. Temperature of bottom water very similar to that of surface water; circulation practically continuous throughout year.

It must be understood that while such a classification may be very useful as a means of organizing the typical cases, there are all sorts of intergrades between the various groups mentioned, even in the same general region. Also circumstances, such as altitude, and special forms of exposure and of protection may set up modifications of the thermal conditions in lakes. This classification is, therefore, useful to the extent that it deals with the general average expectation in different types of lakes.

Attempts have been made in the past to add certain *depth* distinctions to the above classification, as, for example, to attach a general depth value of over 200 ft. to order 1, over 25 ft. to order 2, and under 25 ft. to order 3. So utterly arbitrary are these values and so numerous are the instances in which they would be of no use that not only do they add nothing to the classification but they actually detract from its value.

Heat Budgets of Lakes. Temperature changes in lake water are the result of two sets of processes. The following list is modified from a similar one by Sverdrup, Johnson, and Fleming (1942):

Addition of Heat	Loss of Heat
1. Radiation from sun and sky	1. Evaporation
2. Condensation of water vapor	2. Convection to atmosphere
3. Convection from atmosphere	3. Convection to lake basin
4. Convection from lake basin	4. Back radiation from lake surface to atmosphere
5. Heat from chemical changes	
6. Heat from friction in water movements	

Radiation from sun and sky is by far the most important of the heating processes. On the other hand, quantitative information on heat generated in chemical changes and heat resulting from friction in water movements is obscure or wanting, but the supposition is that these sources of heat are minor and, for limnological purposes, may be disregarded. The other three heat sources are variable, depending upon local and seasonal circumstances. They may be regarded as intermediate in importance. Of the heat-loss processes, evaporation is much more effective than the other three.

Since the heat content of a lake is a matter of vital importance in limnology, methods of determining *heat budgets* are necessary. The following discussion is taken from the work of Birge (1915, 1916).

Three things may be understood by the heat budget of a lake:

1. The amount of heat necessary to raise its water from 0°C. to the maximum temperature found in summer. This may be called the *gross* or *crude heat budget*.

2. The amount of heat necessary to raise its water from the minimum temperature of winter to the maximum summer temperature. This may be called the *annual heat budget*.

3. The amount of heat necessary to raise its water from 4°C. to the maximum summer temperature. This may be called . . . the *wind-distributed heat*, or the *summer heat income*.

Since lakes do not have bottom temperatures so low as 0°C., the first statement is of least importance. The second statement, representing as it does the two limits of heat content for the particular lake under consideration, is fundamentally the most valuable of the three conceptions. It involves, of course, the necessity of having available the necessary winter temperature data which, unfortunately, are often lacking. The third conception is, therefore, useful for those lakes whose winter temperatures are unknown. It applies only to the temperate lakes of Forel's classification and has no significance for polar lakes which do not rise above 4°; furthermore, in the tropical lakes it has certain obvious difficulties. Since the 4°C. point represents a very important position in the temperature cycle of a temperate lake, this method of approaching the heat budgets is of value.

Computation of heat budgets may be made on the following bases (Birge):

1. The number of calories necessary to warm a column of water of unit base in the deepest part of the lake from the selected minimum (0°, 4°, winter minimum) to the summer temperature.

2. The total sum of the calories necessary to warm in a similar way the whole mass of the water of the lake from the selected minimum to the summer temperature.

3. The total number of calories necessary to warm in a similar way a column of water of unit base and a height equal to the mean depth of the lake.

Birge computed heat budgets as follows when the lake is considered as a unit:

Annual heat budget $= Dm(Tm^s - Tm^w)$.

Wind-distributed heat $= Dm(Tm^s - 4)$.

where Dm = mean depth of lake in centimeters.

Tm^s = mean summer temperature in degrees centigrade.

Tm^w = mean winter temperature in degrees centigrade.

The results are expressed in gram calories.

Unfortunately, heat budgets have received far too little attention in the past, and so few lakes have been studied with regard to this matter that dependable conclusions of a general nature are still lacking. That they form an important method of comparing lakes with respect to heat content has already been demonstrated. Lakes, as a group, show wide differences in heat budgets; therefore it is essential that when comparisons are made, only those lakes which are strictly comparable should be considered. Birge, the pioneer in this work in America, chose to approach the problem by selecting a group of lakes which he designated as the "first class" and which he defined as those lakes

. . . whose size and depth are such as to permit the lake to acquire the maximum amount of heat possible under the weather conditions of the season. The lower limits for such lakes in the eastern and central United States seem to be about 10 km. of length with, at least, 2 km. of breadth; and 30 m. of mean depth, which means 50 m. or more of maximum depth. Such lakes must also lie under ordinary conditions of topography and altitude. Lakes whose conditions of climate or location are exceptional, such as those of alpine lakes at considerable elevations, cannot be compared directly with those in lower and more normal situations.

It was found (Birge and Juday, 1914) that such lakes in eastern United States have heat budgets which ordinarily equal or exceed 30,000 g.-cal. per sq. cm. of the lake's surface and ordinarily lie between 30,000 and 40,000 g.-cal. Birge, in a critical comparison of 7 American and 26 European lakes, selected to conform as nearly as possible to the specifications of the first class mentioned above, came to several general conclusions, among them being the following:

1. In a lake of simple form, the mean temperature of the water "may be derived from a single series of observations taken at or near the center of oscillation of the water."

2. It appears that American lakes in the latitude of 43°N. have higher and more uniform heat budgets than corresponding European ones.

3. "There is no evidence that the annual heat budget increases with latitude within the limits of the zone between 40 and 60°N. Still further, the data from these lakes do not show that a temperate lake has a larger heat budget than a tropical lake of comparable area and depth."

It must be remembered that these guarded conclusions were made on the basis of the then available evidence and that, after all, the number of lakes concerned in the comparison was very small, particularly the American lakes. Without doubt, a considerable number of factors enter into the problem as determiners of differences in the heat budgets of lakes. Also, the same is true of the production of variations in the heat budget of a single lake for different seasons. Stromsten (1927) has found evidence that in Lake Okoboji, Iowa, the summer heat income, when considered for a period of several years, seems to follow a sort of cycle, possibly having a certain correspondence with the local climatic conditions which also appear to be more or less cyclic in nature. Other work has been done with heat budgets on American lakes, but it is still too small in amount to be of much service.

Work of the Wind in Warming a Lake. It should be recalled that after the disappearance of the ice cover in spring and after the surface-water temperatures rises above 4°C., the surface water becomes gradually lighter and offers a certain *thermal resistance* to mixing with the colder, heavier

TABLE 4. HEAT BUDGETS OF A SELECTED GROUP OF LAKES
Compiled from Birge, Scott, and others

Lake	Location	Annual heat budget	Wind-distributed heat
Canandaigua...................	New York	......	25,400
Cayuga.......................	New York	37,450	27,750
Keuka........................	New York	......	23,750
Owasco.......................	New York	35,600	27,700
Seneca........................	New York	36,700	31,300
Skaneateles...................	New York	39,100	27,950
Green........................	Wisconsin	34,000	26,200
Karluk.......................	Alaska	33,500	18,900
Manitou......................	Indiana	......	5,361
Big Barbee...................	Indiana	......	10,563
Yellow Creek.................	Indiana	......	11,458
Okoboji......................	Iowa	......	20,849
Bolsena......................	Italy	31,600	
Como.........................	Italy	32,000	
Bourget......................	France	31,950	34,600
Geneva.......................	Switzerland	36,600	
Zürich.......................	Switzerland	21,800	20,200
Constance....................	Switzerland	23,200	22,400
Zug..........................	Switzerland	31,300	38,900
Traun........................	Austria	33,400	32,100
Würm........................	Germany	23,800	20,700
Ness.........................	Scotland	37,200	
Vettern......................	Sweden	32,000	16,200
Ladoga.......................	Russia	33,300	18,000

water underneath. While, as already explained elsewhere, temporary cooling of the surface resulting from cold nights or cold waves in the atmospheric temperatures may produce convection currents and thus accomplish some insignificant mixing, the *warming up* of a lake in spring and early summer is due largely to work which the wind performs in forcing the warmer, lighter, surface water into the colder, heavier, underlying water. This work of the wind is therefore work done against gravity, and its amount depends upon the contrast in temperature (and therefore density) between the surface layer and the underlying one. Water at any depth having a temperature above 4°C. owes its heat to the work of the wind (Fig. 12). This work has been performed in numerous stages, and the "net amount of work may be represented by the amount of energy necessary to push down through the water at its maximum density a stratum of water of the smallest density possessed by the water." Birge has developed methods for computing this work,

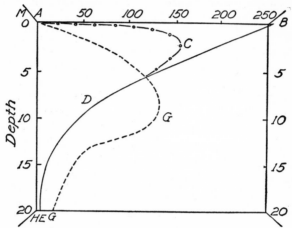

Fig. 12. Work curves of Lake Okoboji, Iowa, showing (1) the direct work, (2) the distributed work, and (3) the effect of the sun in distributing the sun's energy (direct isolation). The vertical axis indicates depth; the horizontal axis shows gram centimeters of work per meter of depth and square centimeters of surface of lake. *AGG* is the curve of direct work. About 130 g.cm. of work, for example, are necessary to carry the heat of the 9–10 meter stratum from the surface and put it in place. *BDE* is the curve of distributed work, derived from *AGG*, and shows the amount of work done in each 1 m. stratum. The entire area enclosed by the curve of distributed work, *ABDEHA*, is equal to that enclosed by the curve of direct work, *AGGHA*. The area *ACDBA* gives the direct effect of the sun, and the area *ACDEHA* that of the wind. (*Redrawn from Birge and Juday*, 1920.)

when the necessary conditions are known, and shows by mathematical analyses that it is *in direct proportion to the difference in density.* It is true that as the temperature of surface water rises, thus decreasing its density, a wind of a selected velocity becomes much more effective in moving the surface water, but the essential feature in this discussion is not the ease or difficulty of moving surface water but, instead, the ease and difficulty of *mixing* the lighter surface water with underlying heavier water or, in other words, of overcoming *thermal resistance*, which is a very different thing. When surface water has risen to 10°C., after the spring overturn when the mean temperature was about 4°C., the thermal resistance is ten times as great as at the overturn; also, the thermal resistance is about twenty-five times as great when the surface temperature rises to 20°C. The relative ease with which the wind circulates the water in spring is thus explained, in spite of the fact that water is heaviest at that time; also, the effectiveness and behavior of the thermocline are thus understandable. Obviously, the steeper the temperature gradient in a thermocline the greater the total work required to produce a mixing with superimposed, lighter waters. Furthermore, it must be remembered that at the junction of epilimnion and thermocline, increase in density is abrupt.

Since water is an exceedingly mobile liquid, it is obvious that if it could undergo changes of temperature without affecting its density, the whole story of thermal relations in lakes would be profoundly different. Change of density with change of temperature constitutes a very effective barrier to unrestricted distribution of surface temperatures.

It must be remembered, at this point, that if difference in density were the only opposing influence to mixing by wind action, water would be a *perfect fluid,* i.e., without internal friction. However, it has already been pointed out that not only does water have a viscosity but this viscosity increases distinctly with falling temperatures. In fact, the viscosity of water just before freezing is about twice that of surface water at ordinary, midsummer temperatures. Thus, it appears that viscosity also offers a certain resistance to movement by wind and thus to mixing; and while the actual amount of viscosity at any temperature is very small compared to that of other more viscous liquids, yet it does have an influence even though a slight one. According to Birge,

. . . it has been impossible to find a quantitative relation between *thermal resistance* and viscosity so as to ascertain exactly how much the increase of the latter at low temperature would affect the influence of the wind. . . . The present question is one of the relative influence of viscosity at different temperatures, and the viscosity plainly increases far more slowly at low temperatures than thermal resistance diminishes . . . Since the influence of the wind will vary as the square of its velocity, the greater amount of wind in the spring will more than compensate for the increase in viscosity.

In consideration of all of these matters, it is imperative that an understanding of the relation of work by wind action (1) to viscosity, (2) to density *per se*, and (3) to thermal resistance (*contrasting* densities) be free from confusion, since they are all very distinct influences.

Warming Due to Penetration of Sun's Rays. While the major part of the warming of a lake is due to the work of wind, it must not be assumed that all warming is thus produced, since some heat is delivered directly into the uppermost layer of water by the penetration of solar radiation and its absorption by the water, a process known as *insolation.* This means that wind-produced currents which transfer heat to deeper waters do not secure this heat at the surface only but find it already delivered at various distances below the surface down to the limit of direct solar heat penetration. Of the large amount of sun's heat available at the surface, some is reflected by the surface film and some of it enters the water. Of that which enters the water, part is consumed in evaporation, part is returned to the air, and part is distributed by wind to underlying layers. Birge and Juday (1931), by the use of a specially devised instrument, the pyrlimnometer, made extensive studies on Wisconsin lakes and found that most of the radiation which enters an inland lake is consumed by the uppermost stratum. In extreme cases, practically none is transmitted deeper than 2 to 4 m., and in such lakes the direct heating effect of the sun is confined to a very thin stratum. Measurements made on 72 lakes showed that the depths at which the total solar radiation was reduced to 1 per cent varied from 1.5 to 29.9 m. The instance of 1 per cent at 29.9 m. was evidently very exceptional, since no other lake showed a maximum of more than 16.3 m. They propose the following tentative classification of 68 Wisconsin lakes on the basis of solar radiation:

TABLE 5. CLASSIFICATION OF WISCONSIN LAKES ON BASIS OF SOLAR RADIATION
From Birge and Juday

Transmission[1]	Lakes	
	Number	Per cent
Low, 0–30	8	12
Low-medium, 31–50	14	20
High-medium, 51–70	34	50
High, 71 and above	12	18

[1] The term *transmission* means the percentage of transmission of radiation through a stratum of water 1 m. thick.

The main factors which determine transmission are

. . . (1) the selective action of water, which is transparent to short-wave radiation and opaque to long waves; (2) the selective effect of stain which acts more strongly on the short-wave radiation and is effective in proportion to the amount and kind present; (3) the action of suspended matter—organic and inorganic—which offers more obstruction to short-wave radiation, but is not definitely selective.

The 1- to 2-m. stratum was almost always found to have a more reduced transmission than the deeper strata, owing, probably, to the greater abundance of plankton in the upper water. Contrary to the usual impression, it was found that waves made no noticeable difference in the amount of reflected energy, as compared with the reflection from the surface of smooth water.

It thus appears that the surface-water stratum of 1 m. depth absorbs a very large part of the incident radiation. The solar radiation below a depth of 1 m. is practically all in the form of light. Even pure water, which does not occur in nature, absorbs more than 50 per cent of the radiation in the first meter of depth. Also, the effect of the water itself, not considering for the moment the additional effects of stain and suspended matters, is to eliminate rapidly all radiation from wave lengths greater than 6000 Å. Therefore, while the sun performs a certain function in warming a lake by direct insolation, it is confined to the surface layers, and often to a thin surface stratum, leaving the great bulk of the work of warming the lower strata to the efforts of the wind. It becomes obvious that the sun, by direct radiation, gives a relatively larger aid in a shallow lake than in a deeper one. In Wisconsin lakes, and possibly to a large extent in all lakes, the transparency or the opacity of the water makes little or no difference in the heat budget, a fact which indicates clearly the preeminence of wind as the means of distributing heat within a lake.

Heat Exchanges between Water and Basin. When water stands in an ordinary laboratory container, the temperature of both water and container tends to become the same; if heat is applied to the exposed surface of the water, and the latter is stirred somewhat to facilitate the distribution of the heat, some heat will, in turn, be transmitted to the container, thereby raising its temperature. If, on the other hand, ice is placed in the water, or much colder water is added, the whole mass of water is cooled, and subsequently heat will pass from the walls of the container into the water. This rough example indicates the general nature of a heat exchange which occurs between the water of a lake and its basin at certain times of year. Since a lake secures its heat at and through its surface, and since, as already described, there is an annual income and outgo of heat in the total water mass, it would be expected that the bottom deposits of a lake, especially those in the shallower parts of the basin, would gain heat from the water during the spring and summer and lose heat to the overlying water during autumn and winter. Bottom deposits have a certain power to pass heat through their materials by conduction. We owe our knowledge of this subject to the work of Birge and Juday, who, by means of a specially devised apparatus known as a *mud thermometer*, have secured an actual measure of these heat exchanges in Lake Mendota, Wisconsin. Temperature records were secured at four stations in the lake, having water depths of 8, 12, 18, and 23.5 m., respectively. Such records were made once, sometimes twice, a month throughout the year and at depths beginning with the surface of the bottom mud and extending through 5 m. at depth intervals of 0.5 to 1 m. The following data selected from the tables of Birge and Juday indicate the nature of these heat changes.

TABLE 6. TEMPERATURE AT DIFFERENT LEVELS IN THE BOTTOM DEPOSITS OF LAKE
MENDOTA, WIS.

The values represent the mean of observations made during 1918, 1919, and 1920

Data from Birge and Juday

Depth of lake at selected station, m.	Date	Surface of mud	Depths in mud, m.						
			0.5	1.0	1.5	2.0	3.0	4.0	5.0
			Temperature, degrees Centigrade						
8	Dec. 15	2.3	5.7	8.3	9.8	11.0	11.5	11.1	10.6
	Aug. 1	22.3	20.1	16.5	13.3	11.6	9.7	9.2	9.4
12	Dec. 15	2.2	5.5	7.9	9.4	10.1	10.1	9.5	9.3
	July 15	15.3	12.8	11.2	9.9	9.0	8.6	8.7	8.8
18	Jan. 1	1.8	4.4	6.4	7.7	8.5	8.8	8.5	8.6
	Oct. 1	12.5	11.0	9.8	9.1	8.6	8.1	7.8	7.8
23.5	Jan. 1	2.8	5.1	7.0	7.9	8.3	8.7	8.6	8.2
	Oct. 1	11.5	10.5	9.6	8.9	8.5	8.0	7.8	7.8

It was found that the *bottom heat budgets* were approximately as follows:
at 8 m., 3,000 cal.; at 12 m., 2,200 cal.; at 18 m., 1,100 cal.; and at 23.5 m.,
1,100 cal. From these results, it was calculated that the mean annual
heat budget for the bottom of Lake Mendota was, in round numbers,
2,000 cal. per sq. cm. of its surface. Since the average annual heat
budget for the water of the lake was found to be 23,000 to 24,000 cal., it
now becomes necessary to add about 2,000 cal. to this amount to represent
the heat which goes into the bottom. About 8 to 9 per cent of the entire
heat budget goes into the bottom. The heat losses of the mud to the
water in late winter can be stated in the same way. The heat lost was as
follows: 8 m., 1,040 cal.; 12 m., 600 cal.; 18 m., 300 cal.; 23.5 m., 300 cal.
The mean result is a loss of approximately 650 cal. per square centimeter
of surface.

Gain of Heat through Ice. Results from Lake Mendota also give
information on the gain of heat through the ice in winter. During the
period of ice cover, this lake gains steadily in heat, the average amount
being about 20 cal. per sq. cm. of surface per day during the winter.
From the foregoing discussion, it appears that a certain part of this gain
in heat comes from the bottom, but Birge and Juday found that the
bottom-heat exchange accounts for only about one-fourth of the total
gain. Of the remaining three-fourths, a small part may possibly be
attributed to inflowing water, but the major part comes from the sun

through the ice, a contributing source which becomes more effective as winter passes into spring.

Light

One of the most obvious and familiar properties of water is its transparency. Natural waters manifest great differences in the degree to which sunlight can illuminate them. The extremely turbid waters of the Missouri River and some of its tributaries offer striking contrast to those mountain lakes in which light penetrates to unusual depths. Also, many natural waters show seasonal and irregular variations, due to several possible causes, in the degree to which they permit passage of light. Light exerts a very profound influence upon a whole series of biological phenomena in water, but, despite its fundamental importance, inherent difficulties involved in the perfection of methods and instruments for measuring light in water, qualitatively and quantitatively, have long resisted solution, and this subject is still among the least satisfactorily known of the important limnological influences.

Light Penetration and Light Absorption. *Methods of Measurement.* Limit of Visibility Methods. Secchi's Disk. In 1865, A. Secchi of Rome, Italy, devised a method for studying the transparency of the waters of the Mediterranean Sea. It consisted in lowering into the water a white plate, 20 cm. in diameter, on a graduated rope, noting the depth at which the plate disappeared, then lifting the plate and noting the depth at which it reappeared. The average of these two readings on the graduated rope was considered the limit of visibility. Later, Forel used the same method, employing either a white zinc disk or a white crockery plate, and pointed out conditions under which such tests should be made to secure best results. This method was subsequently used by many investigators. Whipple modified the method by dividing the disk into quadrants and painting them in such a way that two of the quadrants which were directly opposite to each other were black and the intervening ones white. He also increased the efficiency of the method by viewing the disk, as it sank in the water, through a water telescope held under a sunshade.

This method has come into a wide use as a means of comparing different waters. Obviously, it is not an actual measure of light penetration, but, instead, merely a useful, rough index of visibility when used under standard conditions. It is also useful in making comparisons of the same waters at different times. See Welch (1948) for further information.

Geneva Commission Method. In 1883, the Physical Society of Geneva Switzerland, established a committee for the study of transparency in Lake Geneva. This committee made use of a method the essential feature of which is the substitution of an incandescent lamp for the white disk of Secchi.   The point of disappearance of the bright spot (the lamp) was designated as the *limit of clear vision,* while the subsequent disappearance at a lower level of the last vestige of the surrounding glow of diffused light was specified as the *limit of diffused light.*   This method has the same limitations as that of Secchi's disk, and it has had a very restricted use.

PHOTOGRAPHIC METHODS.   Early Methods.   In 1873, Forel, hoping to make use of the well-known fact that silver chloride (a white precipitate) blackens when exposed to light, tried lowering a bottle of this substance into water for known depths and exposures, but the results were not satisfactory.   He later devised small, square frames which could be suspended horizontally on a rope and in each of which a sheet of sensitized albumen paper was so placed that one-half of its surface was exposed and one-half was protected against light action.   This equipment, lowered into the lake at night and brought up the next night, enabled the observer not only to determine the depth at which no light effect occurred on the photographic paper, but also some effect of light intensity at different depths was distinguishable in the degree of change in the sensitive paper. Not only did the exposed and unexposed portions of the sheet provide means of judging degree of light effect, but an additional aid was devised in the form of a photographic intensity scale made by exposing sheets of the same paper to sunlight, in air, for different lengths of time.   Certain other devices and modifications were employed by Forel, Asper, *et al.,* which need not be reviewed here.

During the three decades succeeding the work of Forel, many photochemical devices were invented the more important of which have been discussed by Klugh (1925).   Many of these early instruments are preserved in the Oceanographical Museum of Monaco and afford an interesting picture of the evolution of effort in this direction.   While increasing perfection and ingenuity of method are exhibited in this early history, all of the devices fell short in one or more respects.   However, it appears that for securing records of that faint light which penetrates to great depths, photographic methods are the best yet known.

Recent Methods.   Knudsen (1922) proposed a method the essential features of which were two spectrophotometers placed on a line, one above the other, the distance between them representing the thickness of the layer of water to be examined.   A system of slits made possible the determination of the coefficient of absorption for each region of the spectrum through the effect on a photographic plate.

Klugh (1925) devised an instrument the principle of which is the use of panchromatic photographic plates "exposed beneath a set of neutral percentage transmission filters, the plates exposed to the lower intensities being read against the plate exposed to the highest intensity, the results being given directly in percentages." The instrument is said to measure both total intensity and the spectral quality of light in water and to be sensitive to radiation representing most of the visible spectrum.

Certain other modifications of the photographic method have been devised during recent years but need not be described here.

PHOTOELECTRIC CELL METHODS. One of the promising developments of recent years is the use of photoelectric cells in measuring penetration of light into water. Shelford and Gail (1922), Atkins and Poole (1930), and others have made extensive use of various forms of instruments in which the photoelectric cell was the essential feature and have, from time to time, made certain improvements. The principle of the photoelectric cell is described by Shelford as follows:

All metals emit electrons under the influence of light. This emission depends upon the kind of metal, upon the condition of the surface, and upon the surrounding conditions. In most cases, the emission is imperceptible. By using a very active metal, such as strontium, rubidium, caesium, lithium, sodium, or postasium, and placing it in a vacuum or, much better, in an atmosphere of helium, hydrogen, or argon, the photoelectric effects become very considerable with a potential of 20 to 300 volts across the cell.

Gas-filled cells are said to be sensitive to all wave lengths except red but only slightly sensitive to yellow and extreme ultraviolet. It appears that the most promising use of these cells is due to their greater sensitivity for the short wave lengths (violet, blue, green). These instruments are undergoing a rapid evolution at the present time, and perhaps their complete possibilities are not yet known. Detailed description of a modern photoelectric cell outfit designed for work in water is given by Welch (1948).

THE PYRLIMNOMETER. Birge and Juday (1929, 1931) developed an instrument known as a pyrlimnometer. The first instrument, described by Birge in 1922, has undergone numerous improvements. In its present form, its essential features are (1) a large-surface Moll thermopile, mounted in a special carrier; this thermopile receives the solar radiation; (2) apparatus for measuring the electrical currents thus caused. Two types of measuring instruments are employed: (a) millivoltmeters to be taken out in the boat with the pyrlimnometer; (b) a galvanometer, for special studies, to be set up onshore and connected by an insulated cable with the boat. The carrier of the thermopile has a rotating shutter, with eight openings, which may be open or may carry opaque disks or light filters. The filters are of Jena glass. The sun's radiation, acting on the thermopile, produces an electrical effect, registered on the recording instrument, which is proportional to the energy of the sun's radiation. Thus, this instrument measures sun's energy penetrating lake water to a given level. It furnishes data on transmission through lake waters of light and heat; it also gives the composition of the visible spectrum in water, in terms of either wave length or color bands, and the changes in composition which the spectrum undergoes as light passes through lake waters. The apparatus is designed for use in small inland lakes and has been much used by Birge and Juday in such waters.

Factors Influencing Light Penetration. Several factors affect the way in which light illuminates natural waters. The following are important:

INTENSITY AT SURFACE. The intensity of illumination at the surface of water varies with a number of circumstances, such as degree of cloudiness or clearness of sky, presence of fog, smoke, dust, or other occasional features of atmospheric condition, time of day, and season of the year. Some of these variations are cyclic, such as the alternation of day and night; others are irregular meteorological phenomena; and still others originate in various ways. Moonlight is known to illuminate water to some extent; also starlight in a much more limited way; but these sources of light are likewise subject to variations in intensity at the surface. Strictly speaking, light intensity at the surface of natural waters is highly variable, and periods of uniform intensity are of limited duration. It should be understood that on a clear day, the light reaching the surface of the water is the sum total of the light coming (1) directly from the sun and (2) from the hemisphere of the sky. Clouds passing across the sun produce alterations in the relative amounts of light from the two sources.

ANGLE OF CONTACT OF LIGHT WITH SURFACE. Light rays meeting the surface of water at right angles pass into it without deviation from the original axis. If, however, the angle of contact is less than 90°, those rays passing into the water are refracted, i.e., bent toward the perpendicular. The refractive index from air to water is about $\frac{4}{3}$, or 1.33. It is therefore evident that the position of the sun with reference to the surface of water is concerned with the depth to which light will penetrate. The greatest penetration in a body of water would result from a zenith sun. As the sun departs from the zenith, the rays on entering the water, even though bent toward the perpendicular, penetrate in a diagonal direction and hence to shallower depths.

In general, when light waves encounter the surface of water, a part of light will be reflected, and another part will enter the water and become refracted. This is true under practically all conditions, but the nature of the reflection depends upon the angle of the rays with the general water surface and also upon the degree of agitation of the water surface. Since water is so commonly in a state of disturbance of some sort, varying from the most gentle swings to severe wave action, at least a part of the reflection is usually a very irregular, momentary feature. Owing to this common motion of the water surface, light at a given time may, in a series of successive moments, meet the surface film momentarily at many different angles of incidence; hence, the irregularity of the reflection. Even in times of greatest calm, there is a certain change of surface level; i.e., it is never absolutely immobile. Therefore, under no circumstances would all of the light impinging upon the surface enter the water; some is always reflected.

Differences in Latitude. Obviously, latitude determines the relation of a lake surface to the general incidence of light from the sun. The more remote a lake is from the equatorial region the greater the departure of the sun's rays from the vertical.

Seasonal Differences. Closely associated with latitude are the seasonal changes in the position of the sun. Only locations at or between the tropics of Cancer and Capricorn (23°28′N. lat. and 23°28′S. lat., respectively) ever have a vertical sun. Beyond this zone (torrid), north or south, not only do locations have an angular sun but the angle changes progressively with the sequence of seasons.

Diurnal Differences. The apparent daily journey of the sun from east to west results in its rise in the sky from the horizon to the meridian for a chosen location and a succeeding drop across the sky to the western horizon. Therefore, the angle of contact of light rays increases, in an east-west plane, from 0 to 90° and then declines to 0 in the evening. The angle of contact of light with the water surface is constantly changing during the day, reaching its nearest approach to the zenith at noon.

DISSOLVED MATERIALS. Natural waters differ from pure water in the way in which they absorb light; also, natural waters differ widely among themselves in this respect. Dissolved materials constitute one of the influences responsible for this difference. Unfortunately, too little is yet known concerning this subject. It has been claimed that chlorides of calcium and magnesium and similar salts diminish light absorption. Traces of ammonia, proteins, and nitrates in solution in pure water are said greatly to reduce its transparency to ultraviolet light, whereas dissolved salts usually have little effect. Differences in light transmission between ordinary "hard-water" and "soft-water" lakes, assignable to the mineral content of their waters, are apparently minimal. That dissolved gases have an influence is probable, but at present little seems to be known about it.

SUSPENDED MATERIALS. Finely divided materials in suspension, organic or inorganic, tend to screen out light. These materials will be discussed more fully under the subject of turbidity. In general, the more suspended matter in water the more completely is light shut out. In very highly turbid waters, light seems to be excluded by a relatively thin stratum at the surface.

Light Penetration in Pure Water. Since natural waters have various substances and circumstances associated with them which affect light penetration, it is better to approach the subject by considering first the phenomena of light penetration and light absorption in *pure* water. In this way, the inherent, unmodified effects of water alone upon entering light may be distinguished.

When light enters pure water, two changes occur: (1) a certain part of the light is *absorbed* by the water, and (2) some of the light undergoes a *scattering* within the water, this scattering being in the form of a deflection in all directions. Absorption is a *selective* performance in which certain wave lengths are absorbed more quickly than others. The general character of this selective absorption in pure water can be seen in Fig. 13.

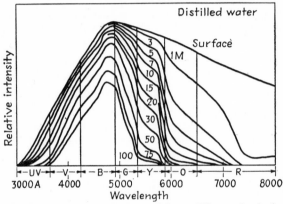

Fig. 13. Graphs showing relative intensity of light at different depths in pure (distilled) water. Relative intensity is indicated along the vertical axis. Differences in spectral distribution are shown along the horizontal axis. Depths are expressed in meters. The uppermost curve represents the spectral distribution of solar energy at the surface. Wave lengths are expressed in Ångstroms (Å). Abbreviations along the horizontal axis represent colors of the spectrum. (From Clarke, 1939.)

It has been estimated (Shelford and Gail, 1922) that very small quantities of the violet, blue, green, and yellow penetrate to a depth of at least 1,800 m. of pure water.

Light Penetration in Natural Waters. QUANTITATIVE DETERMINATIONS. Early Records. Early work on light penetration was concerned, by interest and by limitations of method, with the *depth* to which any light was transmitted, without reference to selective absorption. Also, it was concerned almost wholly with marine waters whose transparencies are greater than those of most fresh waters. Some of the early records will now be mentioned. Forel (1895) found light affecting his photographic apparatus in Lake Geneva at 200 m. depth. Fol and Sarasin, using a photographic-plate method, obtained light effects at a depth of almost 480 m. in the Mediterranean Sea near the Riviera. Petersen, also working in the Mediterranean near Capri, got light influence on a photographic plate at a depth of 550 m. Luksch obtained a photographic effect in the eastern Mediterranean at 600 m.   By means of an improved photographic apparatus (Helland-Hansen photometer) used in the Atlantic Ocean during the Michael Sars Expedition, records of light penetration to a depth of 1,000 m. after an exposure of 80 min. were secured (noon, June 6, 1910, clear sky, near Azores), a depth much greater than had formerly been found; but an exposure of the same apparatus at 1,700 m. for 2 hr. yielded no light effect.   Somewhere between these depths, light, as determined by this type of apparatus, faded out completely. Photographic evidence of light at 1,500 m. has since been found.

Early workers also discovered that the length of "day" in water is very different from that in air; that this day varies in duration with depth; and that the dawn and twilight periods, present in air, are virtually absent in water.   The well-known oceanographer The Prince of Monaco, using Regnard's apparatus in Funchal Harbor, Madeira, in March, found that the day at a depth of 20 m. was 11 hr. long; at a depth of 40 m., it lasted 15 min.   Fol, using a diver's outfit in the Mediterranean Sea just off Nice, France, observed that at 10 m. the solar light disappeared abruptly in the afternoon long before sunset.

Modern Records.   It appears that methods employing photographic plates or photographic paper are probably the best for securing records of that very feeble light which is transmitted to great depths.   However, in modern work, the interest has shifted from a desire to know the depth of final disappearance of *all* light to the more fundamental matters of light absorption in the upper strata.   For that reason, little has been added to the knowledge of greatest depths of penetration.   Beebe reported the disappearance of all color from the spectrum at a depth of 213 m. in the Atlantic Ocean near the Bermuda islands.

There is a general law sometimes employed in estimating the rate of diminution of light with increasing depth in a body of water, viz., that as the depth increases arithmetically the light decreases geometrically. Occasionally, the actual conditions in a lake tend to follow this law, but caution should be exercised in using it as the general expectation since modifying influences are many, and departures from values given by this law are common and often marked.

Because of the various factors and combinations of factors which affect light penetration in natural waters, inland lakes vary widely in the way in which they transmit light.   In the large number of lakes in Wisconsin studied by Birge and Juday, the depth at which the amount of radiation delivered at the surface would be reduced to 1 per cent varied from about 1.5 to 29 m., with various intergradations between them.   Without doubt, even wider variations exist.

QUALITATIVE DETERMINATIONS.   The selective absorption, characteristic of pure water, is manifested by natural waters, modified by those additional factors already mentioned which affect absorption. Since these modifying influences vary so widely in different waters, only a very general statement of the usual character of selective absorption can be given here for fresh-water lakes. A considerable study of this phenomenon in sea water has been made by various investigators, and while in some respects sea water and fresh water behave similarly in light absorption, there are certain inherent differences. In this discussion, attention will be confined largely to the results from fresh water.

Birge and Juday (1930), in their work on more than 30 Wisconsin lakes, found that the general story of changes in the composition of the sun's radiation as it passes through the waters of these lakes is as follows:

1. In lakes containing heavily stained water, very little radiation of wave lengths less than 6000 Å occurs below a depth of 1 m.; the blue is negligible, the amount of green is very small and disappears rapidly as depth increases, and the same is true of the adjacent region of the yellow. The red may be higher than any other color—in fact, it may equal or exceed all other radiation. The red is less affected by stain and by suspended matters, and, in waters where stain and suspended matters are at a maximum, the transmission of red may be higher than any other color. In such lakes, the radiation at and below 1 m. depth comes from that part of the spectrum whose wave lengths are greater than 6000 Å.

2. In lakes of moderate transparency, the central part of the spectrum (about 5500 Å; yellow) has a much greater transmission than either end, although both red and blue are present. Radiation passing through a few meters of water contains very little from the blue or the red, although there is more of the latter.

3. In the most transparent lakes, blue exceeds the red. The short-wave half of the spectrum contributes much at all depths, and radiation from the whole region, extending to wave length 5700 Å, is transmitted through the water at much the same rate.

The following table (Table 7), taken from Birge and Juday (1930), shows the general results and presents not only a summary of their results but what may prove to be the initial step in the formation of a classification of lakes on the basis of relation of transmission of colors to total radiation.

According to Pietenpol (1918), particles suspended in water are non-selective in their absorption of light. This conclusion has been considered doubtful by other workers. Harvey (1928) pointed out that Pietenpol's results show evidence of a selectivity in suspended particles, viz., that the transmission of the short-wave radiations is more affected by suspended particles than is that of the longer wave lengths. Birge and Juday (1930) confirmed this statement.

Some understanding of the composition of the radiation at different depths in different types of lakes can be secured through an inspection of Figs. 14 to 16, taken, without change, from Birge and Juday (1931). The explanation attached to the figures indicates the nature of the diagrams.

TABLE 7. RELATION OF TRANSMISSION OF COLORS TO THAT OF TOTAL RADIATION
The transmission of total is taken as 100 per cent in all cases; that of colors is stated as a percentage of total
From Birge and Juday

Transparency, meters..	1.4–2.9	2.7–3.5	3.5–7.6	6.9–12.2
Color.................	45–132	10–45	0–20	0–4
Transmission of total..	Low, 8–30	Low medium, 31–50	High medium, 51–70	High, 71 and over
Total.............	100 per cent	100 per cent	100 per cent	100 per cent
Blue...............	Very small	50–66	60–90	80–100
Yellow.............	50 or less	100–115	100–117	100–110
Red...............	100–120	90–100	80–98	70–90

In this table, *transparency* indicates depth (in meters) at which Secchi's disk disappeared. *Color* is indicated by the U.S. Geological Survey or platinum-cobalt scale.

Color or stain in water also has a selective effect. Like suspended matters, color offers more obstruction to short wave lengths than to long ones. As already mentioned, radiation from the red end of the spectrum is less affected by color than is that from the other end. In fact, transmission of all parts of the spectrum is affected by color, but the most marked effect is on the short-wave radiation.

Light Penetration through Ice Cover. Ice cover interposes a partial barrier to light penetration, the effectiveness of which depends upon circumstances such as thickness of the ice, its degree of transparency, and the presence or absence of accumulated snow on its surface. It has already been pointed out that a lake accumulates heat during the winter from the sun's rays that pass through the ice. Some of the sun's energy penetrating the ice is in the form of light. Detailed knowledge of this whole subject is still imperfect although a few studies have been made by the use of modern techniques for measuring light transmission, one of the latest being that of Greenbank (1945) from which the following quotation is taken:

It is readily apparent that the penetration of light through ice varies greatly with the condition of the ice. For example, 7½ in. of clear ice transmitted 84 per cent, as against 22 per cent for 7½ in. of "partly cloudy" ice. This ice was full of minute air bubbles, which gave it somewhat the appearance of opal glass, and rendered it probably as opaque as any ice likely to be encountered on natural waters, except that which might have inclusions of dirt or other foreign matter. Similarly, the "clear" ice just mentioned was probably as crystal-clear as any which ever freezes on inland lakes. Between these two extremes, the ice of most lakes, varies greatly in character, and in ability to transmit light, depending on the manner in which it was frozen, on various thaws and refreezings, and so forth.

Greenbank also found that ice may have a differential effect upon qualitative transmission of light, depending upon the physical character

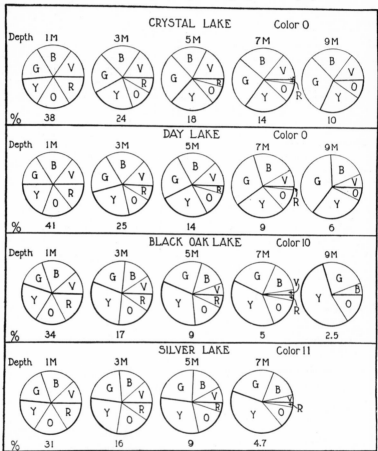

Fig. 14.　Diagrams showing distribution of solar radiation to the several color regions in four Wisconsin lakes and changes which radiation undergoes with increasing depth. The numbers under each diagram following the sign % indicate the amount of total radiation at each depth, stated as a percentage of that delivered to the surface of the lake. Color values for each lake are expressed in terms of the platinum-cobalt scale, increasing numerical values indicating increasing color of the water.　It will be noted that these are relatively clear lakes.　(*Redrawn from Birge and Juday*, 1931.)

of the ice itself.　Clear ice seemed to produce no significant differences in the relative transmission of light of different colors, but turbid ice caused a distinctly lower relative penetration of blue light, a result which he attributed to the effect of air bubbles and other inclusions.

Snow accumulations on the surface of ice are common, and when

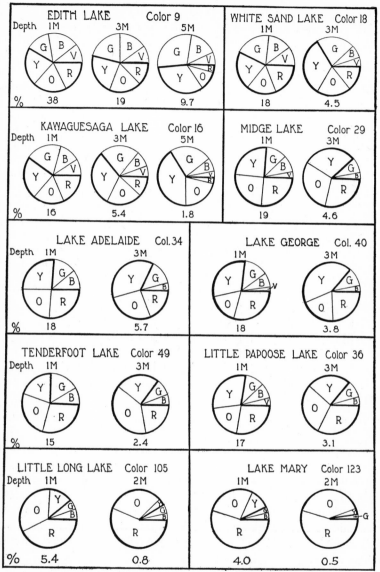

FIG. 15.   Diagrams showing the distribution of solar radiation to the several color regions in 10 Wisconsin lakes and the changes which radiation undergoes with increasing depth. As in Fig. 14, the numbers under each diagram following the sign % indicate the amount of total radiation at each depth, stated as a percentage of that delivered to the surface of the lake.   Color values expressed in terms of the platinum-cobalt scale.   Note that Little Long Lake and Lake Mary are highly colored lakes; also that red yields a very large part of the total in both instances.   (*Redrawn from Birge and Juday, 1931.*)

present they act as an additional and even more effective barrier to light, thus reducing to varying degrees the amount of light which reaches the snow-ice interface. Snow reduces the initial sunlight in two principal ways: (1) reflection from the surface of snow greatly exceeds that from the surface of water or ice; (2) light entering the snow is rapidly shut out. According to Greenbank, only a very small amount of light penetrates

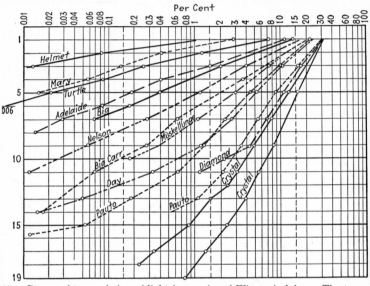

Fig. 16. Curves of transmission of light in a series of Wisconsin lakes. The term *transmission* refers to the passage of solar radiation through the waters of a lake. The unit of depth is 1 m. Depth is indicated by the equally spaced horizontal lines. The curves for Crystal and Pauto Lakes show the general loss of transparency as summer advances, although the character of the curve is altered but little. This series varies from a very opaque lake (Helmet) to a very transparent one (Crystal). (*From Birge and Juday*, 1932.)

through a layer of snow a few inches in thickness. It appears reasonably certain that heavy snow fall, in its ordinary physical state, may for the time practically prevent all light from reaching the underlying ice. Snow is also said to have a differential effect upon the quality of light which penetrates it, apparently effecting a greater reduction in the red and blue portions of the spectrum.

COLOR OF WATER

By color in water is meant those hues which are inherent within the water itself, resulting from colloidal substances or substances in solution. The term *true color* is sometimes used to designate the colors due to these causes. This definition rules out of consideration the *apparent color* due (1) to living or nonliving substances in suspension and (2) to extrinsic conditions, such as sky or color of bottom in shallower water. These causes of *apparent color* in water are sometimes very effective in producing misleading appearances, such as the "yellow" water overlying a clean sandy shoal on a clear day; the bright-green appearance of water superimposed upon the Algae-covered slopes of precipitous depressions; the green appearance of water containing unusual quantities of phytoplankton; and the blue of lake water on a clear, calm summer day which gives place to the dull color with overcast skies. Clayey turbidity usually imparts a yellow color to water. Suspended matters often influence the color of lakes as seen from shore. Marl lakes have a bluish-green shade due, it is thought, in part to the reflection of light from the whitish marl particles. Lakes rich in plankton acquire a brownish tinge when diatoms become abundant, and another color prevails when *Ceratium* appears in large numbers. Filtration eliminates these effects. Drifts of phytoplankton give a deep green to local areas.

Natural waters differ greatly in color. Some are almost colorless, while others are heavily stained, and there is almost every imaginable gradation between these two conditions. The darkest waters are usually those of swamps and bogs, or of streams which drain swamps and bogs, in which the color may be so intense as to give the water the appearance of very dilute coffee or of weak tea. Natural, uncontaminated waters from certain peat bogs in Europe have been reported as being black as ink by reflected light and coffee-brown by transmitted light when observed through a stratum 20 cm. thick. Juday and Birge (1933) found that in 530 lakes in northeastern Wisconsin, the color varied from 0 to 340 on the platinum-cobalt standard.

The following substances are said to play a part in producing color in natural waters: (1) Iron, as ferrous sulphate or as ferric oxide, produces various shades of yellow depending upon the amounts present. (2) Humic matters, originating from peat deposits, produce colors varying, with increasing amounts, from blue through green, yellow, and yellow brown to dark brown. (3) Large quantities of calcium carbonate are claimed to produce a green color. (4) Carbon and manganese are supposed to be involved in color production, but the exact effect is uncertain. Juday and Birge (1933) found a definite correlation between the brown color of bog and marsh waters and the amount of organic carbon in the surface waters. Color production by some of the substances mentioned above has been denied outright by certain investigators. According to James and Birge (1938), all colors found in lake waters, subsequent to settling, are originally colloid in their nature or are associated with colloids; hence such colors are reducible by filtration. It seems certain that the whole matter of color production in water is a very complex one and is still badly in need of critical study.

In some lakes, the color is essentially the same at all depths from surface to bottom; in others, particularly the brown lakes, there may be a very distinct increase in the brown color with increasing depths, increases being due to such causes as the increase of vegetable stain or of iron in the lower waters.

Changes in color with season are well known. Some of these are rhythmic; for example, certain waters have two periods of maximum color (May or June and November or December) and one of minimum color in each of the intervening periods. Other changes are irregular, such as those produced by rainfall.

That colored water bleaches on exposure to direct sunlight seems to be well established. According to Whipple, certain waters lose 20 per cent of the original color by 100 hr. exposure to sunlight, and complete color loss results from long exposure. Such bleaching is most effective in the surface layer and diminishes rapidly with increasing depth. This bleaching, if and when it occurs, bears directly upon several important limnological phenomena. Too little is yet known about it to make extended discussion profitable, but if bleaching of the magnitude indicated above goes on in various colored waters in nature, it is obvious that it has an influential effect on light penetration, since stained waters, as already described, affect light absorption. Furthermore, if bleaching goes on all summer, those lakes whose waters maintain the same color throughout the season must have a source of income of color-producing substances which continually replaces the color lost by bleaching. Presumably, the circulation of the epilimnion makes it possible for this bleaching to influence the whole upper stratum of a lake or even the whole body of a shallow lake. While the effective, diurnal, bleaching period does not seem to be definitely known, it is possible that the actual *bleaching hours* are fewer than those of the nonbleaching period. No study seems to have been made of seasonal differences in the bleaching effect of sunlight.

Color of water is determined by comparing a sample with some form of colorimeter. Long ago, Forel devised a set of color standards by mixing in various proportions two aqueous solutions, one containing copper sulfate and the other potassium chromate. His color chart contained 11 graded colors ranging from the deep blue of the copper sulfate solution alone to a distinct yellow produced by a mixture of the two solutions in which the yellow solution (potassium chromate) predominated. Forel's color scale was the basis for measurement of color in natural waters for many years, and even yet there is an occasional mention of it in the current European literature. Two different methods are commonly used in America at the present time, viz., (1) the platinum-cobalt standards method, the essential feature of which is a series of color standards prepared by the progressive dilutions of a solution containing potassium chloroplatinate; and (2) the U.S. Geological Survey field apparatus in which the color standards are colored glass disks, calibrated individually to correspond to the colors of the platinum-cobalt scale.   It should be noted that in spite of the distinctions commonly made between the *true* and the *apparent* color of water, field practice often consists merely in the measurement of color in a sample taken directly from the water and without change of any sort, such as filtration or centrifuging to remove suspended matter.

TURBIDITY

Turbidity is a condition of water resulting from the presence of suspended matters.   In common parlance, water is turbid only when its load of suspended matter is conspicuous, but, as a matter of fact, all natural waters contain suspended materials, and therefore all are turbid, although they vary widely in the amount.   The clearest of mountain lakes have a very low turbidity, while the Missouri River represents the opposite extreme.   The timeworn statement that "there is not enough silt in the world to make the oceans turbid" is mere fiction, since the oceans are already turbid.

The sources of substances producing turbidity are innumerable.   Any materials, finely divided or later becoming so, which find their way into waters contribute to turbidity, and the great array of materials which may get into a lake and the variety of ways of delivering such materials to a lake are such as almost to defy complete enumeration.   Prominent among these materials are plankton organisms, finely divided substances of organic origin, and silts.

From the point of view of their relation to water, turbidity-producing substances may be divided into two groups, viz., the settling suspended matters and the nonsettling suspended matters.

Settling Suspended Matters.   Those substances which in motionless water will sooner or later settle to the bottom are known as the *settling suspended matters*.   Certain materials settle very slowly; others settle with considerable promptness.   Rate of settling is determined largely by the specific gravity of the particle, by the size of the particle, by the ratio of surface to volume of the particle (shape), and by the viscosity of the water.   Long ago, Stokes constructed the following formula to express the velocity of fall of a spherical body through a liquid:

$$V = \frac{2g(s - s')r^2}{9v}$$

where V = velocity of falling particle.

   g = acceleration due to gravity (32.16 ft./sec.^{2}, or 980 dynes).

   s = specific gravity of body.

   s' = specific gravity of liquid.

   r = radius of body.

   v = viscosity of liquid.

While certain modifications of this law have been proposed for use in physiological work, it expresses, in its original form, the essential factors involved and their general relations. Owing to the fact that Stokes's law as stated involves several fundamental assumptions, its use in determining the rate of settling of particles in lake waters is dependable only as the existing conditions approach the fundamental ones inherent in the formula. To express the sinking velocity of plankton organisms, Ostwald (1902) proposed the following simplified formula:

$$\text{Sinking velocity} = \frac{\text{excess of weight}}{\text{viscosity of water} \times \text{form resistance}}$$

In this formula, excess of weight is the difference in the specific gravity of the body and that of the water; and form resistance is the surface area and shape of the body. Steuer (1910) also presented means of applying this formula to plankton problems. Since particles in water vary widely in shape, size, and specific gravity, and the water itself varies in viscosity, it is not possible to present any satisfactory mathematical statement of the rate of sinking applicable to lakes in general, although certain rather complicated formulas have been proposed. Likewise, specific data on rate of settling of particulate matter in lakes are very meager. Table 8, taken from Whipple (1927), indicates the probable settling rate under the conditions specified. The hydraulic subsiding value of spherical particles possessing a specific gravity of that of quartz sand (2.65) has been estimated as follows:

TABLE 8. RATE OF SETTLING IN PURE, STILL WATER[1]
Temperature of water, 50° F.; specific gravity of particles, 2.65; shape of particles, spherical

Material	Diameter, mm.	Hydraulic subsiding value, mm. per sec.	Time required to settle 1 ft.
Gravel	10.0	1000.0	0.3 sec.
Coarse sand	1.0	100.0	3.0 sec.
Fine sand	0.1	8.0	38.0 sec.
Silt	0.01	0.154	33.0 min.
Bacteria	0.001	0.00154	55.0 hr.
Clay	0.0001	0.0000154	230.0 days
Colloidal particles	0.00001	0.000000154	63 years

[1] Reprinted by permission from Whipple, "The Microscopy of Drinking Water," 4th ed., John Wiley & Sons, Inc., 1927.

The substances mentioned above represent but one class of particles (on basis of specific gravity) and must be regarded largely as suggestive only. In every lake and at all times of year, there is a continuous settling through to the bottom of particulate matter. This continuous rain of material varies in amount from time to time, and without doubt the settling is a differential one depending upon the various conditions expressed in Stokes's law. Furthermore, it may well be that certain additional influences are also operative, as, for example, the effect of surrounding particles upon a single particle in the sinking performance. Unfortunately, almost nothing is known about the interrelation of the various particles as the whole mass settles through the water.

It must not be overlooked that the settling of particulate materials is by no means at a uniform rate, particularly in a deeper lake having considerable difference in temperature (and hence differences in viscosity) between the surface and bottom layers. In the presence of thermal stratification, particles settling through the epilimnion, under conditions of calm, might have a fairly uniform rate until they reach the thermocline, where the rate of settling is abruptly reduced and passage through the thermocline is not only slow but actually diminishes in rate until the lower thermocline limit is reached. Then, since the hypolimnion is usually similar in temperature throughout, the remaining passage to the bottom would be at about a uniform rate, although the rate would be relatively slow, since the deep, cold water has a greater viscosity. There is, however, some counterinfluence due to the fact that decreasing temperature usually increases the specific gravity of the particles. In the absence of thermal stratification, rate of settling would be modified by any inequalities of temperature in the water, whatever their causes and positions. Kindle (1927) studied the effects of thermal stratification on the settling of sediments by developing thermal stratification in a laboratory jar and then slowly adding fresh lake-bottom ooze which had first been carefully mixed with water having the same temperature as that of the artificial epilimnion. The sediment spread "uniformly through the water above and within the thermocline and remained floating on the denser cold water below with a sharply defined base at the contact of the colder water." Owing to the difficulty of maintaining artificial thermal stratification for any considerable time, the subsequent developments in his experiments are probably not a true picture of the natural phenomena, but it seems that these experiments support the conclusion that the sharply contrasted densities and viscosities of the epilimnion and the hypolimnion cause a distinct delay in the settling of finely divided sediments. Kindle also pointed out that there are three general effects of the summer thermal stratification on the finely divided settling matters: (1) Delayed settling of fine, suspended matter in the epilimnion facilitates its oxidation and largely controls the character of other biochemical changes in the sediments which are dependent upon temperatures; (2) delayed settling promotes a sorting and a selecting of sediments, since the various kinds of particles settle through a stratified liquid until they reach a layer approximating their own specific gravity; and (3) in the alkaline epilimnion and the neutral or even acid hypolimnion, the biochemical products and the resulting sediments differ accordingly.

Thus it follows that in the epilimnion of a lake the water may be saturated or nearly saturated with respect to calcium carbonate, and deposits of marl may be formed in the bottom within the limits of the epilimnion zone, while in the deep water the acidity may be sufficient to dissolve shells or other calcareous matter [falling into it].

During the complete overturns of spring and fall, circulation of the water to all depths brings about a temporary, uniform distribution of the suspended matters and may also return into suspension finely divided matters previously settled to the bottom. Some of these materials are so finely divided and the specific gravity so low that any small movement of the water is sufficient to bring them into suspension again. Therefore, the turbidity of a lake may be greatly increased temporarily at overturns, although not all turbidity at those periods is due to the overturn alone. The early portion of the spring overturn may coincide with (1) the spring thaw when the turbidity is further increased by much inflow of surface water bearing large amounts of silt; (2) the spring maximum of plankton; and (3) release into the water of the winter accumulations of wind-blown materials in and upon the ice. Likewise, the autumn overturn may coincide, in part, with (1) the autumnal plankton maximum; (2) a period of increased wind-blown material; and (3) autumn rains. After the overturn is completed, settling out of much of the materials occurs rather quickly, and the water resumes a more transparent condition. In those lakes having either an incomplete overturn or none at all, the permanently stagnant deep waters, although not themselves circulating, become temporarily more turbid by the increased amount of sediment settling through from above at those times when the surface waters become markedly turbid.

Turbidity conditions during the winter stagnation period are usually different from those of other seasons. Ice cover not only shuts out wind-blown particulate matter, but it eliminates all surface disturbance, imposing dead-calm conditions upon underlying water. Furthermore, density-viscosity relationships are altered. The *colder, lighter,* but *more viscous* water is at the top, while the *warmer, heavier,* but *less viscous* water is below. While little is known about the actual facts of settling of particles under these conditions in a lake, it seems likely that those particles at the top which will settle do so at about a uniform rate from top to bottom, since the temperature conditions, operating as they do on the specific gravity of the particles themselves, on density, and on the viscosity, apparently about balance each other. It should also be remembered that the difference in temperature between top and bottom is but 4°C. when bottom water is at maximum density; also, that it is changed viscosity rather than changed density that exercises the major effect upon the rate of settling.

The more or less constant wave action of the upper waters of a lake not only tends to slow down settling of suspended materials but also, as pointed out elsewhere, erodes and transports shore materials some of which are finely divided and become, at least temporarily, suspended matter in the water. Irregularities of turbidity thus arise from that continuously changing character of surface-water disturbance of which there is every possible intergrade from calm to violent storms. Irregularities also arise out of (1) inflowing waters at one side of the basin; (2) floods and droughts affecting inflowing waters; (3) sudden contributions of wind-blown material; (4) plankton swarms and plankton drift; (5) differences in shore configuration; and other possible local circumstances.

Nonsettling Suspended Matters. By *nonsettling suspended matters* are meant either those exceedingly finely divided solids or those materials whose specific gravity is less than water which are in permanent suspension as long as their state remains unchanged. Such materials do not settle out on long standing in undisturbed water. True it is that there are intergrades between the settling suspended matters and the nonsettling matters and that certain of the former settle at an exceedingly slow rate. Also, it is certain that some of the former undergo physical and chemical changes which may convert them into the nonsettling state. Furthermore, materials which will settle slowly in the upper waters may become nonsettling in the deep, denser water; for example, in certain lakes, the bottommost waters are exceedingly turbid owing largely to nonsettling materials.

In a very general way, these nonsettling materials may be divided into two classes:

1. Plankton organisms and coarsely divided, nonliving substances whose specific gravity is such that they are constantly suspended. Certain of these materials are so constituted that only strong centrifuging will pull them down. The plankton Alga *Gloeotrichia,* so common in many lakes, is an excellent example.

2. Very finely divided, nonliving materials and organisms of exceedingly small size, such as some of the very minute nannoplankton.

There is reason for believing that all natural waters contain a certain amount of nonsettling suspended matter, the amounts varying in different waters and varying from time to time in the same water; also, that these materials grade down in size of particle to that of true colloids. Materials in colloidal suspension may undergo flocculation, forming particles sufficiently large to sink eventually under the influence of gravity.

CHAPTER V

CHEMICAL CONDITIONS AND RELATED PHENOMENA

Chemically pure water does not exist in or upon the earth. While natural waters differ widely in their chemical content, it can be said with safety that those with but minimal chemical content are nevertheless chemically complex. Everything conspires to make a lake or stream a catch basin for innumerable materials coming to it from the atmosphere, from drainage, and from its own basin. Combine with these circumstances those qualities of the water itself—its ability to dissolve more substances than any other liquid, its own chemical stability, its ability to combine chemically with a great array of substances, and its ability to interact with some substances in hydrolysis—and the stage is set for one of nature's greatest displays of chemical diversity and chemical dynamics. The existence and continuance of life in water depend upon the presence of that miscellaneous array of substances which natural water contains, and, in a general way, the richer the contained substances the greater the biological productivity. If pure water existed in nature (an impossibility, of course), it would be a biological desert, since no organism could continue to live in it. It follows, therefore, that limnology is concerned in a very important way not only with the water itself but also with its large and varied chemical content. Much yet remains to be discovered in this field. In the following discussions, only those features now known to be important will be considered. Phenomena still little known will either be mentioned only or omitted outright.

DISSOLVED GASES

A dissolved gas is one which so intermingles with water that its extremely minute subdivision extends down to molecular dimensions. For example, by dissolved oxygen is meant oxygen added to already existing water and intermingled with the latter to the degree just mentioned. Gases, originating from the atmosphere, from the lake basin, from substances and organisms within the water, or from drainage, may go into solution in natural waters, and since some of them at least play a far-reaching part in aquatic biology, they must be taken up in some detail.

When a gas is brought into contact with water, it dissolves in the water until a state of equilibrium is reached in which the solution and the emission of the gas are balanced, as, for example, oxygen (gas) $\rightleftarrows$ oxygen (dissolved). Total solubility is expressed in Henry's law: *the concentra-*

tion of a saturated solution of a gas is proportional to the pressure at which the gas is supplied. This tendency to establish equilibrium prevails irrespective of whether the initial excess of the gas occurs outside the water or in solution in it.

Conditions Affecting the Solubility of Gases in Water

When a mixture of two or more gases at the same temperature is in contact with water, each individual gas behaves as if all the other gases were absent and it alone occupied the whole available space. Therefore, in a mixture of 100 cc. of oxygen and 400 cc. of nitrogen, each at a pressure of 1 atmosphere, the resulting mixture occupies 500 cc. at this pressure. The oxygen, however, behaves as if it were under a pressure of only $^{100}/_{500}$, or $\frac{1}{5}$ atmosphere, and the nitrogen behaves as if it were under a pressure of $^{400}/_{500}$, or $\frac{4}{5}$ atmosphere. This relation forms the essence of Dalton's law of partial pressures, which may be stated as follows: *The pressure exercised by each component in a gaseous mixture is proportional to its concentration in the mixture, and the total pressure of the gas is equal to the sum of those of its components.*

Solubility of gases differs widely, even when their pressures are equal. It is therefore necessary to know the solubility constants. Henry's law is sometimes stated as

$$C = Kp$$

where C = concentration of gas in solution.
p = partial pressure of gas.
K = constant of solubility.

Other general conditions affect the solubility of a gas.

1. Rising temperature reduces the solubility.

2. Increasing concentration of dissolved salts diminishes solubility.

3. Rate of solution is greater when the gases are dry than when they contain water vapor.

4. Rate of solution depends upon the degree of undersaturation of the water with the gases concerned. The greater the degree of undersaturation the greater the rate of solution.

5. Rate of solution is increased by wave action and other forms of surface-water agitation.

Since gases are related to natural waters in various ways, these fundamental relations must be kept in mind.

Since the volume of a gas varies inversely with the pressure, the *actual volume* of the gas absorbed, compared with that at standard conditions (0°C. and 760 mm.), will be twice as much under a pressure of 2 atmospheres and only one-half as great under a pressure of $\frac{1}{2}$ atmosphere; i.e., the *actual volume* as indicated above varies directly with the pressure.

Dissolved Gases in Natural Waters

The following dissolved gases are of sufficient frequency in natural waters to require discussion here: oxygen, carbon dioxide, methane, hydrogen sulfide, nitrogen, ammonia, sulfur dioxide, and carbon monoxide.

Oxygen. *Sources of Dissolved Oxygen.* The principal sources of dissolved oxygen in water are (1) directly from the atmosphere through the exposed surface and (2) from the photosynthesis of chlorophyll-bearing plants.

Since the atmosphere is usually in contact with the surface of water, it becomes a consistent source of oxygen. Absorption of oxygen from air is accomplished in two ways: (*a*) by direct diffusion at the surface and (*b*) through the various forms of surface-water agitation, such as wave action, waterfalls, and turbulences due to obstructions.

Direct diffusion from the air through the surface film and into underlying water is a very slow and relatively ineffective form of supplying oxygen to water, even though it is potentially operative twenty-four hours in the day and at all times except when complete ice cover is present. While there is some variation in the rate of diffusion conditioned by temperature and by the relative concentration of the gas in the different water strata, it is always a very slow process. A rough statement often used is that oxygen diffuses at the rate of about 6 m. per year in quiet water having a constant temperature. One authority (Hoppe-Seyler) found that oxygen-free water in the laboratory and at a constant temperature acquired oxygen by diffusion alone to a depth of only 6 m. in a year and then only to the amount of 0.25 cc. per l. Another investigator (Hüfer) calculated that in Lake Constance, Switzerland, 42 years would be required for oxygen to pass from the surface to the bottom, a depth of 250 m., by diffusion alone; furthermore, that it would require 1,000,000 years for the same lake to become saturated with oxygen if the temperature of the water were 10°C., and if it were completely devoid of dissolved oxygen to start with and had to acquire it wholly by diffusion. It therefore appears that, as a means of distributing oxygen in water, diffusion is a minor factor. If natural waters depended upon diffusion alone for the internal distribution of dissolved oxygen, the biology of aquatic environments would be different in many important respects.

The highly effective means of supplying oxygen to water is agitation in its various forms. Many of the familiar aerating devices used in connection with aquariums are based upon this fact. In nature, all forms of surface-water movement function to a greater or lesser extent in this way. In lakes, wave action with its various accompaniments has no rival in effectiveness in incorporating into the upper waters, and often indirectly into the deeper ones, a supply of oxygen, frequently maintaining in the surface waters a condition approaching saturation. During periods of ice cover, this means of supplying oxygen is temporarily eliminated.

Aquatic chlorophyll-bearing plants in their photosynthetic activities release oxygen directly into the water, diffusion and water movements subsequently effecting its wider distribution. Since photosynthesis depends upon an adequate supply of the essential part of sunlight, the depth to which green plants may exist is limited by all of those factors which facilitate or reduce light penetration. The total photosynthetic zone, even in the most transparent waters, is after all confined to the upper strata of deep lakes.

Two zones of production of oxygen by green plants are common in lakes: (1) the littoral, or shore, zone of shallow water which supports the beds of rooted plants and (2) the limnetic, or open-water, zone in which green plants are present only as phytoplankton. Since the phytoplankton occupies the water from shore to shore, the latter zone overlaps the former in deeper lakes, although in the large, extremely shallow ones, both may occupy the whole lake.

The amount of oxygen derived from green plants depends upon a number of things, prominent among which are (*a*) concentration of plants in a given cubic unit of water and (*b*) duration of effective light. In dense vegetation beds or in dense concentrations of phytoplankton, the oxygen evolved is of large amount during the day, although it is often inconspicuous, owing to the fact that the water movements level out the oxygen accumulation by keeping it distributed over an area much wider than that occupied by the vegetation bed. Under conditions of complete calm, the water surrounding dense vegetation beds may show an *oxygen pulse*, i.e., a distinct rise in dissolved oxygen content, which reaches a maximum in late afternoon, this maximum being due to the gradual accumulation during the day. This accumulation begins to fall off with the decline of effective sunlight and with the continued activity of the oxygen-consuming factors to be mentioned later. The duration of effective light varies with the season, being longer in summer. A limited amount of photosynthesis is said to occur in bright moonlight. Ice cover in winter imposes a partial barrier to light (page 81), and while there is evidence that some light gets through into the uppermost water and that a certain amount of photosynthesis is performed by the green plants under the ice, the quantity of oxygen resulting therefrom is much reduced as compared with the amounts so produced in summer. Combined action of the oxygen-supplying sources and special circumstances sometimes produce supersaturations of considerable magnitude.

Reduction of Dissolved Oxygen. An adequate supply of dissolved oxygen is one of the prime requirements of most aquatic organisms. Therefore, oxygen-consuming processes require careful consideration. The principal causes of oxygen decrease in water are:

1. Respiration of animals and plants. This is a continuous activity day and night.

2. Decomposition of organic matter. Dissolved oxygen is used up in decomposition of the mucky bottom materials and the suspended organic matter. Decomposition goes on faster in warm than in cold conditions; therefore, loss of oxygen due to this cause is greater in the shallower waters during the summer. However, it goes on to some extent at all temperatures down to freezing; and, as will be pointed out later, in the cold, profundal waters, it often aids in the deoxygenation of the entire hypolimnion. Obviously, the total loss of oxygen due to decomposition in a lake depends upon the amount and distribution of organic accumulations, upon the prevailing temperatures of the water, and upon the volume of water in the hypolimnion if thermal stratification is present.

3. Reduction due to other gases. It is well known that a gas may be entirely removed from solution by bubbling another gas through the water in which it is dissolved. This is due to the fact that a gas will leave a solution and pass into a space until the rates of emission and return become equal. Bubbles of another gas passing through water furnish the space to receive the emitted, original gas; also, the bubbles present relatively large surfaces so that that process goes on rapidly. Since the bubbles rise to the surface and burst, there is no chance for re-solution of the first gas, since it is expelled into the atmosphere. Actually, it is caught, transported, and eliminated. In nature, decomposition gases (carbon dioxide, methane, and others) often accumulate at the bottom of a lake in such quantities that a certain excess rises through the water in the form of bubbles. In lakes having bottom accumulations of organic matter, it is no uncommon thing to observe, on a calm summer day, masses of bubbles rising and breaking at the surface. Such gases arise from the muck beds in deep water, but even greater quantities may be released in the warmer, shallower regions of a lake where large amounts of organic matter of recent origin are deposited. Since the rise of gases from bottom deposits is a continuous process, day and night, and since such gases are not oxygen, they continually rob the water of some of its dissolved oxygen. The sum total so removed during a year, while not known, is probably of considerable magnitude. Obviously, the amounts so removed depend upon the quantity of bottom gases produced and released.

When organic bottom accumulations are kept largely removed by currents or by other special circumstances, loss of dissolved oxygen by this means is small.

4. Automatic release of dissolved oxygen from the water of the epi-

limnion due to the oncoming of summer temperatures.   As will be shown later, the capacity of water for oxygen increases with decrease of temperature, i.e., the colder the water the greater the amount of oxygen that it can contain before saturation is reached.   Since, therefore, the water of a lake takes on its maximum load of oxygen shortly after the ice cover goes off in spring (during the spring overturn), subsequent warming up of the surface waters reduces the amount which the water can hold, and it may happen that well toward 50 per cent of the oxygen contained in the upper water in early spring may be given back to the air by midsummer, owing to the inability of water to contain it at prevailing midsummer temperatures.   Just at the freezing point, saturation capacity of water is about 10.2 cc. per l.; while at 25°C., the saturation capacity is about 5.8 cc. per l. It must not be assumed that the water of the epilimnion of every lake is continually saturated with oxygen, since circumstances may keep it somewhat below the saturation point.   This, however, does not essentially alter the oxygen reduction just described.   The amount of reduction may vary widely with different lakes.

5. Inflow of subterranean water.   Subterranean waters are usually very low in dissolved oxygen, often showing total absence.   In lakes with considerable inflow of underground water into the deeper parts of the basin, the volume of water with reduced oxygen content may be materially increased in this way.   If such water is delivered near the surface, its effect may not be so significant, since the surface circulation tends to aerate it, but, if delivered below the thermocline, it will aid materially in making the hypolimnion a region of low oxygen content.   Since the deeper underground waters are already cold before they enter a lake, they will tend to remain in the deeper parts of the lake basin.

6. Presence of iron.   It is claimed that in those lakes which contain iron the oxidation of soluble iron compounds to form the insoluble ferric hydrate plays an important part in the exhaustion of the dissolved oxygen.   That iron does occur, in some lakes, dissolved in the water and deposited at the bottom is well known, but the relative importance of its oxygen-consuming power in lakes is at present too little known to make possible any satisfactory general discussion.

Most or all of the causes of oxygen reduction mentioned above commonly act simultaneously, and their combined effect may, in extreme cases, seriously deplete the oxygen supply.   In shallow, plant-filled waters, the dissolved oxygen may be completely eliminated during the night by the oxygen-consuming forces when photosynthesis is temporarily absent.   Fortunately, such extensive reduction is not of common occurrence.   Complete exhaustion of oxygen in the hypolimnion will be discussed later (page 126) in connection with the seasonal physical-chemical cycle.

Solubility of Oxygen.　By volume, air contains about 20.9 per cent oxygen and about 79.1 per cent nitrogen, but this is not the proportion of the two gases when they are dissolved, because they are not equally soluble in water.　In fact, since the oxygen is more soluble than the nitrogen, the air that is dissolved in the water consists of 34.91 per cent oxygen and 65.09 per cent nitrogen.

Temperature affects the quantity of gas which can be absorbed.　Cold water has a greater capacity for gas than does warm water.　When water containing gases in solution is heated, its capacity is decreased (solubility becomes less and less) as the temperature rises, and some of the gas is given off.　If water is boiled for a short time, practically all dissolved gases will be removed.　Table 9 indicates the relation of temperature to solubility of oxygen in water.　More detailed data are available in any standard book of chemical and physical tables.

TABLE 9.　SOLUBILITY OF OXYGEN IN FRESH WATER AT DIFFERENT TEMPERATURES WHEN EXPOSED TO AIR CONTAINING 20.9 PER CENT OXYGEN AND UNDER A PRESSURE OF 760 MILLIMETERS

Temperature, °C.	O_2, p.p.m.	O_2, cc. per l.
0	14.62	10.23
5	12.80	8.96
10	11.33	7.93
15	10.15	7.11
20	9.17	6.42
25	8.38	5.86
30	7.63	5.34

Salinity reduces the solubility of oxygen.　For example, oxygen is about one-fifth less soluble in sea water than in fresh water.　This fact should not be overlooked in studies on the inland saline waters.

Carbon Dioxide.　*Sources of Carbon Dioxide Dissolved in Water.*　1. Directly from air.　Air normally contains some free carbon dioxide. The amount is relatively small in open country regions (about 3.5 parts in 10,000) but may be larger in the vicinity of cities and in volcanic regions. It is readily soluble in water.　Since the partial pressure of carbon dioxide in air is low, the amount which remains in solution at a given temperature is also low.　Therefore, water freely exposed to air may contain, under normal conditions, a small amount of free carbon dioxide by having absorbed it directly from the air.　However, amounts so secured are minor compared with the quantities provided from other sources.

2. From inflowing ground water.　Waters filtering through the soil commonly acquire considerable quantities of carbon dioxide from the decomposing matters with which they come into contact.

3. Decomposition of organic matter. Accumulations of organic matter, common in natural waters, undergo decomposition, one product of which is free carbon dioxide. Active deposition of organic materials on the floor of a lake goes on uninterruptedly, although with somewhat varying rates at different times of year, since fresh, decomposable matter is continually added to the bottom. Decomposition occurs at all times of year, although more slowly when temperatures are low. Other things being equal, the amount of carbon dioxide so produced varies with the amounts of organic matter deposited. Under some circumstances, very large quantities of the gas are produced in this way. Allgeier, Peterson, Juday, and Birge (1932) studied the fermentation of bottom deposits in Lake Mendota, Wisconsin, under laboratory conditions. It was found that carbon dioxide was the second largest decomposition product, constituting 3 to 30 per cent of the total gas evolved.

4. Respiration of animals and plants. Respiratory processes continually produce and release carbon dioxide into the water. Obviously, quantities so formed are governed by the magnitude of the aquatic flora and fauna, the relative size of the individual organisms, and those circumstances which determine the rate of respiration. Without question, quantities so produced are much larger than is ordinarily supposed.

5. In combination with other substances, chiefly calcium and magnesium. Carbon dioxide also occurs in natural waters in two other important forms, viz., (a) a part of the nearly insoluble monocarbonate (such as $CaCO_3$ or $MgCO_3$) and known as *fixed*, *combined*, or *bound* carbon dioxide; and (b) that additional amount required to convert the monocarbonate into the bicarbonate [such as $Ca(HCO_3)_2$ or $Mg(HCO_3)_2$] and known as the *half-bound*. This half-bound carbon dioxide is not in so stable a state as the fixed carbon dioxide and may be regarded as being a sort of intermediate between the *free* and fixed carbon dioxide. In fact, it is in such loose combination that Algae are able to utilize a large part of it (as much as 92 per cent according to Wiebe, 1930) in their photosynthesis. Bound carbon dioxide has been regarded as unavailable to the Algae, but it is now claimed that some can also be used. Water charged with free carbon dioxide is an active agent in converting the monocarbonates, when it meets them in the ground, into soluble bicarbonates, thus transporting them in solution. Such subterranean, inflowing waters may supply considerable quantities of carbon dioxide in this form. Subterranean waters are much more likely to contain larger quantities of bicarbonates than are the surface drainage waters, since surface soils are often low in carbonates.

Reduction of Carbon Dioxide in Natural Waters. Since, as will be shown later, carbon dioxide is an extremely necessary constituent in an aquatic environment, the processes which tend to reduce the carbon dioxide supply, either permanently or temporarily, must be carefully considered. The principal ones are the following:

1. Photosynthesis of aquatic plants. Consumption of free CO_2 in photosynthesis is dependent upon several circumstances, such as the amount of green plants, both phytoplankton and higher plants, which the water supports; duration of effective daylight; transparency of the water; and time of year. Some photosynthesis occurs under the ice cover, although in much reduced amounts, and some photosynthesis is said to occur in the presence of moonlight. Under this heading should be mentioned the utilization of the half-bound carbon dioxide by Algae; also, its indirect release when plants exhaust the free carbon dioxide, and half-bound carbon dioxide becomes detached as free carbon dioxide by difference in tension.

2. Marl-forming organisms. The following groups of aquatic organisms are known to function in the formation of marl (largely calcium and magnesium carbonate): certain rooted, submerged plants; marl-forming Algae; mollusks which form calcareous shells; and some insects. Lime-precipitating bacteria may also be involved. A few other organisms may function similarly in a minor way. That these organisms, except the bacteria, are related to the formation of the insoluble carbonates is well established, but the nature of the various lime-forming processes involved is not definitely known. In some instances, at least, the carbonate is in the nature of a cell product of the organism. In other cases, the process appears to be a form of external precipitation, brought about by the consumption of half-bound carbon dioxide leaving the insoluble carbonate. Marl eventually sinks to the bottom, and, depending upon circumstances, the carbon dioxide involved goes temporarily or permanently out of circulation. Since these events automatically involve the calcium and the magnesium, and since the whole subject has numerous biological ramifications, it will be discussed more fully elsewhere (pages 190, 196). The status of lime-precipitating bacteria is uncertain. Precipitation of large quantities of calcium carbonate in the sea by a bacterium has been both claimed and disclaimed. Also, the presence of lime-precipitating bacteria in fresh-water lakes still remains to be positively demonstrated.

3. Agitation of water. Under certain circumstances, agitation of water is said to release some of the half-bound carbon dioxide with consequent precipitation of calcium carbonate, although it is also claimed that such release may occur in quiet, inflowing water. Bicarbonate brought in by spring water has been described as giving up half-bound carbon dioxide in this way. Agitation is a very effective method of eliminating free carbon dioxide in water. This accounts, in part, for the fact that surface waters usually show, by chemical test, little free carbon dioxide, although the gas may occur in the deeper parts in large amounts. Much

of the free carbon dioxide formed by decomposition of bottom materials is lost into the air by the circulation and wave agitation of the water. This elimination at the surface goes on constantly except under conditions of dead calm and during periods of ice cover. Water, therefore, is automatically prodigal of one of its most important biological assets, and the losses of free carbon dioxide by this means are often great. Such losses would be even greater if it were not for the fact that in many lakes sufficient amounts of the monocarbonates are present to take up some of the free carbon dioxide before it is lost to the air.

4. Evaporation. Evaporation of waters containing bicarbonates results in the loss of half-bound carbon dioxide and the precipitation of monocarbonate. This form of loss is greatest in shallow lakes of large area where evaporation is most effective.

5. Rise of bubbles from depths. Free carbon dioxide often accumulates in decomposing bottom deposits in such quantities that at frequent intervals increasing internal pressure of the gas exceeds the external pressure, and the excess rises in the form of masses of bubbles, some of large size, to the surface and is lost into the air. Mention has already been made (page 96) of this well-known phenomenon in lakes. While not all bubbles which rise to the surface in summer are composed of free carbon dioxide (other gases may be involved), nevertheless in some waters, at least, much free carbon dioxide is lost in this way.

Solubility of Carbon Dioxide. Carbon dioxide dissolves readily in water. It dissolves in its own volume of water at 760 mm. pressure and 15°C. Solubility follows Henry's law (page 92) closely up to pressures of 4 or 5 atmospheres. Table 10 indicates the influence of temperature on solubility.

TABLE 10. INFLUENCE OF TEMPERATURE UPON SOLUBILITY OF CARBON DIOXIDE[1]

Temperature, °C.	Absorption Coefficient
0	1.713
5	1.424
10	1.194
15	1.019
20	0.878
25	0.759
30	0.665

[1] Values selected from "Handbook of Chemistry and Physics," ed. by Hodgman, Chemical Rubber Company.

Classification of Lakes on Basis of Bound Carbon Dioxide. Birge and Juday (1911) offered the following classification of lakes on the basis of bound carbon dioxide present:

1. Soft-water lakes—those whose waters hold small amounts of calcium

and magnesium in solution and in which the average bound carbon dioxide does not exceed 5 cc. per l.

2. Medium-class lakes—those which contain a medium amount of bound carbon dioxide, i.e., those whose bound carbon dioxide falls between 5 and 22 cc. per l.

3. Hard-water lakes—those which contain more than 22 cc. per l. of bound carbon dioxide. The maximum amount of bound carbon dioxide in lakes of this class may approach or possibly exceed 50 cc. per l.

Interrelations of Free, Bound, and Half-bound Carbon Dioxide. Free carbon dioxide, dissolving in water, combines in part with the water to form carbonic acid. In other words, CO_2 exists in natural waters both as free CO_2 and as H_2CO_3. The relation is supposed to be CO_2 (gas) $\rightleftarrows$ $(1 - n)$ CO_2 (dissolved) $+$ (n) H_2CO_3 in which the value of n is said to be greater than 0.5, meaning that *more than one-half* of the CO_2 in solution is in the form of H_2CO_3 and the remaining portion is simple CO_2. The almost insoluble calcium or magnesium monocarbonate reacts with the carbonic acid to form the soluble bicarbonate. Various processes, some of which have already been mentioned, detach, in one way or another, the half-bound carbon dioxide, causing the resulting carbonate to be released in almost insoluble form, and it settles to the bottom as marl, thus taking out of circulation, temporarily at least and sometimes permanently, the bound carbon dioxide. If the marl so deposited is later overlaid by clayey or other relatively nondecomposable materials, it may become permanently removed from circulation; if, however, it is later brought into contact with free carbon dioxide, which in natural waters is commonly being produced, transformation into the soluble bicarbonate will occur, and it will again be available for circulation. If the supply of carbonate formed or brought into a lake is in such excess that the free carbon dioxide supply cannot convert all of it, such a lake will have a permanent deposit of carbonate even though it may be completely exposed to the water and may become a "marl lake" if the marl-forming agencies continue to outrun the free carbon dioxide-forming agencies. On the other hand, in a lake where the reverse conditions (free carbon dioxide production always exceeds the marl deposition) prevail, marl deposits will be absent. Special circumstances may bring about a regular or an irregular alternation of free carbon dioxide production and consumption so that a corresponding conversion of carbonate into bicarbonate and the reverse occurs. It should be noted, however, that the smaller the calcium and magnesium content the less prominent this whole phenomenon becomes, so that in the very soft waters it is virtually absent. Other bicarbonates, such as iron bicarbonate, $Fe(HCO_3)_2$, may be present in water and not only tie up quantities of carbon dioxide but, under some circumstances, may undergo similar reciprocal transformations. Eroding shores occasionally bring to light the existence of marl beds extending out under the land which were laid down in ancient times when the waters covered a greater area. Such beds together with those which occur buried in the bottoms of lake basins and found only by the use of penetrating marl samplers are mute testimony to the great quantities of those two very important production substances—calcium and carbon dioxide—which the water by its own natural processes has eliminated.

Acidity, Alkalinity, and Neutrality of Water. Formerly, it was the practice to define acidity in natural waters as due to the presence of free carbon dioxide; alkalinity, as the absence of free carbon dioxide and of half-bound carbon dioxide; and neutrality, as that condition in which the monocarbonates were just converted into bicarbonates but with no excess of free carbon dioxide. While the various evolutions of free carbon dioxide are intimately involved in these matters, it is now known that carbon dioxide is but one of many substances in natural waters which bring about conditions of acidity, alkalinity, or neutrality. Since these matters are tied up with the subject of hydrogen-ion concentration, further discussion will occur under that heading (page 114).

Other Dissolved Gases. *Methane.* Methane, sometimes called marsh gas, is one of the products of decomposing organic matter at the bottoms of marshes, ponds, and lakes. Lakes having imperfect overturns may show larger amounts at the bottom than would otherwise be expected. Conditions favorable for production of methane appear at about the time the dissolved oxygen content is exhausted. In lakes in which conditions conducive to methane production continue for four or five months in summer, amounts at the bottom may vary from a mere trace at the beginning of the period to more than 10 cc. per l. In fact, there are records of bottom-water samples which showed almost 40 cc. per l. Under favorable circumstances, large quantities are produced over the period of a summer, much of which escapes into the air. Little is known concerning its formation and fate during the period of ice cover. Mention has already been made of the commonly observed rise of gas bubbles from the bottom. Those large submerged accumulations of decomposing vegetable matter which sometimes occur along the margins of lakes and streams in summer may yield prodigious quantities of methane when the mass is stirred with an oar. It rises to the surface in huge bubbles, and by the judicious use of a lighted torch at the surface of the water it is possible to ignite the escaping gas and cause a momentary flame to flash over the surface, since methane is highly combustible.

Information on the quantities of methane produced in lakes is still very scanty. In a study of decomposition gases evolved, under laboratory conditions, by bottom deposits from Lake Mendota, Wisconsin, Allgeier *et al.* (1932) showed that methane was the chief fermentation product, composing 65 to 85 per cent of the gas produced (Fig. 17).   Conger (1943) measured the methane production during late summer in a small, shallow lake and found it to be approximately 90 cu. ft. per acre per day.   Without doubt the amounts produced in nature vary greatly in different waters and under various conditions, but it appears fairly certain that substantial quantities are not uncommon.

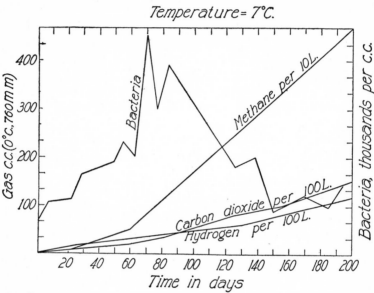

Fig. 17.   Graphs showing the quantities of certain gaseous products of anaerobic fermentation in bottom deposits from Lake Mendota, Wisconsin, evolved over a period of 200 days and of a temperature of 7°C.   (*Modified from Allgeier, Peterson, Juday, and Birge,* 1932.)

Hydrogen Sulfide.   Hydrogen sulfide may appear in the bottom waters of lakes in late summer after anaerobic decomposition has been in action for some time.   It has been discovered that an odor resembling that of sulfuretted hydrogen is not a dependable indication of the presence of hydrogen sulfide, since the odor may be distinct but the chemical test for the gas may show negative results.   When present, it is a product of anaerobic decomposition of organic matter containing sulfur.   It is not uncommon in sewage-contaminated streams.   Lakes and ponds are occasionally found in which the formation of hydrogen sulfide is so great that brass parts of limnological instruments will be heavily tarnished on a single submergence.

Nitrogen.   Nitrogen has a low solubility in water.   It is such an inert gas that the quantities which occur in lake water are not changed by the chemical and biological processes so characteristic of natural waters. The atmosphere usually supplies the greater amounts of nitrogen found in water, although the liberation of elemental nitrogen by the decomposition of lake-bottom deposits has been reported. The maximum amount occurs in winter, since it is more soluble in cold water. Nitrogen-saturated water is common in the epilimnion, and at the conclusion of overturns the entire body of water may be saturated. While the upper water, in the summer, tends to remain at the saturation point, excesses of nitrogen are likely to occur in and below the thermocline. Such excesses are thought to arise in one or both of two ways: (1) The lower water, saturated with nitrogen at the spring overturn, gradually rises in temperature with the advance of summer, thus reducing the absorption capacity of the water and releasing some of the nitrogen. Then the hydrostatic pressure, lack of circulation, and very low rate of diffusion prevent escape of the gas, and supersaturation results. (2) Ground water, frequently bearing an excess of nitrogen, may produce supersaturation in lower waters of lakes.

The autumn overturn provides the lake with a uniform supply of nitrogen from top to bottom. At that time, the water is not only saturated with nitrogen but also has its greatest capacity for dissolved gases. Little seems to be known concerning the dissolved-nitrogen story after the ice cover appears. Much of the lack of specific information concerning free nitrogen in natural waters is due to the fact that because of its inertness, free nitrogen determinations are not a common part of limnological investigations.

Ammonia. Ammonia occurs in small amounts in unmodified natural waters. It is exceedingly soluble, 1 volume of water dissolving 1,300 volumes of ammonia at 0°C. In lakes, it is one of the results of the decomposition of organic matter at the bottom. This accounts, in part, for the fact that in summer free ammonia ordinarily increases with depth and that the bottom ooze may contain a quantity many times that of the layer of water next above it.

In Lake Erie, only small amounts of free ammonia have been reported. In September, surface waters showed 0.038 p.p.m., while at the same time the bottom waters at about 17 m. depth contained only 0.008 p.p.m. Increase in amount in the upper waters with advance of the summer season was found; but the opposite result occurred in bottom waters. The quantities are much lower than those found in Wisconsin lakes.

Sulfur Dioxide. Traces of sulfur dioxide may occur in natural waters.

Hydrogen. Liberation of hydrogen in the anaerobic decomposition of lake-bottom deposits seems likely. It appears, however, that the amounts so formed are small.

Carbon Monoxide. Carbon monoxide may occur in the bottom of the hypolimnion but ordinarily in such small amounts as to be of little significance, supposedly, from the biological standpoint.

DISSOLVED SOLIDS

All waters in nature contain dissolved solids. Water is the universal solvent, dissolving more different materials than any other liquid. This remarkable quality coupled with the many ways by means of which natural waters may come into contact with a great array of soluble substances explains the complexity of a chemical analysis of such waters. Mere contact with its own basin, erosion at shore line, wind-blown materials, inflow of surface waters, inflow of seepage and other forms of subterranean waters, decay of aquatic organisms—these and other sources provide a lake with quantities of solid materials either already

TABLE 11. TOTAL DISSOLVED SOLIDS IN A SELECTED SERIES OF LAKES
Data from Clarke

Name	Total Dissolved Solids, p.p.m.
Moosehead Lake, Maine	16.0
Bass Lake, Vilas Co., Wisconsin	18.3
Tahoe Lake, California	73.0
Crater Lake, Oregon	80.4
Green Lake, Wisconsin	174.5
Utah Lake, Utah	1,165.0
Devils Lake, North Dakota	11,278.0
Soap Lake, Grant Co., Washington	28,200.0
Sevier Lake, Utah	86,400.0
Large Soda Lake, Nevada	113,700.0
Lake Superior	60.0
Lake Michigan	118.0
Lake Huron	108.0
Lake Erie	133.0

in solution or subsequently becoming so. It has been stated that water to the amount of about 6,500 cu. miles runs off the land in a year, carrying with it about 5 trillion tons of dissolved solids. Drainage systems are the transportation avenues for this vast quantity of dissolved material and often deliver it into lakes. As might be expected, these dissolved solids vary markedly, both qualitatively and quantitatively, in different waters; they also vary in the same waters depending upon season, location, and other factors. It is impracticable to attempt here a catalogue of the different kinds of dissolved solids. Almost any complete chemical analysis of lake waters shows how complex the content is. With respect to quantity, rain water usually contains 30 to 40 p.p.m. of dissolved solids, which means that even the very recently fallen rain water which collects in temporary basins already has a certain dissolved content before it has a chance to acquire more from other sources. As a very rough estimate, it might be said that lake waters in general vary in content from about 15 to 300 p.p.m. and sometimes much more, as, for example, in the inland salt lakes.   The brief table (Table 11) on page 106 includes data, selected for illustrative purposes only, from a compilation by Clarke (1924).

DISSOLVED INORGANIC SOLIDS

It seems probable that most if not all of the various dissolved inorganic matters common to natural waters play some part, directly or indirectly, in the biology of aquatic organisms.   However, certain ones are regarded at present as being more immediately significant and have received more attention from investigators.   The more prominent ones will be discussed in the following paragraphs.

Inorganic Nitrogen Compounds.   *Nitrates.*   Nitrates occur in varying amounts in different lakes; also, the supply in a given lake varies with the

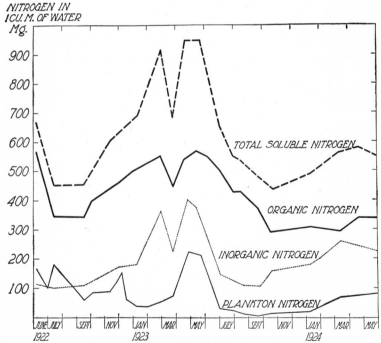

FIG. 18.   Forms of nitrogen found in 1 cu. m. of surface water of Lake Mendota, Wisconsin. (*Redrawn from Domogalla, Juday, and Peterson, 1925.*)

season, as shown in Figs. 18 and 19.   Owing to its relation to the nitrate bacteria and to the nitrate-consuming organisms (page 291), the nitrate content of natural waters is likely to be in a continually changing state. There is reason for believing that in certain waters, at least, the annual variation is of a regular nature, in both fresh and marine situations. Variations in amounts with depth are to be expected, although a temporary condition approaching uniformity may occur at certain times of year, and it may disappear completely in some waters for a certain period. According to studies made on Lake Monona, Wisconsin, the nitrate content at 20 m. conspicuously exceeds that at the surface from March to June inclusive and in December; while from July to September inclusive, the reverse is true. Actual amounts of nitrate are usually small, irrespective of situation, season, or depth, although it is said that considerable quantities occur in the deep water of the Atlantic Ocean and in the north-

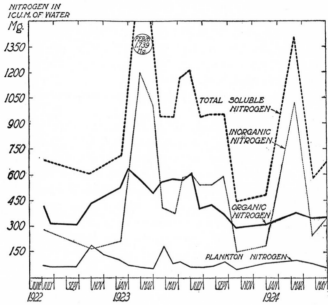

FIG. 19. Forms of nitrogen found in 1 cu. m. of bottom water in Lake Mendota, Wisconsin. (*Redrawn from Domogalla, Juday, and Peterson*, 1925.)

ern part of the North Sea. Whether such amounts ever exist in fresh waters does not seem to be known. Since all of these matters are inseparably tied up with certain biological processes, further consideration will be deferred until later (page 199).

Ammonium Salts. Natural waters contain some ammonium salts. Ammonium carbonate is probably the common form. For further consideration, see the section on bacteria (page 280).

Silicon. Silicon does not occur in nature as a free element. Natural waters commonly contain silicon dioxide in some form of soluble silicate. Silica may also exist in certain waters, particularly in rivers, in colloidal form. The dissolved form, however, is of most direct interest here.

Analyses are commonly expressed in terms of the insoluble silicon dioxide. River waters are relatively rich in silica and often markedly affect the silica content of lakes into which they flow. Quantities may vary with (1) different lakes; (2) season of year; (3) presence or absence of stratification; (4) nature and periodicity of inflowing water; (5) diatom productivity; (6) depth; and (7) other possible factors which need not be mentioned here. A silicon stratification may be present at certain times of the year.

Phosphorus. Much interest has been manifested of recent years in the phosphorus content of waters, both fresh and marine. Free phosphorus does not occur in nature, but in the form of phosphates it is abundant. It has been estimated that roughly 0.12 per cent of the earth's crust is composed of combined phosphorus. Calcium phosphate is the common phosphate, composing the principal part of "phosphate rock." Phosphates are widely distributed in certain soils, certain ores, and the bodies of animals and plants.

Total phosphorus in lake water is usually regarded as divisible into two components: *soluble phosphorus* which is in the phosphate form and *organic phosphorus* which is contained in plankton organisms and other organic matter in the water. Juday and Birge (1931) found that in 479 lakes in northeastern Wisconsin the mean quantity of *soluble phosphorus* in the surface water was 0.003 mg. per l., with a range of zero in nine lakes to a maximum of 0.015 in one; the mean quantity of *organic phosphorus* in surface water was 0.020 mg. per l., with a range of 0.005 to 0.103. Seasonal and vertical differences in distribution of phosphorus within the same lake are common. It now appears that most lakes contain relatively small amounts of phosphorus and are subject to variation.

Since phosphorus is now regarded as of great importance in the determination of biological productivity in water, its source, cycle within the lake, and loss are of vital concern. The ultimate source is the phosphorus-bearing rocks which are near enough to be available. Soluble phosphorus is delivered to a lake by inflowing water which has picked it up in connection with erosive processes. Organic phosphorus, originating elsewhere, may also be brought in by tributaries. Artificial additions may occur in connection with pollution or soil fertilization.

Once within a lake, the phosphorus enters into a complicated cycle involving various physical, chemical, and biological processes. These processes tend to keep the phosphorus in the lake water, either in soluble or organic form, by a continuous series of conversions from one form to the other.

Losses of phosphorus occur through outflowing water which removes both soluble and organic forms. A certain quantity is likely to be lost to the bottom deposits, but it should be noted that while some of this loss may be permanent a certain part of it is returnable to circulation, particularly the organic phosphorus in the uppermost stratum of the bottom. Loss may also occur through artificial removal of fish, mollusks, water plants, or other organisms.

Other Elements. Many other inorganic substances occur in water in amounts which range from substantial quantities down to mere traces. Certain elements, such as calcium, magnesium, manganese, iron, sodium, potassium, sulfur, copper, and others, constitute elements of chemical compounds dissolved in the water and, in one way or another, play very important parts in determining the nature of environments. Greater amounts are found in some lakes than others, and variations, both seasonal and irregular, may exist. As will appear later, certain ones have been regarded as indices of productivity. In addition to the elements named above, there is increasing evidence that many others have environmental functions the value of which is not yet understood.

Dissolved Organic Matter

The presence of organisms of a wide variety, both within a lake and about its margins, insures the more or less continual addition of organic materials to the water, some of which, immediately or later, go into solution. Thus, all waters in nature have a certain content of dissolved organic matter. Such substances may be transient, undergoing further chemical changes, but the supply is maintained in a somewhat irregular fashion by certain continuous processes, such as production of wastes by living animals, death and disintegration of the various organisms, accretions of organic materials due to wind action, inflowing waters bringing extractions from soil and marshes, and wave action at margins. Much remains to be learned concerning dissolved organic materials, their role, and their cycle, in spite of the fact that a large literature on the subject exists. Conflicting statements have been made in the past as to the amounts of dissolved organic matter normally present in water. Analyses of contaminated waters often show a much larger content than normal waters. In the past, more attention has been given to marine waters, but an extensive series of studies of Wisconsin lakes by Birge and Juday has made available valuable information as to the dissolved organic matter in lakes of the type commonly found in northern United States. Among other things, they found (1) that the average amount, for the lakes studied, of dissolved organic matter is 12.8 mg. per l. of water; (2) that the range is 2.9 to 39.6 mg.; (3) that for each lake the dissolved organic matter does not show great quantitative or qualitative variation either with depth or with season; hence, a single analysis reveals the character of the lake; (4) that the great changes of dissolved oxygen content in the hypolimnion have little effect on the total dissolved organic matter; (5) that the quantity of dissolved organic matter is much greater in fresh-water lakes than in the sea; and (6) that the standing crop of dissolved organic matter is ordinarily several times, often many times, greater than the organic matter in the total plankton supported by the same water.

The term *dissolved organic matter* requires some explanation. Since lake waters contain plankton and other materials in suspension, water for analysis of the dissolved matter must first be put through a high-speed centrifuge or some very effective filter in order that these materials may be removed in so far as such removal is possible. If samples of such

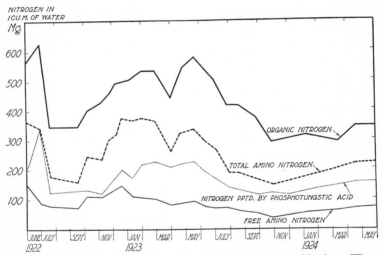

Fig. 20. Forms of organic nitrogen in the surface water of Lake Mendota, Wisconsin. (*Redrawn from Domogalla, Juday, and Peterson, 1925.*)

centrifuged or filtered water be evaporated slowly, the dry residues may be expected to contain contributions from (1) a certain amount of unremoved plankton and organic debris; (2) various colloids; and (3) true solutions. "Probably by far the greater portion of the 'soluble nitrogen' or the 'dissolved carbon' is dissolved only as egg albumen or starch may be said to be dissolved in water" (Birge and Juday).

Kinds of Dissolved Organic Substances. Little seems to be known concerning the specific nature of dissolved organic materials as they occur in natural waters, but without doubt they (1) are of many diverse sorts and (2) contain many compounds which are of great biological significance. Recent studies have centered around the determination of organic nitrogen, organic carbon, and ether extracts (fats).

Dissolved Organic Nitrogen. Table 12 and Figs. 20 and 21 present results obtained from certain Wisconsin lakes.

TABLE 12.   DISSOLVED ORGANIC NITROGEN IN LAKE WATER, MILLIGRAMS PER LITER
From Birge and Juday

Lake	Depth, m.	Maximum	Minimum	Mean
Mendota..............	0	0.484	0.307	0.398
Mendota..............	20	0.559	0.304	0.385
11 others..............	0	0.744	0.219	0.517

Among the same records, one from the surface waters of Lake Michigan in February showed only 0.143 mg. per l., a value much lower than the smallest of the other records.

The existence of amino acids in lake waters has been demonstrated, and Table 13 indicates the kinds and quantities.

In addition to the amino acids mentioned in Table 13, arginine has also been found in certain Wisconsin lakes.

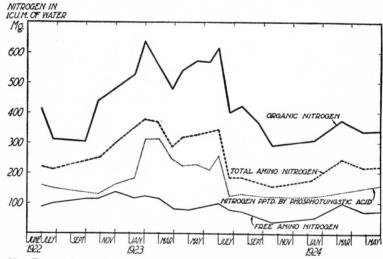

FIG. 21.   Forms of organic nitrogen in the bottom water of Lake Mendota, Wisconsin. (*Redrawn from Domogalla, Juday, and Peterson, 1925.*)

Dissolved Organic Carbon.   Results included in Table 14 represent quantities of organic carbon in certain Wisconsin lakes.

This dissolved carbon is an integral part of certain chemical compounds.   In the residues of certain Wisconsin lakes, obtained by evaporating large samples of water from which the plankton had been removed by centrifuging, the proteins were computed to contain about 53 per cent carbon, the fats about 75 per cent carbon, and the carbohydrates about 54 per cent carbon.   A determination of *total carbon* includes (1) *plankton carbon*, that carbon contained in the organisms (mostly plankton) and the particulate matters which are removed by a high-speed centrifuge;

and (2) dissolved carbon, that carbon contained in substances in true solution or in colloidal state or in such extremely minute organisms as may escape the centrifuge. The average nitrogen-carbon ratio in the plankton was found by Birge and Juday to be about 1 to 6, while in the dissolved matter it was about 1 to 14 or 15.

TABLE 13. CERTAIN AMINO ACIDS IN LAKE WATERS, MILLIGRAMS PER CUBIC METER
From Peterson, Fred, and Damogalla

Amino acid	Method	Lake Mendota surface, June 18, 1924	Lake Mendota bottom, June 25, 1924	Devils Lake, Oct. 10, 1923	Green Lake, July 18, 1923	Lake Michigan, Feb. 28, 1924	Turtle Lake, Jan. 18, 1924
Tryptophane.....	Fürth and Nobel	10.1	13.1	12.2	14.2	5.5	8.6
Tryptophane.....	Folin and Looney	11.0	14.6	12.9	16.4	7.8	10.6
Tryptophane.....	May and Rose	9.9	12.2	.....	16.1	6.1	
Tyrosine.........	Folin and Looney	10.4	12.5	17.6	9.6	8.3	16.7
Histidine.........	Roessler and Hanke	5.7	10.2	14.8	19.2	6.7	22.7
Cystine..........	Folin and Looney	1.5	6.1	3.3	4.4	2.1	7.5
Total organic nitrogen...............		320	357	117	310	143	487

TABLE 14. DISSOLVED ORGANIC CARBON, MILLIGRAMS PER LITER
From Birge and Juday

Lake	Minimum	Maximum	Mean
Mendota...........................	4.00	7.95	5.80
Other lakes........................	3.02	13.22	6.66

Fats (Ether Extract). Under the term *ether extract* are included those substances usually designated as *fats*. In certain Wisconsin lakes, it has been found to differ in amount from about 0.2 to nearly 0.8 mg. per l. of water. These dissolved fats are much greater in amount than those in the plankton from the same amount of lake water, although in spite of this fact they constitute a smaller proportion of the total dissolved matter than they do of the total organic matter in the plankton.

Total Dissolved Organic Matter. As already mentioned, the dissolved organic matter is a mixture of many, often a great many, different substances. But since the knowledge of this field is still so very incomplete, some of the computations of component parts of these materials are, at present, only approximations. In results reported by Birge and Juday, the crude protein was computed as 6.25 times the organic nitrogen; the carbon in the protein was given a value of 53 per cent. Since organic carbon occurs in other dissolved materials, two general sources are involved: (1) from the nitrogenous substances and (2) from the non-nitrogenous substances. The latter were computed as carbohydrates which, in turn, were computed as starch or cellulose and contain an average of about 45 per cent carbon. Sugars occur in very slight amounts. The fats were regarded as having a carbon content of 75 per cent.

HYDROGEN-ION CONCENTRATION

It is now known that an important means of understanding the chemical conditions which prevail in natural waters is through the measurement of hydrogen-ion concentration. In 1887, the Swedish chemist Arrhenius advanced an hypothesis that the molecules of an electrolyte put into solution are largely broken up into their constituent radicals, each radical carrying an electrical charge, positive or negative. These charged portions or radicals are called *ions*, and the hypothesis is known as the *ionic hypothesis*. The fundamental feature of this hypothesis is now accepted as established fact. Among the many subsequent developments of the ionic hypothesis is one which has far-reaching effects, viz., the resolution of *acidity* into two features: (1) the concentration of the hydrogen ions and (2) the amount of acid necessary to furnish a given amount of ionized hydrogen. The conditions known as acidity, alkalinity, and neutrality were long ago recognized by chemists and others as having intimate relations to many biochemical phenomena. Years ago, the commonplace method of determining the reaction of a substance was by the use of litmus, a test now known to be hopelessly inadequate for precise work of many kinds. About thirty-five years ago, Sørensen published results of some important investigations on the effect of the hydrogen ion upon enzyme activity in connection with which he developed very precise methods for measuring hydrogen-ion concentration, methods which led to a remarkable advance in biochemistry. During the past few decades, hydrogen-ion concentration has been studied in almost every field of scientific endeavor, with accompanying development of diverse and highly refined methods. Methods for measuring hydrogen-ion concentration have developed far beyond those for measuring concentrations of other kinds of ions. As will appear later in this discussion, the hydrogen ion is a dissociation product of most of the substances having biochemical significance.

In order to lay the foundation for an understanding of what is meant by hydrogen-ion concentration, it will be necessary to mention briefly, by way of review, certain well-established chemical facts:

1. Ionization is a form of dissociation of a compound in solution and constitutes a true chemical change.

2. Compounds put into solution in water are inherently different from each other to the extent to which they ionize under the same conditions.

3. Strong electrolytes dissociate more completely than do weak electrolytes, under the same conditions.

4. Ionization becomes more complete as the solution becomes more and more dilute.

5. Since complete ionization seldom if ever happens, a compound dissociates into a certain number of positively and negatively charged ions, leaving a residue of the original compound undissociated.

6. Pure water is itself both an extremely weak acid and an extremely weak base, dissociating into the two ions H+ and OH− to an exceedingly small extent (at ordinary temperatures, the fraction is less than 0.000,000,002). It is therefore virtually a nonconductor of electric current.

7. A *base* is any substance furnishing, on ionization, the negatively charged hydroxyl ion OH−. For example, NaOH dissociates to form Na+ and OH−. *Strong bases* ionize more completely than do the *weak bases* under the same conditions.

8. An *acid* is any substance furnishing, on ionization, the positively charged hydrogen ion H+; i.e., an acid yields two kinds of ions, viz., hydrogen ions and some other kind of ion. For example, HCl dissociates to form H+ and Cl− ions. *Strong acids* ionize more completely than do *weak acids* under the same conditions.

9. *Salts* are substances furnishing on ionization a positive ion other than hydrogen and a negative ion other than hydroxyl. With few exceptions, they ionize extensively.

ACIDITY, ALKALINITY, AND NEUTRALITY

The terms *acidity, alkalinity,* and *neutrality* are in common and almost everyday use, but often their exact meaning is not clearly understood. In fact, these terms involve a rather complicated chemical subject which cannot be discussed here. Distinctions given herein stress merely those features which seem necessary for present purposes and make no pretense of satisfying completely all chemical demands.

Acidity. The condition usually known as acidity involves two components: (1) quantity, or total available acid; and (2) intensity, or concentration of hydrogen ions. Thus, it appears that hydrogen-ion concentration is not equivalent to acidity, as is sometimes the loose use of the term, but is only one aspect of it, viz., *acid intensity.* An acid, containing as it does a positive ionizing hydrogen radical, ionizes in aqueous solution, thus increasing the number of free hydrogen ions. Increase of the number of these ions means increase in their concentration, and as the concentration increases the greater becomes the acid *intensity* of the solution. Waters yield both hydrogen ions and hydroxyl ions. According to an important law, the product of the hydrogen-ion concentration and the hydroxyl concentration is a *constant*. This means that the greater the hydrogen-ion concentration the less in the same degree the hydroxyl-ion concentration, and vice versa. In ordinary work, a water solution is called *acid* when the hydrogen-ion concentration exceeds to any degree the hydroxyl-ion concentration.

Alkalinity. Likewise, in ordinary work, a water is described as *alkaline* when the hydroxyl-ion concentration exceeds, to any degree, the hydrogen-ion concentration. Because of the constant mathematical relation of the hydroxyl ions to the hydrogen ions in the same water, the alkaline intensities can also be expressed in terms of the hydrogen-ion concentration.

Neutrality. In chemically pure water, obtained by repeated distillations in insoluble containers, the hydrogen- and hydroxyl-ion concentrations are equal. This condition constitutes *neutrality*.

EXPRESSION OF HYDROGEN-ION CONCENTRATION

Two methods of expressing hydrogen-ion concentration are in common use. They are as follows:

1. The number of moles of ionized hydrogen per liter. Since this method involves the use of the numbers themselves or the expression of these numbers in reduced form by means of an exponent (example, 0.000,000,001, or 1×10^{-9}), thereby becoming unwieldy or inconvenient, this method is in less use than the following one.

2. The pH scale. This scale, originally employed by Sørensen, expresses hydrogen-ion concentration as the "logarithm of the reciprocal of the normality of free hydrogen ions." It may also be expressed by the following formula.

$$\text{pH} = \frac{1}{\log_{10} \text{ H-ion concentration in gram equivalents per liter}}$$

Thus, pH = 8 means that the hydrogen-ion concentration would be 10^{-8}, or $\frac{1}{10^8}$, or $\frac{1}{100,000,000}$, or 0.000,000,01 normal.

Again, pH = 6 indicates a hydrogen-ion concentration of 10^{-6}, or $\frac{1}{10^6}$, or $\frac{1}{1,000,000}$, or 0.000,001 normal.

This scale, as commonly used, extends from pH = 0.0 to pH = 14.0, with three fixed points as follows:

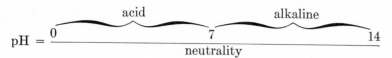

The value pH = 0 represents the pH of a solution normal in hydrogen ions; pH = 14, a solution normal in hydroxyl ions; and pH = 7.0, the pH of a *neutral* solution. All values between pH = 0 and pH = 7 represent acid reactions; between 7 and 14, the reaction is alkaline. It must be carefully noted that as the values *approach* pH = 0, the acidity *increases;* whereas the alkalinity *increases* as pH = 14 is approached. A habit has grown up in some circles of speaking of a "higher pH" or a "lower pH" if the exponent is higher or lower in the numerical scale, but, as a matter of fact, such descriptive expressions are misleading, since the thing being measured is hydrogen-ion concentration, and increase in concentration is expressed by the diminishing numerical value of the exponent. It has also become a common practice to omit the equality sign after the expression pH.

Although it is not necessary to attempt to go into the intricacies of this subject here, it should be noted that the adoption of pH 7 as the point of neutrality on the basis of its being the pH of pure water has certain inherent objections for the biochemist, since the hydrogen-ion concentration of such water has no "general relation to the hydrogen-ion concentration at the equivalence point sought in the 'neutralization' of an aqueous solution of an acid by an aqueous solution of a base," because this exact point is dependent upon such features as the variation of temperature and the salt content of the solution. However, for most limnological purposes, the approximation of neutrality at pH 7 is sufficiently accurate.

The meaning of the symbol pH should be explained. Sørensen, the originator of the symbol, proposed the representation of hydrogen-ion concentration by a negative power of 10 (*"puissance négative de* 10) (*"*10^{-p}*"*), using, however, the *reciprocal* form of the exponent (10^p). Combined with the symbol for hydrogen, the original form was p_H. Therefore, the symbol is sometimes explained as the "power of hydrogen." Also, since it is linked with the potential of a hydrogen electrode in an apparatus in common use, the explanation is sometimes offered as "potential of hydrogen." Typographical convenience has been given as the explanation for changing the original form p_H to pH, the latter now being in general although not exclusive use.

MEASUREMENT OF HYDROGEN-ION CONCENTRATION

Methods of measuring hydrogen-ion concentration are, in general, of two kinds: (1) electrometric and (2) colorimetric. The electrometric methods depend essentially upon determining pH through the measurement of electrical conductivity of the liquid to be tested. Colorimetric methods, on the other hand, depend upon the addition of the proper sensitive indicator solutions to the sample and then comparing the color so produced with graded, colored standards the pH values of which are known. The procedures and equipments for operating both of these methods are at present numerous and varied. Of these two general types, the electrometric has a higher precision.

SUBSTANCES YIELDING HYDROGEN IONS TO INLAND WATERS

Owing to the great variety of substances which occur in water or make contact with it, numerous compounds may be present which contribute ionized hydrogen. They vary greatly both qualitatively and quantitatively and are of many sources. To enumerate them, even if all were adequately known, would not be possible here. Without doubt, natural waters obtain the vast quantity of contained ionized hydrogen from their contacts with the various sorts of soils. In the following statement, Wherry (1920) lists the groups of substances occurring in various soils which yield hydrogen ions to the soil solution:

SOIL CONSTITUENTS YIELDING HYDROGEN IONS

I. Directly (when treated with water alone).
  A. Inorganic:
    1. Strong, highly ionized acids, such as hydrochloric, sulfuric, and nitric.
    2. Weak, slightly ionized acids, especially carbonic.
    3. Acid salts, such as potassium acid sulfate, which may be moderately or slightly ionized (as acids).
    4. Salts of weak bases with strong acids, such as aluminium chloride and ammonium sulfate, which are slightly hydrolyzed and therefore yield a small amount of hydrogen ions.
  B. Organic:
    1. Strong, highly ionized acids, such as oxalic.
    2. Weak, slightly ionized acids, such as acetic.
    3. Acid salts, such as potassium acid sulfate, which may be moderately or slightly ionized (as acids).
    4. Salts of weak bases with strong acids, such as aluminum citrate and ammonium oxalate, which are hydrolyzed as in *A*4.
    5. Amino acids, such as aspartic (aminosuccinic) acid, which may be moderately or slightly ionized.
    6. Humic acids, which, if they exist at all, are all slightly ionized.
II. Indirectly (when treated with solutions of salts).
  A. Inorganic, especially colloidal clay.
  B. Organic, especially colloidal humus.

This analysis will suggest how complex the problem of accounting for the sources of ionized hydrogen in natural waters is; and while it may be that seldom if ever are all of these sources involved in a single body of water, it must be remembered that the collection of waters by any form of drainage may have the effect of mixing waters of diverse origins and diverse exposures to soil conditions.   One tributary may drain a series of bogs; another may collect water of a very different history.   In addition to the relations of inflowing water and to the contacts of the water with the soil, developments within the body of water itself may also help determine the concentration of hydrogen ions.

Range of Hydrogen-ion Concentration in Natural Waters

In various kinds of natural, unmodified waters, hydrogen-ion concentration differs from at least pH 3.2 to 10.5 inclusive.   Water in the outlet of a thermal spring in Japan has been reported to have a pH of 2.2.   The expectation in most ordinary lakes and streams is a range of about pH 6.5 to 8.5.   However, it may happen that the diversity of waters in a relatively small region may be such that the extremes of the total range mentioned above (pH 3.2 to 10.5) may be almost realized; for example, the various lakes, all natural and unmodified, located within a radius of 10 miles of the University of Michigan Biological Station, Douglas Lake, Michigan (extreme northern end of Southern Peninsula), show a mid-summer range of pH 4.3 to 9.4 in the open waters of the different lakes; and if there be included the waters which occur in the *Sphagnum* mats and accumulate in small marginal pools, the range is pH 3.3 to 9.4.   The Great Lakes, the larger inland lakes, and perhaps the majority of the smaller inland lakes of North America are alkaline in reaction.   Many bog lakes are acid in reaction, although numerous exceptions occur. Waters composed mainly of the seepages from coal-bearing strata are likely to be acid.

Changes of Hydrogen-ion Concentration

Annual Changes.   Ordinarily, the surface waters of larger lakes undergo relatively small change in pH from season to season.   Special circumstances surrounding smaller lakes may impose changes of greater magnitude.   In the deeper waters, however, extensive changes are to be expected and have a definite relation to overturns, stagnation periods, duration of ice cover, nature of bottom materials, and other circumstances.   Some indication of these more definite, periodic changes is given in Fig. 22.   Bottom waters may change from alkaline to acid reaction, and there are on record lakes which even in the surface waters swing back and forth, with sequence of seasons, from alkaline to acid conditions, and vice versa.

Seasonal Changes.   In the larger lakes, the hydrogen-ion concentration of the epilimnion often remains surprisingly uniform during the spring, summer, and autumn   During the period 1918–1930, the surface waters of Douglas Lake, Michigan, in summer showed a variation of only pH 7.8 to 8.6.   Progressive changes occur, as already mentioned, in the deep waters at times, such as the stagnation periods and the period of continuous ice cover. In the very small, shallow lakes, irregular changes in pH may be common. In some instances, increased rainfall makes striking changes in pH.

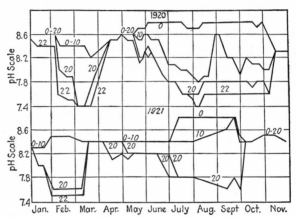

FIG. 22.   Diagram showing hydrogen-ion concentration in Lake Mendota during 1920 and 1921.   Numerals on the curves indicate depths in meters.   (*Adapted by Chapman*, 1921, *from Juday, Fred, and Wilson*, 1924, *McGraw-Hill Book Company, Inc.*)

General Changes.   General changes in pH of a progressive, apparently permanent kind are absent in the large lakes or, if present, are so extremely slight as to be indistinguishable in records now available. Perhaps this is also true of most smaller lakes.   However, a lake is occasionally found which manifests such changes in a striking way.   The following table (Table 15) gives the midsummer changes which the author has witnessed in the surface waters of Vincent Lake, Michigan, a small bog lake.

TABLE 15.   GENERAL CHANGES IN pH IN VINCENT LAKE, MICHIGAN
Midsummer records only

Year	pH	Year	pH
1923	4.4	1928	6.3
1924	4.4	1929	6.6
1925	4.4	1930	6.7
1926	7.1	1931	6.6
1927	6.4	1932	5.7

Diurnal Changes.   In the smaller lakes and in ponds, variations in pH on different days and at different times of the same day may be noticeable. This is especially true of those bays, coves, ponds, and other protected areas which maintain a considerable crop of aquatic plants.   In such situations, these diurnal changes in pH are largely the result of photosynthetic and respiratory processes of the various organisms concerned. Diurnal changes in the large bodies of water, if they occur at all, are so slight as to be difficult of detection. In fact, it has been stated that no significant diurnal changes of pH occur in the open sea, and probably the same is true of the very large lakes. Like oxygen pulses, changes of pH in dense vegetation beds may be easily detected if the water is in a state of complete calm but are almost or quite indistinguishable if the water is in vigorous motion, since the moving water tends to dilute and distribute the products of photosynthesis and respiration. Changes of pH 7.7 to 9.6 have been reported by Philip (1927) in protected waters containing considerable Algae. Other changes of similar magnitude are known.

ABRUPT TRANSITIONS OF HYDROGEN-ION CONCENTRATION

Occasionally, circumstances permit waters of strikingly different pH to exist in close proximity to each other. Instances of this sort occur in certain bog lakes in which the water of the open lake is distinctly *alkaline* while the water in the *Sphagnum* mat which borders the alkaline water is distinctly acid, the two waters separated from each other by a gradient of not more than a few inches. This situation is due without doubt to the fact that the water in the *Sphagnum* mat is so very thoroughly pocketed by the vegetation that no circulation or movement is possible. At the junctions of streams of diverse waters or of streams and lakes whose waters differ widely, similar transitions, although less extensive, may be found.

BUFFER EFFECT

Since natural waters contain a variety of substances, and since these substances vary greatly, both qualitatively and quantitatively, such waters differ not only in the character of the reaction (pH) but also in the *buffer effect*. In some waters, the range of chemical change which may occur without altering the reaction is large, while in others it may be small. If this range is large, the water is said to have high buffer effect; if it is small, the water has little buffer effect. Weak acids and weak bases have greater buffer action in preventing rapid changes in hydrogen-ion concentration because of the fact that the initial ionization is low. When newly entering substances affect the hydrogen-ion concentration at any instant, the remaining undissociated molecules yield ions (become ionized) until a new equilibrium is established which has about the same hydrogen-ion concentration as before. Therefore, a greater amount of the modifying substance is necessary to bring about distinct changes in the reaction of the solution. Waters containing large amounts of dissolved matters are most likely to show high buffer effect, while low buffer effect is to be expected in waters very low in dissolved materials. As an example of substances which influence buffer effect, the action of carbonates may be mentioned. If, in water containing the monocarbonates and bicarbonates of calcium [$CaCO_3$ and $Ca(HCO_3)_2$] and magnesium [$MgCO_3$ and $Mg(HCO_3)_2$], carbon dioxide is withdrawn from solution, as for example by the action of chlorophyll-bearing plants, some of the bicarbonate dissociates at once into the monocarbonate and carbonic acid (H_2CO_3). Ifc arbon dioxide be added, as for example by decomposition of bottom deposits or by respiratory activity of animals and plants, some or all of it combines at once with the monocarbonate to form bicarbonate. In the absence of carbonates, additions or reductions of the free carbon dioxide would result in the increase or decrease respectively of the carbonic acid and would of course alter the hydrogen-ion concentration accordingly; but in the presence of the carbonates, the addition or withdrawal of the carbon dioxide immediately results in the reestablishment of the original equilibrium, and the hydrogen-ion concentration tends to remain the same. It must be understood that this holds only within the inherent limits of the buffer substances. In the example just given, the calcium and magnesium carbonates are *buffer substances*.

The effect of inflowing acids or bases on the pH of a lake will depend upon its buffer action. Soft-water lakes have low buffer action, and the sudden changes in hydrogen-ion concentration which sometimes occur in them following heavy rains, freshets, and the like are often due to this fact. Hard-water lakes, on the other hand, have high buffer action, and a similar inflow would either have a very much smaller effect or possibly have no appreciable effect at all unless the entry of substances were great.

RESERVE pH

Reserve pH, indicated by the symbol RpH, is measured by a second pH determination made after the sample is thoroughly aerated. Aeration of a sample may or may not result in the RpH being of different value from the initial pH; if the total pH is due to substances in the water not releasable by aeration, the RpH will be of the same value; if due in part to substances released by aeration, such as free CO_2, the RpH will have a higher numerical value than the original pH reading. At the present time, the value of this new and somewhat undeveloped measurement seems to rest on the possible ground that the RpH is an index of *alkali reserve* or some other significant feature of water.

ELECTROLYTES

Acids, bases, and salts in solution in water are conductors of electricity and are therefore known as *electrolytes*. Since acids, bases, and salts differ in their solubility in water, they differ in their conductivity of electricity, those with slight solubility being *weak electrolytes* and manifesting low conductivity, while those with high solubility are *strong electrolytes* and show high conductivity. A measure of the total electrolytes in natural waters can therefore be secured by measuring the electrical conductivity of a sample of that water. It has been claimed that, other things being equal, the richer a body of water in electrolytes the greater its biological productivity.

The quantity of electrolytes held in solution in natural, uncontaminated waters differs widely, as shown by conductivity measurements. Michigan lakes are known to have a conductance range of about 10 to 330 reciprocal megohms; doubtless these values do not include the actual range, since but relatively few lakes have been tested. Juday and Birge (1933) determined the conductivity of more than 500 lakes in northeastern Wisconsin and found the range to be 9 to 124 reciprocal megohms.

Conductivity may show diurnal variations, one of the principal causes apparently being the change in electrolyte content due to the assimilation processes of green plants. Annual variations may occur in some lakes; they may be lacking in others.

Vertical distribution of electrolytes differs in different lakes. The various chemical and biological processes may have a conspicuous effect upon the vertical distribution of the electrolytes in some lakes, while in others they seem to result in a uniform vertical distribution throughout the whole summer season. Frequently, lakes show a uniform conductivity value from the surface to the lowermost stratum of water, but in this lowermost stratum the value may be several units higher.

SEASONAL CYCLE OF DISSOLVED GASES AND ESSENTIAL SUBSTANCES

A sufficient amount of chemical background has now been laid so that the complex seasonal cycle can be presented The profound significance of thermal stratification was mentioned previously (page 49). Upon it will now be built another section of the stratification story. It will be assumed at this point that the details of thermal stratification have been mastered and are clearly in mind. The same order of seasonal events presented in the discussion of thermal stratification will serve as the outline of the chemical history, and the situation described first will be that of a *typical temperate lake* of the *second order*.

Temperate Lake of the Second Order

Spring Overturn. *Dissolved Oxygen.* Complete circulation of the water of a lake at the spring overturn, coming as it does at a time when the water is very cold and thereby having its greatest capacity for dissolved oxygen, insures not only equal distribution of dissolved oxygen from surface to bottom but also the taking on by the water of its maximum load of oxygen. Only at one other time during the year, viz., the fall overturn, does the lake hold such a supply of dissolved oxygen. Birge has expressed this fact in a striking way by comparing a lake to the respiration of an organism and describing the overturns as the times when the lake "takes a deep breath." So effective are this stirring and circulation of the water that not only is it usually oxygenated up to or very near saturation for that temperature, but also it is distributed uniformly from top to bottom. At that time, a depth-distribution curve for dissolved oxygen is a straight line. Only in the event of an *incomplete overturn* would the dissolved oxygen history depart from that just described.

Other Dissolved Gases. Decomposition gases, such as free carbon dioxide, methane, hydrogen sulfide, and others, which may have accumulated in the bottom waters during the winter, are redistributed by the overturn and ultimately discharged at the surface, so that at the end of the overturn period, all of these gases are virtually absent. The lake has become completely ventilated. Nitrogen is more uniformly distributed.

Hydrogen-ion Concentration. Since the overturn brings about a uniform mixing of the water, the hydrogen-ion concentration becomes the same at all levels.

Suspended Materials. During the overturn, suspended materials, living or dead and including the plankton, are uniformly distributed to all depths. They may be much increased quantitatively owing to the fact that the movement of the water brings again into suspension and circulation some of the finely divided materials which had previously settled to the bottom. For this reason, the overturn in some lakes is the period of greatest turbidity. Care must be taken, however, not to attribute all of this increased turbidity to overturn action, since this period tends to coincide with the season of spring rains which wash quantities of suspended matters into lakes. Still other circumstances may contribute to the increased turbidity at this season (page 90).

Dissolved Substances. Dissolved substances likewise become uniformly distributed during the overturn. Substances resulting from bottom decompositions during the winter and accumulations of any sort in deeper waters are brought into circulation throughout the lake. This may have the effect, among other things, of enriching the upper waters by bringing into them some essential materials from deeper levels.

Summer Stagnation Period (Fig. 23). *Dissolved Oxygen.* With the gradual establishment of thermal stratification following the spring overturn, there comes a series of events which will be described under the headings of the three principal regions of the lake, viz., epilimnion, thermocline, and hypolimnion.

Since the water of the epilimnion continues to circulate throughout the summer, the only significant event in the dissolved oxygen history is the reduced capacity of the water for this gas, due to the rise in temperature. The influence of temperature on the capacity of water for oxygen is discussed on page 98. By the time that the upper lake waters have warmed to midsummer temperatures, they have given back to the air roughly one-half of the dissolved oxygen which they held at the close of the overturn. Epilimnion waters may not always be completely saturated with oxygen, but they tend to approximate it. Supersaturation, due to unusual circumstances such as luxuriant growths of aquatic plants in times of calm, may occur locally and temporarily but is not common.

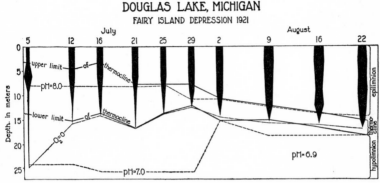

Fig. 23. Chart showing certain midsummer physicochemical conditions in one of the submerged depressions within the main basin of Douglas Lake, Michigan. All data have been plotted quantitatively. The black, vertical columns represent quantities and distribution of dissolved oxygen; the quantities may be compared by use of the following data: dissolved oxygen content *at the surface* for July 5 = 2.58 cc. per liter; for Aug. 2 = 4.88 cc. per liter; for Aug. 16 = 6.77 cc. per liter.

The epilimnion is amply and continuously supplied with oxygen throughout the summer. Oxygen added by circulation more than offsets all oxygen-consuming processes. As air temperatures fall in late summer and early autumn, the water of the epilimnion slowly cools, thus increasing its capacity for dissolved gases, so that oxygen determinations made in autumn, before the onset of the fall overturn, show an increasingly larger dissolved oxygen content. Therefore, some of the loss due to rising water temperatures in spring is regained in the autumn. Also, the gradual fall in the level of the thermocline, especially that of its upper margin, enlarges the oxygenated region in the late summer and in autumn. Largely because of its continuously rich dissolved oxygen supply, the epilimnion constitutes the major part of the *productive volume* of a lake during the summer stagnation period.

Profound changes occur in the hypolimnion. Circulation of the kind operating in the epilimnion is now eliminated by the establishment of the thermocline. Bottom deposits and suspended matters contain organic substances which undergo decomposition even under the conditions of very low temperature. This decomposition begins to consume the dissolved oxygen in the surrounding water, reducing it until it eventually disappears. As the early summer progresses, this oxygenless zone involves an increasingly larger volume of water, ultimately reaching the lower limit of the thermocline and thus converting the entire hypolimnion into a region devoid of dissolved oxygen. The time necessary to accomplish this result varies in different lakes and depends upon (1) the volume of the hypolimnion; (2) the temperature of the hypolimnion water; (3) the kind, quantity, and distribution of organic bottom deposit; (4) the decay of dead organic matter (particulate matter of all kinds) sinking through from the upper waters; (5) respiration of the animals and plants inhabiting the deeper waters until driven out by the oxygen reduction; (6) the bubbling through to the surface of decomposition gases accumulating at the bottom; and (7) the bacterial population. Under special circumstances, the entry below the thermocline of oxygen-free, subterranean waters may accelerate the oxygen decline. In many temperate lakes of the second order, this oxygen exhaustion is completed even by early summer and from that time to the onset of the fall overturn the hypolimnion is virtually removed from the productive volume of the lake, becoming, for the time, a biological desert. Only anaerobic organisms can survive there. Since the extent of oxygenless water is limited by the lower margin of the thermocline, the usual decline in thermocline level, as the summer progresses, converts an upper portion of the hypolimnion into thermocline, sometimes even into epilimnion, so that there may be a certain reclamation of some of the oxygenless region.

As pointed out in another section (page 94), oxygen diffuses in water at a very slow rate; in fact, too slow to be effective. Therefore, the nature of the disappearance of dissolved oxygen in the hypolimnion requires notice. In typical instances, the oxygen disappears from the whole hypolimnion very much sooner than can be explained on the basis of oxygen consumption processes of bottom deposits and the subsequent diffusion and consumption of oxygen in the upper waters of the hypolimnion. Not infrequently, vertical samples, taken in the middle of a basin before complete oxygen exhaustion, show the oxygen content of the whole hypolimnion about equally reduced throughout its entire depth. To explain the behavior of oxygen disappearance from the hypolimnion, Alsterberg (1927) proposed his *microstratification theory,* the essential features of which are as follows: bottom deposits, through their decomposition processes, consume oxygen, exhausting it completely not only within themselves but also in a thin layer of water lying immediately above the bottom, thus producing a "microstratification." Mathematical computations show the impossibility of this microstratification later developing into the *macrostratification* or major stratification of the lake, if diffusion only is operating. Furthermore, even if the diffusion rate were very much greater, the expected result would be a gradual decline of dissolved oxygen content from the top of the hypolimnion to the bottom, which ordinarily is not the case. Actual examinations of Scandinavian lakes showed (1) that in lakes unusually protected against the influence of wind, oxygen stratification below the thermocline followed closely the bottom configuration, while thermal stratification was entirely horizontal, indicating that the original oxygen consumption occurred in the bottom deposits; (2) in exposed lakes with effective wind action, oxygen stratification was of a horizontal nature. Alsterberg explains the condition in exposed lakes as due to the wind which not only circulates the water of the epilimnion but also causes secondary and tertiary horizontal currents *below the thermocline* (Fig. 10) which distribute horizontally the effects of oxygen consumption in bottom deposits, thus producing a more or less uniform oxygen content from one side of the depression to the other. A few other investigators claim to have confirmed, to a certain extent, Alsterberg's theory. Since ice cover in winter eliminates circulation due to wind action, the distribution of the oxygen consumption effects of bottom deposits must rest on other causes. It has been suggested that the conversion of microstratification under the ice sheet may possibly be produced by convection due to the rising temperature of the bottom water by transfer of heat from bottom mud (page 71). It seems likely that the bubbling through of decomposition gases accumulating in the bottom (page 96), which must occur in winter as well as in summer, plays some part not only in reducing the oxygen in the water through which the bubbles pass but also in distributing the oxygen consumption effects of the bottom.

Increasing indications that movements in the hypolimnion are more extensive than has formerly been thought give some additional support to the Alsterberg theory.

Alsterberg's theory, while interesting and having certain supporting evidence, is not without its weaknesses. However, there has appeared another explanation of the diminution of dissolved oxygen content in lowermost waters which seems to meet some of the difficulties in the microstratification theory, namely, direct consumption of oxygen by bacterial activity. As will be discussed in a later chapter (page 284), evidence indicates the existence of a very much greater bacterial population in uncontaminated waters than has hitherto been supposed. Kusnetzow and Karzinkin (1931) present data and computations which indicate that in Lake Glubokoje, U.S.S.R., the bacteria in one liter of lake water will consume about 2.4 mg. of dissolved oxygen in 10 days, leading them to favor the theory that the oxygen reduction of lower waters is due to the continuous oxygen consumption of bacteria within the water itself, and not to bacterial action in bottom mud as supposed by Alsterberg. They also point out a weakness of the Alsterberg theory, namely, the difficulty of applying it to a lake with an irregular bottom relief. It is evident that the quantity of dissolved oxygen consumed by bacterial action in the water itself depends upon (1) size of the bacterial population present; (2) amount of particulate, decomposable matter; and (3) quantities of soluble organic matter and different mineral salts which are necessary for the existence of bacteria.

It is probable that both of these theories have some part in explaining the disappearance of dissolved oxygen in the hypolimnion. Bacterial action goes on both in the bottom and in the water. It is possible that prevailing circumstances in one lake may make bottom decomposition more influential, while in another lake the suspended bacterial population may play a greater part.

The thermocline is, in many respects, the transition zone between epilimnion and hypolimnion. Usually, its upper portions are well supplied with oxygen. When first formed in the spring, the thermocline contains a full load of oxygen but the oxygenless region of the lower waters increases until it reaches the bottom of the thermocline and some loss appears within the thermocline itself. The form of oxygen decline within the thermocline is a very variable feature. Without doubt, the continually generous supply of oxygen in the topmost levels of the thermocline results from proximity to, and from circulation effects of, the superimposed epilimnion. There is reason for believing that oxygen depletion in the midthermocline region is the result of two factors: (1) decomposition of dead organic matter, mostly plankton, which on settling from the less dense epilimnion waters become checked in their descent in the denser and more viscous thermocline water and remain there through the early stages of decay, making inroads upon the dissolved oxygen; and (2) plankton, senile or healthy, which sink into this region and live for some time, consuming oxygen by respiratory processes. Concentrations so formed may produce considerable oxygen reduction. Sometimes the oxygen content within the thermocline becomes less, in the summer and autumn, than in the uppermost part of the hypolimnion.

Other Dissolved Gases. The epilimnion is nearly or quite saturated with nitrogen and, in the lower waters, an excess may occur.

Owing to the ease with which free carbon dioxide escapes from water, particularly when the water is agitated, the epilimnion may contain a minimal amount of this gas. In midsummer, often earlier, free carbon dioxide increases progressively with depth in the hypolimnion, due to its production in the decomposition of bottom deposits and of suspended matters. In some lakes, the bottommost waters show, in summer and early autumn, an acid reaction due mostly to accumulated carbonic acid, H_2CO_3. As mentioned elsewhere, quantities of carbon dioxide bubble through to the surface and escape into the air. This not only helps limit bottom accumulations of this gas but also doubtless helps distribute it through the hypolimnion and thermocline.

Other decomposition gases, such as methane and hydrogen sulfide, accumulate in bottom waters as summer progresses, excess quantities of which may bubble through to the surface as described above for carbon dioxide.

Hydrogen-ion Concentration. Hydrogen-ion concentration tends to remain constant in the epilimnion; usually shows a distinct, progressive increase with increasing depth in or near the thermocline; and in the hypolimnion, becomes still greater although the gradient between its top and bottom is usually slight. The lowermost waters tend to approach neutrality, often attain it, and, in some lakes, become acid in reaction. The condition just described prevails after sufficient time following the spring overturn has permitted decomposition activities within the hypolimnion not only to deplete the dissolved oxygen but also to build up an accumulation of acid-forming substances. The condition of the lower waters may become more or less stabilized at about midsummer so that the pH at a given depth remains approximately uniform for the remainder of the summer stagnation period. This approximate stabilization may occur at different pH values in the same lake for different summers.

Suspended Materials. During the summer stagnation period, suspended materials throughout the epilimnion consist of plankton organisms and miscellaneous debris, organic and inorganic. Ordinarily, it is more or less uniformly distributed, although, as will be shown later, the first meter of water at the surface usually contains less plankton than the waters immediately below, since in the latter the light effect is more favorable. Likewise, the horizontal and seasonal distribution of plankton is not uniform.

Concentrations of suspended matters in the thermocline have already been mentioned (page 89). These concentrations, formed largely from materials settling through from above, vary greatly depending upon the circumstances which determine the supply from the epilimnion. However, the thermocline may contain certain organisms which normally occupy that level.

Suspended matters in the hypolimnion during summer stagnation are largely those which settle through from above and the turbidity of this region is ordinarily rather uniform, although it, like the thermocline, would be varied by any conditions which change the suspended matters in the epilimnion. Water immediately above the bottom, especially a mucky bottom, is likely to have a considerable amount of very finely divided material in suspension. In some lakes, it is not possible to secure a clear sample of water within the last two meters of depth, and others may show an even greater thickness of distinctly cloudy water at bottom. These more or less permanently suspended materials are commonly mixtures of (1) finely divided substances, settled through from above, which are supported in the colder, denser water near the bottom, and (2) materials from the bottom deposits which, due to changes subsequent to their original settling, have come into suspension again. Intermingled with them are the settling suspended matters which are continually sinking through to the bottom.

Dissolved Substances. Dissolved substances are usually more or less uniformly distributed throughout the epilimnion, and in fact, throughout the whole lake, although in some lakes and under certain circumstances greater quantities may occur in the thermocline and in the hypolimnion, especially at and near the bottom of the latter. Concentrations near the bottom have no chance of a general circulation until the fall overturn.

Fall Overturn. Events of the fall overturn practically duplicate those of the spring overturn, with the exception that temperature changes are in the reverse direction. The whole lake circulates; a maximum and uniformly distributed load of dissolved oxygen is taken on; decomposition gases at the bottom are distributed and eliminated at the surface; the hydrogen-ion concentration becomes uniform from top to bottom, and bottom waters have a reaction near that of the summer epilimnion; plankton and other materials in suspension are completely mixed from surface to bottom; some bottom materials are brought up into flotation again and the whole lake becomes more turbid; and any localized accumulations of dissolved substances are spread uniformly throughout the lake.

Winter Stagnation Period. With the advent of permanent ice cover, the whole lake acquires a set of conditions which resembles, to a certain extent, the hypolimnion of the summer stagnation period. The ice cover isolates the water from the atmosphere, completely eliminates surface movement and circulation, and reduces the illumination of the whole lake. Succeeding events parallel closely those of the hypolimnion following the spring overturn. Bottom deposits continue their decomposition with the consumption of dissolved oxygen and the ultimate production of decomposition gases. Other oxygen-reducing processes remain active. As winter progresses, the oxygenless zone increases in volume; the deeper waters change in reaction; and dissolved substances accumulate. Suspended matters gradually sink through, but no longer contain components resulting from wind-blown materials or materials brought into suspension from the littoral bottom regions. Hydrogen-ion concentration increases to a certain level after which a form of stabilization occurs resembling that of the summer stagnation period except that the concentration level may be higher (more acid) than the summer one.   Enough light gets through the ice to make possible the continuance of a limited photosynthesis of phytoplankton and some higher plants, so that the plankton world continues to be active.   In fact, under conditions of transparent ice and little or no snow, the aquatic Algae may, on clear days, perform photosynthesis to the extent of raising the oxygen content of the water just under the ice well above saturation.   The increasing magnitude of the oxygenless zone limits more and more the volume of productive water since those organisms requiring free oxygen must keep in the upper oxygenated strata.   Fortunately, in lakes of the second order, the oxygenless zone very seldom completely engulfs the productive zone, even in winters of unusually prolonged ice cover.   When it does happen, the mortality of flora and fauna is very great.   Decomposition gases probably bubble through from the bottom in much the same way as they do during the summer, although in smaller quantities due to the reduced temperature in the shallower portions of the bottom.

TEMPERATE LAKES OF THE FIRST ORDER

As defined on page 63, a temperate lake of the *first order* is one whose morphological features are such that while two circulation periods (overturns) are possible, one in spring and one in autumn, the depth is usually so great that there are no *complete* overturns.   In such a lake, absence of complete overturns usually means the presence in the summer of (1) an upper circulating zone having the essential features of an epilimnion; (2) a thermocline of the usual sort (except in lakes of great area); and (3) a hypolimnion which is permanently stagnated in its deeper portions. This means the continual presence, in the lowermost waters at least, of chemical conditions similar to those described for the summer and winter stagnation periods of a lake of the second order, except that the stagnation is often more intensified and more severe.   Overturns are of the incomplete type, merely extending the circulation zone to a greater depth but not reaching the bottom.   In those lakes which barely qualify as belonging to the *first order*, complete overturns may occur now and then depending upon the various conditions which alter the depth to which circulation can occur.   At those times when complete overturns do occur, the history of dissolved gases and essential substances closely parallels that of lakes of the second order.

With respect to lakes of great depths and great magnitude, such as the deepest of the Great Lakes, necessary information is still too incomplete to make possible a satisfactory discussion.   One or more localized, discontinuous thermoclines may form during the summer, but the chemical events in the lowermost waters are almost unknown.   It has been pointed out that in the Atlantic Ocean dissolved oxygen occurs in considerable amounts at great depths and even to the bottom, although the percentage of saturation of surface water is greater than that of bottom waters due to the deficient circulation of the latter and to oxygen consuming agencies within them. Oxygen from the atmosphere is distributed to such depths, in part by the much lower levels to which the effects of surface circulation extend, and in part by vertical currents which sometimes play a very important role. In certain relatively deep arms of oceans, protected by narrow, shallow entrances from the main body of water (example: certain Norwegian fiords), bottom water becomes stagnant with consumption of the dissolved oxygen and accumulation of hydrogen sulphide.

TEMPERATE LAKES OF THE THIRD ORDER

In lakes of the third order which circulate completely and continuously during the open seasons, the conditions which prevail are essentially those of a typical epilimnion in a lake of the second order. Ice cover converts it temporarily into a condition which, in a general way, resembles that of the ice-covered lakes of the second order. Therefore, two periods, an open period and an ice cover period, constitute the main annual events. During the open period, the continuous circulation provides (1) ample aeration at all depths; (2) disposal of decomposition gases forming in the bottom deposits so that no lasting stagnation effects can arise; and (3) general distribution of substances passing into solution from chemical changes in the bottom deposits and from the decay of plankton and other suspended organic materials.

During the ice cover period, stagnation conditions become established and, owing to the shallow depth, may involve the greater part of the whole volume of water before the ice disappears in the spring. In the smaller, shallower lakes of this type, an occasional, unusually prolonged ice cover leads to a rather complete stagnation in which the oxygenless zone reaches the ice and decomposition products accumulate, the combined effect of which becomes serious and leads to a great mortality among the trapped organisms.

SUBMERGED DEPRESSION INDIVIDUALITY

Lakes occasionally have isolated depressions in the main basin, separated completely from each other except for the upper stratum of water which is, of course, common to all of them. The number of such depressions varies from the minimum of two to a considerable number. Douglas Lake, Michigan, where the author has made a special study of depression individuality, has seven distinct submerged depressions, several of which are essentially of the same form, position, and depth. It has been found that in summer such a series of similar, comparable depressions within the same lake basin may show a remarkable individuality of chemical, physical, and biological behavior, in spite of the fact that their close similarity might naturally lead to the assumption that they would all present very much the same limnological conditions. In Douglas Lake (Fig. 11), each submerged depression acts independently of the others with respect to: (1) date of thermal and chemical stratification; (2) position, form, and thickness of the thermocline on a given date; (3) seasonal history of stratification, when established; (4) presence or absence of stratification; (5) permanence of stratification when established; (6) bottom deposits; (7) rate of oxygen consumption; (8) bottom temperature; and (9) rate of change of bottom temperature. These facts were established on the basis of studies made on this lake over a period of about 15 years. It was also found that this physical-chemical individuality is accompanied by a biological individuality, the latter manifesting itself in such features as: (1) differences in the vertical distribution of the plankton; and (2) qualitative and quantitative differences in the profundal bottom organisms. The frequency of occurrence of this depression individuality in multidepression lake basins is still uncertain since few studies (Welch, 1927, 1945; Scott, 1931; Yoshimura, 1931, 1936, 1938; Welch and Eggleton, 1932, 1935; Scott, Hile, and Spieth, 1938; Cooper and Fuller, 1945) have as yet been made, but it may be more common than now realized. The underlying causes of this phenomenon are not always clear, especially in those instances in which depressions exist side by side under what appear to be identical conditions. In lakes whose depressions differ in such fundamental respects as depth, protection or exposure to wind action, size, form, relation to shore line, and relation to bottom contours and to shallow-water bottom deposits, explanations seem more obvious. Entry of underground water might have an important influence. Apparently, no investigation of the behavior of multiple depressions within the same lake basin has ever been made during the winter period although such work would be significant since the ice cover eliminates surface disturbance and some measure of the role which wind plays in this depression individuality might be secured. Since different depressions may show striking individuality during the same season, it behooves the limnologist not only to know the form of the basin of the lake which he is studying but also, in the presence of multiple depressions, to make his vertical examinations in at least several of them (preferably all of them) if correct indices of the lake are to be secured. Examinations in but one depression might be very misleading. Furthermore, since this individuality is not constant from season to season, one must not depend upon the results of a single season for any significant conclusion as to the nature of the limnological processes in that body of water.

CHEMICAL STRATIFICATION

As already indicated in the preceding sections, the essential uniformity of distribution of chemical substances which prevails during the spring and autumn overturns of a temperate lake of the second order is usually succeeded by a differentiated condition during the summer and winter stagnation periods, especially during the former, in which certain horizontal strata become quite different chemically from adjacent ones and often with abrupt transitions from one to the other. It is a common practice to refer to this condition as *chemical stratification*. The term is a useful one, but as employed at present it lacks the definiteness of scope and usage of the term *thermal stratification*. Chemical stratification is an expression which is sometimes used to describe a condition in which there is but one chemical substance known to be stratified, and sometimes used to describe a stratification of several substances. Furthermore, no rules or agreements yet exist as to the determining criteria of the presence or absence of chemical stratification. Definite, generally accepted distinctions are badly needed and must be established if investigators are to know clearly what is meant whenever the term is used.

Chemical stratification is not confined to temperate lakes of the second order. It exists in most if not all temperate lakes of the first order and may be present in those of the third order, at least at times. It also occurs in many polar and tropical lakes, depending upon circumstances and upon how chemical stratification is defined.

In temperate lakes of the second order, the close correspondence of the chemical stratification with the thermal stratification is often so very striking during most of the summer stagnation period that the impression is sometimes gained by inexperienced observers that chemical stratification is always the result of thermal stratification. While the two phenomena occur together so commonly and have some important interrelations, they may, under some conditions, exist independently of each other, as for example, occasional instances appear in which well defined thermal stratification exists but chemical stratification of the usual sort is absent, while, conversely, chemical stratification may be found existing in a lake in which there is no thermal stratification.

It must not be assumed that if some of the dissolved gases show a distinct stratification all of the chemical features of the water are likewise stratified since such a conclusion may be far from the truth; as for example, the dissolved oxygen, free carbon dioxide, and certain other factors may show stratification, but the methyl orange alkalinity and the quantity of dissolved organic matter may lack any form of stratification.

CHEMICAL COMPOSITION OF BOTTOM DEPOSITS

As already pointed out (page 25), bottom deposits originate from numerous sources. As a consequence, chemical analyses of such deposits in different lakes show a striking diversity. The following results are taken from the work by Black (1929) on 15 Wisconsin and three Alaskan lakes. Of the Wisconsin lakes, three were hard water lakes, three were soft water lakes, and the remainder, including the Alaskan lakes, were of the medium or intermediate class. Results are expressed in percentages of the dry weight, as follows: SiO_2, 9.35 to 69.42; Fe_2O_3, 1.33 to 9.47; Al_2O_3, 0.80 to 9.56; CaO, 0.60 to 24.70; MgO, 0.11 to 3.01; P_2O_5, 0.18 to 1.44; SO_4, 0.11 to 3.92; CO_2, 0.00 to 16.33; organic carbon, 4.41 to 38.95.

The nature of the organic matter in bottom deposits is still imperfectly known. Allgeier, Peterson, Juday, and Birge (1932) present evidence which seems to indicate that, for Lake Mendota, Wisconsin, at least, the bottom deposit is an organic complex composed largely of protein and lignin.

Lakes with large and diversified basins may exhibit striking differences in the chemical composition of bottom deposits in the different parts of the same basin. In bottom samples from different localities in Lake Balaton, Hungary, it has been reported that the silica varied from 1.5 to 54 per cent; the calcium, from 12 to 52 per cent; and the magnesium, from 0.7 to 4.6 per cent. Bottom deposits in the six major submerged depressions in the basin of Douglas Lake, Michigan, differ considerably in their general composition. There is urgent need for active research in this little-known field.

DECOMPOSITION OF BOTTOM DEPOSITS

Very little precise information is as yet available concerning the character of the decomposition of bottom deposits. Black (1929) reported the following results of experiments (Table 16) undertaken to determine

TABLE 16. NATURE OF DECOMPOSITION OF DEEP-BOTTOM MUD
From Black

Duration of experiment, days	Temperature	Volume of sample, l.	Gas produced				Weight dried mud at end of experiment, g.
			Total, cc.	CO_2, cc.	CH_4, cc.	Remainder	
171	"Room temperature"	5	2,597	297	1,470	H & N	600
171	4°C.	4	593	39	320	H & N	690

decomposition rate and the chemical composition of gases given off during the decomposition of bottom mud taken from Lake Mendota, Wisconsin, at a depth of 24 m., on Oct. 21, 1927.

Allgeier, Peterson, Juday, and Birge (1932) studied the decomposition of bottom deposits of Lake Mendota, Wisconsin (Fig. 17), as it takes place under laboratory conditions and reported, among other things, the following data:

1. The production of gas increased greatly with increase of temperature of incubation.

2. Methane comprised 65 to 85 per cent of the gas; carbon dioxide formed 3 to 30 per cent; hydrogen was present to the extent of 1 to 3 per cent; and nitrogen formed a considerable part of the gas evolved at the lower temperatures. Relative proportions of the various gases produced differed with different temperatures.

3. The rate of decomposition of bottom deposit determined for the temperatures of 7 or 15°C. indicated that it would require a century or more to accomplish the complete destruction of a given quantity of the deposit. There was reason for believing it probable that as the decomposition continues the residues become increasingly more resistant to the action of microorganisms.

4. The original samples of lake deposit contained about 100,000 bacteria per cubic centimeter. This number rose rapidly with increase of temperature, the number for 7°C. being about 400,000, but very much greater for higher temperatures.

PART III

BIOLOGICAL RELATIONS

In Part II, the principal physical and chemical conditions operative in natural waters have been described. These and other possible conditions, in their various combinations and intensities, make up the fundamental environmental structure upon which the occurrence, the distribution, and the success of aquatic organisms depend. Each of these conditions functions in one or more ways in exerting influence upon organisms, and, in addition, the organisms exert influences upon each other; therefore, a third set, viz., the biological relations, are involved. Conditions within an environment are, to a great extent, mutually dependent, and, in nature, factors are always operating in the presence of others; consequently, it must be understood that any consideration of the influence of a single condition or factor on the organisms is merely a necessary method of approach. In the following section, some of the more important limnological influences of these physical and chemical conditions will be discussed, followed by a treatment of the outstanding biological relations and adjustments which constitute an intimate part of limnology.

CHAPTER VI

INFLUENCE OF PHYSICAL CONDITIONS

FORM OF BASIN

Shore Line

Under strictly comparable conditions, the greater the length of the shore line the greater the biological productivity. Increased irregularity of shore line results in (1) greater contact of water with land; (2) increased areas of protected bays and coves; (3) increased areas of shallow water for growths of rooted vegetation; (4) greater diversification of bottom and margin conditions; (5) reduction of the amount of exposed, wave-swept shoal; and (6) increased opportunity for extensive, close superposition of the *photosynthetic zone* upon the *decomposition zone*. These and other possible results combine in various ways to increase the production of animals and plants.

Relation of Photosynthetic and Decomposition Zones

The form of basin of a lake determines, among other things, the relative amounts of shallower waters. Within limits and under strictly comparable conditions, the greater the areas of shallow water the greater the biological productivity. Excluding the diminutive lakes whose greatest dimension is too small to permit severe wave action, those shores which face the prevailing winds will usually present what is commonly called barren, wave-swept shoals. Their exposed nature usually results in (1) the absence of rooted plants; (2) the absence of organic bottom deposits; and (3) the absence of any permanent animal population save those whose burrowing habits make occupancy of position in such a habitat possible. Nevertheless, a fairly substantial but largely concealed population may be present, although of all the shallow-water faunas it is usually the smallest one.

In the protected, shallow waters, however, conditions are more favorable for greater productivity. Protected shoals permit (1) growth of rooted plants; (2) accumulation of organic bottom materials; and (3) the presence of much larger and more diversified faunas. Among the various features contributing to this productivity is the *close superposition of the photosynthetic zone over the decomposition zone*. On these protected shoals, particularly if the bottom slope is slight, accumulating organic matter settles to the bottom forming muck deposits which remain largely

139

where formed. Therefore, the products of these decomposition beds (carbon dioxide; nitrites; nitrates, and others), which are necessary to plants, are immediately available for plant growth. The plant zone, together with its associated animal inhabitants, contributes to the bottom deposits additional decaying organic matter which, remaining directly below the photosynthetic zone, becomes again, through further decomposition, available for the plants above. Thus a cycle of mutual exchange of essential materials takes place between the two zones with the result that a permanent condition of greater fertility is maintained. Also because of the very gentle slope and the restricted water movements of a protected situation, losses of the essential bottom materials due to removal into deeper water are much less than elsewhere. Therefore, it can be stated that in comparable situations, the closer and more permanent the association of the photosynthetic zone with the decomposition zone the greater the biological productivity.

In contrast to conditions described above, the steeper the slope of the basin, or the greater the exposure of shoals, or both, the greater the removal of the decomposition zone to the profundal depths of deeper lakes with the result that much, and in extreme cases practically all, of the essential decomposition materials becomes inaccessible. They settle into the hypolimnion where their products remain locked up except at the overturns when temporarily they participate in the general circulation. In lakes of the first order, they may virtually pass into complete unavailability. A deeper lake with steep basin slope thus tends to automatically and continuously rob itself of its stores of organic matter. Lakes of the third order, because of shallow depth and continuous circulation except during the ice cover period, retain all organic accumulations in available position, the essential decomposition products either remaining immediately beneath the plant beds or else being constantly distributed by the water.

Slope and the Deeper Decomposition Zone

Form of basin also involves the slope of deeper portions of the basin. Upon the nature of this slope depends, to a large extent, the character of the bottom. The influence of gravity, aided by water movements, in pulling to the lowermost bottom the various materials which settle through, is much more effective on a declivitous slope. Some basin slopes are so abrupt that very little of the loose, settling materials can remain on the steep sides. Thus the decomposition zones of such a lake are restricted to (1) those of the shallow, protected shoals (if any are present), and (2) those at the bottoms of the deepest regions, separated by steep sides which maintain little or no decomposing deposits. On the other hand, the basin slopes may be gentle enough, even in the deeper regions, to fall well within the angle of permanence, the loose, finely divided, settling materials remaining mostly where they first fall and thus resulting in the maintenance of a more or less continuous deposit of organic matter all over the sides as well as within the deepest parts.   Portions of such a continuous deposit may be both above and below the thermocline.   The important matter is that the very gentle slope makes possible the existence of a continuous carpet of decomposing deposit which not only presents a much greater area to the superimposed water but also provides greater opportunities for the maintenance, periodic or continuous, of bottom-dwelling organisms.   Greater exposure to the water means more complete exchanges of substances between water and bottom and a more extensive circulation of the dissolved substances throughout the lake.

Alsterberg (1927) claims to have found in these facts one of the chief reasons for the difference between *eutrophic* lakes (rich in nutritive matters) and *oligotrophic* lakes (poor in nutritive matters).   He held that relatively great depth and steep sides are characteristic of most oligotrophic lakes.   In such basins not only can little bottom deposit remain on the sides but also the contact area of a water stratum of given depth with the basin is much smaller on the steep bottom slope than on the more gentle slopes of eutrophic lakes.   Unfortunately for this proposal, not all oligotrophic lakes have basins with very steep sides.

Productive Volume

Form of basin determines the extent of *productive volume*.   By productive volume is meant that portion of water in which virtually all biological production occurs.   In a lake of the *third order*, total volume is productive at least during the open season.   In lakes of the *second order*, productive volume is almost exclusively confined to the epilimnion and the thermocline during most of the summer stagnation period.   During the overturns, the entire lake temporarily becomes productive volume but the duration of these periods may be too short to be of any great consequence. Lakes of the *first order* resemble those of the second order in that they maintain the productive zone in the upper stratum, usually limited by the presence of a thermocline.   In those lakes having no complete overturn, the productive zone, during open season, merely varies in volume with those conditions which determine the depth to which circulation may extend.   During prolonged ice cover, lakes of the *second* and *third orders* undergo gradual reduction of productive volume due to encroachment of the underlying stagnation zone, while lakes of the *first order*, under these conditions, may undergo less change in productive volume due to their size and to the presence of the permanent, deeper stagnation region.   Complete ice cover may not occur in lakes of unusual size and depth, even though located in colder regions.

Without overlooking the fact that both *depth* and *area* of a lake basin combine in innumerable ways to produce a great heterogeneity of lake forms in each of the three orders mentioned above, it seems possible to state that, since inland lakes seldom exceed certain area limits, depth is fundamentally of prime importance in determining productive volume. Certain European limnologists hold that *average depth* is the factor which determines whether a lake is eutrophic or oligotrophic, computing average depth as the quotient of volume of the lake over area of the lake (V/A). They claim that, in oligotrophic lakes, the volume of the hypolimnion is greater than the volume of the epilimnion, and that in eutrophic lakes the reverse occurs. Since this conception is inextricably tied up with dissolved oxygen content and with organic substances in the water, further discussion will be deferred (page 342). It will suffice here to state that while without question depth is a matter of fundamental importance, it alone is not sufficient to explain the phenomena of oligotrophy and eutrophy in general.

PRESSURE

No satisfactory statement can be made concerning the influence of pressure on fresh-water animals. In spite of the fact that pressures in deeper lakes may seem large, they actually are small compared with pressures in the oceans, and possibly for that reason alone it may be that some of the phenomena reported for deep sea animals (absence of cavities which contain gas; complete penetration of the bodies with water; and others) do not appear in the profundal, fresh-water forms. That organisms of a diverse sort live at the bottoms of many of the inland lakes is well known; also it is known that failure to occupy the profundal regions, periodically or permanently, is due to causes other than pressure. Some animals are known to occupy regions in Lake Michigan at a depth of 246 m. (Eggleton, 1936, 1937), and there are records of hydra dredged from depths of 269 m. in Lake Superior. There is evidence that, in lakes having overturns, bottom-dwelling animals in shallow water are often swept down into the profundal regions. At least some of them withstand the abrupt shift into the much greater pressures and live, grow, and reproduce there for protracted periods. There is also evidence that some of the free-swimming animals, such as certain fishes, are occasionally temporary invaders of deep water. Permanent occupancy of the greater depths is made possible by an adjustment of pressures within the animal to equalize the external ones. Reactions of aquatic animals to increasing or decreasing pressures are little known, due to the difficulty of operating gradients for pressure which do not at the same time involve the action of gravity. It seems likely that, within limits, pressure is not a very significant factor in inland waters.

COMPRESSIBILITY, DENSITY, AND VISCOSITY

While compressibility, density, and viscosity are distinct properties of water, their relations to biological processes are so intimately bound together that they may well be discussed in the same section although their inherent distinctions must be kept clearly in mind.

The important relation of *incompressibility* of water to aquatic organisms is their occupancy of water by complete *displacement*. Space occupied by organisms is provided only by pushing the water aside without altering the density of the water adjacent to the invading organisms. Such space is, then, secured only by raising the water level.

A body submerged in water is buoyed up by a force equal to the weight of the water displaced (law of Archimedes) and the weight of the displaced water is directly due to its *density*. The effect of this buoyancy on an aquatic organism depends upon its own specific gravity; some organisms are heavier than water and tend to sink; others have the same weight as the surrounding water and remain in suspension; still others are lighter than water and rise to the surface. Since, as has already been shown (page 34), density of water varies principally with temperature, substances in solution, and substances in suspension, and since the specific gravity of the organisms themselves may vary with such features as life-history changes and development and storage of cell products, this buoyancy relation is not a fixed one.

The unusually low *viscosity* of water accounts for its ease of flow and deformation, in spite of its great density and its incompressibility. It is for this reason that motile aquatic organisms can readily move about in it. Rate of sinking of plankton organisms and similar objects is intimately connected with the viscosity of water. Since, like density, viscosity varies with temperature, its opposition to the tendency of a particle to sink varies, the greater the viscosity the greater the opposition.

Flotation Phenomena

Nonmotile Organisms. In calm water, nonmotile plankton organisms depend entirely upon the relation between their own specific gravity, the density of the water, and the viscosity of the water in maintaining their vertical position; they are passive victims of the interaction between these three circumstances. Nonmotile, attached animals, particularly the colonial forms such as the larger colonies of fresh-water sponges and certain fresh-water Bryozoa (*Pectinatella*), may develop forms and masses of body, which could not be maintained in the absence of the buoyant effect of water, and even the soft-bodied hydra would be helpless without it. It is probably safe to state that all sessile animals depend, to some extent at least, upon the buoyancy of the water. Many higher aquatic plants likewise are dependent upon the supporting effect of the water in order to maintain their proper form and orientation.

Motile Organisms. Those *plankters* (organisms composing the plankton) which possess powers of locomotion vary greatly in the efficiency of their progression, but some change of position in space is possible due to their own activity. While such locomotion may be almost negligible when compared with the shifting and transporting effects of the water, it may nevertheless be vital to the organism in many ways, such as in the capture of food, and in the change of water in contact with respiratory surfaces. Locomotion in water, by animals large or small and by whatever means, possesses a certain advantage when compared with locomotion on land or in air, owing to the fact that, due to the buoyant effect of water, much less energy is consumed in merely maintaining position above the bottom and a proportionately larger amount of the total potential energy is available for propulsion activity. In fact, those organisms whose specific gravity is essentially the same as the surrounding water expend practically no energy in merely keeping up in the water. Certain aquatic animals, because of the possession of air stores or other special means, are distinctly lighter than water and must use a certain amount of energy to keep below the surface when they need to do so, but it is an open question whether this energy requirement ever exceeds the advantage due to the buoyancy effect. Many air-breathing, aquatic insects have air stores so located that not only are they lighter than water but the posterior end is lighter than the anterior, enabling the insect to float at the surface in the proper respiratory position. Without doubt, the admirable ease with which many aquatic organisms swim is, to a considerable extent, due to the fact that the body is partly or wholly adjusted to float in water.

Reduction of Specific Gravity. Protoplasm alone has a specific gravity which closely approaches that of water, but the various cell products which occur in animals and plants may combine to produce bodies which are either heavier or lighter than water. Products which tend to make the body heavier (such as chitinous exoskeletons of arthropods, bones, shells of various kinds) and those which tend to make it lighter are often present in the same body so that the specific gravity of the whole depends upon which of the contrasting materials predominate. The most effective and the most common of those cell products which reduce specific gravity seem to be the following:

1. Gases originate from various sources (metabolic products, external and internal air stores, and others) and remain, at least for a time, enclosed within or attached to the body. These gas accumulations may be of sufficient magnitude to make an otherwise heavy-bodied animal (as, for example, certain aquatic insects) much lighter than water.

2. Fats and oils are commonly produced and stored within aquatic organisms, notably in the plankton Crustacea and in the plankton Algae. Their well-known quality of being lighter than water causes them to act as floats.

3. Gelatinous and mucilaginous secretions of varying amounts are common as matrices and external envelopes. While doubtless serving other functions, they often aid materially in flotation.

Relations of Surface to Volume. *In Different Species.* Since in relatively compact bodies of organisms, the relations between volume and surface tend to conform roughly to the well-known mathematical principle that the surface varies as the square of the dimension while the volume varies as the cube of the dimension, it follows that, in a general way, the smaller the body the greater the relative expanse of surface. If the body has a specific gravity greater than water, it will sink, although resistance to sinking will be offered by the viscosity of the water. The greater the surface compared to the volume the greater will be the friction between water and body. Because of this relation, particles of very small size, even though composed of a substance having a specific gravity greater than 1, may not sink at all; likewise, organisms which would sink promptly if of approximately spherical shape may float if so shaped that a relatively larger surface is exposed to the water; or, if they do not actually float, they may sink very slowly.

Few aquatic organisms, irrespective of size, are spherical in form. Any departure from the spherical form results in relatively increased body surface. Relative increase of surface is accomplished in so many different ways that only a general classification is attempted here.

1. General body form. Main portion of body may present:
   a. Various degrees of attenuation.
   b. Various degrees of compression or depression or general flattening.
   c. Miscellaneous forms of asymmetry.
2. Body surface sculpturing: ridges, furrows, striae, impressed or raised patterns.
3. Extensions and modifications of antennae, tentacles, gills, legs, cerci, and others.
4. Development of special peripheral processes: hairs, setae, spines, bristles, filaments, radial axes, tubercles, cilia, pseudopodia, crests.
5. Formation of colonies: linear, dendritic, radial, lamellate, irregular.
   Combinations of several of these structural features in the same organism may occur, sometimes with remarkable flotation results.

In the Same Species. In certain plankton organisms, a striking seasonal change of body form of a very definite sort occurs. The interpretation of this phenomenon has for a long time been the center of a vigorous controversy. According to one explanation, this change of body form is a response to changes in the viscosity of the water due to seasonal changes in temperatures. However, this subject will be discussed with considerable fullness under another heading (page 261) and is mentioned here merely for the sake of completeness.

Accessory Provisions for Flotation.   Cases and coverings of various kinds composed, in part at least, of foreign materials are constructed by some aquatic organisms.   While such cases often serve several other purposes, certain ones are so constructed that they either increase the tendency of the whole organism to be in suspension or completely support it at the surface.   Instances of this sort are not uncommon among the aquatic insects (certain caddis-fly larvae, certain aquatic caterpillars, and others).

Hydrofuge Structures.   Hydrofuge structures, such as hydrofuge pubescences, hydrofuge caudal filaments, and hydrofuge smooth surfaces, often play an important and sometimes a vital part in the flotation of organisms.   Once at the surface they may provide (1) for the proper orientation of the body into the breathing position and (2) for the ability to remain at the surface in this position without effort during the breathing period.   Examples are not uncommon among aquatic insects.

Certain hydrofuge structures are related directly or indirectly to respiration in some air-breathing aquatic insects.   Gaseous plastrons, held on body surfaces by hydrofuge mechanisms in certain aquatic Coleoptera (*Dryopidae*) and certain Hemiptera (*Naucoridae*), have been studied by modern experimental means (Harpster, 1941, 1944; Thorpe, 1950; Thorpe and Crisp, 1947) and found to be efficient devices in securing dissolved oxygen from water.

Still other functions may be performed by hydrofuge features, and several such functions may act simultaneously.

Precision in Flotation Adjustment.   Among the plankton, flotation at the proper level is sometimes a matter of precise adjustment.   A very small discrepancy in adjustment may result in (1) too great buoyancy, causing the organism to rise to an unfavorable level or even to rise to the surface, either of which contingencies might be fraught with peril, owing to various hazards such as excess light, entanglement with the surface film, and evaporation; or (2) sinking to an unfavorable depth at which such features as reduction of effective light, critical reduction or absence of oxygen, and absence of proper nutritive materials may result seriously. Such nicety of adjustment is thus of vital importance to certain non-motile plankters.   That this adjustment follows the seasonal changes of viscosity and density of water in such a way that organisms may continue to thrive is one of the marvels of aquatic life.

Among the motile plankters, some species, lacking this precise flotation adjustment and yet requiring maintenance of position at a level out of which they would sink, remain at proper levels only by the performance of certain movements.   In some instances, the organism must work constantly to maintain its position. Water fleas swim intermittently but unceasingly, and certain microorganisms occupy proper levels by constant vibrations of flagella or cilia.

Body-form Adjustments

Streamline Form. When a body is either in motion through quiet water or stationary in moving water, it must overcome a resistance which the water imposes; otherwise, it will either fail to make progress or fail to maintain its stationary position. It must be remembered that such a body must occupy space by complete displacement of the water and that when either the body or the water moves, the body continues the process of displacement. Also, under these conditions, not only must the great weight (density) of the water be overcome in pushing it aside, but the internal friction (viscosity) of the water plus the friction of the water against the surfaces of the object must also be overcome. Thus, energy is expended by the object in overcoming these resistances, and, as will be shown later, the amount of this energy depends upon the form of the body when other conditions are the same.

The resistance met by the hull of a ship in motion is due to (1) displacement resistance, (2) frictional resistance of the hull against the liquid, and (3) air resistance. Since but few aquatic organisms swim or maintain their position at or on the surface with the body partly submerged (aquatic mammals, birds, gyrinid beetles, and others), air resistance can be omitted from this discussion, and only conditions of complete and continuous submergence will be considered.

While, as shown in an earlier section (pages 34–36), viscosity and density of water vary with certain conditions, particularly temperature, the resistance met by a moving organism or by an organism maintaining its position in moving water is considerable under all circumstances. Organisms vary greatly in their ability to overcome this resistance, owing to inherent differences, a very important one being the *form of the body*. Obviously, certain forms of body are more effective for locomotion in water than others. That form giving least resistance is the central theme of this discussion.

When water is displaced by a firm, moving object, the result may be interpreted according to the *streamline* theory. Water in motion past a firm, immovable object can be regarded as made up of streams of particles any one of which is called a streamline. These "streams," as they meet and pass a displacing object, may become sinuous, rotational, or eddying, depending upon the conditions established by the form of the object.

Historical. Statistical Studies on Form of Body. Who first regarded the form of a fish as having any significance with reference to the water in which it lives may never be known. It is not unlikely that the fact that fishes are effective swimmers may have been explained as just another instance of the "marvels of nature" or the "wondrous foresight of the Creator." It was not until recent times that serious attempts were made (Thurston, 1887; Parsons, 1884; *et al.*) to apply information secured by mathematical analyses of the form of various kinds of fishes and Cetacea to boat construction. Among other things, it was found that the body consists of two principal parts: (1) the *entrance* or *forebody*, that part from the tip of the snout to the maximum transverse section; and (2) the *run*, or *afterbody*, that portion from the maximum transverse section to the tip of the caudal fin. It was also found that, in all specimens examined, the average position of greatest transverse section occurred at a distance of about 36 per cent of the total length from the snout, the variation being within 2 per cent. Likewise, a *coefficient of fineness* was calculated for each species from the ratio of $\dfrac{\text{displacement of the fish}}{\text{displacement of a circumscribing cylinder}}$, the average being 0.476, which was said to correspond closely to the coefficient of fineness of the then existing vessels of high speed. Some of the early workers also recognized the possibility that the replacement of water following maximum displacement had something to do with the function of the afterbody.

RESISTANCE MEASUREMENTS OF DIFFERENT FORMS OF BODY. As early as 1775, experiments with models of various shapes submerged in water were performed, but little of importance resulted. Much later, Houssay (1908 and later), experimenting with a plastic model (pliable rubber bag filled with a mixture of oil, vaseline, and white lead) to which a known velocity in water was imparted by a line, pulley, and falling-weight system, claims to have found, among other things, that such a model becomes molded into a form, at certain velocities, similar in some respects to that of a fish. Other investigators, experimenting with a similar bag, claim the discovery that such a model cannot move rapidly through water unless it has a rigid forebody which is either spherical or conical in shape.

Houssay also made resistance tests with rigid models of various shapes and at various velocities, these models being constructed of wood, rendered impermeable, ballasted to float at desired depths, and having similar exposed surfaces. The essential results seem to have been (1) that cone-shaped models *with base in advance* were subject to less resistance than were the same models when the apex was in advance; (2) that similar results came from models of other shapes but having a shorter, blunter forebody and a longer, more pointed afterbody; and (3) that the addition of stabilizing appendages (artificial fins) demonstrated the superiority of the "fish form" (streamline form) to that of cone-shaped models with blunt end in advance.

MODERN STUDIES. Clemens (1917) suspended models of various shapes in a stream of known velocity and measured the *pull* (resistance) of the water on the models by means of a delicate spring balance to which the models were attached by a fine wire. The models were all made from 184 g. of grafting wax so that each had the same mass. The results of particular interest in this discussion are exemplified in Table 17.

These results and others indicate clearly that the closer the approach of body shape to the streamline form the greater the reduction of resistance to progress in water and that a body with a rounded, blunter, shorter forebody and a sharper, longer afterbody has less resistance than a body of the reverse shape, although contrary to popular impression. The principle of the streamline body is now extensively used in the construction of submarines, torpedoes, boats of various kinds, air craft, and automobile bodies.

TABLE 17. RESISTANCE OF MODELS OF DIFFERENT SHAPE IN RUNNING WATER
Current rate, 1.65 ft. per sec.; mass of all models, 184 g. of grafting wax
Data from Clemens

Form of model	Position of model	Pull, g. (resistance)
Cone[1]	Base against current	28
Cone	Apex against current	50
Sunfish	Head against current	15
Trout	Head against current	6
Trout	Tail against current	10
May-fly nymph[2]	Head against current	9
May-fly nymph[2]	Caudal end against current	16

[1] Cone without sharp edges on base.
[2] *Isonychia* (= *Chirotonetes*).

Principle of Streamline Form. The efficiency of the streamline form may be explained by means of the following diagrams (Fig. 24). If it is remembered that a body with streamline form moving through standing water and the same body maintaining a fixed position in running water present the same essential conditions, it is evident that the position of maximum transverse section represents the maximum displacement of water. It likewise determines not only the maximum energy expended in displacement but also the termination of virtually all energy expenditure so far as body surface is concerned, since the particles of water, having passed that position, now begin to close in again. If the afterbody of a streamline form were removed (Fig. 24), then the most posterior position of the body would be the level of maximum displacement; beyond it, the water would fall precipitously to occupy the original space, forming eddies at the rear. Such a body would have expended the full amount of

energy required to displace the water, with no recovery of any part of it.
On the other hand, if the body has a sloping afterbody of the proper shape,
the closing in of water, acting as it does on a sloping surface, produces a
force which acts in the direction of the forebody and therefore brings

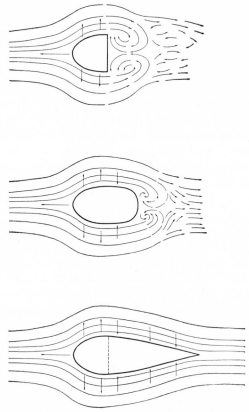

FIG. 24.   Diagrams showing relation of the form of a body, moving in water, to the displacement and return of the water.   The upper diagram represents the behavior of water
displaced by a solid object having the form of the *forebody only* of a typical streamline
form (same as the typical streamline body represented in the lower figure but with the afterbody removed).   Note the vortices produced at the rear, or the so-called dead water.
     The middle diagram represents the same forebody, but with a short, abruptly rounded
rear end, and showing the result of an afterbody which is too short and blunt.
     The lower diagram is that of a typical streamline form and shows the even flow of the
water over the shorter, blunter forebody and its return, without deformation, over the
longer, tapering afterbody.   The broken, vertical line represents the position of maximum
area of transverse section.

about the recovery of a certain fraction of the original energy expended
in displacing the water.   The energy recovered never equals the original
displacement energy—in fact, the difference is considerable—but the
closer it approaches the latter the more effective the body becomes in
the penetration of water.

It has also been claimed that the efficiency of streamline form is due, in part at least, to the fact that the "streams of water" flow over the rounded, sloping surfaces of both forebody and afterbody with minimal deformation, whereas departures from streamline form result in eddies and vortices ("dead water") at the rear, the effect of which is to act as a drag on the moving body.

The forward position of the maximum transverse section requires comment here. Certain early workers claimed that in a fish the maximum transverse section is essentially at the middle of the long axis and that the caudal fin should not be considered, since it is located farther to the rear in order to function without reducing the effective area of the afterbody. There seems reason, however, for believing that within certain limits, the longer the afterbody the greater the exposure to returning water and hence the greater the recovery of expended energy. However, the longer the afterbody the more gentle its slope and also the greater the total friction of water against it. Therefore, any extension of the afterbody beyond a certain effective length would result in declining efficiency.

Another function claimed for the form of the afterbody should be mentioned. If the object displacing the water terminates in a truncated fashion and without any reduction in the maximum transverse section, then the converging water just behind it manifests the maximum amount of eddy formation (area of dead water); and since this region is low in pressure, it tends to pull the body in a rearward direction. The effect of tapering the afterbody is to lessen the tendency to eddy formation and hence to reduce the drag of the dead water. Complete elimination of the dead-water region behind the body is not possible even by the most tapering afterbody, although it can be reduced in this way. It should also be noted that the greater the speed of flow of the water the greater the extent of the dead-water region. Hora (1930) claims that the long, whiplike tails of some of the fishes living in torrential streams have a particular significance in the reduction of the dead-water area at the rear.

With reference to the form of the forebody of the typical streamline form, it may be pointed out that the rounded contours facilitate the flow of the *streams* of water without deformations and that, within limits, the shorter the forebody the less the surface to produce friction with the water.

Prevalence of Streamline Form among Aquatic Animals. Among aquatic animals manifesting rapid locomotion through water, the streamline form of body predominates, at least in the most successful ones. Many fishes exhibit strikingly the streamline form. The same is largely true of aquatic mammals. Some of the finest examples appear among adult aquatic insects, such as the Dytiscidae, Hydrophilidae, Haliplidae, Gyrinidae, Belostomatidae, Corixidae, Notonectidae, and others. In fact, all of the strongest swimmers have this form of body. Larval aquatic insects should also be listed here, especially those with strong swimming powers. It is toward this form of body that the stronger swimmers of all groups of aquatic animals tend to converge, the degree of approach to perfect streamline form varying to a certain extent depending upon various circumstances.

Those animals which regularly live in rapids and maintain their position in the face of plunging waters—black-fly larvae (*Simulium*); certain May-fly nymphs (*Isonychia*); caddis-fly larvae (*Brachycentrus*); stone-fly nymphs; and others—exhibit the streamline form to a marked degree, accomplishing it, in some instances, in unique ways. The larva of the black fly is confined to running water; and since it is usually attached at the posterior end, the flexible body hangs suspended in the water, head downstream. In this position, the usual conditions are reversed so that the head is at the end of the afterbody, the caudal end has become the free end of the forebody, and the maximum transverse section occurs nearer the caudal end. The effect of such reversal of the usual conditions is to preserve the streamline form in the properly oriented position. Another modification of conditions occurs in a certain caddis-fly larva, which constructs its case in such a form that, facing into the current, a shorter forebody, composed of the anterior end of the larva and the anterior end of its case, is followed by a longer sloping afterbody composed of the tapering case.

Conditions existing in streams, on wave-swept beaches, and in other forms of moving, shallow waters approximate, to varying degrees, those of rapids, and these situations commonly present many characteristic animals with body contours more or less of the streamline form (Fig. 25). Some species have tended to develop the typical streamline form. Still others have met the common need in a different way, especially those which cling closely to the supporting surface. The noteworthy departure in form is the development of the *hemistreamline form*, one which might be described as the complete streamline form divided lengthwise in the median plane, with the flat side applied to the supporting surface, thus producing a limpet-like body. In such forms, appendages, when present, are flattened down upon the supporting surface, concealed under the body, or modified in some other fashion so that they offer minimal resistance to the flow of water. As illustrations of this hemistreamline form may be cited the well-known parnid-beetle larva (the so-called water penny, *Psephenus*); the snail *Ferricia* (*Ancylus*); several May-fly nymphs (*Epeorus*, *Rhithrogena*, and others); the *cases* of the microcaddis-fly larva, *Ithytricha confusa;* the pupal shelter of the rapids caterpillar, *Elophyla fulicalis;* and the cases of certain caddis-fly larvae (*Leptocerus ancylus*, *Molanna angustata*, and others). While it must be understood that some of these animals have other structural devices for aiding in their maintenance of position in the face of moving water, possession of this form of body renders them less likely to be washed away; in fact, the moving water may tend to press them against the supporting object.

In the past, it has been supposed that the definitely flattened bodies of certain organisms inhabiting swift streams, wave-washed shores, and similar situations were adaptations for life upon rocks and other supporting objects in such situations, aiding in the maintenance of position.

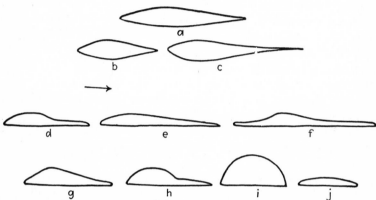

Fig. 25. Diagrams representing body-form profiles of torrent-inhabiting animals. *a, b, c,* forms of animals which dangle freely in the current; *d, e, f, g, h, i, j,* forms of animals which lie closely pressed to the substratum; *d, e, f,* showing progressive modification toward tapering of the form; *g, h, i,* showing progressive modification toward the limpet-like form. *a,* rhyacophilid caddis-fly larva; *b,* form of free-swimming fish, such as *Barbus tor; c,* nymph of May fly *Baetis; d,* a *Balitora* fish; *e,* a *Phractura* fish; *f,* a *Farlowella* fish; *g,* a *Gastromyzon* fish; *h,* nymph of May fly *Iron; i,* a psephenid (Parnidae) larva; and *j,* a planarian. (*Redrawn from Hora,* 1930.)

However, there is some evidence that mere flattening may have another function. Dodds and Hisaw (1924) found that the most successful May-fly nymph in the swift mountain streams is not one with a flattened body but one with a round body (*Baetis*); that only one nymph with flattened form (*Iron*) approached the rounded *Baetis* form in ability to hold its position in swift water; and that all the other flattened forms do not live on exposed surfaces but seek the protection of narrow crevices under stones. Strong adhesive structures aid the nymphs of *Iron* to maintain an exposed position.

Among aquatic animals in general, the streamline type of body form is common. Examples are numerous among the Protozoa (particularly the Mastigophora and Infusoria), the micro-Crustacea (especially the free-swimming Copepoda such as *Cyclops, Diaptomus,* and *Canthocamptus*), and the Rotatoria. Likewise, in various other groups, additional examples may be sought with success.

Inorganic Manifestations of Streamline Form. Various observers (Karrer, 1921; *et al.*) have pointed out what they have interpreted as interesting instances of the streamline form in the inorganic world. These were found in such phenomena as the fundamental curves of snow drifting around obstructions; forms assumed by immobile, wind-eroded boulders, and the shape of the so-called snow "mushrooms" (masses of snow left stranded on the tops of broken trees and other objects which act as pedicels).

Other Forms of Adjustment. Frictional relations between water and obstructing bodies depend much upon the velocity of the former, a fact which is often overlooked. In water velocities of the ordinary ranges, the rounding off of contours of the body and the elimination of surface irregularities of all sorts (i.e., a smoothing of the outer surface) in organisms are not only an advantage but may, in some situations, be a necessity, since by these means the friction between the surface and the water is minimized. However, it is claimed that under conditions of still greater water velocities, surface roughness is an advantage, paradoxical as it may seem. The following explanation is given by Hora (1930). If the velocity of water flowing over or against a solid object is less than a certain critical rate, under conditions of streamline motion there will be no *slip* at the region of contact of water with solid. As a consequence, the physical features of the surface of the object will not have an influence on the resistance to the water flowage. Under these circumstances, the surface of the object is covered with a layer of water in which flowage is absent, and the movement of the main body of water occurs by the formation of a shearing zone in the water itself above the quiet layer resting against the object. At velocities higher than the critical rate mentioned above, the water motion as a whole may be distinctly turbulent; if so, there might still remain a nonturbulent layer of water in contact with the surface of the object, but this layer is now so very thin that any increased roughness of the object's surface increases the resistance by increasing the eddy formation. Under these circumstances, the resistance produced is due, to some minor extent, to the shear in the water but for the most part to the eddy formation. Resistance due to eddy formation is said to depend entirely upon the rate at which kinetic energy is imparted to the eddy system and is also said to be proportional to the density of the water and to the square of the velocity.

Hill and mountain streams are often very rapid and turbulent. In such environments, it would appear that the smoothing off of the bodies of organisms living therein would be an urgent necessity, since, presumably, reduced resistance would thus result. However, some animals living in the strongest currents possess spines on the exposed surface (Blepharoceridae). It would appear, on first thought, that these projecting structures would be detrimental by increasing the resistance. But, strange as it may seem, these roughnesses actually help to *decrease* resistance. In bodies such as spheres and cylinders, the nature of the resistance may change markedly with relatively small changes in the conditions involved; thus, it is said that at certain velocities, the resistance of a sphere may be *reduced* by *roughening its surface.* Hora concludes that it is probable that the various, conspicuously rough backs of blepharocerid larvae have been developed as a means of diminishing the resistance to the fierce currents in which they live; that these spines obstruct the flowage of water against the surface of the larva, thus maintaining against the animal a layer of relatively calm water, over which the very swift, outlying current glides—water gliding over another layer of water with less resistance than if it were gliding over a smooth chitinous surface. According to this interpretation, the spines on such a body would increase the resistance at some water velocities but would decrease the resistance at certain higher rates of flow.

RELATIONS OF ORGANISMS TO MOVEMENTS OF WATER

Movements of water, in their various forms, affect aquatic organisms in a great many ways, directly or indirectly, and often play very important roles in aquatic environments. The following paragraphs cover some of the general and more important relations.

EFFECTS UPON SESSILE ANIMALS

It has frequently been claimed that different growth forms in the same animal, notably the fresh-water sponges, are the result of presence or absence of water currents or movements. However, Old (1932) has found branched and unbranched colonies of *Spongilla lacustris* side by side in both streams and lakes, thus affording double proof against the old idea that one form was the result of living in standing water and the other the result of living in running water. Old contends that the statement made by Carpenter (1928) that the branched form of *Ephydatia fluviatilis* occurs in lakes and the flat type in streams is the result of a confusion of two species, viz., *Spongilla lacustris* and *Ephydatia fluviatilis.* The basis of the production of the two or more forms of certain species of fresh-water sponges is not known. Claims have been made that the unbranched colonies are the result of unfavorable conditions, but this can scarcely be credited when both the branched and the unbranched forms occur side by side in the same water and on similar supports. Bryozoa have also been supposed to develop different growth forms in standing and in moving water. True it is that, in certain species at least, both fresh-water sponges and Bryozoa are highly variable in body form, but it has not as yet been demonstrated satisfactorily that the presence or absence of current is directly responsible for the differences.

EFFECTS UPON MOTILE ANIMALS

Many motile animals show a definite orientation response to current; i.e., they exhibit either positive or negative rheotropism. Orientation reaction may be accompanied by locomotor activities, so that certain animals will not only head upstream but will swim, either maintaining their original position or making progress against the current. It has been claimed that under experimental conditions, certain fishes may exhaust themselves swimming against a current stronger than the optimum. One of the most striking exhibitions of heading into the current and the maintenance of the original position may be seen in fish-hatchery ponds in which trout (brook, rainbow, or brown) arrange themselves with military precision in the face of inflowing water. Sometimes the response to current depends upon some important event in the life history such as sexual maturity. Creaser (1925) described an interesting example in the Atlantic smelt, now established in the upper waters of the Great Lakes, which while essentially a lake-inhabiting fish, becomes positively responsive to current at the onset of spawning season and exhibits spawning "runs" at night into certain adjacent inland waters flowing into the Great Lakes. A great many examples of orientations to current can be accumulated from among the insects, Crustacea, and in fact from almost all of the groups of aquatic, free-moving animals. In some forms, definite, constant reaction seems to be absent. Different animals may manifest current reaction at different current velocities, many tending to respond to that velocity characteristic of the normal environment in which they live.

Water in motion imposes pressure against certain surfaces of the animal, and it has been held that equality or inequality of current pressure on different parts of the body affords the stimulus to orientation of some aquatic animals, which, if true, furnishes an instance of the direct effect of current. Other explanations have been offered in which the current is considered as acting indirectly, as, for example, certain fishes are supposed to orient in response to visual impressions as they float downstream (Clausen, 1931; *et al.*); and still other fishes have been thought to orient in response to the rubbing of parts of the body on the bottom as the current floats them downstream. The visual theory seems ineffective in those instances of runs at night (smelt) or in very turbid waters. By the use of modern experimental means, Brown and Hatch (1929) showed that the orientations of stream-inhabiting Gyrinidae (*Dineutes discolor*) have an exclusively visual basis. All of these orientations are still far too little understood.

Certain phenomena, morphological or physiological, may either be caused by, or correlated with, movements of water and their different velocities. For example, it has been claimed (Altnöder, 1926) that a general correlation exists between the rate of flow and the shape of mussels in eastern Bavaria. Also it has been shown (Fox *et al.*, 1935) that oxygen consumption of certain caddis-fly larvae and May-fly naiads from swift streams is considerably greater than that of comparable species from still water.

CURRENT DEMAND

Certain aquatic organisms exist permanently only in the presence of appropriate movements of water, and it is now known that current is demanded by some of them. For example, practically all animals composing the typical rapids association never occur elsewhere. Among these, black-fly larvae (*Simulium*) of all species (one possible exception in Asia) inhabit only rapidly running water. Wu (1931) has shown, among other things, that these larvae possess an *inherent demand for current* and that their universal absence from standing waters is due directly to the absence of the necessary current and not to the supposed high dissolved oxygen demand so often postulated by earlier workers. Whether other members of the rapids association select their habitat primarily because of a similar demand for current remains for future research to determine. Secondarily, current is also related to *Simulium* larvae in such matters as proper food delivery and respiration (page 163).

RESISTANCE TO WATER MOVEMENT

Maintenance of position in the face of currents, waves, or other forms of water movement determines not only the occupancy of such a situation but, in many organisms at least, is a matter of life or death. In general, animals which meet this problem successfully do so by means of one or more of the following features: (1) body form which offers least resistance, such as the streamline or the hemistreamline form already described (page 151); (2) unusually well-developed burrowing or clinging habit; and (3) special forms of attachment to fixed, supporting objects. Combinations of (1) and (2) or (1) and (3) in the same animal are common. Typical inhabitants of rapids, rocky stream beds, barren stony shores and shoals of lakes, and similar situations where burrowing is difficult or impossible are usually characterized by combinations of suitable body form and clinging habit (*Isonychia* nymphs and others) or of suitable body form and special attachments (*Simulium* larvae and others). A few may maintain their position because of unusually effective attachment devices (powerful adhesive suckers of the larvae of Blepharoceridae).

On exposed, barren, sandy shoals of lakes, practically no animal which does not possess well-developed powers of burrowing can exist permanently. In only a very few instances, such as the clams, is the burrowing habit combined with a more or less appropriate form of body. Not only are the clams the largest of the inhabitants, but they usually do not burrow completely, thus exposing the posterior ends to the wash of waves. Baker (unpublished) found that clams in Douglas Lake, Michigan, vary markedly in their liability to be pulled loose and washed ashore by wave action. Table 18 includes some of his data and indicates the nature of the results. Moffett (1943) conducted similar experiments in Douglas Lake, using the same species. His findings were essentially confirmatory.

TABLE 18. DIFFERENCES IN RESISTANCE TO WAVE ACTION BY CERTAIN CLAMS IN DOUGLAS LAKE, MICHIGAN

Unpublished data by H. B. Baker

Species	Sex	Relative percentage of liability of being washed ashore
Anodonta grandis	Female	100.0
Anodonta marginata	......	34.5
Lampsilis siliquoidea	Female	15.6
Ligumia (Lampsilis) nasuta	Male	11.4
Ligumia (Lampsilis) nasuta	Female	8.9
Lampsilis siliquoidea	Male	7.2

According to these results, distinct resistance differences exist between the sexes of the same species; therefore water movements might have a selective effect. However, it has been claimed (Allen, 1921) that sex is a negligible factor in the distribution of fresh-water clams.

PROVISIONS FOR CLINGING AND ATTACHMENT

Among the numerous, special provisions for increased efficiency in maintaining position in the face of strong water movement are the following:

1. Strong, recurved tarsal claws.

2. Exceedingly flat ventral surface.

3. Strongly depressed body.

4. Lateral margins of head and thorax produced in the form of flat margins for increased contact with the supporting object.

5. Legs, when of large size, flattened horizontally and applied by their sides as well as by the tarsi to the supporting object.

6. Special flattening of gills or the modification of the entire gill series to form a ventral attachment disk (Fig. 26).

7. Special sucking disks. Examples: blepharocerid larvae; leeches; nymphs of May fly, *Ephemerella doddsi* (Fig. 27).

8. Ventral adhesive pads, often bearing recurved spines. Examples: certain stream-inhabiting aquatic Hemiptera and May-fly nymphs.

9. Terminal attachment disks. Example: *Simulium* larvae—posterior disk a combination of a row of hooks with a gelatinous secretion originating from the mouth.

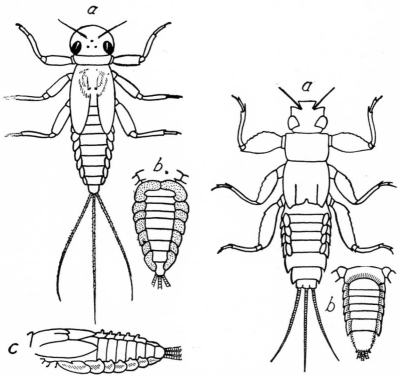

FIG. 26. *a*, dorsal view of the redgill May-fly nymph (*Rithrogena doddsi*); *b*, ventral view of the abdomen showing how the seven pairs of gill plates combine to form an oval sucking disk on the ventral surface; *c*, oblique lateral view of the abdomen showing the gills and the gill plates. (*Redrawn from Needham and Christenson*, 1927.)

FIG. 27. *a*, dorsal view of nymph of the ginger quill May fly (*Ephemerella doddsi*); *b*, ventral view of abdomen showing the special sucking disk. (*Redrawn from Needham and Christenson*, 1927.)

10. Threads which anchor the animal directly to the support. Example: thread used by *Simulium* larvae when shifting position.

11. Threads which anchor case or shelter of animal. Example: certain caddis-fly larvae.

12. Shelters, tubes, or cases which protect against the wash of currents and waves. Examples: sand-constructed case of caddis fly, *Molanna*;

cases of certain midge larvae; egg capsules of leeches; tubes of tubificid worms.

13. Adhesive secretions. Example: common hydra.

Provisions for Burrowing

Burrowing is often accomplished by animals having no special structural provision for that purpose. In such instances, they are merely capable of forcing their way into bottom materials, aided by such features as (1) more or less pointed anterior end; (2) body movements of a penetrating sort; (3) setae; (4) longitudinal contraction and extension of a portion of the body; (5) extensile and protrusible body tubercles; and (6) strongly muscular body walls accompanied by freely-moving, soft, internal organs and fluids. By such means as these, some of the softest-bodied aquatic animals (Oligochaeta and others) penetrate the hard-packed sand of barren, exposed shoals, thus maintaining their position in the presence of the strongest wave action.

Other animals have developed special structural features for effecting partial or almost entire penetration of bottom, such as (1) the flattened, shovel-like, anteriorly directed front legs, the posteriorly directed hind legs appressed to the body and adapted for pushing, and the pointed sloping head of the nymphs of the May flies *Hexagenia* and *Pentagenia*, and the dragon flies *Gomphus;* (2) the long, upturned, mandibular tusks of burrowing May-fly nymphs; (3) the muscular foot of clams and snails; (4) the long, spraddling, spider-like legs of certain dragon-fly nymphs (*Macromia*), so oriented on the body that they rest full length upon the sand and, by wriggling movements, work the sand entirely over them, thus gaining a certain anchorage; and (5) the strikingly flattened, shoal-inhabiting dragon-fly nymphs (*Hagenius*), which weight themselves down by working sand on top of the thin abdominal margins.

Burrowing by some species may be a direct response to excess light, but the end result of maintaining position remains the same.

Habits Facilitating Resistance to Water Movement

In organisms possessing special structural features which aid, in one way or another, in resisting the transporting tendency of water movement, it is perhaps unnecessary to point out that they manifest physiological activities necessary to render these structural features effective. In addition, however, there may be other animals, which, lacking special structural developments, manage to maintain position in current or wave-swept areas by reactions alone. These are exemplified by the habitual seeking of (1) the protected sides of and the interstices between rocks; (2) fissures in bottoms and bottom materials; and (3) the more protected parts of rooted plants.

Influence on Construction Activities

Construction processes of certain animals can be properly performed only in the presence of water movement. A striking instance is that of the net-building caddis-fly larvae which can produce their nets only in moving water; in calm water, the attempt results only in a shapeless mass of threads. Certain stream-inhabiting caddis-fly larvae build portable cases which are heavily ballasted by the attachment of stones. This ballasting is regarded as a provision against being swept away by the current. According to Webster and Webster (1943), the larva of one caddis-fly, *Goera calcarata*, builds significantly heavier cases in running water than it does in standing water.

Distribution of Organisms

Since moving water is an effective transporting agent, movements of water play a very active part in the distribution of many aquatic organisms, particularly those which are relatively small and in partial or complete suspension or those which develop life-history stages or reproductive bodies upon which water motion may have a direct transporting effect. The whole plankton is virtually, by definition, a group in perpetual change of position by the movements of the medium. Not only is plankton constantly subject to water movements, but, under some circumstances, great, temporary concentrations of surface plankton occur alongshore, due to the effect of onshore winds. Equalities and inequalities of plankton distribution, particularly in the upper waters, are largely the result of water motion. Statoblasts of Bryozoa drift widely. Many diverse aquatic animals secure dissemination by the transportation of a supporting object. Pieces of aquatic plants bearing various eggs, larvae, pupae, and even adults of insects, hydra, Bryozoa, Mollusca, and many others break from their attachments and drift with the water. Floating bits of wood, masses of Algae and other nonrooted plants, floating "islands," detached pieces of marginal mats, and other similar materials act as disseminators in the same fashion. In the running-water series, not only are ordinary transportation effects present, but in times of freshets and high waters a partial or virtually complete scouring out and removal of a whole population may occur, particularly in stream beds of considerable slope where erosion effects are extensive. Vigorous wave action on lake shores commonly has a selective elimination effect, as for example on a sandy, exposed shoal practically all animals are eliminated save those with well-developed burrowing habits; on a typical rocky, exposed shoal, all species are eliminated save those with well-developed clinging and attaching provisions and a small group of forms such as crayfish which utilize crevices and crannies among the rocks. There is an occasional exception to the statements made above, such as certain caddis-fly larvae with *floating* cases which seem somehow to stay mostly in shoal waters, but such exceptions are rare. Fishes may wander into shoal waters or, in some instances, come there for breeding purposes, but because of their marked powers of locomotion and wider ranging habits they may be omitted in this connection.

Molar Agents

Moving water is seldom if ever free from substances in suspension. The various conditions under which it transports particles and objects are too well known to justify discussion here. Add to moving water materials in suspension or materials capable of being rolled about on the bottom and the mechanical effects of the water on other objects become greatly increased. Sand, fine gravel, rocks of various sizes, and sometimes even boulders, carried or rolled by the water, become a veritable wearing, grinding, fragmenting machine which constitutes one of the serious menaces to the whole biota of those situations. Conspicuous signs of such molar action are often found on exposed, wave-swept, rocky shoals where the polished, worn, or even broken shells of mollusks and the damaged bodies or mutilated appendages of crayfish constitute mute evidence of the severity of this molar action.

Effects of Turbulence

Waves and currents, especially during storms and sudden high waters in streams are often found to produce fragmenting effects on organisms, especially upon certain aquatic plants and some of the more delicate invertebrates. Such effects, in some instances, are due to the combined action of both the moving water and the accompanying molar agents. However, vigorous or violent water motion alone may be responsible for the fractionating of some of the less resistant organisms, particularly the sessile ones, in the littoral zone.

Knowledge of the mechanical effects of turbulence on plankton in both littoral and limnetic regions is in a very unsatisfactory condition. In the older literature it has been stated that wave action causes fragmentation of filamentous algae and fragile organisms, that colonial plankters may be broken apart, that injury to individual plankters occurs, and that in some instances (*Microcystis aeruginosa*) smaller, more compact colonies are produced in moving water as contrasted with the larger, irregular, more loosely constructed colonies of the same species in quiet water. Recently, Harris (unpublished) studied the mechanical effects of turbulence on several common lake-inhabiting plankters. He found no evidence that the ordinary turbulences in the open water of Douglas Lake, Michigan, produce any fragmentation or separation of parts of plankters.

Fragmentation and destruction of plankters by rapids and waterfalls have been reported by competent observers, but it does not yet seem clear as to how much of the result is due to molar action of suspended particles and the character and roughness of the channel and what part is caused by turbulence of water alone.

Various authors have reported what appeared to be physiological effects of artificially produced turbulences, such as suspension of growth in certain algae, acceleration of movement in *Oscillatoria,* alteration in number of males of *Daphnia,* and decrease in locomotion and ingestion in *Paramecium.* Such information is still too meager and fragmentary to be of service to the limnologist.

INDIRECT EFFECTS OF WATER MOVEMENT

Water movement is indirectly concerned with the life of aquatic organisms in a number of ways, the following being among the most important:

1. Constant shifting of bottom materials on shoals and other shallow waters may prevent the rooting and, therefore, the occupancy of these areas by higher aquatic plants.

2. Erosion or transportation of materials may completely alter the environment, converting it into some very different type to which the organisms are not fitted. The example of the cutting off of a sand-spit beach pool from the body of a lake is merely one of a great many different types which might be mentioned.

3. Circulation, and in some instances the return to circulation, of essential nutritive substances in the water, both dissolved and suspended.

4. Production and maintenance of turbidity, thus affecting the light penetration and certain other relations.

5. Delivery of food to sessile or sedentary animals, particularly when the food is in the nature of suspended, living organisms (plankton) and suspended, finely divided, nonliving materials.

6. Respiratory relations, such as (*a*) renewal of properly oxygenated water to respiratory surfaces and (*b*) renewal of dissolved oxygen supply from the air by the surface agitations incident to water movement.

7. Temporary exposure to air, as in seiches which imitate the ebb and flow of a tide and which, if of sufficient magnitude, may expose for a time a whole set of shallow-water organisms to evaporation and other serious hazards.

SUBSURFACE WAVES AND SUBSURFACE SEICHES

Subsurface waves and subsurface seiches have been studied so little that for the most part their effects can only be surmised. It seems probable that the most direct effect is that of horizontal and vertical transportation of such plankton organisms as occur at the depths involved. Indirect effects may result through changes in the temperature at a given level.

SURFACE-FILM RELATIONS

SUPPORT

When certain conditions are met, the surface film serves as a mechanical support for organisms and miscellaneous particulate materials. Both surfaces of the film may function in this way. The term *neuston,* originally applied to minute organisms, is now commonly extended to include all organisms associated with the surface film. Those related to the upper surface of the film comprise the *supraneuston;* those related to the lower surface, the *infraneuston.*

The larger animals commonly associated with the *supraneuston* are: (1) water striders (Gerridae); (2) broad-shouldered water striders (Veliidae); (3) water measurers (Hydrometridae); (4) hebrids (Hebridae); (5) mesoveliids (Mesoveliidae); (6) whirligig beetles (Gyrinidae); (7) springtails (Collembola); and (8) certain spiders. In all of these instances, utilization of the surface film by running about over it has its basis in the possession of hydrofuge surfaces which make contact with the water. Certain of these forms have the ability to break through the surface film at will and swim below for a brief period.

Hardman (1941) mentions unpublished results of experiments by G. E. Hutchinson dealing with the effect of reduction of surface tension on certain surface-skating insects. When surface tension was reduced experimentally to about 50 dynes per cm., which reduction is within the range of variation observed in Wisconsin lakes, a gerrid would fall through the surface film with legs held rigid in normal position, while *Hydrometra* would first collapse, lying flat on the water. Such preliminary results seem to indicate that the natural variations in surface tension may be great enough to affect members of the supraneuston in a vital way.

The minute components of the supraneuston have been studied by various investigators but are still little known. This assemblage of organisms appears to vary locally and may be complex. Bacteria, Fungi, and certain Algae are said to be common. Various predatory Protozoa and certain Phycomycetes are reported as attacking this stratum and reducing it. Anopheline larvae are known to feed upon the supraneuston. It is probable that it is a much larger biota than is now known.

In addition to the groups mentioned above, the surface film serves to help support certain terrestrial animals, such as field crickets, grasshoppers, and grouse locusts, which accidentally or otherwise get into marginal waters. Mention of these more or less accidental occurrences of animals on the surface might not be justified here were it not for the fact that their relations to water may be connected with the completion of life cycles of certain parasites (Gordius and others) and that certain food relations are involved.

The infraneuston is also but vaguely known. The lower surface of the film often supports temporarily certain representatives of the following groups of animals: the common hydra, planarians, Entomostraca (Ostracoda, Cladocera), insect larvae (larvae of mosquitoes, certain midges, soldier flies, and others), insect pupae (midges, mosquitoes, and others), and pond snails. It has been contended that since this relation to the lower surface of the film by hydra, planaria, and snails is more or less incidental and that they gain no special advantage, they are not true representatives of the infraneuston but are to be regarded merely as occasional visitors. An assemblage of microorganisms occurs on the lower side of the surface film, composed of bacteria, plants, and animals. Possibly this group is more typically an infraneuston although it also has been suspected of being temporary in character.

In this connection, the pleuston (page 221) should be mentioned, especially those components which have parts that float on the surface of the water, such as the leaves of water lilies, certain potamogetons, and others. If these surface-floating parts secure any portion of their mechanical support from surface tension, then it appears that they impose a certain handicap on themselves since Hardman (1941) showed that as beds of water lilies were approached in certain Wisconsin lakes the surface tension was reduced and among the plants the surface tension was depressed by 15 to 20 dynes per cm. The depressant was supposed to be some unidentified substance given off from the leaves.

RESPIRATION

Air-breathing aquatic animals have various relations to the surface film which cannot be completely catalogued here. Conspicuous among them are the following:

1. Some adult insects, typically aerial, descend into the water for purposes of oviposition. They enter the water with safety, since their hydrofuge surfaces cause the surface film to form a more or less complete envelope about the body, inclosing thereby an air space.

2. In certain aquatic insects which carry various, more or less exposed air stores (bubbles at posterior end, air stores under wing covers, plastrons of air on venter, and others), the surface film acts as a diffusion membrane through which gases pass from the air space to the water, and vice versa, thus enabling such an insect to draw upon the dissolved oxygen of the water even though devoid of gills or other special provisions for sodoing. It has been shown (Harpster, 1941, 1944; Thorpe, 1950; Thorpe and

Crisp, 1947) that those very unique aquatic insects (certain Dryopidae and certain Naucoridae) which may be continuously submerged in the adult stage accomplish their respiration by this means.

3. Successful respiratory position of air-breathing aquatic insect larvae often depends upon the spreading out of a tuft of hydrofuge hairs, bristles, or other structures on the surface film, such tuft usually surrounding important spiracles. By this means, hanging to the surface film during exchange of gases is greatly facilitated.

Hazards of Surface Film

The surface film offers certain hazards; for example, it is well known that when certain Entomostraca accidentally find themselves above the surface film, return to submerged condition may be accomplished with difficulty, the unfortunate animal sometimes succumbing to effects of evaporation or to the attack of an enemy. Entanglement with the surface film, particularly by small animals, is not a circumstance to be invited.

Light Reflection

Reduction of light due to surface film reflection has been discussed in an earlier section (page 76), and mention is made here merely for sake of completeness.

TEMPERATURE RELATIONS

The profound influence which temperature exerts upon aquatic life has already been mentioned. This influence, direct and indirect, is of a diversified and complex nature, an understanding of which continually extends into the province of physiology.

General

With the exception of the aquatic birds and mammals, all aquatic animals are cold-blooded (poikilothermous), i.e., their internal temperatures follow, usually within close limits, the temperatures of the surrounding medium. It must be understood, however, (1) that exceptions in the form of unusual deviations from surrounding temperatures may occur, as, for example, the claim that certain fishes may have an internal temperature of as much as 10°C. higher than that of the surrounding water; and (2) that the degree of agreement between body temperature and external temperature may differ with the temperature level of the latter; as, for example, Pirsch (1923) found that in low air temperatures the honeybee, when active, maintains a body temperature somewhat higher than the medium; with medium air temperatures (about 35°C.), the temperatures are practically coincident; while with high air temperatures, the body temperatures are maintained at a somewhat lower level.

Whether any of the aquatic animals exhibit this form of adjustment does not seem to be known, but it appears likely. Some aquatic animals live in surroundings the temperature of which is below freezing (glacier worms and others), but it has usually been supposed that the freezing point of their body fluids is depressed by substances in solution. Even if this is true, there remains to be explained the fact that under those very low temperatures they are not only active but grow, develop, and reproduce.

INFLUENCE ON METABOLISM

Within the ordinary temperature limits for a given cold-blooded animal, decreasing temperatures diminish metabolism, and vice versa, a relation which is opposite that for warm-blooded animals. This means that metabolic rate is, to a large extent, governed automatically by the external temperatures. It also means that the falling temperatures of increasing depths in water or of increasingly northern latitudes inflict lower rates of metabolism. A general rule for this change in metabolism in cold-blooded aquatic animals can be stated as follows: A rise of 1°C. increases the rate of metabolism about 10 per cent; stated otherwise, this means that the rate of oxygen consumption and carbon dioxide output doubles with a temperature increase of 10°C. This rule serves for general purposes only. Precise statement requires certain modifications of this rule, since it is known that in many instances rate of metabolism does not increase uniformly with increase of temperature but, instead, the increase in rate per 1°C. changes as the temperature increases. It has become customary to express this increment in rate by the term Q_{10} which can be described as one plus one-tenth of the percentage increase in rate for a rise of 1°C. Even this statement is subject to refinement, since the value of Q_{10} frequently is not constant but changes with increasing temperature. Further consideration of this matter is unnecessary here, and the reader is referred to works on physiology for additional information.

The temperature influence on metabolism just described presents various limnological relations, one of which relates to food consumption and food supply. In warmer waters, aquatic organisms have a greater daily food requirement; conversely, they have a smaller daily requirement in cold waters. Expressed otherwise, the same standing crop of food will support more animals in the colder regions than in the warmer ones.

INFLUENCE ON DEVELOPMENT AND OTHER BIOLOGICAL PROCESSES

Rising temperature increases the rate of (1) development of animals, (2) respiratory movements, (3) heart beat and comparable circulatory rhythms, (4) enzyme action, and (5) other physiological processes, although the operative limits in each process may differ. A cold-blooded aquatic animal may be expected to complete its life cycle more slowly and to produce fewer generations per unit of time in the northern than in the southern part of its range; likewise, the normal individual life span may be longer. Onset of hibernation, breeding season, changes in reproductive activity, germination of asexual reproductive bodies, and a host of other biological activities too numerous to catalogue here are profoundly influenced by surrounding temperatures.

TEMPERATURE TOLERATION

Each organism has a maximum and a minimum environmental temperature between which life is possible but beyond which conditions are lethal. Even for individual species, these temperature limits are not absolutely fixed, since they may vary with different individuals, with the different sexes, with different life history stages, with different physiological states, and in different parts of the geographic range. In spite of this variation, it is possible roughly to divide animals into two groups: (1) those which are restricted to a narrow range of temperature change (stenothermic animals) and (2) those which tolerate a wide range of temperature change (euthermic animals). As would be expected, there are intergrades between these two groups. It is a well-known fact that acclimatization can shift temperature restrictions as well as those of other environmental factors. Somewhere between the maximum and minimum limits, an *optimum* region occurs, the position and extent of which vary with different animals. It is sometimes stated that the optimum is usually closer to the maximum than to the minimum, but in some instances the reverse condition prevails. Acclimatization may also affect the position of the optimum.

In considering temperature toleration, it should be noted that while some aquatic animals can survive wide extremes of temperature under experimental conditions or during environmental variations, such extremes would not necessarily be selected by the animal if free to choose. However, certain aquatic animals regularly experience wide differences in temperature as a part of the daily program. For example, *Corethra* larvae and those other plankton organisms which migrate from the depths to surface waters during the night, returning to the depths at the onset of dawn, may pass from about 4°C. at the bottom to 20°C. or more at the surface, in the summer time, representing almost the complete annual temperature range of the environment. During the winter, these same organisms are confined to temperatures from about 4°C. at the bottom to near the freezing point at the surface.

In temperate lakes of the first and second orders, only the nonmigrating, profundal bottom organisms live under what approximates a fairly even temperature throughout the year. On the contrary, those surface-water forms which remain active throughout the year must endure the complete range of temperature. Those not active in all seasons have developed various forms of hibernation, and aestivation, as a means of passing over the more rigorous conditions. Many aquatic animals remain active through wide ranges of temperatures, the active period ending only just before the extremes are reached.

Effects of Extremes of Temperature

The specific effect of extremely low temperature is usually considered as being mainly mechanical, involving the water of the body, while that of extremely high temperature is principally chemical, affecting the protoplasm. The chemical effect of excessively high temperature is more severe than the mechanical effect of correspondingly low temperatures. It is true that even in the temperate latitudes, certain aquatic animals (mosquito larvae and others) may be frozen into surface ice and recover on release. This phenomenon seems to be more common in the arctic and subarctic regions. The ever recurring question as to whether the protoplasm of the cells is actually frozen under such circumstances has apparently not been satisfactorily answered, but, at any rate, animals may be surrounded by ice and under conditions of such very low temperature that complete freezing seems unavoidable. On the other hand, temperatures rising to a level dangerous for certain organisms seem to become abruptly lethal. The occasional rise of surface-water temperature to unusual heights (although only a few degrees above the usual summer maximum) in protected bays in times of clear, hot weather and dead-calm water promptly leads to a dying off of surface plankton and certain other shallow-water organisms. However it should be pointed out that in nature the specific effect of excessive heat is difficult to determine since rising temperatures set up other changes in the water which act simultaneously and may profoundly affect the end result.

Recognition of Temperature Differences

Some aquatic animals have a well-developed recognition of changing temperature and, if free to choose, may respond with considerable precision. Under experimental conditions, certain fresh-water animals have been found to recognize temperature differences of 0.2°C. and react to them. According to Ward (1921), salmon migrating upstream in fresh waters choose the cooler water at the river forks. In thermally stratified lakes, it is very difficult to determine the presence or absence of a limiting effect to downward distribution by the steep thermal gradient in the thermocline, since other varying conditions are simultaneously present, such as light, chemical stratification, and viscosity changes.

Freezing-out Effects

The following "freezing-out" phenomena are of interest here:

1. Substances in solution in surface waters freeze out to some extent when ice forms and become more concentrated in the unfrozen water below. The reduction of about 20 per cent of the salt in ice frozen from sea water is often cited as an instance.

2. Bacteria also "freeze out." Ice may contain as little as 1 per cent of the number present in the water from which the ice is formed. It is claimed, however, that this reduction process is not one of a removal of the bacteria but rather a killing off of the bacteria due to lack of food and water and that because of these deficiencies most of the original bacterial population dies off in a short time.

3. Freezing out of dissolved gases also occurs. This may sometimes account for the occasional accumulation of oxygen immediately under the ice.

LIGHT RELATIONS

The various relations of sunlight to aquatic organisms may be classified into two sets: (1) direct influences upon the organisms as a whole and (2) photosynthetic relations.

Direct Influences

Lethal Effects. Many aquatic organisms are sensitive to the higher intensities of sunlight and, in fact, must avoid them by occupying deeper levels in the water; by seeking the shelter offered by shore materials, the higher aquatic plants, or shade of overhanging shore vegetation; or by burrowing into the bottom or into plants. This is particularly true of the small, soft-bodied, nonpigmented forms into and through whose bodies sunlight may pass readily and with serious results. Pigmentation, chitinous coverings, shells, cases constructed of foreign materials, and similar structures provide protection in varying degrees, enabling certain organisms to inhabit well-lighted shoals and other areas from which they would be completely eliminated if their bodies were directly exposed during the day. Eggs of many forms must have similar protection although exceptions exist. Plankton organisms occur in surface waters, exposed to the maximum light intensity. Many are phytoplankton and have photosynthetic relations, but it is a well-established fact that in most natural waters the maximum populations of plankton occur at some depth, one of the important reasons being the more favorable light effects. Klugh (1929) holds that the short-length ultraviolet radiations of the sun are deadly to plankton Crustacea and that this explains why these organisms, in the region of St. Andrews, New Brunswick, remain 27 m. or more under the surface of the sea during the day and come to the surface at night.   Klugh (1930) also found that ultraviolet light alone, submitted to various surface-inhabiting marine species, killed young eels in 18 to 24 hr.; killed amphipods in 2 to 4 days; had little effect on ctenophores; and readily killed animals which live at considerable depths and come to the surface only under weak illumination.   Whipple (1927), summarizing results of experiments on effect of sunlight and ultraviolet light on plankton growth in a pond, reports that the sample kept in the dark changed only slightly from the original sample; that both sunlight and ultraviolet light seemed to devitalize the diatoms (excepting *Synedra*) but stimulated the Chlorophyceae and the Myxophyceae, the ultraviolet light providing a slightly greater stimulus.   Since the ultraviolet light is quickly absorbed in the surface waters, its effects are very restricted.   ZoBell and McEwen (1935) failed to find evidence of lethal influence of sunlight on bacteria in sea water.   Many aquatic organisms, especially bottom-inhabiting forms, live in conditions of almost if not complete darkness and quickly succumb in direct sunlight.   Light is often a powerful factor, sometimes the determining one, in the distribution of organisms in aquatic situations.

Behavior and Orientation.   Responses of aquatic organisms are often due to, or conditioned by, light.   Forms and directions of growth of sessile species, changes in position or orientation, various actions having a true visual basis—these and other groups of responses include a vast, diversified aggregate of light-stimulated activities, details of which are not necessary for present purposes.   One of the most striking results of the alternation of day and night is the migration of certain plankton organisms from deep water to the surface at night and their return to the depths near dawn. This phenomenon will be discussed in some detail later (page 243), but it will suffice here to state that modern work seems to demonstrate that light is the principal motivating influence of this migration.   For some organisms, day is the period of general activity, night the period of quiescence; for other forms, the reverse is true.   The literature on freshwater biology is full of diverse, intriguing examples and modifications of such responses.   Creaser (1925) has shown that the spawning run of the smelt from upper Lake Michigan into certain inflowing waters is at night and that most of the fishes return to deep water during the day or hide under the banks and bridges.   A light held at the mouth of the stream and directed toward the lake will stop a large part of the run.   Return to the lake, when the run is stopped by the arrival of daylight, is accomplished by a curious dropping-back reaction which is essentially a cessation of forward swimming but a maintenance of the original orientation so that they float *tail first* downstream.   In many aquatic animals, the light responses differ markedly with physiological state, age, life history stage. season, and other conditions.

Other Influences. A complete analysis of the various direct influences of light would add others to this discussion such as the effects upon pigments and pigment production, upon growth, upon development, and, in fact, upon many of the conditions involved in the general success of organisms. Shelford (1929) gives a general account of the effects of light on organisms to which the reader is referred for additional information. While there exist certain important contrasts between the sunlight after it enters water and the sunlight on land, due to inherent differences in the two media (water and air), the fundamental light responses of terrestrial and aquatic animals have much in common.

PHOTOSYNTHESIS

One of the most profound influences of sunlight (and of moonlight to a limited extent) in water is its intimate role in the photosynthetic processes of all chlorophyll-bearing, aquatic plants. Like the chlorophyll-bearing plants on land, these plants furnish, directly or indirectly, the carbohydrate and the protein supply for the aquatic world. They occupy that strategic position between the inorganic and the higher organic components which makes the latter their complete dependents. The phytoplankton has been called the *green pasture of the sea*, and it plays a similar role in fresh waters. It has been thought by some that the higher, chlorophyll-bearing, aquatic plants are of minor importance in the direct aquatic food cycle, but further discussion is deferred (page 305). The direct influence of light is upon the plant itself, making possible one of its most important functions. Indirectly, it is deeply involved in the whole matter of aquatic productivity.

Of recent years much research has been done on chlorophyll and on the mechanisms of photosynthesis. The findings belong largely in the provinces of biochemistry and plant physiology. Outstanding among the discoveries are the following: (1) All plants do not possess the same photosynthetic apparatus. For example, chlorophylls and yellow pigments occur in diatoms, brown algae, and red algae which are not the same as the corresponding pigments in higher plants. (2) Chlorophyll in plants is not a single substance but is diversified. Higher plants and green algae contain chlorophyll *a* and chlorophyll *b*, while diatoms, dinoflagellates, and brown algae contain chlorophyll *a* and chlorophyll *c* but lack chlorophyll *b*. It does not seem to have been ascertained as yet whether the products of photosynthesis reflect these differences in the photosynthetic mechanism. Another pigment, bacteriochlorophyll, closely related to the chlorophyll in green plants, occurs in certain bacteria and is said to perform photosynthesis in the presence of appropriate light and other circumstances.

It becomes increasingly clear that the process commonly referred to as photosynthesis is a very complex phenomenon. Light, temperature, solutes, and carbon dioxide affect simultaneously the photosynthetic apparatus. However, it seems certain that light of the appropriate kind and intensity is the supreme factor.

Light Requirements. The light supply has two important aspects: (1) light intensity and (2) effective wave lengths.

Intensity. The rate of photosynthesis increases with the intensity of light; in fact, if certain conditions of temperature and carbon dioxide are met, the rate of photosynthesis is proportional to the intensity of the incident light. However, the rates of photosynthesis differ in different plants.

Wave Lengths. In spite of its importance and the numerous investigations which have been made, this subject is still in an unsatisfactory state. The following statements appear to have some basis:

1. Ultraviolet rays are of little or no consequence in photosynthesis. This has been demonstrated experimentally with terrestrial plants. Considering the fact that ultraviolet waves are completely absorbed in the uppermost, thin layer of the water and that various aquatic plants thrive far below the level of disappearance of these wave lengths, the aquatic situation seems to offer confirmation of the statement.

2. Experimental evidence appears to show that with equal intensity of incident light, photosynthesis is affected by different wave lengths, being greatest in the red and least in the blue-violet. Certain investigators claim that the rate of photosynthesis diminishes with decreasing wave length.

If these statements are well founded, and assuming that it is legitimate to apply them to conditions in water, then certain interesting consequences appear, viz., that the red wave lengths are the most effective, but in some waters red is a region of high absorption so that the effective penetration and intensity are confined to the uppermost waters; that the blue-violet waves are the least effective but constitute a region of relatively low absorption in water (page 78). It has been pointed out (Miller, 1931) that

. . . since there are different degrees of absorption of the different wave lengths by the leaf cells due to specific differences of the cells themselves or to the thickness of the leaves, it would appear to be impossible to find values for the relative rates of photosynthesis in light of different wave lengths which will hold in general for all plants and all conditions.

Add to this situation as it prevails in terrestrial plants the complicating situation of light penetration and absorption in the diverse natural waters with their various modifying substances in solution and suspension, and the picture becomes increasingly difficult.

Effective Light Penetration. The normal existence of healthy chlorophyll-bearing plants at various depth levels in water may be taken as evidence that some of the effective light is present in sufficient intensity to enable these plants to perform photosynthesis. It must not be assumed, however, that the lowest limit of green plants is the lowest limit of effective light penetration, since other circumstances may determine this lower limit of the plant distribution; for example, high position of the thermocline with an underlying, oxygenless hypolimnion, in mid-or late summer, may confine the green plants to a relatively high level, although the effective light penetration would permit a deeper distribution. Where other physiochemical conditions permit, certain plants thrive at considerable depths in some lakes.

The literature contains statements to the effect that Algae have been found in certain mountain lakes below a depth of 400 m. and at greater depths in the ocean, but it remains to be conclusively demonstrated that these plants are performing photosynthesis. Possibly, in some instances, they are but senile material gradually sinking from above. However, it is claimed that certain algal cultures have continued to grow in total darkness for long periods of time when the proper nutrient materials were supplied. Hence, it may be that some Algae exist at great depths as saprophytes and without performing photosynthesis. If so, their presence would indicate nothing as to the depth to which light rays effective for photosynthesis would penetrate.

In excessively turbid waters, the rapid shutting out of effective light may limit chlorophyll-bearing plants to a very thin surface stratum, but in inland lakes at large, there is reason for believing that some effective light penetrates to greater depths than the plants actually inhabit owing to the fact that often their downward distribution is limited by other factors. Not only does this hold for the phytoplankton, but it is especially true of higher aquatic plants which, in the clear northern lakes of the United States, often do not extend beyond 8 to 10 m. depth.

It seems certain that light is a very influential factor in determining the occurrence and distribution of chlorophyll in a lake. Therefore it may be expected that since light conditions differ in different waters the quantity and activity of chlorophyll will be influenced correspondingly. Nevertheless the processes of light penetration and photosynthesis in natural waters are so complex and still so imperfectly known that it is practically impossible to formulate generalizations with any certainty. It has been commonly stated that the maximum rate of photosynthesis in lakes in full sunlight usually occurs somewhere below the surface layer, the exact depth depending upon the light transmission of the water concerned. It has also been claimed that plants inhabiting situations having moderately reduced light intensity usually have more chlorophyll than do those living in full sunlight. Relatively large quantities of chlorophyll have been found in the profundal regions of some lakes, well below the depth of effective light penetration, but it is generally assumed that it is inactive photosynthetically. *Light adaptation* apparently exists in certain Algae (Manning *et al.*, 1938) in which maximum rates of photosynthesis for more than one different light intensity occur; it appears to be absent in the higher aquatic plants. The theory of *chromatic adaptation*—color distribution of plants represents an adaptation to differences in light quality at different depths—seems to have no support in the phytoplankton and the flowering plants of fresh water (Dutton and Juday, 1944). The quantity of chlorophyll is not a strictly dependable index of photosynthetic capacity, for reasons which have been summarized by Manning and Juday (1941), but is generally useful in estimating the photosynthetic process in the uppermost waters of a lake.

That light intensity at which oxygen production in photosynthesis and oxygen consumption by respiration of the plants concerned are equal is known as the *compensation point*, and the depth at which the compensation point occurs is called the *compensation depth*. For a given body of water this depth varies with several conditions, such as season, time of day, degree of cloudiness of sky, condition of the water, and taxonomic composition of the flora involved. As commonly used, the *compensation point* refers to that intensity of light which is such that the plant's oxygen production during the day will be sufficient to balance the oxygen consumption during the whole 24-hr. period. In terms of productivity, the light intensity at the compensation point "is the minimum at which the plant in question could survive in nature, and is still too low to allow for any increase in crop" (Jenkin, 1937). In Lake Erie, Meyer *et al.* (1943) found that the compensation point for a series of submerged vascular plants was about 2 per cent of sunlight intensity on clear summer days. The compensation depth would vary, depending upon differences in turbidity and other factors.

PHOTOCHEMICAL NITRIFICATION

An indirect effect of sunlight is through a possible photochemical nitrification. It has been claimed (ZoBell, 1933) that at least a portion of the nitrification which goes on in the sea is photochemically activated; also, it is reported that some chemical nitrification in soil is activated by sunlight in the absence of the biological agencies. Since nitrates are intimately concerned in plant growth and hence with productivity in general, this discovery, if well founded, is of fundamental importance. As yet no information relating to fresh water is available, but it seems not unlikely that if such a phenomenon exists in marine waters and in soil, it may occur also in inland waters.

RELATIONS OF MATERIALS IN SUSPENSION (TURBIDITY)

Effects through Light Reduction

Perhaps the most general effects of suspended matter on aquatic biota are due to light obstruction. In general, these effects have two aspects, favorable and unfavorable. A favorable effect appears in protection against excess light, thus rendering the surface waters more habitable by light-sensitive species, or in a greater ease of escape from enemies. Unfavorable effects arise out of the restriction of photosynthetic processes in plants; the tendency of those organisms which for reasons, direct or indirect, require some illumination to congest the upper waters; and the general reduction of the more productive volume of water.

Effects upon Temperature of Water

Long ago, Forel pointed out that turbid waters are warmer than clear waters. Particles floating in water absorb heat more rapidly than does the water itself; then these particles radiate their heat to the surrounding water, thereby adding to its heat content. According to Wesenberg-Lund (1930), pond waters containing large quantities of plankton organisms, especially the Myxophyceae, behave thermally like dirty waters. He records such waters in which the temperature, during calm weather, may rise well above the air temperature and 4 or 5°C. above the water of those ponds low in plankton. Higgins (1932), reporting the work of Ellis on the Mississippi River, states that erosion silt produces definite changes in the heat conduction and heat radiation of the water, although the nature of these changes is not described. There is reason to believe that the heat budgets of waters are influenced by substances in suspension and should be taken into account in comparing such budgets.

Food Relations

Since some aquatic organisms feed wholly or in part upon particulate organic matter, the availability of this material not only at the bottom but also in suspension makes it possible for detritus feeders to inhabit the open waters and in some instances to be independent of the bottom. Plankton often constitutes a very important turbidity-producing element. High turbidity due to this cause means the presence of a large food supply for plankton feeders. On the other hand, substances in suspension, especially in conspicuous quantities, may have a detrimental effect upon the feeding activities of some organisms. For example, Ellis (1936) showed that in laboratory experiments with water carrying a large amount of erosion silt, clams suffered from interference with their normal feeding. It also appears that in some other organisms interference with the food supply may take the form of clogging collecting fans, collecting nets, and similar structures.

TOLERATION OF AND SENSITIVITY TO TURBIDITY

Aquatic organisms vary widely in their relations to different degrees of turbidity. Since all natural waters are turbid to some degree, every organism meets some form of turbidity in its environment. Some organisms occupy waters or strata of waters which have low turbidity the year round; others are in waters perpetually muddy. Annual and seasonal variations may be slight or at a maximum, with every intergradation. Certain animals normally occur and thrive in maximum turbidity the year round, possessing morphological and physiological features which fit them for better occupancy of such a situation; others survive the enforced exposure to temporarily high turbidity in times of flood, overturns, freshets, or severe storms but could not permanently endure these conditions; others temporarily invade muddy waters; others (*Corethra* larvae) migrate daily from the very muddy bottom waters to the clear ones at the surface and back again.

Satisfactory information on toleration ranges and sediment reactions of aquatic animals is surprisingly lacking; likewise, little seems to be known concerning the specific effects of turbidity upon the physiological processes of organisms. It is sometimes difficult to determine whether the effect of high turbidity is in the nature of an interference with some particular function or is merely an indirect mechanical effect of some sort. Wu (1931) found that the minimal current rate for *Simulium* larvae in the same stream may be different at different positions within short distances, owing, apparently, to sediment accumulation, the greater the sedimentation about the larvae and their supports the higher the minimal current rate. Without doubt, many organisms smother in prolonged conditions of very high turbidity by a clogging of respiratory mechanisms.

Morphological provisions for protection against respiratory smothering are described by Needham and Lloyd (1930) as being mostly in the form of an inclosure of the respiratory structures into protected chambers, these chambers in some instances (gill chambers of crayfish; rectal gill chamber of dragonfly nymphs; gill chamber of fresh-water mussels) being equipped with a straining device to allow ingress of water but not of the excess of suspended matter. They also describe (Fig. 28*a*, *b*) those remarkable modifications of the gills in the fresh-water crustacean *Asellus* and in the nymph of the May fly, *Caenis*, which are interpreted as adaptations for protection against excess silt, since both live in very turbid situations. In both of these forms, the paired, platelike gills (blood gills in the former and tracheal gills in the latter) have become closely associated into a sort of packet, and the anterior pair has been transformed, in each instance, into a pair of enlarged gill covers which overlie and protect the functional gills.   In addition, the gills have marginal, interlacing fringes of hairs which serve as strainers when the respiratory chamber is open.   The snowflake May-fly nymph, *Tricorythus explicatus* (Needham and Christenson, 1927), has the thin gills covered by a pair of triangular gill plates which occur on the second abdominal segment (Fig. 28*c*), a structural provision which does much to protect the insect against the large amount of silt which is a regular feature of its environment.

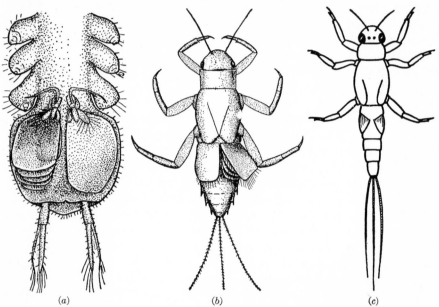

(a)   (b)   (c)

Fig. 28.   Structural adaptations for protection against excessive silt.   *a*, ventral view of abdomen of the crustacean *Asellus* showing the packet of blood gills and the anterior pair of gills modified to form a pair of enlarged opercula or gill covers.   *b*, nymph of the May fly, *Caenis*, showing the dorsal packet of tracheal gills, the anterior pair of which has become developed to form enlarged gill covers.   *c*, dorsal view of the nymph of the snow-flake May fly, *Tricorythus explicatus*, showing the pair of triangular gill plates on the second abdominal segment which covers the thin gills.   (*a and b from Needham and Lloyd's Life of Inland Waters, Chas. C. Thomas, Publisher, 1930; c redrawn from Needham and Christenson, 1927*.)

Recently Wallen (1951) investigated the direct effect upon fishes of turbidity produced by montmorillonite clay, a substance very prominent in muddy waters of Southwestern United States.   It was shown that for the fishes tested turbidity effects did not develop until concentrations of turbidity neared 20,000 p.p.m.   In lethal concentrations opercular cavities and gill filaments were clogged with clay particles.   The reader is referred to this paper for full information and an extensive bibliography.

Particulate matters suspended in moving water constitute *molar agents* whose action depends upon such features as the physical nature of the particles, the concentration of particles, and the type of water motion. Abrading effects of fine silt in suspension are well known, but the action of finer, softer particles on aquatic organisms is still uncertain. Also nothing seems to be known concerning the results of impacts of plankters on each other and on other organisms.

DISTRIBUTIONAL EFFECTS

In addition to influences mentioned above, others may operate indirectly, such as the oxygen-consuming activity of organic turbidity-producing materials. High turbidity tends to modify general productivity, to exercise a selective effect on the biota, and to modify the vertical distribution of organisms. Pearse (1939) has shown that turbid lakes produce their greatest variety and quantity of fish life in the 0- to 5-m. stratum, while in clear lakes more species and greater numbers of fish occur in the 5- to 10-m. stratum.

It has long been known that in turbid waters a process known as *flocculation* may occur in which particles aggregate into masses (flocculi). Both organic and inorganic particles may flocculate. It is thought that flocculation is much retarded when the turbidity is extremely low. Flocculation is conspicuous in waters heavily ladened with organic particulate matter, such as domestic sewage. There is reason for believing that it occurs in all natural waters to an extent determined by the amount and diversity of turbidity-producing materials. These flocculi often, perhaps usually, contain actively growing microscopic organisms of various kinds including bacteria, fungi, and Protozoa. This tendency for fine sediments to attract into aggregates various microscopic organisms and then settle to the bottom results in a significant transportation of the biota from open water to bottom deposits.

Since a large portion of the turbidity-producing materials is usually of the settling type (page 87), such substances are contributors to bottom-deposit formation. If this subsidence is not excessive and is composed substantially of organic matter it may provide a continuous enrichment of the bottom sediments and insure increased productivity of the benthos. However, if such deposition is excessive, it may have the effect of altering the nature of the original bottom conditions, causing extensive changes in, and in extreme instances extinction of, important portions of the biota.

Under certain and somewhat special circumstances, turbidity-producing substances, especially erosion silts, may produce *density currents* (page 36), with resulting effects upon the distribution of some organisms.

CHAPTER VII

INFLUENCE OF CHEMICAL CONDITIONS

RELATIONS OF DISSOLVED OXYGEN

Oxygen Supply

Oxygen supply in air and in natural waters affords a striking contrast. Normally, air contains oxygen to the extent of approximately 21 per cent, which is an abundant supply for the respiration of air-breathing organisms. In fact, there is such a large margin of safety that, except in very special circumstances, lack of oxygen is almost never a threat. In water, however, the situation is very different. A liter of water will contain only about 9 cc. of oxygen when saturated with this gas, whereas a liter of air will have 210 cc. In view of the active interplay of oxygen-producing and oxygen-consuming processes in inland waters (page 94), this small maximum supply sets the stage for serious hazards in aquatic respiration. Sometimes the oxygen supply exceeds the demand so little that the tenuous margin of safety is wiped out by some shift in the environmental processes, thus leading to disaster. Those air-breathing aquatic animals which make respiratory contacts with the atmosphere, directly or indirectly, may thus escape the risks confronting their aquatic associates which depend wholly upon the oxygen dissolved in the water. Surface waters, at least during the ice-free seasons, usually maintain a dissolved oxygen near saturation, but other waters may show oxygen reduction and, at times, even depletion.

Excess of Oxygen

Moderate supersaturations of dissolved oxygen occur in natural waters from time to time, usually owing to the photosynthetic activities of large masses of green plants in very calm water. Under special and rarer circumstances, large accumulations of excess oxygen appear in the upper part of the thermocline or in deeper strata of a lake. Quantities as large as 364.5 per cent saturation have been reported (Birge and Juday, 1911), and even larger amounts are on record although such excesses are rare and the conditions producing them not well understood. Among the large number of limnological records by the writer and his graduate students, made mostly on various lakes in Michigan, no excesses of dissolved oxygen greater than about 195 per cent have been found. That oxygen in excess amounts is toxic to many air-breathing animals has been demonstrated experimentally by Adams (1912), Cleveland (1925), and others. However, thus far the writer has failed to find, either in nature or in limnological literature, positive evidence that such excesses of dissolved oxygen as are known at present to occur in natural unmodified waters either have any serious effect or continue long enough to cause serious effect upon the organisms. Under experimental conditions, increases up to 25 cc. per l. are said to have no marked effect on fishes. In fact, it appears that virtually no effect of any sort results from water supersaturated up to at least 223 per cent (Birge and Juday, 1911). However, Matheson and Hinman (1931) found that mosquito larvae die in 2 to 4 days when submitted to a stream of minute oxygen bubbles and believe that the absence of these larvae in certain ponds in which *Chara fragilis* grows abundantly is due to the small bubbles of oxygen, present in excess amounts, which are ingested and which either have a deleterious effect upon the digestive processes or affect the food supply so as to render it unavailable. Work on pond fishes (Wiebe, 1933) showed no significant effects resulting from high concentrations of dissolved oxygen, but Woodbury (1942) suspected excess oxygen as the cause of mortality of fishes in Lake Waubesa, Wisconsin.

NORMAL DISSOLVED OXYGEN REQUIREMENTS

With the exception of the anaerobic bacteria, that unique group of miscellaneous animals which occurs in the bottoms of deep lakes under anaerobic conditions (page 183), and perhaps certain of the internal parasites occurring in aquatic hosts, all organisms living in fresh waters require an adequate supply of free oxygen. Remembering that, in the dynamics of natural waters, oxygen supplying and oxygen consuming processes are in constant action, the limits of an adequate supply of dissolved oxygen for organisms at large become an important matter.

A large literature now exists on the oxygen requirements of animals. Studies have included various animals from the Protozoa to the vertebrates, many of which have been selected from the aquatic groups. Not all of the work has been equally good, and results are sometimes conflicting and debatable. Out of the accumulated material has come one generalization which appears to be well founded, viz., that many invertebrates find the oxygen supply adequate, showing no visible sign of recognition of declining supply, until that supply has dropped to a very low level. In fact, some animals do not show evidences of response to declining oxygen until it has been reduced to 0.2 to 0.3 cc. per l. Furthermore, it is now known that in many aquatic animals, possibly in most of them, respiration is independent of varying oxygen tensions for the greater part of the normal range of the variations.

Some of the records of supposed oxygen minima have resulted from observations in nature, such as the capture of fishes by deep-set nets and the collection of plankton organisms and of various higher invertebrates at depths through which the dissolved oxygen is declining. In some of the records for fishes, there is doubt as to whether the individuals caught were truly inhabiting those conditions or whether they were caught while on a temporary excursion into waters uninhabitable except for very short periods. Pearse and Achtenberg (1920) state that perch may enter the oxygenless profundal regions and use part of the oxygen supply in the swim bladder for respiration. The case is probably clearer for those carefully conducted field observations on plankton organisms. It should be pointed out that the minimal oxygen requirement may be affected somewhat by other environmental features, e.g., temperature, CO_2, and certain conditions existing within the organism itself such as age or life-history stage. Therefore, any attempt to define precisely a dissolved oxygen minimum for an animal by the examination of its distribution in nature should include a statement of the essential environmental conditions surrounding it at the supposed minimum and the state of the animal itself. Without doubt, some of the discordant results in the literature have been due to differences in circumstances inherent in the observations or experiments. Many of the oxygen minima on record were based upon lethal points only. This is particularly true of such determinations made on lower organisms in which symptoms of the onset of oxygen want are not recognizable or are very uncertain. Information on death points may be valuable, but for limnological purposes the most important need is for means of detecting that threshold of oxygen decline beyond which the organism concerned is suffering from oxygen deficiency.

For both scientific and practical reasons, many studies have been made on fishes. Results for the same species do not always harmonize, probably owing to differences in the conditions of the observation or experiment, also possibly to differences in the oxygen requirements in individuals of the same species in different parts of their geographic range. A certain acclimatization may operate here as well as in other functions. Existing records, even recent ones, are too numerous and diversified to summarize here. Perhaps one of the best generalizations is that of Ellis *et al.* (1946), based upon several thousand field determinations made on inland waters in central United States, viz., that in general "dissolved oxygen at levels of 3 p.p.m. or lower should be regarded as hazardous to lethal under average stream and lake conditions; and that 5 p.p.m. or more of dissolved oxygen should be present in waters, if conditions are to be favorable for freshwater fishes." This statement assumes, of course, that other vital requirements are maintained within their proper limits. It also applies primarily to warm-water fishes. It has been claimed that cold-water fishes require a higher dissolved oxygen content.

Since metabolic rates, inherent degree of activity, expanse of respiratory surfaces, and character of the circulatory system—features affecting the rate of oxygen consumption—vary in different animals, it would seem that some animals might well have a minimum much higher than others. However, many of the older statements of such high minima have been found to be based upon inference only. Too often it has been assumed that animals living in highly oxygenated waters are there because they require the high oxygen pressure provided by such situations. Such an assumption has long existed for the animals restricted to rapids, mountain streams, and other agitated waters, but Wu (1931) showed in her study that *Simulium* larvae live only in running water because of current demand and not because of the often postulated high oxygen requirement. It is possible that the explanation for the occurrence of other components in the rapids association will have a similar fate.

Ruttner (1926) pointed out that the respiration of aquatic organisms depends not alone upon the dissolved oxygen content but also in a significant measure upon the temperature of the surrounding water; that the oxygen consumption is almost doubled by a rise of 10°C.; that the same amount of dissolved oxygen has about twice as great a supply value at 5 as at 15°C.; that in lakes showing a decline of the dissolved oxygen in the deeper waters in summer or winter, the water temperature must be considered in determining the respiratory value of the dissolved oxygen present; and that the practice of expressing the results of dissolved oxygen analyses in percentages of saturation is misleading, since, from the point of view of the oxygen demand by organisms, the respiratory value is not taken into account.

RESISTANCE TO ABSENCE OF DISSOLVED OXYGEN

Organisms Inhabiting the Oxygenless Regions in Lakes. Most temperate lakes of the second order maintain a unique population of organisms in the profundal bottom regions where, during the summer and winter stagnation periods, the dissolved oxygen is absent for many weeks. In some lakes having incomplete overturns and thus maintaining continuous stagnation conditions in the profundal regions, an animal population may be totally absent. Table 19 includes some of the animals now known from North American lakes which exist, during the stagnation periods, in the profundal mud under conditions of no detectable oxygen. Anaerobic bacteria occur in such situations.

The animals named in Table 19 are typical components of the profundal bottom fauna. Such a fauna varies qualitatively and quantitatively both in different lakes and in the deep, submerged, independent depressions within the same lake. It also varies with the progress of the summer or winter stagnation periods, as will be shown later. Certain quantitative

TABLE 19. SOME ANIMALS KNOWN TO OCCUR IN THE PROFUNDAL OXYGENLESS REGIONS OF AMERICAN LAKES

Animal	Lake	Authority
Protozoa:		
Representatives of *Difflugia; Pelomyxa; Monas; Paranema; Caenomorpha* (= *Gyrocoris*); *Coleps; Colpidium; Lacrymaria; Loxodes; Loxophyllum; Metopus; Paramecium; Prorodon; Spirostomum; Stentor; Uronema*	Lake Mendota, Wis.	Birge & Juday (1911)
Enchelys sp	Lake Mendota, Wis.	Juday (1919)
Pelomyxa palustris	Douglas Lake, Mich.	Moore (1939)
Pelomyxa villosa	Douglas Lake, Mich.	Moore (1939)
Coleps hirtus	Douglas Lake, Mich.	Moore (1939)
Cothurnia sp	Douglas Lake, Mich.	Moore (1939)
Frontonia leucas	Douglas Lake, Mich.	Moore (1939)
Spirostomum ambiguum	Douglas Lake, Mich.	Moore (1939)
Stentor coeruleus	Douglas Lake, Mich.	Moore (1939)
Nematoda:		
Anguillula sp	Lake Mendota, Wis.	Juday (1908)
Hydromermis sp	Douglas Lake, Mich.	Eggleton (1931)
Unidentified Nematoda	Douglas Lake, Mich.	Moore (1939)
Oligochaeta:		
Limnodrilus claparedianus	Douglas Lake, Mich.	Eggleton (1931)
Limnodrilus hoffmeisteri	Douglas Lake, Mich.	Eggleton (1931)
Limnodrilus sp	Lake Mendota, Wis.	Juday (1908)
Tubifex sp	Lake Mendota, Wis.	Juday (1908)
Gastrotricha:		
Chaetonotus sp	Lake Mendota, Wis.	Birge & Juday (1911)
Chaetonotus sp	Douglas Lake, Mich.	Moore (1939)
Rotatoria:		
Philodina sp	Lake Mendota, Wis.	Birge & Juday (1911)
Rotaria rotatoria	Douglas Lake, Mich.	Moore (1939)
Rotaria tridens	Douglas Lake, Mich.	Moore (1939)
Crustacea:		
Candona exilis	Douglas Lake, Mich.	Moore (1939)
Candona reflexa	Douglas Lake, Mich.	Moore (1939)
Candona sp	Lake Mendota, Wis.	Birge & Juday (1911)
Cypria exsculpta	Douglas Lake, Mich.	Moore (1939)
Cypria lacustris	Douglas Lake, Mich.	Moore (1939)
Canthocamptus staphylinoides (cysts)	Douglas Lake, Mich.	Moore (1939)
Canthocamptus staphylinoides (active)	Douglas Lake, Mich.	Moore (1939)
Cyclops bicuspidatus (cysts)	Douglas Lake, Mich.	Moore (1939)
Cyclops bicuspidatus (cysts)	Lake Mendota, Wis.	Birge & Juday (1911)
Insecta:		
Corethra punctipennis larvae	Lake Mendota, Wis. and elsewhere	Birge & Juday (1911)
Corethra punctipennis larvae	Douglas Lake, Mich.	Eggleton (1931)
Chironomus tentans larvae	Lake Mendota, Wis.	Muttkowski (1918)
Protenthes choreus larvae	Lake Mendota, Wis.	Muttkowski (1918)
Chironomus plumosus larvae	Douglas Lake, Mich.	Eggleton (1931)
Chironomus plumosus var ferrugineovittatus larvae	Douglas Lake, Mich.	Eggleton (1931)
Chironomus utahensis larvae	Douglas Lake, Mich.	Eggleton (1931)
Chironomus fasciventris larvae	Douglas Lake, Mich.	Eggleton (1931)
Protenthes culciformis larvae	Douglas Lake, Mich.	Eggleton (1931)
Mollusca:		
Pisidium idahoense	Lake Mendota, Wis.	Juday (1908)
Pisidium compressum	Douglas Lake, Mich.	Eggleton (1931)
Pisidium sp	Douglas Lake, Mich.	Eggleton (1931)
Musculium rosaceum	Douglas Lake, Mich.	Eggleton (1931)
Musculium truncatum	Douglas Lake, Mich.	Eggleton (1931)

fluctuations are due to the emergence of the adult stages of the insects (*Corethra*, *Chironomus*, and others). This fauna will be discussed in the chapter on benthos.

Source of Oxygen Supply. During the spring and autumn overturns, bottom waters become as well supplied with oxygen as are the surface waters; also they are freed from excess accumulations of decomposition products. Advancing stagnation gradually exhausts the oxygen at the bottom, and, in time, anaerobic conditions prevail, to continue for many weeks until the next overturn rejuvenates the whole body of water. During this period, the profundal, bottom animals are without an obvious source of oxygen, yet they are often present in great numbers. With the exception of *Corethra* (= *Chaoborus*) larvae which migrate to the surface waters at night and return into the depths during the day, all of these profundal bottom animals are confined to that situation which not only continues without dissolved oxygen but gradually accumulates decomposition products. The source of the oxygen necessary for their metabolism becomes, then, a pertinent question. Various explanations have been offered, some seeking the source in certain processes *within* the animals, others in certain *external* phenomena. The following are some of the theories:

1. Storage of oxygen. Various investigators have proposed explanations based essentially upon the idea that the haemoglobin of the blood may act as a storehouse for oxygen; that such storage at times of abundant free oxygen may furnish the supply in an oxygen deficiency. Since only a few of the profundal bottom animals have haemoglobin, and since it has been shown that the amount of oxygen stored by haemoglobin is utterly inadequate for the requirements of the animals during the long-continued oxygenless period, explanations having this feature as the essential background are worthy of little consideration. It has also been postulated that *Corethra* larvae store air in the "air sacs," when in the surface waters at night, sufficient to provide for their needs during the day's sojourn in the oxygenless, profundal waters. This explanation was based wholly upon inference. In spite of the many studies made upon *Corethra* larvae, the function of the air sacs is still an unsettled question.

2. Internal chemical transformations. These theories have in common the idea of chemical transformations taking place within the animal, such as occur in the utilization of foodstuffs in which oxygen is released and made available for recombination. Some claim a source from the splitting of stored glycogen, such as is said to occur in some parasites; others are content merely to postulate intramolecular respiration. Opponents to explanations of this sort urge that oxygen resulting from such a source would not suffice for the energy exhibited by some of these animals. Another explanation has as its basis the supposed presence in the animal

of an enzyme complex which can synthesize a peroxide and then split off oxygen from it.

3. Catalysts facilitating oxygen absorption. Since it has been shown that many profundal bottom animals have manganese in their tissues, it has been supposed by some that this element may serve as a catalyst, facilitating oxygen absorption at low tensions, but total absence of oxygen does not seem to be provided for in this theory. Attempts to attach significance to a supposedly higher catalase content in profundal bottom animals have yielded nothing.

4. Atomic oxygen from decaying plant tissues. Cole (1921) found that the decomposing plant tissues in the profundal mud, even under anaerobic conditions, gradually liberate small amounts of an oxidizing substance which he postulated to be atomic oxygen and which, it was claimed, could be utilized by the animals living in such close relationship to the decaying plant debris.

None of these explanations is free from objections. The source of the oxygen supply is still uncertain.

Temporary Anaerobiosis. It has long been known that many aquatic organisms can live for longer or shorter periods of time in the absence of free oxygen, although none of the intervals of anaerobiosis (some hours or, at most, several days) compares in length with the period of many weeks in the profundal bottom regions during the stagnation periods. Animals living in the muddy bottoms of shallow water or other similar conditions in which the oxygen exhaustion occurs quickly and for limited times, may be forced to meet these temporarily unusual conditions. Many may succumb, but certain ones are able to survive such a period. These facts have been established both by observations in nature and by experimentation. Certain representatives of Protozoa, nematodes, earthworms, leeches, immature stages of insects, mollusks, fishes, and others exhibit this ability. Explanations of this type of survival are as yet inadequate. In some mollusks, it has been claimed that glycogen reserves disappear during the oxygenless period. Cleary (1948) found that in certain oligochaetes glycogen is used in excess when the worms are subjected to anaerobic conditions. Some investigators claim to have demonstrated that during oxygen lack a certain amount of energy may be released by the splitting of carbohydrates into reduced substances, thus building up an "oxygen debt," this debt being repaid by the increased rate of oxygen consumption when the organism is returned to aerobic conditions. According to another explanation, oxygen lack may be met, at least temporarily, by the simple reduction of oxygen requirements by a slowing down of the vital processes. A certain fresh-water clam which can withstand several days of exposure to oxygenless water was found to contain, according to one investigator, a peculiar enzyme complex which was interpreted as a possible respiratory agent functioning under conditions of oxygen deficiency. Certain biologists have claimed that anaerobic respiration[1] was the primitive fundamental type and that the utilization of free oxygen was a subsequent development in evolution, from which it might be argued that these varying abilities of different animals to withstand anaerobic conditions are persistent remnants of past history.

Alterations of Resistance to Absence of Oxygen. Experiments have indicated that in certain fishes resistance to lack of oxygen is increased by the injection of sodium bicarbonate and that decreasing the alkalinity of the blood by injecting acetic acid into it reduced the resistance; also, that fishes live longer in oxygen-free water if previously injected with carbohydrates such as mannose or glucose; and, furthermore, that the embryos of certain marine fishes lived in oxygen-free water 73 to 141 per cent longer in the presence of glucose, maltose, levolose, and cane sugar, the increase of resistance varying with the different sugars. It is possible that among the innumerable substances in natural waters there may be present, at times and at certain places, substances which facilitate those processes, whatever they are, which enable animals to inhabit oxygenless waters. It has also been pointed out, on the basis of the experimental results mentioned above, that if an organism possesses the ability to change the chemical composition of its blood it might become increasingly capable of occupying oxygenless water. Powers (1922) holds that the alkali reserve of the blood of fishes is intimately related to the problems of absorption of oxygen at different tensions.

Recently, Brand (1946) reviewed extensively the whole subject of anaerobiosis in invertebrates, and his account should be consulted for further details.

SOME EFFECTS OF INSUFFICIENT DISSOLVED OXYGEN

When, for any reason, the dissolved oxygen falls to or below the minimum for any animal, certain eventualities occur. The usual ones are:

1. Attempts to migrate. In lakes, it is usually an upward migration into overlying, better oxygenated waters, and, if the animal can thrive in increasing light intensity, increasing water movement, and the other features of the upper waters, it finds security in this migration, particularly in the summer when the epilimnion is always favorable so far as oxygen supply is concerned. Largely as the result of this upward migration, the whole hypolimnion ultimately becomes devoid of animals save for the occasional temporary invader and the profundal-bottom anaerobic organisms. These upward migrations may account, in part at least, for

---

[1] Some authors hold that the expression "anaerobic respiration" should be replaced by the term "fermentation." See Science, 1945, **101:** 88–89, 352–353, 585–586, for discussions.

certain concentrations of organisms in the thermocline and on the slopes of the basin.

2. Onset of diseases. Various investigators have pointed out definite evidences of a close relation between insufficient dissolved oxygen and diseases of fishes, parasitic and bacterial. Serious epidemics in the fish *Leucichthys artedi*, which seems to occupy the cooler water below the thermocline during summer, have occurred in certain Wisconsin lakes in late August and early September when the hypolimnion is very low in oxygen, resulting in large numbers of dead fish on shore. Similar epidemics among the larger Crustacea are on record.

3. Suffocation beneath ice cover. Shallow waters with bottoms containing large amounts of putrescible matter and occurring in regions where prolonged ice cover in winter is common may, at times, almost or completely exhaust the dissolved oxygen of the unfrozen water with resulting mortality ("winter kill") among the organisms. There are on record many instances in which disappearance of the ice cover was accompanied by great accumulations of dead fish about the shores and by evidence of a similar mortality among some of the other organisms, although, because of their size and distribution in the water, the signs of their mortality were not so conspicuous as those of the fish. Such natural tragedies are not uncommon in small artificial ponds or lakes which have no drainage and which contain an unusual amount of organic bottom deposit. When the small, shallow, muck-bottom lakes at large are considered, it is perhaps surprising that these natural catastrophes are not more common. It is not unlikely that they do occur more frequently than is known, since, in certain classes of small, shallow waters, fishes are virtually or completely absent, and effects on the invertebrates are overlooked. There is reason for believing that winter kill is seldom if ever a simple matter of oxygen lack. As oxygen declines under the ice, decomposition products accumulate. The final killing off of organisms may be due primarily to a suffocation caused by oxygen want, or to the toxic effect of some decomposition product, or to a combination of unfavorable factors. Recently, Greenbank (1945) made an extensive study of winter kill in Michigan lakes with special reference to fish, and the reader is referred to his paper for more details. Artificial fertilization of lakes may increase the danger of winter kill by adding to the water, directly or indirectly, relatively large amounts of putrescible organic matter which continue to reduce oxygen and develop decomposition products during the winter.

4. "Summer kill." Instances of summer kill have been reported (Moore, 1942) in fishes. Critically low dissolved oxygen and unfavorable temperatures have been suspected as causal agents, but the case is not clear since other conditions were probably in a simultaneous state of flux.

RELATIONS OF CARBON DIOXIDE

GENERAL EFFECTS ON ORGANISMS

Carbon dioxide is one of the most important substances in the life of organisms. In fact, it has been stated, with some foundation, that in one sense carbon dioxide is the basis of all living substance. Far too often, it is looked upon by the uninformed as an undesirable waste product and something which should be eliminated both from the animal body and from the environment. It must be noted, however, that the statement made above concerning its far-reaching influence implies its presence under appropriate circumstances and in proper amounts.

Small Quantities. Evidence would indicate that carbon dioxide is necessary for all bacterial growth and development and therefore for life itself, although the minimal quantities required are very small. Small amounts of this gas also appear to be essential for aquatic animals. Usually, the quantities in the air are very small but yet sufficient for the photosynthetic activities of chlorophyll-bearing plants. Likewise, in natural waters, the amounts may be very small in the upper circulating waters, but healthy growths of green plants are standing proof of the sufficiency of these small quantities.

Large Quantities. Large quantities of carbon dioxide usually have a detrimental effect, becoming rapidly fatal if amounts are sufficiently great. Ordinarily, accumulations in unpolluted, natural waters do not reach such lethal amounts, owing to the ease with which they are released into the air or combine chemically. Increasing amounts of free carbon dioxide in association with other decomposition products may gradually render the hypolimnion untenable by all organisms save the resistant anaerobic animals in the bottom, and even these, during prolonged stagnation periods, may succumb. What part of this effect is due to the carbon dioxide is as yet not certain. Such accumulations may render bottom waters acid in reaction and thus affect organisms sensitive to acid waters. High carbon dioxide content seems to be more toxic in the presence of low oxygen content.

Several workers have claimed that free carbon dioxide is very toxic to fishes and that they manifest the avoiding reaction when they encounter as little as 5 cc. per l. Since an excess of dissolved carbon dioxide is usually accompanied by a much reduced dissolved oxygen content and other important conditions, it has been proposed that the carbon dioxide content of the water is probably the best single index of the suitability of water for fishes, strongly alkaline waters excepted. It remains to be shown, however, that these conclusions hold for all fresh water fish.

It is a well-established fact that carbon dioxide has a very definite effect upon the affinity of blood for oxygen in fishes and certain other animals.

In general, very low concentrations of carbon dioxide in the surrounding medium do not prevent blood from becoming approximately saturated with oxygen even when the latter is present in quite reduced amounts. However, as carbon dioxide tension is increased, the capacity of blood for oxygen becomes reduced, the amount of reduction varying with the amount of carbon dioxide and with the species of animal involved. In some fishes the effect of carbon dioxide on oxygen transport is said to be very marked; in certain others it seems to be almost negligible; in still others, the degree of effect lies, to varying extents, somewhere between these two extremes. Fry (1939) found that, for the situations studied by him, sensitivity to carbon dioxide showed a correlation with vertical distribution of fishes in lakes in summer. The most sensitive species were found in the hypolimnion, the least sensitive in weedy shallows. Evidently such correlation must be due to differences in oxygen transport capacity of blood in the species concerned.

Since in nature increases in carbon dioxide are almost invariably associated with other simultaneous chemical changes, its specific effects are usually very difficult to establish. Powers (1938, 1939) reported instances of sudden mortality among fishes in nature which seemed to be caused, not by oxygen shortage, but by abnormally high carbon dioxide tension in the water. He interpreted the deaths to be due to "a derangement brought about by the blood compensating first for a high and then a low CO_2 tension in the water." He stressed the serious effects of fishes encountering wide, abrupt changes in carbon dioxide tension. He also held that fishes may tolerate wide, but not sudden, ranges of carbon dioxide tension of the water by "increasing the alkali reserve of their blood in high carbon dioxide tension water and by lowering the alkali reserve of their blood in low carbon dioxide water."

Relations to Lime-producing Organisms

The potential supply of carbon dioxide is closely linked with those biological activities centering about lime production. Certain fundamental facts relating to combined carbon dioxide have already been presented (page 99). Since various organisms function in the production of lime, and since lime formation involves a tying up, temporarily or permanently, of some of the carbon dioxide supply, these processes will be considered in some detail.

Limnologists commonly refer to lime accumulations in water as *marl*. This term has many definitions. As used in this book, *marl* is a soft, whitish, finely divided to crumbly deposit composed largely of calcium carbonate derived from various sources such as precipitation by plants, remains of calcareous shells of animals, remains of calcareous plants, and certain inorganic processes.

It should be noted that since the carbonates involved are largely compounds of carbon dioxide with calcium or magnesium, all of these substances enter inseparably into the processes to be described. It is well known that calcium is an essential element for most green plants (not essential for many Algae), and magnesium is likewise desirable. It seems also to have been well established that the more calcium and magnesium in water, other things being the same, the greater the productivity. Therefore, processes which lead to the precipitation of calcium and magnesium monocarbonate remove from availability, either temporarily or permanently, quantities of two sets of substances (calcium or magnesium, and carbon dioxide) both of which are indispensable. Calcium is not only a necessity *per se* in plant growth, but, in addition, its ions are said to make physiologically available other equally indispensable nutrient ions.

Lime Precipitation by Bacteria. It has been stated that certain bacteria, occurring in shallow seas, cause precipitation of calcium carbonate on a large scale, but this claim has been disputed. However (Bavendamm, 1931, 1932), the claim has been revived on new evidence. Almost nothing is known concerning such a role for bacteria in fresh waters. No lime-precipitating bacteria have been definitely demonstrated in American inland waters unless it be found that a reported minute lime-precipitating organism in hard-water streams in eastern United States proves to be of a bacterial nature. However, the existence of special lime-forming bacteria has been definitely reported in European literature, and it may be that such organisms will later be found in American waters.

Lime Formation by Algae. A common phenomenon in many of the medium- and hard-water lakes of Northern United States and elsewhere is the formation of calcium carbonate by Algae, sometimes in striking quantities. In fact, in some lakes, large beds of marl are almost exclusively the result of the action of Algae. The principal forms of lime formations so produced are as follows:

1. In sandy, exposed beaches, both above and below water line. Intermixtures of marl and sand on wave-swept, sand shoals and beaches are commonly the product, in part, of certain Algae living in the sand. These so-called "green sands" can easily be demonstrated by removing the thin surface layer. Such sands often contain enough Algae to give the whole a distinctly green color.

2. Incrustations on the surface of rocks and other fixed objects in shallow water. Marl deposits of varying thickness and general form are common over inanimate objects in shoal waters. Since, superficially, the appearance is often brownish, the presence of Algae may be overlooked, but removal of the thin, surface layer permits the green of the Algae to

appear.　Such incrustations occur profusely on rocks exposed to severe wave action, but there is reason for believing that the thickness of such a layer is limited by the waves, the excess accumulations being washed off by the moving water and dropped to the bottom.　Such accumulations vary in general appearance; sometimes they form layers of almost uniform thickness all over and around the supporting objects; sometimes they form tubercle-like aggregations of varying sizes, each aggregation representing a center of growth of the Algae and their products.　In the less

FIG. 29.　Photograph of a bed of marl concretions exposed by an unusual fall in water level of the lake.　Exposure to the air and the wash of waves has caused some alterations of the original shape and sizes of the concretions.　These concretions are produced by marl-forming Algae.　Bass Lake, near Lakeland, Mich.　(*Photograph by J. E. Reighard.*)

exposed, shallow waters, such layers are sometimes quite thick.　Uncovered roots of water plants may acquire a thick covering, and in some situations great masses accumulate on abrupt banks just below the water line.

3. Accumulations on exposed posterior ends of fresh-water mussels. In waters containing marl-forming Algae, the exposed caudal tips of fresh-water mussels are favorite places for these accumulations.　Frequently, every mussel in an undisturbed lake bottom will exhibit algal marl masses, most if not all of which are of a green color.　The thickness of these accumulations varies with the degree of exposure to wave action; those on mussels inhabiting exposed, wave-swept shoals are relatively thin, compact, and dense, while those growing on protected shoals may bear conspicuous, looser masses, 1 to 2 in. in thickness.

4. Marl pebbles and marl concretions. For reasons not fully known, deposition of lime by Algae sometimes takes the form of compact, spherical, or flattened concretions varying in size from that of small pebbles to large masses 6 in. or more in diameter. Formations of the size of pebbles are more common, while the large concretions seem to be more or less rare,

Fig. 30.   Photograph of the beach of a lake which produces unusual quantities of marl concretions.   What appears to be a rocky, gravelly beach and bank is actually the water-worn marl concretions which have been washed up by the waves.   Note that the highest portion of the bank, in the rear of the photograph, is also composed of the same material. Bass Lake, near Lakeland, Mich.   (*Photograph by J. E. Reighard.*)

although when they do occur they may be present in great quantities. Certain lakes in the vicinity of Ann Arbor, Mich. (Figs. 29 and 30), are usually rich in these large concretions, extensive areas of the bottom being completely covered with them.   When viewed from a boat, they give the bottom the appearance of being paved with stones.   In this same region, large, spherical lime concretions, 7 to 8 in. or more in diameter, excavated from the beds of certain rivers, may have been formed in ancient time as the result of algal activity.   Concretions often contain at the center some foreign object, such as a small snail shell, and sometimes they are built about a larger object such as the shell of a mussel; however, concretions are sometimes found which seem to lack any such central object. As they occur on the lake bottom, they are usually of a greenish-brown color, due to the admixture of the Algae, the calcium carbonate, and the extraneous, finely divided materials which have settled into the interstices. In Ore Lake, near Ann Arbor, Mich., such concretions are of a light, brick-red color owing to the presence of a considerable iron content.

5. Lime deposition by *Chara*. *Chara*, a plant commonly listed among the Algae, lives in shallow water and is rooted to the bottom. In certain waters, it grows in great quantities, carpeting large areas. It has a peculiarly characteristic brittleness and a roughness to the touch. Its vernacular name, stonewort, arose from the fact that this plant contains in its tissues and bears on its surface an unusual amount of calcareous deposit. So abundantly may it grow and so high is the calcareous content that in certain lakes it is said to form the chief, or even the sole, source of marl, and that large marl deposits have resulted from *Chara* alone. Analyses indicate an unusually high carbonate content, calcium carbonate composing about 30 per cent of the dry weight of the plant, and magnesium carbonate about 2 per cent. The great windrows of *Chara* fragments sometimes seen along the shores of marly lakes indicate the nature and method of bottom deposition by this plant.

The Algae associated with lime deposition appear to be largely of the blue-green type (Myxophyceae). Thus far, the question of which Algae are most concerned with the actual deposition has remained largely unanswered. It is not impossible that some of the Algae reported as present in the marl masses merely find them a habitat and may be only incidentally concerned. An extensive literature exists on this subject, out of which only a few works can be mentioned here. Wesenberg-Lund (1901) found such deposits in Danish lakes due mostly to representatives of the genera *Schizothrix* and *Rivularia*, with diatoms and certain *Cladophora* producing similar deposits in springs. Pollock (1919) found four species of blue-green Algae to be more constantly present than the others in the marl concretions of Ore Lake, near Ann Arbor, Mich., viz., *Schizothrix fasciculata*, *Lyngbya nana*, *Lyngbya martensiana calcaria*, and *Dichothrix calcarea*. Certain other forms were less regularly and less abundantly associated with those just named. Kindle (1927) reported three species of *Gloeocapsa* as responsible for the original growth of marlyte pebbles in Mink Lake, Canada, with *Tolypothrix tenuis* coming in later; also present were another blue green Alga (*Phormidium tenax*), a green Alga (*Centrosphaeria facciolaea*), and 14 different species of diatoms. Kindle likewise presented some evidence which suggests the deposition of lime by diatoms. In a preliminary examination of the lime deposits on the exposed posterior ends of mussels in Douglas Lake, Michigan, Prof. G. E. Nichols found a representative of *Tolypothrix* to be the chief Alga present in the samples which he examined.

There is good evidence that deposits in connection with Algae are characterized by high percentage of calcium carbonate. Pollock (1919) found that the marl pebbles from Ore Lake were 97.22 per cent soluble in hydrochloric acid (chiefly calcium carbonate); of the remaining 2.78 per cent, 84 per cent (2.34 per cent of the whole pebble) was volatile on incineration (chiefly organic matter).

No satisfactory information seems available as to the rate of deposition of lime by Algae. Obviously, there must be some direct relation between the amount of deposit and the number of Algae present. Pollock estimated that, under the conditions of algal lime deposit on exposed tips of mussels, the maximum rate of deposition would be about 30 cm. of marl for each 50 to 100 years and discussed evidence which suggested that a rate of 4 mm. per year was within the limits of possibility.

Lime Formation by Aquatic Flowering Plants. Various aquatic plants develop incrustations of marl upon leaves, petioles, stems, and other exposed parts. In fact, some investigators of marl formation who prefer to look upon these incrustations as precipitations of lime from the water due to plant activity believe that all of the aquatic plants are either actual or potential lime-precipitation agents. However this may be, certain of the aquatic flowering plants are much more conspicuous in this process than others, prominent among them being various species of *Potamogeton* whose leaves are, in many situations, almost constantly covered on the upper surface by substantial coatings of marl. Absence of such coating may be due to its removal by the wash of waves. Analyses of this material have shown that over 30 per cent is calcium carbonate with a small quantity of magnesium carbonate. It has been claimed that this lime crust becomes thickest, when clear, calm weather permits it to accumulate most rapidly, on those parts of the plant exposed to the strongest light. Leaves may develop and carry a weight of lime crust several times their own weights. The amount of calcium carbonate within the tissues of *Potamogeton* is relatively small. *Ceratophyllum, Myriophyllum, Anacharis, Nymphaea, Vallisneria,* and others function in lime deposition by either surface-crust formation or deposit within the plant tissues or by both.

Lime Formation by Plankton. Plankters are responsible for the formation of calcium carbonate which, on the death of the organisms, may be transferred to the bottom. While it has been shown that the plankton organisms may contain more than fifty times as much calcium as an equal amount of the water in which they occur, it seems likely that in most lakes the plankton is of minor importance in the production of combined carbon dioxide.

Lime Formation by Higher Animals.   Of the higher animals inhabiting inland waters, the mollusks constitute by far the most important lime formers.   The calcium carbonate used in the construction of their shells ultimately finds its way, on the death of the animals, into the bottom, and, in shallow waters supporting large populations of mussels and snails, the contributions to bottom deposits may be considerable.   Old marl beds commonly contain shells of mollusks, often in a surprising state of preservation, and without doubt their prevalence has often in the past been the source of the mistaken conclusion that they alone were responsible for the deposits.   A few other groups of fresh-water animals, such as the larvae of the Stratiomyiidae (Diptera), the crayfishes, and others, deposit calcium carbonate in their exoskeletons and elsewhere, but the additions from these sources are virtually negligible, when compared with the other lime formers described in the preceding pages.

Fate of the Combined Carbon Dioxide and the Calcium

From the foregoing discussion, it is evident that certain processes are going on in many lakes which automatically rob, temporarily or permanently, the water of two of its exceedingly important substances, calcium (and to some extent, magnesium) and carbon dioxide.   The removal of carbon dioxide from circulation in the form of the insoluble carbonate is temporary only if the carbonate deposit remains in direct contact with the overlying water and if periods of free carbon dioxide production make possible the conversion of the monocarbonate into the soluble bicarbonate, thus restoring it to circulation.   This circulation is much more complete in the shallower waters in which water movements may redistribute the soluble bicarbonate; but in the profundal regions, the converted bicarbonate can become distributed only by very slow diffusion and by such small and often negligible water movements as occur in the hypolimnion, the result being that effective circulation must wait for the next overturn.

Permanent removal of great quantities of calcium and of the bound carbon dioxide in the monocarbonates occurs when circumstances are such that the marl is so covered by other sediments that it is no longer in direct contact with the superimposed water.   Various filling processes bury marl permanently.   Vertical samples often reveal successive marl strata in the bottom of shoal waters.   Similar methods of vertical exploration reveal buried marl beds in bogs and other basins which have undergone rapid filling.   Even conditions of ordinary mixing with other bottom materials may be sufficient virtually to eliminate contact of the deposited carbonate with the water.   Inflowing streams which drain clay lands may in times of severe rains, spring thaws, and seasonal heavy precipitation, lay down over the lake bottom layers of more or less impervious materials and in so doing bury any marl deposits which have formed since the previous, sudden silt deposit. Such constant inroads upon and removals of the calcium and the associated carbon dioxide, as well as the magnesium and its associated carbon dioxide, indicate clearly the necessity for a lake to have means of replacing these essential materials if it is to retain even its original productivity. The enormous beds of marl buried under the lands back from lake margins are mute witnesses of the extent to which ancient lakes robbed themselves of some of their own most precious materials. When this robbing process exceeds replacement, the lake begins to decline in productivity, even though other influences tend to increase the availability of other fundamental substances; and, in time, such a lake may become one of those poverty-stricken marl lakes in which the paucity of life is sometimes so conspicuous.

Carbon Dioxide Tension

While the carbon dioxide tension within natural waters and within the atmosphere constantly tends toward an equilibrium, circumstances prevailing in the water (slow diffusion, rapid production of carbon dioxide, insufficient agitation of the water) may be such that at some depths the carbon dioxide tension is greater than in the air.

It has been found (Powers, 1941) that "when a fresh water or a calcium bicarbonate water is mixed with sea water there is an increase in the carbon dioxide capacity of the mixed waters over the total of the capacities of the waters that go to make up the mixture." Powers held that such mixtures of fresh and sea water set up a carbon dioxide tension gradient which is the principal factor determining the migratory movements of salmon. Such results and others have led some investigators to believe that carbon dioxide tension performs a more important role than has heretofore been supposed, a role thought to arise from the existence of simple carbon dioxide along with carbonic acid in the water. Little seems to be known concerning the specific influences of carbon dioxide tension. It has been suggested that possibly they are related in some way to permeability, since carbon dioxide is said to penetrate organisms easily.

RELATIONS OF OTHER DISSOLVED GASES

Methane

No satisfactory statement can be made concerning the effect or effects of methane on organisms. Limnologists have speculated on this matter, arriving at various conclusions. Some have claimed that it is nontoxic; others, that its effects on organisms are minor or that, at most, it may be occasionally toxic to animals or that it may cause them to migrate from particular situations. Possibly methane accumulations in bottom waters may have something to do with the increasingly severe conditions which develop with the progress of stagnation periods.

HYDROGEN SULFIDE

Inherently, hydrogen sulfide is very poisonous. Certain marine fishes are said to be very sensitive to this gas and to avoid water containing it. It has been supposed that in many waters the quantities developed in the profundal regions are too small to be significant, but here, again, such a statement is largely speculative. It has also been supposed to have merely an indirect effect through dissolved oxygen absorption relations. Available evidence indicates that it may be very influential wherever the accumulations are large, a condition under which it is a major factor, if not the determining factor, in the complete elimination of all bottom animals. Beerman (1924) claims to have shown that hydrogen sulfide produces intracellular acidity in acid, neutral, or slightly alkaline media and that it penetrates living cells easily. If these findings are true for the conditions which exist in natural waters, it may be that its effects are more significant than has been thought, even in reduced amounts.

NITROGEN

Free nitrogen has usually been supposed to be the least important of the dissolved gases when it occurs in ordinary quantities. Excess nitrogen is said to cause *gas disease* in fishes. Unusual amounts may produce entry of the gas into the circulatory systems of aquatic animals, causing stoppage. Little is known concerning the minimal excesses required for effects on the organisms, and different investigators have not secured results that are in agreement. Definite information on thresholds of nitrogen effect is needed. In spite of the excesses known to exist in water, there seems to be little evidence that under the natural conditions fatal results occur. In explanation of this supposed fact, it has been assumed that perhaps the effect of excess nitrogen, when present, is slow, requiring several hours or even several days.

Dissolved nitrogen has taken on a new interest with recent, positive evidence of nitrogen fixation by blue-green Algae belonging to various species of Nostocaceae. The nitrogen-fixing system in these plants is physiologically similar to that in other organisms. It now seems almost certain that all plankters belonging to the Myxophyceae not only possess this significant ability but are thus able to flourish in situations, such as open water, where the nitrogen-fixing bacteria cannot grow. Nitrogen so fixed eventually passes into the general circulation, thus becoming available to other organisms unable to fix it for themselves. This subject has been reviewed recently by Fogg (1947).

Ammonia

Scant information is available on the biological relations of gaseous ammonia as produced in natural waters. Indirectly, and in the form in which it occurs in certain chemical compounds to be mentioned later, it is concerned in the supply of the nitrogen so necessary for plant growth. Ellis *et al.* (1946) state that the amount of ammonia and ammonium compounds (chiefly ammonium carbonate) in unmodified natural waters is very small, averaging less than 0.1 p.p.m.; that amounts exceeding 2.5 p.p.m. are generally detrimental or lethal; and that quantities of more than 1.0 p.p.m. usually indicate organic pollution. They also point out that in spite of the general limit just stated various fishes such as carp, buffalo, and some of the sunfishes can tolerate 3.0 to 10.0 p.p.m. of ammonia. According to certain investigators, gas-works ammonia delivered into a stream not only becomes toxic to fishes but has one particularly insidious characteristic; viz., fishes do not seem to recognize its presence when entering water containing it and often succumb without manifesting avoiding reactions.

Carbon Monoxide

In searching for an answer to the question as to whether carbon monoxide has a poisonous action *per se* or the effect is in the nature of an interference with the proper oxygenation of tissues, Macht (1927) found evidence of a *per se* influence, a conclusion contrary to the interpretation usually held. Nothing definite seems to be known concerning the thresholds of this effect in the various aquatic organisms. It has been thought that the quantities present in nature are too small to be significant— probably a faulty inference in the face of no adequate information.

DISSOLVED SOLIDS

Relations of Carbonates and Bicarbonates

Roles of carbonates and bicarbonates have been discussed in connection with the consideration of carbon dioxide (page 190).

Relations of Inorganic Nitrogen Compounds

Ammonium salts, nitrites, and nitrates furnish a supply of nitrogen which is essential in the fundamental food relations of organisms. Ammonium salts ("ammonia nitrogen" or "free ammonia") constitute the first stage in mineralization of organic nitrogen. It is usually considered that nitrates supply nitrogen in more available form, although the other two compounds, particularly ammonium salts, are utilized to some extent. Claims have been made that while some plants seem to prefer nitrates, there are others which grow equally well with both nitrites and ammonium salts; also, that some plants, especially when young, prefer ammonia (Allison, 1931). Variations in the quantities present in water are correlated with the growth seasons of plants and with the temperatures which control, to some extent, the rate of bacterial action. Ordinarily, nitrogen in its final oxidized form as nitrate does not occur in great amounts in natural, uncontaminated waters. As will be shown later (page 359), waters may become enriched or impoverished in nitrates and other essential substances by changes in the drainage areas due to processes accompanying cultivation of the land. It seems likely that constancy of adequate supply of available nitrogen compounds is much more important than large amounts produced periodically. Studies on the ammonia and nitrate contents of certain Wisconsin lakes have shown that the Algae, water weeds, and nitrate-reducing bacteria are the important consumers of nitrogen content and that the nitrifying bacteria aid in increasing the nitrate content.

Nitrogen is considered to be one of the most important limiting factors in the development of phytoplankton. It is one of the nutritive substances necessary for the production of chlorophyll. Formation of chlorophyll ceases very quickly in the presence of nitrate deficiency (Rodhe, 1948).

Certain toxic relations seem to exist. A dilute solution of nitrites is said to be injurious to some plants while beneficial to others, and solutions may be concentrated to the point of injury, the solutions of nitrite being more toxic than those of the same strength of nitrate. Ammonium salts in excess are reported as poisonous to fishes if present with carbonates. Whether these exigencies ever occur in unmodified lakes remains to be demonstrated.

RELATIONS OF SILICON

Since diatoms require silicon for the manufacture of their shells, and since they constitute a very prominent and strategic group in the plankton at large, the available supply of silicon in the water is regarded as a matter of real consequence. Large growths of diatoms draw heavily upon the silicon crop, producing variations in it in the upper waters. In fact, it is claimed that the production of diatoms is directly determined by the silicon supply. According to Conger (1941) the available evidence indicates that silica deposition by diatoms is a one-way process; that silica in the form of diatom shells is highly resistant to passage into solution in water; that diatom shells once formed are practically permanent in many waters; that only in certain bog and marsh deposits were highly corroded shells found, indicating dissolving action of some sort; and that acid bog waters with very low silica and slightly alkaline spring waters with high silica content "exhibit the two extremes of richness in diatom productivity." An opposing view is (Sverdrup *et al.*, 1942) that silicon removed from sea water by diatoms and other organisms may return to solution after they die, or it may sink to the bottom; that the high silicon content commonly found near the bottom is due to resolution of the settled silaceous shells; and that the occurrence of accumulated dissolved silicates in a thermocline is evidence of resolution of slowly settling shells. It appears that the silicon cycle in natural waters is still in a state of partial mystery. Supporting evidence for the resolution view appears in certain laboratory cultures (King and Davidson, 1933) in which complete resolution of diatom shells occurred in about five months. The presence of an enzyme which hastens solution was suggested.

Development and success of the fresh-water sponges depend upon an adequate supply of silicon for the manufacture of spicules. While experiments with higher plants seem to indicate the possibility of growth in the absence of silicon (or in the presence of the merest trace), there is evidence that they profit by its presence and also act as consumers. Indications are on record that the silicon content of water may be of importance to certain plankters other than diatoms, but this matter requires further investigation.

It is still difficult to appraise silica as a possible limiting factor. Oceanographers tend to regard it as having no limiting effect in the sea. In inland waters, however, it varies greatly in different waters and may vary widely in the same water at different times or seasons. Reductions to depletion are recorded, but the limiting effect still seems to be obscure. The exceedingly scant occurrence of diatoms in certain bog lakes has sometimes been attributed to very low silicon content of the water. Studies have been made of the relation of silica content to the quantity of diatoms produced. Some marine investigators have found no evidence that silica ever limits diatom production in the ocean. In Lake Mendota, Wisconsin, a certain correlation between silica and diatoms has been detected by Meloche *et al.* (1938), but since 0.13 mg. per l. was the minimum silica content it seems likely that silica was not a limiting factor. In Cultus Lake, British Columbia, Ricker (1937) found 6.0 mg. per l. of silica, an amount about twenty-five times the quantity of silica present in the diatoms at the time of their greatest abundance.

Some permanent loss of silicon is commonly to be expected, in average situations, owing to transportation by currents, to outlets, and to burial in bottom deposits. In the presence of such losses, a source of renewal is necessary if a body of water is to avoid silicon decline to a critical level.

RELATIONS OF PHOSPHORUS

During the past two decades much attention has been given to the phosphorus content of lakes and streams. Since the amount of soluble phosphorus in natural, unmodified waters is small and since phytoplankton requires an adequate supply of phosphorus, it is now generally regarded as a limiting factor. Extensive studies based upon measurements in natural waters and upon laboratory experiments indicate clearly the vital importance of phosphorus. Nevertheless, inconsistent and discordant results still stand in the way of a satisfactory understanding of phosphorus as a limiting factor.

It is a well-known fact that in both marine and fresh waters there is a more or less definite periodicity in the quantity of plankton present; in some lakes at least, there are well-developed spring and also autumn maxima separated by summer and winter minima. Complete exhaustion of the phosphorus by these maxima has been claimed, thus limiting or even virtually eliminating the Algae. Phytoplankton, occupying the upper waters because of their light requirements, die and sink to the bottom, carrying away a certain amount of the phosphorus. Restoration of phosphorus to the upper waters might be brought about by inflow of waters rich in phosphate or by the return to circulation of the phosphorus contained in the dead phytoplankton or other phosphorus-containing materials, return of which would be facilitated by overturns or other forms of circulation. Juday and coworkers (1928, 1931) found that the waters of lakes in northeastern Wisconsin contain only a small amount of soluble phosphorus; that the amount of soluble phosphorus is not correlated with the amount of carbonate in solution; that in those lakes supporting sizable crops of plankton no decrease occurs in the amount of soluble phosphorus, or at most a very slight one, during the summer; that there is no correlation between the quantity of centrifuge plankton and the quantity of organic phosphorus; and that no convincing evidence was found that soluble phosphorus is a limiting factor in the production of phytoplankton in the lakes studied. On the other hand, Wiebe (1931), reporting results from the Mississippi River, claims that the soluble phosphorus varies considerably; that the minimal values occurred simultaneously with a great increase in the phytoplankton; and that the evidence can be interpreted as supporting the contention that soluble phosphorus may at times become a limiting factor.

Streams pick up and transport quantities of nutrient materials. Riley (1937) states that the Mississippi River delivers into the Gulf of Mexico a quantity of phosphate per unit volume four times that in the Gulf water and that a zone of high phytoplankton production coincides with the area of increased phosphorus.

During recent years a great mass of research data has accumulated. It is difficult to summarize and often not clear as to its complete meaning. It seems to indicate that the role of phosphorus as a limiting factor in the production of plankton Algae is diverse and complicated. Rodhe (1948) has reviewed this subject in some detail. Significant correlations are said to have been found between the phosphorus content and chlorophyll content in water. Seasonal variations of soluble phosphorus may be considerable and even involve periods of disappearance. It has been claimed that a constant ratio exists between the nitrate-nitrogen and the phosphate-phosphorus content of water, but this statement, if true, holds only in a general way.

The Nitrogen–Phosphorus Ratio

Of recent years considerable attention has been given to the ratio of nitrogen to phosphorus. The relation of these two substances is better known for sea water than for fresh water, although the latter has received some study. The importance of this matter arises from the claim, which seems to have some supporting evidence, that the concentrations of the two substances closely parallel each other. In sea water it appears that the ratio tends to approach a constant value, with nitrogen exceeding considerably the phosphorus content, and that as claimed these substances occur in marine plankton in about the same proportions. Deviations from a fixed mean ratio are known to occur, both in special and general oceanic regions. Furthermore, the ratio in inland waters may be different not only in numerical value but also in the range of deviation from proposed mean. This matter is still in the pioneering stage, but is suggestive of basic limnological possibilities and deserves more investigation.

The possible existence of other and somewhat more complicated ratios is now being studied, such as the carbon-nitrogen-phosphorus ratio, or the oxygen-carbon–nitrogen-phosphorus ratio. Work of this sort is too new to justify discussion here, but it may be that ratios of this kind, assuming that they exist in significant form, will lead to increasing insight into the complicated interrelations of essential substances and their relation to productivity.

RELATIONS OF OTHER ELEMENTS

The significance of several other chemical elements appears most prominently in their essential roles in the metabolism of the various groups of aquatic plants. In some cases, it is necessary to assume that the roles demonstrated for certain elements in land plants are similar if not identical in the aquatic plants, since apparently the aquatic plants have not been investigated.

The role of calcium has already been mentioned (page 191). According to Miller (1931), calcium is required by all green plants except some of the lower Algae; is not necessary for the fungi; and while necessary for the nonchlorophyll flowering plants, they usually contain less calcium than do the chlorophyll-bearing ones. It appears to have several physiological roles, such as (1) relation to the proper translocation of the carbohydrates; (2) an integral component of plant tissue; (3) facilitating the availability of other ions; and (4) an antidoting agent reducing the toxic effects of single-salt solutions of sodium, potassium, and magnesium.

Magnesium is a component of chlorophyll and must be present for its proper development. It appears to act as a carrier of phosphorus, at least in some instances. In the past, there has been an impression that quantities of magnesium larger than usual in natural waters may be toxic to some aquatic organisms. It has also been suggested that the apparently well-established fact that Cladocera are wholly absent from certain lakes (Lake Tanganyika, Lake Kivu) may be owing to the excess of magnesium over calcium salts. However, experimental work (Hutchinson, 1932) seems to show that the magnesium content of Lake Tanganyika is less than that tolerated by Cladocera. It is also pointed out that Cladocera are known to occur regularly in lakes in which both the magnesium and the total electrolytes are greater than in Lake Tanganyika.

Iron must be supplied for plant growth and development. It functions in the proper production of chlorophyll, although it does not enter into the chemical composition of chlorophyll. The precise method of functioning is not yet convincingly demonstrated. Some of the theories center about the possibility that it acts as a catalyzer; others, that iron is the oxygen-carrying substance in certain respiratory processes. Both the quantity and the form in which it is presented to the plant are now known to be important, these being conditioned by the features of the environment (hydrogen-ion concentration, organic matters, and others) and the kind of plant involved. Most Algae grow best when the water has a ferric oxide content of 0.2 to 2 mg. per l., but distinct toxicity occurs when the available iron exceeds 5 mg. However, many natural waters may contain more than 5 mg. of iron without being toxic owing to the buffer action of organic compounds or of calcium salts (Smith, 1933). Bog waters possessing high iron content have been reported from both America and Europe. The influence of such high contents is a matter of some doubt. It has been claimed that in some European bogs, high iron content limits the toxicity of bog water to macroplankton. Toxic oxidation products of pyrites are said to be formed in peat deposits. Two other relations of high iron content have received attention in limnological literature: (1) reduction of nitrates to nitrites by ferrous salts in the presence of oxygen and (2) reduction of dissolved oxygen in the presence of iron.

Sodium, while apparently not absolutely necessary for plant growth and development, is evidently a very desirable element. According to Miller (1931), it may serve one or more of the following roles: (1) act as a conserver of potassium, since less is absorbed when sodium is present; (2) replace potassium to a limited extent as a plant-nutritive element; (3)

render soil-adsorbed potassium more available to plants; and (4) be an antidoting agent against certain toxic salts in the medium.

Potassium is a fixed requirement for plants. As mentioned above, sodium may replace it to a certain extent but not completely. Its function is imperfectly known, but it appears to be twofold: (1) a fundamental requirement in food manufacture and (2) a catalyst.

Sulfur must be provided for plant growth and development. It forms a necessary material in the composition of protein and other constituents of the plant.

TRACE ELEMENTS

By trace elements is meant those chemical elements essential to the well-being of animals and plants but required only in extremely small quantities. Knowledge in this field is still in the pioneer stage. It seems clear that, in addition to the normal physiological role played by these elements in the favorable metabolism of animals and plants, pathological manifestations arise, at least in some instances, as the result of either *deficiencies* or *excesses*. Many of the researches have been made on terrestrial organisms, and specific information concerning the aquatic biota is scanty. Possibly a reasonable assumption is that results obtained from terrestrial organisms are, to some extent, applicable to aquatic situations and organisms. The list of trace elements, known to function, or suspected of functioning, in a significant way in organisms, is a long one. For details the reader is referred to a digest of this subject by Stiles (1946). Prominent among these trace elements are copper, manganese, zinc, boron, lead, cobalt, and iodine. The very imperfect and uneven information as to occurrence, cycles, and roles of these elements in inland waters make impracticable a summary here, but enough is known to indicate that some of these substances are of real importance. Future research may show some of these elements to be vital and limiting factors.

DISSOLVED ORGANIC MATTER

The question of the amount and availability of dissolved organic matters in natural waters has long engaged the interest of biologists and particularly of physiologists, oceanographers, and the limnologists. Obviously, it is of great fundamental importance to know what part is played in the aquatic complex by these substances. To what organisms, if any, are these dissolved organic substances directly available as food materials? In what chemical forms do these materials occur? Are there sufficient quantities of these matters in the water to replace or supplement other sources of essential substances? These are questions which deserve critical attention.

It has long been assumed that many of the minute, more or less undifferentiated organisms, such as the bacteria, certain Algae, and certain

Protozoa, must depend upon the dissolved materials in their environment for the substances necessary to growth and development.   At one time, the discovery that many microorganisms use particulate foods cast some doubt on the direct utilization of dissolved substances by many organisms. However, it has since been clearly demonstrated that bacteria, diatoms, most if not all other phytoplankton, and some of the Protozoa normally utilize and depend upon both the dissolved inorganic and the dissolved organic materials in their surroundings.   It likewise seems probable that many other small organisms which lack a digestive tract or other provisions for introducing particulate foods will be discovered to depend upon these materials, wholly or in part.

Much work and controversy have centered about attempts to settle the nature of the relations of dissolved organic matter in natural waters to the higher aquatic organisms.   Like many other controversial matters, the provocative nature of the problems involved and the vigor of the contentions have led to the discovery of many interesting and important matters relating directly or indirectly to the main issues.

In the earlier days of plankton investigations, plankton was conceived to be the *producing class* of the open ocean, i.e., the fundamental source of nutrient matters for the higher marine animals.   Pütter (1907, 1909; and others), in a series of papers, attempted to show (1) that the plankton in the ocean is entirely insufficient in amount to supply the necessary nourishment for those animals supposed to depend upon it and (2) that an abundant supply of food is available in the dissolved organic matter in the water.   In support of these proposals, Pütter assembled an interesting series of data and arguments.   From computations of the minimal carbon requirements of certain marine animals for a given time unit and determinations of the plankton content of the surrounding water, he insisted that the amount of water strained by the animal to secure the minimal amount of carbon was impossibly large.   In this way, he showed that a certain common marine sponge would need to filter 242 l. of sea water per hour (about four thousand times its own bulk) to secure the minimal amount of carbon from the plankton.   However, calculations from the dissolved organic matter in the Bay of Naples, in which he found 65 to 92 mg. of dissolved carbon per liter, enabled him to contend that the necessary amount of water to supply carbon from the dissolved source could easily pass through the sponge in an hour.   Similar evidences were secured from other animals.   Vigorous opposition to Pütter's conclusions arose at once and continued actively for some years.   Opposing arguments stressed the following points:

1. Failure to find in the sea the generous quantities of dissolved organic matter claimed by Pütter.   Other workers reported only about 6 mg. per l. or less in the open sea.

2. The presence of much larger quantities of plankton in the sea than Pütter reported. Variations of plankton with season and with locality may have accounted for some of the disharmony.

3. Inaccuracy of Pütter's computations of food requirements and of his computations of necessary volumes of water strained to secure the required plankton.

4. Food value of the demersion (sinking masses of dead plankton) which constitute an important source of food for animals everywhere in the sea.

5. The insufficiency of both plankton and dissolved organic matter combined for the nutrition of swimming marine animals.

Pütter, using the experimental method, claimed to have kept large marine animals, including fishes, for long periods of time in water free from obvious particulate matter, concluding therefrom that they must have lived on the dissolved organic matter; also, that fishes could obtain from one-half to two-thirds or more of their food requirements from the dissolved organic substances.

Moore and his coworkers (1912) made some interesting and perhaps far-reaching contributions to this subject. Among other things, they repeated the aquarium experiments of Pütter, using large marine animals such as lobsters, octopus, and fish. These animals were never fed; oxygen consumption and carbon dioxide output were measured each day. At the end of several months, the experimental animals showed no serious injury and no loss of weight, a fact which looked superficially like the utilization of dissolved materials. However, examinations of their tissues showed replacement of the used-up organic matter by an equivalent amount of water; the proteins were greatly reduced, the loss being sufficient to account for the metabolic demands of the animals. Obviously, such replacement cannot continue indefinitely.

Later, Dakin and Dakin (1925), carrying on experiments on goldfish and certain other aquatic vertebrates, likewise failed to support the findings of Pütter, the experimental animals undergoing gradual starvation in water containing no solid foods.

Moore and his associates (1920) claimed that the chlorophyll-bearing phytoplankton is not dependent upon nitrogen salts or upon carbon dioxide in water for either nitrogen or carbon but, instead, can utilize atmospheric nitrogen dissolved in the water (nitrogen fixation); that the nitrites, nitrates, and ammonium salts in the water may remain unconsumed; and that bicarbonates of calcium and magnesium can be broken up, the half-bound carbon dioxide furnishing a carbon supply for the green phytoplankton. This reaction, they claimed, is of such magnitude that at the spring plankton maximum, assuming that it occurs to the same extent down to a depth of 100 m., the carbon so provided would be sufficient for a phytoplankton crop of 10 tons or more per acre, wet weight. Thus, another objection to the original Pütter hypothesis was offered, since Pütter assumed the ammonia, nitrites, and nitrates to be the source of the nitrogen, and the dissolved organic carbon the source of the carbon. Mention is made elsewhere (page 198) of the now increasing certainty as to nitrogen fixation by the chlorophyll-bearing phytoplankton, and the detachment of the half-bound carbon dioxide by green plants is well established (page 99). Moore insisted that the dissolved carbon in sea water is such an exceedingly minute quantity that it lies at the limit of detectability by the best known methods.

Birge and Juday (1926, 1927) undertook some very significant studies of the dissolved organic matter in the Wisconsin lakes, the principal findings being as follows:

1. Lake water contains much more organic matter than does the water of the open sea.

2. The quantity of inorganic salts in lake water is far smaller than in the sea.

3. In lake water, there is a large standing crop of organic matter other than that contained in the plankton, viz., the dissolved organic matter; it is ordinarily several times, often many times, greater than that in the plankton.

4. Such indispensable amino acids as tryptophane, cystine, tyrosine, histidine, and arginine occur in the lakes studied, and they seem as well suited for food as is the organic matter of the plankton.

5. In the plankton of Lake Mendota, Wisconsin, the dry organic matter of the two main groups of *eaters* (Crustacea and rotifers) is about one-third that of the organic matter of the entire *net* plankton. The average net plankton is slightly more than one-sixth of the total plankton. Therefore, in the total particulate matter removed from the water by the centrifuge, there is fifteen to twenty times as much organic matter as exists in the Crustacea and the rotifers.

6. The dissolved organic matter in lake water, judging from its quantity and its chemical composition, constitutes a potential food supply several times greater than that contained in the plankton.

These results virtually reopened the question of the role of dissolved organic matter in the food supply by removing, in so far as fresh water is concerned, certain objections offered against the Pütter hypothesis as applied to sea water.

Since 1924, results of a large number of investigations have been published (Chomkovic, 1926; Krizenecky and Podhradsky, 1924; Krizenecky and Petrov, 1927; Esaki, 1926; Koller, 1930; Kostomarov, 1928; Nakajima, 1927; Rauson, 1926–1927; and others), many in the nature of experiments to test the availability and the actual utilization of dissolved organic matters by various animals. Many of these workers claim positive results. Not only have certain animals been kept for long periods of time in water containing dissolved matters only, but also it is claimed that tadpoles have undergone normal metamorphosis in this kind of medium. Other evidences are presented to prove direct utilization by absorption. Criticism of some of the earlier works has been offered on the ground of failure to exclude the very fine particulate matters, such as the bacteria, but later workers have tried to protect their experiments against this objection. The accumulated body of positive results by different workers now seems to require some attention.

In addition, investigations on plankton production (Gaarder and Gran, 1927; and others) and on growth and development of mosquito larvae (Matheson and Hinman, 1931; Hinman, 1932; and others) seem to supply additional evidence of the direct utilization of dissolved organic substances. Krogh and Lange (1931) performed a series of critical experiments bearing directly upon certain vital aspects of this whole matter, and Krogh (1931) reviewed the whole subject rather exhaustively. The following statements taken from Krogh's summary combine his appraisal of the present status of this controversy with the salient results of his own investigations:

1. Organic detritus and living organisms in water usually provide food in necessary quantity for the aquatic animals present. Certain Protozoa and possibly sponges may absorb dissolved substances from the water. That a few animals live mainly upon dissolved substances cannot be denied.

2. The rather large quantities (10 mg. per l. or more) of dissolved organic matter in fresh water include proteins in colloidal solution and several amino acids greatly diluted. Carbohydrates present do not appear to be in readily assimilable form.

3. Dissolved organic matter seems to be principally waste products, some of which are very resistant to bacterial action.

4. Very little of the organic matter produced by living Algae is given off to the water; 90 to 95 per cent of it is stored in the organisms.

5. It is possible that higher animals absorb insignificant quantities of the dissolved substances.

6. Experimental evidence is now available which indicates that tadpoles, mussels, and probably other animals may take up dissolved organic matter from rather concentrated solutions and are thus enabled to thrive and grow, at least for a considerable period of time, in the absence of particulate food.

7. Experiments of certain investigators show that absorption of dissolved organic matter by tadpoles, mussels, and starfish occurs through the intestine and not through gills or integument. The integument and

gills of aquatic animals seem to be, for the most part, impermeable to organic substances.

Adolph (1925) reported penetration of the integument of certain annelids by dissolved substances, although the entrance was faster in marine animals than in fresh-water ones. He also found that the body fluids of fresh-water animals have a lower osmotic pressure than do these of marine animals. Krogh regards the reports of unidirectional permeability of the skin of fishes and Amphibia as based upon artifacts. Bond (1933) concluded that, in general, marine invertebrates are permeable to water, salts, and organic solutes but that teleosts and fresh-water invertebrates have very slight permeability. Gellis and Clarke (1935) found evidence that in *Daphnia magna* organic substances in true solution were not used for food, but organic matter in colloidal form was utilized.

Many of the problems involved in the direct utilization of dissolved organic matter await solution. Future research must decide the extent to which the various fresh-water organisms utilize the potential food store now known to exist in dissolved form. That there is some absorption of substances from the water by the smaller, soft-bodied forms seems established. Possibly, forms as high as the fishes may absorb a slight amount of dissolved substance, but the securing of a large proportion of their nutriment in this way, as has been postulated, appears very doubtful. Nevertheless, if some of these claims, which still seem startling, should become established facts, the present conception of the fundamental sources of food supply in water will require far-reaching alteration.

HYDROGEN-ION CONCENTRATION

During the past three decades, innumerable papers have been published dealing with the hydrogen-ion concentration of natural waters and its possible significance. The same is true in the fields of physiology, bacteriology, medicine, agriculture, and others. In spite of this accumulation of data, much remains to be done before the role of hydrogen-ion concentration is well understood. The variety of conditions determining hydrogen-ion concentration, the complexity and dynamics of the environment in which it may be acting, and the complexity of living substance upon which it acts produce a situation bristling with difficulties for the investigator. Nevertheless, it is known to possess a significance of sufficient importance to require attention.

INFLUENCE UPON PROTOPLASM

That hydrogen-ion concentration has a relation to living matter seems established, but its exact nature is little understood. Possibly, the effect may differ with the tissue and with other conditions; certainly, it seems to be true that different organisms respond differently to various amounts of ionized hydrogen in the medium. The effects of a dilute solution of a strong acid (e.g., hydrochloric acid) on animal tissue as contrasted with those of weaker acids (e.g., acetic or boric) of the same dilution, such as about 3 per cent, have been sometimes used to illustrate the general difference in the effect on tissue based upon differences in degrees of ionization, but aside from the fact that a 3 per cent solution of hydrogen chlorine will produce a "burn" while a 3 per cent solution of acetic acid can be taken in connection with foods and a 3 per cent solution of boric acid may produce no sensation on a very sensitive tissue, the example explains nothing as to what happens in the protoplasm. Various suggestions occur in the literature; as for example, it is thought that pH may have some effect through changing the ability of cells to absorb and utilize oxygen and to give off carbon dioxide; or that it may work through some modification of the permeability of the cell membranes.

Organisms and tissues respond differently to conditions of neutrality, acidity, or alkalinity. In former years, the statement was current that protoplasm must necessarily maintain an essential neutrality, but there is now grave doubt as to the accuracy of such a statement; in fact, it has been claimed that active protoplasm is actually acid in reaction. Internal body fluids of animals are known to differ markedly in their reactions; some are distinctly alkaline, some are near neutrality, and others are acid in reaction. Also, it is now known that, in certain animals at least, the reaction of the body fluid may differ in pH at different times or under different physiological states. In plants, pH is known to have a conditioning influence upon certain enzymes, growth relations, and the performance of some functions.

Probably the greatest difficulty involved in determining the effects of pH upon aquatic organisms is to discover to what extent the effects of an acid are due (1) to its ionized hydrogen, (2) to the negative ions, and (3) to the undissociated molecules.

GENERAL LIMNOLOGICAL INFLUENCE OF HYDROGEN-ION CONCENTRATION

At one period during the past thirty years, the significance of pH was greatly overemphasized by enthusiastic exponents of the idea that it might be the key to the whole ecological situation; that it might be a supreme, controlling factor in determining the presence and distribution of aquatic organisms. This conception met the fate which it deserved, since there is no evidence that in the complex of operative factors in an environment any single factor has complete control. Therefore, of late years, pH has fallen from the somewhat exalted position which it once appeared to occupy, although it is still regarded as playing certain roles sufficiently significant to necessitate continued study. There are two general ways of regarding the limnological value of pH, viz., (1) as a limiting factor and (2) as an index of a general environmental condition.

Hydrogen-ion Concentration as a Limiting Factor. Each organism has its toleration range of pH terminated by a maximum and a minimum and possesses an optimum at some intermediate position. This is in accordance with the usual type of reaction to stimuli in general. In addition to these critical points, it has been found that in many plants there is between the extreme limits of acidity and alkalinity a *third region* where the reaction affects the plant in an injurious way, so that, when the growth is plotted, the curve shows two maxima and three minima. The total result is three regions of reduced growth and two of maximum growth. How widespread this reaction among plants may be is yet uncertain, and little seems to be known concerning the existence of such a phenomenon among animals. It has been found in the ciliates *Colpidium* and *Glaucoma*. Knowledge concerning the limiting effects of pH is in a very unsatisfactory state. In the sense that every species has somewhere its extremes of toleration of acidity and alkalinity, pH can be regarded as limiting the occurrence of organisms, but not infrequently the extremes are so far apart that in nature some other factor or factors may have an eliminating influence before either extreme is reached. The literature contains numerous positive contentions that pH is an important limiting factor for certain organisms. Sometimes, the evidence is conflicting for the same species. Other workers regard pH as of at least secondary importance, and certain investigators have claimed for some organisms no correlations of any sort with the pH range as it occurs in natural, unmodified waters. As nearly as can be determined at the present time, it appears that the true role of hydrogen-ion concentration lies somewhere between these contrasting views. It would appear that hydrogen-ion concentration is so valuable an influence in aquatic life that it must not be ignored, but it is not clear that it occupies any supreme position as an over-all limiting factor.

Hydrogen-ion Concentration as an Index of Environmental Condition. In addition to the possible direct action of pH as a factor, it may also serve as an index of certain existing conditions in water. For example, the proper determination of pH may, in addition to giving a measure of the concentration of the ionized hydrogen, yield indirect information on (1) the free carbon dioxide content, (2) alkalinity, (3) dissolved oxygen content, (4) reserve pH, (5) the dissolved solids content, and probably others. In this respect, it may serve as a test of several environmental conditions. While it has been claimed that carbon dioxide tension is a better index of environmental conditions than pH, the latter is still regarded as of value in this respect.

Hydrogen-ion Concentration Ranges

The literature swarms with records which purport to establish the pH ranges for various organisms. Many of these records are based upon faulty methods or faulty assumptions and are of no value. Many of them depended upon the use of specimens from limited parts of the geographic range of the species, the use of specimens of doubtful identification, or the use of different life-history levels of the same species. These and other similar defects make many records of doubtful value. Far too many field records merely present pH values of waters in which certain organisms are distributed, with little consideration for or, in some instances, complete disregard of the other environmental factors operating simultaneously and possibly exerting a greater local effect than pH. The most usable data are those worked out in the laboratory under controlled conditions and those done in nature which are accompanied by qualitative and quantitative information on other environmental features.

There is some evidence that the different species of a taxonomic group may each have an individual pH range. This seems to be better established for the fishes, since they have been favorite materials for study. Likewise, in species of wide geographic range, both the toleration and the voluntary-selection limits may be different in different parts of the range. Furthermore, it has been shown that acclimatization effects may be manifested not only in individuals from widely separated parts of the geographic range but also in the instances of individuals of the same species which occupy waters closely adjacent but widely different in pH. In so far as natural fresh waters are concerned, the pH range of any species usually cannot be dependably determined from the values of waters in a restricted region unless those waters happen to show a diversity far greater than is usually the case.

Responses to Differences of Hydrogen-ion Concentration. According to published records, animals differ widely with respect to a recognition of and responses to differences in pH. Shelford (1923) found that fishes, with a few exceptions, react definitely to differences of pH, and this conclusion has been confirmed, to some extent, by others. On the other hand, some of the lower, aquatic animals are said to show no reaction to hydrogen ions. How many of the negative records are due to faulty experimentation remains to be determined.

Brown and Jewell (1926) found that in a gradient tank supplied with water from an acid lake (pH 6.4) at one end and with water from a basic lake (pH 8.6) at the other, fishes common to both lakes selected the water with the reaction to which they were accustomed, owing, probably, to the effect of acclimatization. Experiments with fishes from other sources confirmed the selection of water with pH to which they were ordinarily accustomed. From these findings, they concluded that

. . . while it is improbable that pH, as such, plays any important role in the distribution of most species of fresh-water fish, since fish are found in practically the whole pH range ordinarily encountered in natural waters, still the question as to whether or not the fact that fish do tend to avoid a change from the pH to which they are accustomed would tend to limit or retard migration into new areas and confine them to their native waters, as suggested by Shelford and Powers (1915) for marine fishes, merits further study.

Range of Possible Toleration. Survival experiments (Brown and Jewell, 1926) have shown that fishes of several species can be transplanted from natural waters of pH 8.4 to 8.6 to natural waters of pH 4.4, as well as in the reverse order, and survive the transfer for 40 or more days, indicating that "it is not necessary to assume that fishes found in these extreme hydrogen-ion concentrations have gradually developed a resistance or are physiologically different from the fishes of the same species from ordinary waters." Fresh-water mussels, absent from the more acid waters in nature, survived a transplantation to water of pH 4.4 for 46 days, the only observable effect being slight corrosion of the shell. Wiebe (1931) found that certain fishes, under experimental conditions, tolerated rapid and extensive changes of pH in the surrounding water.

In some situations, an important relation exists between the hydrogen-ion concentration and the dissolved oxygen content. This relation is an inverse sort, the hydrogen-ion concentration varying, in a rough way, inversely with the dissolved oxygen in water having a stable alkalinity. Survival experiments have demonstrated increasingly injurious effects on organisms of low dissolved oxygen in the presence of increasing hydrogen-ion concentration. In fact, there is reason for believing that the unfavorable effects sometimes attributed to low dissolved oxygen may be due to an accompanying high hydrogen-ion concentration.

ALKALI RESERVE

The normal alkalinity of water or of an internal body fluid is maintained by the dissolved salts and other substances, these substances being designated collectively as the *alkali reserve*. It has been shown that in human beings, the mechanism of the blood which prevents acidosis is the alkali reserve of the blood. Since fishes and possibly some other organisms are able to survive in waters in which the pH varies greatly, the mechanism enabling them to adjust themselves to such differences in surroundings has been sought by some investigators in the alkali reserve of the blood. The reserve pH (RpH) (the pH of a sample after thorough aeration) is known to be a good index of the alkali reserve and therefore figures prominently in the determinations. Results thus far have been conflicting. Powers (1922) found that certain nonmigratory marine fishes possess the ability to change the alkali reserve of their blood so as to adjust themselves to the variations in the carbon dioxide tension, to the oxygen tension of the sea water, or to both; and Powers and Logan (1925) concluded that the adjusting mechanism in the blood of a certain marine fish to meet changes in the environmental constitution may be of two types: (1) a mechanism for rapid compensation enabling the fish to make marked changes of the alkali reserve in a short time and (2) a slower and more permanent alteration of the blood, referred to as acclimatization. Opposed to these results, Jobes and Jewell (1927), working with freshwater fishes from waters of widely different chemical characters, found (1) that the alkali reserve of the blood of these fish varied within wide limits (RpH 6.9 to 8.1); (2) that there was no correlation of the RpH of the fish blood with the pH of the water; and (3) that the theory that the alkali reserve of fish blood varies with the carbon dioxide tension of the surrounding water is not yet warranted.

ANTAGONISM AND BALANCED ENVIRONMENTAL CONDITIONS

In the preceding pages, attention has been given to the important substances and groups of substances which compose the chemical features of the aquatic environment. That these diverse substances combine to assist in forming a suitable medium for aquatic life is evidenced by the fact that organisms inhabit the various natural waters. It cannot be too strongly emphasized that the *form of the combination* of materials is of prime importance. Many of the individual chemical constituents of the medium, while absolutely necessary, are toxic to the very organisms which use them when *they alone* constitute the only solute. It is often pointed out that marine organisms live successfully in sea water which is in part a mixture of salt solutions, but a solution of *any one* of these salts alone would kill these same organisms in a relatively short time. Many salts possess a counteracting influence or an antidoting effect upon the toxicity of other salts, thus rendering them nontoxic. This hindering effect which one salt may have on the toxicity of another is known as *antagonism*. The exact nature of antagonism is little understood; it seems to be concerned with permeability changes in the protoplasm. Its role in the production of environments as they exist in the natural waters is profoundly important. A certain fundamental balance must not only be established but also maintained between the various chemical components. Maintenance requires that in the complex set of chemical changes which go on constantly in natural waters, enough of the various substances, acting and counteracting, must be supplied to continue the essentially favorable medium. An excess of a salt over its counteracting one leads to the development of toxicity. Single-salt toxicity varies with the salt and with certain other surrounding conditions. That temporarily unbalanced conditions may occur in nature seems likely, and it may be that occasional, large quantities of some substance in water constitute an *excess* which, for the time, exerts some unfortunate effect upon one or more organisms. It is also certain, however, that such circumstances are much more likely in polluted waters than in the unmodified, natural waters.

It is known that some, possibly many, aquatic animals react to the presence of excess, toxic substances. Under experimental conditions, it appears that the reaction is negative (avoiding) in some species, positive in others, and absent in still others. Those manifesting the avoiding reactions may be able to escape the unfavorable conditions.

OTHER ESSENTIAL OR ACCESSORY GROWTH FACTORS

Various indications suggest the existence of certain other essential, or, if not essential, very desirable, substances or conditions in the normal aquatic environment. Such indications usually arise in connection with attempts to synthesize natural waters. As an example of these unknown conditions may be cited the experience of one investigator, who on trying to maintain certain marine microscopic organisms in the most carefully made synthetic sea water found that the culture was only very indifferently successful but that the addition to this culture of a small amount of the natural sea water or extracts of a certain marine Alga converted the culture into a very successful one. Other experiments have yielded similar results with various organisms. There seems to be evidence that some of these substances are complemental to others, i.e., neither performs adequately in the absence of the other. At present, little beyond speculation is possible concerning the nature of these unknowns. It is possible that they are not always required since some investigators report good growths of certain marine diatoms in artificial sea water. The existence of similar essential or stimulating agents in inland waters is at least very probable.

Vitamins. Extensive studies of animal nutrition, especially among terrestrial vertebrates, have yielded a substantial body of information concerning those accessory organic substances known as *vitamins*. For aquatic organisms information is scanty, fragmentary, and very incomplete. It appears that vitamin requirements are somewhat better known in fishes. Phillips and Brockway (1948) list four vitamins which are essential for trout and six others which may be needed. For aquatic invertebrates much less is known. According to Hutchinson (1943) they are rich in *thiamin*. Hutchinson (1943) and Hutchinson and Setlow (1946) found *thiamin, niacin,* and *biotin* present in solution in lake water and also in seston suspended in the same water. These substances showed a rather wide variation. McLaren *et al.* (1947) studied experimentally the vitamin requirements of the rainbow trout. By the use of a purified diet, they determined the optimum levels of 11 vitamins and recorded observations on the relation of vitamins to specific disease symptoms. Phillips and Rodgers (1949) presented evidence that trout (brook, brown, and rainbow) require at least 175.2 micrograms of folic acid per kilogram of trout weight per day. Certain vitamins are important growth factors for various bacteria, also for higher aquatic plants. It is probable that all aquatic organisms are somehow involved in, or related to, the complex of vitamin influence.

OXIDATION-REDUCTION POTENTIALS

A young but growing interest is now evident in the measurement of oxidation-reduction (redox) potentials in inland waters and bottom muds as a possible means of studying the dynamics of these environments. Natural waters and bottom muds contain complexes of substances which are in a state of chemical instability and in the process of undergoing reactions. The term *oxidation* as used in this connection includes those reactions which involve not only the addition of oxygen but also the loss of hydrogen or the loss of electrons. *Reduction* is essentially the opposite of oxidation. Thus there is electron transfer in oxidation-reduction reactions. A single substance can lose electrons, or it can receive them, depending upon the chemical circumstances at the moment. In natural water or bottom mud various, sometimes many, oxidation-reduction "systems" are involved. Since electron transfer is accompanied by measurable changes in potential, it is possible to make quantitative investigations of oxidation-reduction reactions. The oxidation-reduction potential is a direct index of the ability of one "system" to oxidize another.

An oxidation-reduction system must be viewed in two different ways: (1) *intensity*, which is measured by the potential, and (2) *capacity*, or the buffering of the system, which refers to the ability to oxidize or reduce without changing the potential.

Measurements of oxidation-reduction potential are now usually made electrometrically. Some use has been made of colorimetric indicators, but while not without value they are less exact. The development of electrometric equipment for measuring oxidation-reduction potentials *in situ* in lake waters (Allgeier *et al.*, 1941) is an important step in advance.

Oxidation-reduction potentials are related in one way or other to pH, dissolved oxygen, ferrous iron, hydrogen sulfide, and perhaps other substances, but the nature of the relationships is as yet little known. Hutchinson *et al.* (1939) found evidence that redox potentials may be of importance in determining lake typology. Allgeier *et al.* (1941) reported that in the oligotrophic lakes which they studied there was either no decrease in redox potential, or else only a small one, in the lower water, but that in the eutrophic and dystrophic lakes the decrease, in the lower water, was much greater.

With regard to the relation of redox potentials to the distribution of organisms, knowledge is largely in the threshold stage. Dependable information appears to be mostly in the field of bacteria and certain other microorganisms. For example, it is said that only anaerobic forms can occur in mud and water which lack dissolved oxygen and have low potential, whereas aerobic bacteria flourish where the potential is relatively high. It has been claimed (Hutchinson *et al.*, 1939) that the distribution of certain characteristic bottom-dwelling insect larvae (Chironomidae) is in close correspondence with redox potential values in the lake studied.

Much work must be done before dependable conclusions can be drawn concerning the value of redox potentials as an index of environmental dynamics in aquatic situations. Evidence now available seems to encourage the hope that here is another profitable means of studying limnological processes.

CHAPTER VIII

ORGANISMS IN INLAND WATERS

Unmodified inland waters of virtually every form, composition, altitude, and latitude are populated with organisms, both plant and animal. The composition of the biota differs greatly with differences in the various waters. Considered in general, the taxonomic diversity of animals and plants inhabiting inland waters is truly remarkable. With but a very few exceptions, all of the major groups of plants and animals are represented, often by a great array of species. An extended consideration of this biota is beyond the province of this book. Ward and Whipple's "Fresh-water Biology" and other similar works present taxonomic details of the fresh-water organisms. The following abbreviated outline will suffice for present purposes. Certain rare groups are omitted.

GROUPS OF ORGANISMS REPRESENTED IN AMERICAN INLAND WATERS

I. PLANTS

A. Algae[1]

Chlorophyceae—the grass-green Algae. Largest group of fresh-water Algae; representatives in nearly all kinds of aquatic situations.
Charophyceae—the stoneworts. Small group; mostly fresh water.
Euglenophyceae—common in fresh water, sometimes very abundant.
Cryptophyceae—small group; mostly in fresh water.
Dinophyceae—primarily a marine group; representatives of a few genera in fresh water; widely distributed; sometimes common locally.
Xanthophyceae—primarily a fresh-water group.
Chrysophyceae—common, especially in plankton; widely distributed.
Bacillariophyceae—the diatoms; very common and widely distributed.
Myxophyceae (Cyanophyceae)—the blue-green Algae. Very common and widely distributed.
Rhodophyceae—the red Algae. A few scattering representatives in fresh water.

B. Fungi

Schizomycetes—the bacteria. Many genera and species.
Phycomycetes—Algae-like fungi. Common in fresh water.

C. Bryophyta

Hepaticae—the liverworts. A few aquatic species.
Musci—The mosses. Several truly aquatic species.

[1] Classification as given by Smith (1938).

D. *Pteridophyta*

Lycopodiales—club mosses.
Isoëtaceae—the quillworts. A single genus, *Isoëtes*, includes several fresh-water species.

E. *Spermatophyta*

Only the more important aquatic groups are listed below. Certain small and relatively insignificant ones are omitted.

Angiospermae.
Monocotyledoneae.

Typhaceae—the cat-tails. Mostly aquatic.
Sparganiaceae—the burweeds. Essentially aquatic.
Naiadaceae—the pondweeds. Preeminently aquatic.
Alismaceae—the water plantains. Marsh plants.
Hydrocharitaceae—the frog's-bit group. All aquatic.
Poaceae—the grasses. A few aquatic species.
Cyperaceae—the sedges. In part aquatic.
Araceae—the arum group. Certain aquatic species.
Lemnaceae—the duckweeds. All aquatic.
Eriocaulaceae—the pipeworts. Aquatic and marsh species.
Pontederiaceae—the pickerel weeds. All aquatic.

Dicotyledoneae.

Polygonaceae—the smartweeds and others. A very few aquatic species.
Ceratophyllaceae—the hornworts. All aquatic.
Nymphaeaceae—the water lilies. All aquatic.
Ranunculaceae—the crowfoot group. A few aquatic species.
Brassicaceae—the mustard group. A few aquatic species.
Callitrichaceae—the water starworts. Chiefly aquatic.
Lythraceae—the loosestrifes. In part aquatic.
Haloragidaceae—the water milfoils. In part aquatic.
Lentibulariaceae—the bladderworts. Mostly aquatic.

II. Animals

Protozoa—all classes and most orders represented.
Porifera—confined to Demospongiae and to the order Monaxonida.
Coelenterata—hydra; also a few other Hydrozoa.
Platyhelminthes—many representatives in all classes.
Nemertea—only a few species in inland waters.
Acanthocephala—parasites in various hosts.
Rotatoria—almost entirely a fresh-water group.
Gastrotricha—exclusively in fresh water.
Nematomorpha—several species; adults free living in fresh water; immature stages parasitic.
Nematoidea—many species.
Tardigrada—a few species.
Bryozoa—several Ectoprocta and a very few Endoprocta.
Linguatula—a very few species in fresh-water hosts.
Annelida—many Oligochaeta; Polychaeta rare; Hirudinea almost wholly confined to fresh water.

Arthropoda—a few spiders; many mites; Crustacea generously represented in all major groups except Cirripedia; Insecta with many species aquatic in some stage of life history.

Mollusca—many species of Gastropoda and Pelecypoda.

Chordata—Cyclostomata, represented by the lampreys; Pisces, many species; Amphibia, many species aquatic in some life-history stage; Reptilia, certain groups have aquatic habits; Aves, many birds frequent water more or less intimately; Mammalia, certain species have aquatic habits and adaptations.

CLASSIFICATIONS OF ORGANISMS IN WATER

The literature contains a variety of classifications or groupings of the organisms which inhabit water. Such classifications usually apply to both fresh and marine waters and, in addition, sometimes include debris and the remains resulting from once living organisms. Certain workers have proposed very extended, detailed classifications of aquatic organisms, some of which involve artificial criteria and detailed analyses to such an extent that their value may well be in doubt. Such classifications as are included here have gained at least partial acceptance in limnological circles.

According to a time-honored classification, aquatic plants and animals are divided into three groups:

1. Plankton—organisms of relatively small size, mostly microscopic, which have either relatively small powers of locomotion or else none at all and which drift in the water subject to the action of waves, currents, and other forms of water motion.
2. Nekton—organisms of larger size which swim freely and determine independently, to greater or less extent, their distribution in space regardless of the movements of the surrounding water.
3. Benthos—organisms which live in or on the bottom of the basin.

Seston. The term *seston* came into use of recent years. It designates that whole heterogeneous mixture of living and nonliving bodies which float or swim in water. The present conception of seston is indicated in the following outline:

Seston

I. Bioseston—living components of the seston.
   A. Plankton—defined above.
   B. Neuston—organisms which are related to the surface film of water, either (1) by hanging from or floating against the lower side (*infraneuston*) (bacteria, Protozoa, Algae, hydra, certain Entomostraca, certain insect larvae, and others) or (2) by ranging upon the surface film (*supraneuston*) (Gerridae, Veliidae, Hydrometridae, Gyrinidae, certain Collembola, and others).
   C. Pleuston—higher plants which float either upon the surface or within the water.
   D. Nekton—defined above.

II. Abioseston (Tripton)—Nonliving components of the seston.
   A. Autochthonous detritus—detritus produced locally.
      1. Plankton-produced detritus.
      2. Neuston-produced detritus.
      3. Pleuston-produced detritus.
      4. Nekton-produced detritus.
      5. Benthos-produced detritus.
   B. Allochthonous detritus—detritus originating outside a given locality.

Littoral-limnetic-benthic Organisms.   Another grouping of the aquatic biota of long standing is the following:

1. Littoral—organisms inhabiting regions immediately adjacent to the shore.
2. Limnetic, or pelagic—organisms inhabiting the open waters.
   a. True limnetic—organisms characteristic of and thriving in open waters only.
   b. Facultative limnetic—organisms which, in one or more life-history stages, may occupy the open waters although capable of existence in the littoral or benthic zones.
3. Benthos—organisms inhabiting the bottom.

CHAPTER IX

PLANKTON

The term *plankton* was first proposed by the oceanographer Victor Hen-- sen in 1887 to designate that heterogeneous assemblage of minute organisms and finely divided, nonliving materials then known to occur in the waters of the sea and to float about at the will of the waves and other water movements. The term was soon extended to cover all assemblages of such organisms and materials regardless of the nature of the waters which they occupied, and this is the sense in which the term is sometimes used today. Commonly, however, the term *plankton* is restricted to the organisms only, while the associated detritus, which is always present to some extent, is indicated under other terms. A single organism in the plankton is known as a *plankter*.[1]

ORGANISMS COMPOSING PLANKTON

Plankton of the various fresh waters differs widely in quality. The following outline is merely an abbreviated indication of the organisms which may occur in the plankton of fresh waters at large. Those groups most commonly and regularly represented in plankton are in the first list.

A. PLANTS

1. Algae. All of the classes of Algae, are represented, some of them very generously, in the plankton of inland waters.
2. Fungi. Bacteria occur abundantly in the plankton; in fact, it seems likely that no water in nature is free from them. Other fungi also occur widely and often commonly.

B. ANIMALS

1. Protozoa. All of the classes and subclasses of Protozoa, except the Sporozoa, have representatives among the plankton. Often represented by many genera and species.
2. Coelenterata. Hydra is a facultative plankter, occurring at times free in the open water.
3. Rotatoria. One of the most important groups of the zooplankton.

---

[1] The term *planktont* of the older literature should be abandoned because of its faulty word structure.

4. Gastrotricha. Representatives of Gastrotricha occur in the plankton but usually in limited numbers.

5. Bryozoa. The Bryozoa (Polyzoa) may be represented in the plankton by their statoblasts (asexual reproductive bodies); also, in special situations and at certain times, by their free-swimming larvae.

6. Arthropoda.

a. Crustacea. Entomostraca, especially Cladocera and Copepoda, constitute one of the most prominent and significant of the plankton groups.

b. Insecta. Certain insect larvae (*Corethra*) are common plankters in lentic waters.

C. Occasional Plankters

In addition to the groups of organisms mentioned above which are so commonly present in the plankton at large, there is a second group, representatives of which may occur as plankters only occasionally or under somewhat unusual conditions, although when they do appear they are to be regarded as properly belonging to the plankton. The following groups exemplify this class, although it must be understood that other organisms might be added.

1. Flowering Plants. These plants contribute little to the formation of true plankton. Among the more or less exceptional instances, representatives of the Lemnaceae (*Wolffia*) occur at various depth levels and are recorded as plankton organisms, especially in certain rivers.

2. Coelenterata. The fresh-water medusa, *Craspedacusta*, is essentially a plankter whenever it makes one of its rare, sporadic appearances.

3. Platyhelminthes. As a rule, the Turbellaria are of little importance in fresh-water plankton. However, under special conditions and at certain times of year, they may become abundant in the plankton of pools, backwaters, and similar habitats. Certain species are said to be adapted to the limnetic habit and apparently qualify as true plankters when they appear.

Cercariae may appear in plankton, particularly in samples taken in shallow lakes or from shoal waters. However, they are rarely mentioned in plankton records, and in ordinary plankton examinations they are seldom seen. Wesenberg-Lund (1934) insists that fresh-water lakes support a peculiar fauna of pelagic cercariae which live a true planktonic life and that the failure to find them in plankton samples in the past has been due to faults of plankton collection and to peculiarities of seasonal distribution.

4. Insecta. Temporary adoption of the limnetic habit by certain May-fly nymphs may occur in special situations. Adult and nymphal aquatic Hemiptera are occasionally found in the plankton, especially in rivers and ponds. There is some evidence that at times certain chironomid larvae become temporarily limnetic. A few other insect larvae mingle at times in plankton under circumstances which suggest that their presence is not accidental. Considerable quantities of eggs of the aquatic Diptera and of Ephemerida are found in the plankton of some waters, particularly at certain seasons.

5. Arachnida. Water mites are occasionally found in the plankton.

6. Vertebrata. Representatives of the vertebrates occur but rarely in plankton and then only as the small, juvenile stages of fishes.

D. ADVENTITIOUS PLANKTON ELEMENTS

Many littoral and benthic organisms, particularly the small ones, may become accidentally and temporarily incorporated into the plankton. Wave action resulting from violent storms, rising water level, flood periods in running-water systems, seiches, and other water disturbances facilitate the introduction of adventitious components. Certain turbellarians; certain cercariae of trematodes; fresh-water nemerteans; various free-living, aquatic nematodes; representatives of the smaller, aquatic oligochetes, especially species belonging to the Aeolosomatidae and the Naididae; certain nonplankton Crustacea and insects; tardigrades; small snails; glochidia of mussels—these and other organisms may find their way into the plankton adventitiously. In fact, almost any of the smaller littoral and benthic organisms are potential, adventitious plankton elements. Discrimination between true plankters and adventitious forms is relatively simple in some instances; in others, it may be very difficult owing to the rhythms, periodicity, life-history features, and other complicating circumstances which surround and govern the appearance of the occasional plankters.

In addition to the accidental inclusion of the smaller, marginal and bottom organisms in the plankton, the planktonologist not infrequently encounters wind-blown organisms, reproductive bodies, and life-history stages of organisms, all of terrestrial origin. Pollen of various shrubs and trees is often blown into water in considerable quantity.

CLASSIFICATION AND TERMINOLOGY OF PLANKTON

The vast amount of research on plankton has resulted in various classifications. Some of the more important groupings follow:

SOME CLASSIFICATIONS OF PLANKTON

I. On the basis of quality.
   A. Phytoplankton—plant plankton.
      1. Phytoplankton proper—chlorophyll-bearing plankton.
      2. Saproplankton—bacteria and fungi.
   B. Zooplankton—animal plankton.

II. On the basis of size.

    A. Macroplankton—the larger units of plankton, visible to the unaided eye.

    B. Net plankton (mesoplankton)—plankton secured by the plankton net equipped with No. 25 silk bolting cloth (mesh, 0.03 to 0.04 mm.)

    C. Nannoplankton (microplankton)—very minute plankton not secured by the plankton net with No. 25 silk bolting cloth.

III. On the basis of local environmental distribution.

    A. Limnoplankton—lake plankton.

    B. Rheoplankton (potamoplankton)—running-water plankton.

    C. Heleoplankton—pond plankton.

    D. Haliplankton—salt-water plankton.

    E. Hypalmyroplankton—brackish-water plankton.

IV. On the basis of origin.

    A. Autogenetic plankton—plankton produced locally.

    B. Allogenetic plankton—plankton introduced from other localities.

V. On the basis of content.

    A. Euplankton—true plankton.

    B. Pseudoplankton—debris mingled in plankton.

VI. On the basis of life history.

    A. Holoplankton—organisms free floating throughout their life.

    B. Metoplankton—organisms free-floating only at certain times or stages of life cycle.

DISTRIBUTION OF PLANKTON

So far as is known, all natural waters, irrespective of latitude, altitude, and physicochemical characters, are, in the vast majority of instances, normal supporters of a plankton, although it may differ in a great many respects. Statements are sometimes made in the literature to the effect that rapidly running streams and rivers may be devoid of plankton—a statement requiring some qualification. Similar statements are occasionally made concerning certain thermal waters, subterranean waters, spring-fed streams, transient pools, and other special situations, but some of these environments may contain a plankton, even though very much restricted. The almost universal presence of a plankton in natural waters is in itself an indication of the significant position which it occupies in the aquatic complex.

General Geographic Distribution of Plankton

Latitudinal Differences. For a long time it has been claimed by some oceanographers that the polar seas support a much more abundant plankton than do the tropical ones. This contention is based upon very incomplete information and does not meet with universal acceptance. In fact, the evidence is often directly conflicting. Allen (1939) points out that very large areas of the ocean in high latitudes show very light phytoplankton and extensive areas in the tropical seas produce very heavy phytoplankton. It is claimed that certain arctic marine plankters show increased size over their warm-water relatives, a result which is attributed to a thermal effect, but to what extent it influences the mass quantitative plankton production is not known at this time. It seems clear that before any latitude can be rated as the most productive, at least so far as the oceans are concerned, a vastly greater body of information must be available.

Polar and tropical inland waters are still so little known limnologically that their plankton production cannot be compared satisfactorily. It has been claimed that quantitatively there is likely to be less plankton in tropical inland waters than in temperate waters. Certain northern low-lying lakes in countries bordering on the Baltic Sea are said to produce a generous plankton, but whether it is due to latitude or to other circumstances is not clear. High alpine lakes, as a rule, are likely to produce a small plankton. Plankton production in the inland waters of far northern North America is little known. Rawson (1947) found low plankton production in Great Bear Lake, Great Slave Lake, and Lake Athabasca. The plankton of tundra waters is almost unknown. Shelford and Twomey (1941) reported plankton Crustacea very scanty in July in Lake Isabelle located in the tundra country near Churchill, west shore of Hudson Bay, Canada; also, "numerous individuals" of Cladocera and certain plankton Protozoa in a small permanent pond in the same locality. In the face of this great paucity of conclusive information, no profitable comparisons of plankton production at different latitudes can be made. Certainly there is no convincing proof that arctic inland waters are more productive in plankton than are the more southern ones; in fact, it is within the range of possibility that the reverse may be true.

Cosmopolitanism of Fresh-water Plankton. One of the striking features of fresh-water plankton at large is its apparently well-marked cosmopolitanism. Many of the plankton forms in North American lakes and streams are identical with those in Europe and other continents, and many more are closely related species. This is said to hold not only for the continents but also for the oceanic islands. Certain things must be made clear at the outset of this discussion: (1) It must be understood that not *all* fresh-water plankton is alike the world over; such is not the case. (2) Plankton literature contains many records of species from large geographical regions which have not been reported from other regions. (3) Certain groups of plankton organisms may show less cosmopolitanism than others, e.g., the desmids; but even in this group, most species are cosmopolitan. (4) Cosmopolitanism seems to be more marked in the plankton of typical lakes with considerable open water, although exceptions occur, such as in the small bog lakes. (5) Since environmental selection is an active influence among plankton organisms, similar waters must be compared if cosmopolitanism is sought. (6) Absence of cosmopolitanism may be (*a*) real, made known in thoroughly investigated waters; or (*b*) apparent, a possible result of incomplete information. (7) The essence of this cosmopolitanism rests in the striking occurrence, sometimes predominance, of the same or closely related species in similar situations in the other continents, a condition which appears to be unparalleled in all other organic communities either on land or in marine waters. This applies to many of the groups of both fresh-water phytoplankton and zooplankton.

Among the groups of organisms which furnish so many species common to the fresh waters of the whole world are the diatoms; blue-green Algae; green Algae; Protozoa, particularly the Mastigophora; rotifers; copepods; and Cladocera. As illustrative of this situation, the distribution of the rotifers has been described by Jennings (1918) as follows:

Studies on the rotifers of Europe, Asia, Africa, America, and Australia show not different faunas in these regions but the same common rotifers found everywhere, with merely a new form here and there, and it is an extraordinary fact that when a new rotifer is described from Africa or Australia, its next occurrence is often recorded from Europe or America. In stagnant swamps all over the world appear to be found the characteristic rotifers of stagnant water; in clear lake water are found the characteristic limnetic rotifers; in sphagnum swamps everywhere, the sphagnum rotifers. Variation in the rotifer fauna of different countries is probably due mainly to differences in the conditions of existence in the waters of these countries, rather than to any difficulty in passing from one country to another.[1]

Work on tropical lakes (Ruttner, 1931) has yielded a similar story. In the lakes of Java and Sumatra were found the same species of *Cyclops*, the same Cladocera, and the same rotifers as occur in Central European lakes. Certain other groups showed the same cosmopolitanism.

Deviations from this cosmopolitanism may take the form of (1) absence of certain plankton types, such as is said to occur in the high arctic zone; (2) plankton species restricted to limited areas; (3) special plankton components in certain situations, such as the remarkable diatom plankton said to occur in the large African lakes; (4) restricted cosmopolitanism, such as the occurrence of numerous species of Cladocera in southern United States and also in South America but absent in the northern States; (5) absence of cosmopolitanism in certain groups; for example, of the 46 species of the genus *Diaptomus* (Copepoda) known for North America, 43 are restricted to the Western Hemisphere, and but 1 North American species (*D. marshi*) has been recorded from South America (Marsh, 1929).

Space cannot be given here to the great mass of detailed information relating to the numerous species which manifest this striking cosmopolitan distribution. The reader may find more than passing interest in knowing

---

[1] Reprinted by permission from "Fresh-water Biology," by Ward and Whipple. John Wiley & Sons, Inc.

that the familiar *Ceratium hirundinella* occurs from the Arctic regions, where it is free and pelagic for only a few weeks of the year, to the warm, constantly open waters of the tropics where it is perennial; that the easily recognized entomostracans *Cyclops serrulatus, Daphnia longispina, Bosmina longirostris,* and the rotifers *Polyarthra trigla (platyptera)* and *Filinia (Triarthra) longiseta* are merely a few of the plankton inhabitants of American lakes which inhabit fresh waters from the arctics to the tropics, the world over.

Explanations offered to account for this cosmopolitanism are distinctly hypothetical. It will suffice here to state that some of them are based upon the contention that the fresh-water plankton is one of the oldest communities on the earth; others depend upon a claim that fresh-water plankters show an almost unexcelled elasticity and adaptability to various and to varying environmental conditions.

Origin of Fresh-water Plankton. Like many phylogenetic questions, the *ancient origin* of fresh-water plankton rests in the realm of speculation. According to one theory, fresh-water plankton is a very ancient derivative of the primitive ocean, and certain evidences seem to support this view. However, the literature is not without suggestion that life arose in the small, shallow waters where certain postulated electrical disturbances or complex chemical reactions, thought necessary to the origin of living from nonliving matter, would supposedly be more strongly felt than in the great water masses of the oceans. The latter conception might be construed to suggest that ancient fresh water was the original environment for life. On the other hand, if the ancient oceanic origin of plankton be accepted for the moment, the question still remains as to the chemical nature of the original seas. It is supposed by some geologists that the ancient oceans were very much less saline than at present; that the salinity has been gradually increasing through the ages by the accretion of salts added to them from the land masses. Attempts have been made to show that while the general chemical composition of primeval sea water was essentially the same as it is today, the concentration of salts was very much less. In fact, it has been hinted that the primitive oceans were essentially fresh water, a conception that would derive life from fresh-water conditions. It has been argued that while, in time, the ancient oceans may have acquired inorganic salts, provisions for supplying the organic nitrogen were necessary for the rise of a biota and that certain primitive nitrogen-fixing bacteria were probably the first organisms to be evolved. Nitrogen-fixing bacteria are numerous in modern fresh waters, although not confined to them.

All of the simplest types of Protozoa occur in fresh water; in fact, it is contended by some that the entry of the fresh waters by the primitive Protozoa occurred before the subclasses of that phylum had been evolved, and it has been regarded as possible that the whole phylum may have had a fresh-water origin.

If, as has been supposed, the primitive inland waters and most primitive ocean waters were similar in chemical content, then the two classes of water have been gradually diverging in character with the passing ages. If the evidence that the fresh-water plankton is among the oldest communities on the earth is dependable, then the various ancestral components of the present-day fresh-water plankton may have found their way into the inland waters during the early ages when conditions of contrast between the two kinds of water were so slight as to constitute no barrier to migration from one to the other. Since the plankton occupies such an important position in the food cycle of aquatic organisms, its appearance in the primitive fresh waters must have preceded the advent of the higher aquatic animals.

Considerable speculation has centered about the question as to the original entrance route of plankton into fresh waters. The following theories might be mentioned:

1. An old theory proposed the ancient entrance of plankton into fresh waters from the tropical regions, a theory which apparently has little modern support.

2. A polar origin for fresh-water plankton has had, and apparently is still having, some serious consideration. This theory stresses salinity effects, postulating that in the arctic region plankton types would become more accustomed to the wide variations of salinity, due to alternate freezing and thawing of the water, while at the same time continually low temperatures minimize chemical effects. In addition, it is claimed that many of the European fresh-water species have very close "Nordic" affinities, indicating a Nordic origin of the fresh-water plankton, although it has been stated that there are no convincing instances of present-day immigration of arctic forms into European fresh water near the arctic fringe. Associated with this theory is the proposal that certain evidences indicate a separate origin for the arctic and the antarctic fresh-water stocks. Certain adherents to the general theory have regarded the whole fresh-water plankton as an assemblage of forms which immigrated into the inland fresh-water lakes from the Arctic Sea during the ice age.

3. Another theory holds essentially that

. . . the fresh-water plankton could be designated as bottom and littoral forms which have adapted themselves more or less to pelagic life and made themselves independent of bottom and bank where the great majority still pass a shorter or longer period of their life (as resting stages). The home of the fresh-water plankton is to be found on the bottom and in the littoral region of the lakes whence it is still recruited to this very day.[1]

[1] Wesenberg-Lund, 1926.

In connection with this theory, it is contended that the fresh-water plankton greatly antedated the ice age; that while during the ice age the fresh-water plankton may have been driven out of vast areas of its former distribution, it repossessed the old areas after the ice disappeared. Therefore, the influence of the ice age on the history of the fresh-water plankton community has been but a transient one, according to this theory. It has also been contended that the fresh-water plankton is not homologous with the marine plankton; that much of the fresh-water plankton is closely related to the littoral and bottom forms; and that some organisms which are bottom forms in lakes poor in calcium, nitrogen, and phosphorus are plankton forms in lakes containing larger amounts of these substances.

In the production and maintenance of a standing crop of lake plankton, various sources may be involved. The principal ones are: (1) Many species may be open-water forms, developing and reproducing continuously *in situ.* (2) Inflowing water from plankton-producing tributaries may make both qualitative and quantitative additions. (3) Certain organisms occupying the margins, the littoral zone, and the bottom may become plankters. Some workers have claimed that this is the major source of plankton. (4) Various components of the periphyton automatically released into the water or washed off the supports by water movements become a part of the plankton (Young, 1945). For a discussion of the sources of plankton in streams, see Chap. XVII.

HORIZONTAL DISTRIBUTION OF PLANKTON

Lack of Uniformity. One of the principal, well-established facts concerning horizontal distribution of plankton is its irregularity when any area of fair size is considered. Earlier in the history of plankton investigations, it was assumed that, in those areas of the sea in which environmental conditions were essentially the same, the plankton distribution was uniform, an assumption now known to be without basis in either marine or fresh waters. The discovery of this irregularity in horizontal distribution revolutionized certain of the methods of studying plankton. This lack of uniformity extends not only to large areas but also often to relatively small lakes and regions of lakes. In fact, it is imperative to avoid an assumption of uniformity in any area of water. Uniformity is not an impossibility, but it is not the common condition in nature and may be rare. This irregularity involves both the phytoplankton and the zooplankton, although, according to certain investigators, the phytoplankton appears to have a more uniform distribution, in general, than does the zooplankton; also, the zooplankton may show great irregularities which have not been correlated with any variations in the amount of phytoplankton or in the chemical and physical features of the environment.

Causes of Irregularity. *Wind Action.* One of the most common causes of irregularity in horizontal distribution is the wind acting upon surface waters. As is well known, wind not only causes waves but in addition may produce an actual drift of the upper waters. Under certain conditions of drifting water, plankton organisms become concentrated temporarily in the vicinity of the shore which faces into the wind at that time. Such plankton drifts are common in many lakes in summer. Sometimes such a plankton drift, particularly where it meets the shore, becomes so thick that the whole water is altered in color and general appearance. Small bays or coves may become the concentration grounds for surface-water plankton at such times. The writer has witnessed many times veritable windrows of plankton at the water's edge, the main drift being more than one-fourth mile long, many feet wide, and as concentrated as it would seem possible, while beyond this main drift near shore thick accumulations extended much farther out into the lake, diminishing in concentration with the increasing distances from shore. Accumulations of *Gloeotrichia, Anabaena,* and certain other phytoplankton appear in small coves and in boat slips and in such concentrations that the whole water to considerable depths is not only a dense blue-green color but is also distinctly sluggish from its massed content. Surface-water movements all tend to disturb uniformity of distribution, but it appears that these vast shoreward accumulations occur most frequently as the result of a steady but gentle shoreward water drift, rather than the more violent wave actions.

The general effect of such plankton drift is to concentrate, more or less, the plankton of the upper waters throughout one part of a lake with corresponding thinning on the opposite side. Obviously, plankton sampling in the region of the exposed shore would yield results much in excess of the general average for the lake; a sample from the opposite region would be below normal. Under such condition, the closer to the exposed shore the sample is taken the greater the error in the direction of a false magnitude. While the plankton of the uppermost waters is most affected by water drift, it should not be overlooked that surface-water drift may be producing return currents or drift below the shearing plane and just above the thermocline with possibilities of disturbing the distribution of plankton at those levels.

Plankton drifts due to wind action are always temporary, practically all of the accumulations spreading back over the lake when the wind dies down or changes its direction. On occasion, portions of the drift in contact with the shore become washed upon the beach where the plankton may disintegrate. Some of it may get worked into the inner beach materials where it remains moist and continues to live for a time.

Inflowing Streams. Inflowing surface drainage usually produces one or more of several effects, as follows:

1. Increase of plankton, quantitatively, qualitatively, or both, in the region surrounding the mouth of an inflowing stream. Under special circumstances, certain inflowing, sluggish, plant-filled streams may of themselves be greater plankton producers than the lake into which they flow; or they may be in the form of very short, direct outlets of other adjacent lakes which are more productive in plankton. The effect is to pour plankton into the receiving lake. Plankton samples taken opposite the mouths of such drainage yield results which exceed the average for the lake. Such a region is, of course, subject to the plankton variations inherent in the drainage system itself.

2. Dilution. Inflowing water from streams more often bears a scantier plankton than the water into which it flows, thus producing a condition of dilution in the plankton population of the lake water opposite the mouth of the stream. Systems of streams, particularly those which do not drain standing-water units of any sort, usually yield small plankton crops. Many river systems, especially the swifter ones, have been reported as producing very little plankton compared with the standing waters into which they flow.

3. Qualitative variations. Inflowing streams sometimes bring into a lake, regularly or at intervals, plankters which may not ordinarily flourish in the lake receiving them.

4. Physicochemical alteration of the water. The entry of water markedly different, chemically and physically, may deliver plankters not normal to the lake. It may also eliminate locally some of the plankters normal to the lake water.

Irregularity of Shore Line. Irregularities of horizontal distribution may result from a shore line which produces various bays or coves, sufficiently protected to provide better conditions for developing plankton than does the open water, i.e., regions where not only is plankton abundantly produced but in which successive generations of plankters can pile up, producing a greater concentration of plankton population. Such semiinclosed waters may have sufficient protection against the general circulation of the open water to form a more or less permanent region of denser plankton.

Depth of Water. For reasons not well understood, depth of the water has an influence upon certain plankters. It has been shown that, in some situations and at certain seasons at least, growths of diatoms are much greater in the region of deep water than in the shallows. A few other organisms, including the young of some fishes, have been reported as exhibiting this phenomenon.

General Flowage Areas. General flowage areas, particularly shallow-water flowage, often alter horizontal distribution. Proximity of a main inlet to an outlet in the same lake and various other circumstances may produce the flowage of whole fields of surface water. Mass differences, streaked distribution, and other forms of plankton irregularity may be so produced.

Currents. Definite currents of any sort act in various ways to alter the general horizontal distribution. These streams within the lake often have a plankton concentration different from the neighboring, more stationary areas.

Undertow Currents. Undertow resulting from the piling up of waters on one shore by a sudden, vigorous wind may result in bringing about unequal concentrations of plankton.

Plankton Swarms. Oceanographers have often observed local concentrations, sometimes very striking, of certain plankton organisms. Such local aggregations may be so concentrated as to impart a definite color to the water. They also occur in lakes, although perhaps in less striking form. They may be the result of one of several different causes, such as certain peculiar forms of surface drift or the active migration of individuals of a species into a particularly favorable area or the rapid reproduction of a species in a specially favorable region or the tendency of certain forms to be gregarious. Such swarms may be produced by the enormous numerical dominance of a single plankter, such as certain Cladocera, Protozoa, and others. They have been described in inland waters as forming great bands or streaks or as arranged into areas of thick and thin concentrations, simulating cloud effects. As in the sea, they may give the water a strikingly different color in the region of the swarm. These swarms establish thick and thin areas and must be taken into account particularly in quantitative work.

Difference of opinion exists as to the relative significance of plankton swarms in diversifying the horizontal distribution of fresh-water plankton, some workers holding that the swarms are not frequent enough to produce serious lack of uniformity. However, there seems to be evidence that they are sufficiently common to necessitate taking them into account when plankton sampling is planned.

Action of Predators. Aggregations of plankton feeders may greatly reduce the prey locally. Thus, a swarm of predators may leave a wake in which the plankton is greatly depleted.

Indirect Results of Diurnal Migration. Diurnal migration, which will be discussed later (page 243), may contribute indirectly to an irregular horizontal distribution. Winds rising during the night drift the migrating plankters into shoal water, making it impossible for many of them to return to the depths with the oncoming of dawn. Thus trapped in surface water, they must wait for changed conditions in order to have a chance to return to the depths. In the meantime, they produce a temporary irregularity of horizontal distribution.

Concentrations of the limnetic plankton toward the center of a lake are said to occur at times in some situations, causing a diminution of these organisms in the peripheral areas. One explanation which has been offered to account for this phenomenon stresses the indirect effect of vertical distribution in the following way: Plankters which migrate vertically descend with the onset of dawn, those nearer the shore arriving at the bottom at a higher level, and, following down the slope of the basin in order to reach deeper water, tend to concentrate in the depths; on the next trip to the surface, they rise vertically from the profundal area, thus producing at the surface a greater concentration above the deep parts than above the peripheral regions.

General Consequences of Irregularity of Horizontal Distribution. Since there are so many different causes of irregular horizontal distribution, some of them operating simultaneously, the likelihood of a uniform distribution is slight. It has been shown that even in the Sargassa Sea, a region existing under circumstances which might seem ideal for producing uniform horizontal distribution of plankton, the variation may be considerable. It therefore behooves students of plankton to make, in their methods of sampling, proper recognition of this irregularity; otherwise, very serious errors are likely to occur.

In general, horizontal distribution of plankton and alterations in it are largely of a mechanical character and less concerned with profound environmental differences such as are involved in vertical distribution.

Vertical Distribution of Plankton

Since conditions change with increasing depth, some of which have a vital influence, the vertical distribution of plankton is a complicated matter. Various horizontal levels and strata, superimposed upon each other, may exhibit plankton populations (Fig. 31) which differ qualitatively, quantitatively, or both. If deeper regions are provided with a plankton at all, it may show little or no resemblance to that of the upper waters. Under circumstances to be mentioned later, definitely demarked stratifications and concentrations become established. Certain deep regions periodically become devoid of a true plankton, and the uppermost surface layer may, at times, have a very scanty one. In lakes of the second order, an approximation to a uniform vertical distribution of plankton occurs only during spring and fall overturns, after each of which the various stratifications in the vertical distribution are soon reestablished. Lakes of the third order may show a certain difference in vertical distribution at times of calm, although they are subject to a circulation by wind action

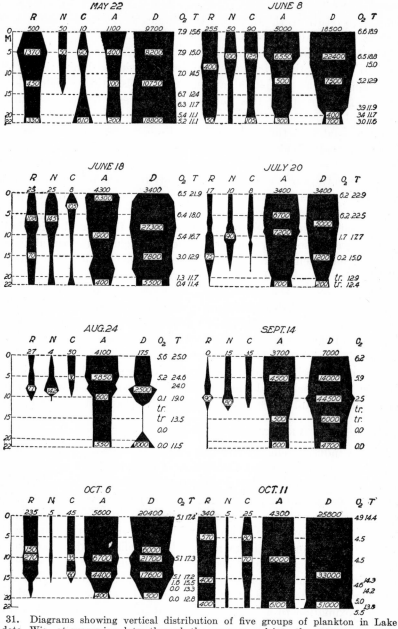

FIG. 31. Diagrams showing vertical distribution of five groups of plankton in Lake Mendota, Wis., at successive dates through the summer and into the autumn overturn, season of 1906. All quantities are expressed in numbers of plankton organisms per liter of lake water. The numerals set within black, vertical areas indicate the numbers of plankton organisms per liter at that level; those set just above the black areas indicate the numbers of plankton organisms per liter in the surface water. The black areas are all

which tends to mix the plankton uniformly. In addition to the general biological stratification which characterizes the total plankton, each plankter, as a rule, has its own level, indicated by the region of its maximum population. Certain plankters are distributed, in reduced or minimal quantities, from the surface to the lowermost limits of habitability, but somewhere in that range a concentration usually occurs. It does not follow, however, that the depth position of the concentration zone is the same in all lakes inhabited by the same organism. The more outstanding features of vertical distribution are presented in the following pages, although it must be understood that the discussion is a very general one.

Distribution of Phytoplankton. The demand by chlorophyll-bearing phytoplankton for sufficient effective light predetermines the depth to which they may be distributed in any lake. That depth, however, may not be attainable at certain times owing to the chemical stratification; e.g., in a very transparent lake, effective light may extend to considerable depths during the summer stagnation period, penetrating into the hypolimnion; but if the upper portions of the hypolimnion are devoid of oxygen and otherwise uninhabitable, the depth distribution is restricted to a smaller region. The uppermost waters are, then, the home of the chlorophyll-bearing plankton; but within this general zone, limitations impinge both from above and below, such as excess light and possibly other less favorable circumstances at the surface and encroachment of hypolimnion conditions from below. Considered from the point of view of general mass distribution, the following statements commonly hold:

1. The blue-green and the green phytoplankton (Myxophyceae and Chlorophyceae) usually have their maximum concentration at a higher

---

drawn to the same scale and are constructed quantitatively.

Abbreviations: R, rotifers; N, nauplii; C, Crustacea; A, Algae other than diatoms; D, diatoms; O_2, dissolved oxygen in cubic centimeters per liter; T, temperature in degrees centigrade; $tr.$, trace; M, depth in meters.

Qualitative changes: May 22—most abundant forms were *Tabellaria, Fragilaria, Cyclops, Keratella* (*Anuraea*) *aculeata, Keratella* (*Anuraea*) *cochlearis,* and *Notholca longispina.* June 8—predominant forms were *Aphanizomenon, Melosira, Keratella* (*Anuraea*) *cochlearis, Daphnia hyalina* in the upper 8 m. and *Cyclops* below that level. June 18—predominant forms were *Staurastrum, Fragilaria, Cyclops, Keratella* (*Anuraea*) *cochlearis* in the upper 10 m. and *Polyarthra* thence to the bottom. July 20—predominant forms were *Staurastrum, Fragilaria, Cyclops,* and *Keratella* (*Anuraea*) *cochlearis* which was responsible for the increased number of rotifers at 15 m. Aug. 24—predominant forms were *Ceratium, Staurastrum, Melosira, Keratella* (*Anuraea*) *cochlearis, Daphnia hyalina* in the upper 5 m. and *Cyclops* thence to the bottom. Sept. 14—predominant forms were *Microcystis, Melosira* (practically the only diatom), *Polyarthra* in the upper 7 m. and *Keratella* (*Anuraea*) *cochlearis* below this depth; Crustacea fairly evenly divided among the several species represented. Oct. 6—predominant forms were *Coelosphaerium, Melosira, Keratella* (*Anuraea*) *cochlearis* and *Cyclops.* Oct. 11—diagram shows the vertical distribution immediately after the autumn overturn; predominant forms were the same as on Oct. 6. (*Diagrams constructed from data taken from graphs of Birge and Juday, 1911.*)

level than do the diatoms. This result has been thought to be due to the heavier weight of the latter.

2. The maximum populations of the total chlorophyll-bearing phytoplankton are usually at some level below the surface stratum, although exceptions occur.

3. The blue-green Algae as a group tend to concentrate toward the surface.

Distribution of Zooplankton. It is difficult to generalize on the vertical distribution of the zooplankton as a whole, and the same is true of the various taxonomic groups composing the zooplankton, the controlling circumstances being so involved and so variable that general statements are scarcely possible. Certain tendencies in vertical distribution appear, such as (1) greater occurrence of the Sarcodina in lower waters; (2) preference of the Dinoflagellata for upper waters; (3) general scattering of the Ciliata; (4) selection of different levels by the young and adult stages of certain Crustacea; and others. However, there are so many departures from these statements that they can scarcely be used with any certainty in advance predictions as to the distribution in any water. The distribution behavior may be very different in different kinds of water. Under conditions of well-developed physicochemical stratification, the levels of maximum population of the Crustacea and the Rotifera often correspond very closely, although such a statement cannot be depended upon, since striking exceptions occur. Distribution, described only in terms of the larger groups of plankters, shifts with the season; and correlations existing between two or more groups may disappear later. Cold-water forms tend to keep to the deeper, colder water unless forced upward by encroachments of the oxygenless zone.

Relation to Physical and Chemical Stratification. In lakes exhibiting physicochemical stratification, vertical distribution of the plankton is profoundly affected by the various events of the stratification. During the overturns in temperate lakes of the second order, the plankton is usually distributed throughout the whole water mass. Progression of the characteristic events of the summer stagnation period is accompanied by a gradual reduction and sometimes a final disappearance of the plankton, in living form, from a part or all of the hypolimnion. On the other hand, striking concentrations and microstratifications sometimes form in the thermocline. In many lakes, the lowermost extent of living plankton, during the latter part of the summer stagnation period, is either the lowest limit of the thermocline or some level within it. Not infrequently, plankton disappears with striking abruptness at some level within the thermocline. In those lakes whose depth and surface-area relations are such that overturns are either absent or incomplete, bottom waters may be perpetually devoid of living, healthy plankton. In describing the deeper waters as devoid of plankton at certain times or under certain conditions, the possible occurrence of some kinds of bacteria should not be overlooked.

Vertical distribution during the winter stagnation period, following as it does a general, virtually uniform distribution during the fall overturn, develops certain similarities to that of the summer stagnation period. Typical thermocline influences are absent, and light relations are modified by ice and snow cover. Depth of effective light penetration is more restricted, and the chlorophyll-bearing plankters may be expected to occupy somewhat higher levels. Under conditions of prolonged ice cover, the whole plankton, in some instances at least, may ultimately be confined to a much thinner stratum of the uppermost waters than is occupied during the summer.

Concentration Zones and Depression Individuality. During periods of thermal and chemical stratification, certain plankters form distinct concentrations of the population at some particular depth. In some instances, the concentration zone may be broad; in others, strikingly thin. Unless care is taken to prevent it, thin concentration zones can be missed in plankton sampling, and since in such zones the population may be densely massed failure to sample it properly would result in serious errors. The depth, position, and thickness of concentration zones differ with the different plankters which form them. It appears that most if not all concentration zones are the result of conditions set up and maintained by physicochemical stratification; they are dispersed during the overturns and re-form with the onset of stratification. Since stratification conditions differ in different waters, it is inevitable that the concentration behavior of a given plankter is not a constant feature in all lakes.

In a multidepression temperate lake of the second order, concentration behavior of some plankters gives additional evidence of depression individuality (page 58). The concentration zone of a plankter may be very different in position and form in the different depressions within the same lake. One of the best contributions in this field is that of Campbell (1941) who found that in Douglas Lake, Michigan, rotifers respond to depression individuality in the following ways: (1) Concentration zones were established on different dates in the several depressions and also disappeared on different dates. (2) Depth positions, widths, and density of concentration zones varied among depressions on corresponding dates. (3) In winter, concentration zones occurred at different depths in different depressions.

Conditions Influencing Vertical Distribution. Among the influences which may operate in the production of various forms of vertical distribution, the following are important: (1) light; (2) food; (3) dissolved gases, principally oxygen, and other dissolved substances; (4) temperature; (5) wind; (6) gravity; and (7) age of individuals of a species.

Light. The various general effects of light have been treated in a previous section (page 170), and only passing reference is necessary here. That it is one of the most important factors in vertical distribution of plankton is well established. Its presence, for various reasons, tends to reduce, sometimes almost to disappearance, the plankton in the surface layer, while its absence, total or ineffective quality and quantity, eliminates the chlorophyll-bearing plankters and many others from the lowermost waters. The annual, diurnal, and other variations of the light, qualitative and quantitative, are potent influences in producing shifts, alterations, or migrations of plankton. These migrations and other forms of diurnal movement will be described in a later section (page 243). During the ice-cover period, the vertical distribution depends much upon the nature and thickness of the ice and upon the presence or absence of an additional snow cover. It has been found that important changes in the vertical position of many plankters can be produced by the removal of the snow which has accumulated on top of the ice, thus admitting more light. Surface water immediately below the ice cover may teem with plankters of various kinds.

Differences in the light reaction of the young and the adult stages of certain plankters lead to a different vertical distribution of the life-history stages in the same species. Instances of this phenomenon are said to be common among the plankton Crustacea, the adults of certain species responding negatively to light and seeking the deeper levels while the young are positively phototropic and occupy the upper waters.

Food. The explanation of certain facts of vertical distribution of plankton seems to involve the relation of food and eater; i.e., the distribution of the eater is determined to some extent by the distribution of its food. In the past, attempts have been made to explain concentrations of Protozoa, micro-Crustacea, and rotifers in the thermocline on the basis of the effect of the temporary checking of settling suspended materials in the thermocline (due to rapid changes in viscosity and density of the water), thus presumably producing a greater concentration of such materials at that level. This being assumed to be true, these substances, together with the included bacteria, would cause their eaters (Protozoa and others) to collect there, and these in turn would cause the Crustacea and rotifers to congregate there to feed upon the Protozoa and other substances. Similarly, the general occurrence of limnetic Algae in the upper waters doubtless has something to do with the distribution of the micro-Crustacea. As will be shown later, attempts have also been made to explain certain plankton migrations on the basis of the eaters' following the changes in position of their food.

In general, it may be stated that, ordinarily, a plankter should be most numerous where its food is most abundant, and vice versa, but the degree to which this food relation determines the habitual distribution of the eater is still a matter of some uncertainty. Furthermore, in the instance of some plankters, the food explanation fails completely. At best, it can be said at present only that it acts simultaneously with other regulating factors and with varying degrees of influence depending upon the plankton group involved.

Dissolved Gases and Other Substances. As pointed out elsewhere (page 125), chemical changes in bottom waters may lead to the development of inimical conditions. Disappearance of the dissolved oxygen is usually the most significant event, although other substances may play, in some lakes, an important part in rendering deeper waters partially or wholly uninhabitable for most of the common plankters. Some plankters are more sensitive than others to the accumulating results of decomposition in underlying waters, so that all which do not die retreat upward at the same rate, and a certain stratification may result. Nevertheless, chemical changes often progress to the lethal point for most or all pelagic plankton organisms, eventually eliminating them from certain underlying strata.

Temperature. Temperature acts both directly and indirectly in influencing vertical distribution of plankton. Direct effects are usually manifested through either (1) selection by some motile plankters of certain favorable temperatures or (2) inability of some nonmotile forms to exist in levels having certain temperatures. Such effects appear to apply only to those plankters which manifest sensitivity to differences in temperature, while apparently many plankters are not influenced at all by any of the vertical temperature differences within a lake. There appears to be good evidence that the temperature characteristics of the thermocline are important in determining the position of certain plankters.

Temperature acts indirectly in causing changes in the density and viscosity of water, such changes altering the flotation levels of those plankters which are delicately adjusted to flotation. It is also said to act indirectly in changing the sensitiveness to light of the limnetic Crustacea; higher temperature increases while lower temperature decreases this sensitivity, thus leading to different degrees of response.

Wind. Wind effect of any significant amount varies with the season. During the summer, it can influence directly only the epilimnion in which during hard blows it may make changes in the vertical distribution of the plankton. However, it is probable that such changes are not so extensive as has been supposed, since active forms, particularly the Crustacea, are to a considerable degree independent of such vertical currents as may be temporarily produced and, in fact, may respond negatively to them.

Furthermore, some of the nonmotile, floating phytoplankton show surprising resistance to such mechanical influences working toward changing their normal levels.   Wind-produced oscillations of the thermocline may cause corresponding changes in the vertical position of the different plankton strata.   During the autumn and the spring overturns, the wind may play a prominent part in disturbing plankton since the water is of the same density and viscosity throughout; is without any significant temperature gradients; circulation of the water is more extensive; the phytoplankton may be at maximum production and widely distributed through the water — these and other circumstances not necessary to list here make various plankters much more apt to be shifted vertically than they are in the summer.   During the period of ice cover, the disturbing influence of the wind is eliminated.   Wind action at any time may affect vertical distribution by keeping certain plankters, such as diatoms, either in flotation or suspended at a higher level.

Gravity.   Gravity relations are intimately involved in the vertical position of many plankters.   Certain phytoplankters, such as *Gloeotrichia*, occupy the surface waters because of a much reduced specific gravity; in fact, they are drawn out of flotation only by vigorous centrifuging.   On the other hand, many plankters, e.g., the pelagic Crustacea, are heavier than water and sink with appreciable speed when momentarily inactive. *Daphnia* regularly maintain their position in water in the following way: Short periods of immobility of the swimming appendages (antennae), during which the animal sinks at about the rate of 20 to 30 cm. per min., are terminated by abrupt resumption of a swimming period in which a few strokes of the antennae restore the animal to the former, higher level. Horizontal change of position by swimming interrupts the routine from time to time, but the alternate sinking and upward swimming are resumed immediately in the new location.   This relation demands a constant continuous expenditure of energy and is responsible for the statement that the animal has no opportunity to sleep.   Other Crustacea (*Diaptomus, Cyclops*, and others) manifest movements less regular than the daphnids but nevertheless must expend energy to maintain their positions.   As the individuals (*Daphnia, Cyclops*) become older and larger, the energy-expenditure demand becomes greater with the result that these older, and sometimes feebler, individuals tend gradually to sink while the younger individuals remain behind.   The sinking rate of newly hatched daphnids is said to be less than one-third as great as that of adults; therefore, less energy is required for maintenance of position against gravity.   Certain other plankton Crustacea (*Diaptomus, Diaphanosoma*), which seldom show this form of sinking, may escape this fate because of the development of a considerable amount of fat within their bodies, thus providing greater flotation.

Age of Individuals of a Species. Reference has already been made to the fact that distinct differences may exist between the young and the adults of certain plankters with respect to their vertical distribution. This phenomenon is perhaps best represented among the plankton Crustacea, some of the important facts of which are as follows:

1. As a general rule, young individuals of a species occur near the surface.

2. The annual spring increase of Crustacea appears in the uppermost water stratum where the population is composed of juvenile forms.

3. Adult individuals tend to sink into deeper strata.

4. Nauplii (Copepoda) do not seem to conform to the rule of age mentioned above but often occur in greatest number in the general vicinity of the thermocline.

Other instances of age effect on vertical distribution will be described subsequently in connection with the subject of diurnal plankton movement.

Diurnal Movements of Plankton. One of the most striking phenomena manifested by plankton is the diurnal, vertical migration of certain prominent plankters. Such movements occur both in the seas and in lakes. They have been the subject of numerous investigations and, while many facts have been accumulated, there still remain features about which information is absent or scanty or about which results of research are in conflict.

Plankters Manifesting Diurnal Movements. In inland waters the plankton Crustacea comprise very largely the species which exhibit diurnal movements. Such movements are widespread among the Cladocera and the Copepoda. Certain rotifers manifest diurnal movement, but apparently the group as a whole is little concerned in these migrations. The larvae of one insect (*Corethra*) perform these movements in a striking way. Diatoms, flagellates, and other organisms with weak locomotion have been observed to manifest diurnal movement but are restricted to narrow limits.

Nature and Extent of Diurnal Movements. Diurnal movements differ greatly under the various environmental conditions and with the various species involved. The following statements indicate, in part, reasons for the lack of uniformity in diurnal movements:

1. Lakes differ widely in their inherent environmental conditions.

2. The various plankters are not equally affected by factors which stimulate and govern these migrations.

3. Close kinship of plankters does not insure similarity of performance.

4. Representatives of any one species do not necessarily behave in the same way in different waters.

5. Nauplii and other juvenile stages may exhibit a performance distinctly different from that of adults of the same species.

An examination of the literature dealing with the whole subject of the summer diurnal movements of plankton in various kinds of lakes and in different geographical situations indicates that certain reasonably distinct types of movement are recognizable of which the following are probably the most important:

Type 1.   A certain portion of a plankter population spreads out into the upper layers of water during the night, producing a more extensive vertical distribution without involving any general upward movement of the whole population.   During the day, the migrating individuals desert the upper waters.   The result is, therefore, a concentration of the population into a more restricted stratum during the day and an extension of the vertical range during the night with corresponding quantitative thinning of the whole population.

Type 2.   Certain plankter populations as a whole migrate to a region at or near the surface at night, returning to the deep water during the day.

Type 3.   Certain plankters characteristic of the hypolimnion show some upward movement at night but find the thermocline a limiting obstacle.

Type 4.   The main body of certain plankter populations manifest little diurnal movement, but a few individuals migrate to the surface waters at night, returning to the deeper water during the day.

Type 5.   Certain plankters come to the surface both at dawn and at twilight but occupy the deeper waters during both the day and the night intervals.

Type 6.   Some species occupy the surface waters in the afternoon but show a distinct downward movement at night.

Type 7.   The adults of certain plankters remain near the surface both day and night, but the juvenile stages migrate into deeper water at dawn.

Type 8.   The young of certain plankters have the usual form of migration, being at or near the surface at night and occupying the bottom waters during the day, while the adult stages manifest the reverse movement, inhabiting the surface waters during the day and the lower waters at night.

It must be clearly understood that in different lakes and under different circumstances, the performance of a single plankter may represent more than one of the types of movement mentioned above.   Likewise, it must be understood that, under certain circumstances, some plankters may be more or less evenly distributed in their particular vertical range and exhibit no recognizable diurnal movement at all.

So complicated are the conditions which determine the performances of migrating plankters that it is difficult to find criteria on which to base dependable predictions as to just what form of diurnal movement a selected plankter will show in an uninvestigated lake.   With knowledge of these phenomena still incomplete, the only safe procedure is to make an actual examination of any new situation.

Vertical diurnal movement, when present, varies greatly in extent, even in lakes having considerable depth. Certain plankters may exhibit a movement of only a fraction of a meter; another plankter in the same lake and at the same season may perform a migration equal to the maximum depth of the lake; while still others move over distances between these two extremes.

No rule, applicable to lakes in general, can be laid down concerning the time of the greatest concentration of plankters at the surface due to the vertical movement, except that it appears that such concentrations occur at night. Published records differ widely as to the period of the night when maximum numbers occur in surface waters, owing, evidently, to the fact that differences in lakes and their contained plankton populations produce a variety of results. In some lakes, the maximum abundance in the surface waters is said to occur late in the night; in others, the maximum appears in the early part of the night. Situations more or less dominated by a movement of the kind described as type 5 are said to have two intervals of maximum concentration, one in early evening and the other in early morning.

In some lakes, perhaps in many, the order of reaching the surface by various migrating plankters is a fairly definite one, at least for the Crustacea; the order of leaving the surface at dawn is essentially the reverse of the order of arrival in surface waters in the evening.

Some Common Examples of Diurnal Movements. CORETHRA PUNCTIPENNIS (Culicidae, Diptera). A common inhabitant of lakes in central North America is *Corethra* (= *Chaoborus*) *punctipennis.* The larvae and pupae are aquatic and, during the summer time, often exhibit a striking form of diurnal movement. During the day, the full-grown larvae occupy the bottom mud in the deepest water, while the younger larvae inhabit the water just above the bottom. With the coming of twilight, some of the larvae, both young and full grown, migrate toward the surface, commonly beginning to arrive there about an hour after sunset and continuing to arrive for some time thereafter. Throughout the night, the surface water may teem with them. Not all of the larvae migrate from the bottom regions, roughly one-half to two-thirds of the population remaining there. Just before sunrise, they begin to desert the surface waters, in some instances practically disappearing from the upper 15 m. in a period of 20 min.

It is interesting to note that the larvae of a close relative, *Corethra plumicornis,* exhibit, in some lakes at least, a curious departure from the performance of *C. punctipennis;* viz., during the day, approximately as many larvae are at the surface as at the bottom so that, the day distribution of *C. plumicornis* larvae is essentially that of the night distribution of *C. punctipennis.*

LEPTODORA KINDTII (Cladocera, Crustacea). This remarkable, transparent cladoceran, limnetic in the lakes of northern United States, migrates into the surface waters at night, arriving there, often in great numbers, from one to two hours after sunset, and disappears into the deeper waters before sunrise. That this performance is not an invariable one is indicated by the reported occurrence in parts of certain river systems of considerable numbers of this crustacean in surface waters during the day. There is also evidence that in other situations where the water is both clear and shallow, it buries itself in the mud during the day.

DAPHNIA LONGISPINA (Cladocera, Crustacea). This cladoceran is an almost world-wide component of lake plankton and has been studied by workers in several continents. In a typical, temperate, deep lake it commonly behaves as follows: Both young and full-grown individuals spend the after part of the night near the surface but descend during the day into the depths remote from the surface. In some situations at least, the thermocline seems to have no effect. A very similar migration occurs in some tropical lakes, such as Victoria Nyanza. In certain Wisconsin lakes, the range of vertical migration of *D. longispina var. hyalina* is from 0.2 to 7 m., although the depths of the lakes are distinctly greater. It has been reported that in Lough Derg, Ireland, the young of *D. longispina* have the usual migration, being at or near the surface during the night and near the bottom during the day but that, strangely enough, the adults perform a reverse type of migration, being in the strongly lighted waters during the day and in the deeper waters during the night. From Japanese lakes and elsewhere come reports that this daphnid is restricted to the hypolimnion; that it tends to move upward during the night; but that not a single individual occurs above the thermocline. It appears that the various *forms* of *D. longispina*, of which there are many, may differ in migration behavior; for example, it was found that in a certain Wisconsin lake the form having rounded crests or helmets did not show diurnal movement, while that form with pointed crests showed such movement; in another lake containing both forms, the migration behavior was exactly the reverse; in still another lake containing both forms, both manifested diurnal movement.

OTHER ENTOMOSTRACA. Among the plankton Crustacea, the following common, widespread species exhibit diurnal movements, at least in some lakes and under certain conditions. The lists are not intended to be complete; there are many other such examples:

Cladocera: *Daphnia retrocurva, Daphnia pulex, Diaphanosoma brachyurum, Bosmina longirostris,* and *Polyphemus.*

Copepoda: *Epischura lacustris, Limnocalanus macrurus,* certain species of *Diaptomus,* and *Cyclops.*

Rotatoria: *Keratella (Anuraea) cochlearis, Ploesoma truncatum,* and others.

Seasonal Differences in Diurnal Movements. This subject is in such an incomplete and confused state that any attempt to construct a condensed, consistent summary of what is known about it is most baffling. That the diurnal movements of some plankters are influenced by the succession of seasons in temperate regions seems to have been demonstrated, but the modifications are very diverse in different lakes and different species. Some of the findings seem to be contradictory. It has been claimed that with the advance of winter conditions the center of population of certain plankters rises toward the surface and then the diurnal movements become restricted to a narrower range during the winter. Certain species of *Daphnia* are said to behave in this way in some lakes. Cessation of diurnal movement in the plankton Crustacea has been reported in certain European lakes during that part of summer in which there is the greatest heating of the water, resumption of the diurnal movements occurring only when the temperature of the water has dropped to a lower level. Plew and Pennak (1949) made a year-round study of the vertical movements of zooplankters in an Indiana lake and found that the copepods (*Cyclops bicuspidatus, Diaptomus birgei,* and nauplii), one Cladocera (*Daphnia longispina*), and one rotifer (*Kellicottia longispina*) show diurnal movements at all seasons; that the amplitude of diurnal movements was much greater in winter than in summer; and that the general population of *Diaptomus birgei* exhibited a slow seasonal drift upward into the surface waters starting in autumn and then reversed this drift beginning in the spring. These are but samples of the many published conclusions.

Speed of Diurnal Movements. Since, in some instances, the diurnal movement of certain plankters covers a large vertical distance, it is a matter of interest to know the speed at which the ascent and descent are made. This speed differs with (1) different plankters, (2) different environmental circumstances, and (3) age of the individual plankter. A satisfactory understanding of the speed of this movement depends upon the determination of (*a*) time of departure from the lowermost position and the time of arrival at the uppermost position, (*b*) distance covered, and (*c*) rate of movement in different parts of the journey. If it is true, as claimed, that certain plankters (Cladocera) do not swim directly in a vertical direction in this diurnal movement but, instead, arrive at their destinations by a diagonal path, then the distance traversed is greater than the depth of the water in a vertical direction. The many computations recorded in the literature show a wide variety of rates of movement. Table 20, taken from one of the most recent contributions on this subject, indicates the speed of diurnal movement of some of the plankton Crustacea in Lake Lucerne, Switzerland.

Influence of Age on Diurnal Movements. The young and adult stages of some plankters behave differently in diurnal migration (Table 20; also Fig. 32). No consistent difference occurs for all plankters showing this feature. The difference in behavior between adult and young sometimes is characteristic for a particular species and may or may not be duplicated in another plankter. This age effect seems to appear frequently in the plankton Crustacea, although it occurs elsewhere, e.g., in the larvae of *Corethra.* Inconsistencies of behavior occur within the same group of

TABLE 20. SPEED OF MOVEMENT OF LAKE LUCERNE PLANKTON
From Worthington

Organism	Extent of migra- tion, m.	Speed of descent, 1 m. in	Speed of ascent	
			Noon till dusk, 1 m. in	Dusk onward, 1 m. in
Daphnia longispina, adults..	10–40	5 min.	25 min.	6.3 min.
D. longispina, young.......	5–60	3.1 min.	17.5 min.	4.3 min.
Bosmina coregoni, adults....	15–15	No movement		
B. coregoni, young.........	7–55	4.5 min.	26 min.	7.5 min.
Diaphanosoma brachyurum..	3–10	10 min.	No movement	12 min.
Diaptomus gracilis, adults...	13–30	12 min.	60 min.	15 min.
D. gracilis, young..........	20–37	20 min.	60 min.	12 min.
D. laciniatus, adults........	25–75(?)	4.6 min.	14 (?) min.	8 min.
D. laciniatus, young........	22–58	4.4 min.	28 min.	8 min.
Cyclops strenuus, young.....	12–46	7 min.	60 min.	5.5 min.
C. leuckarti, adults.........	3–15	20 min.	105 min.	12 min.

plankters in different waters; e.g., Maloney and Tressler (1942) found that in Caroga Lake, New York, in August, nauplii of Copepoda showed no definite diurnal movement, and Pennak (1944) likewise detected no vertical movements of nauplii in five northern Colorado mountain lakes in late summer; but Plew and Pennak (1949) report that in a lake in Indiana nauplii showed diurnal movements throughout the year. Any study of diurnal movements in plankton must make certain that the performance of juvenile forms is not overlooked.

Influence of Sex on Diurnal Movements. The different sexes in some plankters may show a different performance in diurnal movements. This has been reported in both marine and inland-water plankters. These sex differences are still too imperfectly known to make possible a satisfactory analysis. In some instances it has been reported that in certain species and under some circumstances the females of the plankter concerned are the more active migrant. On the other hand, Pennak (1944) found no sex differences in the diurnal movements of Cladocera in certain Colorado mountain lakes.   However, in studies of diurnal migrations, the possibility of sex differences should not be overlooked.

Character of Diurnal Movements.   Far too little is known concerning the kind of path described by the various plankters in the performance of

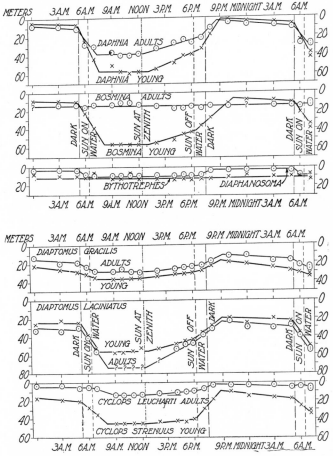

FIG. 32. Graphs showing average diurnal movements of Cladocera and Copepoda in Lake Lucerne, Switzerland in September.   Note difference in the behavior of young and adults of the same species.   (*Modified from Worthington, 1931.*)

diurnal movements.   It is too often assumed that it is a vertical path except as the plankters may be swung out of line by movements of the water, especially near the surface.   Grover and Coker (1940) report indications of a diurnal *horizontal* migration.   However, in some groups at least (Cladocera) the ascending movement is a zigzag one and in a diagonal direction, the angle of the path with the perpendicular depending upon the form of the body and upon the swimming position of the major body axis.   It has recently been found that large *Daphnia* narcotized to eliminate all voluntary movements sink steadily in water at the rate of about 1 m. in 200 sec.   Small *Daphnia*, having much greater surface resistance compared with their volume, sink more slowly.   When these sinking rates are compared with calculations of the actual descent rate of the young active forms in water under normal conditions, it appears that the descent is not a passive sinking but must involve an active downward swimming.

Causes of Diurnal Movements.   The causes of diurnal movements are but partly understood.   Various hypotheses have been proposed, and evidence accumulated in their support, but none has thus far been adequate as a general explanation.   Diurnal migration even within a single species may be difficult to account for when it is found that the behavior of individuals of the same species differs in different lakes.   The different behavior of species in different situations has already been discussed.   It is neither possible nor desirable to review here all of the various attempted explanations; therefore, only a brief account of the present status of this subject will follow.   The reader is referred to the papers of Juday (1904), Russell (1927), Rose (1925), Worthington (1931), Clarke (1933), and others for greater detail.

The best work on this subject indicates rather definitely that not one factor but several factors interact in the production of some, and probably all, forms of diurnal movement.   The principal factors involved appear to be light, temperature, food, and gravity.   It is also possible that still other factors may sometimes influence the reactions.

It seems reasonably certain that light is the most important factor in most forms of diurnal movement, but it is not known whether the response is due to *intensity per se* or to *change* of intensity.   Rise to the upper waters in the evening and descent into deeper waters in the morning coincide with the diurnal light rhythm.   Responses to light changes of less magnitude than those of day and night are found in some of the Crustacea which occur nearer the surface on cloudy days or which may occupy the upper waters on a cloudy day in almost as great a concentration as at night, while totally absent from the upper stratum on a bright, clear day.   Other Crustacea, however, may not show themselves so sensitive to the light changes of cloudy and clear skies.

According to one current theory, each species has its own optimum light intensity to which it will always migrate when possible.   As light declines during the afternoon, the plankter follows this optimum intensity toward the surface.   With the advent of night, the light intensity falls far below this optimum, and, according to this explanation, the stimulus for upward migration being this eliminated, the organism is free to **go** where it will, possibly becoming evenly distributed throughout its diurnal vertical range. With the onset of the following day, this postulated optimum light intensity, appearing first at the surface and then gradually to lower and lower levels, causes a retreat into the deeper water, ultimately reestablishing the more restricted day range of the species. This hypothesis, originally proposed to explain the diurnal movements of certain marine plankters, has been thought by some to hold for some plankters of fresh water. Worthington (1931) tested it in connection with his studies of the vertical movements of the fresh-water macroplankton in Lake Lucerne, Switzerland, and Victoria Nyanza, Africa, and found the following weaknesses: (1) Descent of the migrating plankters is completed well before the sun reaches its zenith; (2) the main upward movement does not start until dusk and continues for several hours after darkness prevails; and (3) there is very little tendency to a random distribution during the late hours of darkness. Other objections to the theory that this movement is purely a light reaction appear, such as (1) the lack, at least in some waters, of a direct relation between the transparency of the water and the depth to which the migrating plankters descend during the day; (2) the fact that certain plankters may leave the surface waters as much as 2 hr. or more before sunrise, at a time when there is little if any increase of the light over the average darkness condition of that particular night; and (3) moonlight is said to have no appreciable effect on the vertical movement of plankton Crustacea. These and other difficulties indicate that while light may be a very important influence in producing diurnal movements, it is conditioned by other factors operating simultaneously in the same environment.

Certain attempts to account for diurnal movements as purely temperature phenomena, resulting from changes in viscosity of the water brought about by temperature changes of day and night, have failed owing largely to the fact that temperature-viscosity changes so often do not correspond with movements of the plankters nor are they always of sufficient magnitude. It seems well established that temperature cannot be regarded as either the direct or the indirect cause of diurnal movement. However, it has been definitely shown, both in field work and in laboratory experimentation, that temperature conditions may affect the nature of light response, one important modification being that a high temperature increases the negative phototropism while a low temperature lessens or even reverses it.

Explanations of diurnal movements on the basis of food relations are founded largely upon the fact that the phytoplankton is most abundant near the surface, thus making such a region rich in food for the migrating forms. The movement of some plankters toward the surface and out of regions in which the food is nearly, if not fully, as abundant as at the surface; occupancy of or movement into regions of greatly reduced food; and other phenomena seem to cast doubt on this explanation.

That response to gravity (geotropism) may be involved in the causes of diurnal movement seems to have some basis. Existence of a geotropism has been demonstrated experimentally, and field observations seem to yield confirmatory evidence. In fact, it has been claimed (Dice, 1914), for example, that the diurnal movements of *Daphnia pulex* are caused chiefly by variations in geotropism induced by changes in light intensity. Increase of light intensity is said to produce a tendency to positive geotropism in some plankters, while a decrease in light intensity results in a tendency to negative geotropism. Temperature also affects this geotropism, high temperatures producing a tendency to positive geotropism and low temperatures a tendency to negative geotropism.

One proposal is that of Worthington (1931) which explains diurnal movements on the interaction of geotropism and heliotropism (phototropism).

The organisms may be regarded as being under the influence of two forces: (1) a negative geotropism, acting persistently from below and causing them to congregate in the upper layers; and (2) a negative heliotropism, acting intermittently from above and causing those species which are susceptible to light to descend during the day. Light forces them down into the lower layers during the morning; after midday, they are free to move upward slowly; but it is not until dusk that negative geotropism has full sway and the organisms start their main upward movement. . . . It is only those organisms which are not capable of adapting themselves completely to changing light intensity *in situ* that must migrate downwards during the day. But why is it that they should prefer the upper water layers and should go to the astonishing expense of energy of swimming upward against gravity through some 50 m. of water every evening? . . . Most species are filter feeders, dependent upon the nannoplankton, which is most abundant in the upper layers; it is suggested, therefore, that hunger is the ulterior reason why they should seek the upper layers. Thus, those species which are less susceptible to light . . . have an advantage in that they spend much more of their time in their food regions.

It will be seen from the foregoing discussion that the diurnal movement of plankton organisms is not a simple phenomenon but is rather one which involves the interaction of several factors, the relative importance of each varying with the particular circumstances operative in different kinds of waters. That the causative factors are environmental and not within the organisms seems certain. A physiological rhythm has been claimed for certain marine plankters which results in an upward and downward migration even after the effects of light and other stimuli are removed. Possibly, physiological rhythm occurs to some extent in certain fresh-water plankters, but such rhythm, if it really exists, may be merely a reflection of the periodic changes of the environment and possibly should be looked upon as a result rather than a cause.

Seasonal Distribution of Plankton

Qualitative Relations. Ordinary unmodified water existing under conditions of approximate biological equilibrium supports a plankton composed of a set of plants and animals, the individual components of which are usually present, somewhere in the water and in some life-history stage, throughout the year and during successive years. Certain plankters apparently disappear at certain periods and reappear during others. Such disappearance is, as a rule, only an apparent one, due to such phenomena as (1) existence of the species in such extremely small numbers of active individuals that plankton collections rarely show them; (2) existence of the species only in an encysted stage, in a resting egg, or in some other form of quiescence; and (3) intervals between broods or generations. The active plankton stage in the life cycle or in the seasonal cycle of a species may thus disappear temporarily from the plankton proper, although existing elsewhere in the same general environment. Under special circumstances, a true disappearance followed by a restocking of the species from some other source may occur, but such a condition is not common. At no time during the year is there an absence of all active plankters from the open water.

Quantitative Relations. *Total Volume of Plankton.* The total volume of plankton varies from season to season in all waters. The form and amount of the variation are not the same in all kinds of aquatic situations, but in the temperate lakes, particularly those of the first and second orders, the total annual production often takes the form of a bimodal curve presenting two maxima, one in the spring and one in the autumn, and two minima, one during the summer and the other during the winter (Fig. 33). This means that the greatest crops of plankton occur in spring and autumn and that the production reaches its lowest condition in late summer and late winter. While seasonal variations in different years may cause the dates of the maxima and minima to shift somewhat, these periods in the lakes of northern United States usually appear as follows: spring maximum, April to May, occasionally early June; summer minimum, usually in August; autumn maximum, late September to October; winter minimum, February to March. While the relative sizes of maxima and minima follow no fixed rule, the spring maximum commonly exceeds the autumn maximum, and the winter minimum is usually somewhat smaller than the summer minimum. It is interesting to note here that plankton production in the temperate seas manifests the same succession of maxima and minima.

Differences in the amounts of plankton (standing crop) at times of maxima and minima vary greatly with various lakes and with environmental circumstances. It is commonplace to find a maximum which shrinks to one-third its original size to form the succeeding minimum. Still greater differences may occur.

It must be understood that the total plankton referred to above includes both nannoplankton and net plankton. In most, if not all, natural waters, the nannoplankton greatly exceeds in quantity the net plankton. Therefore, unless both are included in the examinations, the true nature of this seasonal periodicity may not be discovered. In fact,

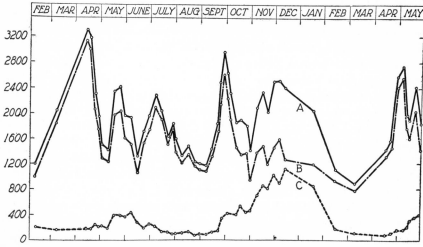

FIG. 33. Curves showing amount of dry organic matter in the net plankton, the nannoplankton, and the total plankton of Lake Mendota, Wisconsin, in 1916 and 1917. Curve *A* represents the *total plankton;* curve *B,* the *nannoplankton;* and curve *C,* the *net plankton.* Quantities are expressed in terms of the number of milligrams per cubic meter of water. (*Redrawn from Birge and Juday,* 1922.)

the net plankton may give a very different and wholly misleading picture; for example, it has been shown in some lakes that the net plankton alone exhibits only a mere hint of a spring maximum, the autumn maximum being the only one indicated in well-defined form, although the actual condition of the *total plankton* is that of the typical maxima and minima, with the spring maximum larger than the autumn one (Fig. 33). Of the two kinds of plankton, the nannoplankton very much more nearly indicates the true nature of the seasonal quantitative changes.

The annual bimodal type of plankton production, as just described, is commonly to be expected in medium to large lakes having considerable depth, but it is important to know that among the various kinds of smaller, shallower lakes the pattern of total annual plankton production may be very different. Some lakes have been reported as manifesting no plankton maxima or minima; some, with three maxima and three minima.

It is suspected that still other forms of annual quantitative production exist. In the absence of dependable information, no lake should be assumed in advance to perform according to any particular type.

Seasonal History of Species and Groups of Species. In order to understand the way in which rhythmic, seasonal changes in total plankton are produced, it is necessary to consider the seasonal history and sequence of the various plankters and groups of plankters. One point can be settled at once, viz., that the maxima and minima described above are not due to simultaneous quantitative increases and declines of *all* of the plankters which compose the plankton of a lake.

While certain groups of plankters sometimes tend to act similarly, it is difficult to make any general statements because of numerous exceptions, deviations, and necessary reservations. Statements are common in the literature that diatoms dominate the whole winter plankton; that the blue-green Algae (Myxophyceae) and the green Algae (Chlorophyceae) virtually disappear during the winter; that the bacteria and fungi show no very definite seasonal periodicity; and so on. Pearsall (1932) reports that in the English lakes (1) diatoms flourish in the winter and spring when the water is richest in nitrate, phosphate, and silica; (2) green Algae and desmids occur in the summer when the nitrates and phosphates are low; and (3) the blue-green Algae have a general correlation with that time of year when the organic matter is high and are able to grow abundantly in minimal quantities of nitrate and phosphate. However, such general statements, when applied to lakes at large, have at most only limited value. Furthermore, each of the groups of plankters is composed of many diverse genera and species, most of which exhibit such an individuality and such an independence of behavior that attempted general statements must be used with care. It is therefore necessary to approach this matter from the standpoint of the individual plankters and the type of water which they occupy. While the plankton is an organic community in which exist many interdependencies, it must be remembered that each component of this heterogeneous assemblage has its own form of life cycle, its own problems of maintenance, and its own characteristic reactions to stimuli; also, that these features may differ even among those species which are most closely related taxonomically. The plankton community is, in this respect, no different from some terrestrial community in which each of the various species, while influencing associated organisms in many ways, has its own individual sequence of life-history stages, generations, and reactions.

Each plankter is directly or indirectly subject to the complex of influences which changes of seasons impose, and the proper responses must be made, some of which result in quantitative changes, i.e., increases or decreases of size of the population. The annual quantitative history of many plankters is a succession of appearances and disappearances or of waves of development followed by decline. These sequences of increase and decline vary greatly in magnitude. In some species, the amplitude of rise and fall in quantity, while distinct, is not great enough to produce more than minimal changes in the total plankton population; in others, the change is so great that a wave of development of a single plankter may be sufficient to dominate numerically a whole plankton population and even produce the greater part of a seasonal maximum. All sorts of intergrades between these two extremes occur. The periods of quantitative increase and decline of the individual plankters do not, in many species, coincide with the seasonal minima and maxima of the total plankton described previously; in fact, certain species may exhibit their maxima during the general seasonal minima, and vice versa. Also, certain plankters may show a considerable number of these waves and depressions. These waves of numerical increase are known as *plankton pulses*. While in some species these *pulses* may approach a certain regularity of appearance, in a great many plankters their occurrence is sporadic, unpredictable, and frequent or infrequent. In some instances, they may be present during one season and absent during the same season of the succeeding year. They also may vary greatly in magnitude in the seasonal history of a single species. They may occur simultaneously with one or more pulses of another plankter at one time and at different times during another season. The rate of development of a pulse varies greatly, some plankters increasing slowly and more or less uniformly to the maximum, while others may show an almost startling burst of development, rising from an apparent absence to a numerical dominance of the whole plankton in a very short period. Disappearance of the pulse may also be deliberate or precipitous. While some plankters may not show pulses at all in particular lakes, there are excellent reasons for believing that every plankter has the potentialities for developing pulses. Without question, the high rate of reproduction and the short life cycles of plankters create the setting for plankton pulses, so that with the advent of more favorable conditions, such as increased abundance of food, more optimum physical-chemical conditions in the water, and greater release from enemies, a plankton pulse is possible. Furthermore, the make-up of a favorable environment for one plankter differs from that of others to greater or less degree; also, the interplay of factors in a body of water is a continually dynamic performance. Thus plankton pulses become inevitable. A reversal of favorable conditions leads to reduction of numbers of individuals and the disappearance of the pulse. The possible frequency and irregularity of plankton pulses necessitate frequent sampling in a body of water if dependable information is to be obtained. Figures 34 and 35 indicate the nature of these plankton fluctuations for certain seasons in

Lake Mendota, Wisconsin, fluctuations which typify but do not necessarily duplicate the similar changes in other comparable lakes of northern United States.

Having described briefly the course of events in individual plankters, it will now be possible to consider the composition of the spring and autumn maxima and the summer and winter minima. Since each plank-

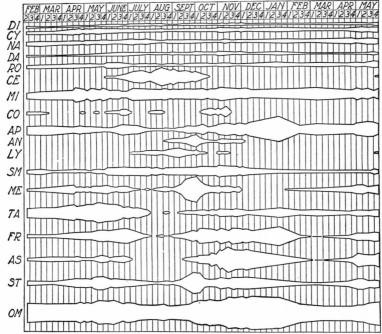

Fig. 34. Diagram showing quantitative seasonal changes in the net plankton of Lake Mendota, Wisconsin, in 1916 and 1917. The following abbreviations indicate the various plankters and materials: *Di, Diaptomus; Cy, Cyclops; Na,* Nauplius; *Da, Daphnia; Ro, Rotatoria; Ce, Ceratium; Mi, Microcystis; Co, Coelosphaerium; Ap, Aphanizomenon; An, Anabaena; Ly, Lyngbya; Sm, Staurastrum; Me, Melosira; Ta, Tabellaria; Fr, Fragilaria; As, Asterionella; St, Stephanodiscus; Om,* organic matter. (*Redrawn from Birge and Juday,* 1922.)

ter manifests its own periods of increase and decline which may or may not coincide with those of the other surrounding plankters, it becomes evident that the big periodic maxima and minima are not the result of the simultaneous increase and decline of *all* of the plankters. Plankters which may show a maximum at the time of the general spring maximum may be absent at the time of the autumn maximum; certain plankters come to their greatest development during the summer or the winter minimum; some plankters may show little quantitative differences throughout the year; some show but one maximum; and still other forms of deviation exist. The large, annual rhythms (maxima and minima) are the result of conspicuous increases and declines in certain, often few, plankters accompanied by others whose quantitative changes have smaller effects on the whole mass. The spring maximum may contain very influential

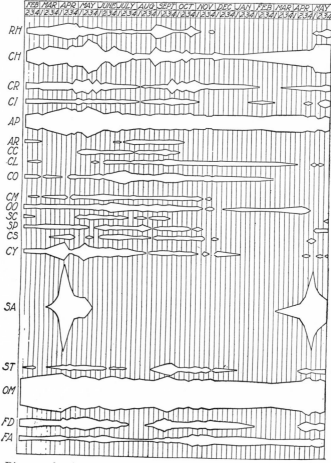

Fig. 35. Diagram showing the quantitative seasonal changes of the various organisms in the nannoplankton of Lake Mendota, Wisconsin, 1916 and 1917. The following abbreviations have been used for the different organisms: *Rh*, Rhizopoda; *Ch*, *Chlorochromonas*; *Cr*, *Cryptomonas*; *Ci*, Ciliata; *Ap*, *Aphanocapsa*; *Ar*, *Arthrospira*; *Cc*, *Chroococcus*; *Cl*, *Closterium*; *Co*, *Coelosphaerium*; *Cm*, *Cosmarium*; *Oo*, *Oocystis*; *Sc*, *Scenedesmus*; *Sp*, *Sphaerocystis*; *Cs*, *Cocconeis*; *Cy*, *Cyclotella*; *Sa*, *Stephanodiscus astraea*; *St*, *Stephanodiscus*; *Om*, organic matter; *Fd*, fragments of diatoms; *Fa*, fragments of *Aphanizomenon*. (*Redrawn from Birge and Juday, 1922.*)

plankters, some of which may participate little if any in the autumn maximum, their places being taken by other species. It may happen that a single plankter dominates conspicuously a whole maximum, although the usual situation is one in which several species participate. Those plankters which exhibit their *maximum* numbers during the summer or the winter minimum are, nevertheless, under such environmental control that they alone cannot markedly influence the minimum level of the plankton population at that time. The striking thing is that this periodic, annual rhythm is so general an occurrence, although produced, to some extent at least, in different ways and by different plankters in different kinds of lakes.

Causes of the Annual Maxima and Minima. The general coincidence of the spring and autumn maxima with the spring and autumn overturns naturally led to a search for causal relations arising out of the overturns. Release of decomposition products at the bottom; complete aeration of the lake, or at least a much larger part of it, as in the lakes of the first order; circulation of nutrient substances previously accumulated at the bottom—these and other effects of the overturns have been interpreted as presenting the most favorable conditions during the year for plankton production, and hence the great quantitative increases which follow on the heels of the overturns by those species which respond most vigorously to these supposedly optimum conditions. It must be constantly kept in mind that the make-up of optimum conditions for one plankter may be and often is different from that of another. Therefore, all that can justly be said of these spring and fall overturn conditions is that it seems evident that they do develop optimum conditions for certain plankters and that among these are the diatoms, which do respond vigorously to the new conditions, with the result that diatoms are often the chief forms concerned in the production of the spring and autumn maxima. Objections have been raised to the overturn explanation on the basis that the spring and autumn maxima occur in lakes which are too shallow to have a thermocline and are therefore presumably in more or less complete circulation throughout the year except at times of ice cover. For these shallow waters, explanations have been offered, based upon seasonal floods (spring and fall) which transport quantities of essential substances (nitrates, silica, and others) into them in a short time. However, for shallow lakes without inflowing surface waters of consequence, this form of explanation has no bearing.

Other explanations have sought to use temperature, light, dissolved oxygen, and certain other environmental factors as the bases for these annual rhythms. One theory holds that phosphorus is the limiting factor. The phytoplankton requires a supply of nitrogen, potassium, and phosphorus; nitrogen and potassium are usually available in natural waters in quantities ample for the demands, but it is held that phosphorus is usually present in such limited amounts that it must act as a limiting substance in the growth of the plankton Algae. According to this theory, the small quantities of soluble phosphorus in the upper waters—that region occupied by the phytoplankton—is soon exhausted by the increasing growth of phytoplankton, thereby converting favorable into unfavorable or limited conditions which prevail throughout the summer or the winter, as the case may be, until there is a renewal of the supply of phosphorus which is supposed to occur in the spring and in the autumn. Serious objections to this theory have come out of work done by Juday, Birge, and coworkers (1928) on Wisconsin lakes in which it was shown that only a small quantity of soluble phosphorus occurs in the upper waters in spring and summer and that in most instances virtually no decrease in the phosphorus content occurred as the summer progressed, and this in spite of the fact that some of the lakes supported a fairly large crop of phytoplankton in July and August. Furthermore, in some lakes there was an actual increase of soluble phosphorus in the upper water between May and July or August. In at least one lake, no trace of soluble phosphorus was found in the upper 3 m. of water in early July, and none in the upper 2 m. in late August, yet an abundant growth of phytoplankton occurred in these strata at both times.

Krogh and Berg (1931) have found a close coincidence of the Cladocera spring and autumn maxima with the spring and autumn maxima of the carbohydrates and crude proteins in the phytoplankton of a Danish lake and consider this coincidence as of causal significance. The fat content was low and showed no outstanding coincidence.

It does not seem possible to designate any single factor or influence as the sole cause of the periodic maxima and minima. Doubtless, they are the result of the interplay of a combination of factors acting at different intensities. There are still reasons for considering the multiple events concerned in the overturns as having some intimate relations to the maxima in lakes manifesting thermal and chemical stratification. It does not necessarily follow that the annual maxima and minima in all kinds of waters are due to the same combination of causes.

Other Forms of Plankton Production. Sometimes and in some waters plankton production lacks any regular periodicity. Maxima and minima may occur sporadically and apparently defy prediction. Such irregularity may manifest itself both in total mass production or in individual plankter performance. Conspicuous among these instances of irregular waves of maxima and minima are the so-called "blooms" of certain phytoplankters in which certain species suddenly appear in the water in tremendous abundance and then subsequently become reduced to modest or sometimes insignificant numbers. Blooms are known almost entirely from summer observations, although there appears to be circumstantial evidence that they may occur in winter. Several blooms may occur in the same lake during a single summer and in what seems to be a completely sporadic sequence. The principal participants in such blooms are certain species of blue-green Algae (Myxophyceae), such as *Aphanizo-*

menon flos-aquae, Microcystis aeruginosa, Microcystis flos-aquae, Gloeotrichia echinulata, and several species of *Anabaena.* These Algae float high in the water and may even form "scums" at the surface. At times they may predominate in plankton drifts (page 232) formed under the influence of onshore winds. Sometimes these blooms are of such a magnitude that they upset the biological balance of a lake, pond, or reservoir, causing the death of fishes and other aquatic organisms. Prescott (1948) recently published an excellent account of this subject. He described experiments which indicate that fish may succumb to toxic products such as hydroxylamine or hydrogen sulfide that are released into the water when great masses of these blue-green Algae decompose. For additional information, the reader is referred to Prescott's account. Pennak (1949) described an unusual bloom in a Colorado mountain lake in which stupendous quantities of certain blue-green Algae were produced and which persisted through one summer. Lackey (1949) presented an excellent general review of the whole subject of blooms, their nature, occurrence, and causes. His statement of causes is as follows:

Highly special or local causes may occur at times, but there seems little reasonable doubt at present that one or more optimal conditions—light, temperature, pH, food—produce them, and perhaps the most compelling of these is the nutrient content of the environment. Many laboratory studies have indicated that nitrogen and phosphorus relationships are perhaps the most critical.

SEASONAL CHANGES OF BODY FORM IN PLANKTON ORGANISMS

One of the most unique phenomena in the biology of plankton organisms is the occurrence, in many plankters, of seasonal changes of form (*cyclomorphosis*) some of which are so striking that the summer and winter forms of the same species would certainly be supposed to represent different species by an observer unacquainted with the facts. While all plankton organisms do not manifest such seasonal changes, they do occur in a large number of plankters, both plant and animal, scattered through the whole taxonomic range of the plankton series. Figure 36 indicates the general character of these seasonal form changes. A great body of information relating to these seasonal variations and to the general biology of the organisms exhibiting them is now available. Much of the work has dealt with the fresh-water Cladocera, since they manifest these seasonal form changes in a conspicuous way and have been found to be especially favorable material for such studies.

Morphological Character of Form Changes. These seasonal changes of body form differ so greatly in the different plankters that there seems to be only one feature common to most of the instances, viz., that the change from the winter to the summer form is in the nature of an increase of body surface compared to the body volume, while the transformation

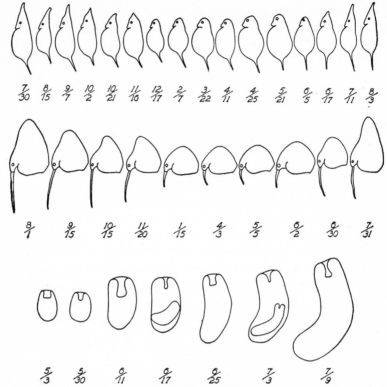

FIG. 36.   Outline drawings of certain plankters which manifest seasonal changes in body form.

The upper series represents seasonal variation in *Daphnia cucullata;* the numbers below each figure indicate the date on which that particular body form was present (the upper numeral represents the month and the lower one the day of the month).   In the summer generations, the crest is much higher than in the winter and the whole body form is more slender.

The middle series represents seasonal variation in *Bosmina coregoni;* the numbers below each figure indicate the date.   During the summer, the body is higher than long, while in the winter it is longer than high; in summer, the antennae are more than twice as long as in winter; also the eye is largest in winter.

The lower series represents seasonal variation in a rotifer, *Asplanchna priodonta.*   The dates are indicated below each drawing.

It should be understood that in the three series the outlines of the animals are all drawn in the same position for purposes of comparison, although actually the normal orientation of the animal in the water differs not only in the different species but also in the same species at different seasons.

(*Redrawn and slightly modified from Wesenberg-Lund, 1910.*)

of summer into winter form is of the reverse sort.   The following instances are offered merely as examples of some of the many types described as occurring in natural waters: (1) the flagellate *Dinobryon* shows a tendency in summer to have longer stalks and more acute angles between the individual branches; (2) the well-known *Ceratium hirundinella* develops in summer a fourth horn or else produces a longer, narrower body form; (3)

among the Cladocera, certain species of *Bosmina* develop a body in summer which is higher than long, with a longer beak and longer posterior spine (mucro), the reverse of these conditions characterizing the winter form; in the *Daphnia* group, the summer form is commonly distinguished by the elongation of the head into an angular crest, a general enlargement and elongation of the trunk, and often an elongation of the caudal spine, while the winter form exhibits a low, rounded head, a smaller trunk, and a shorter, terminal spine; and (4) among the rotifers, those nonloricate species manifesting this seasonal change of form commonly approximate the general features indicated in Fig. 36 (lower row); while the loricate species show changes in body size, changes in number and development of anterior spines, and degree of development of the terminal spine, if present. These changes in rotifers occur mostly in ponds; less frequently in lakes.

General Biological Features. Out of the great body of information which has been built up about the subject of seasonal changes of form, certain general biological considerations should be mentioned here. The following statements are based largely upon the summary by Wesenberg-Lund (1926).

1. Seasonal change of form is best developed among the perennial species; least, if at all, developed among those summer forms which seem to disappear during the winter.

2. Seasonal changes of form may take a different aspect in different lakes due to local variations.

3. Transition from the winter to the summer form does not take place through a gradual series of transformational stages but, instead, occur almost abruptly, often requiring only 2 or 3 weeks; in the autumn, however, the transition from the summer to the winter forms is a gradual one.

4. Regardless of the extent to which local variation may diversify the character of the summer forms of the perennial species in different lakes, winter brings a convergence in all of the species to the same type of body form, which in each species is invariably the same, at least over fairly large regions.

5. The change of form appears in the passage of one generation into one or more succeeding generations and not by growth changes within a single generation.

6. Once the summer body shape has been attained, the form is not appreciably changed during the summer season.

7. Seasonal change of body form among the Cladocera and the Rotatoria seems to be restricted to the female sex.

8. A few plankters exhibit a seasonal change of body form which appears to be a reversal of the usual sequence, e.g., in the rotifer *Keratella* (*Anuraea*) *cochlearis* whose summer form is smaller with reduced spines

and a more compact body, while the winter form shows a larger, more elongated body with greater development of both anterior and posterior spines.

9. Coincident with appearance of the summer forms of the perennial species, the periodic summer species (apparently not present during winter) begin to appear, with the result that early in summer the plankton community takes on a very different appearance from that exhibited during the winter and early spring.

10. It has been claimed that these seasonal forms are not developed in arctic, alpine, and such northern lakes as do not have wide annual variations of temperature but are restricted to the low-lying lakes of the temperate zone.

Causes and Interpretation of Seasonal Changes of Form. The causes and significance of these seasonal form changes have long been of interest to those biologists working with the organisms manifesting them. A great array of investigations has dealt with these matters, yielding much valuable information and conflicting views. Years ago two different interpretations largely monopolized this field, representing two different schools of workers, one led by the Danish limnologist Wesenberg-Lund, and the other by the German limnologist Woltereck. Some of the interpretations of these two eminent leaders and their students are in direct contraposition.

The first serious approach to an interpretation of seasonal changes of form was made by Wesenberg-Lund (1900, 1926) who offered the explanation that these forms were the result of changes in the density of the water arising from seasonal changes of temperature. The essence of his theory was essentially that plankters which must of necessity occupy a certain stratum of water are adjusted to the buoyant power of water at a certain density; that since seasonal temperature changes automatically produce alterations of water density of some magnitude, the plankters must either (1) sink or rise, as the case may be, into layers of water in which they could not commonly live, or (2) alter in some way their floating or swimming ability; and that these seasonal changes of form seemed to develop strongly just those structures and elements of body form which either increase or decrease their flotation. Rising temperatures in spring produce decreasing density values of the water, and the plankters therefore either show a greater tendency to sink or else sink at a more rapid rate. To meet this exigency, some of the plankters, according to Wesenberg-Lund, respond by the rapid development of the summer forms, with their various methods of increasing the exposed surface compared with the body volume, thus readjusting their flotation to the new conditions.

Shortly thereafter, Ostwald (1902) also proposed the origin of these seasonal forms in the physicochemical changes of the water, emphasizing particularly the idea of the regular seasonal variations in the *viscosity* of the water as the main stimulus in the production of these seasonal variations. While he specified a different physical factor, viz., viscosity, it will be recognized at once that Ostwald's explanation has the same general, central idea as had the original Wesenberg-Lund hypothesis; but since the viscosity is more intimately concerned with the sinking rate of submerged objects than is density, it appears that that particular portion of Ostwald's proposal is more nearly correct, a feature which Wesenberg-Lund subsequently conceded. The work of these two investigators thus brought into existence the *buoyancy theory* as it has long been known. The term buoyancy was used in describing the role of those morphological developments which decrease the rate of sinking, so that plankters possessing them were supposed to be able to keep in the proper strata of water. Woltereck and his coworkers championed a different explanation for the origin of the seasonal changes of form, viz., that they are due to seasonal variations in the *nutritive materials* in the water, support for which was derived both from nature and from many laboratory experiments. It was contended, among other things, that the prolongation of the major axis of a body cannot be regarded as a method of augmenting the cross-section resistance of that body; also, that these form changes are intimately concerned in locomotor activities.

As a part of the effort to solve this intriguing problem of change of body form, transplantations of certain plankters were made into geographical regions in which they were not indigenous and in which the seasons and temperature relations are of a different type. As an instance, Woltereck transplanted *Daphnia cucullata* from Denmark into Lake Nemi (Rome, Italy) in 1914. As reported by Ancona (1927), it was recovered in 1922 and 1924–1926. In this Italian lake, the seasonal variation of *D. cucullata* did not follow the temperature directly but was greatest in autumn with low temperature and smallest in spring with high temperature. It was found that the response in the new environment, both in seasonal variation and in the performance of the sexual cycle, was due in part to the external factors and in part to the inherent hereditary factors.

Of later years several American investigators have carried on researches in this field. Coker and Addlestone (1938) and Coker (1939), on the basis of laboratory experiments, hold (1) that changes of form in *Daphnia* are not the simple result of external factors or of any inherent cycle, but instead are due to some combination of internal and external conditions; and (2) that temperature *per se* acting directly upon the embryo is a significant factor. Recently, Brooks (1946) presented an extensive critical review of the literature, the problem of cyclomorphosis in *Daphnia*, and results of his own studies. Among other things, he also found temperature to exercise an important controlling influence. He also reported

(1947) that adult *Daphnia longispina* reared in turbulent water in the laboratory produced helmets larger than those reared in nonturbulent media, thus apparently establishing water turbulence as another environmental factor involved in helmet development.

The causes of cyclomorphosis are still obscure. At the present time it appears that the underlying influences may be very complex and that much critical research is required before they will be revealed in full.

Local Variations in Body Form of Plankters

At this point, it is necessary to indicate more specifically the nature of the local variations which aid in diversifying the appearance of the plank-

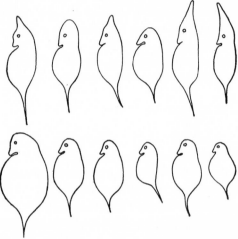

Fig. 37. Outline drawings of *Daphnia hyalina* indicating the nature of its local variations. In the upper row are shown the summer races from different Danish lakes. The lower row represents winter races from the same lakes. The summer races differ greatly from each other; the winter races have much the same appearance. (*Redrawn from Wesenberg-Lund*, 1910.)

ton. The periodic, seasonal variations discussed in the preceding pages develop in the different localities along parallel lines so that their essential features are usually recognizable. However, as already mentioned, these seasonal variations are not identical in appearance in the different localities even in the same region, owing to the existence of *local variations*. These local variations commonly manifest themselves as modifications of the *amount* or *degree* of development of the seasonal variation (Fig. 37). According to Wesenberg-Lund (1910), there are species which manifest local variations so freely that every lake may practically be said to have its own race, and these racial characters seem constant from year to year, especially in some of the daphnids. Irrespective of the degree of diversity produced by the local variations, these plankters (rotifers and Cladocera) are all supposed to return to the one common type which for each species is the same in all localities.

FOOD OF PLANKTON ORGANISMS

Since the plankton contains such a miscellaneous assemblage of organisms of widely diverse taxonomic relationships some of which are fairly high in the animal scale, the food requirements of this community are likewise diverse and can be considered best in connection with each individual group. Much still remains to be learned about the food habits and food demands of the various plankters, and it is likely that any statements such as the following ones represent but a part of the actualities.

GREEN PHYTOPLANKTON

As previously mentioned (page 206), the chlorophyll-bearing phytoplankters utilize organic and inorganic materials dissolved in the water. Certain species, sometimes classified as chlorophyll-bearing Protozoa, have, in addition to the typical algal form of nutrition, means of using also a certain amount of particulate materials. Examples of these combined types are not uncommon among the flagellates.

NONGREEN PHYTOPLANKTON

Those phytoplankters not possessing chlorophyll, such as the bacteria, depend upon the dissolved materials in the water or materials capable of being rendered soluble.

PROTOZOA

In general, protozoan plankters feed upon minute Algae and bacteria. The extent to which detritus is used is uncertain. As mentioned above, certain organisms sometimes classified as Protozoa contain chlorophyll, and, in addition to the ordinary holozoic type of nutrition, photosynthesis is performed. Utilization of dissolved substances has been demonstrated in certain Protozoa, and it may be that some of the plankton Protozoa, possibly all of them, make some use of this additional supply of nutrition.

METAZOA

The determination of the food of zooplankters can be approached in two ways: (1) direct observation of food taking, either in nature or in the laboratory; and (2) examination of contents of the digestive tracts of those plankters having such structures. In many respects, the former is more dependable. The latter method involves many difficulties, an important one of which is the rapidity with which various food materials are digested, often leaving masses of material of which little can be recognized unless hard parts are present and are sufficiently intact to make identification possible. Nevertheless, considerable useful information has been secured by both of these methods with respect to the diet of marine and fresh-water plankton.

In this connection, the work of Naumann (1921, 1923, 1929) deserves attention. He considers the relation of zooplankton as seston feeders to be divisible into four types: (1) grasping type, such as those Rhizopoda which touch and secure seston with the pseudopodia; (2) filtration type—the filtering of seston from water as the animal moves about—the method employed by most Cladocera and by some Copepoda; (3) sedimentation type—the capture of seston by means of induced water currents—the method employed by rotifers; and (4) predatory type—pursuit and capture of other organisms—employed by certain Cladocera and certain Copepoda. A brief summary of some of Naumann's observations and experiments follows.

Rotatoria. The following table (Table 21) includes results of some recent work in the determination of the foods of rotifers.

TABLE 21. COMPOSITION OF MATERIALS IN DIGESTIVE TRACTS OF ROTIFERS TAKEN FROM NATURE

Modified from Naumann

Species examined	Type of water	Composition of digestive-tract contents
Keratella aculeata and *K. cochlearis*	Oligotrophic	Slight yellow to gray, granular mass with minute Algae
K. aculeata and *K. cochlearis*	Eutrophic	Green masses with numerous minute Algae
Notholca longispina.........	Oligotrophic	Same as *Keratella* from oligotrophic situations
Polyarthra trigla (*platyptera*)	Oligotrophic	Same as *Keratella* from oligotrophic situations
P. trigla..................	Eutrophic	Same as *Keratella* from eutrophic situations
Synchaeta (several species)..	Eutrophic	Same as *Keratella* from eutrophic situations
Conochilus unicornis........	Oligotrophic	Yellow-brown, granular mass with minute Algae
Filinia (*Triarthra*) *longiseta*	Eutrophic	Gray-green mass with very few minute Algae
Asplanchna (several species)	Oligotrophic	All of medium-size Algae; also larger zooplankton, such as rotifers and *Bosmina*

Experiments in which both suspensions of carmine and India ink and of Algae were used gave evidences of an ability of some rotifers to discriminate in the choice of food, certain ones (*Asplanchna* and *Polyarthra*)

accepting none of the suspensions, while the others took both readily; also in experiments, in which plankters of different sizes were used, it was found (1) that *Asplanchna* took living plankton which exceeded 15 microns in size; (2) that *Keratella* (*Anuraea*) took only the smaller Algae (up to 10 microns); and (3) that *Conochilus*, *Notholca*, *Polyarthra*, *Synchaeta*, and *Filinia* (*Triarthra*) took only the small Algae of nannoplankton size. Within the last-named group, some differences appeared, the importance of which is not as yet clear.

From all of these results, it appears probable that the rotifers are divisible into two general groups: (1) a group of species in which discrimination occurs in favor of the larger particulate foods and in which a predatory habit exists; and (2) another group, probably the larger, in which food discrimination is greatly reduced or absent, the particulate substances in the water being taken as they come.

Cladocera. Naumann divides the Cladocera into two groups on the basis of the method of securing food: (1) those which obtain food by the active filtration of water and (2) those which are predatory. In this last group, he lists only *Leptodera*, *Polyphemus*, and *Bythotrephes*.

It appears that those Cladocera which filter their food from the water take virtually all particulate matter—inorganic debris, organic debris, living organisms—as it comes, all passing into the digestive tract just as received by the filtering apparatus as the animals swing about. The reader is referred to Naumann's original paper (1921) for detailed description of the filtering devices, three types of which are described. Experiments showed that *Daphnia*, *Ceriodaphnia*, and *Bosmina* took ordinary pond debris, carmine, India ink, Algae, and finely divided humus indiscriminately, soon filling the digestive tract with the mixture. The predatory form *Polyphemus* showed no carmine in the alimentary tract after prolonged exposure to experimental conditions.

The filtering apparatus varies somewhat in form and functioning but is a fine enough device to secure apparently most if not all of the particulate matter of ordinary sizes, only the minute organisms and particles having a chance to escape through it. Some of these very minute materials are caught along with the other substances. An experiment with a species of *Bosmina* showed that in water in which Algae of the "nannotype" (size about 5 to 60 microns) occurred with a frequency of 800,000 to 8,000,000 per cc., the intestine became filled in 15 min.; with bacteria in the water to the amount of 8,000,000 to 9,000,000 per cc., the intestine became filled in 2 to 4 hr. It was shown also that in most of the limnetic Cladocera, food remains in the digestive tract for only a short time (15 to 30 min.); and most of the Algae pass through the intestine without being affected by digestive processes, indicating that Algae function little as food for these animals. They appear to depend upon very minute organisms and very finely divided debris, eliminating in more or less unchanged form the larger materials which have been taken into the digestive tract.

Copepoda. Examinations, by Naumann, of the digestive tracts of certain copepods taken from a lake in Norway, in summer, gave the following results:

1. *Cyclops:* yellow, slightly granular mass; fragments of the exoskeleton of Entomostraca; jaws of the rotifer *Conochilus.*
2. *Diaptomus:* yellow, finely granular mass; minute Algae.
3. *Heterocope:* yellow, granular mass; fragments of exoskeleton of Entomostraca (particularly Copepoda); jaws of the rotifer *Asplanchna;* representatives of the genera *Coelosphaerium, Cyclotella, Gomphosphaeria, Dinobryon, Glenodinium, Gymnodinium, Peridinium, Staurastrum,* and *Tabellaria.* The Algae were apparently intact; discoloration of the chlorophyll was not observed.
4. Nauplii: yellow, granular mass, with minute Algae.

Experiments showed that *Cyclops* and *Heterocope* apparently exercise a certain selection of foods, while *Diaptomus* and *nauplii* do not, the latter seemingly taking anything of dimension greater than 1 μ. Klugh (1927) found (1) that the chief food of certain Entomostraca is the planktonic Chlorophyceae and (2) that some can use fine organic detritus.

Other Materials

Limnology is greatly in need of precise studies which will yield information as to exactly what organisms or substances the different plankters use as food. Great stress is sometimes placed on the value of diatoms as the main food of many plankters, a conclusion which is doubtless true in some instances. One important consideration, viz., the extent to which *detritus* functions as food for plankton, is badly in need of clarification. At present, opinions differ greatly. Lebour (1920) questioned its importance in marine plankton. Pennak (1946) believes that the principal portion of the food of zooplankton consists of detritus and found little evidence that predation by zooplankton has a significant effect on the size of phytoplankton populations in nature. On the other hand, Pennington (1941) found that in fresh water certain zooplankters, when present in sufficient numbers, can reduce the phytoplankton very rapidly. Since all natural waters contain detritus in varying amounts, its role as a source of food is a question of considerable importance.

Quantity of Food Used by Plankton

Although very important in many limnological matters, the quantities of food taken by plankton organisms are little known. The following statement from Birge and Juday (1922) gives a glimpse into some of the problems involved:

Just how much food a rotifer or a crustacean consumes each day is not known, but the following figures show how much water would have to be depleted of its population in order to furnish some of these forms with their own weight of organic matter for food. The average dry weight of some of the constituents of the plankton of Lake Mendota has been determined, and the results are as follows: (1) A large *Asplanchna* weighs 0.000834 mg.; (2) a mature *Cyclops*, 0.0041 mg.; (3) a *Diaptomus*, 0.00858 mg.; (4) an adult *Daphnia longispina hyalina*, 0.02172 mg. Taking the average quantity of organic matter in the nannoplankton of Lake Mendota as a basis for the calculation, viz., 1,630 mg. per cubic meter of water, each of these animals would have to remove all of the nannoplankton from the following quantity of water in order to obtain its own weight of dry organic matter for food: (1) an *Asplanchna*, 0.5 cc.; (2) a *Cyclops*, 2.5 cc.; (3) a *Diaptomus*, 5.2 cc.; and (4) an adult *Daphnia hyalina*, 13.3 cc. These quantities of water seem very small, but when compared with the size of the organisms concerned they are very large. Disregarding temperature and assuming that 1 cc. of water weighs 1 g., the above organisms would have to filter about 600,000 times their own dry weight of water in order to secure their own weight of dry organic matter in the form of nannoplankton. These animals may also feed upon some of the organisms in the net plankton and thereby reduce the above quantities of water proportionately. . . .

Computations based on the numerical data indicate that the Crustacea and the rotifers contribute from 25 per cent to 75 per cent of the organic matter in the net plankton; the maximum percentage is found in late winter and early spring when the Algae and Protozoa reach their lowest points in the net material; the minimum percentage is found in the early summer and in the autumn when the protista flourish most abundantly. Since the maximum percentage of Crustacea and rotifers is correlated in time with one of the minimum periods of the net plankton, it seems probable that these two groups of organisms furnish something like 30 per cent to 40 per cent, or about one-third, of the mean quantity of organic matter in the net plankton, i.e., an average of about 115 mg. out of 343 mg. per meter of water. If the protista of the net plankton are included in the computation, therefore, the quantity of water that a rotifer or a crustacean would have to strain to obtain its own weight of organic matter would be reduced about 12 per cent. . . .

These quantities of water are based on the mean quantity of organic matter in the nannoplankton and in the protista of the net plankton. Whenever the quantity of organic matter in these two groups of organisms is above the mean, the quantities of water would be smaller than the amounts indicated; and whenever it is below the mean, these amounts of water would be larger than indicated above.

Here is another field deserving of precise investigation. The solution of certain fundamental problems of limnology depends upon a knowledge of the quantitative food demands of the various plankters. It is a very common assumption that, other things being the same and favorable, the greater the food supply the greater the production of any group of organisms—an assumption for which there is considerable support—but until the food requirements of the individual plankters are known, a serious obstacle continues to stand in the path of any approach to an understanding of either actual or potential productivity. Too often, portions of the fragmentary information now known are carried over and applied to another situation on the very doubtful assumption that food requirements of the plankters are the same or similar in the two or more places.

PLANKTON PRODUCTIVITY

As has already been stated, the plankton productivity of various waters differs greatly, with every possible intergrade from very high production to an exceedingly scanty plankton population. A quantitative measure of the production of a lake can be expressed in terms of (1) *standing crop*— the total amount of plankton present in the water on a selected date—and (2) *annual crop*—the total quantity of plankton produced during the entire year. The problem of determining the true annual crop is a very complex one, requiring a knowledge of (1) rate of reproduction of each kind of plankter under the different environmental conditions; (2) length of life of each kind of plankter in the different environmental conditions; and (3) the average individual weight of each different kind of plankter in the different environmental conditions. Such detailed knowledge can come only from very elaborate investigations, and it can probably be safely stated that this information is not completely known as yet for any body of water. If rate of reproduction and longevity are known, the *annual overturn* of plankton material can be estimated. Birge and Juday (1922) have estimated that the *annual production* of plankton in Lake Mendota, Wisconsin, would be 12,000 kg. of dry organic matter per hectare of surface (10,700 lb. per acre) *if it be assumed that there are 50 overturns of the plankton stock per year.* The accuracy of this assumption remains to be determined, but it is thought to be roughly correct for Lake Mendota. The great diversity in size of the different plankters necessitates determinations of the average individual weights mentioned above in order to get at the relative importance of each plankter in the whole plankton complex.

It must be remembered that the standing crop is the result of a continual loss-and-replacement process. Losses due to death of plankters, consumption of plankton by other organisms as food, removal by outflowing waters, and other causes must be offset, more or less, by the normal reproduction and growth. Increases or decreases in standing crop are due to excess of production over loss or excess of loss over production, respectively. Sequences of different relations between production and loss may be a normal part of the annual history of plankton production. Such losses and replacements act differentially among the various plankters so that the qualitative and quantitative composition of the plankton is constantly shifting. Losses, whatever their causes, may occasionally exceed replacement to such an extent that a species temporarily fades out of the plankton, while later it may appear and for a time manifest considerable excess of production over the losses. At certain times of year, the plankton may be composed of representatives of many genera, while at another period, it may include representatives of only a small number of genera. However, qualitative losses and replacements do not parallel the quantitative losses and replacements, so that the magnitude of total standing crop does not necessarily vary with the *number of species* of plankters present.

There is no period of time during the year when one crop of plankton ceases and another begins, so that there is no definite starting point for the estimation of the annual crop of plankton, such as one finds for a land crop, for example. Neither is there any exact date of maturity, or harvest season, for the plankton crop as there is for the land crop. The crop of plankton, therefore, represents a continuous stream of life which flourishes at all seasons of the year and which passes on from year to year as long as favorable conditions obtain in a body of water.[1]

Some authors (Smith, 1933; *et al.*) divide the plankton flora into two types, the *Caledonian* and the *Baltic*. The Caledonian type, so named because it was originally described from Scotland, is characterized by (1) reduced total quantities; (2) richness in species; (3) many desmids; and (4) relatively few Chroococcales and Hormogonales. The Baltic type shows (1) few species but considerable quantities of individuals of the species represented; (2) predominance of Chlorococcales and Myxophyceae; and (3) conspicuous paucity of species of desmids. The Caledonian type is said to occur only in waters deficient in calcium.

CHEMICAL COMPOSITION OF PLANKTON

While it is important to know the total mass of plankton produced by a body of water, it is likewise necessary to have information as to the chemical make-up of the plankton if its value as a source of food is to be determined. Birge and Juday (1922) made an extensive chemical study of the plankton of four lakes in the vicinity of Madison, Wis. The following information is taken from their paper, but the reader is referred to the original source for further details.

The chemical analyses of plankton from the four lakes referred to above

. . . showed that, on the average, the crude protein constitutes from a little more than 44 per cent to more than 57 per cent of the dry organic matter in this fresh-water plankton; in this respect, the material compares very favorably

[1] Birge and Juday, 1922.

TABLE 22.　Results of Chemical Analyses of Various Plankton Organisms Stated in Percentages of Dry Weight of Sample

Part I indicates results with the ash included; Part II gives data on an ash-free basis

From Birge and Juday

Lake	Date	Organism	Part I, ash included								Part II, ash free					
			N	Crude protein (N × 6.25)	Ether extract	Pento-sans	Crude fiber	Nitrogen-free extract	Ash	SiO_2	N	Crude pro-tein	Ether extract	Pento-sans	Crude fiber	Nitrogen-free extract
Mendota	9/30/1911	Microcystis	8.60	53.75	4.55		2.11	32.05	7.54	0.38	9.30	58.13	4.92		2.28	34.67
Monona	7/11/1914	Microcystis	9.27	57.94	2.67	4.97	0.26	34.82	4.31	0.13	9.68	60.55	2.79	5.19	0.27	36.39
Monona	10/17/1917	Microcystis	6.32	39.50	2.75		0.65	52.09	5.01		6.65	41.60	2.90		0.68	54.82
Waubesa	7/7/1917	Chiefly Microcystis	8.35	52.19	5.02	7.80		39.40	7.81	1.62	9.05	56.61	5.44	8.46		42.44
Mendota	9/19/1914	Anabaena	8.27	51.69	1.11	4.81	0.63	39.93	7.17	0.95	8.91	55.68	1.20	5.18	0.68	41.89
Devils	10/8/1913	Anabaena and Coelosphaerium	8.35	52.19	2.05	6.15	1.17	30.12	4.66	0.27	8.75	54.74	2.15	6.45	1.22	32.58
Mendota	7/11/1915	Aphanizomenon	9.30	58.12	3.72	2.04	0.53	25.72	7.51	1.16	10.05	62.83	4.02	2.20	0.57	27.62
Mendota	12/3/1913	Aphanizomenon and Anabaena	9.94	62.12	4.34	3.42	1.30	31.24	6.52	0.17	10.63	66.45	4.64	3.66	1.29	33.06
Monona	7/20/1915	Lyngbya	9.17	57.31	2.36	5.25	3.42	34.74	5.67	0.15	9.73	60.81	2.50	5.56	3.63	36.64
Monona	7/24/1915	Lyngbya	8.21	51.31	1.38	3.76	7.39	22.60	5.18	0.20	8.66	54.12	1.45	3.97	7.79	29.55
Culture	5/13/1915	Ankistrodesmus	3.66	22.87	13.60	2.87	1.43	34.30	39.50	30.78	6.05	37.81	22.48	4.74	2.36	37.35
Mendota	8/28/1915	Diatoms	7.61	47.56	5.54	1.00	6.32	12.60	6.28	0.24	8.12	50.75	5.91	1.06	6.74	36.60
Monona	7/6/1916	Volvox	10.38	64.87	8.01		8.58	4.58	5.94		11.03	68.93	8.51		9.12	13.44
Fowler	9/28/1918	Diaptomus	9.57	59.81	19.80		10.07	13.59	5.74		10.15	63.43	21.00		10.68	4.89
Mendota	12/16/1918	Diaptomus and Cyclops	9.27	57.93	16.74		5.92	9.47	5.82	0.36	9.84	61.50	17.77		6.28	14.45
Mendota	5/1/1912	Diaptomus and Cyclops	9.87	61.69	17.68	0.58	5.58	7.16	5.58	0.01	10.45	65.31	18.72	0.60	5.91	10.06
Mendota	5/8/1918	Diaptomus and Cyclops	7.18	44.88	39.90	1.32	3.96	14.67	4.10	0.10	7.49	46.75	41.60	1.78	4.13	7.52
Green	8/22/1913	Limnocalanus	7.45	46.56	3.90	1.92	9.02	12.25	25.85	0.73	10.04	62.75	5.26	2.55	12.16	19.83
Devils	7/2/1913	Daphnia pulex	8.27	51.69	2.82		8.51	24.04	24.73	1.16	10.98	68.62	3.74		11.30	16.34
Devils	10/15/1916	D. pulex	6.55	40.94	4.60		7.25	25.19	23.17	2.84	7.22	45.12	5.98		9.43	31.34
Devils	5/15/1916	D. pulex	5.82	36.38	12.07		6.96	21.77	19.40	1.46	8.52	53.25	14.97		8.63	31.28
Devils	5/25/1917	D. pulex	7.58	47.37	3.10		10.89	13.85	16.87	0.14	9.12	57.00	4.73		13.08	26.19
Devils	8/30/1917	D. pulex	8.63	53.94	21.25	0.80	3.34	23.32	17.62	0.07	9.34	58.38	3.00	0.86	3.62	15.00
Monona	4/4/1914	D. pulex	7.91	49.44	3.45		5.58	15.44	18.21	1.95	9.67	60.43	4.22		6.82	28.53
Monona	6/17/1916	D. pulex and D. hyalina	8.51	53.19	8.42	1.58	8.31	8.25	14.64	0.08	9.97	62.31	9.86	1.85	9.73	18.10
Monona	8/5/1913	D. pulex	7.55	47.19	27.90		4.53	19.02	12.13		8.59	53.70	31.75		5.15	9.40
Waubesa	5/10/1917	D. hyalina and D. retrocurva	8.35	52.19	4.55		8.35	23.72	15.89	0.67	9.92	62.00	5.41	7.26	9.92	22.67
Mendota	8/28/1917	D. pulex														
Kawaguesaga	8/14/1913	Holopedium	8.35	52.19	10.58	6.71	5.80	13.20	7.64	0.28	9.04	56.50	11.53	1.12	6.28	25.69
Monona	8/8/1912	Leptodora	7.69	48.06	25.93	1.03	9.55	8.46	8.00	0.20	8.35	52.19	28.18		10.38	9.25
Monona	8/5/1913	Leptodora	9.28	58.00	8.70	0.72	4.60	13.20	15.50	0.22	10.98	68.62	10.29	0.85	5.44	15.65
Mendota	9/3/1917	Leptodora	9.84	61.50	5.88		8.80	12.51	11.31	0.23	11.09	69.31	6.63		9.92	14.14

with some of the meats that are used for human food. Crude protein constitutes about 47 per cent of the dry organic matter in the edible portion of the hind quarter of beef, for example, and about 37 per cent of that in the hind quarter of mutton. This plankton material, therefore, must be given a high rank as a source of protein food for other organisms. The edible portion of fish, however, contains a higher percentage of protein than either beef, mutton, or plankton; in the black bass, for example, the crude protein makes up about 92 per cent of the dry organic matter of the edible portion; and in the brook trout, about 90 per cent.

The plankton yields a relatively small amount of fat or ether extract, averaging from about 5 per cent to somewhat more than 7 per cent. This is comparable to the percentages in black bass and brook trout, for example, which are, respectively, 8 per cent and 10 per cent of the dry organic matter in the edible portions. The percentage of the fat is much larger in beef and mutton; it amounts to 53 per cent of the dry organic matter in the edible portion of the hind quarter of beef and to 63 per cent in the hind quarter of mutton.[1]

Inspection of Tables 22 to 24 will reveal something of the chemical nature of the total plankton and of some of the different plankters.

TABLE 23. SOME INORGANIC CONSTITUENTS OF ASH AS DETERMINED FOR 18 SAMPLES

Results are stated in percentages of dry weight of the sample

From Birge and Juday

Lake	Date	Organism	Ash	SiO_2	Fe_2O_3 and Al_2O_3	P_2O_5	CaO	MgO
Monona.......	7/11/1914	*Microcystis*	4.31	0.13	0.84	1.18	0.92	0.63
Mendota......	9/19/1914	*Anabaena*	7.17	0.95	1.27	1.21	1.42	0.70
Devils.........	10/8/1913	*Anabaena* and *Coelosphaerium*	4.66	0.27	....	....	0.82	0.63
Monona.......	7/6/1916	*Volvox*	6.28	0.24	0.80	2.50	1.10	0.93
Mendota......	12/10/1918	*Cyclops*	5.74	....	1.43	2.32	0.78	0.75
Green.........	8/22/1913	*Limnocalanus*	4.10	0.10	0.10	1.78	0.53	0.42
Devils.........	5/15/1916	*Daphnia pulex*	23.17	2.84	1.58	3.65	9.89	0.49
Monona.......	4/4/1914	*D. pulex*	7.62	0.07	0.98	3.50	2.25	0.89
Waubesa......	5/10/1917	*D. pulex*	12.13	1.02	2.94	3.37	2.01	0.47
Monona.......	8/5/1913	*Leptodora*	15.50	0.22	1.10	3.52	3.22	0.95

LIMNOLOGICAL ROLE OF PLANKTON

It must be constantly kept in mind that plankton is a heterogeneous assemblage the organisms of which differ widely in taxonomic relationships and in the degree of biological complexity; also, that each plankter has its own individual physiology and ecology. Therefore, the relationships and interdependencies are far too numerous and too complex to dis-

[1] Birge and Juday, 1922.

TABLE 24. GENERAL SUMMARY OF VARIOUS PLANKTON CATCHES FROM FOUR DIFFERENT LAKES

The first four lines show general results for all catches of net plankton from the different lakes. The rest of the table gives a summary of net plankton catches corresponding to nannoplankton, of nannoplankton samples, and also of total plankton. Mean percentages indicated for total plankton are based upon the mean quantity per cubic meter of water in each case

From Birge and Juday

Lake	Plankton	Number of samples	Organic matter, mg. per cu. m.	N		Crude protein (N × 6.25)		Ether extract		Pentosans		Crude fiber	
				Percentage, ash free	Mg. per cu. m.	Percentage, ash free	Mg. per cu. m.	Percentage, ash free	Mg. per cu. m.	Percentage, ash free	Mg. per cu. m.	Percentage, ash free	Mg. per cu. m.
Mendota.....	Net	184	332.5	8.37	27.8	52.31	173.8	11.78	39.2	2.88	9.6	6.54	21.7
Monona.....	Net	47	850.2	9.36	79.6	58.50	497.5	6.02	51.2	5.73	48.7	3.62	30.8
Waubesa.....	Net	18	1,665.8	7.54	125.6	47.12	785.0	4.64	115.8	5.90	98.3	4.70	78.3
Kegonsa.....	Net	1	3,738.0	6.88	257.2	43.00	1,607.5	4.94	184.6	4.36	163.0	5.42	202.6
Mendota	Net	84	343.5	8.34	28.6	52.12	178.7	12.21	41.9	3.38	11.6	5.95	20.4
	Nanno-	87	1,630.5	6.84	111.5	42.75	697.0	6.55	106.8	4.82	78.6	5.19	84.6
	Total	...	1,974.0	7.11	140.5	44.48	878.2	7.53	148.7	4.57	90.2	5.32	105.0
Monona	Net	21	813.8	10.05	81.8	62.81	511.2	7.00	57.0	5.85	47.6	3.17	25.8
	Nanno-	21	2,350.0	8.92	209.6	55.75	1,310.0	4.82	113.3	4.36	102.5	4.76	111.8
	Total	...	3,163.8	9.21	291.4	57.56	1,821.2	5.36	170.3	4.74	150.1	4.35	137.6
Waubesa	Net	16	1,639.2	7.49	122.6	46.81	766.2	5.83	95.5	6.20	101.6	4.35	71.3
	Nanno-	16	3,299.1	7.92	261.6	49.50	1,635.0	4.00	132.0	5.55	183.1	4.45	146.8
	Total	...	4,938.3	7.78	384.2	48.62	2,401.2	4.61	227.5	5.76	284.7	4.41	218.1

cuss here; even if it were desirable, the story would of necessity be incomplete and fragmentary, since much yet remains to be discovered in the biology of plankton. For the purposes of this book, only a brief, and to some extent tentative, appraisal of the role of plankton in the general biological economy of water will be attempted.

One of the most outstanding features in the aquatic complex is the partial or complete food dependence, direct or indirect, of the higher, nonplankton animals upon the plankton. While various reciprocal relations exist between the plankton and the nonplankton animals, there is reason to believe that if all of the nonplankton animals were removed from a lake and kept out, the plankton, with possibly some minor modifications, would continue to exist. It appears that the nonplankton animals represent a zoological stratum superimposed, in part, upon the plankton. While certain nonplankton animals possess the ability to utilize directly the nonliving matter in water as food, either throughout their entire existence or during some stage of the life cycle, they are usually in the minority. Even these forms are not always clearly independent of the plankton, since direct utilization of the nonliving, undissolved matters often automatically includes living plankters (bacteria and others), and it is still an open question as to how much the detritus feeders may depend upon the included plankton organisms; furthermore, it should not be overlooked that the dead bodies of the plankton organisms comprise substantial portions of the detritus. This role of plankton is typical of the limnetic region. In the littoral region where shallow water, bottom materials, higher plant growths, and other characteristic circumstances combine to make a very different environment, various nonplankton animals may manifest an independence of the living plankton, e.g., through the intermediary of the higher chlorophyll-bearing plants. Even in the littoral region, however, the plankton is not without its fundamental food relations to many animals.

In the limnetic regions of a lake, fishes usually comprise the only typical, active, pelagic animals of the nonplankton sort. Some fishes are plankton feeders throughout their whole life; others are plankton feeders at some particular stage of the life cycle; some fishes are carnivorous, at least in certain stages, and therefore are but indirectly concerned with the plankton. Plankton-eating fishes appear to utilize virtually all of the plankton organisms, although the Entomostraca are of special importance in this connection, since it is said that many fresh-water fishes may, at some stage of the life history at least, feed mostly or exclusively upon them. It appears that the Cladocera are more important than the Copepoda, since they are used more extensively as food by the fishes.

In the littoral regions, the animals which feed, to some extent at least, upon plankton comprise a large assembly, including, in addition to those fishes which frequent the shallow waters, many of the higher invertebrates, such as sponges, hydra, annelids, certain insects, Bryozoa, mollusks, and others. Certain insects which have the peculiar habit of burrowing in the sandy inner beach of certain lakes utilize as food the plankton drift which the waves work into the sand. Possibly, other animals which constantly frequent that region just at the water's edge may make some use of the plankton concentrations which occur there.

Even within the plankton assemblage itself, two general strata of life occur: (1) the chlorophyll-bearing organisms and (2) the nonchlorophyll-bearing organisms. For the most part at least, the latter depend upon the former. Within the plankton, there is a series of organisms which lifts potential foodstuffs to different levels of availability, beginning with the inorganic materials and culminating in the small but highly organized plankton animals, such as the Cladocera, which in turn become one of the main sources of food for fishes.

Some attention has been given to the *vitamin* content of marine plankton (Drummond and Gunther, 1930; Russell, 1930), and at least one vitamin (vitamin A) has been found. In fresh-water plankton, *thiamin* and *niacin* have been identified (Hutchinson, 1943; Hutchinson and Setlow, 1946). It seems almost certain that still others await discovery. There is reason for believing that various fresh-water animals depend upon the phytoplankton for their vitamin supply.

Finally, it now seems likely that plankton at large may make a greater use of the dissolved organic matter in water than was once thought. This subject has already received some attention (page 206). That some very simple plankters depend wholly upon dissolved matters seems to be established; that many, if not all, other plankters make some direct use of the dissolved matter in water remains to be positively demonstrated, but accumulating evidence points in that direction. If future investigation should show that all of the plankters draw upon the dissolved materials, the value of plankton in the biological economy of a body of water will take on a still greater significance.

The various ways in which plankton influences the medium in which it lives has been summarized by Rylov (1926) in the following diagrammatic way:

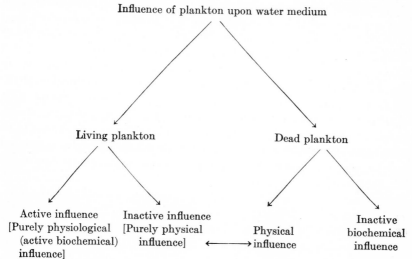

Influence of plankton upon water medium

Living plankton　　　　　　Dead plankton

Active influence
[Purely physiological
(active biochemical)
influence]

Inactive influence
[Purely physical
influence]

Physical
influence

Inactive
biochemical
influence

CHAPTER X

BACTERIA, OTHER FUNGI, AND THE NONPLANKTON ALGAE

BACTERIA IN LAKE WATERS AND THEIR SIGNIFICANCE

All natural waters contain bacteria. Every lake probably has an indigenous bacterial flora which is maintained as a regular part of the biological complex of that lake. In addition, a lake may serve as a sort of catch basin for bacteria which rain water washes out of the atmosphere and for bacteria which run-off water and drainage systems carry from the soils. Pure limnology, as contrasted with applied limnology, is primarily concerned with the normal bacterial populations of uncontaminated waters, and particularly those which may be regarded as of more or less regular occurrence in the waters of different kinds of lakes. Unfortunately, this is a little known field, since bacteriologists and others employing the methods of bacteriology have been mainly concerned in the past with pathogenic bacteria. Only a very few lakes have received any study of the bacteria native to them, and even in these few instances there are many gaps in the available information.

GENERAL DISTRIBUTION IN A LAKE

Bacteria occur in all parts of a lake. The open water contains them at all depths. They constitute an important portion of the nannoplankton. Bottom deposits of all sorts have a bacterial population. Often these deposits are rich in bacteria. The region of the shore line presents conditions, often ideal, for the development and maintenance of these organisms.

KINDS AND CHARACTERISTICS OF BACTERIA IN LAKES

In the past, many studies have been made on the bacteria in margins of lakes and in other bodies of water, especially rivers and streams, with reference to the pathogenic bacteria which may be present because of some form of pollution. Such work has been carried on almost exclusively from the standpoint of sanitation. However, since pollution is an artificial influence, we are concerned in this discussion not so much with those bacteria which come in as a result of it but rather with those which normally occur in natural waters wholly unmodified by the influences of man. For convenience, these bacteria will here be referred to collectively as the *indigenous bacteria*. The existence of such bacteria, normally and regularly inhabiting natural waters, is definitely established, although one occasionally sees in the older literature a persistence of the idea that the clear open waters of unpolluted lakes have few or no bacteria demonstrable by direct microscopic methods. These bacteria are said to be distinctly different from those usually discussed in works on public water supplies, sanitary surveys, and other similar treatises. It should be understood that these indigenous aquatic bacteria do not constitute a single taxonomic unit but represent various taxonomic groups. Furthermore, bacteria from extraneous sources may sometimes be temporarily intermingled with them.

Bacteria indigenous to lake basins may be grouped under three main headings, as follows: (1) planktonic—suspended in the open water; (2) benthonic—living in and on the bottom; and (3) periphytic—attached to submerged objects or submerged vegetation (see periphyton, page 319). The degree to which these groups intermingle seems to be rather uncertain. Some mixture certainly occurs. However, it has been claimed that the benthonic forms are preponderantly bottom dwellers and that certain lake bacteria seem to be definitely adapted to specific habitats.

These aquatic bacteria comprise a great variety of different forms, many of which are imperfectly known; in fact, it is said to be practically impossible, at the present time, to separate taxonomically all of the different forms. True water bacteria and soil bacteria are said (Snow and Fred, 1926) to have many points in common. In 24 Wisconsin lakes, it has been found (Bere, 1933) that nearly all of these bacteria are rod-shaped forms, coccus forms constituting only about 8 per cent of the total. Investigations on Flathead Lake, Montana (Graham and Young, 1934), and on English Lakes (Taylor, 1942) show similar results. The following description presents some of the characteristics of these bacteria in Lake Mendota, Wisconsin:[1]

The bacteria of lake water, taken far out from the shore, show certain well defined characteristics. The kind of microorganisms present in the water is more or less constant. These indigenous forms are present at all seasons and at all depths. As compared with the organisms commonly studied, the majority of them grow slowly on the ordinary culture media and on plate cultures appear as punctiform colonies. About 10 to 25°C. is the optimum temperature for their growth. In general they do not form acid or gas from sugars as was shown by fermentation tests on agar slants containing 1 per cent of the various sugars plus a suitable indicator. They do not curdle milk and the majority of the true lake forms liquefy gelatin slowly. A considerable proportion are chromogenic, but long incubation at comparatively low temperatures is necessary to bring out the deep color. It is in respect to pigment production that the *typical* water flora of Lake Mendota is most easily recognized.

[1] Snow and Fred. 1926.

The student who desires a comprehensive list of specifically identified bacteria (to genera and to species) which compose the water bacteria is doomed to disappointment, since none is available for any unmodified lake in North America or, so far as the writer knows, in other continents. That the forms are very diverse has already been pointed out. Whipple (1927) lists five genera belonging to the order Chlamydobacteriales (iron bacteria: filamentous forms having a thick gelatinous sheath in which iron is commonly deposited) and 24 genera belonging to the order Thiobacteriales (those bacteria distinguished by the presence in the cells of granules of free sulfur or bacteriopurpurin or both, commonly thriving best in the presence of hydrogen sulfide). Just which genera of this list have representatives among the water bacteria is not certain; furthermore, this list does not include the strictly unicellular forms which may be numerous in fresh water.

The water bacteria are as yet too little known to make possible any satisfactory discussion concerning their classification. Henrici (1933) made the following statement based upon his studies of fresh-water bacteria:

It is obvious that, until more completely known, these water bacteria cannot be fitted into existing classifications, but some sort of working classification must be adopted in order to analyze the slides intelligently. The forms encountered so far may be immediately divided into two great groups—those which occur in filaments or chains and those which occur singly or in irregular aggregates, corresponding to the *Trichobacterinae* and *Haplobacterinae*, respectively, of Alfred Fischer. The filamentous types may be further subdivided into those which are continuous and those which are articulated, the latter according to size, shape, and internal structure of the elements. Further noteworthy characters of filamentous types are the presence or absence of sheaths, of true branching, of false branching, and of holdfasts. No true branching filamentous forms have been encountered so far. The nonfilamentous types are of widely varying form and size. There are minute spherical forms, singly or in clusters, larger round or oval cells with a reticulated protoplasm much like Azobacter; there are rods of varying length and thickness, some with deep-staining granules, others uniform in their staining. There are comma-shaped cells and true spirilla varying in size. While it is true that one would hardly be justified in naming these organisms and describing them as species on the basis of their morphologic appearance alone, it is quite evident that the morphology is sufficiently diversified to warrant a tentative classification of the organisms observed which will be sufficient for at least preliminary ecologic surveys.

Bacteria in fresh water may be divided into two groups: (1) aerobic—those usually defined as requiring the presence of free oxygen—and (2) anaerobic—those which can exist in the absence of free oxygen. It has been claimed (Bigelow, 1931) that the important distinction between aerobic and anaerobic bacteria is on the basis of the carbon dioxide tension rather than the oxygen tension.

Bacteria in fresh water may also be grouped on a physiological basis. Some of the most important physiological groups are listed below. It should be understood, however, that these groups as listed are not mutually exclusive; for example, the putrefying bacteria may include representatives of some of the other groups.

1. Putrefying bacteria—bacteria of decay.

2. Denitrifiers—those which function in changing nitrates into gaseous nitrogen.

3. Nitrogen fixers—those having the power to fix free nitrogen.

4. Nitrite producers—those transforming ammonia into nitrites.

5. Nitrate producers—those transforming nitrites into nitrates.

6. Parasitic bacteria—those truly parasitic within the bodies of various aquatic organisms.

Magnitude of Bacterial Populations

Methods of Determination. It has been found that the high-speed centrifuges used in plankton work remove only a small portion of the bacteria from the water. In the past, quantitative studies have been made largely by the use of plate cultures. It has long been known, however, that plate-culture counts are far below those made by direct examination. Improved culture methods have reduced this discrepancy, but it still appears that plate cultures yield only a small fraction of the number found by the direct-count method. Both methods are being employed at present by different workers. Snow and Fred (1926) claimed that direct-count methods, as then developed, were primarily adapted for media in which the bacterial population is very large; that lake populations are so small that it is necessary to concentrate the bacteria in order that the mathematical error involved in computing from the number per unit of the microscopic field to the number per unit of volume of lake water is reduced as much as possible. Since this concentration (by filtration or chemical flocculation) presents difficulties, the direct count was not favored by some investigators. Kusnetzow and Karzinkin (1931) developed a method of direct counting in which the concentration is accomplished by evaporating lake-water samples under diminished pressures and at a temperature not above 35 to 40°C., a method which seems to overcome some of the difficulties and to make the direct count more dependable. They claim that their form of direct count gives a quantity two to four thousand times that found on agar and gelatin plates. In Lake Mendota, the direct counts (Bere, 1933), based upon the same method, varied from twenty to three hundred thirty-five times the plate counts; while in Lake Wingra, the variation was eight to one hundred twenty-five.

Recently, certain bacteriologists have made effective use of a method which consists essentially of submerging microscope slides in water for a period of time. Bacteria accumulate on such slides and grow there. After a period of submergence, the slides are recovered, dried, fixed, stained, and examined microscopically. It is claimed that by this method microscopic counts are facilitated and that species possessing distinct morphological features may be identified by direct examination. This method is discussed by Henrici (1939). The submerged-slide method collects only those bacteria which grow attached to submerged objects, but Henrici believed that they constitute a large part of the entire water group. To this group he applied the term *periphytic*. It is clear that results obtained by the submerged-slide method and expressed as the *number of bacteria per square millimeter per day* cannot be directly compared with values expressed as the *number per unit of volume*. However, Henrici found that for 100 pairs of counts a coefficient of correlation (0.625) was obtainable.

Quantities of Bacteria. Formerly, it was supposed that lake and pond waters were, on the whole, very low in bacterial content, usually not exceeding 200 per cc. and often less than 100 per cc. It is now evident that these values are quite too low. According to Snow and Fred (1926), the bacteria in Lake Mendota varied from 740 to 32,600 per cc. during a period of 14 months, these values being secured by the direct-count method. Kusnetzow and Karzinkin (1931), working with an improved method of making direct counts, report a bacterial population in Lake Glubokoje, U.S.S.R., which varies roughly from 1,000,000 to 6,000,000 per cc. However, it is believed (Henrici, 1939) that these numbers are far too high for any unpolluted lake and that such quantities would produce an obvious turbidity in the water. Bere (1933), investigating certain Wisconsin lakes and using the Kusnetzow and Karzinkin method, found considerable variation in the bacterial content of the surface waters, the range being from about 19,000 to 2,000,000 per cc.

Table 25 shows the bacterial content of several Wisconsin lakes as measured by different methods. It should be pointed out that Brazelle Lake is described as atypical and difficult to classify, is really a brook pond, contains dark-brown bog water, is but 2 m. deep, is surrounded by marshy land, has a bottom composed of a mass of decomposing plant remains, and is very turbid.

There seems to be considerable evidence that a phenomenon perhaps comparable to the blooms of Algae may occur in lake bacteria. It appears to be in the form of sporadic outbreaks of growth of certain bacteria, said to be usually autotrophic, resulting in such quantities as to make the water visibly colored. These upsurges of the bacterial populations are still too little known to justify further discussion here.

TABLE 25. COMPARISON OF NUMBERS OF BACTERIA IN DIFFERENT LAKES
From Henrici (1939)

Lakes	Periphytic bacteria[1]	Plate counts, water[2]	Plate counts, bottom deposit[3]	Microscopic counts, water[4]
Brazelle.....................	3,853	2,963	44,600	2,000,000
Eutrophic lakes:				
Boulder...................	711	.....	47,000	98,000
Alexander................	526	675	144,240	
Little John...............	402	505	39,050	64,500
Mendota..................	375	.....	609,300	975,000
Muskellunge..............	197	133	10,930	400,000
Mean...................	442	438	170,100	384,400
Oligotrophic lakes:				
Weber....................	183	132	2,350	45,000
Trout.....................	177	66	29,790	85,500
Crystal...................	63	80	2,160	36,000
Mean...................	141	93	11,400	55,500
Dystrophic lakes:				
Helmet...................	377	380	120,300	394,000
Mary.....................	24	58	39,450	745,500
Mean...................	200	219	79,880	569,750

[1] Bacteria per square millimeter per day deposited upon slides.
[2] Colonies per cubic centimeter of water on agar plates.
[3] Bacteria per cubic centimeter of bottom mud on agar plates. (*From Henrici and McCoy*, 1938.)
[4] Bacteria per cubic centimeter of water computed from counts of evaporated samples. (*From Bere*, 1933.)

Vertical Distribution of Bacteria. Records are not in agreement as to the character of the vertical distribution of bacteria in lakes. Minder (1927) published data for Lake Zurich, Switzerland, which indicate that the bacteria decrease in number with increase in depth. Lake Zurich is said to be contaminated by sewage and may not be strictly comparable in this respect to unmodified lakes. According to Scott (1916), certain lakes of the Tippecanoe Basin, Indiana, show more bacteria at the surface, at the bottom, and in the thermocline than at other levels, although departures from this type of distribution were found. The works of Fred, Wilson, and Davenport (1924) and Snow and Fred (1926) show that in Lake Mendota, Wisconsin, the bacteria are, in general, uniformly distributed in the different depths, except in the deeper parts of the hypolimnion where the dissolved oxygen content is greatly reduced or absent, thus affecting the aerobic bacteria. Bere (1933) reported that in some Wisconsin lakes the bacteria increase almost continuously from surface to bottom; in others, the reverse condition prevails; in still others, there is an increase at the 5-m. level followed by a steady decrease to the bottom. Henrici (1939) summarized vertical distribution as follows:

Bacteria may be more numerous at the surface of the water in some lakes; this is probably due to the accumulation of floating plankton at the surface, and is most apparent in lakes that bloom. Plate counts do not show marked differences between the epilimion and hypolimnion, but such differences are noted in counts of bacteria on submerged slides, in the case of sharply stratified lakes; they are probably due to temperature differences. There is only slight evidence that bacteria increase in the thermocline. They may show sharp local variations in vertical distribution associated with microstratification. Bacteria are more abundant in the bottom deposit than in the water, and most abundant at the mud-water interface, decreasing at a constant rate below this level. Their abundance is probably due to sedimentation.

Horizontal Distribution. Horizontal distribution of bacteria in lakes is still little known. From the few papers which have been published it appears that the bacteria in the open water remote from shore may have a fairly uniform distribution; that the quantity of bacteria in the open water is less than in the water of the littoral areas, particularly in the protected bays; that the quantity of bacteria tends to be greater and more varied in the vicinity of beds of rooted aquatic vegetation; and that in general the bacteria in the bottom deposits decrease in quantity from the profundal to the littoral zone.

Annual Distribution of Bacteria. Minder (1927) and others have reported for Lake Zurich, Switzerland, two maxima and two minima during the year, the maxima occurring in the spring and autumn, and the minima during the two stagnation periods, thus corresponding in a general way to the annual maxima and minima of the plankton already described (page 253). However, other results are at variance. Earlier work on Lake Mendota, Wisconsin, showed (1) that but one maximum and one minimum appear; (2) that the maximum and the minimum do not necessarily occur at the same time in different years; e.g., in 1920, the maximum was in June and July and the minimum in January and February; in 1921, the maximum was in September and October and the minimum in spring; and in 1922, the maximum came in March and April, and the general minimum during the summer. Bere (1933) found that in three Wisconsin lakes (including Lake Mendota) the maximum occurred in August and that the decline, beginning in September, reaches a very low level in late winter.

Henrici (1939) summarized the situation as follows:

Seasonal fluctuations of bacteria apparently are different in different types of lakes. In high mountain lakes the semi-annual turnover, distributing bottom bacteria through the water, apparently determines the maxima, though the effect of spring thaws and autumn rains may be a factor. Plate counts are probably affected considerably by surface drainage washing bacteria into the lakes. In a highly eutrophic lake the plankton pulses appeared to determine seasonal variations of the bacteria. The activities of periphytic bacteria vary with the temperature, but this is more apparent in open water stations than littoral ones. Periphytic bacteria were found to be unusually abundant in the bottom meter of Mendota during winter stagnation. There are no adequate data on seasonal variations of bacteria in bottom deposits.

Factors Affecting Distribution of Bacteria. *Light.* That strong sunlight may have a lethal effect upon bacteria seems to be regarded as established. This effect is thought to be due to the action of the ultraviolet rays. However, since these rays do not penetrate beyond the superficial layers of surface waters, this action must be greatly limited. Records of actual conditions in lakes are not in agreement. Investigations on Wisconsin lakes showed no indication that sunlight has any reducing effect on the number of bacteria; and Lloyd (1930) found the bacteriocidal effect apparently negligible in the sea, the greater number of bacteria occurring at the surface even on sunny days. Various other workers report a reducing effect of sunlight in both fresh and marine waters. Some have described a diurnal variation of the number of bacteria in the upper waters and have interpreted it as due to the alternation of light and darkness. That such diurnal variation may occur seems possible, but there seems to be evidence that the cause is something more than merely a light effect. Presumably, inhibiting effects of light would reduce greatly the number of surface-water bacteria in the summer time as contrasted with winter, but some of the records furnish opposite results.

Temperature. It is usually stated that temperature has a direct effect upon the number of bacteria, within limits; increase of temperature facilitates growth and multiplication, while the number of bacteria may be reduced by low temperatures. Also, sudden, marked changes of temperature may have a reducing effect, particularly on those species which do not produce spores and which lack a highly resistant cell membrane. This is significant, since the water bacteria are said to be mainly of the small, nonspore-forming type and notoriously sensitive to sudden changes of temperature. In spite of this temperature sensitivity, Fred, Wilson, and Davenport (1924) found that temperature had little or no effect on the multiplication of the bacteria in Lake Mendota, Wisconsin, and, according to Strøm (1928), Netschaeft found denitrifying bacteria in full activity at the freezing point. Possibly, abruptness of temperature change of sufficient magnitude to make this sensitiveness effective does not occur in the surface waters of lakes; possibly, only the very shallow waters of relatively large surface are subject to such an influence.

Sedimentation. Sinking of bacteria, due either to their own specific gravity or to their attachment to suspended particles, has much to do with changes in their number in the upper waters. Since saprophytic bacteria live upon and attached to organic particles, any influence which affects the distribution of such particles automatically affects the distribution of the bacteria. For that reason, saprophytic forms may be abundant at any depth of water where the sinking of particles is temporarily checked or may be particularly abundant at the bottom where these particles finally accumulate. On the other hand, bacteria not attached to particles and whose food materials are derived from the dissolved matters probably sink so slowly that they are less responsible for changes of the number in surface waters.

Other Microorganisms. That bacteria are preyed upon by Protozoa and certain other organisms is well known, and, without doubt, the numbers of bacteria present at a given time are dependent upon this interrelation. It is claimed that in the soil, a numerical relation exists between bacteria and Protozoa, viz., that when Protozoa are abundant, bacteria are scarce, and vice versa. It may be that a similar relation exists in fresh waters, although actual results cannot at present be cited in proof of this suggestion.

Under some circumstances, destruction of bacteria by bacteriophage is now well known. The nature of bacteriophage is still a matter of some uncertainty. According to a generally accepted theory, it is regarded as composed of very minute organisms which parasitize various bacteria. Little seems to be known concerning the existence of bacteriophage in open lake water, but it seems likely that it occurs there. Destruction of bacteria by bacteriophage may be an important influence in their distribution.

Movements of Water. Since bacteria and the suspended particles to which they may be attached sink rather slowly, it is obvious that movements of the surrounding water have a direct effect in their distribution. Both horizontal and vertical variations arise from this cause.

Food Supply. Bacteria, in general, are comparatively sensitive to slight changes in the food supply. Possibly, this is true of the lake bacteria. If so, such phenomena as alterations in food supply and differences in distribution of food materials would produce corresponding effects in the bacterial population.

Other Factors. There are indications that other factors, such as the reaction of the water, aeration, osmotic pressure, and toxic wastes of the bacteria themselves, may enter into explanations of the distribution of bacteria. However, too little is known concerning these possible factors as they operate in nature to make profitable any discussion here.

Effects of Drainage Water on the Number of Bacteria. Drainage waters from the surrounding land areas carry quantities of bacteria into lakes. Such waters from the watershed of a lake are a continual source of contamination, often contributing large quantities of bacteria representing a variety of types, such as the ammonifiers, gelatin liquefiers, and colon forms of both fecal and nonfecal origin. How long such bacterial invaders can persist in lake water is a very significant question. The same question arises in connection with the contaminations of natural waters by sewage. It is said that the disease-producing bacteria of man and the higher animals do not thrive in the open ocean, and there seems to be some evidence that the same is true not only of the Great Lakes and other lakes of large size but also at least of some of the smaller lakes. In Lake Mendota, Wisconsin, it has been found (1) that contaminating bacteria, which enter the lake by means of drainage water, do not seem to persist in the lake water for any great interval of time; (2) that, barring unusual circumstances, they do not spread far into the open water of the lake; and (3) that they disappear rapidly from the water near shore.

It is said to be generally true that a body of standing water contains fewer bacteria than its inflow. Sometimes the contrast is great and the reduction rather abrupt. According to Taylor (1940), bacterial counts of samples taken at the mouth of the principal river entering Lake Windermere, England, were about 200 times greater than the counts in samples of water obtained at a distance of 200 m. offshore from the mouth of the river.

Bacteria in Bottom Deposits. Bacteria occur abundantly and in considerable variety in bottom muds. Doubtless, the bacterial population varies, qualitatively and quantitatively, in different lakes and kinds of bottom deposits. It has been found that in certain marine waters, the number of bacteria in the mud far exceeds that in the water immediately above it, and it is not unlikely that the same may be true in lakes, particularly in the shallower parts of the basins. Increase in number of living bacteria comes about by the reproductive activity of forms already in the mud plus those which settle through from the overlying water and find the bottom muds habitable. In lakes of the third order, especially in those with ample exposure to wind action, it is probable that an abundant bacterial population inhabits the bottom deposits at all times, unless it be during stagnation conditions arising from the presence of prolonged ice cover. Little seems to be known concerning the magnitude of the strictly anaerobic bacterial populations in the bottom deposits. Fred, Wilson, and Davenport (1924) state that while anaerobic bacteria are found in the deep layers of the water and in the bottom muds of Lake Mendota, Wisconsin, their occurrence in large numbers seems highly improbable. According to Allgeier, Peterson, Juday, and Birge (1932), the bottom deposits of Lake Mendota contain 100,000 bacteria per cc., of which about 1,000 per cc. are cellulose-destroying bacteria. The bacterial flora consisted of chromogenics, ammonifiers, denitrifiers, cellulose destroyers, and other typical lake forms.

Information as to the depths in bottom muds to which bacteria occur is scanty. Carpenter (1941) examined vertical core samples taken in Trout Lake, an oligotrophic lake in northern Wisconsin. The samples ranged from zero to 16 ft. mud depth. Aerobic and facultative bacteria varied in number from 4,700 to 250,000 per g. of wet mud at the surface of the bottom deposit, and from 40 to 1,600 in the deepest levels examined. The anaerobic bacteria ranged from 600 to 1,900 per g. in the uppermost samples, and from zero to 45 in the deepest level. In most instances there was a fairly uniform decrease in aerobic and facultative bacteria with increasing depth in the bottom deposit. The anaerobic bacteria decreased at a slower rate with increasing mud depth.

Fundamental Role of Bacteria

Bigelow (1931) reviewed the relations of bacteria to marine biological problems. His statement that the fundamental problems of marine bacteriology center about the ways in which bacteria keep in action the cycle of matter through its organic and inorganic stages in the sea applies equally well to fresh waters. Obviously, the sum total of functions performed by the aquatic bacteria depends upon kinds, quantities, and distribution of these organisms. These features have been discussed in preceding sections (pages 280–284). In a general way, the biological relations of the bacteria involved are of two sorts: (1) relations to the inorganic and to the dead organic matters and (2) direct relations to the higher, living organisms.

Relations to Inorganic and to Nonliving Organic Matters. The relations of aquatic bacteria to the inorganic and the dead organic matters require little more than passing mention here, since they relate to processes already known in a general way to students of biology (Fig. 38). The important general relations are indicated in the following analysis (modified from Henrici, 1933):

I. Autotrophic bacteria—bacteria which secure their nutrition entirely from inorganic sources and are therefore *independent* of all other organisms.
  A. Chemosynthetic autotrophic bacteria—bacteria, such as the true iron bacteria and the white sulphur bacteria, which obtain their necessary energy by the oxidation of certain inorganic compounds, but without the use of sunlight, and utilize only inorganic materials—certain salts, carbon dioxide, and water—for building materials.
  B. Photosynthetic autotrophic bacteria—bacteria, such as the green and purple sulphur bacteria, which obtain their energy from *sunlight* and require only inorganic substances for building materials.

II. Heterotrophic bacteria—bacteria which require *organic* matter for at least a part of their nutrition.
    A. Saprophytic bacteria—bacteria which digest and absorb dead organic matter.
    B. Parasitic bacteria—treated under another heading (page 283).

Bere (1933) found that in about one-half of the lakes examined, the bacterial content was quantitatively proportional to the organic and inorganic constituents of the water and that in about one-third of the lakes, the bacterial content was proportional to the organic material alone.

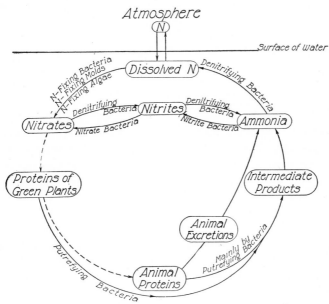

FIG. 38.   Essential features of the nitrogen cycle in natural waters.

Direct Relations to Higher Living Organisms.   The direct relations of aquatic bacteria to the higher organisms are roughly of two sorts: (1) food materials and (2) parasites.

Bacteria as Food Materials.   Many of the Protista (Protophyta and Protozoa) devour bacteria. The same seems true of the metazoan mud feeders and of some of the higher plankton organisms. Beyond these bare facts, far too little is known about this relation in water. Few quantitative data are available. Mention has already been made of the growing indication that the bacterial population is much greater than was formerly supposed. Birge and Juday (1922) mention Lohmann's estimates that one volume of bacteria is equal to six volumes of Protista and to 300 volumes of Metazoa, on *the basis of their ability to produce living matter* in the course of one year, and point out that in Lake Mendota there exists a very much larger proportion of Protista to bacteria than indicated in Lohmann's results. They state, however, that

. . . the value of the bacteria in the plankton economy of Lake Mendota is by no means as small as these figures seem to indicate, because they multiply at a much faster rate than the Protista; the bacteria may pass through a number of generations in the course of a day under favorable food and temperature conditions, while the Protista may not average more than one or perhaps two divisions per day under similar conditions. In spite of this marked difference in reproductive capacity, it appears from the foregoing results that the bacteria do not play nearly as important a role in the plankton complex of Lake Mendota as Lohmann's estimate might lead one to expect.

Bacteria as Parasites. There is reason to suppose that many, possibly all, kinds of aquatic animals suffer from bacterial infections. Evidence of such infections appears at times in certain epidemics mentioned in the literature While such phenomena are usually recognized only among the larger aquatic animals, there is no reason to suppose that even the minute, lower invertebrates are exempt from bacterial diseases, although specific information on such infections is very scanty. However, it should not be assumed that all such "epidemics" are of bacterial origin, since some of them may be due to other parasitic organisms.

OTHER FUNGI AND THEIR SIGNIFICANCE

In addition to the bacteria, water contains a profusion of other kinds of fungi often designated roughly as *water molds.* Not only do they abound in fresh waters of all sorts, but they are also very diverse in kinds, representing many genera and species. They grow freely upon virtually all kinds of organic matter. The dead bodies or fragments of various aquatic organisms are quickly utilized by these fungi. The dead fly which falls upon the surface of water and soon develops a halo of white, radiating filaments is a familiar instance. The student of fresh-water biology is very familiar with those afflictions of fishes, commonly referred to as *Saprolegnia disease.* This malady is due to the entry of a fungus, belonging to the genus *Saprolegnia*, into the tissues of fish, usually through some wound in the skin, often producing conspicuous, surface patches of diseased flesh. Eggs of various aquatic animals are also attacked. Everyone who has occasion to maintain water cultures is certain to meet, sooner or later, the problem of controlling fungus growths Many of the water fungi occur upon other aquatic plants, such as the Algae, and, interestingly enough, some of them live upon other members of the same group; e.g., certain molds are said to affect the saprolegnias.

Kanouse (1925) studied water molds from various types of habitats about Ann Arbor, Mich., such as fresh-water lakes, running water of brooks and rivers, still water in pools near rivers, and stagnant water of semimarshy borders of lakes.

The results indicate that zoospores of *Saprolegniae, Achlyae,* and *Pythiomorpha* are present in all waters. In the clear, rapidly moving water of brooks, rivers, and clear beaches of lakes, these fungi appear almost to the exclusion of other forms. The more quiet waters seem to favor the catching of other forms, also. This may be due to the fact that vegetation accumulating in or near such places offers good substrata for a greater variety of fungi, or it may mean that because of the disintegration of vegetation or other processes, the correspondingly higher concentrations of substances present in solution in water that is being changed slowly favor the growth of fungi of certain genera. At any rate, it was in the waters of this kind that Leptomitus, Apodachlya, Blastocladiae, and Pythia were found. Rhipidia were found in clear water and with one exception, not in rapidly moving water. The Apodachlya and Leptomitus collections came from bait suspended in dirty lake water that must have contained many decomposition products from the plants growing at the marshy edge. The lake bottom at this location was deep mud. Pythia were collected from bait placed in clear quiet water as well as in stagnant water.

The reader is referred to an excellent treatment of the role of the aquatic fungi by Weston (1941). The following statements are taken largely from his account. Among the Fungi only one group is preponderantly aquatic, viz., the aquatic series of the Phycomycetes. In addition, scattering representatives of the Fungi Imperfecti, Basidiomycetes, Ascomycetes, and Laboulbeniales are known from aquatic situations. They possess numerous, effective means for wide distribution. Water fungi are capable of activity and survival under wide ranges of diverse physical and chemical conditions. For example, they may thrive under conditions of light which range from total darkness to brilliant illumination. Temperature, within ranges common in nature, is of minor significance. They show a notable tolerance for the pH of water. Of all the factors which usually influence aquatic vegetation, it is the dissolved oxygen content of the water to which they are most sensitive. Not only are they common in the surface waters, but they are known also from depths of 50 ft. or more, although it is not yet clear whether those in the deeper waters are dormant or active. Little is known concerning seasonal distribution.

The significance of the aquatic fungi in limnology lies chiefly in two roles, viz., as *saprophytes,* and as *parasites.* As saprophytes they perform a very important function in the reduction and transformation of dead animals and plants. In this process they work side by side with the bacteria. As parasites they produce a great array of diseases in both plants and animals. Weston (1941) states that

It is in their parasitism that these fungi attain a significance in limnology far surpassing that of the water bacteria; for but few of the latter are destructively parasitic on aquatic animals and practically none on plants. In contrast there is abundant evidence for the statement that not one of the groups of organisms important in inland water escapes some measure from the attacks of aquatic fungi.

In the light of this statement it is clear that the aquatic fungi exercise an important influence on biological productivity.

NONPLANKTON ALGAE AND THEIR ROLE

Many Algae are never represented in the true plankton. Such plants are largely restricted to the shoal or shallow waters and to the region of the shore line. They are diverse in character, including representatives of nearly all the major groups of the Algae from the simplest to the highest. Some of the simpler ones find lodgment on almost any object in shallow water. Others thrive only in those marginal waters which are pocketed by denser growths of emergent, higher plants. Still others, particularly the filamentous types, may form masses, streamers, draperies, or even great blankets over submerged, rooted vegetation, and other fixed-bottom materials of the quieter shoal waters. The various marl-forming Algae already mentioned (page 191) accumulate on rocks, projecting parts of mussels, and other supporting objects, as well as in and on the bottom itself, especially if it be of a sandy nature. Finally, the Characeae are rooted and, in certain situations, may thrive to the extent of almost completely carpeting the entire bottom. The quantities of nonplankton Algae vary greatly in different waters, being sparse in some and of prodigious quantities in others, with all quantitative intergrades between these extremes. Lakes with large expanses of shallow water are likely to produce generous amounts of such Algae; those with a minimum of shoal or shallow waters, such as the mountain lakes, tend to maintain but minimal quantities. Irregularity of shore line is also an important factor in increasing the production of such plants. As a rule, they are very much reduced in quantity on heavily wave-swept shores.

These Algae perform various functions in the biological complex of which they are a part, one of the most important being that of furnishing food for many aquatic organisms. All of them are fed upon by aquatic animals, in spite of the fact that often this feeding activity is not particularly evident to the casual observer. In some instances, the Algae are consumed outright, e.g., by the Dryopidae (Coleoptera); while in other instances, the cells of the Algae are punctured by the mouthparts, and the contents sucked out, e.g., certain Haliplidae (Coleoptera). Even the Characeae with their large content of calcium carbonate are not exempt from attack. Thus, these Algae, in one way or another, furnish nutrition to many diverse aquatic organisms. When they die and disintegrate, they supply certain substances to the water in dissolved form and others to the bottom deposits in at least temporarily undissolved form. Among the many other services which they may render to organisms are protection from excess light, hiding places and retreats from predatory enemies, and supports for the attachment of eggs. The general functions in connection with the chemical cycle have already been discussed (page 99).

CHAPTER XI

LARGER AQUATIC PLANTS AND THEIR LIMNOLOGICAL
SIGNIFICANCE

CHARACTER OF LARGER AQUATIC PLANTS

As already indicated (page 219), the larger aquatic plants constitute a heterogeneous group composed of a few bryophytes and pteridophytes and a rather imposing array of representatives of many of the families of the spermatophytes. Rare, indeed, are the waters which are completely devoid of some of these plants. In some situations, they are present in great variety and in immense quantities. These plants vary greatly in the degree to which they have become truly aquatic; in fact, they present an interesting series of gradations from those which are little more than amphibious, living at the edge of the water in very moist or water-saturated soil, to those which are completely submerged and which have such adaptations as are necessary to fit them for continuous aquatic existence. They are restricted in distribution to the general vicinity of the shores and to the shallow-water areas. The dividing line between marginal, terrestrial plants and aquatic ones is therefore a very indefinite one, a fact which, among others, has lent support to the interpretation that some if not all of the larger aquatic plants have evolved from terrestrial types. However, the origin of the larger aquatic plants is not clear. Some of them show evidences of a terrestrial ancestry; others show features which have been interpreted by some botanists as evidence of an aquatic ancestry. Restriction to the shallow water should not be stressed too much as evidence of terrestrial origin, since other factors, such as light, doubtless have had much to do with limiting the distribution.

The larger aquatic plants of the United States are said to be mostly indigenous. Muenscher (1944) listed only 19 foreign species which have become established in American waters. The native plants are, for the most part, rather cosmopolitan within the continent, although certain species are highly specific in habitat requirements. The taxonomy of some groups is rendered difficult by the fact that they show a considerable array of growth forms ("varieties," "forms," or other designations), said to be environmentally produced. Hotchkiss (1936) listed about 940 species of marsh and aquatic plants for the United States, exclusive of the Algae and many species characteristic of wooded swamps and peat bogs. Moyle and Hotchkiss (1945) state that in Minnesota the marsh and aquatic plants, exclusive of the smaller Algae and mosses, include about 330 species of which 175 may be classified as aquatic, the remainder being essentially wet-soil species. Available information for Michigan indicates that the aquatic group is of about the same magnitude as that of Minnesota.

In a general way, these aquatic plants can be grouped into three assemblages: (1) Emergent—those rooted at the bottom and projecting out of the water for part of their length, e.g., certain common species of bulrush, *Scirpus*. (2) Floating—those which wholly or in part float on the surface of the water and often do not project above it. Most forms are rooted to the bottom and, except for the leaf blades and flowers, are submerged. The water lilies are examples of this type. However, certain ones are wholly floating and unattached, such as the duckweed, *Lemna*. (3) Submerged—those which are continuously submerged (except sometimes for floating or emergent inflorescences), such as the ellgrass *Vallisneria*, and others. While this grouping is a rough one, it is convenient for general descriptive purposes and has a wide use.

Various more or less elaborate groupings or classifications of the larger aquatic plants have been proposed from time to time, but they cannot be reviewed here. The following classification taken, with some modification, from Arber's work on "Water Plants" (1920) has many points of usefulness:

BIOLOGICAL CLASSIFICATION OF THE LARGER AQUATIC PLANTS[1]

I. Plants rooted in the bottom.
  A. Plants which are essentially terrestrial but capable of living, at least temporarily, as submerged water plants; without any marked adaptation of leaves to aquatic life, e.g., *Achillea ptarmica* (sneezeweed), *Nepeta hederacea* (ground ivy).
  B. Plants sometimes terrestrial; sometimes with submerged leaves markedly different from aerial type; aerial leaves associated with flowering stage, e.g., certain Umbelliferae, such as some of the water parsnips.
  C. Plants which produce three types of leaf: (1) submerged, (2) floating, and (3) aerial.
    1. Plants with aerial type of leaf generally associated with flowering stage, e.g., many Alismaceae, such as certain species of *Sagittaria*.
    2. Plants with floating type of leaf generally associated with flowering stage, e.g., certain representatives of yellow and white water lilies, water buttercups, water starworts, and pondweeds.
  D. Plants which, in certain instances, may occur as land forms but are normally submerged and characterized by a creeping axis bearing long, branching, leafy shoots with no floating leaves or by a plexus of leafy, rooting shoots without a creeping rhizome.
    1. Leafy aerial shoots produced at the flowering period, e.g., *Myriophyllum verticillatum* (water milfoil), *Hippuris vulgaris* (mare's-tail).

[1] Modified from Arber, with permission of the Cambridge University Press.

2. Inflorescence raised out of the water, but no aerial foliage leaves except in the land forms, e.g., *Myriophyllum* (except *M. verticillatum*) (water milfoil), *Hottonia palustris* (water violet), many potamogetons (pondweeds).

3. Inflorescence submerged, but essential organs raised to the surface, e.g., *Anacharis* (= *Elodea*) *canadensis* (water weed).

4. Inflorescence entirely submerged, and pollination occurs below the surface of the water, e.g., *Najas*, *Zannichellia* (horned pondweed), *Zostera* (grass-wrack), *Callitriche hermaphroditica* (water starwort), *Halophila*.

E. Plants which, in some instances, may occur as land forms but which are very commonly submerged and are characterized by an abbreviated axis from which linear leaves arise.

1. Inflorescence raised above the water or borne on a land plant, e.g., *Lobelia Dortmanna* (water lobelia), *Littorella uniflora*, *Sagittaria teres*.

2. Inflorescence sometimes raised above water or sometimes submerged, e.g., *Subularia aquatica* (awlwort).

F. Plants which are entirely submerged as regards the vegetative organs and which have a thallus (morphologically either of root or shoot nature) attached to the substratum. The flowers are aerial. Tristichaceae and Podostemaceae.

II. Plants which are not rooted in the bottom but live unattached in the water.

[A transition between I and II is found in *Stratiotes aloides* (water soldier), which is rooted during part of the year but floats freely during another part. There are also a number of rooted plants, such as *Hottonia palustris* and *Anacharis canadensis*, which are capable of living unattached for considerable periods.]

A. Plants with floating leaves or leaf-life shoots. Flowers raised into the air.

1. Roots not penetrating the bottom, e.g., *Hydrocharis Morsus-ranae* (frogbit), *Spirodela polyrhiza* and *Lemna minor* (duckweeds.]

2. Rootless.

Wolffia (rootless duckweed).

B. Plants entirely or partially submerged.

1. Rooted, but roots not penetrating the bottom; floating shoots, formed at flowering time, raise the flowers into the air.

Lemna trisulca (ivy-leaved duckweed).

2. Rootless.

a. Inflorescence raised out of the water.

Aldrovandia.

Utricularia (bladderwort).

b. Flowers submerged; hydrophilous pollination.

Ceratophyllum (hornwort).

It will appear from the foregoing paragraphs that the larger aquatic plants present various degrees of structural difference from the typical land plants. Needham and Lloyd (1930) give a detailed account of the chief structural characteristics of the vascular aquatic plants, as compared with the land plants, showing that the former possess a variety of differences and modifications, many of which are adaptive, in the structure of the roots, stems, and leaves, as well as in such features as mucilage production, development of vegetative reproductive bodies, and seed production. The reader is referred to their account for detailed information.

ZONATION

One of the most noticeable features of the larger aquatic plants is the distinct tendency to be arranged in more or less parallel zones along the margins of lakes, ponds, and similar bodies of water. In many instances, particularly in the smaller lakes or about the more protected, marginal regions of larger lakes, this zonation may exhibit great regularity, one zone giving place to the next succeeding one with striking abruptness. A transect of a lake margin possessing this typical zonation shows the following sequence:

1. Zone of emergent hydrophytes. This is the zone of those plants which are rooted in the bottom, submerged at their basal portions, and elevated into the air at the tops. It constitutes the shoreward zone, extending from near the edge of the water lakeward to depths which vary with circumstances but roughly about 2 m. These hydrophytes all have one feature in common, viz., the elevation of the principal chlorophyll-bearing portion above water, the submerged portions usually showing less chlorophyll development. In this zone may be found bulrushes (*Scirpus validus* and others), cat-tails (*Typha*), reeds (*Phragmites*), bur reeds (*Sparganium*), wild rice (*Zizania*), arrowheads (*Sagittaria*), pickerel weeds (*Pontederia*), certain sedges (*Carex*), and others. Even within this zone, there may be a certain amount of difference in distribution; for example, the bulrushes may occupy the deeper water, while certain other plants may be restricted to the shallow water at the margin; however, in many situations, the plants are intermingled.

2. Zone of floating hydrophytes. This zone typically occurs next beyond (lakeward) the emergent zone and is composed of plants which are rooted to the bottom but float their foliage upon the surface of the water. The depths occupied vary somewhat but are usually about 10 cm. to 2.5 m. The characteristic plants of this zone are the various water lilies (*Nuphar*, *Nelumbo*, *Nymphaea*), the water smartweed (*Polygonum amphibium*), some of the pondweeds (e.g., *Potamogeton natans*), and others. Some of these plants (e.g., water lilies) have rhizomes at the bottom, sometimes conspicuous in size. Long petioles connect the rooted rhizome with the floating blades. In many instances, the leaves of certain species are lifted somewhat above the surface of the water (e.g. *Nelumbo*).

3. Zone of submerged hydrophytes. Typically, this zone occupies the deeper water beyond the zone of floating plants, extending downward to depths which vary with conditions but in average waters do not exceed 6 m. The characteristic plants are certain species of pondweeds (*Potamogeton*), the water milfoil (*Myriophyllum*), the water weed (*Anacharis*); the eelgrass (*Vallisneria*), the bushy pondweed (*Najas*), and others. They are rooted at the bottom and often form large, dense areas, particularly in

late summer when the growth has reached a maximum. Since these hydrophytes are usually not visible from shore and often are only partially detectable from a boat, the magnitude of the crop of submerged plants produced by a lake is often badly misjudged by the casual observer. Great fields of these plants may be produced in the larger lakes with much shallow water, while a minimum crop will be found in those lakes which have very precipitous slopes and little shallow water. Areas of shallow water remote from shore also commonly support quantities of these plants, the presence of which is often not evident unless special means of collection or examination are employed.

Other submerged plants occur in certain lakes, constituting what some of the older writers have designated as a fourth zone, the *Characetum.* When present, they occupy the water to greater depths, such as 8 to 12 m. or more, although patches of them may appear in the shallower regions. The principal kinds are the stoneworts (Characeae: *Chara* and *Nitella*), bushy pondweed (*Najas*), and certain aquatic mosses (*Drepanocladus pseudo-fluitans*).

The typical zonation described above, while frequently realized, may show various deviations, depending upon prevailing conditions. The form and character of the basin alone may be such as to preclude certain, or even all, of the zones. Intermixtures of zones may occur. Extreme instances are often found in the well-developed, semi-senescent marl lakes in which the larger aquatic plants of the principal zones are virtually absent.

DEPTH LIMITATIONS

Certain environmental factors, such as light, temperature, wave action, and character of bottom, are so inherently involved with differences in depth that it is often difficult to evaluate the effect of any one of them. That depth and its associated influences impose limitations upon the local distribution of the larger plants is obvious. Too little depth may eliminate certain groups; too great depth excludes the larger plants completely. When decreasing light, due to increasing depth, falls below the effective limit, the plants disappear, the critical depth varying greatly in different waters. Changes of temperature at different depth levels are seldom if ever great enough, during the open season, to limit the plant zone. Lower temperatures and low light intensity may retard the growth of the plants, diminishing productivity and producing plants of reduced stature, e.g., those growing near the greatest depth limit (Rickett, 1924).

SEASONAL RELATIONS

In regions having a well-defined winter season accompanied by the development of ice cover, the upper portions of those plants composing the emergent and floating zones usually die down and disintegrate with the onset of winter and are replaced the next spring. However, the extent to which a similar disintegration occurs among the wholly submerged plants is still uncertain, since there is increasing evidence that some of them at least continue in active condition throughout the year even under the ice. Evidently enough effective light penetrates the ice to make continued photosynthesis possible since plants, apparently in good condition, have been found below the ice in late winter.

QUANTITIES PRODUCED

Like the yields of crops on different soils, production of the larger aquatic plants varies greatly with the nature of the water. Detailed quantitative studies by modern methods have thus far been few in number. In this country, probably no better investigation has been made than that of Rickett (1920, 1922, 1924) on certain Wisconsin lakes. By the use of the diving hood, quantitative determinations were made in various depth zones. The following data (Tables 26 to 28) are taken from his papers:

TABLE 26. STANDING CROP OF LARGER AQUATIC PLANTS
Compiled from Rickett

| Lake | Area of plant zone, sq. meters | Yield of lake | | | |
| | | Wet weight | | Dry weight | |
		Kg. per hectare	Lb. per acre	Kg. per hectare	Lb. per acre
Mendota.............	10,040,000	17,788	14,867	2,091	1,801
Green...............	8,573,000	15,180	13,540	1,780	1,590

Tables 26 to 28 indicate clearly not only the difference in general yield of the larger plants in different lakes but also the difference in the quantities of the various plants in the two situations. In Lake Mendota, *Vallisneria americana* (= *spiralis*) constituted about one-third of the total quantity; while in Green Lake, it composed less than 10 per cent. In Green Lake, *Chara* composed roughly one-half of the total quantity; while in Lake Mendota, it amounted to less than 5 per cent. Other differences of a similar sort appear in the tables. There is no reason for believing that the contrasts in Lake Mendota and Green Lake are unusual. In fact, inland waters differ widely, both qualitatively and quantitatively, in the production of the larger plants.

CHEMICAL COMPOSITION

Since in their growth processes the larger plants remove, temporarily at least, certain essential substances from the water and from the bottom deposits, the chemical composition of the plants themselves may give some information as to kinds and amounts of these substances used. On the death and decay of plants, a certain return of the contained materials is made to the lake. Very little is yet known concerning this exchange. Probably the best results of work done in this country come from the researches of Schuette and Hoffman (1922) and Schuette and Alder (1928, 1929). The following table has been assembled from their papers. The analyses of two Algae (*Chara* and *Cladophora*) are also included.

TABLE 27.   ESTIMATED TOTAL WEIGHTS OF VARIOUS LARGER AQUATIC PLANTS IN LAKE MENDOTA, WISCONSIN

Modified from Rickett

Species	Weight, kg.		Percentage	
	Wet	Dry	Wet	Dry
Potamogeton zosteriformis	290,000	50,000	1.5	2.2
P. pectinatus	1,700,000	200,000	9.2	9.0
P. amplifolius	4,200,000	650,000	22.7	29.1
P. Richardsonii	1,600,000	200,000	8.6	9.0
P. lucens	150,000	15,000	0.8	0.7
Heteranthera dubia	200,000	20,000	1.1	0.9
Najas flexilis	400,000	40,000	2.1	1.8
Vallisneria americana	7,500,000	750,000	40.5	33.6
Ceratophyllum demersum	600,000	50,000	3.2	2.2
Myriophyllum verticillatum	700,000	90,000	3.7	4.0
Scirpus validus	100,000	20,000	0.5	0.9
Ranunculus aquatilis	500,000	30,000	2.7	1.3
Lemna trisulca	80,000	10,000	0.4	0.5
Chara crispa	500,000	100,000	2.7	4.5
Cladophora glomerata	60,000	7,000	0.3	0.3
Total	18,580,000	2,232,000	100.0	100.0

It is evident from Table 29 that plants make demands upon the supply of essential materials in the water. From such analyses, it is possible to determine, at least roughly, the amounts of the different substances removed or, in some cases, returned to the water. For example, it has been computed that in Lake Mendota, the annual crop of *Vallisneria* requires a provision of 185,300 kg. of mineral matter and that the annual *Potamogeton* crop requires some 127,000 kg. Substances other than those mentioned in the foregoing analyses also occur in the plants, and a source for them must likewise be provided in lakes. It is evident that the requirements of an annual crop of the larger aquatic plants may be of large magnitude in productive lakes. A certain return of essential substances results from the decay of the plants, but the degree of completeness of return varies with circumstances and the substances involved.

TABLE 28. TOTAL WEIGHTS OF VARIOUS LARGER PLANTS IN GREEN LAKE, WISCONSIN
Modified from Rickett

Species	Weight, kg.		Percentage	
	Wet	Dry	Wet	Dry
Ceratophyllum	2,187,400	152,100	16.8	9.9
Chara	4,897,800	754,000	37.7	49.3
Drepanocladus	165,200	30,400	1.3	2.0
Anacharis	536,500	39,900	4.1	2.6
Myriophyllum	1,557,800	152,600	12.0	10.0
Najas	116,200	11,400	0.9	0.7
Potamogeton amplifolius	199,700	22,800	1.5	1.5
P. foliosus	129,500	13,600	1.0	0.9
P. gramineus	198,600	23,300	1.5	1.5
P. natans	105,300	12,500	0.8	0.8
P. pectinatus	1,257,000	149,700	9.7	10.0
P. Richardsonii	137,600	16,600	1.0	1.1
P. zosteriformis	450,100	52,700	3.5	3.5
Rorippa	22,500	2,200	0.2	0.1
Ranunculus	71,700	7,600	0.5	0.5
Vallisneria	437,100	30,000	3.4	2.0
Heteranthera	132,400	12,700	1.0	0.8
Carex	4,200	400	.....	.....
Nymphaea	24,000	2,000	0.2	0.1
Cladophora	800	100	.....	.....
Nuphar	60,000	4,900	0.5	0.3
Scirpus	311,100	36,500	2.4	2.4
Total	13,002,500	1,528,000	100.0	100.0

DISTRIBUTION IN DIFFERENT WATERS

Qualitative composition of the aquatic flora differs in different kinds of inland waters, the contrasts being striking in some instances. It appears to be reasonably well established that the chemistry of water is the most important influence in determining general distribution, although type of bottom materials and certain physical features also may be very significant. Among the more recent contributions to the subject is that of Moyle (1945), who classified the Minnesota aquatic flora, using water quality (chemistry) as the principal basis, into three major groups: (1) soft-water flora, (2) hard-water flora, and (3) alkali- or sulfate-water flora. Subdivisions of certain of these groups were also proposed. An appraisal of this classification awaits further work in this field.

LIMNOLOGICAL ROLE

It is now necessary to consider the functions which the larger aquatic plants play in the aquatic complex. Their relations, direct and indirect,

TABLE 29. CHEMICAL ANALYSES OF CERTAIN AQUATIC PLANTS
From Schuette and Hoffman, and Schuette and Alder

Constituent	Clado-phora, per cent	Myrio-phyllum, per cent	Vallis-neria, per cent	Potamo-geton, per cent	Nym-phaea odorata, per cent	Najas flexilis, per cent	Chara, per cent
Ash...............	26.53	20.72	25.18	11.42	11.21	19.16	41.22
Crude protein (N × 6.25)............	18.19	18.75	11.80	8.02	17.38	11.62	4.50
Ether extract.......	2.00	2.44	0.73	0.91	2.54	1.63	0.76
Crude fiber........	17.33	15.01	14.00	18.85	19.70	18.41	9.32
Pentosans.........	9.10	7.70	6.88	10.50	11.95	8.45	4.70
Nitrogen-free ex-tract............	26.85	35.38	41.41	50.30	37.22	40.23	39.50
Composition of the ash							
Silica, SiO_2.........	7.08	1.96	5.45	0.78	0.32	1.89	0.83
Ferric oxide, Fe_2O_3..	0.49	0.08	0.81	0.11	0.09	0.40	0.06
Aluminum oxide, Al_2O_3............	1.30	4.25	0.57	0.23	0.08	0.25	0.81
Mangano manganic oxide, Mn_3O_4.....	0.75	Trace	0.52	0.08	0.09	0.05	0.08
Calcium oxide, CaO.	3.35	4.28	8.16	3.38	1.89	8.56	37.82
Magnesium oxide, MgO............	1.62	1.34	1.87	1.38	0.75	1.61	1.19
Sodium oxide, Na_2O.	....	....	0.81	0.26	1.20	1.05	0.35
Potassium oxide, K_2O.............	....	....	5.48	2.08	2.72	2.19	0.58
Chloride, Cl........	0.14	1.62	1.32	0.56	0.40	0.51	0.29
Sulfur, S..........	0.64[1]	1.36[1]	0.85	0.82	0.37	0.48	0.27
Phosphorus, P......	0.32[2]	1.17[2]	0.23	0.13	0.27	0.30	0.06
Carbonate, CO_3.....	....	....	....	....	....	....	39.00

[1] Given in original table as sulfates (SO_4).
[2] Given in original table as phosphorus pentoxide (P_2O_5).

are numerous, but the following ones are probably the most important.

Utilization of Nonliving Matter. Little more than mention of the utilization of the mineral salts and carbon dioxide in the building up of green plant tissue needs to be made here, since it is so well known. As shown in preceding sections, very large crops of such potential food substances are thus transformed out of the inorganic materials of natural waters.

It has been contended (Rice, 1916) that the roots of larger aquatic plants serve primarily as provisions for holdfast or anchorage; that they have very little physiological function in absorbing nitrates and other substances from the bottom; and that absorption of nutrient materials is performed mostly by the body of the plant, securing the necessary substances from the water and not from the bottom. While it is true that in some species the roots are very much reduced, even wanting in some plants, there seems, on the whole, to be some well-founded doubt as to whether the function of absorption is as insignificant as the statement mentioned above would imply. That the function of anchorage has become an outstanding one in these plants seems certain; likewise, the reduction of absorption by these roots, compared with land plants, is also established, but the fact that the roots of several of the genuine aquatic species bear root hairs, together with certain results from experiments, indicates that absorption is still a function of the roots, even though somewhat restricted.

Food for Animals. The fundamental dependence of animals upon green plants holds in water as well as on land and includes not only the chlorophyll-bearing members of the phytoplankton but also the larger aquatic plants. The role of the phytoplankton in the basic food supply has long been admitted, but, in the past, some difference of opinion existed concerning the extent to which the larger aquatic plants functioned as direct food materials for aquatic animals. However, studies made during recent years have shown conclusively that they are a very significant element in the food chain; that a great variety of animals feed directly upon them; and that large quantities of these plants are often consumed. Moore (1915) showed that species of *Potamogeton* are extensively used in this way. Berg (1949, 1950), in studies made on 17 species of *Potamogeton*, found more than two dozen different species of insects which feed regularly and extensively on these plants. Frohne (1938, 1939) reported that various species of *Scirpus, Eleocharis, Carex,* and *Phragmites* serve as foods for a large array of insects. In addition, unpublished work by the writer and certain of his graduate students on Michigan lakes indicates that none of the larger aquatic plants is exempt from the direct feeding activities of animals; that not infrequently feeding is extensive enough to devastate vegetation beds; and that all parts of such plants are potential forage. Feeders on these plants comprise a great array of invertebrates, insects being a large and diversified component. On the other hand, vertebrates are involved only to a lesser extent. That fragments of larger aquatic plants sometimes occur in stomachs of certain fishes is attested by many authentic records. There is reason for believing that in many instances such plant fragments are acquired incidentally. On the other hand, analyses of stomach contents have been reported which, in certain fishes, showed aquatic-plant materials composing up to as much as 50 per cent of the total. Some fishes have been described as "largely vegetarian." The more or less regular occurrence of sizable quantities of plant materials in the stomachs of some fishes may be significant, but the writer has thus far been unable to discover satisfactory evidence that any American fish feeds exclusively upon the larger aquatic plants.

Amphibians and reptiles apparently make no significant use of the larger aquatic plants as food. On the other hand, many aquatic birds, especially ducks and geese, feed extensively upon them (Martin and Uhler, 1939; Bellrose, 1941; Bellrose and Anderson, 1943; Moyle and Hotchkiss, 1945). Of the mammals, but very few species (muskrat, beaver, deer, moose) secure food from these aquatic plants, and, with the exception of the muskrat which is said to depend upon aquatic plants more than any other North American mammal, the use is a very limited and occasional one.

Available evidence seems to indicate that at least some of the larger aquatic plants are more than ordinarily nutritious. Nelson *et al.* (1939) found that *Anacharis, Myriophyllum,* and *Vallisneria* have high protein and carbohydrate content and that they contain several vitamins. Similar results from other species are on record.

Alterations of Bottom. Plant growths alter the character of the bottom to which they are attached in several ways, some of which are (1) the mechanical stabilization of the bottom materials by their root growths and by their mass reduction of wave effects, thus more or less eliminating the shifting of bottom materials due to wave action; and (2) filling due to retention of accumulating materials, some of which are the remains of the plants themselves.

Mechanical Support. These plants function as mechanical support for many different animals. Hydra, Bryozoa, sponges, larval cases and egg masses of insects, rotifers, and others commonly find attachment on the exterior of the plants. They also serve as support for many of the Algae. Clinging forms make temporary use of them in maintaining their position below water or in resisting water movements. Even free-swimming forms with no means of attachment, such as the Naididae (Oligochaeta), may associate themselves with these plants in such a way as to maintain their position even in the face of considerable wave action.

Breeding Places. Not only may the areas within a vegetation bed be used as breeding places, but the plants themselves often serve that purpose. Some aquatic insects deposit their eggs either on or within the tissues of various plants. In many instances, the resulting larvae develop in the leaves, petioles, stems, or root stalks, while larvae of other species develop on the outside of the plants. A great many of the remarkable adaptations of aquatic insects to water involve ingenious methods of making use of the plants for life-history purposes. Various other animals develop here also, such as mollusks, annelids, and many microorganisms.

Relation to Turbidity. One of the newest additions to knowledge of the role of larger aquatic plants is the discovery by Irwin (1945) that, in Oklahoma waters which are commonly very turbid due to colloidal soil particles, (1) new impoundments, which have flooded large areas of vegetation, become clear in the early periods of their existence; (2) impounded waters have much reduced turbidity if their basins support abundant growths of submerged, larger aquatic plants; and (3) removal of larger submerged plants from a lake results in increased and continued turbidity of the water. Irwin suggested that this precipitation of colloidal soil particles from water may have its basis in an ionization process which yields positive ions, making possible the neutralization of negative charges on the particles, thus resulting in the settling of the latter. If this process exists in other situations and in the presence of other kinds of turbidity-producing substances, then it is evident that larger aquatic plants play an important part in the maintenance of clearer water. As indicated on page 165, aquatic plants are known to give off substances which seem to effect surface tension. Possibly among these exudates there are substances which participate in sedimentation processes similar to those described by Irwin.

Other Relations. The larger aquatic plants also function limnologically in the following ways: (1) as shelter from excess light; (2) as refuge from predatory enemies; (3) as materials for abode, such as the cases of certain aquatic insects; (4) in the local reduction of wave action; (5) in the dissemination of certain animals, e.g., the breaking off and floating away of pieces of the plants bearing various life-history stages of different aquatic organisms; (6) in marl formation; (7) in the production of dissolved oxygen; and (8) in the consumption and production of carbon dioxide. Still other functions may occasionally be performed.

Under certain circumstances, growths of the larger aquatic plants may literally capture a part of, or even the whole of, a body of water, ultimately changing its character completely. An instance is that of the water hyacinth, a plant introduced in some of the Florida rivers where it has covered large areas of water by the formation of surface mats. The submerged plants may also choke certain of the more protected waters, to the detriment of some kinds of life and the advangage of others.

Relation to General Productivity. That general biological productivity depends largely upon the plankton seems to be widely accepted at the present time. If this conclusion is correct, then it is obvious that any circumstance which tends either to increase or to decrease the plankton has an important bearing upon the problem of production. Some years ago, Kofoid (1903) concluded that "the amount of plankton produced by bodies of fresh water is, other things being equal, in some inverse-ratio proportional to the amount of its gross aquatic vegetation of the submerged sort." This conclusion, based upon field data taken in certain lakes which are a part of the Illinois River system, referred to the *submerged, unattached vegetation.* It was not contended that all vegetation is inimical to the development of plankton

. . . but only such as successfully competes with the phytoplankton for the available plant food and thus brings by its decay no additional sources of plant nutrition into the water. . . . Where, however, by reason of the local conditions, or the nature of the constituent plants, the aquatic vegetation adds by its decay to the fertility of the water owing to its utilization of sources of food in the soil and the air not available to the phytoplankton, we may expect to find the development of the plankton fostered by such vegetation. These conditions are realized wherever rooted, and especially emergent, vegetation prevails and contributes by its decay to the enrichment of the water. A belt of littoral vegetation of this sort may thus be of considerable effect in maintaining the plankton in a body of water.

This quotation from Kofoid is given here owing to the fact that not infrequently in the past his statement of the inimical effect of the *nonrooted* vegetation on plankton production has been used as if it were a general conclusion for all aquatic vegetation, omitting the qualifications indicated above and leading to the wrong interpretation. Klugh (1926) summarized the literature dealing with the significance of the larger aquatic plants, and the reader is referred to his paper for further details. In general, it appears that the greater the development of the larger aquatic vegetation, the greater the biological productivity of a body of water. When special circumstances prevail, or when the plant crop is restricted to certain species, it is possible that the effect may be of the opposite type. Klugh (1926) has proposed that the amount of rooted submerged vegetation has possibilities as an index character of productivity. Certain lakes, however, abundantly supplied with rooted submerged vegetation, are very low in plankton, and, on the other hand, some lakes with an exceedingly small amount of such vegetation may have what seems to be an unexpected large crop. Raymond (1937), in a study of a marl lake practically devoid of larger aquatic vegetation, found that the plankton was also very scanty, both qualitatively and quantitatively. Recently, Hutchinson and Bowen (1947) have reported competition between certain larger plants and plankton for phosphorus and suggested that possibly this competition may account for certain phytoplankton minima in spring.

Since the nonrooted larger plants do not absorb nutritive substances from bottom deposits, but depend upon those within the water itself, the contention that such plants are in more direct competition with plankton may be well taken. The end result of such competition, if and when it occurs, possibly may not always be in the form of an "inverse ratio," as reported by Kofoid for the Illinois River. It would appear to be within the realm of possibility that in some situations competition for essential nutritive substances by plankton and the larger aquatics might result in a corresponding reduction in both. However, the literature contains instances in which phytoplankton in ponds was lowest when the large aquatic plants were most luxuriant. In a recent paper, Hasler and Jones (1949) present evidence to show that in small ponds studied by them dense growths of large aquatic plants had an inhibiting effect upon phytoplankton and plankton rotifers, although plankton crustaceans were not affected. They suggest that the large aquatic plants may have certain competitive advantages when they reach a certain density of population.

It would appear that as an index character of general biological productivity the larger aquatic vegetation must be employed, for the present at least, with caution, although it does seem evident that in some instances it is indicative of production.

CHAPTER XII

NEKTON

The term *nekton* is used to designate those organisms which swim freely in water and possess an efficiency of locomotion which enables them to be more or less independent of the drifting effects of water movements. The dividing line between plankton and nekton is not always clear, since integrading instances are numerous. Sometimes these border-line cases are adult organisms; sometimes they are some other stage in a life history.

In the limnetic regions of inland waters, the nekton is composed almost entirely of fishes. *Mysis relicta* (Crustacea), a supposed relict form, occurs in some of the Great Lakes and elsewhere at considerable depths and in some situations is known to migrate to the surface at night. It also inhabits certain lakes in Europe. *Pontoporeia hoyi* (Amphipoda) also occurs in the deep water of the Great Lakes but seems to be regarded by some authors (Eggleton, 1937; Eddy, 1943) as a bottom organism. A very few other invertebrates might be mentioned in a general list of limnetic nekton forms, but at least some of them are also border-line instances between the nekton and the benthos. Not all fishes are strictly limnetic in their habits; in fact, this group is usually in the minority when compared with the littoral group; for example, in Douglas Lake, Michigan, only about one-fourth of the species known for the lake might justly be listed as limnetic, and these only in the older stages of the life history. The limnetic nekton animals may inhabit the whole of the open water of a lake and down to its greatest depths, provided the lowermost waters maintain suitable conditions for their existence. Even under stagnation conditions, there are evidences that some of the limnetic fishes make temporary excursions into the underlying hypolimnion.

In contrast to the limnetic region, the littoral area is the zone of greater nekton population. Although this region may constitute little more than a mere fringe about the periphery of a lake, the greatest diversity of species and the largest mass of individuals of nekton are usually concentrated there. In addition to the fishes, young and mature, numerous free-swimming invertebrates occur, of which insects form a sizable part. Vegetation zones, particularly the "pondweed" zone, usually contain the largest nekton population. As will be shown later (page 322), the conditions of the littoral region differ from place to place, and the char-

310

acter of the littoral nekton varies accordingly, being greater and more diverse in some places than others.

Whether any of the other aquatic vertebrates should be considered as nekton is largely a matter of opinion.   Possibly, the clearest case of all is the puzzling occurrence of seals in Lake Baikal, Siberia.   All major groups of the vertebrates, in addition to the fishes (Amphibia, Reptilia, Aves, and Mammalia), have representatives more or less adapted to water and which, at times at least, are free swimming.   In fact, the Amphibia are preeminently aquatic in their developmental activities, and some of them are completely aquatic throughout the whole life cycle, e.g., *Necturus.* Most of them, however, are tied to the water's edge by physiological demands of one kind or another in the adult stages.   Most adult and larval amphibians have the ability to swim in the quieter waters of the littoral region.   Among the reptiles, a few turtles and snakes have acquired certain aquatic habits, often taking to water and swimming about freely but not far from shore; they are, nevertheless, essentially terrestrial, are air breathers, and deposit their eggs on land.   In certain southern regions, alligators and crocodiles occur in fresh waters but, like the other so-called aquatic reptiles, are closely tied to the shore.   Many of the birds, although inherently terrestrial, have developed intimate connections with the water and possess some remarkable adaptations to it, some of which consist of highly efficient swimming and diving activities. Gulls, terns, ducks, and others too well known to mention here may occur on waters, sometimes far from shore, and might be considered among the nekton if the term nekton were interpreted to include temporary swimmers on the surface.   The aquatic mammals (beaver, muskrat, otter, mink, and others) are also temporary inhabitants of the water.   Probably there is little profit in including the aquatic reptiles, birds, and mammals in any consideration of either the nekton or any other assemblage of strictly aquatic organisms, even though they do have complex interrelations with the water populations.

The literature contains attempts to divide the nekton into depth zones; but the position of the proposed lines of separation is somewhat artificial, and the zones often variable.   It appears to be true that certain fishes select the deeper, cooler waters; others, the intermediate regions; and still others, the upper strata.   Such a distribution often depends upon the season, the physiological state of the fish, and the stage in the life history.   It has been claimed (Shelford, 1913) that in the Great Lakes, the whitefish and certain others exhibit a horizontal depth stratification in which some half-dozen species are arranged one above the other in their distribution, with the shallowwater cisco, *Leucichthys artedi,* in the surface waters and the deepwater sculpin, *Triglopsis thompsoni,* confined to depths below 115 m., the other species occupying levels between these extremes. Koelz (1929) made an exhaustive study of the whitefishes of the Great Lakes, and his excellent statement of the essentials of vertical distribution is as follows:

The physical conditions in the lakes vary, and the adaptability of the species also is different, so that it is not possible to generalize too strictly about the habitat selection of any species in the basin. In some lakes, species that regularly inhabit shallow water elsewhere may be driven, by competition on the shoals or by absence of shoals, to find a living in deeper water; and, being adaptable, they may thrive there (Lake Ontario). In other cases, species that regularly inhabit deep water have been known to occur abundantly in shallow water only (Lake Nipigon); but in general, in any lake, there are certain groups of species that are found in shallower water than others. In general, *artedi, clupeaformis,* and *quadrilaterale* are shoal-loving forms; *alpenae, zenithicus, reighardi,* and *hoyi* also like comparatively shallow water; but *johannae, nigripinnis,* and *kiyi* are found chiefly in the deeper waters.

The bathymetric distribution of the species or groups of species is zonal. Each occupies a rather broad zone defined by the depth of water at its margins. At the center of the zone, each has its greatest density of population, and this density diminishes toward the margin of the zone. Only a few stragglers are found beyond their zones, except during the breeding migration. The zones overlap at their margins, so that the different forms intermingle there in relatively small numbers.

There are no data to indicate why these zones have been selected by the various species or groups of species. Nothing is known about their reactions to the various physical and chemical factors of their environment. Possibly, the selection is influenced by the character of the bottom. Throughout the area inhabited by the shoal group, the hydrographic map shows rock, gravel, and sand; and in the deeper parts of the lakes, clay and mud. While each species may range over all of these types of bottom within its zone, of course it is not only possible but probable that there are differences in the character of the areas designated on the chart as mud, clay, etc., and that these differences influence, indirectly, the distribution of the fish. Certainly, all of the forms except *artedi* (which is a plankton feeder and therefore normally takes its food above the bottom), so far as known, are confined to a bottom stratum of water of a thickness of not more than 5 ft. In this stratum, they find their food, which consists (in all forms) chiefly of various species of Crustacea and Mollusca. The character of the food available probably is determined directly by the character of the bottom, and therefore a knowledge of the food regularly taken by each species would be helpful in defining this factor of the habitat.

Spawning grounds of the Great Lakes whitefishes, in so far as they are known, appear to be determined roughly by the vertical distribution of the fish themselves. The shallowwater cisco, *Leucichthys artedi;* the lake whitefish, *Coregonus clupeaformis;* and the round whitefish, *Prosopium cylindraceum quadrilaterale,* spawn on the shoals in November and early December; shortnose cisco, *Leucichthys reighardi,* spawns in Lake Michigan and Lake Huron, in May probably at depths of less than 36 m.; the bloater, *Leucichthys hoyi*, spawns in Lake Michigan and Lake Huron, in March at depths of 36 to 55 m.; while at least three other species spawn in the deep water (110 m.). It is interesting to note that many of the different species in the same Great Lake spawn at different seasons of the year; also, that the spawning season of the same species may differ greatly in the different Great Lakes.

The food of the young of the Great Lakes whitefishes seems to be secured from the plankton, a food habit which may bring the immature fish into the uppermost waters, thus, in some instances, giving them a vertical distribution different from that of the more mature stages.

Other fishes, such as the lake trout, *Cristivomer namaycush,* and the burbot, *Lota lota,* occur in the deeper waters of the Great Lakes. In addition to the fishes of the deep waters and the upper waters remote from shore, there are the numerous species which, in both young and adult stages, occupy the various habitats of the shoreward regions.

In the inland lakes, the strictly limnetic fishes become rapidly reduced with decrease of depth and of surface area, so that, in very small lakes, such a group ceases to exist, and such fishes as do occur constitute merely a littoral nekton. In Douglas Lake, Michigan, a lake about 4 miles long and about 2.3 miles in maximum breadth, with a maximum depth of 28 m., Reighard (1915) found the fishes distributed into four different communities as follows: (1) the community of young fishes which occupy the sandy shoals; (2) the stony-shoal community; (3) the vegetation community; and (4) the deep-water community, this group containing the common sucker (17.8 to 30.5 cm. long); the pike (30.5 to 76.3 cm. long); the small-mouthed black bass (30.5 to 40.7 cm. long); the yellow perch (21.6 cm. long); and the burbot. Earlier stages of these deep-water species occur as regular components of some of the other communities; for example, the young of the yellow perch are conspicuous in the assemblages on the sandy shoals; still older stages form a part of the vegetation community; and finally, with increasing age, the older individuals pass over into the deep-water assemblage. Thus, the community of young fishes is a temporary one in the sense that none of the individuals of any of the species remains there throughout the whole life history, but before their second season they all desert the shoals. On the other hand, the stony-shoal community is permanent except as it was possibly interfered with by winter conditions. Pearse (1921) found that in Green Lake, Wisconsin, the distribution of the fishes, in the summer, shows a definite stratification as follows: 0 to 10 m. depth, all species known for the lake except adult ciscoes; 10 to 20 m. depth, only large pickerel, small-mouthed black bass, and suckers; 20 to 40 m., no fishes caught; 40 to 70 m., ciscoes only, but they were abundant.

Much research has been directed at the bathymetric distribution of fishes in inland lakes. Like plankton, the nekton seldom if ever manifests uniform distribution, this lack of uniformity being due to various causes. Formation of local aggregations, seasonal migrations, diurnal movements, distribution of food, reproductive cycles, presence or absence of shelter, movements of water, oxygen distribution, temperature conditions—these and other limnological circumstances form a complex background for the phenomena of bathymetric distribution of fishes. These potential influences have many interrelationships. They interlace in so many different ways that it seems certain that no single explanation for the various differences in fish distribution will be forthcoming.

CHAPTER XIII

BENTHOS

The term *benthos* includes all bottom-dwelling organisms. This group presents a great assemblage of plants and animals. Among the animals are representatives of most of the phyla. The plants comprise a similar diversified array. It must be understood that the term *benthos* includes organisms of the bottom from the uppermost water-bearing portions of the beach down to the greatest depths. As might be expected, the benthos varies widely with different conditions of bottom, both at the same level and at different depths. In fact, variations are so diverse and so marked that it is difficult to discuss them as a whole. Benthos and nekton intergrade in various ways.

CLASSIFICATION OF BENTHIC REGIONS

Many limnologists recognize three major zones on a lake floor, viz., (1) *littoral*, (2) *sublittoral*, and (3) *profundal*. In addition, a fourth one, the *abyssal*, is sometimes designated in lakes of very unusual depth, this zone beginning at about 600 m. and extending to the deepest regions. Few lakes have depths of such magnitude. While these zones have certain general distinguishing features which can be recognized, it must be understood that they grade into each other and that any lines of demarcation which may be agreed upon are, in certain respects, artificial. The extent of these zones is expressed in terms of depth of the water. Their breadth (depth extent) varies greatly in different lakes, since they are the direct result of the form of lake basins. For example, some lakes may have so shallow a basin that the entire bottom can justly be said to be within the littoral zone, while lakes with basins of considerable depth and very precipitous slope have an exceedingly narrow littoral zone.

As commonly used, the *littoral zone* extends from the water's edge to the lakeward limit of the rooted aquatic vegetation; the *sublittoral zone* extends from the lakeward limit of the rooted vegetation down to about the level of the upper limit of the hypolimnion; and the profundal zone includes all of the lake floor bounding the hypolimnion. If these terms are defined in this way, it is obvious that a lake, irrespective of its area, may be so shallow that its whole bottom comes within the littoral zone; that, similarly, a lake with depths which go beyond the limit of rooted plant growth but which does not stratify thermally and chemically would

TABLE 30. COMPARISON OF SOME OF THE SYSTEMS OF DESIGNATING BENTHIC ZONATION
Modified and extended from Naumann (1930)

Zone	(Shore region)	Thienemann (German lakes)	Wesenberg-Lund (Furesee, Denmark)	Ekman (Vättern, Sweden)	Blomgren, Lundqvist, Naumann; in part, Sernander, Thomasson, Thunmark (Swedish lakes)	Lenz, compromise proposal	Forel (Lake Geneva, Switzerland)	Muttkowski (Lake Mendota, Wisconsin, U.S.A.)
I. Zone above uppermost part of water-level amplitude; never continuously submerged; never subject to splash of waves	Beach	Littoral	Littoral		Epilittoral	Epilittoral		
II. Zone not continuously submerged but at times subject to splash of waves	General shore region				Supralittoral	Supralittoral	(Drier beach)	Shore-shoals zone
III. Zone submerged by high water				Littoral	Eulittoral	Eulittoral (Littoral)	(Wetter beach)	Surf-line zone (rachion)
IV. Permanently submerged zone — 1. Emergent aquatic plants					Sublittoral (Littoral)		Littoral	Upright plant zone
2. Floating-leaf aquatic plants								
3. Submerged aquatic plants			Sublittoral	Macroelittoral			Recumbent plant zone
4. Transition zone		Sublittoral	Sublittoral		Microelittoral (Eulittoral)	Eprofundal (Profundal)		Sublittoral
5. Plantless muddy-bottom deposit — a. Upper part		Profundal	Profundal	Profundal	Profundal	Eprofundal	Deep region	Aphytal
b. Under part						Euprofundal		

Muttkowski headers: Littoral; Eulittoral; Vegetation zone (over Upright plant zone and Recumbent plant zone).

have its whole floor within the littoral and the sublittoral; and that since the extent of the hypolimnion, when present, varies with the progress of the summer season and with other circumstances, the region of separation between sublittoral and profundal zones is not a permanent one. While there is a lack of agreement among limnologists as to the details of this classification (Table 30) or, for that matter, as to the desirability of this particular classification, it appears to be as useful as any thus far proposed. The major zones are occasionally subdivided, e.g., *upper sublittoral* and *lower sublittoral* and *upper profundal* and *lower profundal*, but it does not seem certain as yet that this practice has any great value. Fortunately, most investigators state the depth limits of the major zones which they adopt, thus avoiding, in part at least, some of the confusion which would otherwise result. Application of these terms to lakes may be illustrated from the work of Eggleton (1931) (Table 31).

TABLE 31.   EXTENT OF MAJOR BENTHIC ZONES IN CERTAIN LAKES
Data from Eggleton

Lake	Littoral, m.	Sublittoral, m.	Profundal, m.
Douglas Lake, Mich.................	0–9	9–15	15–28
Third Sister Lake, Mich.............	0–3	3–10	10–18
Kirkville Green Lake, N. Y...........	0–3	3–8	8–61

BEACH ZONES

Formerly it was a common practice to regard the benthic region as beginning at the water's edge and extending to the deepest region. However, it became necessary to change this conception when it was discovered that portions of certain kinds of beaches regularly support a rich and diversified biota. Since the representatives of this biota are almost invariably truly aquatic, living in the water held in the interstices of beach materials, and since this water has a direct continuity with the main body of the lake or stream, the organisms involved are now commonly considered as *benthos* and the environment inhabited by them as a part of the benthic region. For limnological purposes, the beach environment has been subdivided in various ways, sometimes on the basis of natural criteria and at other times apparently on little more than arbitrary convenience. Certain proposals appear in Table 30. A simple, natural, and frequently usable subdivision follows.

Exposed sandy beaches often maintain three parallel environments which, while they grade into one another to some extent, have a certain degree of distinctness depending somewhat upon local conditions. (1) The *inner beach*—that part extending from the water's edge, during periods of calm water, up the slope to the place where the surface of the sand ceases to be saturated with water and shows the first traces of drying. This zone is relatively narrow and is exposed, in part at least, to the slight wash of the gentle waves of calm weather. (2) The *middle beach*— that part occupying space just beyond the inner beach and constituting the region which is subject to the wash of waves only during conditions of ordinary rough weather. In calm weather, this part of the beach, while containing water at lower levels, shows a dry surface. (3) The *outer beach*—that part of the beach which extends from the middle beach to the outer limits of the beach proper. It is washed by waves only during the most violent storms or during times of highest water levels. During the summer season, it is usually dry to some depth, is subject to a certain amount of shifting due to wind action, and may show a scanty encroachment of beach plants.

The degree to which these three regions are developed is largely a matter of the kinds of materials which compose the beach. These zones occur in best developed form on exposed sand beaches with a gentle slope. These three conditions of exposure to wave action exist even on a rocky shore, but the substratum may provide no means of retaining a permanent moisture content above the water line. Mud shores may develop these zones to some degree. Such zones produced on exposed shores are often kept free of debris, although a certain amount of detritus becomes mingled with the sand, and drifts of organic matter may accumulate near the water line during calm weather.

Another subdivision which has received some notice and use of recent years is that of Wiszniewski (1933), who introduced the term *psammolittoral* to designate the sandy zone from an unspecified position in a lake to a region a few meters above the water's edge. He divided the psammolittoral region into (1) the *hydropsammon*—the submerged sandy bottom lakeward from the water's edge; (2) the *hygropsammon*—the zone immediately landward from the water's edge (about 1 m. wide), which is almost constantly saturated with water; and (3) the *eupsammon*—the zone next landward beyond the hygropsammon. In this subdivision, the hygropsammon corresponds roughly to the *inner beach* and the eupsammon to the *middle beach.*

It would seem logical to consider the inner beach and the middle beach as merely an extension of the littoral zone and therefore an integral part of it. Seldom are these zones fixed in position. In lakes whose surface level falls during the summer, areas of submerged bottom near the water's edge become transformed into inner beach by retreat of the water, and simultaneously the earlier inner beach becomes middle beach and middle beach transforms into outer beach. This gradual movement of the zones continues until the lowest surface elevation of the lake is reached; then if surface elevation of the lake rises, the migration of zones described above will be reversed.

PERIPHYTON

The term *periphyton* is now commonly used to designate that miscellaneous assemblage of organisms growing upon free surfaces of objects submerged in water. It frequently takes the form of a slippery brown or green layer. It is commonly found on plants, wood, stones, and various other objects. Periphyton in some form appears to be a constant feature in unmodified inland waters, often conspicuous especially during the summer. Locally it may develop from a few tiny gelatinous plants and in time culminate in a compact felted coat which may be soft and slimy or, in some situations, crusty with contained marl or silt.

Periphyton seems to develop best in littoral and sublittoral regions. In lakes having thermal and chemical stratification, it appears to be confined to bottom areas above the level of the lower limit of the thermocline. It is usually reduced in amount wherever wave action is severe.

Because of its almost universal presence in water and the conspicuous quantities often produced, periphyton must play some important role in limnological processes of a lake or stream. There seems to be at present a tendency among limnologists to regard periphyton as a part of the *benthos*, and it is so treated in this book. However, it must be understood that in some respects the periphyton is not a typical benthos. It may occur generously upon various kinds of supports held up in the water many feet above the bottom. Furthermore, it must be pointed out that a mass of periphyton is likely to contain both plankton and benthic organisms. Plankters are caught and held in the tangle of attached forms. In such a mass, the accidentally entrapped plankters should be regarded as extraneous. But it has been shown (Young, 1945) that even the forms which compose the true periphyton when washed off their supports may become then a part of the plankton.

ZONATION OF BOTTOM DEPOSITS

Considering bottom deposits from the point of view of their most fundamental characteristics, and omitting, for the time, the innumerable, lesser variations, the littoral, sublittoral, and profundal zones present bottom materials of distinctly different sorts. The littoral zone comprises the basic materials which compose the shore itself (sand, gravel, stones, rock, earthy materials, and the like), modified by the action of water, by drift materials, by plant growths, and by organic deposits of more recent origin. The bottom materials of the sublittoral region are of a transitional sort, grading from those of the littoral zone to those of the profundal zone and showing an increasing accumulation of true bottom deposit (materials deposited upon the original basin surface). Finally, the profundal zone is the region of very finely divided, soft oozes which carpet the lowermost parts of a lake basin, sometimes to a great thickness, and which are absent locally only when, under very special conditions, some movement of the deep waters transports them elsewhere as they are formed. Absence of oozes in certain Old World lakes has been theoretically accounted for by assuming that they were subsequently dissolved, an assumption which awaits convincing proof.

DISTRIBUTION OF BENTHOS

The fundamental importance of the benthos in the economy of natural waters has led to a large number of investigations dealing with the qualitative and quantitative aspects of this biota. For the most part, these studies have dealt with inland lakes, while the Great Lakes and others of similar magnitude have as yet received but little attention.

QUALITATIVE DISTRIBUTION

While the different conditions of bottom, exposure to wave action, and other modifying circumstances which diversify the littoral zone bring

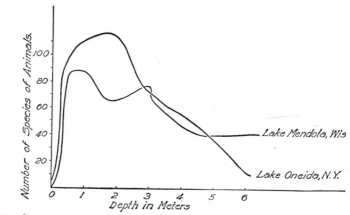

FIG. 39. Graphs showing distribution of the total number of different species of macroscopic animals in the littoral bottom from the water line out to a depth of 6 m., in Lake Mendota, Wisconsin, and in South Bay, Lake Oneida, N. Y., during the summer season. (*Data for Lake Mendota taken from Muttkowski, 1918; data for Lake Oneida from Baker, 1918.*)

about local differences in the fauna, it appears that, as a whole, the littoral zone supports a much greater number of different kinds of animals than do the sublittoral and profundal zones. Figure 39 shows the qualitative depth relations as they occur in two American lakes, indicating that the greatest diversity of life occurs roughly in the region of 0.5 to 3 m. While this is a common type of species distribution in the ordinary inland lakes, it must not be assumed that it is a constant condition. The zone of greatest number of species may vary considerably in position in different lakes, and lakes have been reported in which many species occurred at all levels from the surface to depths of 100 m. or more. Instances are also known of lakes possessing two zones of maximum number of species. Under any circumstances, the number of species of bottom organisms declines abruptly at the lower margin of the thermocline in lakes in which thermal and chemical stratification are well established.

The littoral and sublittoral populations, exclusive of the microscopic forms, contain many insects and mollusks, these two groups often comprising as much as 70 per cent, or even more, of the total number of the different components present. Of these groups, insects often outnumber the different species of mollusks, although the reverse condition may occur. In the latter instance, the number of species of mollusks may truly outnumber the species of insects, but sometimes this relation is merely an apparent one due to the fact that the examinations may have been made at the time when the transformations of bottom-dwelling, immature insects into the aerial, adult stages have temporarily eliminated the more conspicuous instars from the littoral zone.

With increasing depths beyond the littoral zone, the number of different benthic species usually diminishes, often rapidly. The levels at which different species fade out vary with the different lakes and their special circumstances, but it may be expected that in average, temperate lakes of the first and second orders, all species of sponges, Bryozoa, Platyhelminthes, snails, bivalves (except Sphaeridae), and almost all species of nematodes, annelids, and insects will commonly disappear within the first 18 m. of depth. Exceptions occur, e.g., the reported permanent occurrence of snails in the deep waters of certain European alpine lakes; also, the occurrence of Amphipoda to depths of 118 m. in Lake Nipigon, Canada. Since, in many instances, the various species have their own particular zonal distribution, they do not all disappear together but instead drop out in a sequence of single species or groups of species.

The typical profundal benthic population, discussed in another connection (page 184), is a heterogeneous assemblage composed of a very few representatives of widely different animal groups. There is no constancy of composition in different types of lakes. Some lakes have no profundal benthic animal population at all, this circumstance usually arising from decomposition conditions of unusual severity and lacking relief owing to the absence of complete overturns. Even within a single lake basin, differences in the composition of the population may occur at different places, particularly in those lakes which possess a multidepression basin (submerged, isolated depressions within the main basin), thus constituting one of the several evidences of depression individuality. In the multidepression basin of Douglas Lake, Michigan, four of the depressions, during mid- and late summer, show a profundal benthic fauna composed almost exclusively of representatives of insects (*Corethra, Chironomus,* and *Protenthes*) and annelids (Tubificidae), while the other two major depressions contain, in addition, several other kinds of animals.

The nature of the bottom has a selective influence upon the quality of the fauna. Baker (1918) classified bottom materials in the littoral zone (0 to 5.5 m.) of Lake Oneida, N.Y., into six general types, as follows: mud, sand, clay, gravel, boulders, and sandy clay. Of the macroscopic fauna, 26 species lived on all six kinds of bottom; 24 upon three kinds; 16 upon four kinds; 27 upon two kinds; and 77 upon but one kind. Analyzed in another way, 114 species were found upon a mud bottom; 104, upon sand; 83, upon clay; 58, upon gravel; 73, upon boulder bottom; and 72, upon sandy clay. While this example indcates distinct differences in the distribution of the various species, no general conclusion can be drawn from the data or, for that matter, from many other such sets of data which occur in the literature, since (1) classifications of bottom materials for these purposes are as yet too rough and unstandardized to insure that those designated by various authors are sufficiently similar to be comparable; and (2) selective influence of the bottom materials may be modified and even superseded by the influence of other factors in the environment operating simultaneously; for example, Baker points out, in connection with his results mentioned above, that "the effect of the different kinds of bottom is greatly modified by a mass of filamentous algae which covers large areas of the bottom like a blanket and makes a uniform algal habitat over the diverse kinds of bottom." Mud bottoms are often described as supporting the greatest number of different species, but there are records which portray the situation as otherwise, even to the extent of reporting the smallest number on mud bottoms. Bottoms classified as sand vary greatly in the fauna which they support, depending upon whether these bottoms are exposed and wave swept or protected and non-shifting. Krecker and Lancaster (1933) studied the bottom of western Lake Erie at depths of 0 to 2 m. and found the smallest number of different kinds of animals per unit area on sand and the maximum number on flat rubble.

Studies of benthic organisms have thus far dealt very largely with the macroscopic organisms. That a *microfauna* exists in the bottom deposits is established, but very little is as yet known about its composition. These microorganisms are very properly considered as bottom dwellers, since it appears that they (1) are seldom free swimming or (2) are free swimming only in some stage of the life cycle or (3) regularly spend most of the time in or on the bottom materials. Earlier workers (Smith, 1894; Kofoid, 1897; Jennings, 1897; *et al.*) recorded various microorganisms taken from bottom tows and dredgings in both the Great Lakes and inland lakes, but no studies were made of their special relations to the bottom layers or materials. Baker (1918) found 10 species of Cladocera, one copepod, and two ostracods occurring as bottom organisms in Oneida Lake, New York. Bigelow (1928) divided the littoral benthic microorganisms of Lake Nipigon, Canada, into two ecological groups: (1) the ooze-film assemblage and (2) the associated ooze-film assemblage. The ooze-film group comprises those microorganisms living in and on that film of ooze which forms the upper surface of the lake bottom. This assemblage was found to contain the following microscopic organisms: bacteria, 3 green Algae, 13 diatoms, 13 Protozoa, certain rotifers, several Entomostraca (mostly Cladocera), Tardigrada, and certain water mites. The following quotation from Bigelow presents his interpretations of some of the structures and habits of these ooze-film dwellers:

The Cladocera present many striking adaptations to this environment. They seldom swim but creep about by means of their antennae or push themselves through the ooze by means of their postabdomens, which are usually broad and powerful. The eye has a tendency to become small and may even disappear.

Particularly well fitted for their environment are the species of *Ilyocryptus*. Their shells are never completely shed in moulting, but form layers one above the other. The shells are spiny, and ooze clings to them so as to hide the animal entirely. In fact, the animals may be encased in a mass of ooze several times their size. They progress by dragging their way through the ooze film with their antennae, while continually shoving and kicking with their broad, spiny postabdomens. The eye is quite small. *Leydigia quadrangularis* has a similar postabdomen and a small eye, and is quite like *Ilyocryptus* in its habits. In *Monospilus dispar*, the eye has completely disappeared, and only the large pigment spot beside it remains. As in *Ilyocryptus* the shell is retained after moulting and forms layers. The postabdomen is less broad and powerful, but is armed with a powerful claw at its tip and with a large tooth at the base of the claw. Doubtless, this is a very efficient organ for pushing the animal through the ooze. *Rhynchotalona falcata* possesses a short, thick postabdomen with a strong claw and four strong denticles. The rotifers creep about with leech-like movements, but are also able to swim freely in the water.

The water bears (*Tardigrada*) with stumpy legs and long curved claws are well fitted for crawling through the ooze film as are also the horny water mites (*Oribatidae*), which cannot swim, but creep about on the ooze.

The associated ooze-film assemblage was described by Bigelow as composed of those organisms which are

. . . directly dependent upon the ooze film for sustenance and are seldom found far from it. They do not live in the ooze film or creep through it, although they may occasionally rest upon it, but swim about immediately adjacent to it. Most of the organisms are Cladocera.

In addition to 13 species of Cladocera, 5 species of rotifers were listed as belonging to this associated ooze-film assemblage. Members of this group did not show structural modifications, such as appeared in the ooze-film assemblage.

Rawson (1930) studied the benthic microfauna of Lake Simcoe, Canada, at various depths down to 45 m. and listed a population composed of more than 35 Protozoa, 2 Turbellaria, minute nematodes, 2 oligochaetes, 7 rotifers, 8 Cladocera, 2 copepods, nauplii, several ostracods, 1 Gastrotricha, 1 Tardigrada, and 3 water mites, a list which he believed to be quite incomplete. He failed to find the ooze film and the associated ooze-film groups so distinctly separated from each other as had Bigelow in Lake Nipigon. The microfauna was mostly confined to a thin stratum, about 1 cm. thick, at the top of the bottom deposits.

Moore (1939) reported 116 species of microscopic animals from the bottom deposits of Douglas Lake, Michigan, distributed in the following taxonomic groups: Protozoa, 23; Hydrozoa, 1; Rhabdocoela, 6; Nematoda, 1; Rotatoria, 28; Gastrotricha, 2; Oligochaeta, 8; Cladocera, 14; Copepoda, 11; Ostracoda, 11; Acarina, 10; Tardigrada, 1. Further research will certainly extend this list. There are as yet no published records of the microfloral benthos of this lake.

In most if not all natural benthic regions a microflora exists, but so little work has been done on it from the limnological standpoint that no account will be attempted here. The results of Butcher (1932) on the microflora of certain river beds may be some indication of research opportunities in this field.

The benthos of the psammolittoral zone is still only imperfectly known. The first work of consequence in this field was done in Europe only about two decades ago. In this country, two workers (Pennak, 1939, 1940; Neel, 1948) made substantial contributions. Pennak studied the microscopic fauna of the psammolittoral region of 15 Wisconsin lakes and reported a diversified population which included representatives of Protozoa, Tardigrada, Rotatoria, Copepoda, Gastrotricha, Nematoda, Turbellaria, and insects; also other organisms including many bacteria and Algae. Neel investigated the psammolittoral biota, both plant and animal, in the beaches and shoals of Douglas Lake, Michigan, and reported the occurrence of more than 240 species of organisms distributed taxonomically, in part, as follows: Algae, 162; Protozoa, 27; Turbellaria, 1; Rotatoria, 38; Gastrotricha, spp.; Nematoda, spp.; Tardigrada, 1; Oligochaeta, 6; Ostracoda, spp.; Copepoda, 3; Insecta, several kinds of larvae. The works of both Pennak and Neel are but substantial pioneer efforts in a new and very inviting field. Without doubt, present knowledge is but a scant look-in on this aspect of the benthos.

Since the periphyton may be considered a part of the benthos, some reference should be made here to its qualitative composition. There are many papers which deal with periphyton, but only one of consequence (Young, 1945) is concerned with inland waters of the United States. Young found 115 organisms, exclusive of bacteria and Fungi, in the periphyton of Douglas Lake, Michigan. In this highly diversified assemblage, the numerically dominant groups were: Fungi, Rivulariaceae, Chlorophyceae, Bacillareae, Naididae, Cladocera, and Rotatoria. However, in interpreting this census of forms found in periphyton, it should be remembered (page 319) that in this situation components of plankton and benthos come together and intermingle. Here is another new and inviting field in which much work is seriously needed.

It should be noted that representatives of some of the species listed by investigators as being bottom forms are commonly found as plankton forms in the limnetic regions, even though the life-history stage be the same. There is very little known as yet concerning the various interrelations between the plankton organisms and benthic environments. Available evidence seems to suggest that some of the plankters are facultative benthic inhabitants and some of the benthic forms, facultative plankters. Whether, in such instances, the plankton representatives and the benthic representatives of the same species belong to different strains or races, no answer can be made at present. As pointed out elsewhere in this book (page 230), there is some evidence that bottom populations of microorganisms actually produce directly many of the plankters taken in plankton collections. According to one current theory, the original home of fresh-water plankton is the bottom and littoral region of ponds and lakes, from which situation the plankton is still constantly being recruited (Wesenberg-Lund). From these evidences and suggestions, it follows that there may be a large and diversified benthic microbiota in inland waters.

QUANTITATIVE DISTRIBUTION

In Shallow Lakes. In very shallow lakes of the ordinary type (third order), the entire bottom may be more or less uniformly productive if the basin is not exceptionally diversified. Often, such shallow lakes are very productive, although mere shallowness alone does not insure it, and exceptions occur. Every unit area of bottom is situated in a depth zone which facilitates the growth of bottom dwellers; and while the quantities produced at the various depths of even a very shallow lake are not necessarily the same, the differences are of a much smaller magnitude than in the lakes of greater depths. Since, as mentioned in an earlier discussion, the whole benthic region of a very shallow lake belongs essentially to the littoral zone, or possibly to the littoral and the upper sublittoral, the distribution is essentially the same as that on the littoral zone of the deeper lake, assuming that the environmental conditions are comparable.

In Deeper Inland Lakes. From the point of view of quantitative distribution, the deeper inland lakes can be divided into two groups for purposes of discussion: (1) those which do not develop chemical stratification during the summer and (2) those which become chemically stratified and remain so throughout most of the summer period.

Nonstratified Deeper Lakes. In those deeper lakes which do not have permanent chemical stratification during the summer but which continue to circulate and maintain an ample supply of dissolved oxygen, the limiting effects of stratification and the resulting summer stagnation of a hypolimnion are lacking. As a consequence, certain benthic forms extend much deeper into the basin, with resulting greater mass production. The following table (Table 32) represents the nature of the benthic population

TABLE 32. AVERAGE NUMBER OF MACROSCOPIC BENTHIC ORGANISMS AT DIFFERENT
DEPTHS IN LAKE SIMCOE, CANADA
From Rawson

Depth zone, m.	Chironomid larvae	Ephemerid larvae	Gastropoda[1]	Pelecypoda[1]	Amphipoda	Oligochaeta	Corethra	Trichoptera	Miscellaneous	Average number of all organisms per sq. m.	Average dry weight of all organisms,[1] mg. per sq. m.
Shore zone, 0–1	152	48	54	22	28	16	0	1	84	405	1,028
0–5	300	90	124	82	112	36	0	14	30	788	1,280
5–10	450	54	130	78	138	30	2	10	34	926	1,480
10–15	240	52	54	88	94	24	9	4	9	574	654
15–20	540	28	82	118	10	26	15	8	17	844	1,170
20–25	620	0	9	114	2	80	30	0	92	947	1,420
25–30	780	0	8	102	0	106	62	0	10	1,068	1,340
30–35	860	0	7	84	0	98	74	0	11	1,134	1,220
35–40	760	0	5	52	0	118	70	0	7	1,012	950
40–45	740	0	6	34	0	120	72	0	6	978	852

[1] Weight of mollusk shells deducted.

in Lake Simcoe, Canada, during the period of May to October inclusive. According to Rawson (1930), this lake, while showing a certain dissolved-oxygen decline at times during the summer, did not reduce the oxygen below 2 p.p.m., and even this incipient stratification was sometimes lost by renewed circulation.

Thus, it appears that in Lake Simcoe, the greatest average number of organisms occurred in the 25- to 40-m. zone; but in all regions, there was an ample population, the numerical minimum being in the shore zone (0 to 1 m.). In Lake Nipigon, Canada, Adamstone (1924) found that the six most important food organisms for fishes (Mollusca, Chironomidae, Ephemerida, Trichoptera, Amphipoda, Oligochaeta) are so distributed quantitatively that while the Ephemerida and Trichoptera extend only to

TABLE 33. DEPTH DISTRIBUTION OF MACROSCOPIC BOTTOM FAUNA IN THIRD SISTER LAKE, MICHIGAN

Data Selected from Eggleton, 1931

Date	Depth, m.	Number per square meter							Position of thermocline, m.	O₂ Depth, m.	O₂ Cc. per l.
		Corethra	Chironomus	Protenthes	Tubificidae	Hydracarina	All others	Totals			
1927 Sept. 27	5–6	631	151	23	143	107	335	1,410	6–12	4	4.9
	7–8	4,204	6,142	507	1,254	649	720	13,476		6	2.2
	9–10	489	1,733	0	1,510	0	0	3,732		8	0.7
	16–17	1,120	18	0	1,813	0	0	2,950		10	0.0
	18	3,564	0	0	89	0	0	3,653		16	0.0
										18	0.0
Nov. 15	5–6	134	223	667	45	667	311	2,047	Beginning of fall overturn	6	5.7
	7–8	45	667	489	3,422	578	222	5,423		8	4.7
	9–10	3,555	3,083	428	6,789	311	11	11,005		10	4.6
	11.5–13		533	0	11,666	134	0	15,888		12	4.6
	14–15	17,707	90	0	2,580	90	0	20,467		14	4.6
	16–17	21,576	23	0	578	45	0	22,222		16	2.2
	18	21,265	0	0	423	23	0	21,711		17	0.06
Dec. 6	7–8	0	156	311	4,577	0	712	5,756	Temperature uniform	8	5.5
	9–10	667	933	134	7,066	311	0	9,111		12	5.4
	14–15	11,158	911	45	9,400	0	0	21,514		16	5.3
	18	47,818	1,023	0	312	89	0	49,242		18	5.3
1928 Feb. 22	7–8	0	80	276	4,524	400	605	5,485	Temperature almost uniform	18	5.3
	9–10	89	178	89	5,422	112	622	6,800			4.1
	11.5–13	116	1,960	147	11,137	0	8	13,480			
	14–15	9,866	845	45	9,200	0	0	19,950			
	16–17	53,595	90	0	623	0	0	54,308		18	3.6
	18	68,705	0	0	45	0	0	68,750			
Apr. 11	7–8	225	2,848	2,195	5,962	697	1,060	12,987	5–7* Beginning of stratification	‡	5.7
	9–10	727	1,810	742	14,489	225	87	18,080		10	5.6
	11.5–13	523	1,322	456	18,132	89	11	20,533		15	5.0
	14–15	8,157	341	45	6,792	45	0	15,380		17	
	18	36,497	12	12	23	12	0	36,556			
June 6	7–8	445	734	2,755	16,598	23	266	20,821	5–9	5	6.6
	9–10	2,910	689	1,645	7,466	111	0	12,821		10	3.5
	11.5–13	2,022	2,510	178	11,577	67	22	16,376		15	1.2
	14–15	4,888	312	134	4,466	0	0	9,800		17	0.1
	18	6,710	445	67	89	0	0	7,311			

* Data for Apr. 6.
‡ Data in last column (O₂) from unpublished records.

a depth of about 18 m., all of the other groups have representatives which occupy the bottom to depths of 118 m.; and that the zone of greatest production numerically is between 64 and 110 m. Other similar records occur in the literature.

Stratified Deeper Lakes. In deeper inland lakes which develop a well-formed, permanent stagnation zone during the summer, bottom regions exposed to typical hypolimnion conditions become distinctly less productive quantitatively than are the regions directly above them. Eggleton (1931) found, in certain Michigan lakes, that during the summer a benthic *concentration zone* occurs in the upper profundal and lower sublittoral regions in which the population is massed in great numbers and that the total population per unit area of bottom decreased sharply both above and below this zone. There is reason for believing that such a concentration zone exists during the summer in most lakes of the usual type. In Table 33, the records for Sept. 27 are representative of the typical summer condition and show, at a depth of 7 to 8 m., a concentration zone strikingly different from the adjacent zones on either side. With the exception of the Tubificidae, all of the other groups of organisms designated in the table show distinct maxima at that level, and even the Tubificidae are present there in large numbers. Further discussion of this matter will be deferred to the section of seasonal changes (page 334). Physicochemical stratification has a profound effect upon both the quantitative and qualitative distribution of the benthic organisms during the summer and early autumn seasons.

Any summary of the microscopic benthos is difficult because of the paucity and fragmentary nature of available information. As a mere indication of the possible nature of microbenthos, Table 34, taken from the only substantial work (Moore 1939) on American lakes, is included here.

The Great Lakes. Thus far, but few significant investigations have been made on the bottom fauna of the Great Lakes. Shelford (1913) assembled the records then known for Lake Michigan and listed bottom forms (Sphaeridae and Bryozoa) in the depth zone of 25 to 54 m., but it is certain that benthic animals of other kinds occupy not only that zone but greater depths as well. No quantitative data were given. A series of dredgings in Lake Ontario on a line between Toronto and the mouth of the Niagara River (Adamstone, 1924) showed a bottom fauna (1) at all depths down to 125 m., (2) at various distances from shore out to about 25 miles, and (3) on different kinds of bottom. This fauna seems to be relatively rich and varied; likewise, in the greater depths, it appears to exceed that of certain inland lakes. Krecker and Lancaster (1933) found that in the shallow-water bottom (depth, 0 to 6 ft.) of western Lake Erie, the quantitative distribution of the total macroscopic population was

TABLE 34. SUMMARY OF QUANTITATIVE SAMPLES OF MICROBENTHOS IN DOUGLAS
LAKE, MICHIGAN, TAKEN DURING JULY, 1937
Values in body of table indicate the number of organisms per square decimeter of
lake bottom
From Moore

Date	7/7	7/10	7/13	7/20	7/16	7/23	7/28
Water depth, m	20	17	14	11	11	8	5
Transect	AA	AA	AA	BB	AA	AA	AA
Type of bottom	Muck	Muck	Muck	Muck	Sand	Sand	Sand
Area sampled, sq. cm	11.4	19.0	19.0	19.0	15.2	19.0	19.0
Amochaproteus	.....	.....	.....	.....	.....	.....	26
Dileptas gidas	.....	.....	.....	.....	.....	.....	26
Frontonia leucas	106	26	131	236	79	262	
Loxodes rostrum	.....	.....	.....	79	158	210	260
Spirostomum ambiguum	53	26	158	26	185	105	52
Stentor coeruleus	106	26	.....	79	.....	.....	26
Stentor polymorphus	.....	.....	.....	.....	.....	.....	26
Minute ciliates	1,478	4,595	3,780	4,410	4,673	4,856	4,568
Pelmatohydra sp	.....	.....	.....	.....	.....	.....	5
Nematoda	176	2,362	840	525	818	1,129	630
Gyratrix h. hermaphroditus	.....	.....	10	5	20	.....	21
Microstomum sp	.....	.....	.....	.....	.....	.....	16
Unidentified Rhabdocoelida	.....	.....	.....	.....	.....	.....	21
Dissotrocha macrostyla	.....	.....	53	.....	106	.....	53
Rotaria spp	53	26	.....	.....	.....	53	53
Other Rotatoria	.....	.....	.....	.....	26	184	551
Chaetonotus sp	.....	53	.....	.....	53	78	525
Chaetogaster sp	.....	.....	10	10	7	10	105
Other Naididae	.....	.....	.....	.....	.....	5	
Alona quadrangularis	.....	.....	.....	.....	7	26	5
Chydorus piger	.....	.....	.....	.....	.....	10	58
Drepanothrix dentata	.....	.....	.....	.....	.....	5	5
Latona setifera	.....	.....	.....	.....	7	10	
Leydigia quadrangularis	.....	.....	5	.....	7	.....	
Canthocamptus sp	.....	.....	.....	.....	7	31	131
Canthocamptus staphylinoides	9	26	26	.....	33	.....	283
C. staphylinoides (cysts)	.....	2,772	1,082	1,937	205	5	10
Other Harpacticidae	.....	.....	.....	.....	46	84	84
Cyclops bicuspidatus (cysts)	6,890	1,811	.....	5	.....	.....	
Cyclops leuckarti	.....	.....	5	5	40	5	10
Cyclops agilis	.....	5	16	.....	13	37	
Cyclops viridis	.....	.....	.....	.....	7	.....	
Cyclops sp. (immature)	.....	5	37	5	13	.....	16
Diaptomus sp	.....	.....	.....	.....	.....	.....	37
Candona spp	.....	142	42	110	39	36	
Cypria sp	26	105	539	42	7	.....	
Darwinula stevensoni	.....	.....	.....	.....	.....	21	
Limnicythere sancti-patricii	.....	.....	.....	.....	.....	.....	47
Pionocypris obesa	.....	.....	.....	.....	.....	.....	5
Ostracoda (immature)	.....	.....	.....	10	7	10	
Nauplii	.....	.....	105	.....	.....	25	158
Acarina	.....	.....	5	5	13	36	42
Macrobiotes sp	.....	.....	.....	.....	.....	.....	31

roughly as follows: sand, 100 individuals per square yard; pebbles, 400; clay, 800; flat rubble, 900; block rubble, 1,100; and shelving rock, 7,700. In a study of benthos in Lake Michigan, made on widely distributed samples collected during the spring, summer, and autumn, of two successive years, Eggleton (1936, 1937) reported that (1) the benthos is composed of few species but many individuals; (2) a pronounced *concentration zone* existed between 35 and 50 m. depth; also another but smaller concentration was present between 100 and 140 m. depth. Table 35 summarizes the magnitude of these populations.

TABLE 35. DEPTH DISTRIBUTION OF BOTTOM ANIMALS BY STRATA
LAKE MICHIGAN, 1931 AND 1932
Averages of all samples for both years
From Eggleton

Strata, m.	Total number samples	Number different stations	Average number of animals per square meter within strata				
			Ponto-poreia	Pisidium	Tubifi-cidae	All others	All animals
20– 29	11	11	750	80	180	545	1555
30– 39	22	16	830	155	220	395	1600
40– 49	12	9	3165	175	925	220	4485
50– 59	14	10	1020	150	430	45	1640
60– 69	12	11	1140	110	325	30	1605
70– 79	11	11	790	150	200	50	1190
80– 89	14	9	520	30	175	40	765
90– 99	18	12	670	20	235	95	1025
100–109	20	15	670	20	225	65	980
110–119	13	12	1065	15	270	150	1505
120–129	3	3	560	15	85	55	715
130–139	8	7	380	30	170	80	660
140–149	5	5	180	0	85	105	370
170–179	1	1	70	0	35	15	120
180–189	1	1	90	0	70	0	160
220–229	1	1	20	1	0	50	70
240–249	3	3	35	0	15	70	125

Conditions within the Great Lakes, such as the much greater circulation, aeration, and the presence of currents of greater magnitude, make possible the occupancy of more extensive areas of bottom and of much greater depths by organisms which in inland waters are largely confined to the shallows.

Biota of Psammolittoral Zone. On the basis of his work on Wisconsin lakes, Pennak (1939) made the following statement:

If an average 10-cc. sand sample be taken from the surface of a beach at a distance of 150 cm. from the edge of the water, it will be found to contain 4,000,000

TABLE 36. HORIZONTAL AND VERTICAL DISTRIBUTION OF PSAMMOLITTORAL ORGANISMS IN ONE BEACH TRANSECT ON DOUGLAS LAKE, MICHIGAN

Numerals in body of table designate numbers of organisms per cubic centimeter of sand. No organisms were found below the depths listed. In the first column, the zero sign indicates water's edge; numbers not accompanied by a dash represent distance landward from water's edge; numbers preceded by a dash represent distance lakeward from water's edge (submerged sampling stations).

From Neel

Station	Depth, cm.	Diatoms	Blue green algae Chroococcales		Green algae				Rhizopods				Rotifers							
			Merismopedia	Others	Pediastrum	Scenedesmus	Cosmarium	Others	Difflugia Centropyxis	Arcella	Other Testacea	Turbellarians	Lecane	Others	Gastrotrichs	Nematodes	Tardigrades	Oligochaetes	Copepods	Ceratopogonid larvae
2.5 m.	1	600	37	75	8		3		54	10	3									
	2	300		30					6				2							
2 m.	1	3,800	16	91	27	12	14	2	86	50	3		21	2	5	8		10		
	2	500	2	16	10			2	18	2	8					6		2	2	
	3				16	2			62		1					10		3	2	
1.5 m.	1	1,100	2	29	18	6	6	2	14		2		2	2	5	8		11	2	
	2	300	3	37	10	4	3	2	10			3	2		2	3		6		
	3	160		18	3				6		6	2				3				
1 m.	1	2,700	51	34	13		6		102	110			23	6	6	5	5	6		
	2	960	2	26	3				29		2			10	3	10		3	2	
	3	800		14	10		2		16				2	2				2		
0.5 m.	1	6,200	64	46	8	5	3	5	51	6			25	8				3		
	2	2,200	18	29	13	2			18			2	8	3	5	13	3	6		
	3	1,000	6	16	14	3	2		11				2	2	3	6	3	19		
	4	300	6	8	2				6		3					2		2		
0.2 m.	1	8,200	30	69	16	12	5	2	34		2	2	33	26	13	8		18		
	2	2,700	14	56	24	6		8	27			2	2	3	6		3			
	3	160	18	44	27	5	5		22		2			3	6	2		3		
	4		5	19	10	3			8		3				3	3	2	5		
0	1	5,000	14	91	26		2	2	21				16	46						
	2	1,800	30	19	3		2	2	5		13		5	9	2	3		3	2	
	3		13	21	16				24		2		3	6						
-1 m.	1	30,000	77	173	70	26	6	13	154		6		51	32		83	19	6	19	
	2	1,300	6	51	19	25							6			32	6	6		
	3	160		3												2				
-2 m.	1	26,800	102	192	115	115			128		13		13		26	77	26	26		13
	2	2,100	6	26	45	19			6				6			19				
-3 m.	1	16,300	102	371	128	101		26	64		13			13						
	2	3,200	6	109	90	44			19							26				
-5 m.	1	30,400	77	282	217	103			64		26			13	13	64	13	26		
	2	3,200	26	51	38	57			13											
	3	160	2																	

bacteria, 8,000 Protozoa, 400 Rotatoria, 40 Copepoda, 20 Tardigrada, and small numbers of other microscopic Metazoa. The sample will be found to contain from 2 to 3 cc. of water. In this small volume of water, then, is concentrated a great population, finding all conditions necessary for a flourishing existence. So far as the author has been able to discover, there is no other environment which is capable of supporting such a diversified and dense population of microscopic organisms.

More recent work by Neel (1948) on the beaches of Douglas Lake, Michigan, yielded somewhat similar results (Table 36).

It seems apparent that the psammolittoral zone often, possibly usually, supports a prodigious biota. It has already been shown that the populations vary greatly, both in quality and in quantity, with the conditions which prevail in different beaches. Many questions are yet to be answered concerning such things as the fate or behavior of these populations (1) in winter when beaches are frozen, (2) when falling water level causes a gradual migration of the water-saturated beach zone, (3) in the presence of shore erosion by ice, and (4) in the presence of violent storms causing heavy wave action on beaches. The general limnological relation to the main water mass of a lake or stream is still uncertain.

The Periphyton. It is still very difficult to present quantitative measures of periphyton. In some waters and at least during certain seasons of the year, it occurs in great quantities. Large quantities of this felty material are sometimes drifted to the water's edge after a heavy storm has washed it from its supports. On the other hand, it appears to occur in reduced quantities in certain waters and during certain seasons. Table 37 is presented here merely as an indication of the magnitude of periphyton during the summer in one lake and on one kind of support. It must be understood that this analysis is only a partial one since various organisms, such as Fungi and others, are not included; also that these quantities cannot be looked upon as representative of other waters or other kinds of supports.

Relations of Quantity to Kinds of Bottom Deposits. Quantities of life produced differ on different kinds of bottom materials. Unfortunately, the difficulties involved in formulating satisfactory conclusions from published data are essentially the same as mentioned in the discussion on the effect of different bottom materials upon qualitative distribution (page 320), viz., the unstandardized classifications of bottom deposits and the lack of discrimination between effects of bottom materials proper and selective effects of other simultaneously acting factors. Exposure has much to do with quantitative productiveness of various kinds of bottom; for example, Rawson (1930) found in Lake Simcoe the average numbers of organisms per square meter of bottom in the 0- to 1-m. depth zone to be as follows: bare sand, exposed, 43; sand with vegetation, 696;

bare stone, exposed, 227; protected stone, 1,468; and mud with vegetation, 685. Bottoms containing a predominance of gravel, sand, or rocks often show the highest productivity for the waters concerned.

Baker (1933) summarized the quantitative fauna production on different types of bottom in two fresh-water lakes (Table 38).

TABLE 37. AVERAGE NUMBER OF ORGANISMS COMPOSING PERIPHYTON AS IT OCCURRED ON SUBMERGED PORTIONS OF DEAD BULRUSHES (*Scirpus*), DOUGLAS LAKE, MICHIGAN, SUMMER OF 1939

Values in table represent the number of organisms per square decimeter of supporting surface

From Young

Name of organism	6/24	7/8	7/17	7/24	7/31	8/7	8/14	8/19
Gloeotrichia.................	55	110	640	250	730	470	650	410
Pelmatohydra................	0	0	0	12	5	53	5	5
Oligochaeta................	210	140	180	125	180	70	60	70
Crustacea..................	192	130	42	75	280	55	73	185
Diptera (mostly Chironomidae)...	18	15	5	10	22	16	10	17
Total macroscopic animals........	420	240	250	225	490	212	155	280
Diatoms (in millions)............	53	8	9	9	9	13	8	9
Desmids (in thousands)..........	103	68	151	67	67	57	52	78
Nematoda....................	1,400	2,330	660	450	1,340	540	350	1,520
Rotifera......................	3,100	950	1,750	750	2,380	1,400	1,980	2,270
Centrifuged volume, cc..........	3.1	2.4	1.9	2.0	3.2	2.3	2.5	3.3
Dry weight of sample, mg........	100	185	42	78	105	35	58	60

TABLE 38. POPULATIONS ON DIFFERENT KINDS OF BOTTOM IN ONEIDA LAKE, NEW YORK, AND LAKE WINNEBAGO, WISCONSIN

Populations quoted in number of animals per square meter of the littoral zone

From Baker

Kind of bottom	Oneida Lake	Lake Winnebago
Boulder......................	1,945	321
Gravel......................	1,944	1,579
Sand........................	3,421	1,326
Clay and mud................	5,866	1,450
Vegetation..................	263	4,400

The quantity of microbenthos depends much upon the kind of bottom materials in which it develops. Table 34 shows one instance of this effect. Periphyton is also much influenced, both qualitatively and quantitatively, by the substratum on which it grows.

MOVEMENTS AND MIGRATIONS OF BENTHOS

For some time it has been supposed that under certain circumstances the benthos exhibits movements within or on the bottom, but investigations in this field are few and limited in scope. Repopulation of denuded areas has been frequently described.   Movements of certain organisms up and down stream are well known.   Retreat of benthos from advancing unfavorable conditions has been claimed although little of definite nature is known.   Moffett (1943) observed movements of bottom organisms on a large wave-swept shoal and found that some of the changes in space are due to bottom shifting.   Moon (1935) found that (1) the littoral fauna of Lake Windermere is in a continual state of movement, (2) this fauna is very sensitive to changes in surface level of the lake, (3) the more active elements of the fauna move very quickly into the newly inundated portions of the beach, and (4) a rise in surface level of only 2.5 cm. is sufficient to produce a movement of the fauna.   Nothing is known concerning the movements, if they occur, or the fate of the psammolittoral biota after retreat of the water line on sandy beaches.   Researches are badly needed here.

SEASONAL CHANGES IN BENTHOS

Far too little is known concerning seasonal changes in benthic organisms since to date most investigations have dealt only with summer populations.   Continuous, year-round studies, although very necessary for an understanding of seasonal cycles, have thus far been few in number. Changes of a rhythmic sort occur with the succession of seasons in all lakes and other waters and, in most instances at least, at all depths.   In very shallow lakes, seasonal changes in the whole benthic region are, in many respects, essentially the same as those which prevail in the littoral zone of deeper lakes of the same type and region.   It is only in abyssal regions of those deep lakes which never overturn that benthic conditions remain virtually the same throughout the year.   Table 39 represents an attempt to state in condensed form some of the important seasonal changes which might be expected to occur in a typical temperate lake of the second order.   It must be understood that it is not a complete catalogue of all changes which may occur; also that those changes mentioned in the table may show deviations and that certain ones may be absent. The table is an expression of average expectation as based upon the usual behavior of ordinary inland lakes of the second order located in the general region of the Great Lakes.

The profundal bottom fauna of lakes of the second order undergoes striking seasonal changes of a quantitative nature (Fig. 40).   While it may happen that, in some lakes, one or two of the component organisms may compose the overwhelming bulk of the entire population, the significant fact is that each true profundal species manifests similar and corresponding seasonal increases and decreases the magnitudes of which are more or less characteristic of the species in that situation.   There is now reason for believing that, in most typical temperate lakes of the second

TABLE 39. SOME OF THE SEASONAL CHANGES WHICH MIGHT BE EXPECTED IN THE BENTHOS OF AN AVERAGE TEMPERATE LAKE OF THE SECOND ORDER

Zone	Spring	Summer	Autumn	Winter
Littoral	1. Rapid growth of plants 2. Periodic insect emergences 3. Annual migration to shore of *Sialis* larvae 4. Rapid growth of sessile forms (sponges, Bryozoa) 5. Active growth, reproduction and increase in population of various invertebrates 6. Snail migration to shallow water for breeding activities	1. Culmination of plant growth 2. Large insect emergences 3. Shoreward migration of certain May-fly nymphs from plant zone 4. Maximum for various chironomid larvae 5. Major reproductive period of many invertebrates 6. Snail population augmented by late spring migrants from deeper levels	1. Late autumn decline of shallow-water plants 2. General decline of fauna resulting from *a.* Insect emergence *b.* Scouring effects of autumn storms *c.* Downward migration of *Sialis* larvae, snails, and others	1. Minimum of plant growth 2. Reduction in reproduction, growth, and other physiological processes 3. Many forms dormant; some entirely inactive; certain ones hibernating deeper in bottom 4. Certain summer plant dwellers become bottom dwellers 5. Downward migration of leeches, insects, and others to, or below, depth limit of wave action 6. Disintegration of sponges, Bryozoa, and others
Sublittoral	1. Periodic insect emergences 2. Migration of *Sialis* larvae to shore 3. Upward migration of snails which breed in shallow water 4. Active growth, reproduction, and increase in population of various invertebrates 5. Beginning stages of summer concentration zone (in late spring)	1. Fluctuations of population by insect emergences 2. Hatching of eggs and development of larvae of succeeding insect generations 3. Absence of snails having shallow-water breeding habits 4. Continuance of growth and reproduction in various invertebrates 5. Formation of portion of concentration zone	1. Downward migration of snails from summer breeding grounds 2. Obliteration of concentration zone and shifting of massed population downward along lake floor by fall overturn 3. Reductions due to insect emergences 4. Downward migration of *Sialis* larvae 5. Autumn hatching of insect eggs	1. Increase in population due to *a.* Development of insect eggs laid by autumn generations *b.* Culmination of downward migrations of snails, insects, and others 2. No insect emergences 3. Period of growth of winter insect larvae
Profundal	1. Rapid increase in population due to entrance of organisms from littoral and sublittoral zones during spring overturn 2. Marked insect emergence after spring overturn 3. Beginning stages of summer concentration zone at upper margin	1. Formation of portion of concentration zone at uppermost margin 2. Gradual production of minimum population	1. Persistence of annual summer minimum into early autumn 2. Rapid increase of population by *a.* Entrance of organisms from littoral and sublittoral regions during fall overturn *b.* Active reproduction of Tubificidae 3. Autumn insect emergences 4. Hatching of insect eggs laid in late summer	1. Midwinter maximum of Tubificidae and *Corethra* larvae 2. No insect emergences 3. Gradual reduction of benthos to late winter minimum

order, the major seasonal quantitative changes of this profundal bottom fauna are (1) a distinct midsummer minimum and (2) a midwinter maximum. These changes are represented graphically in an annual,

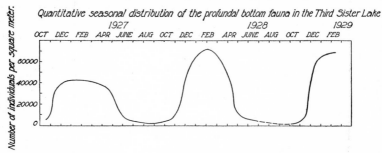

Fig. 40. Graphic representation of quantitative seasonal distribution of the profundal bottom fauna in Third Sister Lake, Washtenaw County, Michigan. The broken portion of the curve represents a period for which no data were secured. (*Drawn by the use of data from Eggleton*, 1931.)

unimodal curve (Fig. 40). The quantitative and chronological character of the annual maximum and minimum differs, to some extent, from year to year.

ORIGIN AND PERMANENCE OF PROFUNDAL BOTTOM FAUNA

The profundal bottom fauna, such as occurs in inland lakes of the second order, is composed of forms which, so far as present knowledge goes, are neither peculiar for nor restricted to the profundal region. In general, they seem to occupy also the sublittoral and, to some extent, the littoral zones.

This bottom fauna is, then, not qualitatively unique for the profundal region but is composed of representatives of a few species belonging to the larger littoral-sublittoral population which can tolerate, for considerable periods of time, the severe stagnation conditions of the profundal region when they find themselves exposed to such conditions. The work of Eggleton (1931) indicates that this profundal population is the result of a selective elimination in which only the few highly tolerant species can survive. During the spring and fall overturns, the population of the sublittoral zone spreads down the lake bottom into the profundal region, bringing into it not only greater numbers of individuals but certain additional species characteristic of the littoral and sublittoral regions—forms which can survive the deeper, bottom conditions during, and for some time after, the overturns. However, the gradual development of stagnation at the bottom brings about a condition which some of the species cannot endure. Consequently, they are either eliminated or are forced to begin a return, upward migration into more favorable surroundings, eventually freeing the hypolimnion in summer and the lower waters in winter of all forms save those which have a much greater endurance for greatly changed environmental conditions.

Occasionally, in unusually deep lakes (some alpine lakes and others), certain animals occur which have been described as constituting a special, abyssal, benthic population—species which are said never to come into the shallower depths above about 50 m., and some of which are usually regarded as glacial relicts.

That continued bottom-water stagnation ultimately begins to have a deleterious effect, even upon those forms sometimes referred to as the true profundal ones, has been demonstrated (Eggleton, 1931) both in nature and by experiment. While the extent of bottom stagnation may vary in different lakes, profundal bottom animals do not seem to be able to withstand indefinitely the conditions of severe summer stagnation, and as a consequence these populations may become greatly reduced, sometimes even to extinction in late summer and early autumn. Different species do not show the same degree of resistance, certain ones outlasting others by a considerable margin. Evidence seems to indicate that the insect larvae succumb first, those of *Corethra* appearing to be less resistant than those of the chironomids. On the other hand, the Tubificidae and the Sphaeridae outlast the other profundal forms, the former apparently being the more resistant. From these results, it appears that profundal bottom forms are not truly a permanent profundal fauna but may themselves be eliminated, wholly or in part, by prolonged exposure to the stagnation. Restocking takes place from egg stages, which may be able to carry over until the next overturn; from the downward migration of the sublittoral population at the time of the overturns; or from both. Eggleton concluded that "evidence now available indicates that the members of the profundal benthic fauna are facultative rather than obligatory 'anaerobes' and that they endure rather than select an anaerobic environment."

VERTICAL DISTRIBUTION OF PROFUNDAL BOTTOM FAUNA

From circumstantial evidence, it has usually been assumed that the profundal bottom fauna is largely confined to the uppermost, thin layer of the bottom deposits. Definite information was secured by Lenz (1931), who, by the use of a specially constructed bottom sampler, was able to bring virtually undisturbed, vertical samples of bottom deposits to the surface and then isolate and examine the various horizontal strata in their unaltered relations to each other. Various horizontal levels were thus studied down to a depth of 24 cm. It appeared that in the north German lakes, this depth was more than adequate. The large part of the fauna occurred in the upper half of the sampler. Some difference appeared in the vertical distribution of the various organisms; for example, it is shown that the Tubificidae tended to be concentrated in the upper portion, while the *Chironomus* larvae were distributed from the surface of the mud down to a depth of 20 cm. or more. Other work dealing with the macroscopic organisms agrees in a general way with the findings of Lenz.

Thus far the most extensive work on the microscopic profundal benthos of an American lake is that of Moore (1939). His findings are indicated,

Strata in cm.	Cyclops bicuspidatus Cysts	Canthocamptus staphylinoides Active	Canthocamptus staphylinoides Cysts	Cypria spp.	Candona spp.	Nematoda (sand)	Nematoda (muck)	Ciliata (minute)	Frontonia leucas
0-1	2771	168	0	120	20	301	571	4774	770
1-2	1902	28	0	54	26	111	366	403	20
2-3	392	11	1	27	23	18	228	156	5
3-4	95	5	5	13	15	24	152	40	0
4-5	41	0	23	3	9	5	111	20	0
5-8	2		222		24		11	0	0
8-11	0		247	4	16		18	0	0
11-14	0		63	0	8		11	0	0
14-17	0		29	0	6		6	0	0
17-20	0		29	0	2		2	0	0
Total	5203	212	619	221	149	459	1476	5393	795
	19 cores	20 cores	20 cores	42 cores	40 cores	14 cores	43 cores	52 cores	20 cores

FIG. 41. Vertical distribution of certain microbenthic organisms in profundal zone of Douglas Lake, Michigan. Each column represents a composite core of bottom deposits, the number of individual cores incorporated into the composite being indicated below each column. Thickness of each stratum and its depth position in core are indicated to left of columns. Number of organisms at each depth level is indicated by values within the columns; total organisms are represented by numbers at bottom of each column. All columns represent profundal bottom positions except that one representing Nematoda which contains values for samples taken from water depths of 5 to 11 m. All samples collected during July and August and from muck bottom with the exception of the one labeled "sand." (*Redrawn from Moore.*)

in part, by Fig. 41. It will be noted that there is an obvious similarity in the vertical distribution of the micro- and macrobenthos.

CLASSIFICATIONS OF LAKES BASED UPON BOTTOM FAUNA

As much as three decades ago certain European limnologists undertook to develop a classification of lakes based upon predominating benthic animals. Bottom faunas differ greatly in various kinds of lakes, and the differences are often numerous and complicated. The numerical dominance of a certain species or group of species does seem, to some extent at least, to be characteristic of certain kinds of lakes, so much so that numerous classifications, using the predominating organisms as indices, have been proposed. All such classifications are as yet of little value, and no attempt will be made here to summarize or appraise them. The reader is referred to Deevey (1941) for a concise account of such classifications. The first edition of this book contains a brief account of some of the earlier attempts. In America, little effort has been made thus far to establish such classifications, although it is known that some lakes have benthic characteristics which resemble, in some respects, those of north European lakes of the same order. Deevey (1941) classified Connecticut lakes as follows: (1) *Chironomus* lakes; (2) Mesotrophic *Chironomus* lakes; (3) *Tanytarsus* lakes; (4) *Trissocladius* lakes; and (5) Unstratified lakes. Certain elements of these attempted classifications seem to have a natural basis, and it may be that further efforts in this direction will lead to some system having substantial value and wide application. Differences in the composition of profundal benthic populations in different parts of the world may, of necessity, prevent the use of one set of names of index organisms for all geographic regions.

CLASSIFICATIONS OF BENTHIC COMMUNITIES

Ecologists make use of certain index organisms to distinguish the various natural benthic assemblages known as communities. As an example, Shelford and Boesel (1942) identified three bottom animal communities in the island area of western Lake Erie, as follows: (1) *Goniobasis-Hydropsyche* community; (2) *Pleurocera-Lampsilis* community; and (3) *Hexagenia-Oecestis* community.

CHAPTER XIV

BIOLOGICAL PRODUCTIVITY

CIRCULATION OF FOOD MATERIALS

That the essential foodstuffs in a lake undergo continuous, more or less definite cycles or changes has already been pointed out in foregoing pages. Taken as a whole, the entire process of circulation of food materials, although very intricate and even yet not fully known, has a certain unity due to the fact that an inland lake is, to some degree, a self-contained institution, enjoying a considerable independence of the adjacent land. This fact was recognized long ago by Forbes (1887) who, in his classical paper "The Lake as a Microcosm," stated that

The animals of such a body of water are, as a whole, remarkably isolated,— closely related among themselves in all their interests, but so far independent of the land about them that if every terrestrial animal were suddenly annihilated, it would doubtless be long before the general multitude of the inhabitants of the lake would feel the effects of this event in any important way. It is an islet of older, lower life in the midst of the higher, more recent life of the surrounding region. It forms a little world within itself—a microcosm within which all the elemental forces are at work and the play of life goes on in full but on so small a scale as to bring it easily within the mental grasp.

The same feature has been stressed by other investigators who have sometimes referred to a lake as a "closed community." However, the student must exercise considerable care that these statements are not overstressed. It is true that the biota of an inland lake composes a "closed community in a stricter sense, perhaps, than the term can be applied to any other nonparasitic assemblage";[1] that in a lake with small inflow and outflow of water, relatively small, slow additions to the food supply are made from outside; and that "the lake is dependent on its own stock of green plants for the stock of organic matter available for food of other organisms; and the possible amount of green plants is limited by the raw material supplied for photosynthesis from the lake itself."[1]

Nevertheless, it must not be assumed that any natural body of water is a completely closed community since there are various direct and indirect

[1] Birge.

influences exerted from the outside even though the sum total of such influences is relatively minor in immediate effect.

In considering the circulation of food materials in a typical lake, the following elementary, fundamental facts must be kept in mind:

1. The ultimate, basic substances are (*a*) inorganic nutritive materials dissolved in the water and (*b*) certain energies and gases from the atmosphere.

2. Only the chlorophyll-bearing plankters, the chlorophyll-bearing littoral flora, and certain bacteria can utilize directly these ultimate basic materials in constructing living matter.

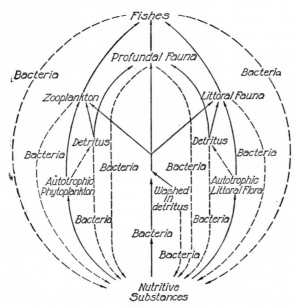

FIG. 42.   Diagram showing circulation of food materials in a lake.   (*Modified from Perfiliew.*)

3. All other organisms, plant or animal, rest as a *dependent* superstructure upon those mentioned in item 2.

4. Every organism of a lake population may, (*a*) by death and disintegration, contribute directly to the dissolved materials and detritus or (*b*) be consumed as food by other organisms.

In the foregoing diagram (Fig. 42), the more prominent features of the internal evolutions are indicated for a typical lake.   Lesser relations are omitted for the sake of simplicity.   No attempt has been made to include the various possibilities of direct utilization of dissolved organic matter by higher organisms, the status of which is still somewhat uncertain (page 305).   Also, that portion of the reduction of dead organisms by autolysis is omitted.

A study of this diagram reveals, among other things, the following relations:

1. Two very general sets of processes: (*a*) constructive, i.e., building upward from the simpler food materials into the higher; and (*b*) reductive, i.e., reducing through bacterial action the various organisms to simpler substances.

2. Circulation of food materials not a simple, single cycle but a combination of complicated cycles.

3. Cycles so interrelated that materials may be built up to the same level in different ways, e.g., the various routes leading to fish production.

4. One cycle through which animals are freed from dependence upon photosynthetic plants, viz., from basic, dissolved, nutritive materials through bacteria which change carbon dioxide to organic carbon in the absence of sunlight to certain animals which consume them.

5. Three basic cycles: (*a*) dissolved nutritive substances → autotrophic phytoplankton → detritus → bacteria → dissolved nutritive substance; (*b*) dissolved nutritive substance → autotrophic littoral flora → detritus → bacteria → dissolved nutritive substances; and (*c*) dissolved nutritive

$$\text{substances} \rightarrow \text{bacteria} \rightarrow \begin{array}{c} \nearrow \text{zooplankton} \searrow \\ \text{littoral fauna} \\ \searrow \text{profundal fauna} \nearrow \end{array} \rightarrow \text{bacteria} \rightarrow \text{dissolved nutri-}$$

tive substances.

Theoretically, at least, the first two cycles might exist in a lake with complete absence of the principal animal groups (zooplankton, littoral fauna, profundal fauna, and fishes). In fact, there are bodies of water which normally contain no fishes and no profundal fauna and in which the zooplankton and the littoral fauna are greatly restricted.

It must be understood that the rate and quantity of this circulation vary (1) for the whole system in different lakes and (2) in the different cycles within the same lake. The various causes and factors are very complex, but as a few out of the great number, the following are listed: influence of surface drainage water bringing about inwash of materials and bacteria; variable production of rooted vegetation in different lakes; differences in the method of and the degree of completeness of phytoplankton utilization; composition of phytoplankton; availability of benthic organisms as food for the nekton; composition of benthic fauna; sedimentation processes; physical features which accelerate or retard food transformations; life-history stages which differ in their food relations; and many others.

CLASSIFICATION OF LAKES ON BASIS OF PRODUCTIVITY

Many attempts to classify lakes on various limnological bases, related in one way or another to productivity, have been made during the past three decades. The combined contributions of a number of these attempts constitute the background of a classification which is now a familiar one in limnological literature, viz., the division of lakes into three major types, the *oligotrophic, eutrophic,* and *dystrophic* types. Fritsch (1931) has reviewed the history of this classification. Many of the proposals are based upon the plankton communities, but plankton is not an infallible index of the general character of a lake. Thienemann, working from the point of view of bottom fauna and the bottom oxygen supply, established the primary division into the *oligotrophic* and *eutrophic* types. Simultaneously, Naumann, working from the point of view of bottom deposits and of biological productivity, also recognized these two main types and added a third, the *dystrophic.* Subsequent investigations by these and other European limnologists did much to introduce this classification. Nevertheless, it still remains to be demonstrated that this classification is a satisfactory one for lakes at large and that these types are natural ones in all lake regions. As might be expected, a great many lakes apparently occupy borderline positions between these types. There are still differences of opinion as to whether the dystrophic type can be regarded as a type of the same rank as the eutrophic and the oligotrophic. It is argued by the chief exponents of this classification that, irrespective of its weaknesses, it is the best which has thus far been developed. Upon this classification, certain European workers attempted to set up rather elaborate subdivisions of the three main types, the scientific value of which remains for the future to determine. They set up long lists of contrasting characteristics for each of these three types, using distinctions which when applied to lakes at large often resulted in confusion. Limnologists have had great difficulty in applying these criteria to American lakes. Peculiarly difficult are the criteria used by European limnologists to distinguish the dystrophic type. These problems have been discussed by Welch (1941). Prescott (1939) presented a revision of the criteria for these three types, based upon his experience with American lakes. Among other departures from the European practice, he separated the *bog lakes* from the *dystrophic* lakes, and the possible importance of the phytoplankton as a diagnostic character is stressed. For a critical discussion of lake classifications and in particular the relation of bottom fauna to lake typology, the reader is referred to the work of Deevey (1941) on certain lakes of Connecticut and New York.

In the classification mentioned above, the fundamental distinction between oligotrophic and eutrophic lakes was on a proposed basis of available nutritive material, the former being poor and the latter rich in such substances. In the dystrophic type, humic substances were regarded as important limiting agencies.

This European proposal that lakes be divided into the three large classes, oligotrophic, eutrophic, and dystrophic, drifted slowly into a certain limited, uncrystallized acceptance in American limnology, although no serious attempts have yet been made to reduce the diagnostic characters to positive specifications valid for American inland waters. The following summary includes some of the more important characterizations of these postulated lakes groups as now employed in a general and somewhat nebulous fashion.

1. Oligotrophic lakes:
   a. Very deep; thermocline high; volume of hypolimnion large; water of hypolimnion cold.
   b. Organic materials on bottom and in suspension very low.
   c. Electrolytes low, or variable; calcium, phosphorus, and nitrogen relatively poor; humic materials very low or absent.
   d. Dissolved oxygen content high at all depths and throughout year.
   e. Larger aquatic plants scanty.
   f. Plankton quantitatively restricted; species many; water blooms rare; Chlorophyceae dominant.
   g. Profundal fauna relatively rich in species and quantity; *Tanytarsus* type; *Corethra* usually absent.
   h. Deep-dwelling, cold-water fishes (salmon, cisco, trout) common to abundant.
   i. Succession into eutrophic type.
2. Eutrophic lakes:
   a. Relatively shallow; deep, cold water minimal or absent.
   b. Organic materials on bottom and in suspension abundant.
   c. Electrolytes variable, often high; calcium, phosphorus, and nitrogen abundant; humic materials slight.
   d. Dissolved oxygen, in deeper stratified lakes of this type, minimal or absent in hypolimnion.
   e. Larger aquatic plants abundant.
   f. Plankton quantitatively abundant; quality variable; water blooms common; Myxophyceae and diatoms predominant.
   g. Profundal fauna, in deeper stratified lakes of this type, poor in species and quantity in hypolimnion; *Chironomus* type; *Corethra* present.
   h. Deep-dwelling cold-water fishes usually absent; suitable for perch, pike, bass, and other warm-water fishes.
   i. Succession into pond, swamp, or marsh.
3. Dystrophic lakes:
   a. Usually shallow; temperature variable; in bog surroundings or in old mountains.
   b. Organic materials in bottom and in suspension abundant.
   c. Electrolytes low; calcium, phosphorus, and nitrogen very scanty; humic materials abundant.
   d. Dissolved oxygen almost or entirely absent in deeper water.
   e. Larger aquatic plants scanty.
   f. Plankton variable; commonly low in species and quantity; Myxophyceae may be very rich quantitatively.
   g. Profundal macrofauna poor to absent; all bottom deposits with very scant fauna; *Chironomus* sometimes present; *Corethra* present.
   h. Deep-dwelling cold-water fishes always absent in advanced dystrophic lakes;

sometimes devoid of fish fauna; when present, fish production usually poor.

i. Succession into peat bog.

The terms *oligotrophic, eutrophic,* and *dystrophic* have also been employed in other classifications, notably those of Strøm (1928) (Tables 40 to 42), in which distinctions rest on other bases. All such classifications are as yet little more than pioneering efforts and should be used with much caution.

TABLE 40

From Strøm

Without humus clear-water lakes		With humus brown-water lakes	
With *pronounced* oxygen consumption	With *slight* oxygen consumption	With *pronounced* oxygen consumption	With *slight* oxygen consumption
Eutrophic "Baltic"	Oligotrophic "subalpine"	Dystrophic the type defined	?Dystrophic not yet investigated; probably many Scotch lochs

Another arrangement might be as follows:

TABLE 41

From Strøm

	Eutrophic	Oligotrophic
With humus................	Humic mud lakes	Dystrophic
Without humus.............	Eutrophic, *s. str.*	Oligotrophic, *s. str.*

Strøm (1928) pointed out that fishery biologists have found some brown-water lakes other than the humic mud lakes which are highly productive in fish and that such lakes may well be characterized as eutrophic even if it does happen that many of the nutritive substances are allochthonous. "It must also be emphasized that we know very little about the humus, and certainly there seems to be a profound difference between the humic substances derived from peaty moors and those derived from decaying leaves, which characterize some lakes in the Baltic region." Stressing the importance of humus, calcium, nitrogen, and phosphorus, Strøm has offered a scheme (Table 42) into which he claims that all of the types now known fit very easily and which has value in showing the relation of the different plankton communities.

In explanation of this analysis, Strøm makes the following statement:

The principal types are in italic. The more aberrant types are the following: The *eutrophic* lake poor in lime has not yet been investigated, but there is much evidence for the belief that some of the shallow lakes situated among cultivated fields on the igneous rocks of the lowlands in Norway and perhaps Ireland may be of this type. The humic mud lakes ("Humusschlammseen") are not uncommon in Holstein, and their humus is derived from the leaves of the surrounding trees. They must generally be regarded as eutroph, and sometimes are exceedingly poor in lime. A few dystrophic lakes rich in lime have been observed in Rügen

TABLE 42

Symbols + and − mean *presence* and *absence*, respectively

From Strøm

	+(N + P) Fundamentally *eutrophic*		−(N + P) Fundamentally *oligotrophic*	
	+Ca	−Ca	+Ca	−Ca
+ humus.........	Not investigated and probably not existing	Humic mud lakes	? Dystrophic lakes in Scotland and Rügen	*Dystrophic*
− humus.........	*Eutrophic*	Not yet investigated but almost certainly existing	a. *Oligotrophic* lakes in the Alps	b. *Oligotrophic* Norwegian lakes

and in Scotland. Their biology will certainly be a very interesting subject for investigation. Probably the lime is bound to humic acids in some colloidal form.

LAW OF THE MINIMUM

Existence and production of animal and plant life depend upon the proper qualitative and quantitative composition of the environment for each component organism. Liebig's *law of the minimum*, originally applied to plants, may be stated as follows: Each organism requires a certain number of food materials, and each of these materials must be present in a certain quantity. If one of these food substances is absent, the organism dies; if not absent but present in minimal quantity, the growth will be minimal. This result holds even though ample amounts of all of the other required substances are present. The yield of a plant or animal, according to this law, is determined by the quantity of that particular, necessary substance which is present in minimal amount as determined by the demands of the organism. According to certain authorities, gradual increase of this minimal substance produces an increase in production in proportion to the amount added until the point is reached where some other substance begins to act as a limiting factor.

In time, this law was extended to cover not only the essential foodstuffs but also all other factors which determine the development of organisms.

While the law of minimum has had a wide acceptance, it has been subject to attack from time to time. Herdman (1923), in discussing the reported discovery by Moore and others that the green phytoplankters are not dependent upon the dissolved nitrogen compounds in the water but that they can obtain elemental nitrogen from the air through the water while the very small quantities of nitrates, nitrites, and ammonia salts in the sea water may remain unconsumed, holds that the law of the minimum breaks down here, at least as regards nitrogen, since the then current interpretations of the law held the supply of nitrogen to be dissolved nitrogen compounds. Other criticisms have been aimed at the statement of proportionality between the amount of a nutritive element and the production, since it has been claimed that, in plants at least, this proportionality occurs only within rather narrow limits and that when the quantity of the given essential substance is gradually increased, the effect upon production ultimately begins to decrease, finally ceasing to affect the production. If this is true, then the dependence of production upon a given limiting substance cannot be expressed graphically by a straight line, as was formerly supposed, but it is claimed by some investigators to be expressible only by a logarithmic curve whose mathematical relations will not be described here. It has also been claimed that deviations from the law of minimum may occur when several factors, instead of one factor, are increasing at the same time, such as the discovery, in certain plant experiments, that increase of one nutritive substance may increase the influence of the other food substances.

The usual statement of the law of minimum must not be allowed to obscure the fact that a factor exercises a controlling influence upon production according *as it is near the optimum or near either the maximum or minimum tolerated by the species.* Also, it is not necessary that only one factor should vary; the result is similar or even accentuated if several factors vary. These are important features in Shelford's *law of toleration* (1913, 1931). Shelford illustrated the action of a factor in the following graphic way:

Minimum limit of toleration		Range of optimum of factor	Maximum limit of toleration	
Absent	← Decreasing	Greatest abundance	—→ Decreasing	Absent

Thienemann (1926) proposed to erect out of the law of the minimum a *law of the operation of environmental factors* as follows: The abundance of an organism is controlled by those environmental factors which, in any particular habitat, impose the most unfavorable effects upon that developmental stage of the organism which manifests the *least ecological valence*. Ecological valence refers to that *range* of influences within which the organism can maintain itself.

Liebig's law of the minimum is the foundation of Blackman's *law of limiting factors*, which refers to the dependence of one factor upon another. Originally, it was supposed that the various environmental factors acted independently, in which case if one factor is present in limiting quantity, an increase of the other factors would effect no change. However, it now seems to be demonstrated that the controlling effect of the minimal factor is not absolute but is only a relative one, slowing down but not completely suppressing the influence of the other factors. The understanding, then, of conditions of biological production depends not only upon the recognition of each of the operative factors and a measure of their quantities or intensities but also upon a knowledge of the way in which they behave in the presence of each other, a fact which further complicates the whole problem.

BIOTIC POTENTIAL AND ENVIRONMENTAL RESISTANCE

The biological productivity of any body of water, or any portion of that body of water, is the end result of the interaction of the organisms present with the surrounding environment. Considerable attention has been directed to the specific quantitative analysis of this interrelation. Chapman (1928) and others have done much in extending our knowledge of this intricate subject.

By *biotic potential* is meant those characteristics and abilities inherent within an organism which enable it to exist and reproduce. It is the sum total of all of those capacities of an organism which determine its relative success in solving all of its problems of maintenance. "It is a sort of algebraic sum of the number of young produced at each reproduction, the number of reproductions in a given period of time, the sex ratio of the species, and their general ability to survive under given physical conditions."[1]

Complete fulfillment of the biotic potential of any species probably never occurs in nature owing to the limiting influence which every environment exerts. Every environment contains active features which work toward the control of production in the various organisms involved. The environment, then, *resists*, to a greater or less extent, the fulfillment of biotic potential. Biological production is the outcome of the struggle between the biotic potential continually pressing toward a greater attainment and the *environmental resistance* continually struggling to suppress

[1] Chapman.

the species.   In the long run, nature acts toward a balance between these two tendencies in which each organism maintains itself in a suitable environment without overpopulation.   Lack of proper balance works inevitably toward one of two ends: if the biotic potential is unduly high or is little opposed, the populations of the species involved will increase to the overpopulation point, while if the environmental resistance is high compared with the biotic potential, the production of the species will diminish, possibly to ultimate extinction.   The lack of fixity of both biotic potential and of environmental resistance accounts for the variations in production which are more or less normal to successive generations and seasons.   In addition to the usual variations of small magnitude, there are those occasional, more or less unpredictable interruptions of the balance which result either (1) in the "outbreaks" of the economic biologist, due to the unusual reduction of some controlling influence, or (2) in the sudden and unexpected reduction, sometimes to apparent disappearance, of a species commonly present in appreciable numbers.   For further discussion of these phenomena and their quantitative aspects, the reader is referred to Chapman (1931).   There is some evidence that mathematical treatment of this whole subject may ultimately become possible; and if future researches bear out this promise, these intricate relations will become much more understandable.

The principles of biotic potential and of environmental resistance, together with all of their associated features, are just as pertinent in aquatic biology as in terrestrial situations.   Biological productivity of any aquatic community is a general measure of all of the adjustments between biotic potential and environmental resistance existing within it. At the present time, it is difficult to give these matters specific, detailed application to conditions in lakes owing to the newness of the subject and the relatively small amount of data sufficiently well worked out to make them usable for such a purpose.

QUANTITATIVE RELATIONSHIPS IN A STANDING CROP

In a general way it can be said that usually a body of water maintains a certain standing crop of organisms composed primarily of five large groups, viz., phytoplankton, bottom flora, bottom fauna, zooplankton, and fishes.   This series composes a nutritional chain in which, by processes well known to students of biology, the first two constitute a *producing* class and the other three are the *consumers*.   Taken as a whole, these organisms are an expression of the productivity of the water concerned. In such a dependency chain, as maintained in nature, it is highly important that the ability of the supporting classes to maintain the dependent groups be known if productivity is to be understood.   In unmodified waters the standing crop of organisms, measured quantitatively, is the visible evidence of the degree of success of the nutritional chain concerned. One of the best studies in this field is that of Juday (1943), from which the following material is taken. Figure 43 shows graphically the relationships, determined gravimetrically, of the various components of the aquatic population in Weber Lake, Wisconsin, a soft-water lake, as they existed in midsummer. The actual values expressed in this "pyramid of aquatic life" are different to some extent in different lakes, but some form of pyramid is the rule. In Fig. 43 the dissolved organic matter

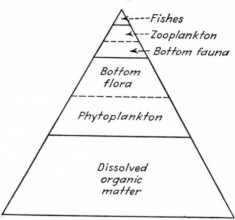

FIG. 43. Diagram showing weight relationships of biota and dissolved organic matter in Weber Lake, Wisconsin, in midsummer. The weight of each group is proportional to total area of triangle. (*Redrawn, with slight modification, from Juday,* 1943.)

composes approximately 60 per cent of the total diagram; the fish, only one-half of one per cent; and the other animals, slightly less than 5 per cent. Juday found that the *ratio* of the weight of plants to that of animals (excluding fishes) was much smaller in soft-water lakes than in the hard-water lakes and interpreted the difference to mean that the former was about 2.5 times more efficient in the conversion of plants into animals.

Differences in the summer standing crop in different kinds of lakes are shown in Table 43 in which two soft-water lakes (Weber and Nebish) are compared with two hard-water ones (Green and Mendota). It should be noted that the data in the lower part of the table were not all taken during the same summer (Weber, 1940; Nebish, 1941; Green, avg., 1921–1924; Mendota, avg., 1915–1916).

TROPHIC DYNAMICS

In the trophic dynamics of an ecological system, basic processes are in the nature of transfers of energy. The ultimate source of such energy is solar radiation. Somewhat recently, certain investigators, notably Lindeman (1942), have attempted to analyze the events within a food complex in terms of energy. Because of great paucity of detailed information basic to dependable formulation of such concepts, any discussion at present is largely hypothetical and must be regarded as suggestive only. Hints that these complex interrelations may eventually yield to mathematical analyses appear in the work of Lindeman and others. Entry into the speculative aspects of this subject will not be undertaken here.

TABLE 43. SUMMER STANDING CROP OF PLANTS AND ANIMALS IN FOUR WISCONSIN LAKES

In upper part of table, conductivity is expressed in reciprocal megohms; dissolved substances in milligrams per liter of water. In lower part of table, all quantitative results are stated in kilograms per hectare of lake surface, on a wet weight, ash-free basis.

Modified from Juday (1943)

	Weber Lake	Nebish Lake	Green Lake	Lake Mendota
Conductivity........................	10	19	275	270
pH.................................	6.4	7.0	8.5	8.6
Bound CO_2...............	1.3	4.0	75.2	69.0
SiO_2.................................	0.1	0.2	8.4	0.5
Ca.................................	0.7	2.3	21.2	22.4
Mg.................................	0.6	1.7	25.7	24.2
Sol. P.....	0.003	0.002	0.004	0.005
NO_3.................................	0.014	0.014	0.024	0.025
Dissolved organic matter..............	2,866	3,829	27,901	15,201
Total plankton.......................	1,143	650	2,944	1,995
Phytoplankton....................	1,069	608	2,767	1,875
Zooplankton......................	74	42	177	120
Bottom flora........................	553	590	4,218	4,600
Bottom fauna.......................	147	122	138	414
Fish................................	23	35		
Total weight of plants................	1,622	1,198	6,985	6,475
Total weight of animals...............	244	199		
Total weight of animals, excluding fish...	....	....	315	534
Ratio of plants to animals.............	6.6	6.0		
Ratio of plants to animals, excluding fish.	7.3	7.3	22.2	12.1
Ratio of other animals to fish....... ..	9.6	4.7		

However, out of the pioneering work done thus far, there have arisen biological conclusions which seem to have a certain validity, viz., (1) food cycles rarely have more than five trophic levels; (2) the greater the separation of an organism from the basic source of energy (solar radiation), the less the chance that it will depend solely upon the preceding trophic level for energy; (3) at successively higher levels in the food cycle, the consumers seem to be progressively more efficient in the utilization of the food supply; and (4) in lake succession, productivity and photosynthetic efficiency increase from oligotrophy to a prolonged eutrophy and then decline in lake senescence.

SUCCESSIONAL PHENOMENA

That all environments are dynamic and undergoing change is a fundamental principle of ecology. Excluding the minor variations of different factors within an environment, these fundamental changes are in the nature of progressive, more or less predictable alterations usually involving considerable expanses of time and having a generally definite course. These changes may be due (1) to the action of predominating inorganic factors in the environment, e.g., erosion; (2) to the action of organisms in modifying the environment; or (3) to combinations of (1) and (2). Whatever the underlying causes are, one fact common to all situations exists, viz., that the various components of the biota must meet the changing conditions in one of the following ways: (1) adaptation, (2) migration, (3) extinction. It is not possible or desirable to enter here upon a discussion of the fundamental and very important subject of ecological succession. When necessary, the reader should consult certain of the standard treatises on ecology (Chapman, 1931; Clements and Shelford, 1939; *et al.*) for a general presentation. Ecological successions of various kinds go on in lakes and other inland waters just as certainly as they do on land, although our knowledge of the former is at the present time much less satisfactory. The great underlying movement in the evolution of the units of the lentic series is in the direction of extinction by the filling of the basins; in the lotic series, it is in the direction of an extension of stream length and a cutting of the stream bed to base level. Associated with these long-time, physiographic progressions are series of biological successions which constitute the progress of the accompanying biotic changes.

Eutrophication. In general and within limits, productivity increases with the age of a lake. Strøm (1928) has stated the process as follows:

The natural process of the maturing of a lake is that of eutrophication. The original state of all lakes must be assumed to be oligotroph, but during the course of time there will always be a surplus of organic sediments accruing from the life processes of a lake, and the originally *oligotroph* lake is changed to a eutroph. The quantities of plankton, oxygen curves, and average depths are the first features to be changed; the bottom fauna, the last. Many of the North German lakes are now in this stage of changing, and it is clear that a supply of nitrogen compound and phosphates from cultivated fields can do much to accelerate the change, even if it be not the main cause. When a lake has reached the real eutroph stage, the changes towards a greater degree of eutrophy are very speedily effected, indeed; the character of a lake can be materially changed within a generation. Wesenberg-Lund has given a vivid picture of the changes going on in the shallow Danish lakes. That the influence of the very highly developed Danish agriculture compared with the rather primitive methods with large poorly manured areas for grazing, formerly prevalent in Denmark and still in Holstein, has something to do with the acceleration of the process seems certain. Finally, the *eutroph* lake disappears as a lake when the littoral vegetation has gained foothold throughout its bottom, and in the very last stage it is transformed into low moors.

The large *oligotroph* lakes such as the Swiss and Norwegian are as yet very far from the eutroph stage if only biological causes are working. Some of the lakes are filled up with inorganic deposits, and at the current rate of yearly sedimentation we can calculate when they will be shallow enough to approach the eutroph stage. The Lake of Constance will be filled up in 12,000 years by sediments from the Rhine; that is, it has already run through more than the half of its life. Those lakes where no such sedimentation takes place, such as many of the Norwegian, will have nearly an infinite life if only natural causes continue to operate in the future.

It must be clearly understood that the maturing process takes place at very different rates in different lakes. In northern United States, for example, the vast majority of the multitudinous inland lakes had their basins formed essentially at the same time, i.e., during the glacial period, and therefore, from that standpoint, are all of the same age. However, they have matured (aged) at vastly different rates, and in fact many of the small basins have long ago passed through all of the succession stages into old age and have become dry land. It is thus possible to find, in those regions where a large number of lakes are massed together in the same general area, gradations from those which, for one reason or another, still retain their oligotrophic character through the matured eutrophic ones to those in the final stages of disappearance. Thus, the story can (1) be read backward in these gradating stages; (2) it can be predicted in advance from these same stages; and (3) its progress can actually be observed, in part and sometimes through to complete extinction, during a single human generation. Obviously, the smaller the lake the more rapid the eutrophication and subsequent extinction, other things being equal. An average lake whose history is such as to permit eutrophication will be expected to pass from an original oligotrophic stage, during which the productivity is relatively low, into the eutrophic stage, in which the productivity reaches the maximum; and finally into the senescent changes, in which the aquatic productivity declines to the stage of complete extinction.

It should be noted, however, that while the order of progress is, in general, from oligotrophy to eutrophy, the opposite order of development may occasionally be found.

Gams was the first to call attention to the fact that many of the lakes which in sub-boreal time had a very low water level, and consequently very often an average depth that determined them as eutroph, have increased very much during the great Atlantic climate change and are now oligotroph. The palaeolimnological investigations by Lundqvist confirms Gams's statements; and Lundqvist declares that for a large number of Swedish lakes the process of evolution has been from eutrophy to oligotrophy, where that process has not been checked or reversed by contamination, as he shows to be the case with quite a number of them.[1]

Thienemann concluded that oligotrophy passes over into eutrophy when the volume of the epilimnion exceeds that of the hypolimnion. If this conception turns out to be as dependable as some European limnologists believe, then it is obvious that when any circumstance either so greatly raises the surface elevation or so greatly depresses the bottom of an eutrophic lake that the hypolimnion exceeds the epilimnion in volume, a reversal either from eutrophy to oligotrophy or from some stage of oligotrophy to a more primitive stage of oligotrophy will occur. The character of such a reversal will depend upon the degree of advance in the evolution of the lake previous to the deepening of the water.

Mention should be made of the fact that certain lakes fail to go through the usual evolution from oligotrophy to eutrophy even though natural filling may render the hypolimnion smaller (or even eliminate it) than the epilimnion as required by Thienemann's rule. Such failure arises from some special development, e.g., the generous formation of marl, covering the bottom to such an extent that the production of benthic organisms and of rooted plants is exceedingly low. Such lakes may go through to complete extinction without having fulfilled, at any time, the conditions of true eutrophy. A more or less perpetual state of oligotrophy may also result in those lakes in which the normal bottom deposits are removed, in part at least, as they are formed, e.g., by the flow of bottom currents such as are said to occur in certain foothill lakes into one end of which a cold mountain stream flows, the cold, heavy water sinking below the upper, warmer, lighter water of the lake and flowing along the bottom to the outlet at the opposite end.

Dystrophication. The dystrophic lakes of today had their beginnings in primitive basins and went through their initial stages as lakes of very low productivity, i.e., essentially oligotrophic. These primitive basins varied greatly in size and depth, many of them covering considerable areas, and many possessing depths which insured a hypolimnion greatly exceeding the epilimnion. Special circumstances, physical and biotic, resulted in *incomplete decay* of plants and the accumulation of humic materials. Thus appeared the beginnings of dystrophication.

After the initiation of dystrophy, the succession progressed by marginal plant encroachment or by bottom accumulations of incompletely decayed plant materials or by both, eventually passing through the senescent

[1] Strøm.

stages into a peat bog. In the lake country of northern United States, one may find, often in relatively small areas, all gradations from typical dystrophic lakes of fair size and depth through the senescent stages to the formation of dry flats. While the end result is the same, viz., formation of dryland, the succession processes of eutrophy and dystrophy are very different.

INDICES OF PRODUCTIVITY IN LAKES

Limnologists have long sought *indices* of general biological productivity in lakes. It has apparently been the hope that there might be discovered a single index to the richness of a lake which would serve as a means of measuring its production and of comparing it with other lakes. Two considerations are involved here and must be kept clearly distinguished: (1) the inherent capacity of a lake to support life—the biotic potential— and (2) the actual productivity at a given time. Indices for both considerations have been postulated. Obviously, one or two indices of productivity, actual or potential, which would give a dependable evaluation would prove of great use in limnology and related subjects. However, thus far, all of the various so-called indices have shown serious weaknesses, and there is reason for believing that it is very unlikely that any such single index exists. Only a few of the more recent proposals will be considered here.

Average Depth. The proposal that the *average depth* of a lake is the determining factor for productivity originated from Thienemann whose theory is based upon the following arguments: The dissolved oxygen content of the various layers of a lake is the indicator of richness or poverty in the fundamental nutritive substances because the organic substances produced in the epilimnion ("trophogenous layer"), which he arbitrarily defines as the 0- to 10-m. stratum, find their way, more or less, into the "trophylitic" layers (10-m. level to the bottom) and, in the disintegration processes, use up the dissolved oxygen. Therefore, oxygen consumption in the hypolimnion is a measure of the production in the upper strata. Computing the depth of individual lakes as $\frac{\text{volume of the lake}}{\text{surface of the lake}}$, and the volume relations between epilimnion and hypolimnion as $\frac{H}{E} = \frac{\text{volume of water from 10-m. depth to bottom}}{\text{volume of water from surface to 10-m. depth}}$, and the dissolved oxygen relations between epilimnion and hypolimnion as $O_2 \frac{H}{E} = \frac{O_2 \text{ content of water from 10-m. depth to bottom}}{O_2 \text{ content of water from surface to 10-m. depth}}$, Thienemann claims to have shown that in oligotrophic lakes the volume of the epilimnion is less than that of the hypolimnion; while in eutrophic lakes, the reverse is true; therefore, the average depth is the determining factor in such lakes. Also, stated in another way, in oligotrophic lakes the dis= solved oxygen content of the hypolimnion is greater than that of the epilimnion, while in eutrophic lakes, the reverse condition prevails.

Certain difficulties appear at once. It is very doubtful whether the 10-m. depth can justly be designated as the dividing line between epilimnion and hypolimnion, since it is well known that the true dividing line varies greatly in position in different lakes. Furthermore, lakes are known in both America and Europe which do not conform to this average depth index, irrespective of whether the *actual* dividing line between epilimnion and hypolimnion or that of Thienemann is used, and which cannot be explained as exceptions due to contamination. Certain other features, such as the degree of development of the littoral regions, constitute very important influences which, in some instances at least, might be more important in determining the production of the lake.

Rooted Submerged Vegetation. Klugh (1926) urged that the amount of rooted, submerged vegetation may be an index character of lake productivity. This view, in guarded form, is shared by Roelofs (1944). As pointed out before (page 308), there seems to be no relation between the plankton production and the quantity of rooted submerged vegetation sufficient to make this a dependable criterion. It is a well-known fact that the amount of rooted submerged vegetation is governed by a number of factors, such as the degree of exposure and slope of the submerged shelf. Large lakes, as for example, Lake Nipigon, may maintain a great fish production which could not be predicted from the scanty vegetation about its shores (Rawson, 1930). Likewise, even in some of the small lakes, the development of the submerged vegetation does not always tell the story of the productivity. Much remains to be learned about the role of the submerged, rooted plants in fresh waters; and until our knowledge of their relations is more exact, they must be used very guardedly as an index of general productivity.

Plankton. The fundamental position which plankton occupies between the nonliving and the living components of an aquatic complex has naturally led to the supposition that plankton should be an index of general production, and claims to that effect have been made. According to Thienemann's scheme, eutrophic lakes are characterized by a quantitatively rich plankton, while oligotrophic lakes have a plankton poor in quantity. It has been claimed that abundance of plankton is usually associated with a rich bottom fauna, while a paucity of plankton accompanies a poor bottom fauna. It may turn out that these relations hold in general, but exceptions occur. Even if it were true that the plankton constitutes a dependable index of the richness of a lake, certain difficulties in its satisfactory use would still remain, e.g., the various fluctuations of the plankton which would require carefully planned and extensive seasonal collections before any appraisal could be made or the difficulties inherent in the determinations of the nannoplankton. The best that can be stated at present is that the plankton is, on the average, an indication of the general nutritive condition of the water.

Bottom Fauna. Much attention has been given to the bottom fauna. That it plays a very important part in the nutrition cycles of a lake is certain. Some European workers have stressed the *quality* of the bottom fauna, particularly that of the deeper water, as an indication of the production character of a lake. As shown in Table 39, seasonal cycles also affect the benthic organisms, sometimes strikingly, so that the difficulties of sampling, both seasonal and at any single time, detract from the usefulness of such an index even if it were a dependable one, which apparently it is not. Form of basin, character of bottom and of bottom deposits, water movements, and other features may be such as to militate against the development of a bottom fauna which would be a true index of the general richness of the lake. When a rich benthic fauna is present, high total productivity is common, but not necessarily insured.

Organic Content of Water. As previously mentioned (page 208), it has been shown that, in many Wisconsin lakes, at least, the standing crop of dissolved organic matter is ordinarily much greater than the total organic matter in the plankton supported by the same water. It has also been shown that there is a fairly constant relation between the plankton and the total organic matter in the water. The dissolved organic matter is said to be so constant in quantity and composition that the character of a lake may be determined from a single sample. This whole subject is as yet too new to justify any predictions as to how satisfactory a general index to the productivity of a lake the dissolved organic matter will turn out to be.

Chlorophyll Content. It has been proposed that if the chlorophyll content of a sample of water can be measured and if the chlorophyll so determined may be used as an index of the photosynthetic capacity, then such a measurement might be used as a convenient method of evaluating biological productivity. Somewhat recently, methods for measuring chlorophyll in water have been devised and considerable attention has been directed to determining the possible value of chlorophyll as a production index. Results of such investigations (Riley, 1940; Manning and Juday, 1941; Gessner, 1944; *et al.*) are not in full agreement. Certain weaknesses appear to be inherent in the idea that quantity of chlorophyll is a dependable index of photosynthetic capacity. This field has not been adequately explored as yet, and only future work will determine whether such a measurement has any significant index value.

Other Proposed Indices. The organic content of bottom deposits is important as food for benthic organisms, but Rawson (1930) seems to have shown that it is not always indicative of the productivity of a lake. In general, hard-water lakes are more productive than are the soft-water lakes, but all hard-water lakes are not highly productive. Moyle (1949) claims that in Minnesota waters total alkalinity and total phosphorus appear to be the most valuable indices of productivity. Hypolimnial oxygen deficits as indices find both support (Hutchinson, 1938) and opposition (Rawson, 1939). Strøm (1933) contended that the relation $\dfrac{\text{water volume}}{\text{surface of bottom}}$ largely determines the productivity of stagnant lakes. Other influences known to be important in natural waters have been examined as possible indices, but no conclusive results are available.

Conclusion. Thus far, no single, satisfactory *index* of productivity has been found, and present understanding of the conditions involved in productivity in nature seems to indicate that no such single criterion exists. Any appraisal of productivity must come, for the present at least, from an examination and measurement of several dominating influences, the particular category of factors to be determined on the basis of the merits of the lake or class of lakes under examination. The search for single indices of production of certain specified kinds of organisms, especially fish production, has met with much the same fate. Degree and area of river overflow have been held to affect markedly fish production but fail as a general index owing to differences in the kinds of lands overflowed, nature of the overflow, and other variables. Alm's *Fb coefficient* (relation of fish caught per hectare to the live weight of bottom fauna per hectare) has not proved wholly satisfactory because of several limitations, two of which are (1) its failure to take into account the plankton-feeding fish or (2) those species of fish which purposely or otherwise are not caught in the usual fishing practices. While from certain utilitarian standpoints, the interest in productivity may center about the fish production of waters, the character and quantities of fishes present are not always satisfactory criteria of the general biological productivity of the water under consideration. As already pointed out in connection with the discussion of the cycle of essential food substances (page 340), fishes are not necessary components of a complex and, in some natural waters, are totally absent. When present, they may fail, for various reasons, to give the correct picture of productivity conditions as a whole. For example, conditions of parasitism in the fishes may be such that their ability to reproduce and grow is greatly impaired. Reighard (1929) reports such an instance in certain northern lakes with much restricted fish faunas in which the small-mouthed black bass were under size and under weight for their ages, were heavily parasitized, and in one of the lakes, all of the specimens examined were believed to have been rendered sterile by the presence of an immature stage of a tapeworm (*Proteocephalus* sp.) in the gonads.

ARTIFICIAL ENRICHMENT

That man has done much, purposely or incidentally, to affect the conditions prevailing within many inland waters is well known. The waste products of his own life or his industries often find their way into natural waters and produce contaminations. Removal of the forests and tilling of the land introduce changes through the medium of the drainage which are not of the nature of contaminations. In very sparsely settled regions, these influences may be negligible, while in some of the thickly settled parts of the Old World, the effects may be marked. Contaminations of natural waters and their results constitute a highly specialized and complicated subject which is outside the province of this book. It will suffice, however, to point out here that certain kinds of contaminations are not always wholly undersirable; in fact, from the standpoint of productivity, they may be distinctly desirable. This kind of enrichment of the water is due to the addition of substances which, either as they are when they enter or after subsequent chemical changes, increase the amounts of essential nutritive materials. Among the contaminations most likely to function in this way are the domestic sewages, downwash from manured fields, and other similar forms of organic matter. In some instances, the concentrations of contaminating materials may be so great at the region of inflow that conditions lethal to the original flora and fauna may prevail, but the ensuing dilution and the subsequent chemical changes may result in some enrichment, although care should be used in making generalizations, since, it must be remembered, not only do the contaminating substances vary immensely in their composition, but the natural waters themselves differ so widely in the conditions which they present; therefore, the greatest caution should be exercised in any attempt to predict the outcome of a contamination.

Enriching effects due to contaminations are more to be expected in the smaller lakes than in the larger ones, although it may occur in the latter, a good example of which seems to be Lake Zurich, Switzerland, which, according to European writers, has been entrophied by sewage materials during the last 65 years. Strøm (1928) makes the interesting statement that in some of the smaller lakes of Sweden, Finland, and Norway, the tracks of the sledges in the winter can be traced later in the richer development of the bottom fauna beneath those paths. In fact, some limnologists have regarded eutrophy as the result mainly of contamination, but such a generalization is without satisfactory foundation. There is some evidence that the sewage from certain large cities when poured into one of the Great Lakes acts in a lethal way over the area of greatest concentration but that, as it spreads farther and farther into the open lakes and dilution becomes greater and greater until the lethal conditions are eliminated, a zone of enrichment may occur in which the biota is distinctly increased.

For many years, fertilizers have been used in Europe to increase fish production in ponds. Latterly, considerable research has been done in America on the application of fertilizers to inland waters. However, this is still a pioneering field. That the proper addition of certain fertilizers may have a favorable effect upon fish production seems to be established, but there is still much to be learned about the addition of fertilizers to different kinds of waters, constituents added, seasonal relations, and other critical matters. European work has centered largely about three chemical elements, viz., nitrogen, phosphorus, and potassium. Substantial and significant work has been done in southern United States on the problem of the application of fertilizers to fish ponds. However, it appears that caution must be exercised in transplanting these results, in unmodified form, to similar waters in other regions, as, for example, to the lake country of northern United States. Even in the same region it is difficult to establish a dependable practice in the small-area waters. Neess (1949) points out that "the principle seems to hold that the smaller the body of water, the more aberrantly it behaves and the more difficult it is to understand." Ball (1949) points out that in his work on the experimental use of fertilizers on certain Michigan "ponds which have been chosen for similarity of physical, chemical, and biological detail will often react quite differently to the stimulus of an application of fertilizer." Ball found that in the Michigan waters studied the volume of fish-food organisms could often be greatly increased by the addition of fertilizer, leading in most instances to an increased growth of the fish. This effect on fish may result in the production of larger game fish, or it may mean an increase in the number of young fish, leading to an overpopulation of the latter. Ball also found an indication that "the closer the feeding habits of the fish concerned are to the base of the food chain, the more the effects of fertilizer are reflected in total weight of fish produced."

Inherent in the problems of application of artificial fertilizer to natural waters are dangers of unfavorable effects. Some misstep in the procedure or some unanticipated effect may lead to disaster. In northern United States, fertilization may lead to winter kill in lakes which normally escape this cataclysm. In work of this kind, sight must never be lost of the fact that a body of water is an exceedingly complex physical-chemical-biological entity balanced by nature into an approximate but uneasy sort of stability, ready to explode into imbalance on slight interference. Injudicious introduction of fertilizing substances may set up some sort of chain reaction, effects of which may be most unfortunate and difficult to interpret.

Thus far the most progress has been made in fertilization programs for small, enclosed waters—ponds, reservoirs, very small lakes. For large lakes much less is known about the possibilities of artificially increasing production with fertilizers. At the present time, it is scientifically uncertain and economically impractical. Experiments on certain open arms of the sea (Gross *et al.*, 1946) give evidence of beneficial effects of fertilizers on plankton, bottom fauna, and fish growth, but such results can as yet be viewed only as exploratory. For a critical discussion of the fertilization of natural inland water, the reader is referred to a recent paper by Hasler and Einsele (1948).

The possible enrichments by various organic contaminations must not be allowed to conceal the various devastations which pollutions may produce. How to make the best use of man's great organic wastes in the enrichment of waters and how to protect waters against the ravages of uncontrolled contaminations constitute very important problems for the future.

DEPTH AND AREA RELATIONS TO PRODUCTIVITY OF BOTTOM FAUNA

That the form of a lake basin has a profound effect upon the various life processes within it is well known. Rawson (1930) proposed some relations of depth and area to the production of bottom faunas which, though relatively undeveloped at present, deserve some mention. He concludes that

1. In general, a lake of large area supports a smaller benthic population per unit area than does a smaller lake.

2. Deep lakes generally support a smaller biota than do the shallow lakes.

3. Since there is a limit to the range over which this increase of area and of depth continues to be accompanied by a decrease of the benthic population, an area of 40 sq. miles is suggested as the tentative limit beyond which the area no longer exercises a significant control over the quantity of bottom fauna, and a depth of 30.5 m. (100 ft.) is suggested as the tentative limit of effective control over the bottom population.

4. Minimal depths and areas probably exist, beyond which this control of the amount of bottom fauna is no longer significant. Rawson presents a curve (Fig. 44) which has been constructed by plotting the average quantity of bottom fauna in each of the lakes included, expressed in pounds dry weight per acre and area in square miles and depths in feet, against the product of the depth and area of each, explaining that the product of the area and depth is not considered as volume, since each

represents separate factors. In lakes having areas greater than 40 sq. miles, the depth is multiplied by the proposed limiting area (40 sq. miles); and in those instances in which the depths exceed 100 ft., the area is multiplied by the proposed limiting depth (100 ft.). Rawson points out that the curve representing the relation between quantity of bottom fauna and depth times area is not expressible by any single mathematical

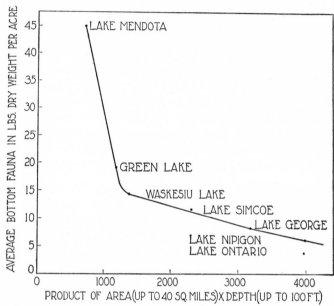

Fig. 44. Graph showing the relation between the amounts of bottom fauna and the product of the depth and the area (within limits) of lakes. (*Redrawn from Rawson*, 1930.)

equation but maintains that such a result is to be expected because of the complexity of the causal factors and the heterogeneity of the fauna itself.

The value of this curve as well as the form of the curve must at present be regarded as tentative. Its author states that the relations portrayed are not universal but expresses the expectation that as the mass of comparable quantitative data on lake-bottom faunas increases, a closer approach to the true form of the curve will result. Many of the bottom-fauna data now available are either fragmentary or are, for some reason, not comparable; therefore, they cannot be worked into this conception with any accuracy.

PART IV
SOME SPECIAL TYPES OF LENTIC ENVIRONMENTS

Among the various lentic environments are some which are sufficiently common and distinct to justify special treatment here, even though the general limnological features presented in the foregoing sections apply to lakes at large. No attempt will be made to include all of the more special types, but the discussion will be confined to two, viz., ponds and bog lakes.

CHAPTER XV

PONDS

In a previous section of this book (page 15), some attention was given to the difficulties of distinguishing between lakes and ponds. Possibly, a way out of the dilemma would be to follow Forel in regarding all bodies of standing water, irrespective of size, as *lakes*. However, the term *pond* has such universal use, and the general conception of a pond is so widely understood, that it seems best to employ the term pond for that class of very small, shallow bodies of standing water in which relatively quiet water and extensive plant occupancy are common characteristics.

That the great diversity of lakes is also represented in ponds goes without saying, since not only are the conditions of origin, distribution, and general status similar, but also ponds are often themselves the evolutionary successors of previously existing lakes. In most respects, limnological knowledge of lakes is much more advanced than is that of ponds; in fact, for ponds it is fragmentary, often altogether lacking in some aspects, and widely scattered in the literature. Much has been learned about fish ponds of various kinds; also about open, water-supply reservoirs. However, in both instances, man's influence is usually a potent modifying factor; and while many of the facts worked out in these more or less artificial situations are applicable in an understanding of pond life, nevertheless, these waters cannot qualify as natural, unmodified ponds.

Ponds are mainly of three general classes: (1) those which represent the pond stage in the extinction of previously existing lakes; (2) those whose basins have never been large or deep (not preceded by a lake) but instead have been small of area from the start and, because of recent origin or for some special reason, have persisted in the pond stage; and (3) those whose basins are the results of man's activities (excavations, quarries, impoundments, etc.). Natural processes alone are constantly forming new pond basins (cut-offs from streams, solution basins, beach ponds, and many others), some of which are never more than temporary ponds from the beginning; others qualifying as permanent ponds at least for a period in their existence.

With respect to seasonal duration, ponds are customarily divided into two general classes: (1) permanent—those which contain some water the year round; and (2) temporary—those in which the basin contains water at certain times or seasons and becomes dry at others. Those which occur for but a limited period in spring are called *vernal* ponds; those which contain water in spring, dry up during summer, and again contain water in the autumn are called *vernal autumnal* ponds; and those which contain some water throughout the open season but freeze to the bottom in winter have been called *aestival* ponds.

PHYSICAL CONDITIONS

WATER MOVEMENTS

Owing to the small areas involved, water movements in ponds are minimal. Even in the most exposed ones, wave action is very slight, while other forms of water movement, such as currents, are present in appreciable form only in those so-called ponds which are expanded portions of stream systems. Luxuriant plant growths, which are often accompanying features of ponds, do much to further restrict water movements. Many ponds are so thoroughly protected by closely surrounding forests, hills, and similar features that even in times of high winds they may maintain an approximate calm. These conditions of almost constant calm in highly protected ponds tend to favor the development of stagnation conditions in the bottom levels, even during the summer, although most ponds of the less protected situations have a more or less complete circulation during the entire open season.

TEMPERATURE

Because of the shallow depth and the large expanse of surface as compared with the volume, pond waters in general tend to follow the temperatures of the atmosphere. This tendency is manifested in both the annual and the diurnal variations. Very shallow ponds may freeze almost or entirely to the bottom in the more northern latitudes, while during the summer the temperatures may rise, on occasion, to 30°C. or above. In northern United States, where at times during summer the days may be warm and the nights cool, the daily variation of water temperature may be wide. However, so many variables enter into the temperature relations of ponds at large that few general statements can be made. The observer constantly finds unexpected temperature features of which the following are but a few. Almost continuous calm, due to unusually protected conditions, may, even in hot weather, result merely in a warm, thin, upper layer (due to the poor conduction of the water itself) while the lowermost water may remain relatively cold. Plant growths tend to reduce any mechanical mixing of the water by wind and often help maintain sharp temperature contrasts between the surface and the bottom water in summer. The writer has found situations, in midsummer, in which within a depth of about 0.6 m. there was a difference of more than 6°C. and a diminutive thermal stratification was present.   He has also found in some of the larger beach ponds a difference of as much as 17°C. in the temperature of the whole mass of water during midsummer when air temperatures varied sufficiently to make such differences possible.

In general, ponds acquire ice cover long in advance of the date of freezing of lakes, and all of the ponds of a given region are likely to freeze over at about the same time.   Ponds protected from wind will usually develop ice cover before those exposed to wind action, if the wind is blowing and other conditions are the same in the two kinds.   This time difference, however, is relatively slight.   In contrast to this almost simultaneous freezing over of ponds in late autumn or early winter, the date of loss of ice cover in spring may differ widely among ponds of similar size in the same region.   Ponds which are shaded and protected from wind action lose the ice cover last.   Especially is this true of forest ponds.   There are records of a difference of three weeks in the thawing of forest ponds and those of open lands.   Usually, the ice disappearance in ponds occurs well in advance of that event in lakes.

TURBIDITY

Turbidity, due either to plankton growths or to suspended nonliving matters, varies greatly with the circumstances of season, productivity, nature of the basin, degree of exposure, inflowing sediment, and other similar features.   Some ponds are clear; others, extremely muddy.   Between these extremes exist all possible intergrades.   Settling suspended matters usually drop rather quickly to the bottom because of the shallow depth and the relatively quiet water of most ponds, although much of it may be so light and flocculent that the ordinary locomotor movements of the various swimming animals keep some of it in suspension much of the time.   Ponds with mucky bottoms maintain, more or less permanently, a layer of cloudy water just above the bottom, due largely to finely divided materials which are virtually nonsettling.   Ponds with clay bottoms or those receiving inflowing, clay-bearing waters are likely to have high turbidity.   Those ponds whose bottoms are composed of substances in which sand, gravel, and humus predominate are likely to have very low turbidity, and the same is true of those with rock basins such as occur in mountain regions and areas of extensive rock outcrop.   Sudden variations of turbidity, due to rains, are not uncommon.

LIGHT

The shallow depths of ponds usually make possible an illumination of the bottom by effective light so that plants may occupy the entire basin. Luxuriant growths of plants produce much shading of underlying waters.

Woodland ponds are often subject to shading by the surrounding forest, especially during the summer. Unshaded ponds with clear water may be illuminated throughout with an intensity almost as great as that at the surface. Light penetration is much affected by the irregular and sometimes abrupt variations in turbidity. Since the small depths allow such complete illumination, it follows that ponds in general are subject to the greatest range of the daily and seasonal variations in light supply.

CHEMICAL CONDITIONS

DISSOLVED GASES

No general statement can be made concerning the usual expectation as to the dissolved gas content of ponds. It has sometimes been supposed that pond water is well supplied with dissolved oxygen and relatively low in the decomposition gases, since frequent circulation of the water and maximum exposure to air were thought to keep it well aerated. Such may be the condition in larger, much exposed ponds in which wind action is vigorous, but circulation in ponds is much reduced, and many ponds circulate little if at all. Therefore, the full range of dissolved gas variation is to be expected and is actually often realized. Obviously, the nature of the bottom has a profound influence upon the gas content of the superimposed water. In protected ponds with mucky bottoms, a well-defined chemical stratification may exist in summer, even in the shallow ones, in which the oxygen is abundant in the thin surface layer but totally absent in the deepest layer, and in which the free carbon dioxide and some other decomposition gases may occur abundantly in the lower water. Shelford (1911) studied a series of ponds at the south end of Lake Michigan and found the dissolved oxygen content of the uppermost water as shown in Table 44.

TABLE 44.   OXYGEN IN CUBIC CENTIMETERS PER LITER IN WATER OF PONDS AT SOUTH
END OF LAKE MICHIGAN
Samples taken at 10 to 12 cm. below surface of open water
Modified from Shelford

Date	Pond 1	Pond 5c	Pond 7a	Pond 14b
July 22, 1910.............	6.99	4.68	7.44	6.20
Apr. 26, 1911.............	6.87	7.25	6.96	6.27

These ponds showed considerable amounts of oxygen in the surface waters; but at greater depths and in proximity with different kinds of bottoms, very dissimilar results were obtained, particularly in the older ponds. Table 45 indicates the nature of the findings.

TABLE 45. DISSOLVED OXYGEN CONTENT AND FREE CARBON DIOXIDE CONTENT OF
WATERS IN CERTAIN PONDS AT SOUTH END OF LAKE MICHIGAN
All results expressed in cubic centimeters per liter. Samples taken at depths of
35 to 40 cm. Ponds indicated in order of age, pond 1 being the youngest and
pond 14*b* the oldest
Modified from Shelford

	Dissolved oxygen									
Pond	Over sandy bottom				Over vegetation		Over bottom with vegetation removed			
	6/27	7/22	4/26	5/10	6/27	7/22	6/27	7/22	4/26	5/10
1....	6.57	6.37	5.91	6.32	....	....	3.34	5.91		
5c...	7.36	8.18	7.31	6.60	....	....	6.52	6.74		
7a...	....	....	....	....	4.42	2.52	0.00	0.00	6.36	3.36
14b...	....	....	....	....	3.33	2.24	0.00	0.00	1.38	1.93
	Free carbon dioxide									
1....	0.0	0.0	....	....	....	....	4.1	0.0		
5c...	0.0	0.0	....	....	....	....	0.0	0.0		
7a...	4.4	2.5	....	....	....	....	21.0	9.6		
14b...	....	....	....	....	3.3	2.4	6.6	4.0		

These results show (1) that over sandy bottoms of younger ponds, abundant dissolved oxygen prevails during the open season; (2) that the water over vegetation has a moderate dissolved oxygen supply at least during the day; (3) that in the older ponds the lowermost waters show an oxygen supply during the spring months but during the summer are devoid of oxygen; and (4) that the free carbon dioxide content of the deeper water is greater in the older ponds. These conditions are doubtless duplicated, more or less, in a great many ponds during the open season.

In some ponds, certain decomposition gases may become quite prominent during the summer, especially methane and hydrogen sulfide. Either of these gases may be evolved from bottom materials in conspicuous amounts.

Mention has already been made (page 97) of the reported fact that in some plant-filled ponds, lagoons, and similar waters, complete exhaustion of the dissolved oxygen supply may occur at night, owing to the combined consumption activities of animals, plants, and bottom deposits. So few studies of this phenomenon have been made that the extent of its occurrence is little known. Without doubt, oxygen reduction goes on at night during the open season to varying extents, and it may be that this extreme reduction is more common than is now realized. Return of effective light at dawn restores oxygen through photosynthesis to the water and rescues the biota from the threat of suffocation.

Concerning conditions within natural ponds during the winter and under ice cover, little definite information is yet available. In more northern latitudes, it would seem that long, continuous ice cover would bring about such complete loss of dissolved oxygen and such accumulations of decomposition products that the contained life would be destroyed. That such tragedies do occur, at times, to at least some of the biota is known, but in many ponds in which it would seem certain that such fatalities would occur, they do not appear but instead, the ice fades off in spring, and the pond resumes its open-season activities with the usual succession of organisms. A satisfactory explanation for the apparent protection of the biota against the effects of complete, prolonged, winter stagnation in ponds at large or for the common failure of such complete stagnation to occur is not yet available. Encystments, hibernation stages or conditions, special behavior, and life-history phenomena may save the day for many species.

Petersen (1926) studied seasonal phenomena in a *Chara*-cat-tail pond in which the water did not exceed 76 cm. in depth and found that the oxygen rose to about 13 cc. per l. in early January; dropped precipitously to about 5 cc. per l. in mid-January; declined to about 2 cc. per l. in March; rose abruptly to about 10 cc. per l. in late March; gradually declined from early July to about 0.7 cc. per l. in mid-August; and then began to rise rapidly in September. In midwinter when but 5 to 7.5 cm. (depth) of water remained under the ice cover, no animals were found, although one week before the thaw they began to reappear. No explanation is given as to the nature of this disappearance. Petersen's figure (Fig. 45) shows the nature of the seasonal changes in oxygen and certain accompanying features.

DISSOLVED SOLIDS

Available data on dissolved solids in ponds are so meager that satisfactory statement is not possible. Shelford (1911) found that in a series of ponds at the south end of Lake Michigan there was a notable decrease in total solids in the older ponds, although he points out that the statement is based upon a single set of analyses and therefore subject to reservation. Chapman (1931) mentions unpublished work by Transeau which showed that in certain ponds the water maintains the same relative concentration irrespective of water level. Examinations of the various scattering analyses of pond waters yield little more in general conclusions than (1) that such a content exists in all ponds; (2) that ponds differ qualitatively and quantitatively in dissolved solids; and (3) that the various dissolved materials show a quantitative seasonal variation, which often differs markedly in different ponds, even in those which are closely adjacent. Obviously, the whole matter of dissolved solids depends much upon such circumstances as the geological history of the basin; nature and source of bottom deposits; presence or absence of outlets; presence or absence of

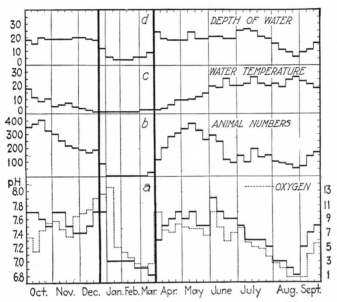

FIG. 45. Graphs showing seasonal changes in certain environmental factors and in the number of animals during the year in a *Chara*-cat-tail pond. In section *a*, dissolved oxygen content in cubic centimeters per liter is indicated by the dotted line and pH values by the solid line. In section *b*, numbers at the left indicate the total number of animals found. In section *c*, numbers at the left indicate water temperatures in degrees centigrade. In section *d*, numbers at the left indicate the depth of water in inches. The spaces between the vertical heavy lines indicate the time during which ice covered the pond. (*Redrawn from Petersen, 1926.*)

inflowing water, either surface streams or subterranean water; area of drainage; rainfall; wind-blown material; and character of the biota.

HYDROGEN-ION CONCENTRATION

As might be expected, the various bodies of water commonly designated as ponds differ as widely in reaction as do all the various kinds of lakes and manifest a range practically equal to the entire range known for unmodified, natural waters. In an examination of 39 ponds in Denmark, Wesenberg-Lund (1930) reported a range of pH 4.4 to 9.4, and there is reason for believing that a variation of this magnitude may be equaled, if not exceeded, in many regions of North America where ponds are common and diversified. Reaction of pond water is normally subject to variation, often of wide range, in the same pond, and various ponds differ greatly in this respect.

Data given in Table 46 illustrate to a limited extent the pH in different pond waters, although the records chosen do not represent known extremes.

TABLE 46. SOME SELECTED RECORDS OF pH VARIATION IN PONDS

Pond	Variation, pH	Period of observation	Authority
Chara-cat-tail pond.............	6.8–7.9	12 months	Petersen (1926)
Granite pond...................	6.2–6.8	2 seasons	Reed & Klugh (1924)
Limestone pond................	7.6–9.2	2 seasons	Reed & Klugh (1924)
Pond *A*.......................	6.6–9.2	Aug. 5–25	Darby (1929)
Pond *B*.......................	6.5	Aug. 5–17	Darby (1929)
Staddon Reservoir.............	7.5–9.3	2 years	Atkins & Harris (1924)
Quarry pond..................	6.0–8.7	14 months	Atkins & Harris (1924)

In some ponds, the pH remains practically constant over considerable periods of time; in others, it may change progressively and more or less uniformly; in still others, it may shift irregularly, often rather abruptly and over considerable range; e.g., ponds have been reported in which a change of pH from 9.2 to 6.6 occurred from one day to the next. It is claimed that heavy rains may produce marked alterations in the pH of some ponds, especially those in which the buffer action is low. Rain water itself may produce some change; however, it has been claimed that since rain water is only slightly acid and is completely unbuffered, it cannot account for some of the larger changes which occur but that these must be due to certain substances which the rain water picks up in running over the soil of the drainage basin and delivers into the pond. While decreasing volume of water due to evaporation is often accompanied by progressive changes in pH, instances have been reported in which the shrinkage from normal water level to subsequent dryness showed no alteration in the hydrogen-ion concentration.

ELECTROLYTES

Very few measurements of conductivity have as yet been made in unmodified pond water. Atkins and Harris (1924) report values of 121, 170, and 263 reciprocal megohms in three similar adjacent ponds in England. They found that the electrical conductivity is high when the pH is low, and vice versa, and suggest that this may be due to the precipitation of the calcium and magnesium carbonates owing to the decrease of carbonic acid in solution, and that the reduction in conductivity may be the result, at least in part, of the removal by Algae of electrolytes necessary for their growth. There is reason to believe that in various ponds, wide differences in conductivity occur; also, that ponds may show fluctuations in conductivity at different times of year and at different times of day.

BIOLOGICAL CONDITIONS

Typical ponds differ from lakes in the absence of most truly limnetic animals and plants. Pond organisms, therefore, are essentially of the littoral and benthic types. Another difference exists; viz., the usual diversification of the littoral area of lakes into different habitats has no counterpart in ponds, since the littoral area of the latter is practically uniform. It must be kept constantly in mind that nature provides all possible gradations between ponds and lakes many of which manifest mixtures of those features which characterize lakes and ponds.

PLANT GROWTHS

Ponds may be divided roughly into two general classes: (1) those with bare bottoms and (2) those with bottoms composed of soft, accumulated deposits. In general, those with bare bottoms are sometimes virtually devoid of the larger vegetation, while in those with bottom sediments, abundant growths of higher plants are to be expected. Ponds representing transitions between these two classes show plant growths of various kinds and quantities. The qualitative composition of the flora differs in different latitudes.

Pond vegetation of a well-developed sort tends to be arranged in zones more or less parallel to the shore line. In general respects, this zonation resembles that of the bordering aquatics in the protected bays and coves of lakes (page 299). Typically, the usual three zones are to be expected, viz., (1) the marginal zone of emergent plants; (2) the middle zone of floating plants, which includes (*a*) rooted forms whose leaves float on the surface and (*b*) completely floating, unattached plants; and (3) the zone of submerged forms. Obviously, all of these zones can occur only in those ponds which have depths sufficient for the development of such a zonation.

In the older and more productive ponds, algal growths, in which representatives of virtually all of the groups of fresh-water Algae may participate, often become conspicuous.

PLANKTON

With the possible exception of the exceedingly small and the highly transient pools, ponds maintain a plankton. Certain ponds, according to statements in the literature, have very few true plankters, the implication being that the microscopic organisms which occupy the more open portions of the water are essentially of the same nature as the strictly littoral ones which occur about the margins and constitute a different group of organisms. However, it is an open question whether such a distinction has any important natural basis. Many of the lake plankters also occur in the plankton of ponds. Pond plankton may also contain still other species usually found only in such situations. Furthermore, true littoral and bottom forms intermingle. Such a mixture is the inevitable result of the very restricted areas and depths so characteristic of ponds. If pond plankton is to be considered as a distinct type (heleoplankton), as is contended by some authors, it is a distinct type merely because it contains *additional components* not found in lake plankton and not because lake plankton types are wholly absent. If there is foundation for the vigorous insistence of Wesenberg-Lund that the home of the fresh-water plankton is to be found on the bottom and in the littoral region of lakes and ponds, "whence it is still recruited to this very day," then the plankton of ponds and that of lakes are so genetically related that they should show a composition gradient from a more qualitatively diversified pond biota to a less diversified lake plankton biota, with no significant dividing lines.

Knowledge of pond plankton is yet so fragmentary that it is very difficult to generalize in a satisfactory way. Certain European limnologists stress the much richer representation of the Chlorophyceae in pond plankton as compared with lake plankton, the ponds maintaining species not found in lake plankton. Records of 90 or more different species of Algae in one pond appear in the literature. It has been claimed that in Danish ponds, the Rhizopoda are of distinctly secondary importance, but this conclusion does not hold for ponds at large. In the permanent ponds and, perhaps to some extent, in the temporary ones, the plankton may be expected to show two annual maxima (spring and autumn) resembling similar maxima in lakes (page 253), although the occurrence of but one maximum, in some instances in the spring and in others in the autumn, is on record.

Wesenberg-Lund (1930) made extensive comparisons of the plankton in Danish lakes with that of Danish ponds and arrived at conclusions among which are the following:

1. Pond plankton differs in composition from lake plankton in several respects, some of which are: (*a*) Diatoms, common in lakes, are almost absent in ponds; (*b*) ponds are much richer in flagellates; (*c*) ponds maintain a greater production of Myxophyceae; (*d*) desmid production is greater in ponds; (*e*) Protozoa play a much more prominent role in ponds; (*f*) all rotifers from the pelagic regions of lakes also occur in ponds, although often exhibiting somewhat different growth forms; and (*g*) the

Entomostraca probably include the largest number of species which either belong exclusively to the lake plankton or occur exceptionally in ponds, although certain genera (example, *Ceriodaphnia*) are very largely composed of typical pond plankters.

2. Lakes, as a group, show a greater uniformity of plankton composition (qualitative) than do the ponds. Species known only from one lake are few, while the reverse is true of the ponds. This diversification of pond plankton, however, occurs only during the summer, disappearing shortly before the formation of the ice cover.

3. Winter plankton in Danish lakes includes both phytoplankton and zooplankton, the former predominating during mild winters. Winter plankton of ponds is often almost exclusively zooplankton.

4. The perennial plankton daphnids of lakes manifest striking seasonal and local variations, while in the pond plankton these phenomena are much restricted or even absent. In the rotifers, however, the reverse is true; it is the pond plankters which have pronounced seasonal and local variations, while, with few exceptions, it appears that seasonal variation is unknown in rotifers from the pelagic regions of the larger lakes.

Variations in the composition of the plankton from year to year are much greater in ponds.

It should be kept in mind that these generalizations are based upon a long-continued study of the ponds and lakes of a relatively small and limited region (Denmark) and may hold only in part for different and more diversified areas.

Faunal Characteristics

There is no occasion for giving here a census of the various faunas found in ponds. Certain general characteristics only will be mentioned.

1. Among the vertebrates, amphibians constitute the important group. Fishes are either reduced to minor quantities or are absent except in the larger, permanent ponds.

2. Of the invertebrates, the Protozoa, rotifers, insects, crustaceans, and snails are most important.

3. Pond faunas, particularly those of temporary ponds, are largely composed of species which may pass a part of the life cycle out of water, as an active aerial or a terrestrial stage or in some quiescent condition.

4. Surface-film animals and those which must come to the surface for breathing are often abundant.

5. A few species occur almost exclusively in temporary ponds, a typical example being the common fairy shrimp, *Eubranchipus vernalis*, while, on the other hand, some species occur only in permanent ponds, e.g., certain gammarids (Chapman, 1931).

6. Insects usually manifest the greatest number and diversity of species.

Faunal Variations

Pond faunas are extremely variable. The following quotation from Wesenberg-Lund (1939) deals directly with Danish ponds, but general features of the description hold for ponds at large.

Nowhere do the variations in the composition of the fauna seem to be so great from year to year as in ponds. It is a well-known fact that Phyllopods may one year be very numerous in a given pond; in the next year or even in a series of years, not a single specimen can be found. This holds good especially for *Branchipus* and *Apus*. In North Seeland, we can speak of *Limnetis* years, i.e., years when *Limnetis* is found in numerous ponds; then for a series of years it will be impossible to get a single one; my studies on Planaria (*Mesostoma lingua*), Cladocera, Rotifera, Flagellata, Ostracoda, *Diaptomus* species, Hydrachnida have all shown the same fact. A species may be abundant in a pond one year, disappear for three or four years, and then suddenly reappear. Furthermore, explorations carried on year after year in the same pond show that species which are constant temporally may live their life in the same locality in different manners in the different years. One year, the species will propagate monocyclically; the next, dicyclically; in another again the formation of resting eggs is almost stopped; the sexual period may be much displaced, in one year forward; in another backward. Owing to the great variation in the composition of the pond plankton from year to year, especially of the nannoplankton, the diet differs enormously and exerts its influence upon the ripening of the sexual products. In one year species have completed their development before the ponds are covered with ice, in others, they are forced to hibernate as larvae below the ice (frogs, salamanders) resulting in tendency to Neotaeni in one year, but not in others.

Seasonal Succession

The procession of seasons in temperate latitudes brings about seasonal successions among the biota of ponds which are quite definite and often very striking. While the details of these phenomena differ in different regions and in various kinds of ponds, some features are sufficiently general to deserve mention here and are illustrated by results taken from certain papers selected from the large but scattered American literature.

In certain permanent, old forest ponds, Allee (1912) found a well-defined, qualitative and quantitative seasonal succession. The number of species present at any one time was greatest in midsummer (64 in August) and smallest in winter (5 in January). Among the fauna, the Crustacea, with *Asellus communis* as the predominant species, were numerically dominant at two times during the year, viz., in spring and in autumn, while the pond snails, with *Lymnaea reflexa* the predominant form, were numerically dominant in midsummer only.

Petersen (1926) studied the seasonal succession of animals in a permanent *Chara*-cat-tail pond and found that

Each species of animal had two periods of maximum abundance, one in autumn and one in spring. Each tended to decrease during the fall, some early and others late. Some, such as the mud minnow, *Umbra limi;* the pond snail, *Physa;* the water strider, *Gerris remegis;* the dragonfly nymphs, Libellulidae; and the damsel-fly nymphs, Agrionidae; disappeared in November, when the pH, oxygen, temperature, and depth of the water were all high; others, such as the isopod, *Mancasellus danielsi;* the amphipod, *Hyalella knickerbockeri;* the small-gilled snail, *Amnicola* (two sp.); and the flat pond snail, *Planorbis deflectus*, disappeared after the ice covered the pond, when pH, oxygen, and temperature were low. Those last to disappear were the first to appear in the spring as soon as the pond was free of ice, when oxygen, pH, and water were very high, but the temperature was low. No animals were found in midwinter, when there was very little available water, low pH and oxygen, and low temperature.

All groups increased in numbers as the temperature rose in spring. *Planorbis deflectus, Amnicola, Hyalella knickerbockeri*, and *Mancasellus danielsi* reached a maximum early in the season, in April and May, when the oxygen and pH were high, temperature moderate and rising, and water deep. *Physa, Umbra limi, Plea*, the *Ephemeridae, Agrionidae*, and *Libellulidae*, on the other hand, reached a maximum through May and June when the oxygen, pH, water temperature, and depth were high. With the exception of *Gerris*, all of the animals were decidedly scarce at the end of August, when the pH and oxygen were extremely low, temperature of water high, and depth of water very low.

It was concluded that the general seasonal succession of the animals was directly due to the temperature and water-level conditions and that pH and dissolved oxygen content were accompanying factors rather than causal ones.

Other investigators (Scott, 1910; Jewell, 1927; *et al.*) have found a spring and autumn maximum among pond-plankton organisms; also, a great reduction of plankton during midwinter and midsummer.

Seasonal successions occur in the temporary ponds as well as in the permanent ones, although differences in the fauna and the various exigencies imposed by the alternate presence and absence of water in the basins alter the general features of the succession. An example of this form of seasonal sequence appears in a study by Shelford (1919) of the spring and early summer succession, up to the disappearance of the water, of a temporary pond near Chicago, Ill., with special reference to five of the larger animals of the fauna. Figure 46 and its accompanying legend indicate the character of the succession. Various organisms other than the five mentioned must have been present.

GENERAL ECOLOGICAL SUCCESSION

It has already been pointed out that the usual, general succession of standing waters is from lake to pond, from pond to swamp, and from swamp to dry land. Since, however, not every pond is the remnant of a lake, the successional history of all ponds is not the same. Ponds which arise from senescent lakes are already *old* when they become ponds and usually have the various characteristics of old ponds, such as a relatively rich flora and fauna. On the other hand, in those ponds which have their initial beginnings, natural or artificial, *as ponds*, the usual succession is from bare bottom and minimal biota to vegetation-covered bottom with increasing biota, finally to swamp, and then dry land. These final stages involve a shrinking, changing biota, one feature of which is a definite increasing of those animals which respire at the surface over those which use the dissolved oxygen of the water.

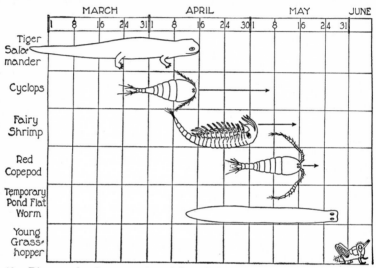

Fig. 46.   Diagram showing succession of five of the animals in a temporary pond on a vacant Chicago lot, from early March to June.   The length of the animal's body plus the length of the arrow indicates the dates between which adults of the five species may be found.   The appearance of the grasshopper, which is a dry land form, coincides with the drying up of the pond.   (*Modified from Shelford*, 1919.)

It is evident that the age of a pond is of fundamental importance in determining its character. The influences and accompanying features of increasing age are numerous, and published results do not always agree. Shelford (1911) studied a remarkable series of chronologically graded ponds and formulated certain conclusions among which are the following: (1) Bacteria, plankton, vegetation, and the larger animals increase quantitatively as a pond grows older; (2) mucky bottom deposits increase, and dissolved oxygen decreases with the age of a pond; (3) animal succession in ponds results from an unused increment of excretory and decomposition products which bring about an increase of vegetation, a reduction of oxygen at the bottom, and a general alteration of the surroundings, all of which primarily affect breeding.

Krecker (1919) investigated the influence of age upon the faunas of five rock-bottom ponds formed in deserted limestone quarries, all occurring in the same region and representing ages of one, five, ten, fifteen, and thirty years. In summer, the oldest and the youngest (thirty years and one year old, respectively) ponds had almost the same number of species of insects, the abundance in the youngest pond being both qualitative and quantitative, while in the oldest pond it was qualitative only. The plankton showed a progressive diminution in the total number of individuals of all kinds from the youngest to the oldest pond, although it should be noted that in the youngest pond Protozoa and rotifers comprised 99 per cent of the total zooplankton, while in the oldest pond the Entomostraca comprised 85 per cent of the total.

In a study of sink-hole ponds in Illinois, Eddy (1931) found that as long as a pond remains in the permanent stage, the plankton shows little change, once it becomes established, but that with decreasing depth and the onset of temporary pond conditions, plankton organisms mingle with those from the bottom to form an assemblage characteristic of very shallow water. He points out that certain pond plankters persist almost as long as any water remains.

In spite of published results to the contrary, it appears that in the large majority of instances and within certain limits, increasing age of a pond brings about a progressive qualitative and quantitative increase of the biota. However, this result becomes reversed after a pond passes its maximum production stage and enters upon its senescence.

The best opportunities for the study of succession in ponds are usually found in those inland ponds which *originate as ponds* and appear in a definite chronological order, so that in the same restricted region the investigator may find various stages of the succession in basins formed by the same processes and subject to the same environment. Under certain circumstances, lakes form series of beach ponds, more or less parallel to each other, the youngest being at the lake margin. Back of the most recent one are successively older ones, the last recognizable pool probably succeeded on the landward side by some pools which have long ago been transformed into dry land. Such a series, beginning at the lake beach, may present the following general stages and in the order named: (1) young, exposed, permanent, bare-bottom ponds; little or no marginal vegetation; little or no vegetation on the bars which separate them; little biota; (2) adolescent, permanent ponds; increasingly muddy bottoms; invading aquatic vegetation; certain amphibious vegetation (sedges, *et al.*), low shrubs, seedl'ngs of forest trees, etc., on the bars; an increasingly diverse and abundant biota; (3) mature, muck-bottom, permanent ponds; abundant growths of aquatic vegetation, often arranged in the typical marginal zonation; young forest trees or some other mature vegetation on the old bars; the biota at its peak of qualitative and quantitative development; (4) senescent ponds; becoming temporary; invading vegetation gradually effecting complete capture of the entire basin; a bounding row of trees or other vegetation of mature type now marking the original margins; with a rapidly declining fauna; (5) marsh ponds; becoming increasingly dry, with standing water disappearing, possibly present only at times of unusually high lake level or following periods of greatest rainfall; completely carpeted by vegetation which is a mixture of remnants of the old marginal, emergent, aquatic plants and the invading amphibious species; surrounded by a high wall of trees or by some other type of mature vegetation; original aquatic biota virtually absent; (6) dry, almost completely filled depressions; marked off by the row of larger trees—the first ones to grow on the original margins; basin devoid of aquatic plants and possibly with merest hints of the old amphibious plants; now invaded by the marginal shrub zone and by certain dryland types of ground plants; all traces of the old aquatic fauna gone. On undisturbed, forested lake shores, it is sometimes possible to locate very ancient beach ponds remote from the shore by tracing the rows of large trees and noting the much younger type of forest occupying what was once the basin, no other surface evidences of the basin remaining. Vertical subsurface samples taken with a soil sampler will also indicate the position of the old basins and, if properly used, will also determine the original depth, since the deposits are usually markedly different from the materials of the original basin. In regions underlaid by limestone, solution ponds are not only common but also often provided a series grading from recently formed ones to those in late senescent stages. Such series offer inviting opportunities for the study of successional phenomena. Similar opportunities arise out of other natural and artificial processes which produce graded age series of basins in the same area.

PRODUCTIVITY FEATURES OF PONDS

Correlations and Limiting Factors. In the numerous attempts to solve the production problems of ponds, various factors and conditions have been proposed as the major determiners of productivity. Unfortunately for any discussion of the limnological aspects of these problems, most of the intensive studies to date have been made on experimental fish ponds; and while some fish ponds practically duplicate conditions in nature, most of them involve, one way or another, the modifying influences of man and are artificial to varying extents. The whole subject is still so immature that little more can be done here than refer briefly to results reported in certain selected, literature.

Schneberger and Jewell (1928) found an important relation existing in certain Kansas hatchery ponds between turbidity and fish production, viz., that a decrease in turbidity was accompanied by an increase in fish production until the turbidity fell below 100 p.p.m., after which the number of fish was controlled by other factors. All of the ponds with high fish production had 10 to 90 per cent of the bottom covered by vegetation, but exceedingly dense plant growths and the opposite extreme (absence of vegetation) both resulted in low fish yields. Results obtained in studies made on certain fish ponds in Europe have been reported as showing that phosphorus compounds and the nitrogen-fixing bacteria are the principal limiting factors of the fauna, particularly the fishes. Atkins and Harris (1924) hold the view, based upon work done on certain ponds in England, that the lack of phosphate rather than lack of nitrate or ammonium salts limits, as a general rule, the plankton in fresh water just as it is thought to do in the sea. Wiebe (1930) concluded from studies on experimental, artificial fish ponds at Fairport, Iowa, that the soluble phosphorus was a limiting factor but possibly not the only one. He also concluded that temperature, transparency, pH, free carbon dioxide, dissolved oxygen, dissolved chloride, and inorganic nitrogen were not limiting factors.

While there exists at present a considerable emphasis on phosphorus as a possible limiting factor, this idea does not have the full support of all investigators. There is reason for doubting if any particular limiting factor is the common and exclusive limiting agent in any pond; also, for doubting that the limiting factor or factors are necessarily the same in different ponds.

Biotic Potential and Environmental Resistance. Chapman (1931), who made extensive investigations on biotic potential in general, stated that the high biotic potential of a pond fauna is probably the most prominent single characteristic of that taxonomically diverse population. The reproductive potential is very high and particularly so in the faunas of temporary ponds. The speed with which suddenly restored temporary ponds are repopulated is, in part at least, an expression of this high reproductive potential.

Chapman also pointed out that small environments, especially transient ones, offer great resistance to the biota. Such factors as temperature, spacial demands, silt, availability of the necessary gaseous content, competition for food, enemies, accumulations of an organism's own wastes, and other similar features become particularly severe in the restricted volume of water in a pond, resulting in the keenest competitions and struggles for existence.

CHAPTER XVI

BOG LAKES

Bogs are best developed in the north temperate, glaciated regions where precipitation is abundant throughout the year, atmospheric humidity is great, soil temperatures are rather low, evaporation is reduced, run-off water is minimized, and abundant growths of plants are possible. They have long been studied by botanists and others, and an extensive literature exists. In the past, research on bogs dealt largely with such features as peat and its origin, bog plants and bog-plant succession, geological history of basin (when a basin is involved), methods of filling and the different kinds of deposits, character of the water in the surface mats and in the deposits, and so on. Considerable attention has been given to the study of the fossil pollen and other plant remains in the various strata of the bog deposits and their significance in the history of bog formation. Thus research has been concerned almost entirely with the bog mat to the neglect, largely, of the limnology of the open water.

Unfortunately, there exists a considerable difference in the use of the term *bog* and certain other terms which are, to some extent, equivalent (swamp, moor, fen, and others). The writer chooses to use the term bog to include those situations in which (1) the water manifests different reactions (acid to alkaline) in different areas; (2) a marginal, semifloating mat often exists (or may have existed at some time), composed of an aggregation of characteristic plants; and (3) *deposits of peat* are invariably present. In European literature, the term *moor* is used extensively to designate bogs. For a discussion of this subject and citations to the literature, see Gates (1942).

Of the many classifications of bogs which have been proposed, the fundamental analyses by Davis (1907) of the various types of Michigan bogs have a general usefulness. They are given below in slightly modified form.

PEAT DEPOSITS CLASSIFIED ACCORDING TO THE FORM OF THE LAND SURFACE UPON WHICH THEY HAVE BEEN ESTABLISHED

I. Depressed surfaces or hollows:
   A. Lake basins of the tarn type.
   B. Shallow lake basins of the ordinary type.
   C. Hollows not permanently filled with water.
   D. Hollows in sand dunes.
   E. Hollows formed by dams of various sorts.

382

II. Surfaces not hollowed out:
   A. Poorly drained till plains.
   B. Broad divides.
   C. Floors of glacial drainage valleys.
   D. Lake and stream terraces.
   E. Deltas of streams.
   F. Slopes over which seepage spring waters flow.
   G. Northern bogs in which peat forms on slopes ("climbing bogs"); often referred to as *raised bogs*.

PEAT DEPOSITS CLASSIFIED ON BASIS OF METHOD BY WHICH DEPOSIT WAS DEVELOPED

I. Those built up by successive generations of plants, starting from what is now the bottom of the peat.
II. Those which have been formed by growth at the sides or at the top of the basin or both:
   A. Inwash of dead and decaying vegetation from the shores into the deeper parts of the lake basin.
   B. Drifting of such materials from tributary streams.
   C. Vegetation may grow out from shores to form floating mats, which ultimately cover entire water surface.
   D. Floating, rootless plants which may develop abundantly at or near water surface.

PEAT DEPOSITS CLASSIFIED ACCORDING TO SURFACE VEGETATION

   I. Elm and black-ash swamps.
   II. Tamarack swamps and bogs.
   III. Cedar (arbor vitae) swamps or bogs.
   IV. Spruce swamps or bogs.
   V. Willow and alder swamps.
   VI. Heath (blueberry, cranberry, and Chamaedaphne) swamps, marshes, or bogs.
   VII. Grass and sedge marshes and bogs.
   VIII. Rush marshes (cat-tail and bulrush marshes).
   IX. Moss bogs (including sphagnum bogs).

A discussion of bogs from the geological and botanical standpoints cannot be attempted here. The reader is referred to the works of Davis (1907), Nichols (1915, 1919), Rigg (1916, 1925, 1926, 1940), Dachnowski-Stokes (1933), Auer (1933), Gates (1942), and others for information on American bogs. For European bogs, see Rigg (1926) and Harnish (1929).

DEFINITION OF BOG LAKES

Except in the final stages of senescence, water is a prominent feature of all true bogs. In a very rough way, bogs may be divided into two groups with respect to the nature of the water distribution: (1) those which have an area of open water (lake or pool) surrounded wholly or in part by water-soaked bog margins or mats and (2) those which have no area of open water but which hold generous quantities of water in the mats of vegetation and the bog deposits. While the latter contain much of interest for the limnologist, space limitations require that the discussion be largely restricted to the type with open water. Also, the discussion will deal largely with the bog lakes of the Great Lakes region.

A typical *bog lake* is here defined as an area of open water, commonly surrounded, either wholly or in part, by true bog margins; possessing peat deposits about the margins or in the bottom or both; usually with a false bottom composed largely of very finely divided, flocculent, vegetable matter; containing considerable amounts of colloidal materials; and so constituted genetically that in time it may become completely occupied by bog vegetation. Owing to differences in degree of development or to certain special circumstances, bog lakes do not always possess all of these characteristics at all times during their history. For example, a bog lake may have once possessed a narrow marginal mat and accompanying marginal peat deposits, but failure of the mat to keep pace with rapidly falling water level may have led to the complete separation of water and mat, with subsequent disappearance of the latter. Bog lakes are also known in which no marginal mat has been formed and in which the peat deposits have originated from the remains of the submerged, rooted aquatic vegetation within the lake itself. Other forms of deviation from the typical condition described above occur. However, in every instance, a deposit of peat is present.

Bog lakes of the Great Lakes region are usually small in area, seldom exceeding two miles in maximum dimension. Often, the areas of open water are only of the magnitude of ponds. In this discussion, no attempt is made to establish size groups, but bodies of water of every size are here included under the general designation of bog lakes. In these lakes, the peat deposits or the typical bog vegetation or both control the character of the open water. They may be almost completely sealed off from surrounding ground water so that but little mineral or other matter is brought into them from outside. Many lakes of large area having bog-margined bays or limited expanses of boggy, protected shores do not qualify as bog lakes, for the reason that the bog influence on the total volume of open water is negligible. Certain extensive regions about the Great Lakes teem with bog lakes representing all of the various stages in their development and senescence. Bog margins vary from a mere fringe about the periphery of an original basin to those extensive mats which have encroached upon the water to such an extent that their area now greatly exceeds that of the open water. Final stages of complete closing over of the open water and the gradual grounding of the entire mat are not difficult to find. Advancing (lakeward) margins of the bog mat usually float on the water and are very treacherous. Shoreward, the mat becomes increasingly firm and compact.

Floral composition of the mat varies in different bog lakes, depending upon the type of bog, the stage of ecological succession, and certain other circumstances. A common condition is one sometimes referred to as a *sphagnum* mat in which sphagnum growths are a conspicuous but not exclusive component of the mat, particularly in the lakeward portions. Further discussion is deferred to a later section (page 392). Not only does the bog vegetation comprise a distinct, unique assemblage, strikingly unlike surrounding terrestrial vegetations, but the inclosed water, both that of the mat and that of the lake portion, possesses characteristics wholly different from the waters of other kinds of lakes and swamps. The bog mat, especially the lakeward portions, is notable for its great water-holding ability; in fact, the mat may correctly be likened to a huge, completely water-saturated sponge.

A common characteristic of the northern bog lakes is the development of a *false bottom*. In such lakes, the open water, often with a depth of but a few feet, is terminated by what appears to be a more or less continuous bottom. Actually, this is a false bottom through which an oar or pole will pass with little more resistance than that offered by the water itself, while a sounding lead may drop many feet below the surface of this false bottom before it reaches a bottom sufficiently resistant to stop its settling. The color of this false bottom varies in the different types of bog lakes; in the sphagnum-bog lakes, it is almost invariably light coffee-brown. It is composed, for the most part, of very finely divided material of plant origin held in suspension in the water. On slight disturbance, this material speedily clouds the superimposed clear water in a striking way, slowly settling out when the water becomes quiet again and apparently dropping to the same level previously occupied. While in some bog lakes this false-bottom material occupies all of the space between its upper surface and the true bottom, in others it floats at some distance above the true bottom with a stratum of reasonably clear water between. What determines its level is not definitely known. According to Needham and Lloyd (1930), it was long ago shown that by the addition of colloidal substances to a vessel of water, the entire contents of the vessel can be broken into strata and these strata made to circulate each at its own level independent of the other strata; also, that settling suspended solids may be floated upon each stratum. On the basis of these statements, they suggest the possibility that the false bottoms of northern bog lakes are produced by certain colloids which determine the strata upon which the different false-bottom materials float. That bog lakes do contain colloidal matters in some abundance is certain, and it may be that the hypothesis just stated has some foundation.

Accumulating decomposition gases, forming in or below a false bottom, sometimes cause masses of it to break loose and rise to the surface where they float for a time, ultimately breaking up and settling back to former levels. Under some circumstances, the entire false bottom may rise to the surface of the water. In advanced senescent stages of a bog lake, continued accumulation of materials causes the false bottom to become increasingly firm and thick; and this process, unless antedated by a complete marginal encroachment, may lead to the ultimate extinction of the lake by entire grounding of the false bottom. Although exceedingly tenuous, the false bottom may, under some conditions, offer just enough consistency to serve as anchorage for certain aquatic plants, such plants maintaining their vertical position mainly by surface flotation of leaves or by the buoyant effect of the water upon submerged parts.

PHYSICAL CONDITIONS

WATER MOVEMENTS

Since bog lakes are relatively small and commonly protected by surrounding hills and forests, water movements due to wind action are usually reduced to a minimum. Those which have inlets or outlets may show some flowage in a definite direction, but a great many bog lakes occupy undrained basins, and currents are absent. The water of the bog mat is so completely pocketed that it is wholly free from consequential movements of any sort.

MOLAR AGENTS

In general, molar action in bog lakes is minimal, owing to (1) the soft, finely divided materials in suspension and in the false bottom; (2) the soft deposits at the shore line; and (3) the marginal bog-vegetation mats. Furthermore, in the very small lakes, size and protection provide an almost dead calm water.

TEMPERATURE

Temperatures of the open water show no features significantly different from other lakes of similar area and depth. In those having sufficient depth, a typical thermal stratification occurs; in others, temporary stratification may appear. In small sphagnum bog lakes, temperatures at the various depths may differ during one season, while at the same time in a succeeding year they may be almost uniform from surface down to the vicinity of the false bottom. While surface temperatures of the smaller lakes tend to be somewhat higher than those of larger lakes, the differences do not appear to be important. Lakes having large areas and very shallow depths show a daily variation greater than the deeper ones. It has been reported that in European moor waters the temperatures are astonishingly variable, often as great as 32°C. during a single day. No such variations have been found in northern bog lakes by the author or his associates; in fact, diurnal variations in temperature have not been found to be particularly different from those of other forms of standing water similar in location and morphology.

TURBIDITY

In smaller bog lakes which maintain a condition of almost complete calm, the water is usually very clear, the very slight turbidity being due to plankton and to a small amount of finely divided peaty matter which is essentially nonsettling. Those large enough to have periods of wind disturbance may, at such times, have high turbidity due to the extreme ease with which materials of the false bottom rise into the superimposed water. Turbidity due to living plankton seems never to be more than moderate, since plankton production in these lakes is seldom if ever high.

COLOR

Typical bog-lake water is usually characterized by a distinct brown color often described as tea color or very dilute coffee color. It is sometimes referred to as *stained water*. This color is due to substances contributed by the peat deposits of the bottom and margins. Until somewhat recently, it was supposed that these color-producing substances were in the nature of true dissolved materials extracted from the peat deposits and associated vegetation. Gorham (unpublished) and others have found that when such waters are put through an ultrafilter, the color is removed, and the filtrate is as clear as distilled water, indicating that this coloring material is in a colloidal state and not in true solution.

LIGHT

In smaller, quieter bog lakes, the clear water above the false bottom, as a rule, is well illuminated. Periods of very high turbidity, when they occur, interfere seriously with light penetration. It has already been pointed out (page 80) that in lakes containing heavily stained water, very little radiation of wave lengths less than 6000 Å occurs at depths below 1 m. The blue is negligible. The green and the adjacent region of the yellow are very small in amount and disappear rapidly with increasing depth. The striking feature is that the red may equal or exceed all other radiation.

CHEMICAL CONDITIONS

DISSOLVED GASES

There is a common impression that bog-lake waters are very low in dissolved oxygen. This may be an inference carried over from what is known concerning the low dissolved oxygen of the water in the sphagnum mat. Also, it has been stated by certain European workers that in the open waters of "moors," the dissolved oxygen is always low and may be completely absent at a depth of only a few centimeters. Such statements do hold for the water which saturates the floating mats; there the water is very commonly devoid of oxygen. But the studies made thus far by the writer on the *open water* of bog lakes in northern United States have failed to reveal any such general condition. It is true that, on corresponding dates and at the same depth levels, bog-lake water usually shows a lower oxygen content than do the nonbog lakes of the same region; nevertheless, the quantities of oxygen are usually not near disappearance. Values of 2.5 to 6 cc. per l. are common for the surface waters, and even higher contents have been found. Oxygen pulses are known to occur in some bog lakes. When depths are sufficient to provide thermal stratification, dissolved oxygen disappears in the hypolimnion in the usual manner.

The free carbon dioxide content seems to vary greatly in different bog lakes. In some, the content appears to be relatively small at all times in spite of the fact that considerable decomposition is going on constantly both in the mat and in the bottom. In others, sizable quantities have been reported and free carbon dioxide pulses have been described. Very little is known concerning the other decomposition gases as they occur in American bog lakes. That they are present is certain, since often great quantities of gas, much of which is methane, can be dislodged from the bottom materials by the mere insertion of an oar. It is likely that they are similar in quality to those developed in other kinds of waters.

Dissolved Solids

So few chemical analyses of the dissolved solids in bog lakes are available that general discussion is difficult. Those which have been made in Europe (see Harnish, 1929, for summary and references) are largely concerned with *Hochmoor* and other moor waters, and it is not yet certain how nearly or remotely those waters resemble bog lakes in North America. The following mineral analysis (Table 47), made for Jewell and Brown (1929) by the Illinois State Water Survey laboratory, is probably one of the most complete.

It will be noticed in this analysis that the amounts of dissolved matter are very small; also, that these waters are very soft.

Gorham (unpublished) made quantitative determinations of ferrous and ferric iron in six northern Michigan bog lakes and found only small quantities in any of them (0.25 to 1.5 p.p.m.). Bog waters having high iron content have been reported both in this country (New Jersey) and in Europe (Russia). Apparently, bog waters differ widely in iron content.

The statement is commonly made in discussions of bog waters that they are poor in available nitrogen, and analyses seem to confirm it. In Table

47, the small quantities of ammonia and nitrate are evident. In some bogs, nitrates have been reported as totally absent. Evidences from other researches show that extractives from marsh and peat materials contain relatively small amounts of nitrogen. During the summer, strata

TABLE 47. ANALYSIS OF WATER OF TWO BOG LAKES, CHEBOYGAN COUNTY, MICHIGAN

All results expressed in p.p.m.

From Jewell and Brown (1929)

Constituents	Vincent Lake	Penny Lake
Iron, Fe	0.2	0.2
Manganese, Mn	0.0	0.0
Silica, SiO_2	1.2	1.8
Nonvolatile	0.4	0.3
Alumina, Al_2O_3	0.0	0.5
Calcium, Ca	1.1	1.7
Magnesium, Mg	1.8	1.5
Ammonia, NH_4	0.1	0.6
Potassium, K	1.9	2.2
Sodium, Na	2.4	2.5
Sulfate, SO_4	0.6	5.0
Nitrate, NO_3	1.8	0.7
Chloride, Cl	2.0	2.0
Alkalinity as $CaCO_3$, methyl orange	10.0	8.0
Residue	26.0	30.0

Hypothetical combinations of the ions given above		
Potassium nitrate, KNO_3	2.9	1.1
Potassium chloride, KCl	1.6	3.3
Sodium chloride, NaCl	2.0	0.7
Sodium sulfate, Na_2SO_4	0.9	7.0
Sodium carbonate, Na_2CO_3	3.0	...
Ammonium carbonate, $(NH_4)_2CO_3$	0.4	1.3
Magnesium carbonate, $MgCO_3$	6.2	5.2
Calcium carbonate, $CaCO_3$	2.7	4.3
Iron oxide, Fe_2O_3	0.3	0.3
Silica, SiO_2	1.2	1.8
Nonvolatile	0.4	0.3
Alumina, Al_2O_3	0.0	0.5
Ammonium sulfate, $(NH_4)_2SO_4$	20.0	0.4

of water nearer the bottom may show an increase of organic nitrogen over the surface waters, although the amounts in both instances are likely to be low.

Birge and Juday (1927) report that in certain Wisconsin bog lakes, the organic carbon comes, in large part, from sources outside the lake; that the organic carbon is relatively high, exceeding 10 mg. per l. of water and being eighteen to twenty-seven times the amount of nitrogen present. They also found that in bog lakes having a carbon-nitrogen ratio (C/N) of 25 or more, there was a content of about 11 per cent crude protein. The same investigators (1931) found very small amounts of phosphorus in such lakes.

TABLE 48. PHYSICAL AND CHEMICAL DATA FROM CERTAIN NORTHERN MICHIGAN (CHEBOYGAN AND EMMET COUNTIES) BOG LAKES
All values from upper strata of water. Summer measurements. Areas represent free, open water only. Compiled from records of several summers

Lake	Area, acres	Depth, ft.	Color	pH	O_2, p.p.m.	Free CO_2, p.p.m.	Methyl orange alkalinity, p.p.m.	Phenolphthalein alkalinity, p.p.m.	O_2 consumed, p.p.m.	Conductivity, reciprocal megohms
Smith.........	0.05	2	224	4.3–6.8	4.2–5.1	8	34	0	47	45
Bryant........	0.1	2–3	56–112	4.0–6.0	1.6–12	0.6–24	2–12	0	32	10–22
Livingstone....	0.4	4	102	4.2–6.4	3.2–9.2	5–9	2–18	0	..	16–23
Penny.........	1	1–2	96–192	4.8–5.2	6.1–8.2	4–7	6–20	0	..	23–50
Nichols........	1.5	3	152	4.6–6.1	4.4–4.5	7–10	6–23	0	44	55–90
West..........	6	2	51	6.0–6.3	6.3–6.4	5–6	0–12	0	..	36–175
Maloney.......	10	2	76	5.7–6.2	1.4–7.9	1–7	7–25	0	31	27–50
East..........	20	3	40	6.3–6.8	4.8–8.1	1–3	8–24	0	33	40–85
Mud..........	25	1–3	28–102	6.5–9.0	6.5–10	1–13	20–138	0–3	46	8–160
Vincent.......	30	20	27–31	4.2–7.8	4.5–6.4	0–3	1–11	0	29	18–40
Lancaster......	52	58	78–83	7.6–8.3	7.1	0–7	154–171	8–10	..	240–275
Munro........	514	13	20	7.8–8.5	5.3–6.4	5.3–8.5	97–125	4–13	..	175–190

HYDROGEN-ION CONCENTRATION

In the past, bog waters were considered to be always strongly acid in their reaction, owing to the accumulation of that group of substances often referred to as humic acids. While it is true that many bog lakes have an acid reaction, true bog lakes are now known in which the reactions are strongly basic. In fact, bog lakes at large show reactions which cover much of the whole known range of hydrogen-ion concentrations for natural, uncontaminated waters. Reference (pages 118–122) has already been made to certain features of the pH of bog lakes, and those pages should be consulted again in this connection.

The source of the acidity, when it occurs, is still incompletely understood, although various theories have been advanced. In many bog lakes, pH does not change on aeration of the sample, indicating that the acidity is not due to the presence of free carbon dioxide. Jewell and Brown (1929) showed that the acidity of certain northern Michigan bog lakes was not due either to the free carbon dioxide or to mineral acids and decided that the source was organic acids produced in the bog margins. Gorham (unpublished) made the interesting discovery that when the bog waters which he studied were put through an ultrafilter, the filtrate lost its acidity or its basic reaction, respectively, and became essentially neutral. When the filtered material was dried and then returned to the same quantity of neutral water, the original reaction was restored. Incineration of the filtered matter showed it to be of an organic nature. Jewell and Brown attributed the acidity to organic acids produced in bog margins and carried into the lake by seepage; in the alkaline bog lakes, however, they believe that the alkalinity is due to other causes, such as the inflow of already alkaline water through tributaries without traversing an acid-producing part of the bog margin. Gessner (1929) postulated the origin of bog lake-water reaction in the bottom materials. Gorham (unpublished) presents evidence to show that in the bog lakes which he studied, the colloidal matter producing the reaction, basic or acid, *arises from the bottom deposits* and that organic acids from old, outlying peat deposits are not carried into the lakes. Therefore basic bog lakes which are surrounded by extensive acid margins, and which have no tributaries, can thus be accounted for. That the materials composing the false bottom in various bog lakes differ strikingly in color, texture, qualitative composition, origin, reaction, and other features can be easily demonstrated. Since the water of the lake is in immediate contact with these bottom deposits, the relations between water and bottom are such that the former may be effectively conditioned by the latter.

While the essential causal distinctions between the acid and the alkaline bog-lake waters are still vague, there seems to be good evidence that the chemical composition of a peat deposit depends not upon the region, topography, and history of the bog but upon the nature and chemical composition of the vegetation from which the deposit originated and upon the conditions under which the decomposition has been effected (Waksman and Stephens, 1929). This may explain why in the bottom deposits derived from bog mat sources the reaction of the water is strongly acid; whereas in the sedge, forest, and sedimentary peat deposits the reactions are of a totally different sort, often, and perhaps usually, alkaline.

Seasonal variation of pH in bog lakes seems to be a common phenomenon, but too little is yet known concerning it to make any generalization possible. Some bog lakes may manifest a definite, progressive, seasonal change during one year, then maintain a virtual uniformity of reaction throughout the open season during the succeeding year. Seasonal changes are sometimes of considerable magnitude. In some instances, it has been supposed that seasonal changes were the result of falling water levels during the summer, but these relations have not yet been satisfactorily demonstrated. Irregular and abrupt changes may also occur, the nature of which is little understood.   Some bog-lake waters contain so little dissolved matter that they have very low buffer action and are therefore subject to easy changes of reaction.   It seems likely that this is a common and widespread character of such waters.   Sudden rains, for example, are known to produce abrupt, temporary alterations in pH in certain bog lakes.

ELECTROLYTES

Much is yet to be learned about the electrical conductivity of bog-lake waters.   Some indication of the values to be expected appears in Table 48.   Striking variations may occur in the same lake.   Apparently very low values are common.

BIOLOGICAL CONDITIONS

Biologically, a bog lake differs in many respects from other lakes, these differences relating to both their plant and their animal populations. While bog lakes are of different types, depending upon such features as vegetational composition of the bog margin, origin and nature of the false bottom, and stage in ecological succession, most of them have certain general features in common, of which the following are prominent: (1) absence, or poor development, of a bottom fauna; (2) a marginal flora peculiar to such situations; (3) partial decomposition of plant remains to form peat; (4) definite qualitative zonation of the vegetation forming the marginal mats; and (5) generally low biological productivity.

PLANT GROWTHS

The flora may be divided into two groups, viz., (1) those plants which compose a portion of the margin or mat and (2) those which grow in the open water of the lake.

For a detailed account of the vegetational features of marginal mats, the reader is referred to various botanical treatises (see Gates, 1942) on this subject.   For present purposes, the essential facts are somewhat as follows: The quaking and partially floating mats which characterize the partly or wholly surrounded bog lakes are built up largely by the grasslike sedge *Carex lasiocarpa*, the low evergreen shrub *Chamaedaphne calyculata*, and various species of sphagnum moss.   In the formation of some mats, the sedge is the important pioneer; in others, the shrub plays the initial part.   In both instances, the plants grow out into the open lake water in the form of a loose tangle which floats on the surface like a raft.   In some regions, certain shrubs belonging to the genus *Decodon* are the principal pioneers of the mat formation.   The sphagnum plays a subordinate part in the formation of sedge mats.   Often it is absent.   It is especially important in mats, where it establishes itself on the framework of branches, spreading throughout the whole mass and binding it together. The surface vegetation on the mat is notable, among other things, for the dominance of xerophytic shrubs and the presence of such bizarre forms as the pitcher plant and the sundew. Sphagnum is often very abundant, and this explains why the term *sphagnum bog* is so often used.

Below this mat of densely massed, living plants is the bed of brownish peat. Beneath the lakeward margin of the mat, the water extends back for some distance, making that portion floating, shaky, and treacherous.

In some bog lakes, a very few plants, such as the water lilies, certain pond weeds, and others, manage to secure the necessary anchorage in the tenuous false bottom. When the false bottom rises to within a few feet of the surface, certain very attenuated plants (e.g., *Scirpus subterminalis*) may find their remarkably slight anchorage requirements fulfilled on its upper surface. The phytoplankton will be discussed in a subsequent section. Filamentous Algae and certain floating plants (*Ultricularia*) are often common about the periphery of the open water.

Plankton

Statements are common in the literature to the effect that bog lakes are very poor in plankton. Such statements have been largely based upon European bogs (see Harnish, 1929, for summary and literature citations). The following discussion is based largely upon the preliminary work of Gorham (unpublished) and subsequent work of the writer on northern Michigan bog lakes. This work dealt wholly with the summer net plankton. The nannoplankton is as yet virtually uninvestigated, and very little is known about it in the similar waters of Europe. It must therefore be understood that the following statements hold only for the net plankton; also, that, at best, these statements are tentative and probably will receive some modifications when more information is available.

Owing to the relatively small size of many bog lakes, the nature of overgrowing mats, the common proximity of the false bottom to the surface, and certain other circumstances, it is often necessary to distinguish carefully between the true plankters and those other microorganisms which may be taken in plankton collections. In fact, such plankton collections may contain representatives of three groups, viz., (1) *euplankters*, (2) *facultative plankters*, and (3) *tychoplankters* (forms originating from the bottom or the margins; do not multiply in the plankton proper).

Qualitative Features. From the qualitative standpoint, the bog lakes of the Great Lakes region seem to manifest the following general characteristics: (1) As compared with other kinds of lakes, bog-lake plankton may be somewhat restricted in the number of species present. However, this reduction in the number of species is not as great as statements in the older literature seem to imply. In each of certain northern Michigan bog lakes, more than 130 plankters have been identified. (2) With the exception of the desmids and a few other Algae, there is a striking diversity of genera compared with the number of species; i.e., there are very few species in any one genus. (3) There is a striking preponderance of phytoplankters over zooplankters.

Qualitatively, the phytoplankton shows the following features: (1) There is a marked preponderance of desmids. (2) The number of diatom species, as compared with other waters, is very small. (3) Most of the genera of fresh-water dinoflagellates (if they be listed with the Algae) known for central North America are represented. (4) The Chlorophyceae predominate in the number of species, with Myxophyceae occupying second place.

Qualitatively, the zooplankton shows the following features: (1) Rotifers are the greatest contributors to the plankton. (2) The Copepoda are greatly reduced in species, there being only about six species in all of the bog lakes examined in northern Michigan. (3) Among the Protozoa, the Sarcodina seem to predominate.

Cosmopolitanism. Since limnological conditions in bog lakes outside this country and Europe have been studied but little, it is evident that North American bog-lake plankton can, at present, be compared only with that of the European bog lakes. Lack of sufficient data makes even that comparison unsatisfactory. It has already been pointed out (page 227) that cosmopolitanism is characteristic of many fresh-water plankters. The Desmidaceae constitute the only group which manifests any outstanding evidence of endemism. It might, therefore, be expected that bog-lake plankton would contain at least some species common to such situations in other continents. As a matter of fact, many phytoplankters of northern Michigan bog lakes have been reported from similar European bog lakes, while all of the rotifers except one listed by Harnish (1929) as characteristic of European bog (moor) lakes are known to occur in Michigan bog lakes. The same is virtually true of the plankton Crustacea. Both European and American bog lakes are as yet too little known to make possible any satisfactory statement as to the completeness of their plankton similarity, but it is probable that the resemblance in this respect may be even greater than the present records indicate.

Plankton Similarities in Different Bog-lake Types. In spite of the fact that bog lakes may differ markedly in certain physicochemical respects, some plankters seem to be common to all of them. In northern Michigan bog lakes, for example, more than 100 species occur in two or more of four different types of bog lakes, and about 20 or more of these organisms are present in all types (acid to alkaline). In the latter instances, the wide differences in hydrogen-ion concentration do not exclude these highly tolerant species.

Nature of Bog-lake Plankton. With the possible exception of certain desmids and some closely allied Algae, few of the species represented in bog-lake plankton seem to be confined exclusively to the open water of bog lakes. On the other hand, available evidence suggests that many (possibly most) of the plankters of bog lakes occur in other waters of the same general region. It is possible that bog-lake plankton is a *selection biota*, i.e., an assemblage composed of those organisms, out of larger and much more widely distributed population, which can withstand the severe conditions of bog waters. It has been contended (Gorham, unpublished; Wesenberg-Lund, 1930) that only cosmopolitan relict and outstandingly resistant forms can withstand such conditions; and that it is the *absence* of many different species rather than the *presence* of a certain few species which constitutes the peculiar feature of bog-lake plankton.

Quantitative Features. Because of physicochemical diversity of bog lakes and the relatively small amount of work which has been done on bog-lake plankton, it is difficult to generalize on the quantitative features. The writer's studies indicate that the net plankton of Michigan bog lakes seems to have the following quantitative characters common to all such waters: (1) common preponderance of phytoplankton at least during certain seasons, (2) low quantity of zooplankton, (3) numerical dominance of rotifers in the zooplankton, (4) very small quantities of Cladocera and Copepoda, and (5) quantitatively reduced total net plankton. It should be noted that the statements just made are based upon *net plankton* only. The nannoplankton is so little known that no statements concerning total plankton are possible.

While it seems to be true generally that quantitatively the total plankton of bog lakes is quite restricted, nevertheless a differential abundance is sometimes striking. For example, Vincent Lake (see page 390), summer of 1936, maintained a *Staurastrum* spp. population of 200,000 to 458,500 individuals per liter of lake water, a number which vastly exceeded the total of all other net plankters. Munro Lake (see page 390), summer of 1932, maintained a *Microcystis* spp. population of 15,750 to 20,200 individuals per liter of lake water, also a number greatly in excess of all other net plankters present at the same time. The occurrence of greatly dominating quantities of some one plankter or group of plankters is apparently not uncommon in bog lakes although the numbers involved are often smaller than those just mentioned.

Seasonal Distribution. No adequate studies of plankton in American bog lakes have extended throughout the year. Winter conditions are almost unknown; therefore, little can be stated concerning seasonal successions.   Preliminary evidence indicates that many if not all of the plankters have their individual seasonal cycles of rise and fall; of appearance and fading.   Work done in Europe points to a definite spring and autumn maxima for certain boglake plankters.   In some of the bog lakes of the Great Lakes region, there appears a falling off of plankton production during summer with signs of a recovery in autumn.

FAUNAL CHARACTERISTICS

Very few faunal surveys of American bog lakes have been made. Therefore, only generalizations of a tentative nature are possible at present.   Since the conditions and biota of the marginal mat are so different from those of the open water, the two must be carefully distinguished.   Unfortunately, discussions in the literature often intermingle them in such a way as to make the proper separation very difficult. The following statements apply only to the fauna of the open water.

1. Bog lakes support a fauna characterized by a limited variety of species.

2. While differing considerably among themselves, bog lakes as a class are very low in faunal productivity.

3. Small bog lakes (roughly less than 5 acres in size) which are completely surrounded by a *Carex-Chamaedaphne* mat, which lack inlets or outlets, which are strongly acid in reaction, and which are supplied with bottom materials mainly from their own peat deposits usually show a total absence of fishes, Malacostraca, oligochaetes, mollusks, Ephemerida, and coelenterates.   Certain lakes of this type also lack sponges, nematodes, and flatworms.

4. The larger bog lakes as a class, whether acid or basic, may contain representatives of most of the major aquatic groups, including those absent from the small "sphagnum" bog lakes, although any individual bog lake has a fauna restricted both qualitatively and quantitatively.

5. Representatives of the Amphibia appear to be universally present as marginal forms.

6. Aquatic insects representing several orders (Hemiptera, Odonata, Trichoptera, Diptera, Coleoptera, and possibly others) are always present.

7. The strongly acid waters eliminate all Mollusca, with the possible exception of certain Sphaeridae which may be abundant.

8. True benthic faunas (exclusive of the microscopic species) (*a*) are virtually absent in the small "sphagnum" bog lakes; (*b*) may be present in the larger bog lakes but restricted as to both kind and quantity.

MAT-IMPOUNDED WATER

In addition to the open water of a bog lake, the fringing mat, if present, also contains great quantities of impounded water.   Since the mat and its contained water may exert various direct and indirect influences upon the surrounded lake, some consideration should be given here to the limnological features of this situation.

As already indicated (page 384), bog lakes in the Great Lakes region are commonly surrounded, wholly or in part, by marginal mats which vary in kind and differ in extent from mere peripheral fringes to those many acres in size. These mats advance upon the enclosed lakes by overgrowing the surface in such a way that the lakeward portions usually float in and on the water surface while shoreward they become increasingly firm, compact, and grounded. Because of their peculiar floral structure and their relation to the lakes which they surround, these mats usually impound, upon and within themselves, great quantities of water, forming a unique aquatic environment. The surface level of the lake is usually highest in early spring and declines gradually through the summer and autumn. The floating portion of the mat rises and falls with changes in lake level (Gates, 1940; Buell and Buell, 1941), thus keeping it saturated with water. The size of the water-filled spaces within the mat depends upon exigencies of growth of the mat-forming plants. Ordinarily such spaces are very small because of the closely interwoven condition of the mat-forming materials.

Except for a narrow zone at the mat-lake interface, mat-impounded water is completely immobilized. Molar action is absent, turbidity very low, color often high, and temperature variable. Illumination diminishes very rapidly with increasing depth in the mat. Chemical features of mat-impounded water vary considerably, depending upon the composition of the mat. In typical "sphagnum" mats (Welch, 1945), the following chemical features are likely to prevail: pH, on acid side; dissolved oxygen, very low, in thin uppermost layer, absent in lower strata; free carbon dioxide, present, variable; methyl orange alkalinity, none or only mere trace; conductivity, variable and low.

The water-filled interstices of a bog mat support a diversified and often abundant biota. All components of this population are microscopic or semimicroscopic in size and truly aquatic in habit. The composition differs in various kinds of mats. In a typical *sphagnum* mat, the following principal elements usually occur: Algae—diversified; often abundant; desmids common. Protozoa—common and diversified; Sarcodina predominate. Rotatoria—common to abundant; many species representing wide variety of genera may be dominant element in fauna. Other animals—scattered representatives such as Gastrotricha, Tardigrada, and Nematoda; more or less rare.

The size of the interstices in mats constitutes a distinct limiting condition. Irwin (1942) found these interstices too small to meet the space requirements of mosquito larvae. A few representatives of Cladocera and Copepoda live in small pools of free water on top of the mat in spring or early summer but do not occur (Welch, 1945) in the tiny spaces within the mat.

Very little is known concerning seasonal relations of the mat biota. In early spring when conditions of very high water in the lake lead to partial inundation of portions of the mat, temporary pools may develop on top of it and become inhabited by various larger animals, as, for example, mosquito larvae, but when later these pools are eliminated by declining water level, such animals disappear. Nothing seems to be known concerning the effects of winter upon the mat-inhabiting organisms.

GENERAL ECOLOGICAL SUCCESSION

In the Great Lakes region, the innumerable bog lakes occupy basins formed almost exclusively by glacial action. At the outset, these basins contained no bottom deposits save for whatever ice-borne sediments may have been deposited when the glacial ice melted. The original lake therefore filled the entire basin, probably to a higher level than now, and contained no peat deposits. Subsequently, characteristic bog vegetation became established along the shore line. The conditions which initiated bog formation in a basin have been matters of considerable speculation, and various causes have been postulated (Rigg, 1916, 1925; and others) none of which is yet definitely established.

An understanding of the past history of a bog lake, particularly one with a well-developed marginal mat and peat deposits, may be secured by the use of two different methods, either singly or in combination, viz., (1) a survey of the horizontal zonation of the different plant communities as they succeed one another from the free-floating margin of the mat to the outermost rim of the original basin; and (2) analyses of vertical sections of the total bottom deposits from the present surface to the bottom of the original basin and taken at various positions from the edge of the mat to the original shore line. These methods will be discussed in the order mentioned.

One of the most conspicuous floral features of a well-developed bog lake, particularly a "sphagnum" bog lake, is the definite, approximately concentric zonation of the plant communities, each community having different, characteristic plant components. In a typical case, starting from the open lake and proceeding landward, the following sequence of plant communities occurs: (1) In the open water and rooted to the bottom are (a) submerged aquatics—in particular, certain species of *Potamogeton;* (b) aquatics with floating leaves, such as *Nymphaea* and *Nuphar.* (2) Occupying the lakeward border of the mat are (a) sedges, chiefly *Carex lasiocarpa;* or (b) the low shrub *Chamaedaphne*, growing intermingled with sphagnum moss; or (c) a mixture of sedges, *Chamaedaphne*, and sphagnum moss; followed to the landward by (*d*) tall shrubs, such as *Nemopanthus;* and, finally, (*e*) black spruce and other bog trees in increasing abundance toward the outer margin. These communities, while in general quite distinct, commonly intermingle in different degrees and in various ways; also, certain trees (tamarack, spruce, and others) may invade the more solid portions of the mat. Plant ecologists who have made analyses of northern bogs recognize the various communities as different associations. Figure 47 shows in abbreviated form the usual

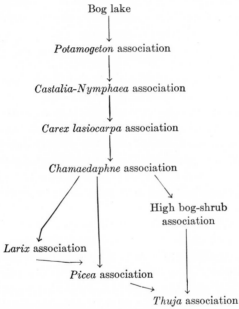

Bog lake

Potamogeton association

Castalia-Nymphaea association

Carex lasiocarpa association

Chamaedaphne association

High bog-shrub
association

Larix association

Picea association

Thuja association

Fɪɢ. 47. Diagram showing the usual successional relationships between plant associations in bogs in the region about Douglas Lake, Michigan. (*From Gates*, 1926.)

successional relationships between plant associations in bogs in northern Michigan. A more detailed diagram appears in a later paper by Gates (1942).

It is usually considered that the conditions described above have come about in the following manner: The open-water associations are not restricted to bog lakes but may be expected in virtually all kinds of lakes and doubtless occurred in the shoal waters of these lakes before they possessed any bog margins. Subsequently, however, a mat-forming association developed at the water's edge and, as time went on, these mat-forming plants (1) slowly began to advance on to the surface of the water to form the beginnings of the floating mat and (2) began to deposit peat in the water below. Continued extension of the mat over the open water (*a*) pushed the open-water associations farther and farther into the lake, (*b*) was accompanied by a gradual grounding of the shoreward portion of the mat, and (c) allowed succeeding associations of bog plants to come in behind in their proper sequence. This process continued, ultimately forming a mature bog condition in which the various associations are represented in a concentric series and in which many of the older portions of the mat have become firm (completely grounded) and invaded, to some extent, by upland plants at the original margin. A horizontal transect of a mature bog, from the remaining portion of the lake to the ancient, original shore line, thus tends to give a chronological picture of the history of the bog. Peat formation is an exceedingly slow process and has much to do with determining the rate of mat advance over the water, since apparently there are limitations to the amount of mat which can float in advance of the grounded portions. In the smaller, shallower basins, these events progressed with greater speed; the mat finally covered the last vestige of open water; filling processes finally grounded the whole mat; conditions became increasingly drier; the rearward associations encroached successively upon those in advance of them; and, at the conclusion of the senescence period, the bog became completely forested. In northern regions where bogs are prevalent, many stages in this history can be found at the present time, varying from young bogs to extinct, forested ones.

In the type of bog history described above, two processes are simultaneously involved: (1) mat encroachment or marginal encroachment upon the water and (2) bottom encroachment due to filling of the deeper parts of the basin. The race between these two processes for the final extinction of the lake may be won by either, and occasionally both participate in the final step of senescence. It should be noted here that instances are known in which the gradual extinction of the lake is virtually accomplished by bottom encroachment exclusively, bog-marginal development either being absent or remaining at a minimum.

In contrast to the horizontal vegetational analysis described above which gives something of the history of a bog lake, analyses of vertical borings may give evidence of a much longer succession. Borings, extended from the bog surface to the bottom of the original basin, make possible qualitative and quantitative examinations of the various deposits and in the chronological order of formation. Such evidences have shown conclusively that some lakes now existing as bog lakes had a long history before any bog formation occurred. It is now known, for example, that some lakes passed through an initial period during which marl deposits were laid down over the floor of the basin; later, when the lake had acquired the bog characteristics, layers of peat were deposited upon the marl stratum. The superimposed layers of peat and associated materials yield interesting and important evidences of the successive changes through which the lake and its surroundings passed. Since a prominent characteristic of peat formation is partial decay, many of the materials in peat strata are remarkably preserved and often can be identified with certainty. Of recent years, much attention has been given to the analyses of pollen deposits in peat beds, with resulting additions to knowledge not only of the past history of the bogs themselves but also of the succession of plant communities and of events on adjacent areas. Evidently, some bog lakes have passed from an early, clear, alkaline, hard-water condition into a subsequent stained, acid, soft-water one, with profound changes in the flora and fauna.

Productivity Features of Bog Lakes

Bog lakes as a class belong to the dystrophic type already discussed in an earlier section (page 344). Low productivity, both qualitative and quantitative, is characteristic of such lakes.

Much attention has been directed by European workers to the question of correlations and limiting factors, with the hope of discovering the influence or influences which determine the peculiar nature of the flora and fauna of bog lakes, but the various proposals must be regarded as tentative. Iron, phosphates, calcium, hydrogen-ion concentration, temperature, dissolved oxygen, and others have each been assigned a limiting role by various investigators. In his work on the macroplankton of northern Michigan bog lakes, Gorham (unpublished) came to the following conclusions, based upon the lakes which he studied:

1. No correlation was found between the macroplankton populations and dissolved oxygen, free carbon dioxide, hydrogen-ion concentration, color, or dissolved inorganic salts.

2. Temperature was a factor only in limiting the Copepoda and Cladocera to northern and widespread species.

3. Iron was present in very small amounts and did not seem to have a limiting effect by exerting a toxic action, as has been claimed for European lakes.

4. Contrary to previous claims, hydrogen-ion concentration was not found to have a limiting effect, many of the organisms occurring in both highly acid and highly basic conditions.

5. Colloidal decomposition products, originating from bottom deposits, eliminate by toxic action certain plankters, thus qualitatively limiting the population.

6. Quantitative production is limited by the small amounts of inorganic nutritive substances.

Surveys of American bog lakes have not yielded enough qualitative or quantitative data on the total biota to make possible any dependable comparisons. However, certain features seem evident; viz., (1) the biota is very restricted qualitatively; (2) quantitative production is usually low for all of the component species; and (3) food relations are restricted and growth rates are often slow.

PART V
LOTIC ENVIRONMENTS

CHAPTER XVII

RUNNING WATERS IN GENERAL

In an earlier section (page 13), certain general features of lotic environments (running-water series) have been discussed. While the main portions of this book deal with many fundamental characteristics common to
all inland waters, the main stress has been placed upon lakes and similar
situations. Since, in the broader sense, limnology is conceived to include
the fundamental production problems of all inland waters, standing or
running, some consideration will now be given to the latter, although it
must be understood at the outset that only general matters can be considered here and that lotic environments will be treated as a whole.

Streams vastly outnumber units of the standing-water series. They
are among the most familiar, ever-present features of all larger land areas
save deserts and the frozen polar regions. They vary in size from the
tiny rivulets at the innermost reaches of surface-drainage systems to
mighty rivers, such as the Mississippi. They are more numerous in
regions of abundant rainfall. Many are intermittent; many are permanent. It has been estimated that streams deliver about 6,500 cu. miles
of water to the sea annually, an uncertain value, but it is clear that the
total water capacity of stream systems of the earth is very great. According to Brown (1944), there is an average of 438 miles of permanent stream
for each county in the state of Michigan and a grand total of 36,350 miles
of permanent stream for the entire state. These figures do not include
the vast mileage of small intermittent network at the heads of various
drainage systems.

Investigation of the running-water series, particularly from the limnological standpoint, has lagged behind that of lakes. In only a few
instances have intensive, long-time researches been conducted. In
America, but one comprehensive study has been made, viz., that extensive
and prolonged (over 50 years) investigation of the Illinois River carried
on by the institution formerly known as the Illinois State Laboratory of
Natural History, under the direction of the late S. A. Forbes. Of the
many outstanding publications resulting from these investigations, that
monumental work by Kofoid (1903, 1908) on the plankton of the Illinois
River is deserving of special mention. Limited and isolated researches
have been undertaken on a number of other American streams. Any
general limnological account must, at the present time, merely be

an attempt to patch together some of the results of widely scattered investigations.

Lotic environments differ from lakes and similar waters in the following fundamental respects:

1. *Depth.* As a rule, the depths of all running-water units are small compared to lakes.

2. *Width of basin.* Aside from those channel expansions sometimes designated as river lakes, the water is confined to a relatively narrow channel.

3. *Current.* The whole volume of water flows in one direction.

4. *Condition of gradient from source to mouth.* All conditions, physical, chemical, and biological, gradually change with distance along the main channel and in a definite direction.

5. *Extension of channel with age.* Stream systems increase their length, width, and depth (to base level) with increasing age. This is in distinct contrast to the reduction processes characteristic of all standing-water units.

6. *Permanent removal of eroded and transported materials.* At any position along the course of a running-water unit, materials eroded at that point and all materials momentarily suspended or dissolved at that level are transported downstream, with no opportunity of return. In lakes, such materials commonly remain within the same basin.

7. *Absence of prolonged stagnation.* Constant flowage with accompanying mixing of the water usually eliminates prolonged summer stagnation of the bottom waters such as occurs in the deeper waters of lakes. Only in intermittent streams when extreme fall of water level converts the deep holes of the channel into a series of isolated ponds may any summer stagnations occur, and then this condition can well be excluded from consideration, since, temporarily, running-water conditions no longer exist. In certain respects, the same is true whenever midwinter, ice-cover conditions suspend stream flowage.

8. *Relative influence of physical factors.* Physical factors of the environment are often relatively more important than they are in lentic situations.

9. *Basic food materials.* Most streams manufacture within themselves little basic food materials but depend much more upon the contributions from the surrounding land than do most lakes.

PHYSICAL CONDITIONS

WATER MOVEMENTS

Current in one direction only is the outstanding feature of lotic environments. Its velocity varies with many circumstances most of which are familiar to the reader. It attains its greatest velocity in the abrupt, precipitous waterfalls and finds its minimum in those situations where for long distances the slope of channel becomes negligible, where stream pools are formed, or where the channel approaches base level. Extremes of current velocity may occur within a single stream or river. Some streams are slow and sluggish throughout their length; others are swift throughout their whole course. The stream systems of the plains and prairie regions are, for the most part, of the slow, steady type; those of the mountains are rapid and turbulent. Except in large, wide rivers, wave action due to wind effect is minimal.

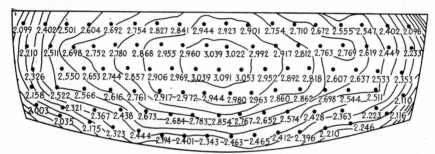

Fig. 48. Distribution of velocities of water flow in a conduit. Figure represents a cross section of conduit. Numerals indicate velocities at points where measurements were made. Contours within the figure are lines of equal velocity. (*From "Hydrology" by King, Wisler, and Woodburn, 1948, with permission of John Wiley & Sons, Inc.*)

Current velocity is not uniform in all parts of the transverse section of a stream but is reduced at and near the surface because of surface tension and diminishes as the bottom and sides of the channel are approached, owing to frictional effects. The maximal velocity is usually found somewhere within the first one-third of the depth. The nearest approach to the ideal pattern of flowage is usually found in certain artificial channels such as conduits. Figure 48 shows the distribution of velocities in an open conduit. Such uniformity of velocity distribution in natural streams may be expected only as a rarity; therefore such a uniformity must be looked upon as merely that pattern which natural streams tend to approach in varying degrees.

The distribution of velocities in natural streams is determined by several different factors operating simultaneously, such as shape of channel, roughness of channel, size of channel, and slope of channel. The maximum velocity is usually found somewhere within the first one-third of the depth of the water. Its distance from the surface is dependent upon depth. In shallow streams the region of maximum velocity is quite near the surface; in very deep streams it may be close to one-third of the depth. It must also be remembered that the velocity pattern of a stream may be altered by strong winds blowing either upstream or downstream. Figure 49 shows the distribution of velocities in a certain natural stream and at a selected location. It is presented here for illustrative purposes only. The numerals within the figure and their distribution hold only for that position on the stream where the vertical measurements were made. At other positions on the same stream or on other streams, different values and patterns may be expected. If vertical velocities are plotted, the resulting curve has approximately the form of a parabola.

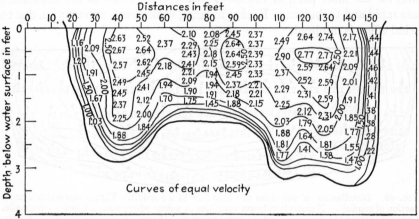

FIG. 49. Distribution of velocities of water flow in a certain natural stream and at a selected cross section. Numerals represent velocities, expressed in feet per second, at points where measurements were made. Contours within the figure are lines of equal velocity. (*From "Hydrology" by King, Wisler, and Woodburn, 1948, with permission of John Wiley & Sons, Inc.*)

On occasion, limnologists may make good use of certain features of vertical velocity curves as worked out by hydraulic engineers and used in their practices. According to King, Wisler, and Woodburn (1948):

The mean velocity in the vertical is ordinarily at 0.55 to 0.65 of the depth. The velocity at 0.6 depth is usually within 5 per cent of the mean velocity. . . . The mean of velocities at 0.2 and 0.8 depth usually gives the mean velocity in the vertical within 2 per cent. . . . The mean velocity in the vertical is ordinarily 0.80 to 0.95 of the surface velocity. The smaller percentage applies to the shallower streams.

Ice cover reduces the surface velocity because of the greater retarding effect of ice as compared with air, the average position of maximum velocity under ice being nearer mid-depth. For very rough ice it may be below mid-depth (Liddell, 1927). Therefore the mean velocity in the vertical would not be at 0.6 depth, but it is claimed that the mean of velocities at 0.2 and 0.8 depth gives approximately the mean velocity just as for a stream without ice cover.

For biological purposes, it is often important to know not only the current velocity at different depth but also the velocity variations resulting from stream obstructions and bottom materials. For example, the current rate may vary markedly at positions on the front, top, sides, and rear of submerged stones; likewise, the same is true of the gaps, channels, and interstices between stones and similar objects. Such differences often determine the position of organisms. For methods of measuring water current in such restricted locations, the reader is referred to Welch (1948).

Erosion, transportation, and sedimentation are inseparable accompaniments of stream currents. The character and rate of erosion depend much upon the volume of water, velocity of current, and character of the channel materials. The transporting powers of running water are well known. Materials if not actually carried in suspension are often rolled downstream. It is sometimes stated that the transporting power of streams varies as the sixth power of their velocities; thus, even slight changes in current rate have important effects.

Since current is the principal characteristic of lotic environments, it follows that *molar agents* are ever present and prominent influences, often creating very severe conditions.

TEMPERATURE

In lotic environments, temperature phenomena are, as a rule, very different from those in lentic situations. The principal features are: (1) tendency toward a uniform temperature at all depths, even in the deeper rivers; in many instances, the difference between the surface and bottom is virtually negligible; (2) tendency to follow air temperatures more closely than do lake waters. Small streams follow the air temperatures much more closely than do the large streams; (3) thermal stratification usually absent. Thermal stratification has been reported from certain regions in streams, but it is apparently not a common phenomenon. It is probably temporary and plays no such role as it does in lakes.

In streams, especially those with considerable length and slow current, temperature variations are common. They are the result of several possible influences, more than one of which may be operating simultaneously. Some of the principal circumstances leading to such temperature variations are differences in (1) depth of water, (2) current velocity, (3) bottom materials, (4) temperature of entering tributary water, (5) exposure to direct sunlight, (6) degree of shading, (7) time of day. The writer has records of temperature differences of as much as 11°C. at various stations along a stream which is about 30 miles long. Entrance of any considerable volume of cold spring water anywhere along a stream will produce a local temperature deviation. In long stretches of shallow, unshaded, slow-moving current it is likely that appreciable gains in temperature occur during the clear days of midsummer, but the water at the same position may have quite a different temperature at night.

Turbidity

The greatest extremes of turbidity occur in the running-water series. In mountain streams and others having rock beds, turbidity is minimal, while in some streams of the plains region of North America, such as the Missouri River, Kansas River, and certain of their tributaries, turbidity is very high. The general effects of current facilitate the production of turbidity, and, under circumstances essentially similar, the lotic environments will maintain a greater turbidity than the lentic situations of the same region. In some stream systems, high turbidity is a permanent feature throughout the year; in others, it occurs only at times of unusual precipitation. Turbidity in streams is due largely to silt, detritus, and other nonliving materials. Since plankton production is commonly restricted, it usually plays a minor role in turbidity production. Domestic sewage and other forms of stream pollution commonly increase turbidity, sometimes markedly.

A general discussion of turbidity has already been presented (pages 87 to 91), and many of the relations indicated there hold for streams. In many regions, erosion silt is the preponderant substance in the production of turbidity. Ellis (1936), in an extensive study of erosion silt in a large number of streams, found that it affects such situations principally by (1) screening out light, (2) changing heat radiation, (3) blanketing stream bottoms, and (4) retaining organic material and other substances which set up unfavorable conditions at the bottom. The possible influences of other kinds of turbidity-forming substances in streams differ according to their origin and their physical and chemical character. It has been claimed that some are directly toxic to various organisms. Effects of contaminations are not within the province of this discussion.

Light

Data on light penetration in streams are still so scattered and fragmentary that an adequate discussion is scarcely possible. Without doubt, the most important factor in the determination of light penetration is turbidity, the influence of which may be so great in certain waters as to reduce markedly the development of plants. Under conditions of temporary turbidity, plants and other organisms requiring considerable illumination may be able to withstand the greatly reduced light for a time.

In certain turbid rivers the decrease of light by suspended silt is in excess of 90 per cent in the first 25 mm. of water depth. This suspended material serves as a screen to all wave lengths of visible light although very muddy waters are slightly selective in favor of the transmission of scarlet-orange light (Ellis, 1936).

CHEMICAL CONDITIONS

Dissolved Gases

Owing to the mechanical conditions involved in current, the dissolved oxygen supply of uncontaminated streams is often high at all levels, often well toward saturation for the existing temperature.   Only in deep holes in slow streams, under special conditions of ice cover, or in instances of pollution does the dissolved oxygen supply show significant decline.

Contrary to what appears to be the general condition, a diurnal variation in the dissolved oxygen has been described (Butcher, Pentelow, and Woodley, 1930; and others) in certain European streams in which the oxygen content begins to increase soon after sunrise, reaches a maximum shortly after midday, and then declines to a minimum.   This variation, which may extend from a considerable supersaturation to a substantial reduction (167 to 36 per cent in some instances), is attributed to the oxygen production by green plants during the day and to oxygen consumption by respiration of the biota and by decay of organic matter during both day and night.   Obviously, such a diurnal cycle could occur only in streams supporting sizable crops of aquatic plants.   It has usually been supposed that in running-water units any oxygen pulse is smoothed out by the current; but it is now known that, under some circumstances at least, some rivers may show very distinct diurnal oxygen pulses, and the dissolved oxygen content may rise to 200 per cent saturation or more. *Oxygen exhaustion* at night and oxygen replacement during the day in plant-choked lagoons, ponds, and similar waters is well known, but the frequency of similar phenomena in lotic situations is yet unknown.

Among the various factors which have to do with the quantity levels of dissolved oxygen in unmodified streams, it appears that ordinarily the most important ones are: character of stream flow, slope of channel, temperature, oxygen released by chlorophyll-bearing plants, oxygen consumed in respiration of the biota, and oxygen consumed in the decay of organic deposits on the bottom.

Decomposition gases of all kinds tend to be minimal owing to the circulation effects of the current.   Only under the special stagnation conditions mentioned above would such gases become significant.

Dissolved Solids

The dissolved solids vary greatly, depending upon the regional characteristics of the drainage basin.   In this respect, lotic and lentic environments have few general differences; in fact, they commonly influence each other markedly because of the intimate way in which they may be related by direct connections, such as inlets and outlets.   There seems to be some evidence that, in general, lotic water contains more salts and less soluble nitrogen than lentic waters (Chapman, 1931), but there are probably many exceptions to this statement. There is reason to believe that flood waters dilute and droughts concentrate, particularly in those instances in which subterranean water is the more steady source of water supply, since subterranean waters usually contain a larger content of dissolved matter. The dissolved content is often subject to changes by dilution or addition at stream junctions. For specific data on the composition of many river waters of the United States, the reader is referred to the large work by Clarke (1924).

TABLE 49. DISSOLVED SOLIDS IN RIVER WATERS OF THE UNITED STATES
Based upon many measurements. Most analyses made during 1906–1907. All values expressed in parts per million
Summarized from Clarke (1924)

Distribution of Rivers	Range of Dissolved Solids
St. Lawrence Basin	50–539
North Atlantic Slope	14–170
Middle Atlantic Slope	36–190
South Atlantic Slope	52–194
Southern Florida	38–338
Mississippi Basin	51–2,908
Rivers of Texas	219–1,136
Rio Grande Basin	52–1,023
Colorado Basin	426–1,234
Interior Basin of California	189–339[1]
South Pacific Slope	145–3,062[1]
Middle Pacific Slope	42–216[1]
North Pacific Slope	30–246[1]
Great Basin	63–637

[1] Expressed in original as "total solids."

While results summarized in Table 49 are based upon a large number of measurements, it must be understood that the ranges given can be looked upon only as a general indication. Also it should be noted that the immense host of small streams is not included in the values. It would appear that the widest ranges and highest values occur in the mid-Continent, the low ranges and low maxima, on the Atlantic and Pacific slopes.

The widespread prevalence of various kinds of contaminations in streams often presents difficulties in appraising the effects of the artificially introduced substances. It appears that at least some of them produce an increase in the quantity of the dissolved solids. Without doubt some of the marked and abrupt changes in the dissolved solids which occur here and there along the courses of streams are caused by localized inflowing contaminations.

Regional differences in the load of solids in streams are common. An example is found when the two parts of the state of Michigan are compared. According to McNamee (1930), the range of total solids in 13 river systems in the Upper Peninsula is 100 to 200 p.p.m.; in 29 river systems in the Lower Peninsula, 200 to 500 p.p.m.

HYDROGEN-ION CONCENTRATION

Aside from the relations of hydrogen-ion concentration to stagnation processes in standing waters, the general features of pH in lotic environments are not different from those of lakes and similar waters. Current tends to keep the pH uniform over considerable distances; likewise, it keeps any acidity due to accumulating free carbon dioxide reduced. In general, it would seem that streams do not develop the more intense acidities, such as occur in some bog lakes, unless they are contaminated or receive heavy seepages from certain mineral deposits.

TABLE 50. RANGES OF HYDROGEN-ION CONCENTRATION IN A SELECTED SERIES OF RUNNING-WATER SYSTEMS

Streams	pH range	Authority
Big Muddy River, Illinois.................	5.8–7.3	Jewell (1922)
Puget Sound and Columbia River drainage...	6.5–8.5	Shelford (1925)
Salt Lake, Colorado, and Rio Grande drainage.	6.4–8.4	Shelford (1925)
Mississippi and Great Lakes drainage.......	6.4–8.2	Shelford (1925)
Trout streams, upper part of Lower Peninsula, Michigan.............................	7.1–8.2	Creaser and Brown (1927)
Blue River System, Nebraska..............	7.3–8.3	Canfield and Wiebe (1931)
Certain Ontario streams, Canada...........	6.5–8.0	Ricker (1934)
Inland streams of United States, Southern Canada, and Northern Mexico...........	6.3–9.0	Ellis (1937)
North Shore Watershed, Lake Superior.......	6.0–8.0	Smith and Moyle (1944)
New River watershed, Virginia..............	6.0–8.2	Shoup (1948)
Surface streams of Tennessee..............	3.0–8.6	Shoup (1950)

Big Muddy River (Table 50) and its tributaries occur in southern Illinois coal fields and receive not only ground water which is frequently acid in reaction but also strongly acid waters pumped from mines.

Tributaries of a stream system may have a different reaction from that of the main stream; also, the upper reaches of a system may have a pH distinctly different from that of the opposite end.

CLASSIFICATIONS OF LOTIC ENVIRONMENTS

Various attempts (Shelford, 1913; Klugh, 1923; Pearse, 1939; Muttkowski, 1929; Hora, 1930; Ricker, 1934; *et al.*) have been made to analyze the lotic environments and associations. From these works, valuable suggestions can be secured and a temporary scheme formulated, but so little is yet known about the running-water series from the modern ecological standpoint that any such efforts may be regarded as nothing more than tentative, and much work must be done in the future before such a classification can approach a permanent basis. Certain lotic associations or communities are so clean cut and well defined (e.g., the rapids community) that there can be little difference of opinion concerning their natural status, but these are outstanding instances and are in the minority. For these reasons, no general classification is attempted here. The reader is referred to the literature indicated above for further information.

BIOLOGICAL CONDITIONS

Since the current conditions of rivers and streams at large vary from turbulent rapids to those in which the current is virtually imperceptible, lotic environments exhibit all intergrades from the very swift, rushing waters in narrow channels to situations which are essentially lentic. This range of conditions is reflected in the biota, which varies from the distinctly characteristic organisms of falls and rapids to lentic floras and faunas of the almost immobilized portions of the system. Sometimes lotic assemblages of various kinds occupy the upper, more elevated portions of the stream system but fade out to give place to lentic assemblages, or at least mixtures of lotic and lentic assemblages, in the low reaches near the mouth of the stream. In other instances, lotic and lentic biotas alternate along the course where wider, level portions of channel interrupt the stretches of more rapid running water or where various types of obstructions producing damming effects sometimes referred to as *ponding*. Back waters, which, by origin and integration, are organic portions of a stream system, often qualify as lentic environments and maintain true lentic biotas. It is therefore very difficult, and perhaps not practicable, to try to lay down fundamental distinguishing differences between all lotic and all lentic biotas. In a rough way, it may be said that the greater the current velocity the greater the divergence of lentic and lotic populations, although sight should not be lost of the fact that a certain general resemblance exists between wave-swept shoals and rapid streams, particularly when the materials composing the bottom of the shoal and the channel are similar, e.g., a stony bottom. However, the similarities should not be overstressed, since the fauna of a wave-swept, stony shoal of a lake and that of a stony, rapid stream are not identical, although similar in certain qualitative, quantitative, and physiological respects.

Certain groups of animals are typically and sometimes exclusively lotic. Stone-fly larvae (Plecoptera) are preeminently lotic; black-fly larvae (Simuliidae) are confined exclusively to distinctly running water; net-building caddis-flies (Hydropsychidae) are typically lotic, although they may occur abundantly on exposed, stony lake shoals. Many other groups of insects are typically lotic. Specific and generic differences in the lentic and lotic faunas are very common, e.g., those of the lake and stream clams, fishes, and others. In a general way, it has been thought that lotic populations are more restricted in the number of species, but such a generalization is of doubtful value because of the great differences which exist in the various lotic and lentic situations.

INFLUENCES OF CURRENT

According to a time-worn statement, the lotic fauna is composed typically of animals whose dissolved oxygen demand is such that it can be fulfilled only by the highly oxygenated waters of streams. That such is not always the case can be shown both by certain observations in nature and by experiment. In some forms (Simuliidae; Wu, 1931), the requirement is an inherent current demand, not a high oxygen demand. It is possible that current demand may also be the preeminent factor in other typically lotic species. Support for the older conception has been seen by some in the work of Dodds and Hisaw (1924) who found that the gill area of May-fly nymphs in mountain streams varied inversely with the dissolved oxygen content but showed no very close correlation with the current rate. Also, Hubault (1927) has claimed, from a study of swift streams in eastern France, that invertebrates inhabiting those situations are more dependent upon the increased amount of dissolved oxygen and the mineral salts in solution than upon current, a generalization which is certainly too sweeping.

On the basis of work done in England, it is claimed (Fox, *et al.*, 1935) that certain May-fly nymphs and caddis-fly larvae from a swift stream have a considerably higher dissolved oxygen consumption than do certain closely related and equal-sized ephemerid nymphs and caddis-fly larvae from a pond; also that the same situation exists within a single species of aquatic crustacean (*Asellus aquaticus*), viz., that the individuals from a swift stream consume more dissolved oxygen than do those from sluggishly flowing water. Also certain swift-water ephemerid nymphs were found to be less resistant to oxygen deficiency than those in quiet water. Washbourn (1936) reported that trout fry from swift water consume significantly more dissolved oxygen than do those from slow water.

Hubault proposed that all running-water animals are forced by inherent necessities to seek certain indispensable physicochemical conditions and in order to find them they are compelled to tolerate current as a mechanical, inconvenient, and even detrimental condition against which they must struggle, emphasis being placed on the idea that the relation of all stream animals to current is an *enforced* one. Obvious weaknesses to such a contention make it of doubtful value as a generalization. Dodds and Hisaw (1925) concluded that most caddis-fly larvae inhabiting the swift Rocky Mountain streams in Colorado live there in spite of the current, not on account of it; also, that some of these larvae not only tolerate the current but have utilized it in such a manner as to make it necessary for their existence. This whole subject should be studied further by modern experimental methods.

Current imposes the problem of maintenance of position, a problem which has been discussed in the general section (page 157). With the exception of the plankton, practically all other members of the biota have developed means of maintaining themselves, except during floods, in that region of a stream for which they are adapted and in which they must remain if they are to thrive or even exist. Since a stream is usually a sequence of different environments from the uppermost waters to the lowermost reaches, a species having definite and limited toleration limits must avoid the ever-present hazard of being swept out of its normal surroundings into the lower waters where conditions may become limiting and even lethal.

Among organisms composing the biota of running waters, characters facilitating maintenance of position are numerous and diversified. It will suffice here merely to mention, as a specific example, the ballasting of cases of certain insects which live in running water during the larval stage. Not only are instances of this sort known to occur in nature, but also it has been demonstrated experimentally (Webster and Webster, 1943) that larvae of the same species (*Goera calcarata;* Trichoptera) build significantly heavier cases in running water than in quiet water.

An accompanying feature of current is molar action which in running water is always an ever present influence. The character and severity of this action vary widely with current velocity, the nature of the bottom materials, and other circumstances. Injury and mortality may be very high at times of flood, an interesting instance of which is reported by Needham (1930) as follows:

A net was used to strain the material being carried downstream during a high flood in Six Mile Creek near Ithaca, N.Y. The results were most illuminating. Practically every kind of aquatic organism which had been collected from this stream during the previous summer was taken in the net. The great majority were dead or injured by the grinding action of rocks and gravel which were being carried downstream. Many parts of insect larvae such as heads, legs, tails, and abdomens offered evidence of the destructive action of the high waters. Many aquatics such as black-fly larvae, Simulium, which are never taken drifting free in the current under normal circumstances, were collected, bruised and battered as they were carried downstream. Bottom studies made after the flood had subsided showed but a fraction of a gram of organisms remaining per unit area.

In addition to molar action, the eroding and scouring-out action of flood waters often has the effect of almost depopulating portions of streams so that restocking is necessary. Nature has numerous and effective means of restoring populations to these denuded situations, such as upstream or downstream migration of animals from adjacent waters, transportation by currents of water, transportation by other organisms, reproduction by the few individuals surviving the floods, spread of aerial adults from nearby waters, and transportation as wind-blown materials.

The speed and completeness of natural restocking after scouring-out effects of a flood depend upon the kind of stream, composition of the biota, time of year, severity of flooding, and certain other circumstances. The conditions surrounding the problem of restocking are so diversified that at present it is impracticable to attempt to formulate any general statements concerning average expectations. Recovery following flooding has been studied in various more or less isolated researches dealing with scattered types of streams, and certain features of natural restocking for the streams involved have been described. For example, Moffett (1936) found that in the bottom fauna of a certain Utah stream (1) those species having the shorter life cycles became reestablished first, (2) recovery was rapid (3 months), and (3) removal of the carnivores among the bottom fauna by the flooding lessened their influence on the herbivores. It seems to have been demonstrated that in a stream subject to population loss by flooding the presence of unaffected areas along the channel do much to speed up recovery, also that the recovery period is much shorter if it occurs during seasons favorable for reproduction. Migration habits of some organisms aid in recovery. The occurrence and extent of such migrations among various species of the nekton-benthos are still little known, but scattered instances appear in the records. For example, it has been shown that in certain European streams populations of *Planaria* are constantly either moving upstream or downstream, depending upon controlling conditions. Other instances of a somewhat similar kind are known.

The production of *drift materials* in a stream is one of the almost invariable effects of current, even in the absence of floods. Flowing water is constantly picking up objects from the channel and transporting them downstream. Mingled in this drift, there are likely to be certain aquatic organisms which have been swept into suspension. The quality and quantity of this *drift biota* will depend upon the conditions which prevail in the stream concerned. Dendy (1944) reviewed the literature relating to this subject and presented results of his investigations on macroscopic drift animals in three northern Michigan streams in which floods never occur. Among other things, he found, in the streams studied, that (1) 71 different kinds of macroscopic animals representing

7 phyla occurred in the drift during the summer months; (2) the presence of macroscopic animals, although highly variable in kind and quantity, was a constant feature; (3) in one of the streams all species represented in bottom-fauna samples were sooner or later found in the drift of that stream; (4) large quantities of drift biota are delivered into the lakes into which the streams emptied; (5) most animals drifting from a stream into a lake survive for but a limited time in the new environment. The work of Dendy and others demonstrates clearly that streams reduce their populations by washing animals away in the drift, such loss being a continuous one, even in the absence of floods.

A phenomenon arising out of current action is the deposition of erosion silt. The various physiographic processes involved are too familiar to justify discussion here. In some lotic situations, e.g., in steep, rock-bed streams, such deposits are virtually absent; in the slower portions of systems draining large areas of the softer types of surface formations, it may be of considerable magnitude. Certain organisms regularly occupy regions of silt deposit with no detriment to themselves, some of them having certain mechanical means of avoiding suffocation by the mud. That silt deposition is a hazard and even a lethal influence to certain benthic organisms is well known, the deleterious influence commonly affecting the animal by interfering with respiration. It has been reported by Ellis (1931) that in various streams of the Mississippi, Ohio, and Tennessee drainage systems, erosion silt is destroying a large proportion of the mussels by (1) directly smothering them by a thick deposit; (2) smothering the juveniles in localities where the adults can manage to maintain themselves; and (3) blanketing the organic matter so that an oxygen deficiency is produced locally, to the detriment of those mussels which require well-aerated water. According to Ellis, very young mussels are particularly sensitive to low dissolved oxygen content. Without doubt, silt deposition has an eliminating effect, directly or indirectly, upon various other organisms and is probably a much more important biological influence than has hitherto been supposed.

The influence of current upon plankton is discussed under another heading (see page 420).

Another influence of current is the elimination of surface breathers, except in the very slow-moving regions. This elimination is virtually complete in very swift streams; in those less vigorous, a few surface breathers may manage to occupy the more protected, marginal regions.

Plant Growths

Larger Plants. The larger aquatic plants (see Chap. XI) usually do not occur in conspicuous quantities in streams except where the current is greatly reduced. Occasionally, certain rooted plants of low stature (*Chara* and others) may be found in rapid streams. It has been claimed that there is a distinct tendency to dwarfing in plants that grow in mountain streams. Certain water mosses (*Fontinalis* and others) may be found in rapid current, especially in streams not subject to severe floods. On the other hand, some of the very slow, sluggish streams may become literally plant choked, maintaining a luxuriant flora composed principally of the submerged and floating types. In the slower water of stream edges, a narrow margin of aquatic plants may occur but usually with but limited success. Occasionally, streams which arise as surface upwelling of subterranean water and which are little subject to floods, droughts, or extensive sedimentation develop abundant growths of submerged rooted plants and certain types of Algae. Back waters and similar situations often produce great quantities of the larger plants, but, although more or less an organic part of a stream system, they are actually more lentic than lotic in character.

Limnological relations of larger aquatic plants are discussed in Chap. XI. It should be mentioned here that they play an important role in stream productivity. Their relationships to limnological processes are numerous and basic. Perhaps the most obvious benefits arise from their influence on fish production. Among various things, they supply shelter, protection, materials for abode, food, and support for a multitude of aquatic invertebrates that in turn serve directly or indirectly as food for fishes. Heavy production of larger plants is said to be favorable for trout production. It has been claimed that one of the favorable results of stream-improvement programs of certain types is the resulting extension of weed beds.

Algae. According to Tiffany (1938), the characteristic Algae of swift streams are those possessing the so-called holdfast cells or other structures which make it possible for them to adhere to various kinds of supports on the bottom and to remain there in the face of strong current. *Lemanea*, a fresh-water red alga, is said to be rather closely restricted to turbulent water and usually found only in rapids or waterfalls. *Batrachospermum*, also a red alga, occurs frequently in rapid streams. A very common green alga (*Cladophora*) attaches to stones and other supports in slow streams. Certain other Algae which lack holdfasts may successfully resist current action because of abundant mucous secretion in which the cells are enclosed and which seal the mass to the substrata. Strands of *Tetraspora* and *Draparnaldia*, globular colonies of *Chaetophora*, certain desmids, blue-greens, and others are said to be similarly attached in rapid streams. On occasion, these plants may be pulled loose from their moorings and become adventitious plankters.

PLANKTON

The literature contains statements to the effect that streams or portions of stream systems are devoid of plankton, or, if the statements do not go so far as to deny the existence of plankton, they stress the presence of only a very limited one. According to Eddy (1932), no plankton occurs in the upper 50 miles of the Sangamon River, Illinois, although bottom organisms, especially diatoms and protozoans, occasionally appeared in the collections. In the lower portions of the same river, a plankton is present. While much remains to be learned about these matters, it seems likely that if there are any parts of stream systems in which a true plankton is absent, they are the uppermost, swift ones; and that if a stream is of sufficient length, plankton will appear at least in the lower reaches. Mountain streams may show very little plankton even in their lower courses. The various negative statements concerning the plankton of running waters have sometimes been allowed to obscure the fact that many streams maintain a true plankton, often in considerable quantity.

Qualitative Features. In his extensive studies of the plankton of the Illinois River, Kofoid (1908) found (1) that the river plankton was a polymixic one, owing to the mingling of the planktons from the various portions of the drainage basin, especially from connected backwaters, and the consequent seeding of the channel waters with a great variety of organisms; (2) that the river plankton is subject to extreme fluctuations in quality; and (3) that this plankton does not contain any species peculiar to it, nor is it characterized by any definite assemblages of eulimnetic organisms, but the whole plankton may be distinguished, in a very general way only, by the greater quantities of littoral or benthic forms which mingle with the typical plankters. In this connection, it should be noted that the Illinois River has a very slow current throughout much of its course; also has much back water and a considerable number of adjacent "lakes" which empty into it. Therefore, the conditions of this river are, in some respects, not typical.

Krieger (1927) holds that the organisms which make up a river plankton originate from (1) the area surrounding the headwaters of the river; (2) the heleoplankton from pools along the river; (3) the limnoplankton from lakes along the river; and (4) tributary streams and drains. Butcher (1932) has shown that, in rivers which he studied, all of the plankton organisms, with very few exceptions, can be found at one time or another on the river bed and among the submerged and littoral macrophytes. Some of the plankters have been caught or entangled there; but many of them, particularly algal plankters, are sessile forms growing on the bottom. The current washes free from attachment individuals and portions of colonies, thus adding them to the plankton. Butcher makes the following analysis of the river plankton and its origin: (1) River phytoplankton contains two groups: (*a*) diatoms; *Fragilaria* and *Synedra* are most common; and (*b*) small green and blue-green Algae; *Scenedesmus* and *Pediastrum* are most frequent and widely distributed. (2) The small green and blue-green Algae become the more important as the river becomes larger. (3) The most common of the potamoplankters develop in various habitats, such as in ponds, lakes, marshy places, and river beds. (4) In large rivers, the relation between the potamoplankton and its sources of supply (lakes, pools, bogs, back-waters, and river beds) is still unknown. (5) In smaller streams, the sessile Algae appear to constitute the most important source of the phytoplankton. Steuer (1910) regarded the lotic plankton (potamoplankton) as an ecological group of organisms (biocoenose) living and breeding in running water and consisting principally of diatoms (*Melosira, Asterionella, Synedra, Fragilaria, Stephanodiscus*) and rotifers [*Asplanchna, Brachionus, Keratella (Anuraea), Gastropus, Polyarthra, Synchaeta*]. Galtsoff (1924) claims that the preponderance of these genera in river plankton may be regarded as characteristic of lotic plankton, since this particular combination has been observed in almost all rivers. However, all of these genera are commonly represented in lakes and ponds. The lotic plankton is not a special community of organisms adapted exclusively for life in running water. According to Galtsoff, only certain Schizomycetes (*Micrococcus rhenanus, Sarcina alba,* and *Microspira danubica*) seem to be restricted to streams. For further discussion of the origin of stream plankton, see page 427.

That stream plankton is not restricted to the diatoms and rotifers mentioned in the above paragraph is now well known. It has been claimed that certain rivers carry only zooplankton, and, in fact, some rivers have been described as having a plankton composed, in midsummer, of rotifers only. Whether in such rivers the phytoplankton is absent throughout the year remains to be shown, but it seems unlikely. Unfortunately, much of the river plankton work has dealt only with the net plankton, and little information is available as to the nannoplankton. Kofoid (1908) reported a total of 529 plankters for the Illinois River of which 83 were phytoplankters and 446 were zooplankters. Allen (1920) found 396 plankters in the San Joaquin River, California, of which the phytoplankters were somewhat fewer than the zooplankters. Galtsoff (1924) listed 36 phytoplankters from the upper Mississippi River and about 80 zooplankters; while Reinhard (1931), also working in the upper Mississippi, found 190 plankters of which 115 were phytoplankters and 73 were zooplankters. In the Illinois River, the predominating group among the phytoplankton was the Chlorophyceae (33 species), with the diatoms occupying second place (29 species); among the zooplankton, the Protozoa led, with 185 species; while the rotifers followed next with 104 species; the Ento-

mostraca included only 43 species.   In the San Joaquin River, diatoms
were considerably in excess of other phytoplankton groups; among the
zooplankton, Protozoa usually led, with the largest number of species,
followed by the rotifers; Entomostraca were represented by a very small
number of species.   In the upper Mississippi River (Galtsoff, 1924), the
Chlorophyceae contained the largest number of phytoplankters, followed
next by the blue-green Algae, the diatoms occupying third place; among
the zooplankton, the rotifers considerably exceeded the other groups,
while the Protozoa ranked second; but Reinhard (1931) reported the
diatoms greatly in the majority.   How typical these results are for the
larger American rivers remains to be demonstrated.   The special conditions which prevail in some rivers, such as high turbidity and special
chemical content, may possibly produce a different plankton composition.
It appears that diatoms are almost universally the most important constituents of river plankton.   Rivers, in general, being more laden with
silt than are lakes, would thus contain more diatoms on the basis of a
greater amount of available silicon (Reinhard, 1931).

Cilleuls (1928), in making a general survey of the literature dealing with
large stream plankton, subdivided the larger units of the lotic series into
two categories on the basis of rate of current: (1) those with slow current
and possessing lacustrine characters and (2) those having rapid current.
Obviously, all kinds of intergrades occur between these two groups.
However, in a general way, significant differences exist between the very
slow and the very rapid waters.   He lists the following general characteristics of the plankton of rivers having rapid flow:

1. Presence of mineral and organic detritus which nearly always sur-
passes the plankton in quantity.

2. Small number of species of phytoplankton.

3. Predominance of diatoms at all times, both in the number of species
and in the number of individuals.

4. Rarity or absence of typical, stream-produced plankters.

5. Materials constantly furnished to the main channel by the shore and
from the various kinds of tributaries.

6. General dominance of the phytoplankton over the zooplankton.

Pennak (1943) made a year-round study of Boulder Creek, Colorado,
a typical cascading mountain stream which arises near the Continental
Divide and flows eastward to the plains.   The net plankton was restricted
wholly to diatoms and *Ulothrix* spp.   Over the period of study (15
months), the diatoms showed a quantitative variation of 9,000 to 2,547,600
cells per liter; the *Ulothrix* spp., 0 to 16,630 cells per liter.   A sizable portion of the former and all of the latter were derived from the surface of
stones in the stream bed.   The very restricted zooplankton was composed
only of one species of Copepoda, three species of Cladocera, and six

species of Rotatoria. Quantitatively, the total zooplankton varied from zero to 36 individuals per liter. It was believed that this zooplankton originates largely from the deeper, quiet pools along the stream course. It was pointed out that the features of the phytoplankton agree with the generalizations of Cilleuls. Since Pennak's sampling station was at the base of the foothills, it is estimated that less than 15 hr. are required for the water from the highest reaches of Boulder Creek to arrive at the point of examination. The water at that point is therefore very "young" (see Eddy's results, page 420).

Quantitative Features. Quantitative production of plankton varies greatly with the stream system, with the various portions of the same system, with the time of year, with the water level, and with other possible circumstances (Table 51). Kofoid (1903) laid down a series of

TABLE 51. ILLINOIS RIVER; TOTAL PLANKTON PASSING HAVANA, SEPTEMBER, 1909–AUGUST, 1910

Modified from Richardson (1921)

Season	Net plankton, cc. per cu.m.	Total plankton, cc. per cu.m.	Ratio of total plankton to net plankton	Water discharge, cu.m. per 24 hr.	Plankton passing per 24 hr., tons	Plankton passing during entire period, tons
Dec.–Feb., 90 days..	0.20	1.37	6.87:1	48,090,240	72	6,536
Mar.–June, 122 days	13.98	27.82	1.99:1	48,090,240	1,474	179,916
July–Nov., 153 days.	0.87	3.43	3.95:1	24,045,120	91	14,025

conclusions for the Illinois River which, in a general way, are applicable to lotic situations, especially the larger, slower systems. Certain ones of very general bearing are as follows:

1. Area and depth, within limits of our environment, show little relation to plankton production.

2. Age of the water is an important factor in determining production of streams. Young waters from springs and creeks have but little plankton, and even such tributaries as the Spoon River (drainage basin, 1,870 sq. miles) contain but little plankton, principally of the more rapidly developing organisms. This barren water, impounded for 10 to 30 days in the backwater reservoirs such as Phelps Lake, develops an abundant plankton. The rate of run-off and replacement of impounded waters determines to some extent the amplitude of production. This is greatest where run-off is least and rate of renewal slowest.

3. Fluctuations in hydrographic conditions constitute the most immediately effective factor in the environment of the potamoplankton. Rising levels usually witness a sharp decline in plankton content (per cubic meter) as barren storm waters mingle with or replace plankton-rich waters of channel and reservoir backwaters. Falling levels are periods of recovery and increase in plankton.

Stability in hydrographic conditions conduces to rise in production at all seasons of the year, and instability is always destructive. Winter floods tend to lower plankton production; spring floods increase it.

4. Temperature affects production profoundly. Below 45°F., the plankton content in the river is only about 9 per cent of that present above this temperature; and in backwaters, but 29 to 40 per cent. Minimum production is at times of minimum temperature.

5. Light affects plankton production. The half year with more illumination and fewer cloudy days produces from 1.6 to 7 times as much plankton as that with less illumination and more cloudy days. Seasons of unusual cloudiness are accompanied by depression in production.

6. The plankton of the Illinois River is largely autonomous. Seepage and creek waters are diluents of its plankton and add little to its diversity. Even Spoon River is generally a diluent, reducing the plankton content 10 per cent and adding but few diversifying species to its population. The reservoir backwaters, on the other hand, generally contain a more abundant plankton than the channel, the amount, on the bases of monthly averages, being from 1.3 to 17 times as great. At all levels, waters from impounding areas in the bottom lands are drawn into the channel, mingled with the plankton-poor contributions of tributaries, and further enriched by the growth of indigenous channel plankton. The reservoir backwaters are thus of great importance both as a source of the channel plankton of the Illinois River and in its maintenance.

7. Filter-paper catches indicate the presence, on the average, of a plankton 3.3 times the volume of that taken by the silk net. Leakage through the silk is therefore a matter of some volumetric importance.

8. The annual production of plankton and of the fisheries of the Illinois River show some correlation in their changes from year to year.

While these conclusions apply primarily to the Illinois River, it has been shown by various investigations made since that time on other river systems, American and European, that they hold more or less generally for similar situations. Definite, quantitative values expressed above are, of course, subject to considerable change in other rivers. Certain comments on the Kofoid conclusions, based upon recent work, follow.

The importance of *age* of water seems to be well grounded. Shelford and Eddy (1929) reported that in the upper reaches of the Sangamon River, Illinois, water approximately 9 days old contained practically no plankton and that plankton did not begin to appear abundantly until the water was at least 20 days old.

The amount of current has a profound effect upon plankton production. According to the so-called Schröder's law, the amount of plankton in a river varies inversely as the slope of the channel. It is not clear that any such constant relation holds in all running water; but within certain limits, the greater the current the less the plankton. Allen (1920) found that water currents above a very moderate speed are distinctly inimical to plankton development, and various other workers have shown that the amount of plankton decreases as the water velocity increases. The influence of current becomes manifest where lake waters containing plankton flow into an outlet (see page 428). That the plankton quantities begin to drop rapidly seems to be well established, especially if the outlet has distinct current. Rapids apparently have a serious effect upon plankton. Galtsoff (1924) found that, in the Mississippi River, the water below Rock Island Rapids carried only about 40 per cent as much plankton as that above the rapids. It was computed that the trip through these rapids required about eight hours. Galtsoff assumed that the plankters are destroyed not directly by the turbulent water itself but by the friction against sand grains suspended in the flowing water and possibly by impacts with the various materials composing the bottom. Pennak (1943) found that in a Colorado mountain stream the remains of both mature and immature zooplankters occurred abundantly in plankton samples. He believed this fragmentation to be due to the turbulence of the stream and resulting contact of organisms upon the stream bed and upon suspended particles.

Seasonal Distribution. Here, again, Kofoid's generalizations for the Illinois River are quoted, since it appears that they apply in a general way, particularly to large rivers with slow current.

1. There is little correlation between the seasonal flux in chemical conditions (as shown in data of sanitary analyses) and the seasonal course of plankton production (as shown in catches of the silk net). The nitrogenous matters are influenced by the plankton pulses, especially when diatoms are multiplying rapidly, but the changes are not uniform or proportional.

2. The course of plankton production in channel and backwaters throughout the year exhibits a series of recurrent pulses, culminating in maxima and separated by minima, which give the planktograph the appearance of a series of "frequency-of-error" curves of varying amplitudes. These pulses generally have a duration of three to five weeks and tend to coincide in their location in all localities coincidentally examined by us. This similarity in the direction of movement in production amounts quantitatively to 65 per cent of the possible comparisons in our records. This cyclic movement in production is plainly influenced, accelerated or retarded, or its amplitude extended or depressed, by environmental factors, but is not itself traceable to any one or any combination of them. A brief interval of examination—not more than one week—is essential to a demonstration of the existence of these pulses.

3. The vernal pulse in production attends the vernal rise in temperature and culminates at about 60 to 70°. With the establishment of the midsummer temperatures (about 80°), production falls from 44 to 87 per cent, in channel and backwaters. It *rises*, however, 68 per cent in Phelps Lake, so that other causes than temperature may be operative in producing the midsummer decline. The autumnal decline in temperatures is accompanied by decline in production in the channel and in Quiver Lake, but by an increase in other backwaters, which

exhibit a tendency toward an autumnal pulse. The decline to winter minimum occurs in December.

An early spring accelerates, and a late spring retards, the vernal pulse, and a late autumn prolongs the autumnal production. Summer heat pulses often attend plankton increases. Minimum temperatures are not prohibitive of large plankton production. The December production in Phelps Lake in 1898 (43.14 cm^3.) exceeds the *vernal* maximum elsewhere in all localities but one, but falls much below the summer production in Phelps Lake. The ice sheet is not inimical to a considerable plankton production unless stagnation conditions occur.

4. In the main, but two types of plankton are found in the Illinois River—the summer, and the winter assemblage. The vernal and autumnal types are only transitions between the two when organisms from both are present. The winter plankton is characterized by a small number of species peculiar to that season, and a number of perennial forms; the summer, by a large number of summer organisms with the perennial types.

Kofoid's results showed that in the channel waters of the Illinois River, there was usually one *total plankton maximum* at some time during the open season; it tended to appear during the spring but sometimes occurred as late as September and occasionally in February, indicating that in this river at least these plankton changes follow the causative changes in the environment and not the calendar. However, it is interesting to note that his curves for the Chlorophyceae, diatoms, Mastigophora, and Crustacea show a general summer maximum and a winter minimum, while rotifers exhibit a tendency toward the bimodal production curve, with maxima in spring and in autumn. Reinhard (1931) reported one spring plankton maximum and one midwinter minimum for the upper Mississippi River. Diatoms constituted the bulk of the plankton at all seasons. The San Joaquin River, California, has but one plankton maximum (Allen, 1920), viz., in the autumn, and the various general groups of plankters (chlorophyll bearers, Entomostraca, Protozoa, and Rotatoria) all show increases at that time, although not of the same magnitude. Some tropical rivers manifest two annual plankton maxima, those maxima being both qualitative and quantitative and depending, apparently, upon the quantity of food material.

Horizontal and Vertical Distribution. Since increasing current means decreasingly favorable conditions for plankton, plankton organisms are commonly more abundant near the banks than in the midchannel, although special conditions may intervene to bring about another type of distribution. If, for example, the waters along one or both banks become stagnant and unfavorable for plankton, the midchannel will contain the larger quantities. In some waters, it appears that the differences between midchannel and marginal distribution are almost insignificant.

Since plankton organisms are victims of the drift of water, their vertical distribution depends much upon current. In some running waters and under some circumstances, the plankton quantities of the deeper strata exceed those of the upper strata. Sometimes, the vertical distribution is uniform; in other waters, especially during the warmer months, the distribution is much the same as would occur in a lake of similar depth. Actually, vertical distribution of plankton in running waters is very variable not only in different systems but also in different portions of the same system.

Origin of Stream Plankton. The origin of running-water plankton has been a much debated question. Various explanations have been proposed, based upon different water systems, some of which are as follows: (1) River plankton arises in the upper tributaries and is not developed in the main portion of the river. According to Galtsoff (1924), Schütt claimed this origin for the plankton of the Amazon River. (2) River plankton arises in the slow-moving sections of the channel, in the bayous, and in the lakes which are either widened regions of the rivers themselves or those closely connected with them. Kofoid (1908) concluded that the plankton of the Illinois River channel is not derived directly from the tributaries but rather largely from the impounding backwaters and that at low water stages, it is almost exclusively indigenous in the channel itself; and Galtsoff (1924) came to similar conclusions concerning the upper Mississippi River. Reinhard (1931) found that, in the upper Mississippi region, plankters peculiar to the tributary waters invariably declined numerically when introduced into the main stream and insisted that tributary forms capable of thriving in the main channel are already established there, while the forms peculiar to tributaries are those not fitted for life in the main stream. He further pointed out that, because of the possibility of passive transportation of plankton for long distances, certain features of a plankton collection may sometimes show little correspondence to the channel environment at the sampling position. Other work on the origin of river plankton (Krieger, 1927; Butcher, 1932) has been discussed on page 420.

It seems now reasonably well established that the plankton of streams (potamoplankton) is not composed of plankters confined exclusively to running water. Allowing for the great variety of special circumstances which may surround streams and parts of stream systems, it appears that the plankton of many streams is a composite of plankters from several sources, some of which may be the limnetic and benthic zones as well as contributing lentic environments, with relatively few species characteristic only of the lotic situation. In fact, some limnologists seem to deny the existence of exclusively lotic plankters, especially in rivers. Positive conclusions on this matter must wait further investigations. Since so many of the available data are based upon the study of net plankton only, the status of nannoplankton cannot be appraised at this time.

Fate of Typical Lake Plankton in Streams.   It has long been believed that a typical lake supports a plankton fundamentally different from that of a river or any other flowing water.   The term *potamoplankton* seems to have been originally proposed to designate a group of plankton organisms thought to exist only in running water, and at the present time it is often used in that sense.   It is also commonly believed that the supposed characteristic differences between lake plankton and running-water plankton are the result of the contrasting environmental conditions in the two different kinds of environments, current being the conspicuous feature in running waters and being responsible, directly or indirectly, for the differences in the plankton.   Many lakes have streams as their outlets, and, as a result, lake plankton, especially that of the surface waters, passes out of the conditions characteristic of a lake into those characteristic of running water.   It therefore becomes important to know what, if anything, happens to the typical lake plankton after its arrival in the running water.   Chandler (1937) made an extensive study of the problem in three different situations in each of which typical lake water, bearing its characteristic plankton, flowed into streams none of which had tributaries in the region studied or had any pollution.   Among the various results of this investigation, the following are significant in this connection: (1) The plankton underwent a progressive, quantitative decrease as it passed downstream.   (2) The decrease in plankton was not uniform in all parts of each stream but varied with the presence or absence of certain environmental factors.   (3) The greatest plankton decrease per unit of distance invariably occurred in the most heavily vegetated sections of the stream.   Decreases of as much as 50 per cent occurred with a distance of 20 m. in heavily vegetated regions. When the plants were removed, plankton decrease almost completely disappeared in that portion of the water.   The plankton may be strained out of the water by thick accumulations of plants, e.g., by a *Lyngbya* mat; likewise, it may also adhere to the accumulated materials on the submerged stems and leaves of the submerged, rooted macrophytes. Plankton thus removed by vegetation settled ultimately to the bottom, forming conspicuous accumulations of very finely divided bottom deposits.   (4) Various kinds of submerged debris and other objects may possess surfaces favorable for plankton accumulation and thus function in reducing the amount of lake plankton.   (5) Plankters settling to the bottom, either alone or in association with inanimate materials, may result in a decrease of lake plankton in running water.   The specific effect of *current* upon lake plankton is still inadequately investigated.   Chandler's work was done on situations in which the current rate was relatively slow. Various investigators (Allen, 1920; Galtsoff, 1924; Van Oye, 1926; and others) have found current related directly to plankton scarcity in rivers, but whether or not this also holds for inflowing lake plankton remains for future research to determine.

It is evident that the quantitative lake-plankton decrease exhibited by the streams investigated by Chandler is not caused by any one factor but by several (aquatic vegetation, debris, subsidence of inanimate materials, and others). One factor may be more important in one section of a river than in another, but the total lake-plankton decrease occurring between the outlet of the lake and some remote station on the stream is the result of the combined effect of several factors. It seemed that the greatest plankton decrease was produced by the collection of plankters on the surfaces of objects with which they come into contact.

Plankton Decrease. It seems certain that the longitudinal distribution of plankton along the course of a river from its origin to its mouth

TABLE 52. LOSS OF PLANKTON IN THE LOWER REACHES OF THE ILLINOIS RIVER
Modified from Richardson (1921)

Reach	Plankton volumes, percentage of volumes in reach I		
	May, 1899	June, 1910	Aug., 1910
I. Chillicothe[1] to Havana; 60.5 miles (middle section of river; most productive in plankton)...................	100	100	100
II. Havana to Lagrange; 42.5 miles........	44	38	8
III. Lagrange to Grafton,[2] 77.5 miles.......	7	12	3

[1] Chillicothe is 146.5 miles downstream from Lake Michigan.
[2] Grafton is at the mouth of the river.

depends upon various circumstances, such as the character, number, and distribution of tributaries; the rate of current; nature, amount, and distribution of back waters; character of the channel; and so on. Longitudinal distribution of plankton in long rivers is still too imperfectly known to permit any generalizations. It should be stated here, however, that certain rivers have been described in which the longitudinal distribution is roughly as follows: the head-water section in which there is little or no true plankton; a next succeeding section in which the plankton is increasing; a middle or submiddle section in which the plankton attains its maximum; and finally a lower section of the course in which there is a distinct *decline* in the plankton, with increasing distance downstream to the river mouth. Table 52 contains a few of the numerous data for the Illinois River and indicates something of the character of the plankton decline in the lower course. Forbes (1928) reported a similar decline in the plankton in the lower course of the Rock River, some of the features of which are given in Table 53. Another instance of the same phenomenon is described by Eddy (1932) in the Sangamon River and is illustrated in

TABLE 53. PLANKTON DECREASE IN LOWER REACH OF THE ROCK RIVER
Ratios of numbers of plankton organisms per cubic meter in the two portions of the river
Data from Forbes (1928)

Plankton groups	Upper reach of river (Beloit to Dixon)	Lower reach of river (Sterling to Colona)
Diatoms...............	1.17	1
Other Algae............	8.7	1
Protozoa...............	7.6	1
Rotifers...............	2.4	1
Entomostraca..........	4.0	1

TABLE 54. SUMMARY OF PLANKTON COLLECTIONS, SAGAMON RIVER, 1929
Modified from Eddy (1932)

Location	Volume, cc. per cu. m.			Number of species represented		
	June 25–27	July 26–28	Sept. 10–12	June 25–27	July 26–28	Sept. 10–12
Monticello[1].............	0.08	0.08	0.05	9	8	16
Lake Decatur[2]..........	15.20	9.50	9.60	36	47	25
Harristown.............	6.00	8.00	10.00	22	34	27
Illiopolis...............	9.00	8.00	8.40	23	31	26
Riverton...............	3.00	3.90	3.60	17	35	35
Springfield.............	.....	0.80	12.60	..	28	36
Petersburg.............	2.20	0.40	17.00	22	22	39
Chandlerville[3]..........	0.50	0.30	6.00	24	22	30

[1] First appearance of plankton; more than 50 miles from source.
[2] Lake formed by damming of main channel of river.
[3] Very near mouth of river.

Table 54. Still other examples occur in the literature. A satisfactory explanation of this plankton decline in the lower reaches of certain rivers is yet lacking. Unfortunately, in some of the rivers in which this decline has been studied, present or previous pollution in the upper portions makes an understanding of this complex phenomenon much more difficult. How common this form of plankton decline is in rivers at large future research must determine.

Nekton–Benthos Characteristics

Since shallowness is a preponderant characteristic of streams in general, no organism inhabiting them is remote from the bottom. Only in deep parts of large rivers are there deviations from this statement. In most streams a sharp dividing line between nekton and benthos on a natural basis does not exist. Of the vast array of organisms involved, fishes are the only group which might justly be called nektonic, and even here the case is not always clear, as, for example, the central mudminnow (*Umbra limi*) whose habits might justify classifying it as a bottom organism. Intergrades between benthos and nekton are so numerous that it is impracticable to consider them separately. Therefore, for purposes of general discussion, they will be treated together in this account.

Temporary and Headwater Streams. The most remote extensions of a lotic system (gullies, rivulets, brooks) are often intermittent. During the dry season, the channel is either completely devoid of water or, at most, contains but a few isolated pools. While such waters often appear, on casual examination, to be almost devoid of life, actually they are usually occupied by certain assemblages of organisms which, in part at least, possess the following features:

1. Life histories requiring water only in a portion of the cycle; therefore, such a stream has no permanent aquatic residents other than those which may persist in the isolated pools of the dried-up water course.

2. Virtually no development of the higher aquatic plants, and hence there are very few direct plant eaters among the fauna.

3. A preponderance of forms which are either carnivorous or which feed upon detritus and microscopic organisms.

4. Positive rheotropism in some of the motile forms; clinging and attachment a common feature of others.

5. Wide toleration of environmental changes by those species which may carry over in the pools from one period of flowing water to the next. Not only must the original lotic organisms inhabit lentic conditions, but also the lentic conditions themselves may become more and more severe during the pool period.

6. Linear sequence distribution of fishes. According to Shelford (1913), the fishes, in many such streams, occur in a very regular linear sequence. For example, in the region of Chicago, Ill., the creek chub (horned dace), *Semotilus atromaculatus*, occupies the farthest upstream position; the redbelly dace, *Chrosomus erythrogaster;* the blacknose dace, *Rhinicthys atratulus;* the young of the white sucker, *Catastomus commersonii;* and others following in the order named (Fig. 50). With the onset of drought, these fishes move downstream; with rise of water level, they go up stream but maintain their general linear distribution.

Somewhat similar phenomena have been reported from European streams.

7. Aquatic insects form the most diversified group of the fauna.

Streams in General. There seems to be a rather general agreement (Pearse, 1939; Shelford and Eddy, 1929; and others) that, in a very broad way, two large types of stream communities can be recognized: (1) those characteristic of swift waters with hard, stable bottoms and (2) those characteristic of slowly moving waters with soft, unstable bottoms. Shelford and Eddy describe these general communities, in part, as follows:

1. Swift-water type. No pelagic communities; the fishes and insects present are preeminently bottom dwellers or else are involuntary drift forms from the pools above; essentially only one type of rapid-water bottom community at low altitude in central North America, viz., the *Cladophora-Hydropsyche-Ethiostominae* communities, in which the dominating positive reactions are to strong current and to rock bottom, and which possess a fair permanence due to minimized shifting effect of floods upon the rock bottom.

2. Sluggish-water type. Depends upon soft bottom and slow current; decaying organic matter, accumulated on bottom, supports large quantities of bacteria and, in addition, Protozoa, Rotatoria, Gastrotricha, nematodes, and Annelida; the microfauna so composed occurs either scattered or in isolated assemblages and is probably important to larger forms; pelagic communities composed of pelagic fishes and plankton; plankton does not constitute a complete area-occupying community; pelagic communities motile and remain in no fixed position in relation to bottom.

In addition to the characters indicated above, the swift stream type contains many organisms showing (1) strong positive rheotaxis; (2) a definite requirement for current; (3) dependence upon firm, immobilized bottom materials for anchorage and construction; and (4) relatively sedentary habits (foods brought to them by current).

In the sluggish-water type, the rooted, higher vegetation comes into prominence, and, among other things, it functions as support for many components of the biota. Pelagic and bottom faunas become more abundant and diversified; also, are relatively active and usually must seek their foods.

Considering streams at large, it is possible to divide them into two general types, viz., intermittent and permanent. Intermittency is more common among the smaller streams but may occur even among streams large enough to be called rivers. Unfortunately, the biology of intermittent rivers of those regions having dry seasons during which rivers may disappear temporarily, to reappear with onset of the wet season, is still so imperfectly known that no discussion will be attempted here.

River faunas, in general, are composites of (1) components from tributaries, (2) ubiquitous species, and (3) true river species, found in rivers only. The typical river organisms are, for the most part, (*a*) fishes and turtles which are strong swimmers; and (*b*) heavy-bodied mussels and other burrowers which can resist strong currents, shifting bottoms, and accumulating drift (Pearse, 1939). Of the running-water series, only the rivers develop large fishes.

Many studies of macroscopic bottom organisms of streams have been made, but the microscopic benthos is still, to a considerable extent, an unknown field. This lack of information is not the result of any failure to recognize the basic importance of the microbiota but rather is in part due to the newness of the subject and to the difficulties inherent in this kind of investigation. There is great need for work in this field.

General Ecological Succession

It is a well-known physiographic fact that the headwater region of any running-water unit or system migrates. Streams, in general, extend their length, as erosion proceeds, by continually cutting back at their source. Therefore, as time goes on, the *young-stream conditions* migrate upstream with the migration of the headwaters, and the next older set of environmental conditions likewise move upstream to occupy the level once occupied by the young-stream environment. In a similar way, all of the linear series of environmental conditions found in a stream or river of today have been and are still (barring special circumstances) moving along upstream. This migration is accompanied by a similar migration of the organic communities characteristic of each set of environmental conditions in the procession, since, when a particular environmental complex has shifted upstream and a different kind is following in its wake, the organisms occupying that particular level of the channel, finding themselves in increasing disharmony with the changing environment, solve the situation by following the migration of the particular habitat for which they are best fitted. In this way, the location of the upper portion of the series of environments and the corresponding series of organic communities has, in some stream and river systems, migrated long distances in past ages. The speed of such a migration is dependent largely upon the rate of erosion and transportation of materials at the source and is a very slow process even when erosion and transportation are most active. Figure 50 and the accompanying explanation exemplify this phenomenon. While the diagram deals specifically with the linear series of fishes, it must be understood that the changes in the fish communities involved simultaneous similar changes in the assemblages of other animals living with the various fishes. The following section quoted from Shelford describes the general dynamics represented in the figure.

When Bull Creek was at the stage represented by the first stage in our diagram (which is represented by the present Glencoe Brook), its fish, if any were present, were ecologically similar to those now in Glencoe Brook in their relations to all factors except climate. This ecological type is represented by the horned dace alone. As Bull Creek eroded its bed . . . the fish community of stage 1 was succeeded by a fish community ecologically similar to the fish communities at the localities marked 2. . . . The fish now ecologically representing this community are the horned dace and the red-bellied dace.   The community of the single species, the horned dace, had at such a period moved inland. . . . As

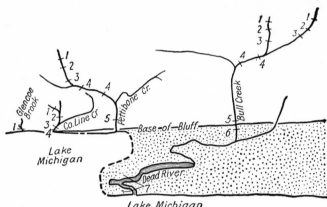

Lake Michigan

Fɪɢ. 50. Diagrammatic arrangement of the North Shore streams. The streams are mapped to a scale of 1 mile to the inch, and the maps are placed as closely together as possible in the diagram.   The intermediate shore lines are shown in broken lines which bear no relation to the shore lines which exist in nature.   Toward the top of the diagram is west.   Each number on the diagram refers to the pool nearest the source of the stream which contains fish, as follows: 1, the creek chub (horned dace); 2, the redbelly dace; 3, the blacknose dace; 4, the suckers and minnows; 5, the pickerel and bluntnose minnow; 6, the sunfish and bass; 7, the pike, chubsucker, etc.   The bluff referred to is about 60 ft. high. The stippled area is a plain just above the level of the lake. (*From Chapman, "Animal Ecology,"* 1931, *after Shelford; "Animal Ecology,"* McGraw-Hill Book Company, Inc.)

erosion continued, the fish community ecologically represented by the horned dace and red-bellied dace moved gradually inland and was succeeded by a fish community . . . ecologically similar to that now found at the point 3. [On continued erosion] fish community 3 was then succeeded by a fish community ecologically similar to the fish community now present at point 4. . . . The fish communities 1, 2, 3 have meanwhile moved inland and are arranged in the order which their ecological constitution required.

The continuation of the process resulted in displacing a fish community ecologically similar to the fish community 4 by a fish community ecologically similar to the present fish community 5. This is represented in the lower waters of Bull Creek.

An interesting development in the subject of the succession of stream communities centers about the contention of Shelford and Eddy (1929) that, contrary to the current belief of plant ecologists, "permanent stream communities exist, undergo successional development, reach and maintain a quasi-stable condition, and manifest seasonal and annual differences, as do terrestrial and marine communities." They insist that it is only the abandoned positions of the stream communities that develop ultimately into land communities; that streams are permanent just so long as the existing climate continues, which is the condition under which land communities form a climax.

Productivity Features of Lotic Environments

The quantitative features of plankton in lotic environments have already been presented (page 423). Productivity of the macroorganisms now deserves some comment. Work in this field, particularly in America, is so scanty and fragmentary that any broad discussion is impossible. Some of the general results of certain recent work will be presented, since they seem to have the possibility of wider application in the field of stream and river productivity. They may also offer suggestions as to the nature of some of the important problems which await more intensive work.

Brooks and Creeks. P. R. Needham (1930) published results of work done on the ecology of the smaller streams in central New York, and among other things the following general features are stressed:

1. Ordinarily, the distribution of aquatic animals in brooks and creeks is dependent largely upon (1) temperature of the water, (2) nature of the bottom, and (3) velocity of current.

2. In general, smaller streams from source to mouth present two distinct types of habitats, (1) pools, and (2) riffles.

3. Riffle bottoms greatly exceed the pool bottoms in productivity.

4. Fishes in brooks and creeks tend to seek the pools. The pools also act as catch basins for animals swept down from the riffles, these drift animals serving as food for the pool fishes.

5. Of the various types of bottom which lack the higher aquatic vegetation, silt bottom is most productive of small organisms; rubble, coarse gravel, fine gravel, hardpan, and bedrock produced successively less in the order mentioned.

6. Plant beds in smaller streams, when they occur, markedly affect productivity. Stream bottoms supporting growths of aquatic plants were found to be over seven times more productive than were stream bottoms bare of vegetation.

7. Small, cold, head-water streams less than 7 ft. in width were found to be twice as productive *per unit area* as were streams which exceeded that width.

8. In streams exceeding 18 ft. in width, the weight of the bottom organisms per unit area *decreased* 12 per cent from the maximum at shore line to the middle of the channel; in streams with widths less than 18 ft.,

the organisms *increased* approximately 12 per cent from shore line to middle of channel; in streams with width of 18 ft., the bottom organisms were quite evenly distributed over the entire bottom.

These findings are, in some respects, not in complete agreement with similar work in other regions but indicate some of the important relations which exist in the region studied. It is probable that modifications of some of these conclusions will be necessary in order to make them apply to stream conditions at large.

In a detailed study of the distribution and abundance of fishes in the small streams of Champaign County, Illinois, Thompson and Hunt (1930) found that the number of fish per unit area varies from seven per square yard in the extreme headwaters to two per square yard in the larger streams. However, this shrink in the number of fish downstream is more than counterbalanced by an increase in the average size of the individual fishes.

Intensive, critical work on the fundamental problems of total stream productivity is greatly needed in America. There seems to be a basis for believing that, in a general way, the *physical* features of stream environments are relatively more influential in streams than they are in lakes, but great care must be exercised in applying such a conclusion, since under some conditions the chemical features modify the whole composition of a stream or portions of a stream.

Rivers. The discussions in this book have dealt, in so far as it has been possible, with the unmodified, uncontaminated natural waters. Unfortunately for any fundamental limnological consideration of rivers, practical interests have directed virtually all of the river investigations toward pollution problems. This is particularly true of the long-continued, intensive researches, which, had they been done on uncontaminated rivers, would have yielded much of fundamental limnological interest. These investigations are full of extremely valuable results, but it is usually impossible to isolate the pollution influences sufficiently to reconstruct the original conditions. The Illinois River has received the most extensive and long-continued investigation of any large American river. In many respects, it is better known biologically than any other river in the world; but the pollution of this river is of such an age and of such a magnitude that most of the vast accumulation of information deals with an already contaminated water. Nevertheless, since the productivity of this river has been more extensively studied than any other, it seems desirable to consider it briefly here. Table 55 presents data on the production of the bottom fauna and weed fauna in the middle section of the river which is approximately the most productive section. A portion of Richardson's summary (1921) of extensive researches on the Illinois River is quoted here at length, since not only are the salient results so clearly and adequately stated but also the summary includes a statement of many of the fundamental production influences and would be important in directing, in part, an approach to limnological examinations of similar rivers or even, to some extent, of other types of rivers.

The *upper* Illinois River is, under present conditions, mainly a mass of plant and animal weeds—forms which occupy the polluted waters to the practical exclusion of everything useful to human kind—but the current of this section carries elements of a normal fertility to the lower reaches of the river, depositing a large part of them finally in the silts and sediments of river and lake in forms available for the nutrition of normal aquatic life, but bearing also an immense quantity to the mouth of the stream where it escapes unutilized into the Mississippi.

TABLE 55. BOTTOM AND WEED FAUNA, ILLINOIS RIVER
Middle section, Copperas Creek Dam to Lagrange; distance, 59.3 miles (1915)
Modified from Richardson (1921)

Areas	Approximate acreage	Bottom and weed fauna, lb. per acre			Total stocks bottom or weed animals, lb.	Hypothetical fish yield, lb. at 5:1[1]	
		Bottom	Weed	Bottom and weed		Total	Per acre
River, all zones............	5,900	705	.....	.....	4,159,500	831,900	141
Lakes,[2] all zones (bottom fauna only)..............	52,760	255	.....	.....	13,453,800	2,690,760	51
Lakes, 0–4 ft. (weed fauna only)....................	29,700	...	2,118	.....	62,904,600	12,580,920	423
All lake area (bottom and weed fauna).............	52,760	...	.....	1,447	76,358,400	15,271,680	289
Total acreage...........	61,900	...	.....	1,300	80,517,900	16,103,580[3]	260[3]

[1] Feeding ratio (5:1) is the estimate of Walter for carp and carplike fishes and is close to estimates for trout.
[2] Lakes referred to are those immediately associated with the river.
[3] Actual catch in this district in 1908 was 11,050,000 lb., or 178 lb. per acre.

The river system below Chillicothe varies enormously in the productiveness of its different parts, the richest of them being the weedy margins of the shallower lakes, and the poorest those sections of the river channel which are swept comparatively bare of sediments by a relatively swift flow. In the river itself, much the most abundant product is found where the current is most sluggish, and the bottom sediments are consequently deepest and are most heavily charged with organic materials originally washed into the stream by rains or poured into it by sewers of cities and towns and transformed by oxidation into compounds suitable for the nutrition of clean-water plants and animals.

In a stretch of the river above Havana, which, with its adjacent lakes, is the richest part of the Illinois River system, the inshore and bottom fauna of the lakes averages in weight to the acre about twice as much as that of the river, and it is in the lakes that the fisheries give their highest yield. The bottom soils of the lakes are, indeed, richer in organic matter, as a rule, than are those of the river opposite, and the muds of the marginal waters of these lakes are richer than those of their deeper parts—facts traceable, in part, no doubt, to the more abundant light and higher temperature of the shallower waters and the consequent greater growth of plants whose decay enriches the soil from which they sprang.

At ordinary high-water levels, the current of the river from Chillicothe to the mouth varies from 1 to 2 miles per hour, according to the slope of the bottom, the width of the bed, and the presence or absence of obstructions; and at the highest water it does not much exceed 3 miles per hour for any important distance. At ordinary midsummer levels, the current rate per hour varies in different sections from ½ a mile to 1 mile. At lowest water, it drops, between Chillicothe and the foot of Peoria Lake, to as little as 0.29 miles per hour.

Above Havana the bottom, both along the shores and in the channel, is, with some exceptions, a rather deep black mud; but below Havana, this shades gradually into hard clay or sand and shells, soft mud failing completely in the channel for long distances. The quantity of inshore vegetation is negligible in the river proper, even in the driest seasons, since the opening of the sanitary canal of the Sanitary District of Chicago in 1900. The bottom-land lakes between Copperas Creek and Lagrange are gradually filling with river silt and a growth of plants. A few have sandy beaches next the eastern bluffs, but the bottoms of all are otherwise of deep black mud, mixed in the shallow water along shore with coarse rotting vegetation. In midsummer, the margins of all the deeper lakes, to a depth of 4 to 6 ft., are well supplied with vegetation, while the shallower lakes are in many cases weedy over their entire acreage.

From Chillicothe to Lagrange, the animal life of both channel and shore waters is almost wholly mollusks (86 to 99 per cent in collections made); but below Lagrange, insect larvae (caddis worms and May-fly larvae) were more abundant than above in the shore muds, the ratio of mollusks falling to 31 to 65 per cent. In the deeper, opener lakes, mollusks made 77 to 96 per cent of the collections; and in the shallower, more weedy lakes, 36 to 79 per cent.

Speaking generally, the richest sections of the river floor are those with the least average slope and the slowest current and, therefore, with the most abundant sediments. The quantity of the bottom fauna diminishes rapidly downstream from Chillicothe, averaging 555 lb. to the acre for the upper 60 miles (the weight of the shells of the mollusks being in all cases deducted), 88 lb. for the 42½ miles next following, and 10.4 lb. for the lower 77 miles. The general average for the river channel from Chillicothe to the mouth was 261 lb. per acre. That for Copperas Creek to Lagrange, within which section lay the 12 principal lakes studied, was 705 lb. per acre; and the highest sectional yield was 2,693 lb. per acre between Copperas Creek and Havana. The highest local yield was found in the lower half of this Copperas Creek–Havana section, whose channel product rose to 5,196 lb. per acre. These enormous yields in the stretch above Havana were evidently due, at least in great measure, to the sluggish current and consequent heavy sedimentation and to the great predominance (99 per cent) of relatively large, thick-shelled snails, edible only by the larger fishes, armed with a powerful crushing apparatus in jaws and throat.

In the muddy section of river above Havana, the channel yields approximated or even surpassed those of the shallow water alongshore; but below Havana, where mud is largely replaced by sand, clay, or shells, the channel yields were only 5 to 10 per cent those of the longshore zone.

Comparing river and lakes between Copperas Creek and Lagrange (59.3 miles), we find that the average bottom yield per acre of 12 lakes examined was about one-third that of the river opposite them but that it was practically the same as the average for the entire river from Chillicothe to the mouth. The deeper lakes with sandy beaches at one side yielded about twice as much per acre as the shallower lakes with mud banks all around.

In the deeper bottom-land lakes surrounded by mud banks, the shore belt, to a depth not exceeding 6 ft., yielded about three times as much bottom fauna per acre as the deeper open water of these lakes; but in the sand-beach lakes, this relation was reversed, the deeper bottom yielding five or six times as much as that within the 6-ft. line.

The foregoing statements all apply to the animals living in or on the bottom muds; but in the shallow, *weedy areas* of lakes and backwaters, the small invertebrate animals living on and among the weeds greatly exceed both in number and in weight per acre the fauna of the bottom itself, aggregating in many collections made near Havana in 1914 from 1,100 to nearly 2,600 lb. per acre, with an average of 2,118 lb.—quantities to be compared with an average of 255 lb. of *bottom fauna* per acre from the lakes of the same district.

Combining weed and bottom faunas of our collections and applying their joint averages to the entire area of lake and backwater between Copperas Creek and Havana, we get a yield of 1,447 lb. per acre, to be compared with 705 lb. per acre for the unusually rich sections of the river opposite.

From analyses of the bottom muds of the river channel and estimates of the nitrogen content of total bottom fauna per acre, it appears that the nitrogen in the river sediments is many hundred times the nitrogen of the flesh of the animals living in them and that the total dry organic matter in the channel muds is several thousand times the dry weight of this bottom fauna.

Chemical analyses show that the bottom soils of the lakes are richer in organic matter than those of the river opposite them and that in the lakes themselves the bottom soil is richer near the shore than at the center.

The plankton of the river passing Havana in a year amounts to about 200,-000 tons live weight, equivalent to 4,000 to 10,000 tons dry weight. This is, roughly, 20 to 50 times the total dry weight of the flesh of the animals of the bottom muds of the lakes from Copperas Creek to the mouth, a distance of 138 miles.

An estimated total of 600,000 tons dry weight of organic matter, suspended and dissolved, passed Chillicothe in 1914. This is 60 to 150 times the dry weight of the plankton that passed Havana in 12 months (1909 and 1910) and 3,000 times the dry weight of the total bottom fauna of 1915 from Copperas Creek to the mouth of the river. The dry weight of nitrogen in the above organic matter was sufficient to replace the nitrogen in the plankton of a year from 92 to 232 times.

The plankton per cubic meter of water was greater throughout the year in

Thompson Lake than in the river opposite in 1909 and 1910, the difference being greatest at times of lowest production (midsummer and winter) in both river and lake.

The river plankton is constantly settling to the bottom to an important degree, as is shown by the composition of the bottom ooze and by the stomach contents of small invertebrates living on and in it. In June, 1914, living, moribund, or recently dead limnetic plankton was more abundant in the upper layers of the ooze than the normal bottom plankton or old organic detritus, as was shown by the food of Sphaeriidae, Trichoptera, and Chironomidae, and it made also an important part of the food of large detritus-eating gastropods (Viviparidae, Pleuroceridae, etc.).

There is a much greater loss of plankton downstream than can be explained by dilution merely. The falling off in plankton per cubic meter between Havana and Grafton amounted, during nine months of the growing season, to approximately 62 per cent, notwithstanding the normal rate of multiplication of the planktons as they passed downstream. These losses were greatest when the current was slowest and settling consequently easiest. They were not due to lack of food, because the percentage of nitrogen and the nitrates increased from Havana downward.

In a later paper, Richardson (1928) presented further studies on the productivity of various sections of the Illinois River. Increasing pollution had caused clean-water conditions to recede much farther downstream. As a result, various marked changes were taking place in the bottom fauna of the various parts of the river affected, and these changes were studied in detail. He concluded that, except where the pollution is very heavy, the small bottom animals, on the whole, constitute a better index of the fundamental or permanent sanitary conditions of the water than does the frequently rapidly changing dissolved oxygen or the plankton.

It should be pointed out that owing to the very slow current in much of its course, to the associated lakes and other extrachannel waters, and to other circumstances, the Illinois River is, in some respects, not typical of rivers in general. It must not be expected that its features of productivity will be commonly repeated in all rivers at large. However, the splendid work of Forbes, Richardson, and others on this river is outstanding and will serve as a background and a guide to investigations on rivers for some time to come.

The reader who desires to go further into the productivity of rivers is referred to the bibliography (page 505) for citations.

Rivers wholly free from pollution are now either difficult to find or remote from the more populated regions. Contaminations commonly mask or modify the original productivity. It is hoped that the future will produce some fundamental research on unmodified running waters of true river magnitude.

TABLE 56. FOOD OF BOTTOM INVERTEBRATES, ILLINOIS RIVER CHANNEL, AT HAVANA, JULY, 1914

Food found in the stomachs of plankton feeders

Modified from Richardson (1921)

Species examined	Fine organic detritus (dead matter)	Bacteria in detritus or dead plankton	Settling limnetic and normal-bottom plankton			Attached microorganisms
			Diatoms	Algae	Protozoa, Rotifera, etc.	
Mollusca: Sphaerium striatinum	Trace	Abundant	Cyclotella (common) Navicula (common) Melosira (common), etc.	Scenedesmus Coelastrum	Chlamydomonas Colorless flagellates[1] Synchaeta pectinata	
Lampsilis parvus	Trace	Very abundant	Cyclotella (common) Navicula (common) Melosira (common), etc.	Pediastrum	Chlamydomonas Colorless flagellates and ciliates[1]	
Campeloma subsolidum	Very abundant	Abundant	Navicula Synedra Cyclotella Melosira (common)	Pediastrum Coelastrum Scenedesmus (common)	Chlamydomonas (common) Pandorina	Pleurococcus (?) (common)
Viviparus contectoides	Abundant	Abundant	Navicula Synedra Cyclotella Melosira (common)	....	....	Pleurococcus (?) (common) Rhizoclonium
Insecta: Larva of caddis-fly (Hydropsyche sp.)	None	Some	Cyclotella Melosira Navicula, etc.	Scenedesmus (common)	Chlamydomonas (common)	
Chironomid larva, ½ in. red	None	....	Many species	Scenedesmus (common)		
Crustacea: Asellus aquaticus	Abundant	Abundant				
Bryozoa: Urnatella gracilis	None	....	Navicula Cyclotella Melosira Fragilaria Surirella	Scenedesmus	Eudorina Pandorina	
Annelida: Tubificid worm	Very abundant	Very abundant				
Platyhelminthes: Planarian	None	A few	Melosira	Coelastrum	Chlamydomonas	

[1] Normal protozoan inhabitants of the thin-bottom ooze.

Biotic Potential and Environmental Resistance

The subject of biotic potential and environmental resistance in lotic situations is as yet unorganized and almost unknown. Therefore, only certain very general comments can be made here. The severity of most lotic situations is self-evident. The hazards of current, molar agents, floods, droughts, varying water level, ice action, and other exigencies characteristic of running waters in general must result in great mortality in the biota. A high biotic potential seems certainly to be a necessity for any organism which is to maintain itself permanently in lotic surroundings. Where the environmental severity imposes such a resistance to the success of organisms, only a biotic potential sufficiently high to insure an excess over the mortality can make possible a biota for these situations. Since, in some surroundings at least, the productivity of running waters is fairly high, the biotic potential is evidently of high magnitude.

BIBLIOGRAPHY

This bibliography includes not only lists of literature specifically referred to in the text but also many additional references selected principally because of their usefulness in making general entry into the subjects involved, in supplementing material given in the text, and in supplying important special bibliographies. Completeness is not attempted in any of the sections. In this revised edition many older references have been omitted, not because of lost value, but in the interests of economy of space and to make room for recent works.

BIBLIOGRAPHIES ON LIMNOLOGY

In addition to the comprehensive general bibliographies, such as the Zoological Record, Concilium Bibliographicum, Bibliographica Zoologica, Biological Abstracts, and others, the following special bibliographies on limnology and closely related subjects are useful.

Bericht über die Literatur der Binnengewässerkunde für die Jahre 1926 und 1927. Arch. f. Hydrobiol., Lit. Suppl. III, 1931, 638 pp.

Bibliographia Hydrobiologica Rossica. In each number of the Russ. Hydrobiol. Zeit., 1921–.

Bibliographie limnologique. Ann. biol. lacustre, **2**: 403–479. 1908 (literature for 1906–1907).

CHUMLEY, J. 1910. Bibliography of Limnological Literature. In Murray and Pullar's Bathymetrical Survey of the Scottish Fresh-water Lochs, **1**: 659–753.

Die Binnengewässer. (Literature lists at end of each vol.; 18 vols., 1925–1950).

Die Limnologische Literatur des Jahres 1923. Arch. f. Hydrobiol., Lit.-Suppl. I, 1925, 165 pp.

Die Limnologische Literatur der Jahre 1924 und 1925, sowie Nachträge für 1923. Arch. f. Hydrobiol., Lit.-Suppl. II, 1927, 317 pp.

FRITSCH, F. E. 1920. Bibliography of English and American Papers on Hydrobiology, 1910–1919. Rev. d'hydrol., **1**: 351–364.

Jahresübersicht der Hydrographischen und Hydrobiologischen Literatur für das Jahr 1908. Int. Rev. d. ges. Hydrobiol. u. Hydrogr., Suppl. Bd. 1, 76 pp.

KLEEREKOPER, H. 1944. Introducão ao Estudo da Limnologia. Rio de Janeiro, 329 pp. (Bibliography on pp. 269–304.)

LAMPERT, K. 1925. Das Leben der Binnengewässer. 3 Auf. Lit.-Verz., pp. 798–892.

Literatur-Supplement für 1908. Int. Rev. d. ges. Hydrobiol. u. Hydrogr., **2**: 77–233.

WARD, H. B. 1899. Freshwater Investigations during the Last Five Years. Trans. Am. Micr. Soc., **20**: 261–336.

JOURNALS AND OTHER PUBLICATIONS DEVOTED LARGELY OR WHOLLY TO LIMNOLOGY

1. General

American Society of Limnology and Oceanography, Special Publications, No. 1–20, 1936–1949 (formerly Limnological Society of America).

Annales de biologique lacustre. 1906–1927. 15 vols.

Archiv für Hydrobiologie. 1905–. Stuttgart. (Formerly, Forschungsberichte aus der Biologischen Station zu Plon; later, Archiv für Hydrobiologie und Planktonkunde.)

Folia Limnologica Scandinavica. Copenhagen. 1943–.

Hydrobiologica. Hague. 1948–.

Internationale Revue d. ges. Hydrobiol. u. Hydrogr., Leipzig. 1908–.

Japanese Journal of Limnology. Tokyo. 1931–1944; 1949–.

Russische Hydrobiologische Zeitschrift. Biol. Wolga-Station, Saratov (vol. 1 in 1921).

Schweizerische Zeitschrift für Hydrologie (Revue suisse d'hydrologie). Zurich. 1920–. (Formerly Zeitschrift für Hydrologie; Revue d'hydrologie.)

Verhandlungen der Internationalen Vereinigung für Theoretische und Angewandte Limnologie. Stuttgart. 1923–.

2. Publications of Inland Biological Stations

Arbeiten der Biologischen Station zu Kossino. Moscow (vol. 1 in 1924).

Arbeiten der Biologischen Oka-Station. Muron (vol. 5 in 1928).

Arbeiten der Hydrobiologischen Station der Swenigorod und der Moskova. Moscow (vol. 6 in 1930).

Arbeiten der Biologischen Wolga-Station. Saratov (vol. 10 in 1930).

Archiva Biologica Hungarica. (Formerly, Arbeiten des Ungarischen Biologischen Forschungsinstitutes; Archivum Balatonicum.) Tihany. 1926–.

Archivum Hydrobiologji i Rybactwa (Arch. d'hydrobiol. et d'ichthyol.). Lake Wigry Station, Poland (vol. 1 in 1926).

Bulletin de l'Institut des recherches biologiques et de la Station biologique à l'Université de Perm. Perm (vol. 6 in 1928).

Folia Zoologica et Hydrobiologica. Organ des Systematisch-Zoologischen Instituts und der Hydrobiologischen Station der Lettländischen Universität. Riga (vol. 4 in 1932).

Reports of the Lake Sevan Station. Elenowka, Armenia (No. 1 in 1927).

Report of the Reelfoot Lake Biological Station. Nashville. 1937–.

Travaux de la Station biologique de Dniepre. Kiew (No. 4 in 1928).

Travaux de la Station biologique du Caucase du Nord. Kaukasus (vol. 3 in 1930).

Travaux de l'Institut des recherches biologiques et de la Station biologique à l'université de Perm. Perm (vol. 1 in 1928).

BOOKS DEALING WITH LIMNOLOGY OR WITH CLOSELY RELATED SUBJECTS

ALLEE, W. C., O. PARK, A. E. EMERSON, T. PARK, and K. P. SCHMIDT. 1949. Principles of Animal Ecology. Philadelphia, 837 pp.

BAUMANN, E. 1930–1931. Limnologische Terminologie. In Abderhalden's Handbuch der biol. Arbeitsmeth., Teil. 8, Heft 1–5. Berlin, 776 pp.

BREHM, V. 1930. Einführung in die Limnologie. Berlin, 261 pp.

CARPENTER, K. E. 1928. Life in Inland Waters. New York, 267 pp.

CHAPMAN, R. N. 1931. Animal Ecology. New York, 464 pp.

CLEMENTS, F. E., and V. E. SHELFORD. 1939. Bio-ecology. New York, 425 pp.

FOREL, F. A. 1892–1904. Le Léman. Monographie limnologique. Lausanne, 3 vols.

―――. 1901. Handbuch der Seenkunde. Allgemeine Limnologie. Stuttgart, 249 pp.

HENTSCHEL, E. 1923. Grundzüge der Hydrobiologie. Jena, 221 pp.

KAWAMURA, T. 1918. [Freshwater Biology.] (In Japanese.) 2 vols. Tokyo, 616 pp.

KLEEREKOPER, H. 1944. Intradução ao Estudo da Limnologica. Rio de Janeiro, 329 pp.

LAGLER, K. F. 1949. Studies in Freshwater Fishery Biology. Ann Arbor, Mich., 240 pp.

LENZ, F. 1928. Einführung in die Biologie der Süsswasserseen. Berlin, 221 pp.

Limnological Aspects of Water Supply and Waste Disposal. 1949. (Symposium; various authors.) Publ. Am. Assoc. Adv. Sci., 87 pp.

MELLANBY, HELEN. 1938. Animal Life in Fresh Water. London, 296 pp.

MURRAY, SIR JOHN, and L. PULLAR. 1910. Bathymetrical Survey of the Scottish Fresh-water Lochs. Edinburgh, 6 vols.

NEEDHAM, J. G., and J. T. LLOYD. 1930. The Life of Inland Waters, 2d ed. Springfield, 438 pp.

PEARSE, A. S. 1939. Animal Ecology. 2d ed. New York, 642 pp.

RUTTNER, F. 1940. Grundriss der Limnologie. Berlin, 167 pp.

SHELFORD, V. E. 1929. Laboratory and Field Ecology. Baltimore, 608 pp.

THIENEMANN, A. 1926. Limnologie. Breslau, 108 pp.

UENO, M. 1935. [An Introduction to Limnological Biology.] (In Japanese.) Tokyo, 276 pp.

WARD, H. B., and G. C. WHIPPLE. 1918. Fresh-water Biology. New York, 1111 pp.

WELCH, P. S. 1948. Limnological Methods. Philadelphia, 381 pp.

WHIPPLE, G. C. 1927. The Microscopy of Drinking Water. 4th ed., rev. by G. M. Fair and M. C. Whipple. New York, 586 pp.

YOSHIMURA, S. 1937. [Limnology.] (In Japanese.) Tokyo, 451 pp.

ZERNOY, S. A. 1934. [General Marine and Fresh-water Biology.] (In Russian.) 503 pp.

GENERAL LIMNOLOGICAL SURVEYS

BIRGE, E. A., and C. JUDAY. 1914. A Limnological Study of the Finger Lakes of New York. Bull. U.S. Bur. Fish., **32**: 525–609.

———. 1920. A Limnological Reconnaissance of West Okoboji. Univ. Iowa Studies in Nat. Hist., **9**: 3–56.

———. 1921. Further Limnological Observations on the Finger Lakes of New York. Bull. U.S. Bur. Fish., **37**: 210–252.

EVERMANN, B. W., and H. W. CLARK. 1920. Lake Maxinkuckee, a Physical and Biological Survey. Dept. Conserv., State of Ind., 2 vols.

FISH, C. J. 1929. Preliminary Report on the Cooperative Survey of Lake Erie. Season of 1928. Bull. Buffalo Soc. Nat. Sci., **14**: 7–220.

———. 1929. A Preliminary Report on the Joint Survey of Lake Erie. Suppl. to 18th Ann. Rept. State of N.Y. Conserv. Comm., pp. 39–106.

MURRAY, SIR JOHN, and L. PULLAR. 1910. Bathymetrical Survey of the Scottish Fresh-water Lochs. Edinburgh, 6 vols.

NEEDHAM, J. G., C. JUDAY, E. MOORE, C. K. SIBLEY, and J. W. TITCOMB. 1922. A Biological Survey of Lake George, N.Y. State of N.Y. Conserv. Comm., pp. 3–78.

OVER, W. H., and E. P. CHURCHILL. 1927. A Preliminary Report of the Biological Survey of the Lakes of South Dakota. South Dakota Geol. Nat. Hist. Surv., Circ. 29, ser. 27, pp. 2–18.

PENNAK, R. W. 1941. An Introduction to the Limnology of Northern Colorado. Univ. Colo. Studies, Ser. D, **1**: 203–220.

Progress in Biological Inquiries, U.S. Bur. Fish. Appendices to the Report of the Commissioner of Fisheries. (Annual issues containing résumés of limnological work on the Great Lakes, inland lakes, and rivers.)

Scott, F. M. 1927. Introduction to the Limnology of Searsville Lake. Stanford Univ. Publ., Biol. Sci., **5**: 3–83.

Scott, W. 1916. Report on the Lakes of the Tippecanoe Basin (Indiana). Indiana Univ. Studies, **3**: 3–39.

———. 1931. Investigations of Indiana Lakes. 3. The Lakes of Northeastern Indiana. Dept. Conserv., State of Ind., Publ. 107, pp. 59–145.

Shantz, H. L. 1907. A Biological Study of the Lakes of the Pike's Peak Region. Trans. Am. Micr. Soc., **27**: 75–98.

Stromsten, F. A. 1927. Lake Okoboji as a Type of Aquatic Environment. Univ. Iowa Studies in Nat. Hist., **12**: 1–52.

Thienemann, A. 1926. Die Binnengewässer Mitteleuropas. Eine limnologische Einführung. Die Binnengewässer, Bd. I, 255 pp.

Thienemann, A., and others. 1930–1931. Tropische Binnengewässer. Arch. f. Hydrobiol., Suppl. Bd. 8, Heft. 1–4, 802 pp.; Suppl. Bd. 9, Heft 1–4, 764 pp.

Ward, H. B. 1904. A Biological Reconnoissance of the Elevated Lakes in the Sierras and Rockies. Trans. Am. Micr. Soc., **25**: 127–154.

Young, R. T. 1924. The Life of Devils Lake, North Dakota. Publ. N.D. Biol. Sta., 116 pp.

INTRODUCTION

Adams, C. C. 1913. Guide to the Study of Animal Ecology. New York, 183 pp.

Agassiz, L. 1850. Lake Superior: Its Physical Character, Vegetation, and Animals, Compared with Those of Other and Similar Regions, with a Narrative of the Tour by J. E. Cabot. Boston, 428 pp.

Bigelow, H. B. 1931. Oceanography. Boston, 263 pp.

Chumley, J. 1910. Bibliography of Limnological Literature. In Murray and Pullar's Bathymetrical Survey of the Scottish Fresh-water Lochs, **1**: 659–753.

Deevey, E. S. 1940. Limnological Studies in Connecticut. V. Contribution to Regional Limnology. Am. Jour. Sci., **238**: 717–741.

———. 1942. A Re-examination of Thoreau's "Walden." Quart. Rev. Biol., **17**: 1–11.

———. 1942. Some Geographic Aspects of Limnology. Sci. Monthly, **55**: 423–434.

Fish, C. J. 1929. Preliminary Report on the Cooperative Survey of Lake Erie. Season of 1928. Bull. Buffalo Soc. Nat. Sci. **14**: 7–220.

———. 1929. A Preliminary Report on the Joint Survey of Lake Erie. Suppl. to 18th Ann. Rept., State of N.Y. Conserv. Comm., pp. 39–106.

Forbes, S. A. 1893. A Preliminary Report on the Aquatic Invertebrate Fauna of the Yellowstone National Park, Wyoming, and of the Flathead Region of Montana. Bull. U.S. Fish Comm. for 1891, pp. 207–258.

Forel, F. A. 1892–1904. Le Léman. Monographie limnologique. Lausanne, 3 vols.

———. 1901. Handbuch der Seenkunde. Allgemeine Limnologie. Stuttgart, 249 pp.

Herdman, Sir W. A. 1923. Founders of Oceanography and Their Work. London, 340 pp.

Johnstone, J. 1928. An Introduction to Oceanography. London, 368 pp.

Juday, C. 1910. Some European Biological Stations. Trans. Wis. Acad. Sci., Arts, Let., **16**: 1257–1277.

KOFOID, C. A. 1898. The Fresh-water Biological Stations of America. Am. Nat., **32**: 391–406.

———. 1910. The Biological Stations of Europe. U.S. Bur. Ed., Bull. 4, 360 pp.

LENZ, F. 1927. Limnologische Laboratorien. Abderhalden's Handb. d. biol. Arbeitsmeth., Abt. 9, Tiel 2, Heft 2, Lief. 232.

MILNER, J. W. 1874. The Fisheries of the Great Lakes. Rept U.S. Fish Comm., 1872–1873, pp. 1–75.

NEEDHAM, J. G. 1941. Fragments of the History of Hydrobiology. In A Symposium on Hydrobiology. Univ. Wis. Press, pp. 3–11.

NEEDHAM, J. G., and J. T. LLOYD. 1930. The Life of Inland Waters, 2d ed. Springfield, 438 pp.

PENNAK, R. W. 1945. Some Aspects of the Regional Limnology of Northern Colorado. Univ. Colo. Studies, ser. D, **2**: 263–293.

REIGHARD, J. E. 1894. A Biological Examination of Lake St. Clair. Preliminary Account of Work Done during the Summer of 1893 by the Party Maintained by the Michigan Fish Commission. Bull. Mich. Fish Comm., No. 4, 60 pp.

SHELFORD, V. E. 1929. Laboratory and Field Ecology. Baltimore, 608 pp.

STIMSON, W. 1870. On the Deep-water Fauna of Lake Michigan. Am. Nat., **4**: 403–404.

WARD, H. B. 1896. A Biological Examination of Lake Michigan in the Traverse Bay Region. Bull. Mich. Fish. Comm., No. 6, 100 pp.

———. 1899. The Fresh-water Biological Stations of the World. Science, **9**: 497–508. Also in the Smithsonian Rept. for 1898, pp. 499–513.

LAKES, THEIR ORIGIN AND DIVERSITY

BIRGE, E. A., and C. JUDAY. 1914. The Inland Lakes of Wisconsin. The Hydrography and Morphometry of the Lakes. Wisconsin Geol. Nat. Hist. Surv., Bull. 27, Sci. ser. 9, 137 pp.

BROUGHTON, W. A. 1941. The Geology, Ground Water and Lake Basin Seal of the Region South of the Muskellunge Moraine, Vilas County, Wisconsin. Trans. Wis. Acad. Sci., Arts, Let., **33**: 5–20.

BROWN, C. J. D. 1943. How Many Lakes in Michigan? Michigan Conserv., **12**: 5–6.

CARPENTER, K. E. 1928. Life in Inland Waters. New York, 267 pp.

CASPERI, W. A. 1910. Deposits of the Scottish Fresh-water Lochs. In Murray and Pullar's Bathymetrical Survey of the Scottish Fresh-water Lochs, **1**: 261–274.

CHAPPIUS, P. A. 1927. Die Tierwelt der unterirdeschen Gewässer. Die Binnengewässer, Bd. III, 176 pp.

COLEMAN, A. P. 1922. Glacial and Post-glacial Lakes in Ontario. Univ. Toronto Studies, Publ. Ont. Fish. Res. Lab., No. 10, pp. 5–76.

FOREL, F. A. 1892–1904. Le Léman. Monographie limnologique. Lausanne, 3 vols.

HARDING, S. T. 1942. Lakes. Chap. VI, pp. 220–243. In Hydrology by O. S. Meinzer. New York, 712 pp.

JOHNSON, D. W. 1919. Shore Processes and Shoreline Development. New York, 584 pp.

JUDAY, C., and W. W. MELOCHE. 1944. Physical and Chemical Evidence Relating to the Lake Basin Seal in Certain Areas of the Trout Lake Region of Wisconsin. Trans. Wis. Acad. Sci., Arts, Let., **35**: 157–174.

KINDLE, E. M. 1925. The Bottom Deposits of Lake Ontario. Trans. R. Soc. Canada, 3d ser., **19**: 47–102.

LUNDQVIST, G. 1927. Bodenablagerungen und Entwicklungstypen der Seen. Die Binnengewässer, Bd. II, 124 pp.

MEINZER, O. E. 1942. Hydrology. New York, 712 pp.

MURRAY, J. 1910. Characteristics of Lakes in General and Their Distribution over the Surface of the Globe. In Murray and Pullar's Bathymetrical Survey of the Scottish Fresh-water Lochs, 1: 514–658.

MUTTKOWSKI, R. A. 1918. The Fauna of Lake Mendota—A Qualitative and Quantitative Survey with Special Reference to the Insects. Trans. Wis. Acad. Sci., Arts, Let., 19: 374–482.

NAUMANN, E. 1929. Die Bodenablagerung der Seen. Verh. d. Int. Ver. f. theor. u. angew. Limn., 4: 32–106.

PESTA, O. 1929. Der Hochgebirgssee der Alpen. Die Binnengewässer, Bd. VIII, 156 pp.

POTZGER, J. E., and I. T. WILSON. 1941. Post-Pleistocene Forest Migration as indicated by Sediments from Three Inland Lakes. Am. Midl. Nat., 25: 270–289.

ROELOFS, E. W. 1944. Water Soils in Relation to Lake Productivity. Tech. Bull. 190, Mich. State Coll. Agr. Exp. Sta., 31 pp.

SCOTT, I. D. 1921. Inland Lakes of Michigan. Michigan Geol. Biol. Surv., Publ. 30, Geol. ser., 25: 383 pp.

SELLARDS, E. H. 1914. Some Florida Lakes and Lake Basins. 6th Ann. Rept. Fla. State Geol. Surv., pp. 115–160.

THIENEMANN, A. 1926. Die Binnegewässer Mitteleuropas. Die Binnengewässer, Bd. I, 255 pp.

TOLMAN, C. F. 1937. Ground water. New York, 610 pp.

TWENHOFEL, W. H., and W. A. BROUGHTON. 1939. The Sediments of Crystal Lake, an Oligotrophic Lake in Vilas County, Wisconsin. Am. Jour. Sci., 237: 231–252.

VEATCH, J. O. 1931. Classification of Water Soils Is Proposed. Quart. Bull., Mich. State Coll. Agr. Exp. Sta., 14: 20–23.

WILSON, I. T. 1936. A Study of Sedimentation of Winona Lake. Proc. Ind. Acad. Sci., 45: 295–304.

———. 1938. The Accumulated Sediment in Tippecanoe Lake and a Comparison with Winona Lake. Proc. Ind. Acad. Sci., 47: 234–253.

———. 1943. Varves in Sandusky Bay Sediments. Ohio Jour. Sci., 43: 195–197.

———. 1945. A Study of the Sediment in Douglas Lake, Cheboygan County, Michigan. Papers Mich. Acad. Sci., Arts, Let., 30: 391–419.

WILSON, I. T., and J. E. POTZGER. 1943. Pollen Studies of Sediments from Douglas Lake, Cheboygan County, and Middle Fish Lake, Montmorency County, Michigan. Proc. Ind. Acad. Sci., 52: 87–92.

PHYSICAL CONDITIONS AND RELATED PHENOMENA

ATKINS, W. R. G. 1925. On the Thermal Stratification of Sea Water and Its Importance for the Algal Plankton. Jour. Marine Biol. Assoc., 13: 693–699.

———. 1932. Solar Radiation and Its Transmission through Air and Water. Jour. cons. perm. int. l'expl. mer., 7: 171–211.

ATKINS, W. R. G., G. L. CLARKE, H. PATTERSON, C. L. UTTERBACK, and A. ÅNGSTROM. 1938. Measurement of Submarine Daylight. Jour. du conseil, 13: 37–57.

ATKINS, W. R. G., and H. H. POOLE. 1930. The Photochemical and Photoelectrical Measurement of Submarine Illumination. Jour. Marine Biol. Assoc., 16: 509–514.

BANCROFT, W. D. 1919. The Color of Water. Jour. Franklin Inst., 187: 459–485.

BARNES, T. C., and T. L. JAHN. 1934. Properties of Water of Biological Interest. Quart. Rev. Biol., **9**: 293–341.

BIRGE, E. A. 1904. The Thermocline and Its Biological Significance. Trans. Am. Micr. Soc., **25**: 5–33.

———. 1915. The Heat Budgets of American and European Lakes. Trans. Wis. Acad. Sci., Arts, Let., **18**: 1–47.

———. 1916. The Work of the Wind in Warming a Lake. Trans. Wis. Acad. Sci., Arts, Let., **18**: 341–391.

———. 1922. A Second Report on Limnological Apparatus. Trans. Wis. Acad. Sci., Arts, Let., **20**: 533–552.

BIRGE, E. A., and C. JUDAY. 1914. A Limnological Study of the Finger Lakes of New York. Bull. U.S. Bur. Fish., **32**: 525–609.

———. 1920. A Limnological Reconnaissance of West Okeboji. Univ. Iowa Studies in Nat. Hist., **9**: 1–56.

———. 1929. Transmission of Solar Radiation by the Waters of Inland Lakes. Trans. Wis. Acad. Sci., Arts, Let., **24**: 509–580.

———. 1929. Penetration of Solar Radiation into Lakes as Measured by the Thermopile. Bull. Nat. Res. Council, **68**: 61–76.

———. 1930. A Second Report on Solar Radiation and Inland Lakes. Trans. Wis. Acad. Sci., Arts, Let., **25**: 285–335.

———. 1931. A Third Report on Solar Radiation and Inland Lakes. Trans. Wis. Acad. Sci., Arts, Let., **26**: 383–425.

———. 1932. Solar Radiation and Inland Lakes, 4th Report. Observations of 1931. Trans. Wis. Acad. Sci., Arts, Let., **27**: 523–562.

BIRGE, E. A., C. JUDAY, and H. W. MARCH. 1928. The Temperature of the Bottom Deposits of Lake Mendota. Trans. Wis. Acad. Sci., Arts, Let., **23**: 187–231.

CHANDLER, D. C. 1942. Limnological Studies of Western Lake Erie. II. Light Penetration and Its Relation to Turbidity. Ecology, **23**: 41–52.

CHRYSTAL, G. 1910. Seiches and Other Oscillations of Lake Surfaces, Observed by the Scottish Lake Survey. In Murray and Pullar's Bathymetrical Survey of the Scottish Fresh-water Lochs, **1**: 29–90.

CHURCH, P. E. 1942. The Annual Temperature Cycle of Lake Michigan. I. Cooling from Late Autumn to the Terminal Point, 1941–42. Univ. Chicago, Inst. Meteor., Misc. Rept. No. 4, 48 pp.

———. 1945. The Annual Temperature Cycle of Lake Michigan. II. Spring Warming and Summer Stationary Periods, 1942. Univ. Chicago, Inst. Meteor., Misc. Rept. No. 18, 100 pp.

CLARKE, G. L. 1939. The Utilization of Solar Energy by Aquatic Organisms. Publ. Am. Assoc. Adv. Sci., No. 10, pp. 27–38.

COKER, R. E. 1938. Life in the Sea. Sci. Monthly, **46**: 299–322.

———. 1947. This Great and Wide Sea. Chapel Hill, N.C., 325 pp.

COLEMAN, A. P. 1922. Glacial and Post-glacial Lakes in Ontario. Univ. Toronto Studies, Publ. Ont. Fish. Res. Lab., No. 10, 67 pp.

CORNISH, V. 1934. Ocean Waves and Kindred Geophysical Phenomena. Cambridge, 164 pp.

DAVIS, F. J. 1941. Surface Loss of Solar and Sky Radiation by Inland Lakes. Trans. Wis. Acad. Sci., Arts, Let., **33**: 83–93.

DOODSON, A. T., R. M. CAREY, and R. BALDWIN. 1920. Theoretical Determination of the Longitudinal Seiches of Lake Geneva. Trans. R. Soc. Edinburgh, **52**: 629–642.

DORSEY, E. D. 1940. Properties of Ordinary Water-substances. New York, 673 pp.

EDDY, S. 1943. Limnological Notes on Lake Superior. Proc. Minn. Acad. Sci., **11**: 34–39.

EMERY, K. O. 1945. Transportation of Marine Beach Sand by Flotation. Jour. Sed. Pet., **15**: 84–87.

EVANS, O. F. 1938. Transportation of Sediments on Fresh-water Surfaces by Flotation. Jour. Sed. Pet., **8**: 33–35.

FOREL, F. A. 1895. Le Léman. Monographie limnologique. Vol. II. Lausanne, 651 pp.

GATES, F. C. 1926. Sand Flotation in Nature. Science, **64**: 595–596.

GREENBANK, J. 1945. Limnological Conditions in Ice-covered Lakes, Especially as Related to Winter-kill of Fish. Ecol. Monogr., **15**: 343–392.

HARDMAN, Y. 1941. The Surface Tension of Wisconsin Lake Waters. Trans. Wis. Acad. Sci., Arts, Let., **33**: 395–404.

HARVEY, H. W. 1928. Biological Chemistry and Physics of Sea Water. Cambridge, 194 pp.

————. 1945. Recent Advances in the Chemistry and Biology of Sea Water. Cambridge, 164 pp.

HELLSTRÖM, B. 1941. Wind Effects on Lakes and Rivers. Proc. R. Swedish Inst. Eng. Res., **158**: 1–191.

HENRY, A. J. 1902. Wind Velocity and Fluctuations of Water Level on Lake Erie. U.S. Dept. Agr., Weather Bur. Bull. 262.

HERDMAN, W. A. 1923. Founders of Oceanography and Their Work. London, 340 pp.

HUTCHINSON, G. E. 1941. Limnological Studies in Connecticut. IV. Mechanism of Intermediary Metabolism in Stratified Lakes. Ecol. Monogr., **11**: 21–60.

JACOBS, W. C. 1942. On the Energy Exchange between Sea and Atmosphere. Jour. Marine Res., **5**: 37–66.

JAMES, H. R., and E. A. BIRGE. 1938. A Laboratory Study of the Absorption of Light by Lake Waters. Trans. Wis. Acad. Sci., Arts, Let., **31**: 1–154.

JOHNSON, D. W. 1919. Shore Processes and Shoreline Development. New York, 584 pp.

JOHNSTONE, J. 1928. An Introduction to Oceanography. London, 368 pp.

JUDAY, C., and E. A. BIRGE. 1933. The Transparency, the Color and the Specific Conductance of the Lake Waters of Northeastern Wisconsin. Trans. Wis. Acad. Sci., Arts, Let., **28**: 205–259.

————. 1941. Hydrography and Morphometry of Some Northeastern Wisconsin Lakes. Trans. Wis. Acad. Sci., Arts, Let., **33**: 21–72.

KEMMERER, G., J. F. BOVARD, and W. R. BOORMAN. 1923. Northwestern Lakes of the United States: Biological and Chemical Studies with Reference to Possibilities in Production of Fish. Bull. U.S. Bur. Fish., **39**: 51–140.

KINDLE, E. M. 1927. The Role of Thermal Stratification in Lacustrine Sedimentation. Trans. R. Soc. Canada, **21**: 1–36.

KLUGH, A. B. 1925. Ecological Photometry and a New Instrument for Measuring Light. Ecology, **6**: 203–237.

————. 1927. Light Penetration into the Bay of Fundy and into Chamcook Lake, N.B. Ecology, **8**: 90–93.

KNUDSEN, M. 1922. On Measurement of the Penetration of Light into the Sea. Cons. perm. int. l'expl. mer, publ. circ., **76**: 1–16.

KRECKER, F. H. 1928. Periodic Oscillations in Lake Erie. Ohio State Univ., Franz Theodore Stone Lab., Contr. 1, pp. 1–22.

————. 1931. Vertical Oscillations or Seiches in Lakes as a Factor in the Aquatic Environment. Ecology, **12**: 156–163.

KREITMANN, L. 1935. Contribution à l'étude experimentale des courants lacustres. Rev. des eaux et fôrets, pp. 1–11.

McKELVEY, V. E. 1941. The Flotation of Sand in Nature. Am. Jour. Sci., **239**: 594–607.

MEINZER, O. E. 1942. Hydrology. Physics of the Earth. IX. New York, 712 pp.

NEWCOMBE, C. L., and J. V. SLATER. 1948. The Occurrence of Temperatures Unusual to American Lakes. Science, **108**: 385–386.

————. 1949. Temperature Characteristics of Sodon Lake. A Dichothermic Lake in Southeastern Michigan. Hydrobiologia, **1**: 346–378.

————. 1950. Environmental Factors of Sodon Lake—A Dichothermic Lake in Southeastern Michigan. Ecol. Monogr., **20**: 207–227.

NEWCOMBE, C. L., and P. S. DWYER. 1949. An Analysis of the Vertical Distribution of Temperature in a Dichothermic Lake of Southeastern Michigan. Ecology, **30**: 443–449.

OSTWALD, W. 1902. Zur Theorie des Planktons. Biol. Zentralbl., **22**: 596–605.

PARMENTER, R. 1929. Hydrography of Lake Erie. In Prelim. Rept. on the Cooperative Survey of Lake Erie, Season of 1928, by C. J. Fish. Bull. Buffalo Soc. Nat. Sci., **14**: 25–50.

PIETENPOL, W. B. 1918. Selective Absorption in the Visible Spectrum of Wisconsin Waters. Trans. Wis. Acad. Sci., Arts, Let., **19**: 562–593.

RUTTNER, F. 1931. Die Schichtung in Tropischen Seen. Verh. d. Int. Ver. f. theor. u. angew. Limn., **5**: 44–67.

SANDSTRÖM, W. J. 1919. The Hydrodynamics of Canadian Atlantic Waters. In Investigations in the Gulf of St. Lawrence and Atlantic Waters of Canada. Canadian Fisheries Expedition, 1914–15. Dept. Naval Serv., pp. 221–343.

SCHMIDT, W. 1936. Cause of "Oil Patches" on Water Surfaces. Nature, pp. 137–777.

SHELFORD, V. E. 1928. The Penetration of Light into Puget Sound Waters as Measured with Gas Filled Photoelectric Cells and Ray Filters. Publ. Puget Sound Biol. Sta., **7**: 151–168.

————. 1929. Die Messung der Eindringens von Licht in Wasser mit photoelektrischen Zellen. In Abderhalden's Handbuch d. biol. Arbeitsmeth., Abt. 9, Teil 2, Heft 3, pp. 1495–1524.

————. 1929. Use of Photoelectric Cells for Light Measurement in Ecological Work. Ecology, **10**: 298–311.

————. 1930. The Use of Photo-electric Cells in Biological Work. Phys. Opt. Soc. Joint Discussion, pp. 187–193.

SHELFORD, V. E., and F. W. GAIL. 1922. A Study of Light Penetration into Sea Water Made with the Kunz Photo-Electric Cell with Particular Reference to the Distribution of Plants. Publ. Puget Sound Biol. Sta., **3**: 141–176.

SHELFORD, V. E., and J. KING. 1926. The Use of Photo-electric Cells of Different Alkali Metals and Color Screens in the Measurement of Light Penetration into Water. Trans. Wis. Acad. Sci., Arts, Let., **22**: 283–298.

SMITH, L. L. 1941. A Limnological Investigation of a Permanently Stratified Lake in the Huron Mountain Region of Northern Michigan. Papers Mich. Acad. Sci., Arts, Let., **26**: 281–296.

STEUER, A. 1910. Planktonkunde. Leipzig, 723 pp.

STROMSTEN, F. A. 1927. Lake Okoboji as a Type of Aquatic Environment. Univ. Iowa Studies in Nat. Hist., **12**: 3–52.

SVERDRUP, H. U. 1937. On the Evaporation from the Ocean. Jour. Marine Res., **1**: 3–28.

SVERDRUP, H. U., M. W. JOHNSON, and R. H. FLEMING. 1942. The Oceans. New York, 1087 pp.

THORNTHWAITE, C. W., and B. HOLZMAN. 1942. Measurement of Evaporation from Lake and Water Surfaces. U.S. Dept. Agr., Tech. Bull. 817, 143 pp.

TOLMAN, C. F. 1937. Ground Water. New York, 593 pp.

UTTERBACK, C. L. 1941. The Penetration and Scattering of Solar and Sky Radiation in Natural Water Bodies of the Pacific Northwest. In A Symposium on Hydrobiology. Univ. Wis. Press, pp. 45–59.

WALLIS, A. H. 1920. An Investigation of Evaporation over Free Surfaces of Water in Inland South Africa, **8**: 283–292.

WEDDERBURN, E. M. 1910. Temperature of Scottish Lakes. In Murray and Pullar's Bathymetrical Survey of the Scottish Fresh-water Lochs, **1**: 91–144.

WELCH, P. S. 1948. Limnological Methods. Philadelphia. xviii + 381 pp.

WHIPPLE, G. C. 1927. The Microscopy of Drinking Water. 4th ed., rev. by Fair and Whipple. New York, 586 pp.

WHITNEY, L. V. 1937. Microstratification of the Waters of Inland Lakes in Summer. Science, **85**: 224–225.

———. 1938. Continuous Solar Radiation Measurements in Wisconsin Lakes. Trans. Wis. Acad. Sci., Arts, Let., **31**: 175–200.

———. 1938. Transmission of Solar Energy and the Scattering Produced by Suspensoids in Lake Waters. Trans. Wis. Acad. Sci., Arts, Let., **31**: 201–221.

WOODCOCK, A. H. 1941. Surface Cooling and Streaming in Shallow Fresh and Salt Waters. Jour. Marine Res., **4**: 153–161.

WORTHINGTON, E. B., and L. C. BEADLE. 1932. Thermoclines in Tropical Lakes. Nature, **129**: 55–56.

WRIGHT, S. 1931. Bottom Temperatures in Deep Lakes. Science, **74**: 413.

YOSHIMURA, S. 1932. Summer Temperatures in Deep Japanese Lakes. Proc. Imp. Acad. Tokyo, **8**: 79–82.

———. 1937. Abnormal Thermal Stratification of Inland Lakes. Proc. Imp. Acad. Tokyo, **13**: 316–319.

CHEMICAL CONDITIONS AND RELATED PHENOMENA

ADENEY, W. E. 1926. On the Rate and Mechanism of the Aeration of Water under Open-air Conditions. Sci. Proc. R. Dublin Soc., **18**: 211–217.

ALLGEIER, R. J., W. H. PETERSON, and C. JUDAY. 1934. Availability of Carbon in Certain Aquatic Materials under Aerobic Conditions of Fermentation. Int. Rev. d. ges. Hydrobiol. u. Hydrogr., **30**: 371–378.

ALLEGEIER, R. J., W. H. PETERSON, C. JUDAY, and E. A. BIRGE. 1932. The Anaerobic Fermentation of Lake Deposits. Int. Rev. d. ges. Hydrobiol. u. Hydrogr., **26**: 444–461.

ALSTERBERG, G. 1927. Die Sauerstoffschichtung der Seen. Botan. Notiser, pp. 255–274.

———. 1930. Die Thermischen und Chemischen Ausgleiche in den Seen zwischen Boden- und Wasserkontakt sowie ihre Biologische Bedeutung. Int. Rev. d. ges. Hydrobiol. u. Hydrogr., **24**: 290–327.

ATKINS, W. R. G. 1930. Seasonal Changes in the Nitrite Content of Sea Water. Jour. Marine Biol. Assoc., **16**: 515–518.

BARNES, T. C., and T. L. JAHN. 1934. Properties of Water of Biological Interest. Quart. Rev. Biol., **9**: 293–341.

BEADLE, L. C. 1932. Scientific Results of the Cambridge Expedition to the East African Lakes, 1930–1931. 4. The Waters of Some East African Lakes in Relation to Their Fauna and Flora. Jour. Linn. Soc., **38**: 157–211.

BIRGE, E. A. 1907. The Oxygen Dissolved in the Waters of Wisconsin Lakes. Rept. Wis. Comm. Fish, pp. 118–139.

———. 1907. The Respiration of an Inland Lake. Trans. Am. Fish. Soc., pp. 223–241.

———. 1910. Gases Dissolved in the Waters of Wisconsin Lakes. Bull. U.S. Bur. Fish., **28**: 1275–1294.

BIRGE, E. A., and C. JUDAY. 1911. The Inland Lakes of Wisconsin. The Dissolved Gases of the Water and Their Biological Significance. Wisconsin Geol. Nat. Hist. Surv., Bull. 22, Sci. ser. 7, 259 pp.

———. 1926. The Organic Content of Lake Water. Proc. Nat. Acad. Sci., **12**: 515–519.

———. 1926. Organic Content of Lake Water. Bull. U.S. Bur. Fish., **42**: 185–205.

———. 1927. The Organic Content of the Water of Small Lakes. Am. Phil. Soc. Proc., **66**: 357–372.

BLACK, C. S. 1929. Chemical Analyses of Lake Deposits. Trans. Wis. Acad. Sci., Arts, Let., **42**: 127–133.

BRÖNSTED, J. N., and C. WESENBERG-LUND. 1911. Chemisch-physikalische Untersuchungen der Dänischen Gewässer. Int. Rev. d. ges. Hydrobiol. u. Hydrogr., **4**: 251–492.

BUTCHER, R. W., F. T. K. PENTELOW, and J. W. A. WOODLEY. 1927. Diurnal Variation of Oxygen in River Water. Biochem. Jour., **21**: 945, 1423–1435.

CASPARI, W. A. 1910. Chemical Composition of Lake-waters. In Murray and Pullar's Bathymetrical Survey of the Scottish Fresh-water Lochs, **1**: 145–155.

CHANDLER, D. C. 1942. Limnological Studies of Western Lake Erie. II. Light Penetration and Its Relation to Turbidity. Ecology, **23**: 41–52.

CLARK, W. M. 1928. The Determination of Hydrogen Ions. 3d ed. Baltimore, 717 pp.

CLARKE, F. W. 1924. The Composition of the River and Lake Waters of the United States. U.S. Geol. Surv., Prof. Paper 135, 199 pp.

CLEMENS, W. A. 1923. The Limnology of Lake Nipigon. Univ. Toronto Studies, Biol. ser., Publ. Ont. Fish. Res. Lab., No. 11, pp. 1–31.

———. 1924. The Limnology of Lake Nipigon in 1923. Univ. of Toronto Studies, Biol. ser., Publ. Ont. Fish. Res. Lab., No. 22, pp. 1–14.

CONGER, P. S. 1943. Ebullition of Gases from Marsh and Lake Waters. Chesapeake Biol. Lab., State of Maryland, Publ. 59, 42 pp.

COOPER, G. P. and J. L. FULLER. 1945. A Biological Survey of Moosehead Lake and Haymock Lake, Maine. Fish Surv. Rept. 6, Maine Dept. Inland Fish and Game, 160 pp.

DOMOGALLA, B. P., and E. B. FRED. 1926. Ammonia and Nitrate Studies of Lakes near Madison, Wisconsin. Jour. Am. Soc. Agron., **18**: 897–911.

DOMOGALLA, B. P., E. B. FRED, and W. H. PETERSON. 1926. Seasonal Variations in the Ammonia and Nitrate Content of Lake Waters. Jour. Am. Water Works Assoc. **15**: 369–385.

DOMOGALLA, B. P., C. JUDAY, and W. H. PETERSON. 1925. The Forms of Nitrogen Found in Certain Lake Waters. Jour. Biol. Chem., **63**: 269–285.

FREEMAN, S., V. W. MELOCHE, and C. JUDAY. 1933. The Determination of the Hydrogen Ion Concentration of Inland Lakes. Int. Rev. d. ges. Hydrobiol. u. Hydrogr., **29**: 346–359.

GROTE, A. 1934. Der Sauerstoffhaushalt der Seen. Die Binnengewässer, Bd. XIV, 217 pp.

HARVEY, H. W. 1925. Oxidation in Sea Water. Jour. Marine Biol. Assoc., **13**: 953–969.

————. 1928. Biological Chemistry and Physics of Sea Water. Cambridge, 194 pp.

————. 1945. Recent Advances in the Chemistry and Biology of Sea Water. Cambridge, 164.

HÜLSEN, K. K. 1918. Sur la formation de l'hydrogène sulfhydrique (H_2S) au fond du lac Onega. Bull. acad. sci. russe (6), No. 18, pp. 2233–2240.

HUTCHINSON, G. E. 1930. On the Chemical Ecology of Lake Tanganyika. Science, **71**: 616.

————. 1938. Chemical Stratification and Lake Morphology. Proc. Nat. Acad. Sci., **24**: 63–69.

————. 1947. A Direct Demonstration of the Phosphorus Cycle in a Small Lake. Proc. Nat. Acad. Sci., **33**: 148–153.

JEWELL, M. E. 1927. Ground Water as a Possible Factor in Lowering Dissolved Oxygen in the Deeper Water of Lakes. Ecology, **8**: 142–143.

JUDAY, C., and E. A. BIRGE. 1931. The Second Report on the Phosphorus Content of Wisconsin Lake Waters. Trans. Wis. Acad. Sci., Arts, Let., **26**: 353–382.

————. 1932. Dissolved Oxygen and Oxygen Consumed in the Lake Waters of Northeastern Wisconsin. Trans. Wis. Acad. Sci. Arts, Let., **27**: 415–486.

————. 1933. The Transparency, the Color and the Specific Conductance of the Lake Waters of Northeastern Wisconsin. Trans. Wis. Acad. Sci., Arts, Let., **28**: 205–259.

JUDAY, C., E. A. BIRGE, G. I. KEMMERER, and R. J. ROBINSON. 1928. Phosphorus Content of Lake Waters of Northeastern Wisconsin. Trans. Wis. Acad. Sci., Arts, Let., **23**: 233–248.

JUDAY, C., E. B. FRED, and F. C. WILSON. 1924. The Hydrogen Ion Concentration of Certain Wisconsin Lake Waters. Trans. Am. Micr. Soc., **43**: 177–190.

KUSNETZOW, S. I., and G. S. KARZINKIN. 1931. Direct Method for the Quantitative Study of Bacteria in Water and Some Consideration on the Causes Which Produce a Zone of Oxygen-minimum in Lake Glubokoji. Zentralbl. f. Bakt., Parasit. u. Infektionskr., **83**: 169–174.

LUNDEGÅRDH, H. 1923. Über die Kohlensäureproduktion und die Gaspermeabilität des Bodens. Ark. f. Bot., **18**: 1–36.

MAUCHA, R. 1932. Hydrochemische Methoden in der Limnologie. Die Binnengewässer, Bd. XII, 173 pp.

MINDER, L. 1922. Studien über den Sauerstoffgehalt des Zürichsees. Arch. f. Hydrobiol., **3**: 107–155.

————. 1926. Biologisch-Chemische Untersuchungen im Zürichsee. Zeit. f. Hydrol., **3**: 1–69.

MONTI, R., A. MONTI, and N. MONTI. 1926. Le Variazioni del Residuo e dei Gas Disciolti nelle Acque del Lario in Rapporto con la Biologia Lacustre. Real. Ist. Lomb. di Sci. e. Let., **59**: 1–11.

MOORE, W. G. 1942. Field Studies on the Oxygen Requirements of Certain Freshwater Fishes. Ecology, **23**: 319–329.

PETERSON, W. H., E. B. FRED, and B. P. DOMOGALLA. 1925. The Occurrence of Amino Acids and Other Organic Nitrogen Compounds in Lake Water. Jour. Biol. Chem., **63**: 287–295.

PHILIP, C. B. 1927. Diurnal Fluctuations in the Hydrogen Ion Activity of a Minnesota Lake. Ecology, **8**: 73–89.

PIA, J. 1933. Kohlensäure und Kalk. Die Binnengewässer, Bd. XIII, 183 pp.

PIETENPOL, W. B. 1918. Selective Absorption in the Visible Spectrum of Wisconsin Lake Waters. Trans. Wis. Acad. Sci., Arts, Let., **19**: 562–593.

POWERS, E. B. 1928. The Behavior of Sea Water, Lake Water and Bog Water at Different Carbon Dioxide Tensions. Publ. Puget Sound Biol. Sta., **6**: 271–281.

———. 1928. The Carbon Dioxide Tension, Oxygen Content, the pH and the Alkali Reserve of Natural Waters Mostly of the Western Portion of the United States. Publ. Puget Sound Biol. Sta., **5**: 381–391.

———. 1929. Fresh Water Studies. I. The Relative Temperature, Oxygen Content, Alkali Reserve, the Carbon Dioxide Tension and pH of the Waters of Certain Mountain Streams at Different Altitudes in the Smoky Mountain National Park. Ecology, **10**: 97–111.

POWERS, E. B., and T. A. HICKMAN. 1928. The Carbon Dioxide Tensions of the Fraser River and Its Lower Tributaries and of Certain Tributaries of the Columbia River. Publ. Puget Sound Biol. Sta., **5**: 373–380.

POWERS, E. B., and L. M. SHIPE. 1928. The Rate of Oxygen Absorption by Certain Marine Fishes as Affected by the Oxygen Content and Carbon Dioxide Tension of the Sea-Water. Publ. Puget Sound Biol. Sta., **5**: 365–372.

PURDY, W. C. 1937. Experimental Studies on Natural Purification in Polluted Waters. X. Reoxygenation of Polluted Waters by Microscopic Algae. Pub. Health Repts., U.S. Treas. Dept., **52**: 945–978.

RAWSON, D. S. 1936. Physical and Chemical Studies in Lakes of the Prince Albert Park, Saskatchewan. Jour. Biol. Bd. Canada, **2**: 227–284.

———. 1939. Some Physical and Chemical Factors in the Metabolism of Lakes. Publ. Am. Assoc. Adv. Sci., No. 10, pp. 9–26.

RICKER, W. E. 1937. Physical and Chemical Characteristics of Cultus Lake, British Columbia. Jour. Biol. Bd. Canada, **3**: 363–402.

RILEY, G. A. 1951. Oxygen, Phosphate, and Nitrate in the Atlantic Ocean. Bull. Bingham Oceanographic Collection, **13**: 1–126.

ROSSOLIMO, L. L. 1928. Zur Frage der Sauerstoffschichtung der Seen. Arch. f. Hydrobiol., **19**: 731–741.

RUTTNER, F. 1931. Hydrographische und hydrochemische Beobachtungen auf Java, Sumatra und Bali. Arch. f. Hydrobiol., Suppl. Bd., **8**: 197–460.

SAUNDERS, J. T. 1926. The Hydrogen-ion Concentration of Natural Waters. I. The Relation of pH to the Pressure of Carbon Dioxide. British Jour. Exp. Biol., **4**: 46–72.

SCOTT, W. 1924. The Diurnal Oxygen Pulse in Eagle (Winona) Lake. Proc. Ind. Acad. Sci., **33**: 311–314.

———. 1931. Investigations of Indiana Lakes. III. The Lakes of Northeastern Indiana. Dept. Conserv. State of Ind., Div. Fish and Game, pp. 57–145.

SCOTT, W., R. HILE, and H. T. SPIETH. 1938. The Bottom Fauna of Tippecanoe Lake. Investigations of Indiana Lakes and Streams. Indiana Dept. Conserv., pp. 3–16.

SENIOR-WHITE, R. 1928. On the Relationship Existing between Carbonates and pH Conductivity in Natural Waters. Indian Jour. Med. Res., **15**(4): 989–996.

SHELFORD, V. E. 1923. The Determination of Hydrogen-ion Concentration in Connection with Fresh-water Biological Studies. State of Ill. Dept. Reg. Ed., Div. Nat. Hist. Surv., **14**: 379–395.

———. 1925. The Hydrogen Ion Concentration of Certain Western American Inland Waters. Ecology, **6**: 279–287.

STRÖM, K. M. 1927–1928. Recent Advances in Limnology. Proc. Linn. Soc. London, **140**: 96–100.

———. 1930. Limnological Observations on Norwegian Lakes. Arch. f. Hydrobiol., **21**: 97–124.

THIENEMANN, A. 1928. Der Sauerstoff im eutrophen und oligotrophen See. Die Binnengewässer, Bd. 4, 176 pp.

WELCH, P. S. 1927. Limnological Investigations on Northern Michigan Lakes. I. Physical-chemical Studies on Douglas Lake. Papers Mich. Acad. Sci., Arts, Let., **8**: 421–451.

———. 1945. More Data on Depression Individuality in Douglas Lake, Michigan. Papers Mich. Acad. Sci., Arts, Let., **33**: 379–390.

WELCH, P. S., and F. E. EGGLETON. 1932. Limnological Investigations on Northern Michigan Lakes. II. A Further Study of Depression Individuality in Douglas Lake. Papers Mich. Acad. Sci., Arts, Let., **15**: 491–508.

———. 1935. Additional Data on Submerged Depression Individuality in Douglas Lake, Michigan. Papers Mich. Acad. Sci., Arts, Let., **20**: 737–750.

WHERRY, E. T. 1920. Soil Acidity and a Field Method for Its Measurement. Ecology, **1**: 160–173.

WIEBE, A. H. 1930. Investigations on Plankton Production in Fish Ponds. Bull. U.S. Bur. Fish., **46**: 137–176.

———. 1931. Dissolved Phosphorus and Inorganic Nitrogen in the Water of the Mississippi River. Science, **73**: 652.

YOSHIMURA, S. 1931. Water Temperature and Dissolved Oxygen in Several Sub-aqueous Basins of Lake Akimota, Fukushima. Arch. f. Hydrobiol., **23**: 279–283.

———. 1938. Dissolved Oxygen of the Lake Waters of Japan. Sci. Repts. Tokyc Bunrika Daigaku, Dec. C, No. 8, Geogr. Inst., pp. 63–277.

———. 1936. A Contribution to the Knowledge of Deep Water Temperatures of Japanese Lakes. Part I. Summer Temperature. Jap. Jour. Astron. Geophys., **13**: 61–120.

ZOBELL, C. E. 1933. Photochemical Nitrification in Sea Water. Science, **77**: 27–28.

INFLUENCE OF PHYSICAL CONDITIONS

ALLEN, W. R. 1921. Studies of the Biology of Freshwater Mussels. III. Distribution and Movements of Winona Lake Mussels. Proc. Ind. Acad. Sci., pp. 227–238.

———. 1923. Studies of the Biology of Freshwater Mussels. II. The Nature and Degree of Response to Certain Physical and Chemical Stimuli. Ohio Jour. Sci., **23**: 57–82.

ALSTERBERG, G. 1927. Die Sauerstoffschichtung der Seen. Botan. Notiser, pp. 255–274.

ALTNÖDER, K. 1926. Beobachtungen über die Biologie von Margaritana margaritifera und über die Okologie ihres Wohnorts. Arch. f. Hydrobiol., **17**: 423–491.

ATKINS, W. R. G. 1925. On the Thermal Stratification of Sea Water and Its Importance for the Algal Plankton. Jour. Marine Biol. Assoc., **13**: 693–699.

BROWN, C. R., and M. H. HATCH. 1929. Orientation and "Fright" Reactions of Whirligig Beetles (Gyrinidae). Jour. Comp. Psych., **9**: 159–189.

BURR, G. O. 1941. Photosynthesis of Algae and Other Aquatic Plants. In A Symposium on Hydrobiology. Univ. Wis. Press, pp. 163–181.

CARPENTER, K. E. 1928. Life in Inland Waters. New York, 267 pp.

CLAUSEN, R. G. 1931. Orientation in Fresh Water Fishes. Ecology, **12**: 541–546.

———. 1934. Body Temperature of Fresh Water Fishes. Ecology, **15**: 139–144.

CLEMENS, W. A. 1917. An Ecological Study of the Mayfly Chirotenetes. Univ. Toronto Studies, Biol. ser. 17, pp. 5–43.

COKER, R. E. 1933. Influence of Temperature on Size of Fresh-water Copepods (Cyclops). Int. Rev. d. ges. Hydrobiol. u. Hydrogr., **29**: 406–436.

CREASER, C. W. 1925. The Establishment of the Atlantic Smelt in the Upper Waters of the Great Lakes. Papers Mich. Acad. Sci., Arts, Let., **5**: 405–424.

DEMOLL, R. 1922. Temperaturwellen (= seiches) und Planktonwellen. Arch. f. Hydrobiol., **13**: 313–320.

DOAN, K. H. 1942. Some Meteorological and Limnological Conditions as Factors in the Abundance of Certain Fishes in Lake Erie. Ecol. Monogr., **12**: 293–314.

DODDS, G. S., and F. L. HISAW. 1924. Ecological Studies of Aquatic Insects. I. Adaptations of Mayfly Nymphs to Swift Streams. Ecology, **5**: 137–148.

———. 1924. Ecological Studies of Aquatic Insects. II. Size of Respiratory Organs in Relation to Environmental Conditions. Ecology, **5**: 262–271.

———. 1925. Ecological Studies on Aquatic Insects. III. Adaptations of Caddisfly Larvae to Swift Streams. Ecology, **6**: 123–137.

DUTTON, H. J., and C. JUDAY. 1944. Chromatic Adaptation in Relation to Color and Depth Distribution of Freshwater Phytoplankton and Large Aquatic Plants. Ecology, **25**: 273–282.

EGE, R., and A. KROGH. 1914. On the Relation between Temperature and the Respiratory Exchange in Fishes. Int. Rev. d. ges. Hydrobiol. u. Hydrogr., **7**: 48–55.

EGGLETON, F. E. 1936. The Deep-water Bottom Fauna of Lake Michigan. Papers Mich. Acad. Sci., Arts, Let., **21**: 599–612.

———. 1937. Productivity of the Profundal Benthic Zone in Lake Michigan. Papers Mich. Acad. Sci., Arts, Let., **22**: 593–611.

ELLIS, M. M. 1931. Some Factors Affecting the Replacement of the Commercial Fresh-water Mussels. U.S. Bur. Fish., Fishery Circ. 7, 10 pp.

———. 1931. A Survey of Conditions Affecting Fisheries in the Upper Mississippi River. U.S. Bur. Fish., Fishery Circ. 5, 18 pp.

———. 1936. Erosion Silt as a Factor in Aquatic Environments. Ecology, **17**: 29–42.

EMBODY, G. C. 1921. Concerning High Water Temperatures and Trout. Trans. Am. Fish. Soc., **51**: 58–64.

FOX, H. M., B. G. SIMMONDS, and R. WASHBOURN. 1935. Metabolic Rates of Ephemerid Nymphs from Swiftly Flowing and from Still Waters. Jour. Exp. Biol., **12**: 179–184.

GELEI-SZEGED, J. v. 1928. Zum Physiologischen Formproblem der Wasserorganismen. Arch. Balatonicum, **2**: 24–35.

GOLDACRE, R. J. 1949. Surface Films on Natural Bodies of Water. Jour. Animal Ecology, **18**: 36–39.

GREGORY, W. K. 1928. Studies on the Body-forms of Fishes. Zoologica, **8**: 325–421.

HARDMAN, Y. 1941. The Surface Tension of Wisconsin Lake Waters. Trans. Wis. Acad. Sci., Arts, Let., **33**: 395–404.

HARPSTER, HILDA T. 1941. An Investigation of the Gaseous Plastron as a Respiratory Mechanism in *Helichus striatus* Leconte (Dryopidae). Trans. Am. Micr. Soc., **60**: 329–358.

———. 1944. The Gaseous Plastron as a Respiratory Mechanism in *Stenelmis quadrimaculata* Horn (Dryopidae). Trans. Am Micr. Soc., **63**: 1–26.

HARRIS, J. P. 1941. Mechanical Effects of Water Turbulence on Certain Freshwater Plankters. Unpublished doctoral dissertation, University of Michigan.

HATHWAY, E. S. 1927. The Relation of Temperature to the Quantity of Food Consumed by Fishes. Ecology, **8**: 428–434.

————. 1928. Quantitative Study of the Changes Produced by Acclimatization in the Tolerance of High Temperatures by Fishes and Amphibians. Bull. U.S. Bur. Fish., **43**: 169–192.

HIGGINS, E. 1932. Progress in Biological Inquiries, 1931. Appendix to Rept. of U.S. Comm. Fish. for fiscal year 1932, pp. 441–529.

HORA, S. L. 1930. Ecology, Bionomics and Evolutions of the Torrential Fauna, with Special Reference to the Organs of Attachment. Phil. Trans. R. Soc. London, **218**: 171–282.

HOUSSAY, F. 1908. Notes préliminaires sur la forme des poissons. Arch. zool. exp. gen., **8**(4): xv–xxxi.

————. 1909. Sur les conditions hydrodynamiques de la forme chez poissons. A. R. acad. sci. Paris, **148**: 1076–1078.

————. 1909. Carènes et poissons. Stabilisation par les mageoires. Rev. gen. sci., **20**: 617–624.

————. 1909. Nouvelle expérience sur la forme et la stabilité des poissons. Rev. gen. sci., **20**: 943–948.

————. 1910. La Morphologie dynamique. Paris, 29 pp.

————. 1912. Forme, poussance et stabilité des poissons. Paris, 372 pp.

————. 1915. The Effect of Water Pressure upon the Form of Fishes. Sci. Am. Suppl., **78**: 376–378.

HUBAULT, E. 1927. Contribution à l'étude des invertébrés torrenticoles. Bull. biol. France et Belg., **9**: 1–390.

IRWIN, W. H., and J. H. STEVENSON. 1951. Physiochemical Nature of Clay Turbidity with Special Reference to Clarification and Productivity of Impounded Waters. Bull. Okla. Agr. and Mech. Coll., **48**, Biol. ser. 4, 54 pp.

JENKIN, P. M. 1937. Oxygen Production by the Diatom *Coscinodiscus excentricus* Ehr. in Relation to Submarine Illumination in the English Channel. Jour. Marine Biol. Assoc., **22**: 301–343.

JUDAY, C. 1921. Observations on the Larvae of Corethra punctipennis Say. Biol. Bull., **40**: 271–286.

JUDAY, C., J. M. BLAIR, and E. F. WILDA. 1943. The Photosynthetic Activities of the Aquatic Plants of Little John Lake, Vilas County, Wisconsin. Am. Midland Nat., **30**: 426–446.

KARRER, E. 1921. The Shape Assumed by a Deformable Body Immersed in a Moving Fluid. Jour. Franklin Inst., **192**: 737–756.

KLUGH, A. B. 1929. The Effect of the Ultra-violet Component of Sunlight on Certain Marine Organisms. Can. Jour. Res., **1**: 100–109.

————. 1930. Effect of Sunlight on Aquatic Organisms. Can. Jour. Res., **3**: 104–106.

MANNING, W. M., and R. E. JUDAY. 1941. The Chlorophyll Content and Productivity of Some Lakes in Northeastern Wisconsin. Trans. Wis. Acad. Sci., Arts, Let., **33**: 363–393.

MANNING, W. M., C. JUDAY, and M. WOLF. 1938. Photosynthesis of Aquatic Plants at Different Depths in Trout Lake, Wisconsin. Trans. Wis. Acad. Sci., Arts, Let., **31**: 377–410.

MEIER, F. E. 1932. Lethal Action of Ultra-violet Light on a Unicellular Green Alga. Smithsonian Misc. Coll., **87**: No. 10, 11 pp.

MEYER, B. S., F. H. BELL, L. C. THOMPSON, and E. I. CLAY. 1943. Effects of Depth of Immersion on Apparent Photosynthesis in Submersed Vascular Aquatics. Ecology, **24**: 393–399.

MILLER, D. E. 1936. A Limnological Study of *Pelmatohydra* with Special Reference to their Quantitative Seasonal Distribution. Trans. Am. Micr. Soc., **55**: 123–193.

MILLER, E. C.   1931.   Plant Physiology.   New York, 900 pp.

MOFFETT, J. W.   1943.   A Limnological Investigation of the Dynamics of a Sandy, Wave-swept Shoal in Douglas Lake, Michigan.   Trans. Am. Micr. Soc., **62**: 1–23.

NEEDHAM, J. G., and R. O. CHRISTENSON.   1927.   Economic Insects in Some Streams of Northern Utah.   Utah Agr. Exp. Sta., Bull. 201, 36 pp.

NEEDHAM, J. G., and J. T. LLOYD.   1930.   The Life of Inland Waters, 2d ed.   Springfield, 438 pp.

OLD, M. C.   1932.   Taxonomy and Distribution of the Fresh-water Sponges (Spongillidae) of Michigan.   Papers Mich. Acad. Sci., Arts, Let., **15**: 439–477.

PARRY, D. A.   1949.   The Swimming of Whales and a Discussion of Gray's Paradox.   Jour. Exp. Biol., **26**: 24–34.

PARSONS, H. DE B.   1884.   The Displacements and the Area-curves of Fish.   Trans. A.S.M.E., **9**: 679–695.

PEARSE, A. S.   1939.   Animal Ecology.   2d ed. New York, 642 pp.

PIRSCH, G. B.   1923.   Studies of the Temperature of Individual Insects, with Special Reference to the Honey Bee.   Jour Agr. Res., **24**: 275–288.

POWERS, E. B.   1920.   Influence of Temperature and Concentration on the Toxicity of Salts to Fishes.   Ecology, **1**: 95–112.

SCOURFIELD, D. J.   1896.   Entomostraca and the Surface Film of Water.   Jour. Linn. Soc., Zoology, **25**: 1–19.

SHELFORD, V. E.   1916.   Physiological Differences between Marine Animals and Different Depths.   Puget Sound Marine Sta. Publ., **1**: 157–174.

――――.   1929.   Laboratory and Field Ecology.   Baltimore, 608 pp.

SHELFORD, V. E., and F. W. GAIL.   1922.   A Study of Light Penetration into Sea Water Made with the Kunz Photo-electric Cell with Particular Reference to the Distribution of Plants.   Puget Sound Biol. Sta. Publ., **3**: 141–176.

THOMPSON, D. W.   1943.   On Growth and Form.   New York, 1116 pp.

THORPE, W. H.   1950.   Plastron Respiration in Aquatic Insects.   Biol. Rev., **25**: 344–390.

THORPE, W. H., and D. J. CRISP.   1947.   Studies on Plastron Respiration.   I. The Biology of *Aphelocheirus* [Hemiptera, Aphelocheiridae (Naucoridae)] and the Mechanism of Plastron Retention.   Jour. Exp. Biol., **24**: 227–269.

――――.   1947.   Studies on Plastron Respiration.   II. The Respiratory Efficiency of the Plastron in *Aphelocheirus*.   Jour. Exp. Biol., **24**: 270–303.

――――.   1949.   Studies on Plastron Respiration.   IV. Plastron Respiration in the Coleoptera.   Jour. Exp. Biol., **26**: 219–260.

THURSTON, R. H.   1887.   The Form of Fish and of Ships.   Trans. Inst. Naval Architects, **28**: 415–436.

VAN OOSTEN, J.   1948.   Turbidity as a Factor in the Decline of Great Lakes Fishes with Special Reference to Lake Erie.   Trans. Am. Fish. Soc., **75**: 281–322.

WALLEN, I. E.   1951.   The Direct Effect of Turbidity on Fishes.   Bull. Okla. Agr. and Mech. Coll., **48**, Biol. ser. 2, 27 pp.

WARD, H. B.   1921.   Some of the Factors Controlling the Migration and Spawning of the Alaska Red Salmon.   Ecology, **2**: 235–254.

WEBSTER, D. A., and P. C. WEBSTER.   1943.   Influence of Water Current on Case Weight in Larvae of the Caddisfly, Goera calcarata Banks.   Can. Entomologist, **75**: 105–108.

WELCH, P. S., and H. A. LOOMIS.   1924.   A Limnological Study of Hydra oligactis in Douglas Lake, Michigan.   Trans. Am. Micr. Soc., **43**: 203–235.

WESENBERG-LUND, C.   1909.   Über die praktische Bedeutung der jahrlichen variation in der Viskositat des Wassers.   Int. Rev. d. ges. Hydrobiol. u. Hydrogr., **2**: 231–233.

————. 1930. Contributions to the Biology of the Rotifera. II. The Periodicity and Sexual Periods. Mém. l'Acad. R. Sci. Let. Danemark, 9me ser., **2**: 3–230.

WHIPPLE, G. C. 1927. The Microscopy of Drinking Water. 4th ed., rev. by Fair and Whipple. New York, 586 pp.

WU, YI FANG. 1931. A Contribution to the Biology of Simulium (Diptera). Papers Mich. Acad. Sci., Arts, Let., **13**: 543–599.

ZoBELL, C. E. 1933. Photochemical Nitrification in Sea Water. Science, **77**: 27–28.

ZoBELL, C. E., and G. F. McEWEN. 1935. The Lethal Action of Sunlight upon Bacteria in Sea Water. Biol. Bull., **68**: 93–106.

INFLUENCE OF CHEMICAL CONDITIONS

ABERG, B., and W. RODHE. 1942. Über die Milieufactoren in einigen Sudschwedischen Seen. Symbolae Botanicae Upsalienses, **5**: 1–256.

ADAMS, A. 1912. The Effects of Atmospheres Enriched with Oxygen upon Living Organisms. (*a*) Effects upon Micro-organisms. (*b*) Effects upon Mammals Experimentally Inoculated with Tuberculosis. (*c*) Effects upon the Lungs of Mammals, or Oxygen Pneumonia. Biochem. Jour., **6**: 297–313.

ADOLPH, E. F. 1925. Some Physiological Distinctions between Fresh-water and Marine Organisms. Biol. Bull., **48**: 327–335.

ALLEE, W. C., O. PARK, A. E. EMERSON, T. PARK, and K. P. SCHMIDT. 1949. Principles of Animal Ecology. Philadelphia, 837 pp.

ALLGEIER, R. J., B. C. HAFFORD, and C. JUDAY. 1941. Oxidation-reduction Potentials and pH of Lake Waters and of Lake Sediments. Trans. Wis. Acad. Sci., Arts, Let., **33**: 115–133.

ALLISON, F. E. 1931. Forms of Nitrogen Assimilated by Plants. Quart. Rev. Biol., **6**: 313–321.

BARNES, H., and K. A. PYEFINCH. 1947. Copper in Diatoms. Nature, **160**: 97.

BAVENDAMM, W. 1931. The Possible Role of Microorganisms in the Precipitation of Calcium Carbonate in Tropical Seas. Science, **73**: 597–598.

————. 1932. Die microbiologische Kalkfallung in der tropischen See. Arch. f. Microbiol., **3**: 205–276.

BEERMAN, H. 1924. Some Physiological Actions of Hydrogen Sulphide. Jour. Exp. Zool., **41**: 33–43.

BIRGE, E. A., and C. JUDAY. 1911. The Dissolved Gases of the Water and Their Biological Significance. Wisconsin Geol. Nat. Hist. Surv., Bull. 22, 259 pp.

————. 1926. The Organic Content of Lake Water. Proc. Nat. Acad. Sci., **12**: 515–519.

————. 1926. Organic Content of Lake Water. Bull. U.S. Bur. Fish., **42**: 185–205.

————. 1927. The Organic Content of the Water of Small Lakes. Proc. Am. Phil. Soc., **66**: 357–372.

BLACK, E. C. 1940. The Transport of Oxygen by the Blood of Fresh-water Fish. Biol. Bull., **79**: 215–229.

BOLD, G. C. 1942. The Cultivation of Algae. Bot. Rev., **8**: 69–138.

BOND, R. M. 1933. A Contribution to the Study of the Natural Food-cycle in Aquatic Environments. Bull. Bingham Oceanographic Collection, **4**: 1–89.

BREDER, C. M. 1927. On the Temperature-oxygen Toleration of Brook Trout. Copeia, **163**: 36–39.

BRESSLAU, E. 1926. Die Bedeutung der Wasserstoffionenkonzentration für die Hydrobiologie. Verh. d. Int. Ver. f. theor. u. angew. Limn., **3**: 56–108.

BROWN, H. W., and M. E. JEWELL. 1926. Further Studies on the Fishes of an Acid Lake. Trans. Am. Micr. Soc., **45**: 20–34.

CHOMKOVIC, G. 1926. Über die Permeabilität der Haut bei Fischen für Lösung von Organischen Nährsubstanzen, Glucose, Saccharose, Pepton. VI. Mitteilung der Studien über die Funktion der im Wasser gelösten Nahrsubstanz im Stoffwechsel der Wassertiere. Pflügers Arch. f. ges. Physiol., **211**: 666–681.

CHU, S. P. 1942. The Influence of the Mineral Composition of the Medium on the Growth of Planktonic Algae. Jour. Ecology, **30**: 284–325.

CLARKE, G. L. 1939. The Utilization of Solar Energy by Aquatic Organisms. In Problems of Lake Biology, Publ. A.A.A.S., No. 10, pp. 27–38.

CLEARY, M. B. 1948. The Anaerobic Glycogen Consumption and the Question of Post-anaerobic Glycogen Resynthesis in Some Invertebrates. Catholic Univ. of Am., Biol. Studies No. 7, 18 pp.

CLEVELAND, L. R. 1925. Toxicity of Oxygen for Protozoa in Vivo and in Vitro: Animals Defaunated without Injury. Biol. Bull., **48**: 455–468.

COKER, R. E. 1925. Observations of Hydrogen-ion Concentration and of Fishes in Waters Tributary to the Catawba River, North Carolina (with Supplementary Observations in Some Waters of Cape Cod, Massachusetts). Ecology, **6**: 52–65.

———. 1938. Life in the Sea. Sci. Monthly, **46**: 299–322.

COLE, A. E. 1921. Oxygen Supply of Certain Animals Living in Water Containing No Dissolved Oxygen. Jour. Exp. Zool., **33**: 293–320.

———. 1926. Physiological Studies on Fresh-water Clams. Carbon-dioxide Production in Low Oxygen Tensions. Jour. Exp. Zool., **45**: 349–360.

CONGER, P. S. 1941. Fixation of Silica by Diatoms. In A Symposium on Hydrobiology. Univ. Wis. Press, pp. 395–396.

CREASER, C. W. 1930. Relative Importance of Hydrogen-ion Concentration, Temperature, Dissolved Oxygen, and Carbon-dioxide Tension, on Habitat Selection by Brook-trout. Ecology, **11**: 246–262.

CREASER, C. W., and H. W. BROWN. 1927. The Hydrogen-ion Concentration of Brook Trout Waters of Northern Lower Michigan. Ecology, **8**: 98–105.

DAKIN, W. J., and C. M. G. DAKIN. 1925. The Oxygen Requirements of Certain Aquatic Animals and Its Bearing upon the Source of Food Supply. British Jour. Exp. Biol., **2**: 292–322.

DEEVEY, E. S. 1941. Notes on the Encystment of the Harpacticoid Copepod *Canthocamptus staphylinoides* Pearse. Ecology, **22**: 197–200.

EDDY, S. 1928. Succession of Protozoa in Cultures under Controlled Conditions. Trans. Am. Micr. Soc., **47**: 283–319.

EGGLETON, F. E. 1931. A Limnological Study of the Profundal Bottom Fauna of Certain Fresh-water Lakes. Ecol. Monogr., **1**: 231–332.

ELLIOTT, A. M. 1933. Isolation of Colpidium striatum Stokes in Bacteria-free Cultures and the Relation of Growth to pH of the Medium. Biol. Bull., **65**: 45–56.

ELLIS, M. M., A. D. MERRICK, and M. D. ELLIS. 1931. The Blood of North American Fresh-water Mussels under Normal and Adverse Conditions. Bull. U.S. Bur. Fish., **46**: 509–542.

ELLIS, M. M., B. A. WESTFALL, and MARION D. ELLIS. 1946. Determination of Water Quality. Fish and Wildlife Service, U.S. Dept. Interior, Res. Rept. 9, 122 pp.

ESAKI, S. 1926. Zur Frage der Ernährung von Amphibienlarven durch im Wasser gelöste Nährstoffe und andere Lösung. Fol. Anat. Jap., **4**(1): 1–12.

FOGG, G. E. 1947. Nitrogen Fixation by Blue-green Algae. Endeavour, **6**: 172–175.

FOX, M. 1949. Blood-pigments. Endeavour, **8**: 43–47.

FRY, F. E. J. 1939. The Position of Fish and Other Higher Animals in the Economy of Lakes. In Problems of Lake Biology, Publ. A.A.A.S. No. 10, pp. 132–142.

GAARDER, T., and H. H. GRAN. 1927. Investigations of the Production of Plankton in the Oslo Fjord. Cons. perm. int. l'expl. mer., rapp. proc. verb. reun., **42**: 1–48.

GALTSOFF, P. S. 1924. Limnological Observations in the Upper Mississippi, 1921. Bull. U.S. Bur. Fish., **39**: 347–438.

GARDINER, A. C. 1937. Phosphate Production by Planktonic Animals. Jour. du conseil, **12**: 144–146.

GELLIS, S. S., and G. L. CLARKE. 1935. Organic Matter in Dissolved and Colloidal Form as Food for Daphnia magna. Physiol. Zool., **8**: 127–137.

GREENBANK, J. 1945. Limnological Conditions in Ice-covered Lakes, especially as Related to Winter-kill of Fish. Ecol. Monogr., **15**: 343–392.

GUTSELL, J. S. 1929. Influence of Certain Water Conditions, Especially Dissolved Gases, on Trout. Ecology, **10**: 77–96.

HAYES, F. R. and C. C. COFFIN. 1951. Radioactive Phosphorus and Exchange of Lake Nutrients. Endeavor, **10**: 78–81.

HINMAN, E. H. 1932. The Role of Solutes and Colloids in the Nutrition of Anopheline Larvae. Am. Jour. Trop. Med., **12**: 263–271.

———. 1932. The Utilization of Water Colloids and Material in Solution by Aquatic Animals with Special Reference to Mosquito Larvae. Quart. Rev. Biol., **7**: 210–217.

HOFFMAN, C. E. 1940. The Relation of Donacia Larvae (Chrysomelidae: Coleoptera) to Dissolved Oxygen. Ecology, **21**: 176–183.

HUTCHINSON, G. E. 1930. On the Chemical Ecology of Lake Tanganyika. Science, **71**: 616.

———. 1932. Experimental Studies in Ecology. I. The Magnesium Tolerance of Daphnidae and Its Ecological Significance. Int. Rev. d. ges. Hydrobiol. u. Hydrogr., **28**: 90–108.

———. 1941. Ecological Aspects of Succession in Natural Populations. Am. Nat., **75**: 406–418.

———. 1943. Thiamin in Lake Waters and Aquatic Organisms. Arch. Biochem., **2**: 143–150.

HUTCHINSON, G. E., and V. T. BOWEN. 1947. A Direct Demonstration of the Phosphorus Cycle in a Small Lake. Proc. Nat. Acad. Sci., **33**: 148–153.

HUTCHINSON, G. E., E. S. DEEVEY, and ANNE WOLLACK. 1939. The Oxidation-reduction Potentials of Lake Waters and Their Ecological Significance. Proc. Nat. Acad. Sci., **25**: 78–90.

HUTCHINSON, G. E., and JANE K. SETLOW. 1946. Limnological Studies in Connecticut. VIII. The Niacin Cycle in a Small Inland Lake. Ecology, **27**: 13–22.

JEWELL, M. E. 1922. The Fauna of an Acid Stream. Ecology, **3**: 22–28.

———. 1927. Aquatic Biology of the Prairie. Ecology, **8**: 289–298.

JOBES, F. W., and M. E. JEWELL. 1927. Studies on the Alkali Reserve of the Blood of *Ameiurus nebulosus* from Acid and Basic Waters. Trans. Am. Micr. Soc., **46**: 175–186.

JUDAY, C. 1908. Some Aquatic Invertebrates that Live under Anaerobic Conditions. Trans. Wis. Acad. Sci., Arts, Let., **16**: 10–16.

———. 1919. A Freshwater Anaerobic Ciliate. Biol. Bull., **36**: 92–95.

JUDAY, C., and E. A. BIRGE. 1931. A Second Report on the Phosphorus Content of Wisconsin Lake Waters. Trans. Wis. Acad. Sci., Arts, Let., **26**: 353–382.

JUDAY, C., E. A. BIRGE, G. I. KEMMERER, and R. J. ROBINSON. 1928. Phosphorus Content of Lake Waters of Northeastern Wisconsin. Trans. Wis. Acad. Sci., Arts, Let., **23**: 233–248.

JUDAY, C., E. A. BIRGE, and V. W. MELOCHE. 1935. The Carbon Dioxide and Hydrogen Ion Concentration of the Lake Waters of Northeastern Wisconsin. Trans. Wis. Acad. Sci., Arts, Let., **29**: 1–82.

———. 1938. Mineral Content of the Lake Waters of Northeastern Wisconsin. Trans. Wis. Acad. Sci., Arts, Let., **31**: 223–276.

JUDAY, C., W. H. RICH, G. I. KEMMERER, and A. MANN. 1932. Limnological Studies of Karluk Lake, Alaska. Bull. U.S. Bur. Fish., **47**: 407–436.

JUDAY, C., and G. WAGNER. 1908. Dissolved Oxygen as a Factor in the Distribution of Fishes. Trans. Wis. Acad. Sci., Arts, Let., **16**: 17–22.

KEMMERER, G., J. F. BOVARD, and W. R. BOORMAN. 1923. Northwestern Lakes of the United States: Biological and Chemical Studies with Reference to Possibilities in Production of Fish. Bull. U.S. Bur. Fish., **39**: 51–140.

KEYS, A. B. 1930. The Relation of the Oxygen Tension in the External Respiratory Medium to the Oxygen Consumption of Fishes. Science, **71**: 195–196.

KINDLE, E. M. 1927. The Role of Thermal Stratification in Lacustrine Sedimentation. Trans. R. Soc. Canada, **21**: 1–36.

KING, E. J., and VIOLA DAVIDSON. 1933. The Biochemistry of Silicic Acid. IV. Relation of Silica to the Growth of Phytoplankton. Biochem. Jour., **27**: 1015–1021.

KINKEL, A. J., and W. C. ALLEE. 1940. The Effect of Traces of Tin on the Rate of Growth of Goldfish. Am. Jour. Physiol., **130**: 665–670.

KOLLER, G. 1930. Versuche an Marinen Wirbellosen über die Aufnahme gelöster Nahrstoffe. Zeit. f. vergl. Physiol., **11**: 437–447.

KOSTOMAROV, B. 1928. Studien über die Funktion der im Wasser gelösten Nährsubstanzen in Stoffwechsel der Wassertiere. X. Mitt. Die Bedeutung der gelösten Nährsubstanzen für den Stoffwechsel der Karpfenbrut. Arch. f. Hydrobiol., **19**: 331–365.

KRIZENECKY, J., and I. PETROV. 1927. Studien über die Funktion der im Wasser gelösten Nährsubstanzen im Stoffwechsel der Wassertiere. VIII Mitt. Zeit f. vergl. Physiol., **6**: 1–35.

KRIZENECKY, J., and J. PODHRADSKY. 1924. Studien über die Funktion der im Wasser gelösten Nährsubstanzen im Stoffwechsel der Wassertiere. Mitt. I, II, III, and IV. Pflügers Arch. f. ges. Physiol., **203**: 129–140; **204**: 1–24, 25–41, 471–476.

KROGH, A. 1931. Dissolved Substances as Food of Aquatic Organisms. Biol. Rev. and Biol. Proc. Cambr. Phil. Soc., **6**: 412–442.

———. 1941. The Comparative Physiology of Respiratory Mechanisms. Philadelphia, 192 pp.

KROGH, A., and K. BERG. 1931. Über die chemische Zusammensetzung des Phytoplanktons aus dem Frederiksborg-Schlosssee und ihre Bedeutung für die Maxima der Cladoceren. Int. Rev. d. ges. Hydrobiol. u. Hydrogr., **25**: 204–218.

KROGH, A., and E. LANGE. 1931. Quantitative Untersuchungen über Plankton, Kolloide und gelöste organische und anorganische Substanzen in den Furesee. Int. Rev. d. ges. Hydrobiol u. Hydrogr., **26**: 20–53.

LINDEMAN, R. L. 1942. Experimental Simulation of Winter Anaerobiosis in a Senescent Lake. Ecology, **23**: 1–13.

MACHT, D. I. 1927. The Toxicology of Carbon Monoxide. Science, **66**: 198–199.

MALOEUF, N. W. R. 1937. The Energy Source of the Mussel (Mytilus edulis) during Oxygen Lack. Zeit. f. vergl. Physiol., **25**: 43–46.

MARSH, M. C. 1910. Notes on the Dissolved Content of Water in Its Effect upon Fishes. Bull. U.S. Bur. Fish., **28**: 891–906.

MARSH, M. C., and F. P. GORHAM. 1905. The Gas Disease in Fishes. App. Rep. Comm. Fish., pp. 343–376.

MATHESON, R., and E. H. HINMAN. 1931. Further Work on *Chara* spp. and Other Biological Notes on Culicidae (Mosquitoes). Am. Jour. Hyg., **14**: 99–108.

MAUCHA, R. 1931. Sauerstoffschichtung und Seetypenlehre. Verh. d. Int. Ver. f. theor. u. angew. Limn., **5**: 75–102.

McLAREN, BARBARA A., E. F. HERMAN, and C. A. ELVEHJEM. 1946. Nutrition of Rainbow Trout; Studies with Purified Rations. Arch. Biochem., **10**: 433–441.

McLAREN, BARBARA A., ELIZ. KELLER, D. J. O'DONNELL, and C. A. ELVEHJEM. 1947. The Nutrition of Rainbow Trout. I. Studies of Vitamin Requirements. Arch. Biochem., **15**: 169–178.

MELOCHE, V. W., G. LEADER, L. SAFRANSKI, and C. JUDAY. 1938. The Silica and Diatom Content of Lake Mendota Water. Trans. Wis. Acad. Sci., Arts, Let., **31**: 363–376.

MILLER, E. C. 1931. Plant Physiology. New York, 900 pp.

MOORE, B., E. S. EDIE, E. WHITLEY, and W. J. DAKIN. 1912. The Nutrition and Metabolism of Marine Animals in Relation to (*a*) Dissolved Organic Matter and (*b*) Particulate Organic Matter of Seawater. Biochem. Jour., **6**: 255–296.

MOORE, B., and T. A. WEBSTER. 1920. Studies of Photo-synthesis in Fresh-water Algae. 1. The Fixation of Both Carbon and Nitrogen from the Atmosphere to Form Organic Tissue by the Green Plant Cell. 2. Nutrition and Growth Produced by High Gaseous Dilutions of Simple Organic Compounds, Such as Formaldehyde and Methylic Alcohol. 3. Nutrition and Growth by Means of High Dilutions of Carbon Dioxide and Oxides of Nitrogen without Access to Atmosphere. Proc. R. Soc. London, (B) **91**: 201–215.

MOORE, B., E. WHITLEY, and T. A. WEBSTER. 1921. Studies of Photosynthesis in Marine Algae. 1. Fixation of Carbon and Nitrogen from Inorganic Sources in Sea Water. 2. Increase of Alkalinity of Sea Water as a Measure of Photosynthesis. Proc. R. Soc. London, (B) **92**: 51–58.

MOORE, G. M. 1939. A Limnological Investigation of the Microscopic Benthic Fauna of Douglas Lake, Michigan. Ecol. Monogr., **9**: 537–582.

MOORE, W. G. 1942. Field Studies on the Oxygen Requirements of Certain Freshwater Fishes. Ecology, **23**: 317–329.

MORTIMER, C. H. 1941–1942. The Exchange of Dissolved Substances between Mud and Water in Lakes. Jour. Ecology, **29**: 280–329; **30**: 147–201.

MOYLE, J. B. 1945. Some Chemical Factors Influencing the Distribution of Aquatic Plants in Minnesota. Am. Midl. Nat., **34**: 403–420.

NAKAJIMA, A. 1927. Über die Ernährung von Urodelen- und Anurenlarven durch im Wasser gelöste Nährstoffe und andere Lösungen. Fol. Anat. Jap., **5**(3): 213–224.

NAUMANN, E. 1921. Spezielle Untersuchungen über die Ernährungsbiologie des tierischen Limnoplanktons. I. Über die Tecknik des Nahrungserwerbs bei den Cladoceren und ihre Bedeutung für die Biologie der Gewässertypen. Lunds Univ. Arsskr., N.F., **17**: 3–26.

———. 1923. Spezielle Untersuchungen über die Ernährungsbiologie des Tierischen Limnoplanktons. II. Über den Nahrungserwerb und die natürliche Nahrung der Copepoden und die Rotiferen des Limnoplanktons. Lunds Univ. Arsskr., N.F., **19**: 3–17.

———. 1925. Methoden der experimentallen Aquarienkunde. Abderhalden's Handbuch der Biol. Arbeitsmeth., Abt. 9, Teil 2, Heft 1, pp. 622–652.

NOLAND, L. E. 1925. Factors Influencing the Distribution of Fresh Water Ciliates. Ecology, **6**: 437–452.

PACKARD, W. H. 1905. On Resistance to Lack of Oxygen and on a Method of Increasing this Resistance. Am. Jour. Physiol., **15**: 30–41.

————. 1907. The Effect of Carbohydrates on Resistance to Lack of Oxygen. Am. Jour. Physiol., **18**: 164–180.

————. 1908. Further Studies on Resistance to Lack of Oxygen. Am. Jour. Physiol., **21**: 310–333.

PEARSALL, W. H. 1922. A Suggestion as to the Factors Influencing the Distribution of Free Floating Vegetation. Jour. Ecology, **9**: 241–253.

————. 1930. Phytoplankton in the English Lakes. I. The Proportions in the Waters of Some Dissolved Substances of Biological Importance. Jour. Ecology, **18**: 306–320.

————. 1932. Phytoplankton in the English Lakes. II. The Composition of the Phytoplankton in Relation to Dissolved Substances. Jour. Ecology, **20**: 241–262.

————. 1934. Light Penetration into Fresh Water. III. Seasonal Variations in the Light Conditions in Windermere in Relation to Vegetation. Jour. Exp. Biol. **11**: 87–93.

PEARSALL, W. H., and C. H. MORTIMER. 1939. Oxidation-reduction Potentials in Waterlogged Soils, Natural Waters and Muds. Jour. Ecology, **27**: 483–501.

PEARSE, A. S., and H. ACHTENBERG. 1920. Habits of Yellow Perch in Wisconsin Lakes. Bull. U.S. Bur. Fish., **36**: 295–366.

PENNINGTON, W. 1942. Experiments on the Utilization of Nitrogen in Fresh Water. Jour. Ecology, **30**: 326–340.

PHILLIPS, A. M., and D. R. BROCKWAY. 1948. Vitaminology. Progr. Fish-Culturist, **10**: 117–124.

PHILLIPS, A. M., and E. O. ROGERS, 1949. The Folic Acid Requirements of Trout. Progr. Fish-Culturist, **11**: 141–145.

POLLOCK, J.B. 1919. Blue-green Algae as Agents in the Deposition of Marl in Michigan Lakes. 20th Rept. Mich. Acad. Sci., pp. 247–260.

POWERS, E. B. 1920. Antagonism and Its Possible Utility in Polluted Waters. Proc. Am. Fish. Soc., pp. 293–296.

————. 1921. A Comparison of the Electrical Conductivity of Electrolytes and Their Toxicities to Fish. Am. Jour. Physiol., **55**: 197–200.

————. 1922. The Physiology of the Respiration of Fishes in Relation to the Hydrogen Ion Concentration of the Medium. Jour. Gen. Physiol., **4**: 305–317.

————. 1922. The Alkali Reserve of the Blood of Fish in Relation to the Environment. Am. Jour. Physiol., **61**: 380–383.

————. 1923. The Absorption of Oxygen by the Herring as Affected by the Carbon Dioxide Tension of the Sea Water. Ecology, **4**: 307–312.

————. 1930. The Relation between pH and Aquatic Animals. Am. Nat., **64**: 342–366.

————. 1934. Certain Conditions of Existence of Fishes, Especially as Concerns Their Internal Environment. Ecology, **15**: 69–79.

————. 1938. Factors Involved in the Mortality of Fishes. Trans. Am. Fish. Soc., **67**: 271–281.

————. 1939. Chemical Factors Affecting the Migratory Movements of the Pacific Salmon. In The Migration and Conservation of Salmon. Publ. A.A.A.S., No. 8, pp. 72–85.

————. 1941. Physico-Chemical Behaviors of Waters as Factors in the "Homing" of the Salmon. Ecology, **22**: 1–16.

POWERS, E. B., and G. A. LOGAN. 1925. The Alkaline Reserve of the Blood Plasma of the Viviparous Perch (Cymatogaster aggregatus Gib.) in Relation to the

Carbon Dioxide Tension, the Oxygen Tension and the Alkalinity of the Sea Water. Publ. Puget Sound Biol. Sta., **3** : 337–360.

POWERS, E. B. 1932. The Relation of Respiration of Fishes to Environment. Ecol. Monogr., **2** : 386–473.

POWERS, E. B., A. R. SHIELDS, and MARY E. HICKMAN. 1939. The Mortality of Fishes in Norris Lake. Jour. Tenn. Acad. Sci., **14** : 239–260.

PÜTTER, A. 1907. Die Ernährung der Wassertiere. Zeit. allg. Physiol., **7** : 283–320.

———. 1909. Die Ernährung der Wassertiere und der Stoffhaushalt der Gewässer. Jena, 168 pp.

———. 1909. Die Ernährung der Fische. Zeit. allg. Physiol., **9** : 147–242.

———. 1909. Vergleichende Physiologie. Jena, 721 pp.

———. 1924. Die Ernährung der Copepoden. Arch. f. Hydrobiol., **15** : 70–117.

———. 1924. Der Umfang der Kohlensäurerreduktion durch die Planktonalgen. Pflügers Arch. f. ges. Physiol., **205** : 293–312.

RAUSON, G. 1926. La nutrition chez les aninaux aquatique. Compt. rend. acad. sci. Paris, **182** : 1102–1104.

———. 1927. L'absorption de matière organique dissoute par la surface exterieure du corps chez les animaux aquatique. Ann. inst. oceanogr., **4** : 49–169.

RAWSON, D. S. 1939. Some Physical and Chemical Factors in the Metabolism of Lakes. In Problems of Lake Biology, Publ. A.A.A.S., No. 10, pp. 9–26.

RICKER, W. E. 1937. Physical and Chemical Characteristics of Cultus Lake, British Columbia. Jour. Biol. Bd. Canada, **3** : 363–402.

RILEY, G. A. 1937. The Significance of the Mississippi River Drainage for Biological Conditions in the Northern Gulf of Mexico. Jour. Marine Res., **1** : 60–74.

———. 1939. Limnological Studies in Connecticut. Ecol. Monogr., **9** : 53–94.

RODHE, W. 1948. Environmental Requirements of Fresh-water Plankton Algae. Symbolae Botanicae Upsalienses, **10** : 1–149.

ROELOFS, E. W. 1944. Water Soils in Relation to Lake Productivity. Michigan State Coll., Agr. Exp. Sta., Tech. Bull. 190, 31 pp.

ROHLICH, G. A., W. B. SARLES, and L. H. KESSLER. 1941. Oxidation-reduction Potentials in Activated Sludge. In A Symposium on Hydrobiology. Univ. Wis. Press, pp. 288–302.

RUTTNER, F. 1926. Bemerkungen über Sauerstoffgehalt der Gewässer und dessen respiratotischer Wert. Naturwiss., **14** : 1237–1239.

SCHUETTE, H. A., and H. ALDER. 1929. A Note on the Chemical Composition of *Chara* from Green Lake, Wisconsin. Trans. Wis. Acad. Sci., Arts, Let., **24** : 141–145.

SHELFORD, V. E. 1923. The Determination of Hydrogen Ion Concentration in Connection with Fresh-water Biological Studies. State of Illinois. Div. Nat. Hist. Surv., **14** : 379–395.

SKADOWSKY, S. 1926. Über die aktuelle Reaktion der Süsswasserbecken und ihre biologische Bedeutung. Verh. d. Int. Ver. f. theor. u. angew. Limn., **3** : 109–144.

SLATER, W. K. 1928. Anaerobic Life in Animals. Biol. Rev. and Biol. Proc. Cambr. Phil. Soc., **3** : 303–328.

SMALL, J. 1946. pH and Plants: An Introduction for Beginners. New York, 223 pp.

SMITH, F. 1925. Variation in the Maximum Depth at Which Fish Can Live during Summer in a Moderately Deep Lake with a Thermocline. Bull. U.S. Bur. Fish., **41** : 1–7.

SMITH, G. M. 1951. The Fresh-water Algae of the United States. 2d ed. New York, 719 pp.

STILES, W. 1946. Trace Elements in Plants and Animals. New York, 189 pp.

SVERDRUP, H. U., M. W. JOHNSON, and R. H. FLEMING. 1942. The Oceans, Their Physics, Chemistry, and General Biology. New York. 1087 pp.

THOMPSON, D. H. 1925. Some Observations of the Oxygen Requirements of Fishes in the Illinois River. State of Ill. Div. of Nat. Hist. Surv., **15**: 423–437.

———. 1933. The Migration of Illinois Fishes. State of Ill. Div. of Nat. Hist. Surv., Biol. Notes 1, 25 pp.

TRUE, R. H. 1922. The Significance of Calcium for Higher Green Plants. Science, **55**: 1–6.

VON BRAND, T. 1946. Anaerobiosis in Invertebrates. Normandy, Mo., 328 pp.

VON BRAND, T., H. D. BAERNSTEIN, and B. MEHLMAN. 1950. Studies on the Anaerobic Metabolism and the Aerobic Carbohydrate Consumption of Some Fresh-water Snails. Biol. Bull., **98**: 266–276.

WESENBERG-LUND, C. 1901. Studier over Søkalk, Bønnemalm og Søgytje. 1 Danske Indsøer. Saertryk Af Meddelelser Fra Dansk Geologisk Forening 7, 180 pp.

WIEBE, A. H. 1931. Notes on the Exposure of Several Species of Fish to Sudden Changes in the Hydrogen-ion Concentration of the Water and to an Atmosphere of Pure Oxygen. Trans. Am. Fish. Soc., pp. 216–224.

———. 1931. Dissolved Phosphorus and Inorganic Nitrogen in the Water of the Mississippi River. Science, **73**: 652.

———. 1931. Notes on the Exposure of Several Species of Pond Fishes to Sudden Changes in pH. Trans. Am. Micr. Soc., **50**: 380–393.

———. 1933. The Effect of High Concentrations of Dissolved Oxygen on Several Species of Pond Fishes. Ohio Jour. Sci., **33**: 110–126.

WOODBURY, L. A. 1942. A Sudden Mortality of Fishes Accompanying a Supersaturation of Oxygen in Lake Waubesa, Wisconsin. Trans. Am. Fish. Soc., **71**: 112–117.

WORTHINGTON, E. B. 1930. Observations on the Temperature, Hydrogen-ion Concentration, and Other Physical Conditions of the Victoria and Albert Nyanzas. Int. Rev. d. ges. Hydrobiol. u. Hydrogr., **24**: 328–357.

WU, YI FANG. 1931. A Contribution to the Biology of Simulium (Diptera). Papers Mich. Acad. Sci., Arts, Let., **13**: 543–599.

ZOBELL, C. E. 1940. Some Factors which influence Oxygen Consumption by Bacteria in Lake Water. Biol. Bull., **78**: 388–402.

ORGANISMS IN INLAND WATERS

I. COMPREHENSIVE TREATISES

BOARDMAN, E. T. 1939. Field Guide to Lower Aquarium Animals. Cranbrook Inst. Sci., Bull. 16, 186 pp.

BRAUER, A. 1909–1912. Die Süsswasserfauna Deutschlands. Heft 1–19. Jena. (32 authors.)

CARPENTER, K. E. 1928. Life in Inland Waters. New York, 267 pp.

FURNEAUX, W. 1906. Life in Ponds and Streams. New York, 406 pp.

HENTSCHEL, E. 1909. Das Leben des Süsswassers. Munich, 336 pp.

LAMPERT, K. 1925. Das Leben der Binnengewässer. 3 Auf. Leipzig, 892 pp.

MORGAN, A. H. 1930. Field Book of Ponds and Streams. New York, 448 pp.

MURRAY, JAMES. 1910. Biology of the Scottish Lochs. I. The Biology in Relation to Environment. II. Census of the Species. In Murray and Pullar's Bathymetrical Survey of the Scottish Freshwater Lochs, **1**: 275–334.

NEEDHAM, J. G., and J. T. LLOYD. 1930. The Life of Inland Waters, 2d ed. Springfield, 438 pp.

NEEDHAM, J. G., and P. R. NEEDHAM. 1938. Guide to the Study of Fresh-water Biology, 4th ed. Springfield, 90 pp.

PASCHER, A. 1913–1936. Die Süsswasserflora Deutschlands, Osterreichs und Schweiz. Jena. Heft 1–15 (No. 8 not issued); 2d ed. issued under name "Die Süsswasserflora Mitteleuropas" (only Heft 9, 10, 14 issued). Parts by various authors.

PRATT, H. S. 1935. Manual of the Common Invertebrate Animals, 2d ed. Chicago, 854 pp.

SCHOENISCHEN, W. 1925–1927. Einfachste Lebensformen des Tier- und Pflanzenreiches. 5th ed. Bd. I, 519 pp.; Bd. II, 522 pp.

SCHULZE, P. 1922–1932. Biologie der Tiere Deutschlands, 34 Lief. Berlin.

WALTON, L. B. 1930. Studies concerning Organisms Occurring in Water Supplies. Part I. Bull. 24, Ohio Biol. Surv., 84 pp.

WARD, H. B., and G. C. WHIPPLE. 1918. Fresh-water Biology. New York, 1111 pp. (27 authors.)

WESENBERG-LUND, C. 1937. Ferskvandsfaunaen biologisk belysk. Invertebrata. 2 vols. Copenhagen, 837 pp.

———. 1939. Biologie der Süsswassertiere wirbellose Tiere. Wien, 1138 pp.

WHIPPLE, G. C. 1927. The Microscopy of Drinking Water. 4th ed., rev. by Fair and Whipple. New York, 586 pp.

ZACHARIAS, O. 1891. Die Tiere- und Pflanzenwelt des Süsswassers. Leipzig, Bd. I, 380 pp.; Bd. II, 369 pp.

ZSCHOKKE, F. 1900. Tierwelt den Hochgebirgsseen. Neue Denkschr. Schweiz. naturf. Ges., 37, 400 pp.

———. 1911. Tiefseefauna der Seen Mitteleuropas. Eine geographisch-faunistische Studie. Leipzig, 246 pp.

II. SPECIAL WORKS

A. Aquatic Plants

ANDERSON, E. N., and E. R. WALKER. 1920. An Ecological Study of the Algae of Some Sandhill Lakes. Trans. Am. Micr. Soc., **39**: 51–85.

ARBER, A. 1920. Water Plants. A Study of Aquatic Angiosperms. Cambridge, 436 pp.

BAUMANN, E. 1911. Die Vegetation des Untersees (Bodensee). Arch. f. Hydrobiol., Suppl. Bd. I, 554 pp.

BESSEY, C. E. 1914. Synopsis of the Conjugate Algae—Zygophyceae. Trans. Am. Micr. Soc., **33**: 11–49.

BROWN, H. J. 1929. The Algal Family Vaucheriaceae. Trans. Am. Micr. Soc., **48**: 86–117.

———. 1930. The Desmids of the Southeastern Coastal Plain Region of the United States. Trans. Am. Micr. Soc., **49**: 97–139.

CONN, H. W., and L. W. WEBSTER. 1908. A Preliminary Report on the Algae of the Fresh Waters of Connecticut. State of Conn., State Geol. Nat. Hist. Surv., Bull. 10, 78 pp., 44 plates.

DENNISTON, R. H. 1922. A Survey of the Larger Aquatic Plants of Lake Mendota. Trans. Wis. Acad. Sci., Arts, Let., **20**: 495–500.

EDDY, S. 1925. Fresh Water Algal Succession. Trans. Am. Micr. Soc., **44**: 138–147.

———. 1927. A Study of Algal Distribution. Trans. Am. Micr. Soc., **46**: 122–138.

FASSETT, N. C. 1930. The Plants of some Northeastern Wisconsin Lakes. Trans. Wis. Acad. Sci., Arts, Let., **25**: 157–168.

————. 1940. A Manual of Aquatic Plants. New York. 382 pp.

FERNALD, M. L. 1932. The Linear-leaves North American Species of Potamogeton, Section Axillares. Mem. Am. Acad. Arts Sci., **17**: 5–183.

HODGETTS, W. J. 1921–1922. Periodicity of Freshwater Algae in Nature. New Phytol., **20**: 150–164, 195–227; **21**: 15–33.

HÖPPNER, H. 1926. Hydrobiologische Untersuchungen an niederrheinischen Gewässern. II. Die Phanerogamenflora der Seen und Teiche des unteren Niederrheins. Arch. f. Hydrobiol., **17**: 117–158.

HOTCHKISS, N. 1936. Check-list of Marsh and Aquatic Plants of the United States. U.S. Dept. Agr., Bureau of Biol. Surv., Wildlife Res. Manag. Leaflet BS-72, 27 pp.

HYLANDER, C. J. 1928. The Algae of Connecticut. State of Conn., State Geol. Nat. Hist. Surv., Bull. 42, 245 pp.

LOWE, C. W. 1923. Freshwater Algae and Freshwater Diatoms. Rept. Can. Arctic Exped., 1913–1918, **4**: 3–53.

MUENSCHER, W. C. 1944. Aquatic Plants of the United States. Ithaca, N.Y., 384 pp.

PEARSALL, W. H. 1920. The Aquatic Vegetation of the English Lakes. Jour. Ecology, **8**: 163–201.

PIETERS, A. J. 1894. The Plants of Lake St. Clair. Bull. Mich. Fish Comm., No. 2, pp. 3–10.

————. 1901. The Plants of Western Lake Erie with Observations on Their Distribution. Bull. U.S. Fish Comm., **21**: 57–79.

POND, R. H. 1905. The Biological Relation of Aquatic Plants to the Substratum. U.S. Fish Comm. Rept. for 1903, pp. 483–526.

PRESCOTT, G. W. 1951. Algae of the Western Great Lakes Area. Cranbrook Inst. Sci., Bull. 31, 946 pp.

RICKETT, H. W. 1920. A Quantitative Survey of the Flora of Lake Mendota. Science, **52**: 641–642.

————. 1922. A Quantitative Study of the Larger Aquatic Plants of Lake Mendota. Trans. Wis. Acad. Sci., Arts, Let., **20**: 501–527.

————. 1924. A Quantitative Study of the Larger Aquatic Plants of Green Lake, Wisconsin. Trans. Wis. Acad. Sci., Arts, Let., **21**: 381–414.

SCHUETTE, H. A., and H. ALDER. 1928. Notes on the Chemical Composition of Some of the Larger Aquatic Plants of Lake Mendota. II. Vallisneria and Potamogeton. Trans. Wis. Acad. Sci., Arts, Let., **23**: 249–254.

————. 1929. Notes on the Chemical Composition of Some of the Larger Aquatic Plants of Lake Mendota. III. Castalia odorata and Najas flexilis. Trans. Wis. Acad. Sci., Arts, Let., **24**: 135–139.

SCHUETTE, H. A., and A. E. HOFFMAN. 1922. Notes on the Chemical Composition of Some of the Larger Aquatic Plants of Lake Mendota. I. Cladophora and Myriophyllum. Trans. Wis. Acad. Sci., Arts, Let., **20**: 529–531.

SMITH, G. M. 1920. Phytoplankton of the Inland Lakes of Wisconsin. Part I. Wis. Geol. Nat. Hist. Surv., Bull. 57, 243 pp.

————. 1924. Phytoplankton of the Inland Lakes of Wisconsin. Part II. Wis. Geol. Nat. Hist. Surv., Bull. 57, 227 pp.

————. 1938. Cryptogamic Botany. New York, vol. I, 545 pp.; vol. II, 380 pp.

————. 1951. The Fresh-water Algae of the United States. 2d ed. New York, 719 pp.

SPARROW, F. K. 1943. Aquatic Phycomycetes. Univ. Mich. Press, 785 pp.

STROEDE, W. 1932. Oekologie der Characeen. Berlin, 118 pp.

TIFFANY, L. H. 1922. Some Algae Statistics Gleaned from the Gizzard Shad. Science, **56**: 285–286.

————. 1926. The Filamentous Algae of North-western Iowa with Special Reference to the Oedogoniaceae. Trans. Am. Micr. Soc., **45**: 69–132.

————. 1928. The Algal Genus Bulbochaete. Trans. Am. Micr. Soc., **47**: 121–177.

————. 1938. Algae, the Grass of Many Waters. Springfield, 171 pp.

TILDEN, J. 1910. Minnesota Algae. Rept. Minn. Survey, Bot. ser. VIII, vol. 1, 328 pp.

————. 1917. Synopsis of the Blue-green Algae—Myxophyceae. Trans. Am. Micr. Soc., **36**: 179–266.

————. 1935. The *Algae* and Their Life Relations. Univ. Minn. Press, 550 pp.

TRANSEAU, E. N. 1913. The Periodicity of Algae in Illinois. Trans. Am. Micr. Soc., **32**: 31–40.

————. 1916. The Periodicity of Freshwater Algae. Am. Jour. Bot., **17**: 121–133.

VIVIAN, E. L. 1932. Report on the Myxophyceae of Nebraska. Trans. Am. Micr. Soc., **51**: 79–128.

WEST, G. 1910. An Epitome of a Comparative Study of the Dominant Phanerogamic and Higher Cryptogamic Flora of Aquatic Habit, in Seven Lake Areas in Scotland. In Murray and Pullar's Bathymetrical Survey of the Scottish Fresh-water Lochs, **1**: 156–260.

WEST, G. S., and F. E. FRITSCH. 1927. A Treatise on the British Freshwater Algae, rev. ed. Cambridge, 534 pp.

WEST, W., and G. S. WEST. 1904–1908. A Monograph of the British Desmidiaceae. Ray Soc. Publ., vol. I, 224 pp.; vol. II, 204 pp.; vol. III, 273 pp.

WOLF, F. A., and F. T. WOLF. 1947. The Fungi. New York, vol. I, 438 pp.; vol. II, 538 pp.

WOLLE, F. 1887. Fresh-water Algae of the United States. Bethlehem, Pa., vol. 1, 364 pp.; vol. 2, 210 plates.

————. 1892. Desmids of the United States. Bethlehem, Pa., 182 pp., 64 plates.

————. 1894. Diatomaceae of North America. Bethlehem, Pa., 45 pp., 112 plates.

WOOD, R. D. 1949. The Characeae of the Woods Hole Region, Massachusetts. Biol. Bull., **96**: 179–203.

B. Aquatic Animals

1. PROTOZOA

BLOCHMANN, F. 1895. Die Mikroscopische Thierwelt des Süsswassers. Abt. I. Protozoa. Hamburg, 134 pp.

CALKINS, G. N. 1926. The Biology of the Protozoa. Philadelphia, 623 pp.

CASH, J., G. H. WAILES, and J. HOPKINS. 1905–1921. The British Freshwater Rhizopoda and Heliozoa. Ray Society. London, 5 vols.

CONN, H. W. 1905. A Preliminary Report on the Protozoa of the Fresh Waters of Connecticut. State of Conn., State Geol. Nat. Hist. Surv., Bull. 2, pp. 5–69.

EDDY, S. 1928. Succession of Protozoa in Cultures under Controlled Conditions. Trans. Am. Micr. Soc., **47**: 283–319.

————. 1930. The Fresh-water Armored or Thecate Dinoflagellates. Trans. Am. Micr. Soc., **49**: 277–321.

EDMONDSON, C. H. 1906. The Protozoa of Iowa. Proc. Davenport Acad. Sci., **11**: 1–124.

————. 1912. Protozoa of High Mountain Lakes in Colorado. Univ. Colo. Studies, **9**: 65–74.

————. 1920. Protozoa of Devil's Lake Complex, North Dakota. Trans. Am. Micr. Soc., **39**: 167–198.

HYMAN, L. H. 1940. The Invertebrates: Protozoa through Ctenophora. New York, 726 pp.

KEISER, A. 1921. Die sessilen peritrichen Infusorien und Suctorien von Basel und Umgebung. Rev. suisse zool., **28**: 221–341.

KENT, W. S. 1880–1882. A Manual of the Infusoria. London, 3 vols.

LEIDY, J. 1879. Fresh-water Rhizopods of North America. U.S. Geol. Surv. Rept., vol. 12, 324 pp., 48 plates.

WALTON, L. B. 1915. A Review of the Described Species of the Order Eugleniodina Bloch Class Flagellata (Protozoa) with Particular Reference to Those Found in the City Water Supplies and Other Localities in Ohio. Ohio State Univ., Bull. 4, Ohio Biol. Surv., **1**: 343–459.

WENYON, C. M. 1926. Protozoology. 2 vols. London, 1,563 pp.

2. PORIFERA

GEE, N. G. 1930–1931. A Contribution towards an Alphabetical List of the Known Fresh-water Sponges. Peking Nat. Hist. Bull., **5**: 31–52.

OLD, M. C. 1932. Environmental Selection of the Fresh-water Sponges (Spongillidae) of Michigan. Trans. Am. Micr. Soc., **51**: 129–136.

———. 1932. Taxonomy and Distribution of the Fresh-water Sponges (Spongillidae) of Michigan. Papers Mich. Acad. Sci., Arts, Let., **15**: 439–477.

———. 1933. Contribution to the Biology of Fresh-water Sponges (Spongillidae). Papers Mich. Acad. Sci., Arts, Let., **17**: 663–679.

POTTS, E. 1887. Fresh-water Sponges: A Monograph. Proc. Acad. Nat. Sci. Phil., **39**: 158–279.

SMITH, F. 1921. Distribution of the Fresh-water Sponges of North America. State of Ill., Div. Nat. Hist. Surv., **14**: 9–22.

3. COELENTERATA

CLEMENS, W. A. 1922. Hydra in Lake Erie. Science, **55**: 445–446.

GRIFFIN, L. E., and D. C. PETERS. 1939. A New Species of Hydra, *Hydra oregona*. Trans. Am. Micr. Soc., **58**: 256–257.

HYMAN, L. H. 1929. Taxonomic Studies on the Hydras of North America. I–IV. Trans. Am. Micr. Soc., **48**: 242–255; **49**: 322–333; **50**: 20–29; 302–315.

———. 1938. Taxonomic Studies on the Hydras of North America. Am. Museum Novitates, No. 1003.

MILLER, D. E. 1936. A Limnological Study of *Pelmatohydra* with Special Reference to Their Quantitative Seasonal Distribution. Trans. Am. Micr. Soc., **55**: 123–193.

PAYNE, F. 1924. A Study of the Fresh-water Medusa, Craspedacusta ryderi. Jour. Morphology, **38**: 387–430.

———. 1926. Further Studies on the Life History of Craspedacusta ryderi, a Fresh-water Hydromedusan. Biol. Bull., **50**: 433–443.

SMITH, F. 1910. Hydroids in the Illinois River. Biol. Bull., **18**: 67–68.

WELCH, P. S., and H. A. LOOMIS. 1924. A Limnological Study of Hydra oligactis in Douglas Lake, Michigan. Trans. Am. Micr. Soc., **43**: 203–235.

4. TURBELLARIA

HIGLEY, R. 1918. Morphology and Biology of Some Turbellaria from the Mississippi Basin. Ill. Biol. Monogr., **4**: 5–94.

HYMAN, L. H. 1928. Studies on the Morphology, Taxonomy, and Distribution of North American Triclad Turbellaria. I–X. Trans. Am. Micr. Soc., **47**: 222–255; **48**: 406–415; **50**: 124–135; 316–335; 336–343; **54**: 338–345; **56**: 298–310; 457–477; **58**: 264–275; 276–284.

KENK, R. 1944. The Fresh-water Triclads of Michigan. Misc. Publ., Mus. Zool., Univ. Mich., No. 60, 44 pp.

STANKOVIC, S., and J. KOMAREK. 1927. Die Süsswasser-Tricladen des Westbalkans und die zoogeographischen Probleme dieser Gegend. Zool. Jahrb., Abt. Syst., Ökol., u. geogr. Tiere, **53**: 591–674.

5. ROTATORIA

BEAUCHAMP, P. DE. 1928. Coup d'œil sur les recherches récentes relatives aux rotifères et sur les méthodes qui leur sont applicables. Bull. biol. France et Belg., **42**: 51–125.

EDMONDSON, W. T. 1940. The Sessile Rotatoria of Wisconsin. Trans. Am. Micr. Soc., **59**: 433–459.

————. 1949. A Formula Key to the Rotatorian Genus Ptygura. Trans. Am. Micr. Soc., **68**: 127–135.

HARRING, H. K. 1913. Synopsis of the Rotatoria. Bull. U.S. Nat. Museum, No. 81, 226 pp.

————. 1921. The Rotatoria of the Canadian Arctic Expedition, 1913–1918. Rept. Can. Arctic Exped., 1913–1918, vol. 8, Part E, 23 pp.

HARRING, H. K., and F. J. MYERS. 1922. The Rotifer Fauna of Wisconsin. Trans. Wis. Acad. Sci., Arts, Let., **20**: 553–662.

————. 1924. The Rotifer Fauna of Wisconsin. II. Trans. Wis. Acad. Sci., Arts, Let., **21**: 415–549.

————. 1926. The Rotifer Fauna of Wisconsin. III. Trans. Wis. Acad. Sci., Arts, Let., **22**: 315–423.

————. 1928. The Rotifer Fauna of Wisconsin. IV. Trans. Wis. Acad. Sci., Arts, Let., **23**: 667–808.

HUDSON, C. T., and P. H. GOSSE. 1889. The Rotifers or Wheel Animalcules. 2 vols. London. 336 pp.

JENNINGS, H. S. 1894. A List of the Rotatoria of the Great Lakes and of Some of the Inland Lakes of Michigan. Bull. Mich. Fish Comm., No. 3, pp. 3–34.

————. 1900. Rotatoria of the United States with Especial Reference to Those of the Great Lakes. Bull. U.S. Fish Comm. for 1899, pp. 67–104.

————. 1901. Synopses of North-American Invertebrates. XVII. The Rotatoria. Am. Nat., **35**: 725–777.

MYERS, F. J. 1930. The Rotifer Fauna of Wisconsin. Trans. Wis. Acad. Sci., Arts, Let., **25**: 353–413.

WESENBERG-LUND, C. 1923. Contributions to the Biology of the Rotifera. I. The Males of the Rotifera. Mém. l'Acad. R. Sci. Let. Danemark, 8me ser., **4**: 191–345.

————. 1930. Contributions to the Biology of the Rotifera. Part II. The Periodicity and Sexual Periods. Mém. l'Acad. R. Sci. Let. Danemark, 9me ser., **2**: 3–230.

6. GASTROTRICHA

BRUNSON, R. B. 1949. The Life History and Ecology of Two North American Gastrotrichs. Trans. Am. Micr. Soc., **68**: 1–20.

————. 1950. An Introduction to the Taxonomy of the Gastrotricha with a Study of Eighteen Species from Michigan. Trans. Am. Micr. Soc., **69**: 325–352.

MURRAY, J. 1913. Gastrotricha. Jour. Quekett Micr. Cl., **12**: 413–447.

PACKARD, C. E. 1936. Observations on the Gastrotricha Indigenous to New Hampshire. Trans. Am. Micr. Soc., **55**: 422–427.

REMANE, A. 1936. Gastrotricha. Klass. u. Ord. d. Tier., **4**: 1–242.

WARD, H. B. 1918. Gastrotricha. In Fresh-water Biology, pp. 621–631. New York.

7. NEMATOIDEA

COBB, N. A. 1913. New Nematode Genera Found Inhabiting Fresh Water and Non-brackish Soils. Jour. Wash. Acad. Sci., **3**: 432–444.

———. 1914. The North American Free-living Fresh-water Nematodes. Trans. Am. Micr. Soc., **33**: 69–134.

———. 1914. Nematodes and Their Relationships. Yearbook of U.S. Dept. Agr. for 1914, pp. 457–490.

GOODEY, T. 1951. Soil and Freshwater Nematodes. London, 390 pp.

HOEPPLI, R. J. C. 1926. Studies of Free-living Nematodes from the Thermal Waters of Yellowstone Park. Trans. Am. Micr. Soc., **45**: 234–255.

MAY, H. G. 1919. Contributions to the Life Histories of *Gordius robustus* Leidy and *Paragordius varius* (Leidy). Illinois Biol. Monogr., **5**: 7–118.

MICHOLETZKY, H. 1922. Zur Nematodenfauna des Bodensees. Int. Rev. d. ges. Hydrobiol. u. Hydrogr., **10**: 491–512.

SCHNEIDER, W. 1922. Freilebende Süsswassernematoden aus Ostholsteinischen Seen. Arch. f. Hydrobiol., **13**: 696–753.

STEINER, G. 1913–1914. Freilebende Nematoden aus der Schweiz. Arch. f. Hydrobiol., **9**: 259–276, 420–438.

WELCH, P. S., and L. P. WEHRLE. 1918. Observations on Reproduction in Certain Parthenogenetic and Bisexual Nematodes Reared in Artificial Media. Trans. Am. Micr. Soc., **37**: 141–176.

8. TARDIGRADA

CURTIN, C. B. 1948. The Tardigrade Fauna of the District of Columbia. Jour. Wash. Acad. Sci., **38**: 251–254.

MARCUS, E. 1929. Tardigraden. Klass. u. Ord. d. Tier., **5**: 1–608.

MATHEWS, G. 1938. Tardigrada from North America. Am. Midl. Nat., **19**: 619–627.

9. BRYOZOA (POLYZOA)

ALLMAN, G. J. 1856. A Monograph of the Fresh-water Polyzoa, Including All the Known Species, Both British and Foreign. Ray Society, London, 119 pp.

BRAEM, F. 1890. Untersuchungen über die Bryozoen des süssen Wassers. Berlin, 134 pp.

BROWN, C. J. D. 1933. A Limnological Study of Certain Fresh-water Polyzoa with Special Reference to Their Statoblasts. Trans. Am. Micr. Soc., **52**: 271–316.

DAVENPORT, C. B. 1904. Report on the Fresh-water Bryozoa of the United States. Proc. U.S. Nat. Museum, **27**: 211–221.

GEISER, S. W. 1934. The Distribution of Pectinatella magnifica Leidy in the United States. Field and Lab., **2**: 56–59.

HARMER, S. F. 1913. The Polyzoa of Waterworks. Proc. Zool. Soc. London, pp. 426–457.

KRAEPELIN, K. 1887–1892. Die deutschen Süsswasser-Bryozoen. I. Anatomischsystematischer Teil, 168 pp.; II. Entwickelungsgeschichtlicher Teil. Hamburg, 67 pp.

MARCUS, E. 1926. Boebachtungen und Versuche an lebenden Süsswasserbryozoen. Zool. Jahrb., Abt. Syst. Ökol. Geogr. Tiere, **52**: 279–350.

———. 1942. Sôbre Bryozoa do Brazil II. Univ. de São Paulo, Bol. d. Fac. d. Fil., Cien., e Letr., **25**: 57–105.

ROGICK, M. D. 1934. Additions to North American Freshwater Bryozoa. Ohio Jour. Sci., **34**: 316–317.

———. 1937. Studies on Fresh-water Bryozoa. V. Some Additions to Canadian Fauna. Ohio Jour. Sci., **37**: 99–104.

———. 1945. Studies on Fresh-water Bryozoa. XV. Hyalinella punctata Growth Data. Ohio Jour. Sci., **45**: 55–79.

ROGICK, MARY D., and H. VAN DER SCHALIE. 1950. Studies on Fresh-water Bryozoa. Ohio Jour. Sci., **50**: 136–146.

WESENBERG-LUND, C. 1896. Biologiske Studier over Ferskvandsbryozoer. (With French résumé.) Viddensk. Medd. Nat. For., pp. 252–363, I–XXXVI.

WILLIAMS, S. R. 1921. Concerning "Larval" Colonies of *Pectinatella*. Ohio Jour. Sci., **21**: 123–127.

10. OLIGOCHAETA

ALTMAN, L. C. 1936. Oligochaeta of Washington. Univ. Wash. Publ. in Biol., **4**: 1–137.

GOODNIGHT, C. J. 1940. The Branchiobdellidae (Oligochaeta) of North American Crayfishes. Illinois Biol. Monogr., **17**: 1–75.

MICHAELSEN, W. 1900. Oligochaeta. Das Tierreich, Lief 10. Berlin, 575 pp.

SMITH, F. 1928. An Account of Changes in the Earthworm Fauna of Illinois and a Description of One New Species. State of Ill. Div. Nat. Hist. Surv., **17**: 347–362.

SMITH, F., and P. S. WELCH. 1919. Oligochaeta Collected by the Canadian Arctic Expedition, 1913–1918. Rept. Can. Arctic Exped., 1913–1918, vol. 9, Part A, 19 pp.

STEPHENSON, J. 1930. The Oligochaeta. Oxford, 978 pp.

WALTON, L. B. 1906. Naididae of Cedar Point, Ohio. Am. Nat., **40**: 683–706.

WELCH, P. S. 1914. Studies on the Enchytraeidae of North America. Bull. Ill. State Lab. Nat. Hist., **10**: 123–212.

———. 1920. The Genera of the Enchytraeidae (Oligochaeta). Trans. Am. Micr. Soc., **39**: 25–50.

11. HIRUDINEA

BENNIKE, S. A. B. 1943. Contributions to the Ecology and Biology of the Danish Fresh-water Leeches (*Hirudinea*). Folia Limn. Scand., No. 2, 109 pp.

BERE, R. 1931. Leeches from the Lakes of Northeastern Wisconsin. Trans. Wis. Acad. Sci., Arts, Let., **26**: 437–440.

MOORE, J. P. 1901. The Hirudinea of Illinois. Bull. Ill. State Lab. Nat. Hist., **5**: 479–547.

———. 1912. The Leeches of Minnesota. III. Classification of the Leeches of Minnesota. Geol. Nat. Hist. Surv. Minn., ser. 5, pp. 65–143.

———. 1923. The Control of Blood-sucking Leeches with an Account of the Leeches of Palisades Interstate Park. Roosevelt Wild Life Bull., **2**: 9–53.

12. CRUSTACEA

CREASER, E. P. 1930. The Phyllopoda of Michigan. Papers Mich. Acad. Sci., Arts, Let., **11**: 381–388.

———. 1931. The Michigan Decapod Crustaceans. Papers Mich. Acad. Sci., Arts, Let., **13**: 257–276.

———. 1932. The Decapod Crustaceans of Wisconsin. Trans. Wis. Acad. Sci., Arts, Let., **27**: 321–338.

DODDS, G. S. 1915. A Key to the Entomostraca of Colorado. Univ. Colo. Studies, **11**: 265–298.

FURTOS, N. C. 1933. The Ostracoda of Ohio. Ohio Biol. Surv. (Bull. 29), **5**: 413–524.

GURNEY, R. 1931–1933. British Fresh-water Copepoda. Ray Society, London, vols. I–III. 958 pp.

HATCHETT, S. P. 1947. Biology of the Isopoda of Michigan. Ecol. Monogr., 17: 47–79.

HENRY, M. 1922. A Monograph of the Freshwater Entomostraca of New South Wales. I. Cladocera. Proc. Linn. Soc. N.S.W., 47: 26–52.

———. 1922. A Monograph of the Freshwater Entomostraca of New South Wales. II. Copepoda. Proc. Linn. Soc. N.S.W., 47: 551–570.

HERRICK, C. L., and C. H. TURNER. 1895. Synopsis of the Entomostraca of Minnesota. Geol. Nat. Hist. Surv. Minn., Zool. Ser. II. 525 pp.

HOFF, C. C. 1942. The Ostracods of Illinois. Illinois Biol. Monogr., 19: 1–196.

JOHANSEN, F. 1922. Euphyllopod Crustacea of the American Arctic. Rept. Can. Arctic Exped., 1913–1918, vol. 7, Part G, 34 pp.

JUDAY, C. 1920. The Cladocera of the Canadian Arctic Expedition, 1913–1918. Rept. Can. Arctic Exped., 1913–1918, vol. 7, Part H, 8 pp.

MARSH, C. D. 1895. On the Cyclopidae and Calanidae of Lake St. Clair, Lake Michigan, and Certain of the Inland Lakes of Michigan. Bull. Mich. Fish Comm., No. 5, 24 pp.

———. 1920. The Fresh Water Copepoda of the Canadian Arctic Expedition, 1913–1918. Rept. Can. Arctic Exped., 1913–1918, vol. 7, Part J, 25 pp.

———. 1929. Distribution and Key to the North American Copepods of the Genus Diaptomus, with the Description of a New Species. Proc. U.S. Nat. Museum, 75: 1–27.

UÉNO, M. 1927. The Freshwater Branchiopoda of Japan I. Mem. Col. Sci., Kyoto Imp. Univ., ser. B, 2: 259–311.

VAN NAME, W. G. 1936. The American Land and Freshwater Isopod Crustacea. Bull. Am. Museum Nat. Hist., 71: 1–535.

WECKEL, A. L. 1907. The Fresh-water Amphipoda of North America. Proc. U.S. Nat. Museum, 32: 25–58.

———. 1914. Free-swimming Fresh-water Entomostraca. Trans. Am. Micr. Soc., 33: 165–203.

WILSON, C. B. 1932. The Copepods of the Woods Hole Region, Massachusetts. Bull. 158, U.S. Nat. Museum, 635 pp.

WRIGHT, S. 1927. A Revision of the South American Species of Diaptomus. Trans. Am. Micr. Soc., 46: 73–121.

YEATMAN, H. C. 1944. American Cyclopoid Copepods of the Viridis-Vernalis Group (including a Description of Cyclops carolinianus n.sp.). Am. Midl. Nat., 32: 1–90.

<h3>13. HYDRACARINA</h3>

KOENIKE, F. 1912. A Revision of My "Nordamerikanische Hydranchniden." Trans. Can. Inst., pp. 281–296.

LUNDBLAD, O. 1920. Süsswasseracarinen aus Dänemark. Mém. l'Acad. R. Sci. Let. Danemark, Copenhagen, 6: 135–258.

MARSHALL, R. 1924. Water Mites of Alaska and the Canadian Northwest. Trans. Am. Micr. Soc., 43: 236–255.

———. 1927. Hydracarina of the Douglas Lake Region. Trans. Am. Micr. Soc., 46: 268–285.

———. 1929. Canadian Hydracarina. Univ. Toronto Studies, Publ. Ont. Fish. Res. Lab., No. 39, pp. 57–93.

———. 1931. Preliminary List of the Hydracarina of Wisconsin. I. The Red Mites. Trans. Wis. Acad. Sci., Arts, Let., 26: 311–319.

————. 1932. Preliminary List of the Hydracarina of Wisconsin. Part II. Trans. Wis. Acad. Sci., Arts, Let., **27**: 339–358.

————. 1933. Water Mites from Wyoming as Fish Food. Trans. Am Micr. Soc., **52**: 34–41.

————. 1933. Preliminary List of the Hydracarina of Wisconsin. Part III. Trans. Wis. Acad. Sci., Arts, Let., **28**: 37–61.

SOAR, C. D., and W. WILLIAMSON. 1925. British Hydracarina. Vol. I. London, 214 pp.

————. 1927. British Hydracarina. Vol. II. London, 215 pp.

UCHIDA, T. 1930–1932. Some Ecological Observations on Water Mites. Jour. Faculty Sci., Hokkaido Imp. Univ., **1**: 143–165.

WALTER, C. 1922. Hydracarinen aus den Alpen. Rev. suisse zool., **29**: 227–411.

14. INSECTA

General References

ALEXANDER, C. P. 1925. An Entomological Survey of the Salt Fork of the Vermillion River in 1921, with a Bibliography of Aquatic Insects. State of Ill. Div. Nat. Hist. Surv., **15**: 439–535.

DODDS, G. S., and F. L. HISAW. 1925. Ecological Studies on Aquatic Insects. IV. Altitudinal Range and Zonation of Mayflies, Stoneflies and Caddisflies in the Colorado Rockies. Ecology, **6**: 380–390.

HART, C. A. 1896. On the Entomology of the Illinois River and Adjacent Waters. Bull. Ill. State Lab. Nat. Hist., **4**: 149–273.

KARNY, H. H. 1934. Biologie der Wasserinsekten. Vienna, 320 pp.

NEEDHAM, J. G., and C. BETTEN. 1901. Aquatic Insects in the Adirondacks. New York State Museum, Bull. 47, pp. 383–612.

NEEDHAM, J. G., and R. O. CHRISTENSON. 1927. Economic Insects in Some Streams of Northern Utah. Utah Agr. Exp. Sta. Bull. 201, 36 pp.

NEEDHAM, J. G., A. D. MACGILLIVRAY, A. O. JOHANNSEN, and K. C. DAVIS. 1903. Aquatic Insects in New York State. New York State Museum, Bull. 68, Ent. 18, pp. 199–517.

PENNAK, R. W. 1947. Keys to the Aquatic Insects of Colorado. Univ. Colo. Studies, ser. D, **2**: 353–384.

PETERSON, A. 1951. Larvae of Insects. Part II. Columbus, 416 pp.

ROUSSEAU, E. 1921. Les Larves et nymphes aquatiques des insectes d'Europe (morphologie, biologie, systématique). Brussels, **1**: 1–967.

WESENBERG-LUND, C. 1913. Wohnungen und Gehäusebau der Süsswasserinsekten. Fortsch. d. Naturwiss. Forsch., **9**: 55–132.

————. 1915. Insektlivet I Ferske Vande. Copenhagen, 524 pp.

————. 1943. Biologie der Süsswasserinsekten. Berlin, 682 pp.

Ephemerida

EATON, A. E. 1883–1888. A Revisional Monograph of Recent Ephemeridae or Mayflies. Trans. Linn. Soc. London, Zool., (2)**3**: 1–352, 65 plates.

KIMMINS, D. E. 1942. Keys to the British Ephemeroptera with Keys to the Genera of the Nymphs. Freshwater Biol. Assoc. Brit. Emp., Sci. Publ., No. 7. 64 pp.

MORGAN, A. H. 1913. A Contribution to the Biology of May-flies. Ann. Ent. Soc. Am., **6**: 371–413.

MURPHY, H. E. 1922. Notes on the Biology of Some of Our North American Species of May-flies. I. The Metamorphosis of May-fly Mouth Parts. II.

Notes on the Biology of May-flies of the Genus Baetis. Bull. Lloyd Libr. Bot., Nat. Hist., Pharm., Mat. Med., No. 22, pp. 3–46.

NEEDHAM, J. G. 1920. Burrowing Mayflies of Our Larger Lakes and Streams. Bull. U.S. Bur. Fish., **36**: 267–292.

Odonata

BYERS, C. F. 1930. A Contribution to the Knowledge of Florida Odonata. Univ. Fla. Publ., Biol. Sci. ser., **1**: 9–327.

GARMAN, P. 1917. The Zygoptera, or Damsel-flies, of Illinois. Bull. Ill. State Lab. Nat. Hist., **12**: 411–587.

———. 1927. Guide to the Insects of Connecticut. V. The Odonata or Dragon-flies of Connecticut. State of Conn., State Geol. Nat. Hist. Surv. 39, pp. 7–331.

HAYES, W. P. 1941. A Bibliography of Keys for the Identification of Immature Insects. Part II. Odonata. Ent. News, **52**: 52–55; 66–69; 93–98.

NEEDHAM, J. G., and H. B. HEYWOOD. 1929. A Handbook of the Dragonflies of North America. Springfield, 378 pp.

TILLYARD, R. J. 1917. The Biology of Dragonflies (Odonata or Paraneuroptera). Cambridge, 396 pp.

WALKER, E. M. 1941. List of the Odonata of Ontario with Distributional Data. Trans. R. Can. Inst., **23**: 201–264.

WESENBERG-LUND, C. 1913. Odonaten-Studien. Int. Rev. d. ges. Hydrobiol. u. Hydrogr., **6**: 155–228, 373–422.

WILSON, C. B. 1920. Dragonflies and Damselflies in Relation to Pond Culture, with a List of Those Found near Fairport, Iowa. Bull. U.S. Bur. Fish., **36**: 182–264.

WRIGHT, M., and A. PETERSON. 1944. A Key to the Genera of Anisopterous Dragonfly Nymphs of the United States and Canada (Odonata, suborder Anisoptera). Ohio Jour. Sci., **44**: 151–166.

Plecoptera

CLAASEN, P. W. 1931. Plecoptera Nymphs of America (North of Mexico). Thomas Say Foundation. Vol. III. Springfield, 199 pp.

———. 1939. A Catalogue of the Plecoptera of the World. Cornell Univ., Agr. Exp. Sta., Mem. 232, 235 pp.

FRISON, T. H. 1929. Fall and Winter Stoneflies, or Plecoptera, of Illinois. State of Ill. Div. Nat. Hist. Surv., **18**: 345–409.

———. 1935. The Stoneflies, or Plecoptera, of Illinois. State of Ill., Div. Nat. Hist. Surv., **20**: 281–471.

———. 1942. Studies of North American Plecoptera with Special Reference to the Fauna of Illinois. Bull. Ill. Nat. Hist. Surv., **22**: 235–355.

NEEDHAM, J. G., and P. W. CLAASEN. 1926. A Monograph of the Plecoptera or Stoneflies of America North of Mexico. Thomas Say Foundation, vol. II. Lafayette, 397 pp.

Hemiptera

BRITTON, W. E., and others. 1923. Guide to the Insects of Connecticut. Part IV. The Hemiptera or Sucking Insects of Connecticut. State of Conn., State Geol. Nat. Hist. Surv., Bull. 34, 807 pp.

HUNGERFORD, H. B. 1919. The Biology and Ecology of Aquatic and Semiaquatic Hemiptera. Univ. Kansas Sci. Bull., **11**: 3–341.

———. 1922. The Nepidae in North America North of Mexico. Univ. Kansas Sci. Bull., **14**: 425–469.

————. 1933. The Genus Notonecta of the World. Univ. Kansas Sci. Bull., **21**: 5–195.

————. 1948. The Corixidae of the Western Hemisphere. Univ. Kansas Sci. Bull., **32**: 1–827.

Coleoptera

BERTRAND, H. 1928. Les larves et nymphes des dytiscides, hygrobiides et haliplides. Vol. 10, Encyclopédie entomologique. Paris, 366 pp.

BLATCHLEY, W. S. 1910. An Illustrated Descriptive Catalogue of the Coleoptera of Beetles (Exclusive of the Rhynchophora) Known to Occur in Indiana. Indianapolis, 1386 pp.

BÖVING, A. G., and F. C. CRAIGHEAD. 1931. An Illustrated Synopsis of the Principal Larval Forms of the Order of Coleoptera. Ent. Am., **11**: 1–351.

BROCHER, F. 1912. Observations biologique sur quelques curculionides aquatiques. Ann. biol. lacustre, **5**: 180–186.

HATCH, M. H. 1925. An Outline of the Ecology of Gyrinidae. Bull. Brook. Ent. Soc., **20**: 101–114.

HICKMAN, J. R. 1930. Life-histories of Michigan Haliplidae (Coleoptera). Papers Mich. Acad. Sci., Arts, Let., **11**: 399–424.

————. 1931. Contribution to the Biology of the Haliplidae (Coleoptera). Ann. Ent. Soc. Am., **24**: 129–142.

HOFFMAN, C. E. 1940. Morphology of the Immature Stages of Some Northern Michigan Donaciinae (Chrysomelidae; Coleoptera). Papers Mich. Acad. Sci., Arts, Let., **25**: 243–290.

RICHMOND, E. A. 1920. Studies on the Biology of the Aquatic Hydrophilidae. Bull. Am. Museum Nat. Hist., **42**: 1–94.

WESENBERG-LUND, C. 1912. Biologische Studien über Dytisciden. Int. Rev. d. ges. Hydrobiol. u. Hydrogr., Biol. Suppl., IV ser., pp. 1–129.

WILSON, C. B. 1923. Water Beetles in Relation to Pondfish Culture, with Life Histories of Those Found in Fishponds at Fairport, Iowa. Bull. U.S. Bur. Fish., **39**: 231–345.

————. 1923. Life History of the Scavenger Water Beetle Hydrous (Hydrophilus) triangularis, and Its Economic Relation to Fish Breeding. Bull. U.S. Bur. Fish., **39**: 9–38.

Trichoptera

BETTEN, C. 1934. The Caddis Flies or Trichoptera of New York State. Bull. N.Y. State Museum, No. 292, 576 pp.

LEONARD, J. W., and FANNIE A. LEONARD. 1949. An Annotated List of Michigan Trichoptera. Occ. Papers Mus. Zool., Univ. Mich., No. 522, 35 pp.

LLOYD, J. T. 1921. The Biology of the North American Caddis Fly Larvae. Bull. Lloyd Libr. Bot., Pharm., Mat. Med., No. 21, 124 pp.

NIELSEN, A. 1942. Über die Entwicklung und Biologie der Trichopteren. Arch. Hydrobiol., Suppl. Bd., **17**: 255–631.

————. 1948. Postembryonic Development and Biology of the Hydroptilidae. Det Kongelige Danske Videnskabernes Selskab, Biol. Skr., Bind 5, 200 pp.

NOYES, A. A. 1914. The Biology of the Net-spinning Trichoptera of Cascadilla Creek. Ann. Ent. Soc. Am., **7**: 251–272.

ROSS, H. H. 1944. The Caddis Flies, or Trichoptera, of Illinois. Bull. Ill. Nat. Hist. Surv., **23**: 1–326.

WESENBERG-LUND, C. 1911. Biologische Studien über Netzspinnende Trichopterenlarven. Int. Rev. d. ges. Hydrobiol. u. Hydrogr., Biol. Suppl., **3**: 1–64.

Lepidoptera

AINSLIE, G. G. 1922. Biology of the Lotus Borer (*Pyrausta penitalis* Grote). U.S. Dept. Agr., Bull. 1076, 14 pp.

BERG, C. O. 1950. Biology of Certain Aquatic Caterpillars (Pyralididae: *Nymphula* spp.) Which Feed on *Potamogeton*. Trans. Am. Micr. Soc., **69**: 254–266.

BERG, K. 1941. Contributions to the Biology of the Aquatic Moth Acentropus niveus (Oliv.). Vidensk. Medd. fra Dansk naturh. Foren., **105**: 57–139.

FORBES, W. T. M. 1910. The Aquatic Caterpillars of Lake Quinsigmond. Psyche, **17**: 219–228.

LLOYD, J. T. 1914. Lepidopterous Larvae from Rapid Streams. Jour. N.Y. Ent. Soc., **22**: 145–152.

WELCH, P. S. 1914. Habits of the Larva of Bellura melanopyga Grote (Lepidoptera). Biol. Bull., **27**: 97–114.

———. 1916. Contribution to the Biology of Certain Aquatic Lepidoptera. Ann. Ent. Soc. Am., **9**: 159–187.

———. 1919. The Aquatic Adaptations of Pyrausta penitalis Grt. (Lepidoptera). Ann. Ent. Soc. Am., **12**: 213–226.

———. 1924. Observations on the Early Larval Activities of Nymphula maculalis Clemens (Lenidoptera). Ann. Ent. Soc. Am., **17**: 395–402.

WELCH, P. S., and G. L. SEHON. 1928. The Periodic Vibratory Movements of the Larva of Nymphula maculalis Clemens (Lepidoptera) and Their Respiratory Significance. Ann. Ent. Soc. Am., **21**: 243–258.

Diptera

ALEXANDER, C. P. 1919. The Crane-flies of New York. I. Distribution and Taxonomy of the Adult Flies. Cornell Univ. Agr. Exp. Sta., Mem. 25, pp. 767–993.

———. 1920. The Crane-flies of New York. II. Biology and Phylogeny. Cornell Univ. Agr. Exp. Sta., Mem. 38, pp. 695–1133.

BERG, K. 1937. Contributions to the Biology of Corethra Meigen (*Chaoborus* Lichtenstein). Det Kgl. Danske Vidensk. Selskab., Biol. Medd., **13**: 1–101.

BRUNDIN, L. 1949. Chironomiden und andere Bodentiere der Südschwedischen Urgebirgsseen. Inst. Freshwater Res., Drottingholm. Rept. No. 30, Fishery Board of Sweden. 915 pp.

DYAR, H. G. 1922. The Mosquitoes of the United States. Proc. U.S. Nat. Mus., **62**: 1–119.

DYAR, H. G., and R. C. SHANNON. 1927. The North American Two-winged flies of the Family Simuliidae. Proc. U.S. Nat. Mus., **69**: 1–54.

HAYES, W. P. 1938–1939. A Bibliography of Keys for the Identification of Immature Insects. Part I. Diptera. Ent. News, **49**: 246–251; **50**: 5–10; 76–80.

JOHANNSEN, O. A. 1922. Stratiomyiid Larvae and Puparia of the North Eastern States. Jour. N.Y. Ent. Soc., **30**: 141–153.

———. 1934, 1935, 1937, 1938. Aquatic Diptera. Parts I–V. Cornell Univ. Agr. Exp. Sta., Mem. 164, 71 pp.; Mem. 177, 61 pp.; Mem. 205, 84 pp.; Mem. 210, 80 pp.

KITAKAMI, S. 1931. The Blepharoceridae of Japan. Mem. Col. Sci., Kyoto Imp. Univ., ser. B., **6**: 53–108.

LEATHERS, A. L. 1922. Ecological Study of Aquatic Midges and Some Related Insects with Special Reference to Feeding Habits. Bull. U.S. Bur. Fish., **38**: 1–61.

MALLOCH, J. R. 1915. The Chironomidae, or Midges, of Illinois, with Particular Reference to the Species Occurring in the Illinois River. Bull. Ill. State Lab. Nat. Hist., **10**: 275–543.

———. 1917. A Preliminary Classification of Diptera, Exclusive of Pupipara, Based upon Larval and Pupal Characters, with Keys to Imagines in Certain Families. Bull. Ill. State Lab. Nat. Hist., **12**: 161–409.

MATHESON, R. 1944. Handbook of the Mosquitoes of North America. 2d ed. Ithaca, N.Y., 322 pp.

METCALF, C. L. 1932. Black Flies and Other Biting Flies of the Adirondacks. Bull. N.Y. State Museum, No. 289, pp. 5–58.

PHILIP, C. B. 1931. The Tabanidae (Horseflies) of Minnesota with Special Reference to Their Biologies and Taxonomy. Univ. Minn. Agr. Exp. Sta., Bull. 80, pp. 3–132.

ROGERS, J. S. 1933. The Ecological Distribution of the Crane-flies of Northern Florida. Ecol. Monogr., **3**: 1–74.

SMART, J. 1944. The British Simuliidae. Freshwater Biol. Assoc. Brit. Emp., Sci. Publ., No. 9. 57 pp.

THIENEMANN, A. 1936. Alpine Chironomiden. Arch. f. Hydrobiol., **30**: 167–262.

TWINN, C. R. 1936. The Blackflies of Eastern Canada (Simuliidae, Diptera). Can. Jour. Res., **14**: 97–150.

WELCH, P. S. 1912. Observations on the Life History of a New Species of Psychoda. Ann. Ent. Soc. Am., **5**: 411–418.

———. 1914. Observations on the Life History and Habits of *Hydromyza confluens* Loew (Diptera). Ann. Ent. Soc. Am., **7**: 135–147.

———. 1917. Further Studies on *Hydromyza confluens* Loew (Diptera). Ann. Ent. Soc. Am., **10**: 35–45.

WU, YI FANG. 1931. A Contribution to the Biology of Simulium (Diptera). Papers Mich. Acad. Sci., Arts, Let., **13**: 543–599.

Hymenoptera

HENRIKSEN, K. L. 1918. De europaeiske Vandsnyltehvepse og deres Biologi. (The Aquatic Hymenoptera of Europe and Their Biology.) Ent. Medd., **12**: 137–252.

MATHESON, R., and C. R. CROSBY. 1912. Aquatic Hymenoptera in America. Ann. Ent. Soc. Am., **5**: 65–71.

15. MOLLUSCA

BAKER, F. C. 1911. The Lymnaeidae of North and Middle America Recent and Fossil. Chicago Acad. Sci., Spec. Publ. 3, 539 pp.

———. 1922. The Molluscan Fauna of the Big Vermillion River, Illinois. Ill. Biol. Monogr., **7**: 1–126.

———. 1927. Molluscan Associations of White Lake, Michigan: A Study of a Small Inland Lake from an Ecological and Systematic Viewpoint. Ecology, **8**: 252–370.

———. 1928. The Fresh Water Mollusca of Wisconsin. Part I. Gastropoda. Bull. 70, Part I, Wis. Geol. Nat. Hist. Surv., 507 pp.

———. 1928. The Fresh Water Mollusca of Wisconsin. Part II. Pelecypoda. Bull. 70, Part II, Wis. Geol. Nat. Hist. Surv., 495 pp.

———. 1931. The Classification of the Large Planorboid Snails of Europe and America. Proc. Zool. Soc. London, pp. 575–592.

BAKER, F C., and A. R. CAHN. 1931. Freshwater Mollusca from Central Ontario. Ann. Rept., 1929, Nat. Mus. Can., pp. 41–64.

BERRY, E. G. 1943. The Amnicolidae of Michigan: Distribution, Ecology, and Taxonomy. Univ. Mich. Mus. Zool., Misc. Publ., 57, 68 pp.

CHURCHILL, E. P., and S. I. LEWIS. 1924. Food and Feeding in Fresh-water Mussels. Bull. U.S. Bur. Fish., **39**: 439–471.

COKER, R. E., A. F. SHIRA, H. W. CLARK, and A. D. HOWARD. 1921. Natural History and Propagation of Fresh-water Mussels. Bull. U.S. Bur. Fish., **37**: 77–181.

GOODRICH, C. 1932. The Mollusca of Michigan. Univ. Museums, Univ. Mich., Mich. Handbook ser. 5, 120 pp.

GOODRICH, C., and H. VAN DER SCHALIE. 1944. A Revision of the Mollusca of Indiana. Am. Midl. Nat., **32**: 257–326.

HENDERSON, J. 1924. Mollusca of Colorado, Utah, Montana, Idaho, and Wyoming. Univ. Colo. Studies, **13**: 65–223.

———. 1929. Non-marine Mollusca of Oregon and Washington. Univ. Colo. Studies, **17**: 47–190.

MORRISON, J. P. E. 1932. A Report on the Mollusca of the Northeastern Wisconsin District. Trans. Wis. Acad. Sci., Arts, Let., **27**: 359–396.

VAN DER SCHALIE, H. 1938. The Naiad Fauna of the Huron River, in Southeastern Michigan. Univ. Mich. Mus. of Zool., Misc. Publ., 40, 83 pp.

WALKER, B. 1918. A Synopsis of the Classification of the Freshwater Mollusca of North America, North of Mexico, and a Catalogue of the More Recently Described Species, with Notes. Univ. Mich. Mus. Zool., Misc. Publ. 6, pp. 3–213.

16. VERTEBRATES

A List of Common and Scientific Names of the Better Known Fishes of the United States and Canada. Spec. Publ. No. 1, Am. Fish Soc., 1948, 45 pp.

ADAMS, C. C., and T. L. HANKINSON. 1928. The Ecology and Economics of Oneida Lake Fish. Roosevelt Wild Life Animals, **1**: 241–548.

BENT, A. C. 1919. Life Histories of North American Diving Birds. Bull. U.S. Nat. Museum, No. 107, 245 pp. (reprinted, 1946).

———. 1921. Life Histories of North American Gulls and Terns. Bull. U.S. Nat. Museum, No. 113, 345 pp.

———. 1922. Life Histories of North American Petrels and Pelicans and Their Allies. Bull. U.S. Nat. Museum, No. 121, 343 pp.

———. 1923. Life Histories of North American Wild Fowl. Bull. U.S. Nat. Museum, No. 126, 250 pp.; No. 130, 376 pp.

———. 1926. Life Histories of North American Marsh Birds. Bull. U.S. Nat. Museum, No. 135, 490 pp.

———. 1927. Life Histories of North American Shore Birds. Order Limicolae. Part I. Bull. U.S. Nat. Museum, No. 142, 420 pp. Part II. No. 146, 412 pp.

BISHOP, S. C. 1943. Handbook of Salamanders. Ithaca, N.Y., 569 pp.

CAHN, A. R. 1927. An Ecological Study of Southern Wisconsin Fishes. Illinois Biol. Monogr., **11**: 1–151.

DEAN, B. 1916–1923. A Bibliography of Fishes. 3 vols. New York, 2,126 pp.

FORBES, S. A., and R. E. RICHARDSON. 1920. The Fishes of Illinois, 2d ed. (and accompanying atlas). State of Ill. Div. Nat. Hist. Surv., i + cxxxvi, 357 pp.

HAMILTON, W. J. 1943. The Mammals of Eastern United States. Ithaca, N.Y., 448 pp.

HOWELL, A. B. 1930. Aquatic Mammals: Their Adaptations to Life in Water. Baltimore, 332 pp.

HUBBS, C. L., and K. F. LAGLER. 1947. Fishes of the Great Lakes Region. Cranbrook Inst. Sci., Bull. 26, 186 pp.

KOELZ, W. 1929. Coregonid Fishes of the Great Lakes. Bull. U.S. Bur. Fish., **43**: 297–643.

NOBLE, G. K. 1931. The Biology of the Amphibia. New York, 577 pp.

RADFORTH, I. 1944. Some Considerations on the Distribution of Fishes in Ontario. Contr. R. Ont. Mus. Zool., No. 25, 116 pp.

ROBERTS, T. S. 1932. The Birds of Minnesota, vol. I, 691 pp.; vol. II, Minneapolis, 821 pp.

WRIGHT, A. H. 1949. Handbook of Frogs and Toads. 3d ed. Ithaca, N.Y., 640 pp.

PLANKTON

AHLSTROM, E. H. 1936. The Deep-water Plankton of Lake Michigan, Exclusive of the Crustacea. Trans. Am. Micr. Soc., **55**: 286–299.

ALLEN, W. E. 1939. Surface Distribution of Marine Plankton Diatoms in the Panama Region in 1933. Bull. Scripps Inst. Ocean., Tech. Ser., **4**: 181–196.

ANCONA, J. V. D'. 1927. Ulteriore osservazioni sulla Daphnia cucullata del Lago di Nemi. Int. Rev. d. ges. Hydrobiol. u. Hydrogr., **18**: 261–295.

AYCOCK, D. 1942. Influence of Temperature on Size and Form of *Cyclops vernalis* Fischer. Jour. Elisha Mitchell Sci. Soc., **58**: 84–93.

BERG, K. 1929. Ecological Studies on the Zooplankton in the Lake of Fredericksborg Castle. Det. 18. Skand. Naturforsk., 5 pp.

———. 1929. A Faunistic and Biological Study of Danish Cladocera. Vid. Medd. fra Dansk Naturh. For., **88**: 31–111.

———. 1931. Studies on the Genus Daphnia O. F. Müller with Special Reference to the Mode of Reproduction. Vid. Medd. fra Dansk Naturh. For., **92**: 1–222.

———. 1932. Ist das Alter der Latenzeier der Daphnien ein geschlechtsbestimmender Faktor? Arch. f. Hydrobiol., **24**: 497–508.

BIGELOW, N. K. 1923. The Plankton of Lake Nipigon and Environs. Univ. Toronto Studies, Publ. Ont. Fish. Res. Lab., No. 13, pp. 41–66.

———. 1928. The Ecological Distribution of Microscopic Organisms in Lake Nipigon. Univ. Toronto Studies, Publ. Ont. Fish. Res. Lab., No. 35, pp. 59–74.

BIRGE, E. A., and C. JUDAY. 1922. The Inland Lakes of Wisconsin. The Plankton. I. Its Quantity and Chemical Composition. Wisconsin Geol. Nat. Hist. Surv., Bull. 64, Sci. ser., No. 13, pp. 1–222.

BIRGE, E. A., O. A. OLSEN, and H. P. HARDER. 1895. Plankton Studies on Lake Mendota. I. The Vertical Distribution of the Pelagic Crustacea during July, 1894. Trans. Wis. Acad. Sci., Arts, Let., **10**: 421–484.

BOND, R. M. 1933. A Contribution to the Study of the Natural Food-cycle in Aquatic Environments. Bull. Bingham Oceanographic Collection, **4**: 1–89.

BRITTON, M. E. 1944. A Catalog of Illinois Algae. Northwestern Univ. Studies in Biol. Sci. and Med., No. 2, 177 pp.

BROOKS, J. L. 1946. Cyclomorphosis in Daphnia. I. An Analysis of *D. retrocurva* and *D. galeata*. Ecol. Monogr., **16**: 409–447.

———. 1947. Turbulence as an Environmental Determinant of Relative Growth in Daphnia. Proc. Nat. Acad. Sci., **33**: 141–148.

BROOKS, J. L., and E. G. HUTCHINSON. 1950. On the Rate of Passive Sinking of Daphnia. Proc. Nat. Acad. Sci., **36**: 272–277.

CAMPBELL, R. S. 1941. Vertical Distribution of the Plankton Rotifera in Douglas Lake, Michigan, with Special Reference to Depression Individuality. Ecol. Monogr., **11**: 1–19.

CHANDLER, D. C. 1940. Limnological Studies of Western Lake Erie. I. Plankton and Certain Physical-chemical Data of the Bass Islands Region, from September, 1938, to November, 1939. Ohio Jour. Sci., **40**: 291–336.

————. 1942. Limnological Studies of Western Lake Erie. III. Phytoplankton and Physical-chemical Data from November, 1939, to November, 1940. Ohio Jour. Sci., **42**: 24–44.

————. 1944. Limnological Studies of Western Lake Erie. IV. Relation of Limnological and Climatic Factors to the Phytoplankton of 1941. Trans. Am. Micr. Soc., **63**: 203–236.

CHANDLER, D. C., and O. B. WEEKS. 1945. Limnological Studies of Western Lake Erie. V. Relation of Limnological and Meteorological Conditions to the Production of Phytoplankton in 1942. Ecol. Monogr., **15**: 435–457.

CLARKE, G. L. 1933. Diurnal Migration of Plankton in the Gulf of Maine and Its Correlation with Changes in Submarine Irradiation. Biol. Bull., **65**: 402–436.

————. 1939. The Relation between Diatoms and Copepods as a Factor in the Productivity of the Sea. Quart. Rev. Biol., **14**: 60–64.

COKER, R. E. 1939. The Problem of Cyclomorphosis in Daphnia. Quart. Rev. Biol., **14**: 137–148.

COKER, R. E., and H. H. ADDLESTONE. 1938. Influence of Temperature on Cyclomorphosis of Daphnia longispina. Jour. Elisha Mitchell Sci. Soc., **54**: 45–75.

COKER, R. E., and W. J. HAYES, JR. 1940. Biological Observations in Mountain Lake, Virginia. Ecology, **21**: 192–198.

CUNNINGTON, W. A. 1910. On the Nature and Origin of Fresh-water Organisms. In Murray and Pullar's Bathymetrical Survey of the Scottish Fresh-water Lochs, **1**: 354–373.

DAILY, W. A. 1938. A Quantitative Study of the Phytoplankton of Lake Michigan Collected in the Vicinity of Evanston, Illinois. Butler Univ. Bot. Studies, **4**: 65–83.

DAMANN, K. E. 1945. Plankton Studies of Lake Michigan. I. Seventeen Years of Plankton Data Collected at Chicago, Illinois. Am. Midl. Nat., **34**: 769–796.

DEEVEY, E. S. 1939. Arctic-Alpine Limnology. Am. Jour. Sci., **237**: 830–833.

DICE, L. R. 1914. The Factors Determining the Vertical Movements of Daphnia. Jour. Animal Behavior, **4**: 229–265.

DODDS, G. S. 1917. Altitudinal Distribution of Entomostraca in Colorado. Proc. U.S. Nat. Mus., **54**: 59–87.

————. 1920. Entomostraca and Life Zones. Biol. Bull., **39**: 89–107.

DRUMMOND, J. C., and E. R. GUNTHER. 1930. Vitamin Content of Marine Plankton. Nature, **126**: 398.

EDDY, S. 1927. The Plankton of Lake Michigan. State of Ill. Div. Nat. Hist. Surv., **17**: 203–232.

————. 1930. The Fresh-water Armored or Thecate Dinoflagellates. Trans. Am. Micr. Soc., **49**: 277–321.

————. 1934. A Study of Fresh-water Plankton Communities. Ill. Biol. Monogr., vol. 12, No. 4, 93 pp.

EGGLETON, F. E. 1932. Limnetic Distribution and Migration of Corethra Larvae in Two Michigan Lakes. Pap. Mich. Acad. Sci., Arts, Let., **15**: 361–388.

GODWARD, M. 1937. An Ecological and Taxonomic Investigation of the Littoral Algal Flora of Lake Windermere. Jour. Ecology, **25**: 496–568.

GROVER, W. W., and R. E. COKER. 1940. A Study of Depth Distribution of Certain Net Plankters in Mountain Lake, Virginia. Ecology **21**: 199–205.

GUNTER, G., R. H. WILLIAMS, C. C. DAVIS, and F. G. W. SMITH. 1948. Catastrophic Mass Mortality of Marine Animals and Coincident Phytoplankton Bloom on the West Coast of Florida, November 1946 to August 1947. Ecol. Monogr., **18**: 309–324.

HARDY, A. C. 1947. Experiments on the Vertical Migration of Plankton Animals. Jour. Marine Biol. Assoc., **26**: 467–526.

HOOPER, F. F. 1947. Plankton Collections from the Yukon and Mackenzie River Systems. Trans. Am. Micr. Soc., **66**: 74–84.

HUBER-PESTALOZZI, G. 1938. Das Phytoplankton des Süsswassers. Die Binnengewässer, Bd. 16, 342 pp.

HUNTSMAN, A. G. 1943. Fisheries Research in Canada. Science, **98**: 117–122.

HUTCHINSON, G. E. 1943. Thiamin in Lake Water and Aquatic Organisms. Arch. Biochem., **2**: 143–150.

———. 1944. Limnological Studies in Connecticut. VII. Examination of the Supposed Relationship between Phytoplankton Periodicity and Chemical Changes in Lake Waters. Ecology, **25**: 3–26.

HUTCHINSON, G. E., and J. K. SETLOW. 1946. Limnological Studies in Connecticut. VIII. The Niacin Cycle in a Small Inland Lake. Ecology, **27**: 13–22.

JENNINGS, H. S. 1918. The Wheel Animalcules (Rotatoria). Chap. XVII in Ward and Whipple's Fresh-water Biology, pp. 553–620.

JØRGENSEN, E. G. 1948. Diatom Communities in Some Danish Lakes and Ponds. Det Kong. Dan. Vidensk. Sel., Biol. Skr., Bd. 5, 140 pp.

JUDAY, C. 1904. The Diurnal Movement of Plankton Crustacea. Trans. Wis. Acad. Sci., Arts, Let., **14**: 534–568.

———. 1921. Observations on the Larvae of Corethra punctipennis Say. Biol. Bull., **40**: 271–286.

JUDAY, C., E. A. BIRGE, G. I. KEMMERER, and R. J. ROBINSON. 1928. Phosphorus Content of Lake Waters of Northeastern Wisconsin. Trans. Wis. Acad. Sci., Arts, Let., **23**: 233–248.

KIKUCHI, K. 1927. Notes on the Diurnal Migration of Plankton in Kizaki Lake. Jour. Col. Agr. Imp. Univ. Tokyo, **9**: 177–198.

———. 1930. A Comparison of the Diurnal Migration of Plankton in Eight Japanese Lakes. Mem. Col. Sci., Kyoto Imp. Univ., ser. B, **5**: 27–74.

———. 1930. Diurnal Migration of Plankton Crustacea. Quart. Rev. Biol., **5**: 189–206.

KLUGH, A. B. 1927. The Ecology, Food-relationships and Culture of Fresh-water Entomostraca. Trans. R. Can. Inst., **16**: 15–98.

KOFOID, C. A. 1903. The Plankton of the Illinois River, 1894–1899, with Introductory Notes upon the Hydrography of the Illinois River and Its Basin. Part I. Quantitative Investigations and General Results. Bull. Ill. State Lab. Nat. Hist., **6**: 95–629.

———. 1908. The Plankton of the Illinois River, 1894–1899, with Introductory Notes upon the Hydrography of the Illinois River and Its Basin. Part II. Constituent Organisms and Their Seasonal Distribution. Bull. Ill. State Lab. Nat. Hist., **8**: 1–354.

KRAATZ, W. C. 1941. Quantitative Plankton Studies of Turkeyfoot Lake, near Akron, Ohio. Ohio Jour. Sci., **41**: 1–22.

KROGH, A., and E. BERG. 1931. Über die chemische Zusammensetzung des Phytoplanktons aus dem Fredericksborg-Schlosssee und ihre Bedeutung für die Maxima der Cladoceren. Int. Rev. d. ges. Hydrobiol. u. Hydrogr., **25**: 204–218.

LACKEY, J. B. 1949. Plankton as Related to Nuisance Conditions in Surface Water. In Limnological Aspects of Water Supply and Waste Disposal, Am. Assoc. Adv. Sci., pp. 56–63.

LANGFORD, K. R. 1938. Diurnal and Seasonal Changes in the Distribution of the Limnetic Crustacea of Lake Nipissing, Ontario. Univ. Toronto, Biol. ser. 45, Publ. Ont. Fish. Res. Lab., No. 56, pp. 1–142.

LEBOUR, M. V. 1920. The Food of Young Fish. Jour. Marine Biol. Assoc., 12: 261–324.

LIND, E. M. 1940. Literature on the Ecology of Freshwater Algae Published since 1930. Jour. Ecology, 28: 491–494.

MACKENTHUN, K. M., E. F. HERMAN, and A. F. BARTSCH. 1948. A Heavy Mortality of Fishes from the Decomposition of Algae in the Yahara River, Wisconsin. Trans. Am. Fish. Soc., 75: 175–180.

MALONEY, M. T., and W. L. TRESSLER. 1942. The Diurnal Migration of Certain Species of Zooplankton in Caroga Lake, New York. Trans. Am. Micr. Soc., 61: 40–52.

MARSH, C. D. 1899. The Plankton of Fresh Water Lakes. Trans. Wis. Acad. Sci., Arts, Let., 13: 163–187.

―――. 1929. Distribution and Key to the North American Copepods of the Genus Diaptomus with a Description of a New Species. Proc. U.S. Nat. Museum, 75: 1–27.

McKEE, P. W., and R. E. COKER. 1940. Notes on Plankton Entomostraca of the Carolinas. Jour. Elisha Mitchell Sci. Soc., 56: 177–187.

MEIER, F. E. 1940. Plankton in the Water Supply. Ann. Rept. Smithsonian Inst. for 1939, pp. 393–412.

MUENSCHER, W. C. 1928. Plankton Studies of Cayuga, Seneca and Oneida Lakes. Suppl. to 17th Ann. Rept., State of N.Y. Conserv. Comm., pp. 140–157.

―――. 1930. Plankton Studies in the Lake Champlain Watershed. Suppl. to Ann. 19th Rept., State of N.Y. Conserv. Comm., pp. 146–163.

―――. 1931. Plankton Studies in Some Northern Adirondack Lakes. Suppl. to 20th Ann. Rept., State of N.Y. Conserv. Comm., pp. 145–160.

NAUMANN, E. 1918. Über die naturliche Nahrung des limnischen Zooplanktons. Ein Beitrag zur Kenntnis des Stoffhaushalts im Süsswasser. Lunds Univ. Årsskr. n. f., Avd. 2, 14: 1–48.

―――. 1921. Spezielle Untersuchungen Über die Ernährungsbiologie des Tierischen Limnoplanktons. I. Über die Technik des Nahrungserwerbs bei den Cladoceren und ihre Bedeutung für die Biologie der Gewässertypen. Lunds Univ. Årsskr. n. f., Avd. 2, 17: 3–27.

―――. 1923. Spezielle Untersuchungen über die Ernährungsbiologie des Tierischen Limnoplanktons. II. Über den Nahrungswerb und die natürliche Nahrung der Copepoden und der Rotiferen des Limnoplanktons. Lunds Univ. Årsskr. n. f., Avd. 2, 19: 3–17.

―――. 1925. See und Teich (Plankton und Neuston). Abderhalden's Handbuch d. biol. Arbeitsmeth., Abt. 9, Teil 2, Heft 1: 139–228.

―――. 1927. Zur Kritik des Planktonbegriffes. Arch. f. Botan., 21A: 1–18.

―――. 1929. Grundlinien der experimentellen Planktonforschung. Die Binnengewässer, Bd. VI. 100 pp.

NYGAARD, G. 1945. Dansk Plante Plankton. Kobenhavn, 52 pp.

OSTWALD, W. 1902. Zur Theorie des Planktons. Biol. Zentralbl., 22: 596–605, 609–638.

PATRICK, R. 1948. Factors Effecting the Distribution of Diatoms. Bot. Rev., 14: 473–524.

PEARSALL, W. H. 1923. A Theory of Diatom Periodicity. Jour. Ecology, 11: 165–183.

————. 1932. Phytoplankton in the English Lakes. II. The Composition of the Phytoplankton in Relation to Dissolved Substances. Jour. Ecology, **20**: 241–262.

PENNAK, R. W. 1944. Diurnal Movements of Zooplankton Organisms in Some Colorado Mountain Lakes. Ecology, **25**: 387–403.

————. 1946. The Dynamics of Fresh-water Plankton Populations. Ecol. Monogr., **16**: 340–355.

————. 1949. An Unusual Algal Nuisance in a Colorado Mountain Lake. Ecology, **30**: 245–247.

PENNINGTON, W. 1941. The Control of the Numbers of Fresh-water Phytoplankton by Small Invertebrate Animals. Jour. Ecology, **29**: 204–211.

————. 1941. Plankton as a Source of Food. Nature, **148**: 314.

PLEW, W. F., and R. W. PENNAK. 1949. A Seasonal Investigation of the Vertical Movements of Zooplankters in an Indiana Lake. Ecology, **30**: 93–100.

PRESCOTT, G. W. 1939. Some Relationships of Phytoplankton to Limnology and Aquatic Biology. Am. Assoc. Adv. Sci., Publ. 10, pp. 65–78.

————. 1942. The Fresh-water Algae of Southern United States. II. The Algae of Louisiana, with Descriptions of Some New Forms and Notes on Distribution. Trans. Am. Micr. Soc., **61**: 109–119.

————. 1948. Objectionable Algae with Reference to the Killing of Fish and Other Animals. Hydrobiol., **1**: 1–13.

PRESCOTT, G. W., and A. M. SCOTT. 1942. The Fresh-water Algae of Southern United States. I. Desmids from Mississippi, with Descriptions of New Species and Varieties. Trans. Am. Micr. Soc., **61**: 1–29.

PÜTTER, A. 1924. Die Ernährung der Copepoden. Arch. f. Hydrobiol., **15**: 70–117.

RAWSON, D. S. 1942. A Comparison of Some Large Alpine Lakes in Western Canada. Evol., **23**: 143–161.

————. 1947. Great Slave Lake. Bull. Fish. Res. Bd. Can., **72**: 45–68.

————. 1947. Lake Athabasca. Bull. Fish, Res. Bd. Can., **72**: 69–85.

RAYMOND, M. R. 1937. A Limnological Study of the Plankton of a Concretion-forming Marl Lake. Trans. Am. Micr. Soc., **56**: 405–430.

REIGHARD, J. E. 1894. Some Plankton Studies in the Great Lakes. Bull. U.S. Fish Comm. for 1893, pp. 127–142.

RICKER, W. E. 1937. Seasonal and Annual Variations in Quantity of Pelagic Net Plankton, Cultus Lake, British Columbia. Jour. Fish. Res. Bd. Can., **4**: 33–47.

RILEY, G. A. 1940. Limnological Studies in Connecticut. III. The Plankton of Linsley Pond. Ecol. Monogr., **10**: 279–306.

————. 1942. The Relationship of Vertical Turbulence and Spring Diatom Flowerings. Jour. Marine Res., **5**: 67–87.

RILEY, G. A., H. STOMMEL, and D. F. BUMPUS. 1949. Quantitative Ecology of the Plankton of the Western North Atlantic. Bull. Bingham Oceanographic Collection, Peabody Mus. Nat. Hist., Yale Univ., **12**: 1–169.

ROSE, M. 1925. Contribution a l'étude de la biologie du plankton; le problème des migrations journalières. Arch. zool. exp. et gén., **64**: 397–542.

RUSSELL, F. S. 1927. The Vertical Distribution of Plankton in the Sea. Biol. Rev. and Biol. Proc. Cambridge Phil. Soc., **2**: 213–262.

————. 1930. Vitamin Content of Marine Plankton. Nature, p. 472.

RUTTNER, F. 1914. Die Verteilung des Planktons in Süsswasserseen. Fortschr. Naturw. Forschung, **10**: 273–336.

————. 1931. Hydrographische und hydrochemische Beobachtungen auf Java, Sumatra und Bali. Arch. f. Hydrobiol., Suppl. Bd. VIII, pp. 197–460.

RYLOV, W. M. 1926. Einige Gesichtspunkte zur Biodynamik des Limnoplanktons. Verh. d. Int. Ver. f. theor. u. angew. Limn., **3**: 405–423.

——. 1935. Das Zooplankton der Binnengewässer. Die Binnengewässer, Bd. 15, 272 pp.

SHELFORD, V. E., and A. C. TWOMEY. 1941. Tundra Animal Communities in the Vicinity of Churchill, Manitoba. Ecology, **22**: 47–69.

SMITH, G. M. 1918. A Second List of Algae Found in Wisconsin Lakes. Trans. Wis. Acad. Sci., Arts, Let., **19**: 614–654.

——. 1920. Phytoplankton of the Inland Lakes of Wisconsin. Part I. Wisconsin Geol. Nat. Hist. Survey, Bull. 57, Sci. ser. 12, 243 pp.

——. 1924. Phytoplankton of the Inland Lakes of Wisconsin. Part II. Bull. Univ. Wis., ser. 1270, 227 pp.

——. 1924. Ecology of the Plankton Algae in the Palisades Interstate Park, Including the Relation of Control Methods to Fish Culture. Roosevelt Wild Life Bull., **2**: 98–195.

——. 1926. The Plankton Algae of the Okoboji Region. Trans. Am. Micr. Soc., **45**: 156–233.

——. 1951. The Fresh-water Algae of the United States. 2d ed., New York, 719 pp.

——. 1938. Cryptogamic Botany. 2 vols. New York, 545 + 380 pp.

SPOONER, G. M. 1933. Observations on the Reactions of Marine Plankton to Light. Jour. Marine Biol. Assoc., **19**: 385–438.

STEHLE, M. E. 1923. Surface Plankton Protozoa from Lake Erie in the Put-in-Bay Region. Ohio Jour. Sci., **23**: 41–54.

TAFALL, B. F. O. 1941. Materiales para el Estudio del Microplancton del Lago de Patzcuaro (Mexico). Sobr. An. Esc. Nac. Cien. Biol., **2**: 331–383.

TAFT, C. E. 1942. Additions to the Algae of the West End of Lake Erie. Ohio Jour. Sci., **42**: 251–256.

THOMPSON, R. 1938. A Preliminary Survey of the Fresh-water Algae of Eastern Kansas. Univ. Kansas Sci. Bull., **25**: 1–83.

THOMPSON, R. H. 1947. Fresh-water Dinoflagellates of Maryland. Chesapeake Biol. Lab., Publ. 67, 28 pp.

THUNMARK, S. 1945. Zur Soziologie des Süsswasserplanktons. Folia Limn. Scand., No. 3, 66 pp.

TIFFANY, L. H. 1938. Algae, The Grass of Many Waters. Springfield, 171 pp.

TIFFANY, J. H., and E. H. AHLSTROM. 1931. New and Interesting Plankton Algae from Lake Erie. Ohio Jour. Sci., **31**: 455–467.

TRESSLER, W. L. 1939. The Zooplankton in Relation to the Metabolism of Lakes. Publ. Am. Assoc. Adv. Sci., No. 10, pp. 79–93.

TUCKER, A. 1948. The Phytoplankton of the Bay of Quinte. Trans. Am. Micr. Soc., **67**: 365–383.

UNTERMÖHL, H. 1925. Limnologische Phytoplanktonstudien. Arch. f. Hydrobiol., Suppl. Bd. 5, 527 pp.

VELASQUEZ, G. T. 1939. On the Viability of Algae Obtained from the Digestive Tract of the Gizzard Shad, Dorosoma cepedianum (Le Sueur). Am. Midl. Nat., **22**: 376–412.

——. 1940. A List of the Filamentous Myxophyceae from Michigan. Am. Midl. Nat, **23**: 178–181.

WAILES, G. H. 1939. The Plankton of Lake Windermere, England. Ann. Mag. Nat. Hist., **3**(11): 401–414.

WESENBERG-LUND, C. 1900. Von dem Abhängigkeitverhältnis zwischen dem Bau der Planktonorganismen und dem spezifischen Gewicht des Süsswassers. Biol. Centralbl., **20**: 606–619; 644–656.

————. 1908. Plankton Investigations of the Danish Lakes. Copenhagen, 389 pp.

————. 1910. Summary of Our Knowledge Regarding Various Limnological Problems. In Murray and Pullar's Bathymetrical Survey of the Scottish Fresh-water Lochs, **1**: 374–438.

————. 1926. Contribution to the Biology and Morphology of the Genus Daphnia with Some Remarks on Heredity. Mém. l'Acad. R. Sci. et Let. Danemark, 8me ser., **11**: 91–250.

————. 1934. Contributions to the Development of the Trematoda Digenea. Part II. The Biology of the Freshwater Cercareae in Danish Freshwaters. Mém. l'Acad. R. Sci. et Let. Danemark, 9me ser., **5**: 1–223.

WOLTERECK, R. 1925. Notizen zur Biotypenbildung bei Cladoceren. I. Experimentalle Untersuchung der Ceresio-Daphnien. Int. Rev. d. ges. Hydrobiol. u. Hydrogr., **14**: 121–127.

————. 1929. Sinkgeschwindigkeit, Ernährungszustand und pelagische Form. Zool. Jahrb., Abt. f. all. Zool. u. Physiol. Tiere, **46**: 209–213.

————. 1930. Alte und neue Beobachtungen über die geographische und die zonare Verteilung der helmlosen und helmtragenden Biotypen von Daphnia. Int. Rev. d. ges. Hydrobiol. u. Hydrogr., **24**: 358–380.

————. 1932. Races, Associations and Stratification of Pelagic Daphnids in Some Lakes of Wisconsin and Other Regions of the United States and Canada. Trans. Wis. Acad. Sci., Arts, Let., **27**: 487–522.

WORTHINGTON, E. B. 1931. Vertical Movements of the Fresh-water Macroplankton. Int. Rev. d. ges. Hydrobiol. u. Hydrogr., **25**: 394–436.

YOUNG, O. W. 1945. A Limnological Investigation of Periphyton in Douglas Lake, Michigan. Trans. Am. Micr. Soc., **64**: 1–20.

BACTERIA, OTHER FUNGI, AND THE NONPLANKTON ALGAE

ALLGEIER, R. J., W. H. PETERSON, C. JUDAY, and E. A. BIRGE. 1932. The Anaerobic Fermentation of Lake Deposits. Int. Rev. d. ges. Hydrobiol. u. Hydrogr., **26**: 444–461.

BERE, R. 1933. Numbers of Bacteria in Inland Lakes of Wisconsin as Shown by the Direct Microscopic Method. Int. Rev. d. ges. Hydrobiol. u. Hydrogr., **29**: 248–263.

BIGELOW, H. B. 1931. Oceanography. Boston, 263 pp.

BIRGE, E. A., and C. JUDAY. 1922. The Inland Lakes of Wisconsin. The Plankton. I. Its Quantity and Chemical Composition. Wisconsin Geol. Nat. Hist. Surv., Bull. 64, Sci. ser. 13, 222 pp.

BURKE, V. 1933. Bacteria as Food for Vertebrates. Science, **78**: 194–195.

————. 1934. Interchange of Bacteria between the Fresh Water and the Sea. Jour. Bact., **27**: 201–205.

CAREY, C. L., and S. A. WAKSMAN. 1934. The Presence of Nitrifying Bacteria in Deep Seas. Science, **79**: 349–350.

CARPENTER, P. L. 1941. Bacterial Counts in Deep Deposits of Trout Lake, Wisconsin. In A Symposium on Hydrobiology. Univ. Wis. Press, pp. 393–394.

COKER, W. C. 1923. The Saprolegniaceae, with Notes on the Other Water Molds. North Carolina, 201 pp.

FRED, E. B., F. C. WILSON, and A. DAVENPORT. 1924. The Distribution and Significance of Bacteria in Lake Mendota. Ecology, **5**: 322–339.

GRAHAM, V. E., and R. T. YOUNG. 1934. A Bacteriological Study of Flathead Lake, Montana. Ecology, **15**: 101–109.

HARDMAN, Y., and A. T. HENRICI. 1939. Studies of Freshwater Bacteria. V. The

Distribution of Siderocapsa treubii in Some Lakes and Streams. Jour. Bact., **37**: 97–104.

HENRICI, A. T. 1933. Studies on Freshwater Bacteria. I. Direct Microscopic Technique. Jour. Bact., **25**: 277–286.

———. 1934. The Biology of Bacteria. New York, 472 pp.

———. 1938. Studies of Freshwater Bacteria. IV. Seasonal Fluctuations of Lake Bacteria in Relation to Plankton Production. Jour. Bact., **35**: 129–139.

———. 1939. The Distribution of Bacteria in Lakes. Am. Assoc. Adv. Sci., Publ. 10, pp. 39–64.

———. 1947. Molds, Yeasts and Actinomycetes. 2d ed., New York, 409 pp.

HENRICI, A. T., and ELIZ. McCOY. 1938. The Distribution of Heterotrophic Bacteria in the Bottom Deposits of Some Lakes. Trans. Wis. Acad. Sci., Arts, Let., **31**: 323–361.

HINMAN, E. H. 1933. The Role of Bacteria in the Nutrition of Mosquito Larvae. The Growth-stimulating Factor. Am. Jour. Hyg., **18**: 224–236.

KANOUSE, B. B. 1925. On the Distribution of the Water Molds, with Notes on the Occurrence in Michigan of Members of the Leptomitaceae and Blastocladiaceae. Papers Mich. Acad. Sci., Arts, Let., **5**: 105–114.

———. 1927. A Monographic Study of Special Groups of the Water Molds: I, Blastocladiaceae; II, Leptomitaceae and Pythiomorphaceae. Am. Jour. Bot., **14**: 287–306; 335–357.

———. 1932. A Physiological and Morphological Study of Saprolegnia parasitica. Mycologia, **24**: 431–452.

KUSNETZOW, S. I., and G. S. KARZINKIN. 1931. Direct Method for the Quantitative Study of Bacteria in Water and Some Considerations on the Causes Which Produce a Zone of Oxygen-minimum in Lake Glubokoji. Zentralbl. f. Bakt., Parasit. u. Infektionskr., **83**: 169–174.

LLOYD, B. 1930. Bacteria of the Clyde Sea Area: A Quantitative Investigation. Jour. Marine Assoc., **16**: 879–907.

LUCK, J. M., G. SHEET, and J. O. THOMAS. 1931. The Role of Bacteria in the Nutrition of Protozoa. Quart. Rev. Biol., **6**: 46–58.

MINDER, L. 1927. Über den Bakteriengehalt des Zürichsees. Vierteljahrssch. d. Naturforsch. Gesellsch. in Zürich, **72**: 354–366.

NAUMANN, E. 1930. Die Eisenorganismen. Int. Rev. d. ges. Hydrobiol. u. Hydrogr., **24**: 81–96.

PERFILIEV, B. W. 1929. Zur Mikrobiologie der Bodenablagerungen. Verh. d. Int. Ver. f. theor. u. angew. Limn., **4**: 107–143.

PETERSEN, H. E. 1910. An Account of the Danish Freshwater Phycomycetes with Biological and Systematic Remarks. Ann. Mycology, **8**: 494–560.

PRESCOTT, S. C., and C. E. A. WINSLOW. 1946. Water Bacteriology. 6th ed., New York, 368 pp.

PÜTTER, A. 1923. Der Stoffwechsel der Copepoden (zugleich ein für die Verwendung der Korrelationsmethode in der Physiologie). Pflügers Arch. f. Physiol. d. Men. u. Tiere, **201**: 503–536.

———. 1924. Die Atmung der Planktonbakterien. Pflügers Arc. f. Physiol. d. Men. u. Tiere, **204**: 94–126.

RADZIMOVSKY, D. O. 1930. Vorläufige angaben über die Dichtigkeit der Bakteriellen besiedelung einiger Gewässer. Trav. Sta. Biol. d. Dniepre, No. 5, pp. 401–402.

REUZNER, H. W. 1933. Marine Bacteria and Their Role in the Cycle of Life in the Sea. III. The Distribution of Bacteria in the Ocean Waters and Muds about Cape Cod. Biol. Bull., **65**: 480–497.

Scott, W. 1916. Report of the Lakes of the Tippecanoe Basin (Indiana). Indiana Univ. Studies, **3**: 1–39.

Snow, L. M., and E. B. Fred. 1926. Some Characteristics of the Bacteria of Lake Mendota. Trans. Wis. Acad. Sci., Arts, Let., **22**: 143–154.

Stark, W. H., and Eliz. McCoy. 1938. Distribution of Bacteria in Certain Lakes of Northern Wisconsin. Zentbl. Bact., Parasit. u. Infektionsk., **98**: 201–209.

Strøm, K. M. 1928. Production Biology of Temperature Lakes. Int. Rev. d. ges. Hydrobiol. u. Hydrogr., **19**: 329–348.

Taylor, C. B. 1939. Bacteria of Lakes and Impounded Waters. Brit. Waterworks Assoc., Annual General Meeting at Nottingham, 7 pp.

——. 1940. Bacteria of Fresh Water. I. Distribution of Bacteria in English Lakes. Jour. Hyg., **40**: 616–640.

——. 1941. The Distribution of Bacteria in Lakes and Their Inflows. Proc. Soc. Agr. Bact. (Abstracts), pp. 1–3.

——. 1942. Bacteria of Fresh Water. III. The Types of Bacteria Present in Lakes and Streams and Their Relationship to the Bacterial Flora of Soil. Jour. Hyg., **42**: 284–296.

——. 1948. The Bacteriology of Lakes. Endeavour, **7**: 111–115.

Waksman, S. A. 1934. The Role of Bacteria in the Cycle of Life in the Sea. Sci. Monthly, **38**: 35–49.

——. 1941. Aquatic Bacteria in Relation to the Cycle of Organic Matter in Lakes. In A Symposium on Hydrobiology. Univ. Wis. Press, pp. 86–105.

Waksman, S. A., M. Hotchkiss, and C. L. Carey. 1933. Marine Bacteria and Their Role in the Cycle of Life in the Sea. II. Bacteria Concerned in the Cycle of Nitrogen in the Sea. Biol. Bull., **65**: 137–167.

Waksman, S. A., H. W. Renszer, C. L. Carey, M. Hotchkiss, and C. E. Renn. 1933. Studies on the Biology and Chemistry of the Gulf of Maine. III. Bacteriological Investigations of the Sea Water and Marine Bottoms. Biol. Bull., **64**: 183–205.

Werkman, C. H., and H. G. Wood. 1942. On the Metabolism of Bacteria. Bot. Rev., **8**: 1–68.

Weston, W. H. 1941. The Role of the Aquatic Fungi in Hydrobiology. In A Symposium on Hydrobiology. Univ. Wis. Press, pp. 129–151.

Whipple, G. C. 1927. The Microscopy of Drinking Water, 4th ed., rev. by Fair and Whipple. New York, 586 pp.

ZoBell, C. E. 1940. The Effect of Oxygen Tension on the Rate of Oxidation of Organic Matter in Sea Water by Bacteria. Jour. Marine Res., **3**: 211–223.

——. 1940. The Factors which Influence Oxygen Consumption by Bacteria in Lake Water. Biol. Bull., **78**: 388–402.

——. 1942. Changes Produced by Microorganisms in Sediments after Deposition. Jour. Sed. Petr., **12**: 127–136.

——. 1942. Bacteria of the Marine World. Sci. Monthly, **55**: 1–11.

——. 1943. The Effect of Solid Surfaces upon Bacterial Activity. Jour. Bact., **46**: 39–56.

——. 1946. Marine Microbiology. Chronica Botan., vol. 17, 240 pp.

ZoBell, C. E., and Catherine B. Feltham. 1942. The Bacteria Flora of a Marine Mud Flat as an Ecological Factor. Ecology, **23**: 69–78.

ZoBell, C. E., and C. W. Grant. 1943. Bacterial Utilization of Low Concentrations of Organic Matter. Jour. Bact., **45**: 555–564.

ZoBell, C. E., and Janice Stadler. 1940. The Effect of Oxygen Tension on the Oxygen Uptake of Lake Bacteria. Jour. Bact., **39**: 307–322.

LARGER AQUATIC PLANTS AND THEIR LIMNOLOGICAL SIGNIFICANCE

ALLISON, F. E. 1931. Forms of Nitrogen Assimilated by Plants. Quart. Rev. Biol., **6**: 313–321.

ANDREWS, F. M. 1927. Deposition of Material by Water Plants. Proc. Ind. Acad. Sci., **37**: 327–329.

ARBER, A. 1920. Water Plants. A Study of Aquatic Angiosperms. Cambridge, 436 pp.

BARNEY, R. L., and B. J. ANSON. 1920. Relation of Certain Aquatic Plants to Oxygen Supply and to Capacity of Small Ponds to Support the Top Minnow (Gambusia affinis). Trans. Am. Fish. Soc., pp. 268–278.

BELLROSE, F. C. 1941. Duck Food Plants of the Illinois River Valley. Bull. Ill. Nat. Hist. Surv., **21**: 237–280.

———. 1950. The Relationship of Muskrat Populations to Various Marsh and Aquatic Plants. Jour. Wildlife Manag., **14**: 299–315.

BELLROSE, F. C., and H. G. ANDERSON. 1943. Preferential Rating of Duck Food Plants. Bull. Ill. Nat. Hist. Surv., **22**: 417–433.

BERG, C. O. 1949. Limnological Relations of Insects to Plants of the Genus *Potamogeton*. Trans. Am. Micr. Soc., **68**: 279–291.

———. 1950. Biology of Certain Chironomidae Reared from Potamogeton. Ecol. Monogr., **20**: 83–101.

———. 1950. Biology of Certain Aquatic Caterpillars (Pyralididae: Nymphula spp.) which feed on *Potamogeton*. Trans. Am. Micr. Soc., **69**: 254–266.

———. 1950. Hydrellia (Ephydridae) and Some Other Acalyptrate Diptera Reared from Potamogeton. Ann. Ent. Soc. Am., **43**: 374–398.

BROWN, C. J. D. 1940. Water Weeds—Their Value and Control. Michigan Conserv. for August, 6 pp.

DANSEREAU, P. 1945. Essai de Corrélation Sociologique entre les Plantes Supérieures et les Poissons de la Beine du Lac Saint-Louis. Rev. Can. d. Biol., **4**: 369–417.

DENNISTON, R. H. 1922. A Survey of the Larger Aquatic Plants of Lake Mendota. Wisconsin Geol. Nat. Hist. Surv., **20**: 495–500.

FASSETT, N. C. 1930. The Plants of Some Northeastern Wisconsin Lakes. Trans. Wis. Acad. Sci., Arts, Let., **25**: 157–168.

———. 1940. A Manual of Aquatic Plants. New York, 382 pp.

FROHNE, W. C. 1938. Contribution to Knowledge of the Limnological Role of the Higher Aquatic Plants. Trans. Am. Micr. Soc., **57**: 256–268.

———. 1939. Semiaquatic Hymenoptera in North Michigan Lakes. Trans. Am. Micr. Soc., **58**: 228–240.

———. 1939. Biology of Certain Subaquatic Flies Reared from Emergent Water Plants. Papers Mich. Acad. Sci., Arts, Let., **24**: 139–147.

———. 1939. Biology of *Chilo forbesellus* Fernald, an Hygrophilus Crambine Moth. Trans. Am. Micr. Soc., **58**: 304–326.

———. 1939. Observations on the Biology of Three Semiaquatic Lacustrine Moths. Trans. Am. Micr. Soc., **58**: 327–348.

GRUCHY, J. H. B. DE. 1938. A Preliminary Study of the Larger Aquatic Plants of Oklahoma with Special Reference to Their Value in Fish Culture. Okla. A. and M. Coll., Agr. Exp. Sta., Tech. Bull. 4, 31 pp.

HASLER, A. D., and ELIZ. JONES. 1949. Demonstration of the Antagonistic Action of Large Aquatic Plants on Algae and Rotifers. Ecology, **30**: 359–364.

HOPKINS, E. F. 1931. Manganese and the Growth of Lemna. Science, **74**: 551–552.

HOTCHKISS, N. 1936. Check-list of Marsh and Aquatic Plants of the United States. U.S. Dept. Agr., Bur. Biol. Surv., Wildlife Res. and Manag. Leaflet, BS-72, 27 pp.

———. 1941. The Limnological Role of the Higher Plants. In A Symposium on Hydrobiology. Univ. Wis. Press, pp. 152–162.

HUTCHINSON, G. E., and V. T. BOWEN. 1947. A Direct Demonstration of the Phosphorus Cycle in a Small Lake. Proc. Nat. Acad. Sci., **33**: 148–153.

IRWIN, W. H. 1945. Methods of Precipitating Colloidal Soil Particles from Impounded Waters of Central Oklahoma. Bull. Okla. A. and M. Coll., **42**: 1–16.

IRWIN, W. H. and J. H. STEVENSON. 1951. Physiochemical Nature of Clay Turbidity with Special Reference to Clarification and Productivity of Impounded Waters. Bull. Okla. Agr. and Mech. Coll., **48**, Biol. ser. No. 4, 54 pp.

KLUGH, A. B. 1926. The Productivity of Lakes. Quart. Rev. Biol., **1**: 572–577.

KOFOID, C. A. 1903. The Plankton of the Illinois River, 1894–1899, with Introductory Notes upon the Hydrography of the Illinois River and Its Basin. Part I. Quantitative Investigations and General Results. Bull. Ill. State Lab. Nat. Hist., **6**: 95–628.

KRECKER, F. H. 1939. A Comparative Study of the Animal Population of Certain Submerged Aquatic Plants. Ecology, **20**: 553–562.

LOHAMMER, G. 1938. Wasserchemie und Hohere Vegetation Schwedischer Seen. Symbol. Bot. Upsal., **3**: 1, 252 pp.

MARTIN, A. C., and F. M. UHLER. 1939. Food of Game Ducks in the United States and Canada. U.S. Dept. Agr., Tech. Bull. 634, 156 pp.

MCATEE, W. L. 1939. Wildfowl Food Plants. Ames, Iowa, 141 pp.

MCGAHA, Y. J. 1951. The Limnological Relations of Insects to Certain Aquatic Flowering Plants. Unpub. thesis, Univ. Mich.

MISRA, R. D. 1938. Edaphic Factors in the Distribution of Aquatic Plants in the English Lakes. Jour. Ecology, **26**: 411–451.

MOORE, E. 1915. The Potamogetons in Relation to Pond Culture. Bull. U.S. Bur. Fish., **33**: 251–291.

———. 1920. Some Plants of Importance in Pond-fish Culture. Bull. U.S. Bur. Fish., Doc. 881, pp. 5–20.

MOYLE, J. B. 1944. Wild Rice in Minnesota. Jour. Wildlife Manag., **8**: 177–184.

———. 1945. Some Chemical Factors Influencing the Distribution of Aquatic Plants in Minnesota. Am. Midl. Nat., **34**: 402–420.

MOYLE, J. B., and HOTCHKISS, N. 1945. The Aquatic and Marsh Vegetation of Minnesota and Its Value to Waterfowl. Minnesota Dept. Conserv., Tech. Bull. 3, 122 pp.

MUENSCHER, W. C. L. 1944. Aquatic Plants of the United States. Ithaca, N.Y., 374 pp.

NAUMANN, E. 1924. Die höhere Wasservegetation des Bach- und Teichgebietes bei Anaboda. Ark. f. Botanik, **19**: 1–31.

NEEDHAM, J. G., and J. T. LLOYD. 1930. The Life of Inland Waters, 2d ed. Springfield, 438 pp.

NELSON, J. W., L. S. PALMER, A. N. WICK, W. M. SANDSTROM, and H. V. LINDSTROM. 1939. Nutritive Value and Chemical Composition of Certain Fresh-water Plants in Minnesota. Minnesota Agr. Exp. Sta., Tech. Bull. 136, 47 pp.

PEARSALL, W. H. 1920. The Aquatic Vegetation of the English Lakes. Jour. Ecology, **8**: 163–201.

PENFOUND, W. T., and T. T. EARLE. 1948. The Biology of the Water Hyacinth. Ecol. Monogr., **18**: 447–472.

PENFOUND, W. T., T. F. HALL, and A. D. HESS. 1945. The Spring Phenology of Plants in and around the Reservoirs in North Alabama with Particular Reference to Malarial Control. Ecology, **26**: 332–352.

PIETERS, A. J. 1894. The Plants of Lake St. Clair. Bull. Mich. Fish Comm. No. 2, pp. 3–10.

POND, R. H. 1905. The Biological Relation of Aquatic Plants to the Substratum. U.S. Fish Comm. Rept. for 1903, pp. 483–526.

———. 1918. The Larger Aquatic Vegetation. In Ward and Whipple's Fresh-water Biology, pp. 178–209.

RAYMOND, M. R. 1937. A Limnological Study of the Plankton of a Concretion Forming Marl Lake. Trans. Am. Micr. Soc., **56**: 405–430.

RICE, T. B. 1916. A Study of the Relations between Plant Growth and Combined Nitrogen in Winona Lake. Proc. Ind. Acad. Sci., pp. 333–362.

RICKETT, H. W. 1920. A Quantitative Survey of the Flora of Lake Mendota. Science, **52**: 641–642.

———. 1922. A Quantitative Study of the Larger Aquatic Plants of Lake Mendota. Trans. Wis. Acad. Sci., Arts, Let., **20**: 501–527.

———. 1924. A Quantitative Study of the Larger Aquatic Plants of Green Lake, Wisconsin. Trans. Wis. Acad. Sci., Arts, Let., **21**: 381–414.

SCHUETTE, H. A., and H. ALDER. 1928. Notes on the Chemical Composition of Some of the Larger Aquatic Plants of Lake Mendota. II. Vallisneria and Potamogeton. Trans. Wis. Acad. Sci., Arts, Let., **23**: 249–254.

———. 1929. Notes on the Chemical Composition of Some of the Larger Aquatic Plants of Lake Mendota. III. Castalia odorata and Najas flexilis. Trans. Wis. Acad. Sci., Arts, Let., **24**: 135–139.

———. 1929. A Note on the Chemical Composition of Chara from Green Lake, Wisconsin. Trans. Wis. Acad. Sci., Arts, Let., **24**: 141–145.

SCHUETTE, H. A., and A. E. HOFFMAN. 1922. Notes on the Chemical Composition of Some of the Larger Aquatic Plants of Lake Mendota. I. Cladophora and Myriophyllum. Trans. Wis. Acad. Sci., Arts, Let., **20**: 529–531.

SMITH, E. V., and H. S. SWINGLE. 1942. The Use of Fertilizer in Controlling Several Submerged Aquatic Plants in Ponds. Trans. Am. Fish. Soc., **71**: 94–101.

SPEIRS, J. M. 1948. Summary of Literature on Aquatic Weed Control. Can. Fish Culturist, **3**: 20–32.

VEATCH, J. O. 1932. Some Relationships between Water Plants and Water Soils in Michigan. Papers Mich. Acad. Sci., Arts, Let., **27**: 409–413.

WILSON, L. R. 1935. Lakes Development and Plant Succession in Vilas County, Wisconsin. Ecol. Monogr., **5**: 207–247.

———. 1937. A Quantitative and Ecological Study of the Larger Aquatic Plants of Sweeney Lake, Oneida County, Wisconsin. Bull. Torrey Bot. Club, **64**: 199–208.

———. 1939. Rooted Aquatic Plants and Their Relation to the Limnology of Fresh-water Lakes. In Problems of Lake Biology, Publ. Am. Assoc. Adv. Sci., No. 10, pp. 107–122.

———. 1941. The Larger Aquatic Vegetation of Trout Lake, Vilas County, Wisconsin. Trans. Wis. Acad. Sci., Arts, Let., **33**: 135–146.

NEKTON

EDDY, S. 1943. Limnological Notes on Lake Superior. Proc. Minn. Acad. Sci., **11**: 34–39.

EGGLETON, F. E. 1937. Productivity of the Profundal Benthic Zone in Lake Michigan. Papers Mich. Acad. Sci., Arts, Let., **22**: 593–611.

HANKINSON, T. L. 1933. Distribution of the Fishes in the Inland Lakes of Michigan. Papers Mich. Acad. Sci., Arts, Let., **17**: 553–574.

HASLER, A. D., and J. E. BARDACH. 1949. Daily Migrations of Perch in Lake Mendota, Wisconsin. Jour. Wildlife Manag., **13**: 40–51.

HILE, R., and C. JUDAY. 1941. Bathymetric Distribution of Fish in Lakes of the Northeastern Highlands, Wisconsin. Trans. Wis. Acad. Sci., Arts, Let., **33**: 147–187.

JUDAY, C., and E. A. BIRGE. 1927. Pontoporeia and Mysis in Wisconsin Lakes. Ecology, **8**: 445–452.

KENNEDY, W. A. 1941. The Migration of Fish from a Shallow to a Deep Lake in Spring and Early Summer. Trans. Am. Fish. Soc., **70**: 391–396.

KOELZ, W. 1929. Coregonid Fishes of the Great Lakes. Bull. U.S. Bur. Fish., **43**: 297–643.

MORROW, J. E. 1948. Schooling Behavior in Fishes. Quart. Rev. Biol., **23**: 27–38.

PEARSE, A. S. 1921. Distribution and Food of the Fishes of Green Lake, Wis., in Summer. Bull. U.S. Bur. Fish., **37**: 254–272.

REIGHARD, J. 1915. An Ecological Reconnoissance of the Fishes of Douglas Lake, Cheboygan County, Michigan, in Midsummer. Bull. U.S. Bur. Fish., **33**: 219–249.

SHELFORD, V. E. 1913. Animal Communities in Temperature America. Chicago, 362 pp.

THIENEMANN, A. 1925. Mysis relicta. Fünfte Mitteilung der Untersuchungen über die Beziehungen zwischen dem Sauerstoffgehalt des Wassers und der Zusammensetzung der Fauna in Norddeutschen Seen. Zeit. f. Morph. u. Ökol. Tiere, **3**: 389–440.

———. 1928. Mysis relicta im sauerstoffarmen Tiefenwasser der Ostsee und das Problem der Atmung im Salzwasser und Süsswasser. Zool. Jahr., Abt. f. all. Zool. u. Physiol. d. Tiere, **45**: 371–384.

VAN OOSTEN, J., R. HILE, and F. JOBES. 1946. The Whitefish Fishery of Lakes Huron and Michigan with Special Reference to the Deep-trap-net Fishery. Fisheries Bull. 40, U.S. Fish and Wildlife Service, pp. 297–394.

BENTHOS

ADAMSTONE, F. B. 1924. The Distribution and Economic Importance of the Bottom Fauna of Lake Nipigon with an Appendix on the Bottom Fauna of Lake Ontario. Univ. Toronto Studies, Biol. ser., Publ. Ont. Fish Res. Lab., No. 24, pp. 35–100.

ADAMSTONE, F. B., and W. J. K. HARKNESS. 1923. The Bottom Organisms of Lake Nipigon. Univ. Toronto Studies, Biol. ser., Publ. Ont. Fish. Res. Lab., No. 15, pp. 123–170.

ANDREWS, J. D., and A. D. HASLER. 1944. Fluctuations in the Animal Populations of the Littoral Zone in Lake Mendota. Trans. Wis. Acad. Sci., Arts, Let., **35**: 175–186.

BAKER, F. C. 1918. The Productivity of Invertebrate Fish Food on the Bottom of Oneida Lake, with Special Reference to Mollusks. New York State Coll. Forestry, Tech. Publ. 9, 264 pp.

———. 1933. Studies on the Bottom Fauna of Fresh-water Lakes. Science, **78**: 190–191.

BERG, K. 1938. Studies on the Bottom Animals of Esron Lake. Mem. Acad. R. Sci. et Lett. d. Danemark, Sec. Sci., 9me ser. t. 8, 255 pp.

BIGELOW, N. K. 1928. The Ecological Distribution of Microscopic Organisms in Lake Nipigon. Univ. Toronto Studies, Biol. ser., Publ. Ont. Fish. Res. Lab., No. 35, pp. 59–74.

BUTCHER, R. W. 1932. Studies in the Ecology of Rivers. II. The Microflora of Rivers with Special Reference to the Algae on the River Bed. Ann. Botany, **46**: 813–862.

CRONK, M. W. 1932. The Bottom Fauna of Shakespeare Island Lake, Ontario. Univ. Toronto Studies, Biol. ser., Publ. Ont. Fish Res. Lab., No. 43, pp. 29–65.

DEEVEY, E. S. 1941. Limnological Studies in Connecticut. VI. The Quantity and Composition of the Bottom Fauna of Thirty-six Connecticut and New York Lakes. Ecol. Monogr., **11**: 413–455.

EDDY, S. 1943. Limnological Notes on Lake Superior. Proc. Minn. Acad. Sci., **11**: 34–39.

EGGLETON, F. E. 1931. A Limnological Study of the Profundal Bottom Fauna of Certain Fresh-water Lakes. Ecol. Monogr., **1**: 231–332.

———. 1932. Limnetic Distribution and Migration of Corethra Larvae in Two Michigan Lakes. Papers Mich. Acad. Sci., Arts, Let., **15**: 361–388.

———. 1936. The Deep-water Bottom Fauna of Lake Michigan. Pap. Mich. Acad. Sci., Arts, Let., **21**: 599–612.

———. 1937. Productivity of the Profundal Benthic Zone in Lake Michigan. Papers Mich. Acad. Sci., Arts, Let., **22**: 593–611.

ENTZ, B. 1947. Qualitative and Quantitative Studies in the Coatings of Potamogeton perfoliatus and Myriophyllum spicatum in Lake Balaton. Arch. Biol. Hungarica, ser. II, **17**: 17–37.

HUMPHRIES, C. F. 1936. An Investigation of the Profundal and Sublittoral Fauna of Windermere. Jour. Animal Ecology, **5**: 29–52.

JENNINGS, H. S. 1897. Biological Examination of Lake Michigan in the Traverse Bay Region. Appendix III. Bull. Mich. Fish. Comm., No. 6, pp. 85–93.

JUDAY, C. 1922. Quantitative Studies of the Bottom Fauna in the Deeper Waters of Lake Mendota. Trans. Wis. Acad. Sci., Arts, Let., **20**: 461–493.

KOFOID, C. A. 1897. A Report upon the Protozoa Observed in Lake Michigan and the Inland Lakes in the Neighborhood of Charlevoix, during the Summer of 1894. Bull. Mich. Fish. Comm., No. 6, pp. 76–84.

KOL, E. 1938. Bodenalgen des Balaton-sees. I. Arb. Ungar. Biol. Forsch., **10**: 161–169.

KRECKER, F. H., and L. Y. LANCASTER. 1933. Bottom Shore Fauna of Western Lake Erie: A Population Study to a Depth of Six Feet. Ecology, **14**: 79–93.

LENZ, F. 1931. Intersuchungen über die Vertikalverteilung der Bodenfauna im Tiefensediment von Seen. Ein neuer Bodengreifer mit Zerteilungsvorrichtung. Verh. d. Int. Ver. f. theor. u. angew. Limn., **5**: 232–260.

LUNDBECK, J. 1926. Die Bodentierwelt Norddeutscher Seen. Arch. f. Hydrobiol., Suppl. **7**: 1–473.

LUNDQVIST, G. 1927. Bodenablagerungen und Entwicklungstypen der Seen. Die Binnengewässer, Bd. II, 124 pp.

MILLER, R. B. 1941. A Contribution to the Ecology of the Chironomidae of Costello Lake, Algonquin Park, Ontario. Univ. Toronto Studies, Biol. Ser. No. 49, Publ. Ont. Fish. Res. Lab. No. 60, 63 pp.

MOFFETT, J. W. 1943. A Limnological Investigation of the Dynamics of a Sandy, Wave-swept Shoal in Douglas Lake, Michigan. Trans. Am. Micr. Soc., **62**: 1–23.

MOON, H. P. 1935. Flood Movements of the Littoral Fauna of Windermere. Jour. Animal Ecology, **4**: 216–228.

————. 1940. An Investigation of the Movements of Fresh-water Invertebrate Faunas. Jour. Animal Ecology, **9**: 76–83.

MOORE, G. M. 1939. A Limnological Investigation of the Microscopic Benthic Fauna of Douglas Lake, Michigan. Ecol. Monogr., **9**: 537–582.

NAUMANN, E. 1928. Die eulimnische Zonation einige terminologische Bemerkungen. Arch. f. Hydrobiol., **19**: 744–747.

————. 1930. Einführung in die Bodenkunde der Seen. Die Binnengewässer, Bd. IX, 126 pp.

NEEL, J. K. 1948. A Limnological Investigation of the Psammon in Douglas Lake, Michigan, with Special Reference to Shoal and Shoreline Dynamics. Trans. Am. Micr. Soc., **67**: 1–53.

NEWCOMBE, C. L. 1949. Attachment Materials in Relation to Water Productivity. Trans. Am. Micr. Soc., **68**: 355–361.

————. 1950. A Quantitative Study of Attached Materials in Sodon Lake, Michigan. Ecology, **31**: 204–215.

PENNAK, R. W. 1939. The Microscopic Fauna of the Sandy Beaches. Am. Assoc. Adv. Sci., Publ. No. 10, pp. 94–106.

————. 1940. Ecology of the Microscopic Metazoa inhabiting the Sandy Beaches of Some Wisconsin Lakes. Ecol. Monogr., **10**: 537–615.

RAWSON, D. S. 1928. Preliminary Studies of the Bottom Fauna of Lake Simcoe, Ontario. Univ. Toronto Studies, Biol. ser., Publ. Ont. Fish Res. Lab., No. 36, pp. 76–102.

————. 1930. The Bottom Fauna of Lake Simcoe and Its Role in the Ecology of the Lake. Univ. Toronto Studies, Biol. ser., Publ. Ont. Fish Res. Lab., No. 40, pp. 1–183.

RICHARDSON, R. E. 1921. The Small Bottom and Shore Fauna of the Middle and Lower Illinois River and Its Connecting Lakes, Chillicothe to Grafton: Its Valuation; Its Sources of Food Supply and Its relation to the Fishery. State of Ill. Div. Nat. Hist. Surv., **13**: 363–522.

————. 1925. Changes in the Small Bottom Fauna of Peoria Lake, 1920–1922. State of Ill. Div. Nat. Hist. Surv., **15**: 327–388.

————. 1925. Illinois River Bottom Fauna in 1923. State of Ill. Div. Nat. Hist. Surv., **15**: 391–422.

————. 1928. The Bottom Fauna of the Middle Illinois River, 1913–1925. State of Ill. Div. Nat. Hist. Surv., **17**: 387–475.

SCOTT, W., R. O. HILE, and H. T. SPIETH. 1928. Investigations of Indiana Lakes. I. A Quantitative Study of the Bottom Fauna of Lake Wawasee (Turkey Lake). Dept. Conserv., State of Ind., Div. Fish and Game, 25 pp.

SCOTT, W., and D. F. Opdyke. 1941. The Emergence of Insects from Winona Lake. Invest. Indiana Lakes and Streams, vol. II. Indiana Dept. Conserv. and Dept. Zool., Indiana Univ., pp. 5–15.

SEBESTYEN, OLGA. 1947. Cladocera Studies in Lake Balaton. I. Mud-living Cladocera and Muddy Bottom as Environment. Arch. Biol. Hungarica, ser. II, **17**: 1–16.

————. 1948. Cladocera Studies in Lake Balaton. II. Littoral Cladocera from the Northeastern Shores of the Tihany Peninsula. Arch. Biol. Hungarica, Ser. II, **18**: 101–116.

SHELFORD, V. E. 1913. Animal Communities in Temperature America. Chicago. 362 pp.

SHELFORD, V. E., and M. W. BOESEL. 1942. Bottom Animal Communities of the Island Area of Western Lake Erie in the Summer of 1937. Ohio Jour. Sci., **42**: 179–190.

SILVEY, J. K. G. 1936. An Investigation of the Burrowing Innerbeach Insects of Some Fresh-water Lakes. Papers Mich. Acad. Sci., Arts, Let., **21**: 655–696.

SMITH, F. 1894. List of the Protozoa and Mollusca Observed in Lake St. Clair in the Summer of 1893. Bull. Mich. Fish Comm., No. 4, pp. 42–44.

WISZNIEWSKI, J. 1933. Remarques sur les conditions de la vie du psammon lacustre. Verh. Int. Ver. f. theor. u. angew. Limnol., **6**: 263–274.

YOUNG, O. W. 1945. A Limnological Investigation of Periphyton in Douglas Lake, Michigan. Trans. Am. Micr. Soc., **64**: 1–20.

BIOLOGICAL PRODUCTIVITY

ALSTERBERG, G. 1924. Die Nahrungszirkulation einiger Binnenseetypen. Arch. f. Hydrobiol., **15**: 291–338.

BAKER, F. C. 1918. The Productivity of Invertebrate Fish Food on the Bottom of Oneida Lake, with Special Reference to Mollusks. Tech. Publ. 9, N.Y. State Coll. Forestry, **18**: 1–264.

———. 1918. The Relation of Shellfish to Fish in Oneida Lake, New York. New York State Coll. Forestry, Circ. 21, 34 pp.

BALL, R. C. 1948. Relationship between Available Fish Food, Feeding Habits of Fish and Total Fish Production in a Michigan Lake. Tech. Bull. 206, Mich. State Coll., Agr. Exp. Sta., 59 pp.

———. 1948. Fertilization of Lakes—Good or Bad. Michigan Conserv., **17**: 7–14.

———. 1949. Experimental Use of Fertilizer in the Production of Fish-food Organisms and Fish. Tech. Bull. 210, Mich. State Coll., Agr. Exp. Sta., 28 pp.

———. 1951. The Biological Effects of Fertilizer on a Warm Water Lake. Tech. Bull. 223, Mich. State. Coll., Agr. Exp. Sta., 32 pp.

CHAPMAN, R. N. 1928. The Quantitative Analysis of Environmental Factors. Ecology, **9**: 111–122.

———. 1931. Animal Ecology. New York, 464 pp.

CLARKE, G. L. 1946. Dynamics of Production in a Marine Area. Ecol. Monogr., **16**: 321–335.

CLEMENTS, F. E., and V. E. SHELFORD. 1939. Bio-ecology. New York, 425 pp.

COMPTON, L. V. 1943. Techniques of Fish-pond Management. U.S. Dept. Agr., Misc Publ. 528, 22 pp.

DEEVEY, E. S. 1941. Limnological Studies in Connecticut. VI. The Quantity and Composition of the Bottom Fauna of Thirty-six Connecticut and New York Lakes. Ecol. Monogr., **11**: 413–455.

EDMONDSON, W. T., and Y. H. EDMONDSON. 1947. Measurements of Production in Fertilized Salt-water. Jour. Marine Res., **6**: 228–246.

EGGLETON, F. E. 1939. Role of the Bottom Fauna in the Productivity of Lakes. In Problems of Lake Biology, Publ. Am. Assoc. Adv. Sci., No. 10, pp. 123–131.

FORBES, S. A., and R. E. RICHARDSON. 1913. Studies on the Biology of the Upper Illinois River. Bull. Ill. State Lab. Nat. Hist. **9**: 481–574.

———. 1919. Some Recent Changes in Illinois River Biology. State of Ill. Div. Nat. Hist. Survey, **13**: 139–156.

———. 1925. The Lake as a Microcosm. State of Ill. Div. Nat. Hist. Surv., **15**: 537–550. (Originally published in 1887.)

FRITSCH, F. E. 1931. Some Aspects of the Ecology of Fresh-water Algae. Jour. Ecology, **19**: 233–272.

GESSNER, F. 1944. Der Chlorophyllgehalt der Seen als Ausdruck ihrer Produktivität. Arch. Hydrobiol., **40**: 687–732.

GROSS, F. 1947. An Experiment in Marine Fish Cultivation. V. Fish Growth in a Fertilized Sea-loch (Loch Graiglin). Proc. R. Soc. Edinburgh, Sec. B (Biol.), **63**: 56–95.

GROSS, F., J. E. G. RAYMONT, S. R. NUTMAN, and D. T. GAULD. 1946. Application of Fertilizers to an Open Sea Loch. Nature, **158**: 187.

HASLER, A. D. 1938. Fish Biology and Limnology of Crater Lake, Oregon. Jour. Wildlife Manag., **2**: 94–103.

———. 1947. Eutrophication of Lakes by Domestic Drainage. Ecology, **28**: 383–395.

HASLER, A. D., and W. G. EINSELE. 1948. Fertilization for Increasing Productivity of Natural Inland Waters. Trans. 13th No. Am. Wildlife Conf., pp. 527–555.

HERDMAN, W. A. 1923. Founders of Oceanography and Their Work. London, 340 pp.

HUBBS, C. L., and R. W. ESCHMEYER. 1938. The Improvement of Lakes for Fishing. Inst. Fish. Res., Bull. 2, Mich. Dept. Conserv., 233 pp.

HUTCHINSON, G. E. 1938. On the Relation between the Oxygen Deficit and the Productivity and Typology of Lakes. Internat. Rev. d. ges. Hydrobiol. u. Hydrogr., **36**: 336–355.

JUDAY, C. 1924. Summary of Quantitative Investigations on Green Lake, Wisconsin. Int. Rev. d. ges. Hydrobiol. u. Hydrogr., **12**: 2–12.

———. 1924. The Productivity of Green Lake, Wisconsin. Verh. d. Int. Ver. f. theor. u. angew. Limnol., pp. 357–360.

———. 1943. The Utilization of Aquatic Food Resources. Science, **97**: 456–458.

———. 1943. The Summer Standing Crop of Plants and Animals in Four Wisconsin Lakes. Trans. Wis. Acad. Sci., Arts, Let., **34**: 103–135.

KLUGH, A. B. 1926. The Productivity of Lakes. Quart. Rev. Biol., **1**: 572–577.

KOZMINSKI, Z. 1938. Amount and Distribution of the Chlorophyll in Some Lakes of Northeastern Wisconsin. Trans. Wis. Acad. Sci., Arts, Let., **31**: 411–438.

LINDEMAN, R. L. 1942. The Trophic-dynamic Aspect of Ecology. Ecology, **23**: 399–418.

LINDQVIST, G. 1927. Bodenablagerungen und Entwicklungstypen der Seen. Die Binnengewässer, Bd. II, 124 pp.

MANNING, W. M., and R. E. JUDAY. 1941. The Chlorophyll Content and Productivity of Some Lakes in Northeastern Wisconsin. Trans. Wis. Acad. Sci., Arts, Let., **33**: 363–393.

MANNING, W. M., C. JUDAY, and M. WOLF. 1938. Photosynthesis of Aquatic Plants at Different Depths in Trout Lake, Wisconsin. Trans. Wis. Acad. Sci., Arts, Let., **31**: 377–410.

MARSHALL, S. M. 1947. An Experiment in Marine Fish Cultivation: III. The Plankton of a Fertilized Loch. Proc. R. Soc. Edinburgh, Sec. B (Biol.), **63**: 21–33.

MOYLE, J. B. 1949. Some Indices of Lake Productivity. Trans. Am. Fish. Soc., **76**: (1946): 322–334.

NAUMANN, E. 1925. Notizen zur experimentellen Morphologie des pflanzlichen Limnoplankton. I–II. Botan. Notiser, pp. 47–51.

———. 1926. Notizen zur Ernährungsbiologie der Limnischen Fauna. Ark. f. Zool., **16**: 1–14.

———. 1929. Einige neue Gesichtspunkte zur Systematik der Gewässertypen. Arch. f. Hydrobiol., **20**: 191–198.

———. 1931. Limnologische Terminologie. Abderhalden's Handbuch d. biol. Arbeitsmeth., Abt. IX, Teil 8, Heft 1–5, 776 pp.

NEEDHAM, P. R. 1928. A Quantitative Study of the Fish Food Supply in Selected Areas. Suppl. to 17th Ann. Rept., State of N.Y. Conserv. Comm., pp. 192–206.

———. 1929. Quantitative Study of the Fish Food Supply in Selected Areas. Suppl. to 18th Ann. Rept., State of N.Y. Conserv. Comm., pp. 220–232.

———. 1930. Ecology of Streams. Biol. Lab., L.I. Biol. Assoc., **2**: 3–6.

NEESS, J. C. 1949. Development and Status of Pond Fertilization in Central Europe. Trans. Am. Fish. Soc., **76** (1946): 335–358.

ORR, A. P. 1947. An Experiment in Marine Fish Cultivation: Some Physical and Chemical Conditions in a Fertilized Sea-loch (Loch Craighlin, Argyll). Proc. R. Soc. Edinburgh, Sec. B (Biol.), **63**: 1–20.

PATRIARCHE, M. H., and R. C. BALL. 1949. An Analysis of the Bottom Fauna Production in Fertilized and Unfertilized Ponds and Its Utilization by Young-of-the-year-fish. Tech. Bull. 207, Mich. State Coll., Agr. Exp. Sta., 35 pp.

PEARSE, A. S. 1921. Distribution and Food of the Fishes of Green Lake, Wis., in Summer. Bull. U.S. Bur. Fish., **37**: 253–272.

———. 1934. Ecology of Lake Fishes. Ecol. Monogr., **4**: 475–480.

PRESCOTT, G. W. 1939. Some Relationships of Phytoplankton to Limnology and Aquatic Biology. In Problems of Lake Biology, Publ. Am. Assoc. Adv. Sci., No. 10, pp. 65–78.

RAWSON, D. S. 1930. The Bottom Fauna of Lake Simcoe and Its Role in the Ecology of the Lake. Univ. Toronto Studies, Publ. Ont. Fish. Res. Lab., No. 40, pp. 1–183.

———. 1939. Some Physical and Chemical Factors in the Metabolism of Lakes. In Problems of Lake Biology, Publ. Am. Assoc. Adv. Sci., No. 10, pp. 9–26.

REIGHARD, J. 1929. A Biological Examination of Loon Lake, Gogebic County, Michigan, with Suggestions for Increasing Its Yield of Small-mouth Bass (Micropterus dolomieu). Papers Mich. Acad. Sci., Arts, Let., **10**: 589–612.

RICKER, W. E. 1932. Studies of Trout Producing Lakes and Ponds. Univ. Toronto Studies, Publ. Fish Res. Lab., No. 45, pp. 111–167.

———. 1946. Production and Utilization of Fish Populations. Ecol. Monogr., **16**: 373–391.

RILEY, G. A. 1940. Limnological Studies in Connecticut. III. The Plankton of Linsley Pond. Ecol. Monogr., **10**: 279–306.

ROELOFS, E. W. 1940. Available Plant Nutrients in Lake Soils. Michigan Agr. Exp. Sta. Quart. Bull., **22**: 247–254.

———. 1944. Water Soils in Relation to Lake Productivity. Tech. Bull. 190, Mich. State Coll. Agr. Exp. Sta., 31 pp.

SAWYER, C. N. 1947. Fertilization of Lakes by Agricultural and Urban Drainage. Jour. New Eng. Water Works Assoc., **61**: 109–127.

SHELFORD, V. E. 1913. Animal Communities in Temperate America. Chicago, 362 pp.

———. 1914. Suggestions as to the Indices of the Suitability of Bodies of Water for Fishes. Trans. Am. Fish. Soc., pp. 27–32.

———. 1931. Some Concepts of Bioecology. Ecology, **12**: 455–467.

STRØM, K. M. 1928. Recent Advances in Limnology. Proc. Linn. Soc. London, pp. 96–110.

———. 1928. Production Biology of Temperate Lakes. A Synopsis Based upon Recent Literature. Int. Rev. d. ges. Hydrobiol. u. Hydrogr., **19**: 329–348.

———. 1933. Nutrition of Algae. Arch. f. Hydrobiol., **25**: 38–47.

SWINGLE, H. S. 1950. Relationships and Dynamics of Balanced and Unbalanced Fish Populations. Bull. No. 274, Alabama Polytechnic Inst., Agr. Exp. Sta., 73 pp.

SWINGLE, H. S., and E. V. SMITH. 1942. Management of Farm Fish Ponds. Alabama Agr. Exp. Sta., Bull. **254**: 1–23.

THIENEMANN, A. 1926. Der Nahrungskreislauf im Wasser. Verh. deutschen Zool. Gesell., **31**: 29–79.

TRESSLER, W. L., L. G. WAGNER, and R. BERE. 1940. A Limnological Study of Chautauqua Lake. II. Seasonal Variation. Trans. Am. Micr. Soc., **59**: 12–30.

WELCH, P. S. 1941. Dissolved Oxygen in Relation to Lake Types. In A Symposium on Hydrobiology. Univ. Wis. Press, pp. 60–70.

PONDS

ALLEE, W. C. 1912. Seasonal Succession in Old Forest Ponds. Trans. Ill. Acad. Sci., **4**: 126–131.

ATKINS, W. R. G., and G. T. HARRIS. 1924. Seasonal Changes in the Water and Heleoplankton of Fresh-water Ponds. Sci. Proc. R. Dublin Soc., **18**: 1–21.

———. 1925. Seasonal Changes in the Water and Heleoplankton of Freshwater Ponds. Jour. Marine Biol. Assoc., **13**: 750–754.

BROWN, H. E. 1908. Algal Periodicity in Ponds and Streams. Bull. Torrey Bot. Club, **35**: 223–248.

BUELL, HELEN F. 1938. The Taxonomy of a Community of Blue-green Algae in a Minnesota Pond. Bull. Torrey Bot. Club, **65**: 377–396.

———. 1938. A Community of Blue-green Algae in a Minnesota Pond. Ecology, **19**: 224–232.

CHAPMAN, R. N. 1931. Animal Ecology. New York, 464 pp.

COKER, R. E. 1918. Principles and Problems of Fish Culture in Ponds. Sci. Monthly, **7**: 120–129.

DAKIN, W. J. 1927. The Fresh Water Pond as an Animal Community. Chap. 18 in Dakin's Elements of General Zoology, pp. 391–414.

DYKE, L. L. 1914. Ponds, Pond Fish and Pond Fish Culture. 1910–1914, Kansas State Dept. Fish and Game, Bull. 1, 208 pp.

EDDY, S. 1925. Fresh Water Algal Succession. Trans. Am. Micr. Soc., **44**: 138–147.

———. 1931. The Plankton of Some Sink Hole Ponds in Southern Illinois. State of Ill. Div. Nat. Hist. Surv., **19**: 449–467.

FRITSCH, F. E., and F. RICH. 1909. Studies on the Occurrence and Reproduction of British Freshwater Algae in Nature. 2. A Five Years' Observation of the Fish Pond, Abbot's Leigh, near Bristol. Proc. Bristol Nat. Soc., (2), pp. 27–54.

———. 1913. Studies on the Occurrence and Reproduction of British Fresh-water Algae. Chap. III. A Four-year Observation of a Fresh-water Pond. Ann. biol. lacustre, **6**: 33–115.

FROHNE, W. C. 1939. Anopheline Breeding: Suggested Classification of Ponds Based on Characteristic Desmids. Pub. Health Reps., U.S. Pub. Health Serv., **54**: 1363–1387.

GRIFFITHS, B. M. 1936. The Limnology of the Long Pool, Butterby Marsh, Durham: An Account of the Temperature, Oxygen-content, and Composition of the Water, and of the Periodicity of the Phyto- and Zooplankton. Linn. Soc. Jour. (Bot.), **50**: 393–416.

HOFF, C. C. 1943. Seasonal Changes in the Ostracod Fauna of Temporary Ponds. Ecology, **24**: 116–118.

HÖPPNER, H. 1926. Hydrobiologische Untersuchungen an Niederrheinischen Gewässern. III. Die Phanerogamenflora der Seen und Teiches des unteren Niederrheins. Arch. f. Hydrobiol., **17**: 117–158.

JEWELL, M. E. 1927. Aquatic Biology of the Prairie. Ecology, **8**: 289–298.

KENK, R. 1949. The Animal Life of Temporary and Permanent Ponds in Southern Michigan. Univ. Mich. Mus. Zool., Misc. Publ., 71, 66 pp.

KLAK, G. E. 1937. A Comparative Study of Summer Plankton from Twenty-one Bodies of Water in the Vicinity of Minneapolis and St. Paul, Minnesota. Trans. Am. Micr. Soc., **56**: 196–202.

KRECKER, F. H. 1919. The Fauna of Rock Bottom Ponds. Ohio Jour. Sci., **19**: 427–474.

KRUMHOLZ, L. A. 1948. Variations in Size and Composition of Fish Populations in Recently Stocked Ponds. Ecology, **29**: 401–414.

LAURIE, E. M. O. 1942. The Dissolved Oxygen of an Upland Pond and Its Inflowing Stream, at Ystumtuen, North Cardiganshire, Wales. Jour. Ecology, **30**: 357–382.

LIND, EDNA M. 1938. Studies in the Periodicity of the Algae in Beauchief Ponds, Sheffield. Jour. Ecology, **26**: 257–274.

———. 1940. Experiments with Pond Muds. Jour. Ecology, **28**: 484–490.

LUND, J. W. G. 1942. The Marginal Algae of Certain Ponds with Special Reference to the Bottom Deposits. Jour. Ecology, **30**: 245–283.

MEEHEAN, O. L. 1937. The Relative Importance of Plankton Constituents in Bass Ponds as Measured by the Organic Content. Int. Rev. d. ges. Hydrobiol. u. Hydrogr., **36**: 131–137.

MOORE, E. 1915. The Potamogetons in Relation to Pond Culture. Bull. U.S. Bur. Fish., **33**: 251–291.

———. 1920. Some Plants of Importance in Pond-fish Culture. U.S. Bur. Fish., Doc. 881, pp. 5–20.

MORGAN, A. H. 1930. Field Book of Ponds and Streams. New York, 448 pp.

MOZLEY, A. 1932. A Biological Study of a Temporary Pond in Western Canada. Am. Nat., **66**: 235–249.

———. 1944. Temporary Ponds, a Neglected Natural Resource. Nature, **154**: 490.

MURRAY, J. 1911. The Annual History of a Periodic Pond. Int. Rev. d. ges. Hydrobiol. u. Hydrogr., **4**: 300–310.

NAUMANN, E. 1914. Beiträge zur Kenntnis des Teichnannoplanktons. Biol. Zentralbl., **34**: 581–594.

———. 1917. Beiträge zur Kenntnis des Teichnannoplanktons. II. Über das Neuston des Süsswassers. Biol. Zentralbl., **37**: 98–106.

———. 1925. See und Teich (Tiefe): Abderhalden's Handbuch d. biol. Arbeitsmeth., Abt. 9, Teil 2, Heft **1**: 103–138.

NYGAARD, G. 1938. Hydrobiologische Studien über dänische Teiche und Seen. Archiv f. Hydrobiol., **32**: 523–692.

———. 1949. Hydrobiological studies on some Danish Ponds and Lakes. Part II. Det Kongelige Danske Videnskabernes Selskab. Biol. Skr. Vol. VII, No. 1, 293 pp.

PEARSE, A. S. 1939. Animal Ecology. 2d ed. New York, 642 pp.

PETERSEN, W. 1926. Seasonal Succession of Animals in a Chara Cattail Pond. Ecology, **7**: 371–377.

PLATT, E. L. 1916. The Population of the "Blanket-Algae" of Fresh Water Pools. Am. Nat., **49**: 752–762.

PYEFINCH, K. A. 1937. The Fresh and Brackish Waters of Bardsey Island (North Wales): A Chemical and Faunistic Survey. Jour. Animal Ecology, **6**: 115–137.

REED, G., and A. B. KLUGH. 1924. Correlations between Hydrogen Ion Concentration and Biota of Granite and Limestone Pools. Ecology, **5**: 272–275.

RICKER, W. E. 1932. Studies of Trout Production Lakes and Ponds. Univ. Toronto Studies, Publ. Ont. Fish. Res. Lab., No. 45, pp. 115–167.

RODECK, H. G. 1941. Distribution Problems in Some Moraine Ponds. Univ. Colo. Studies, ser. D., 1: 193–201.

SCHNEBERGER, E., and M. E. JEWELL. 1928. Factors Affecting Pond Fish Production. Kansas Forestry, Fish and Game Comm., Bull. 9, pp. 5–14.

SCHULTZ, V. 1950. A Selected Bibliography on Farm Ponds and Closely Related Subjects. Progressive Fish-Culturist, 12: 97–104.

SCOTT, W. 1910. The Fauna of a Solution Pond. Proc. Ind. Acad. Sci., pp. 1–48.

SHELFORD, V. E. 1911. Seasonal Succession. II. Pond Fishes. Biol. Bull., 21: 127–151.

———. 1911. Seasonal Succession. III. A Reconnaissance of Its Causes in Ponds with Particular Reference to Fish. Biol. Bull., 22: 1–38.

———. 1919. Nature's Mobilization. Nat. Hist., 19: 205–210.

STEEGER, A. 1925. Hydrobiologische Untersuchungen an niederrheinischen Gewässer. II. Die Seen und Teiche des unteren Niederrheingebietes. Arch. f. Hydrobiol., 15: 467–480.

SWINGLE, H. S., and E. V. SMITH. 1941. The Management of Ponds for the Production of Game and Pan Fish. In A Symposium on Hydrobiology. Univ. Wis. Press, pp. 218–226.

TITCOMB, J. W. 1909. Aquatic Plants in Pond Culture. U.S. Bur. Fish., Doc. 643, pp. 3–31.

TRANSEAU, E. N. 1914. Seasonal Variations of the Osmotic Pressure of Pool, Pond, and Stream Waters. Science, 39: 260.

TREMBLEY, F. J. 1931. A Tentative Classification of the Ponds and Lakes of the Grass, St. Regis, Salmon and Chateaugay Systems. Suppl. to 20th Ann. Rept., State of N.Y. Conserv. Comm., pp. 161–166.

WALKER, E. R. 1908. Observations on the Microfauna of an Oregon Pond. Trans. Am. Micr. Soc., 28: 75–84.

WALTER, E. 1927. Die Versuche 1926 in bäyerischen teichwirtschaftlichen Versuchsstation Wielenbach. All. Fisch. Zeit., pp. 171–178.

WARD, E. B. 1940. A Seasonal Population Study of Pond Entromostraca in the Cincinnati Region. Am. Midl. Nat., 23: 635–691.

WESENBERG-LUND, C. 1930. Contributions to the Biology of the Rotifera. II. The Periodicity and Sexual Periods. Mém. l'Acad. R. Sci. et Let. Danemark, 9me ser., 2: 3–230.

WHITNEY, R. J. 1942. Diurnal Fluctuations of Oxygen and pH in Two Small Ponds and a Stream. Jour. Exp. Biol., 19: 92–99.

WIEBE, A. H. 1930. Investigations on Plankton Production in Fish Ponds. Bull. U.S. Bur. Fish., 46: 137–176.

WIMMER, E. J. 1929. A Study of Two Limestone Quarry Pools. Trans. Wis. Acad. Sci., Arts, Let., 24: 365–399.

BOG LAKES

ALM, G. 1943. Beiträge zur Kenntnis der Limnologie kleiner Schwingferseen. Arch. f. Hydrobiol., 40: 555–575.

AUER, V. 1933. Peat Bogs in Southeastern Canada. Handbuch d. Moorkunde, 7: 141–221.

BIRGE, E. A., and C. JUDAY. 1927. The Organic Content of the Water of Small Lakes. Proc. Am. Phil. Soc., 66: 357–372.

BROWN, H. W., and M. E. JEWELL. 1926. Further Studies on the Fishes of an Acid Lake. Trans. Am. Micr. Soc., 45: 20–34.

BUELL, M. F., and H. F. BUELL. 1941. Surface Level Fluctuations in Cedar Creek Bog, Minnesota. Ecology, **22**: 317–321.

BURNS, G. P. 1911. A Botanical Survey of the Huron River Valley. VIII. Edaphic Conditions in Peat Bogs of Southern Michigan. Bot. Gaz., **52**: 81–104.

CAIN, S. A. 1928. Hydrogen Ion Studies of Water, Peat, and Soil in Relation to Ecological Problems in Bacon's Swamp, Marion Co., Indiana. Proc. Ind. Acad. Sci., **37**: 395–401.

————. 1939. Pollen Analysis as a Paleo-ecological Research Method. Bot. Rev., **5**: 627–654.

COBURN, H., D. DEAN, and G. M. GRANT. 1933. An Ecological Study of Bryant's Bog, Cheboygan County, Michigan. Papers Mich. Acad. Sci., Arts, Let., **17**: 57–65.

CONWAY, V. M. 1949. The Bogs of Central Minnesota. Ecol. Monogr., **19**: 173–206.

COWLES, R. P., and C. E. BRAMBEL. 1936. A Study of the Environmental Conditions in a Bog Pond with Special Reference to the Diurnal Vertical Distribution of Gonyostomum semen. Biol. Bull., **71**: 286–298.

DACHNOWSKI, A. 1912. Peat Deposits of Ohio. Geol. Surv. Ohio, 4th ser., Bull. 14, 424 pp.

DACHNOWSKI-STOKES, A. P. 1933. Peat Deposits in U.S.A. Their Characteristic Profiles and Classification. Handbuch d. Moorkunde, **7**: 1–140.

DAVIS, C. A. 1907. Peat, Essays on Its Origin, Uses and Distribution in Michigan. Rept. State Bd. Geol. Surv. Mich. for 1906, pp. 95–395.

EDMONDSON, W. T. 1940. The Sessile Rotatoria of Wisconsin. Trans. Am. Micr. Soc., **59**: 433–459.

————. 1944. Ecological Studies of Sessile Rotatoria. Part I. Factors Affecting Distribution. Ecol. Monogr., **14**: 31–60.

EGGLETON, F. E. 1935. A Comparative Study of the Benthic Fauna of Four Northern Michigan Lakes. Papers Mich. Acad. Sci., Arts, Let., **20**: 609–644.

FROHNE, W. C. 1942. Reconnaissance of Anopheline Larval Habitats and Characteristic Desmids of the Okefenokee Swamp, Georgia. U.S. Pub. Health Reps., **57**: 1209–1217.

GATES, F. C. 1926. Plant Successions about Douglas Lake, Cheboygan County, Michigan. Bot. Gaz., **82**: 170–182.

————. 1940. Bog Levels. Science, **91**: 449–450.

————. 1942. The Bogs of Northern Lower Michigan. Ecol. Monogr., **12**: 213–254.

GESSNER, F. 1929. Die Biologie die Moorseen. Untersuch anderen Moortalsperren des Isergebirges. Arch. f. Hydrobiol., **20**: 1–64.

GOE, L., E. ERICKSON, and E. WOOLLETT. 1924. An Ecological Study of Mud Lake Bog, Cheboygan County, Michigan. Papers Mich. Acad. Sci., Arts, Let., **4**: 297–310.

GORHAM, W. C. 1931. A Limnological Study of Certain Bog Lakes with Special Reference to the Macroplankton. (Unpub. doctorate diss., Univ. Mich.)

HANSEN, H. P. 1947. Postglacial Forest Succession, Climate, and Chronology in the Pacific Northwest. Trans. Am. Phil. Soc., 37, 130 pp.

HARNISH, O. 1929. Die Biologie der Moore. Die Binnengewässer, Bd. VII, 146 pp.

HENRICI, A. T. 1936. Studies of Freshwater Bacteria. III. Quantitative Aspects of the Direct Microscopic Method. Jour. Bact., **32**: 265–280.

IRWIN, W. H. 1942. The Role of Certain Northern Michigan Bog Mats in Mosquito Production. Ecology, **23**: 466–477.

Jewell, M. E., and H. W. Brown. 1924. The Fishes of an Acid Lake. Trans. Am. Micr. Soc., **43**: 77–84.

———. 1929. Studies on Northern Michigan Bog Lakes. Ecology, **10**: 427–475.

Jones, C. H. 1941. Studies in Ohio Floristics. I. Vegetation of Ohio Bogs. Am. Midl. Nat., **26**: 674–689.

Juday, C., and E. A. Birge. 1931. A Second Report on the Phosphorus Content of Wisconsin Lake Waters. Trans. Wis. Acad. Sci., Arts, Let., **22**: 353–382.

Kurz, H. 1928. Influence of Sphagnum and Other Mosses on Bog Reactions. Ecology, **9**: 56–59.

Lewis, I. F. 1929. Peat Bogs of Southeastern Canada. Ecology, **10**: 155–157.

Lindeman, R. L. 1941. The Developmental History of Cedar Creek Bog, Minn. Am. Midl. Nat., **25**: 101–112.

———. 1941. Seasonal Food-cycle Dynamics in a Senescent Lake. Am. Midl. Nat., **26**: 636–673.

———. 1942. Seasonal Distribution of Midge Larvae in a Senescent Lake. Am. Midl. Nat., **27**: 428–444.

Moore, B., and N. Taylor. 1921. Plant Composition and Soil Acidity of a Maine Bog. Ecology, **2**: 258–261.

Needham, J. G., and T. J. Lloyd. 1930. Life of Inland Waters. Springfield, 438 pp.

Nichols, G. E. 1915. The Vegetation of Connecticut. IV. Bull. Torrey Bot. Club, **42**: 169–217.

———. 1919. Raised Bogs in Eastern Maine. Geog. Rev., **7**: 159–167.

Peus, F. 1932. Die Tierwelt der Moore. Handbuch der Moorkunde. III. Berlin, 277 pp.

Powers, W. E. 1932. Recent Advances in the Study of Peat. Bull. Nat. Res. Council, **89**: 53–60.

Rigg, G. B. 1916. A Summary of Bog Theories. Plant World, **19**: 310–325.

———. 1922. The Sphagnum Bogs of Mazama Dome. Ecology, **3**: 321–324.

———. 1925. Some Sphagnum Bogs in the North Pacific Coast of America. Ecology, **6**: 260–278.

———. 1926. The Bogs of Finland. A Review. Ecology, **7**: 505–510.

———. 1940. The Development of Sphagnum Bogs in North America. Bot. Rev., **6**: 666–693.

———. 1940. Comparisons of the Development of Some Sphagnum Bogs of the Atlantic Coast, the Interior, and the Pacific Coast. Am. Jour. Bot., **27**: 1–14.

Rigg, G. B., and C. T. Richardson. 1938. Profiles of Some Sphagnum Bogs of the Pacific Coast of North America. Ecology, **19**: 408–434.

Rigg, G. B., T. G. Thompson, J. R. Lorah, and K. T. Williams. 1927. Dissolved Gases in Waters of Some Puget Sound Bogs. Bot. Gaz., **84**: 264–278.

Schmidt, H. 1928. Beiträge zur Ökologie und Biologie der Moore-gewässer. Zool. Jahrb., Abt. all. Zool. u. Physiol., **45**: 361–370.

Schreiber, H. 1927. Moorkunde. Berlin, 192 pp.

Sears, P. B. 1930. Common Fossil Pollen of the Erie Basin. Bot. Gaz., **89**: 95–106.

———. 1931. Pollen Analysis of Mud Lake Bog in Ohio. Ecology, **12**: 650–655.

Smith, A. M. 1942. The Algae of Miles Rough Bog, Bradford. Jour. Ecology, **30**: 341–356.

Transeau, E. N. 1905–1906. The Bogs and Bog Flora of the Huron River Valley. Bot. Gaz., **40**: 351–375, 418–448; **41**: 17–42.

Waksman, S. A. 1930. Chemical Composition of Peat and the Role of Micro-organisms in Its Formation. Am. Jour. Sci., **19**: 32–54.

WAKSMAN, S. A., and K. R. STEVENS. 1929. Contribution to the Chemical Composition of Peat. V. The Role of Microorganisms in Peat Formation and Decomposition. Soil Sci., **28**: 315–340.

WELCH, P. S. 1936. A Limnological Study of a Small Sphagnum—Leather-leaf—Black Spruce Bog Lake with Special Reference to Its Plankton. Trans. Am. Micr. Soc., **55**: 300–312.

————. 1936. Limnological Investigation of a Strongly Basic Lake Surrounded by an Extensive Acid-forming Bog Mat. Papers Mich. Acad. Sci., Arts, Let., **21**: 727–751.

————. 1938. A Limnological Study of a Retrograding Bog Lake. Ecology, **19**: 435–453.

————. 1938. A Limnological Study of a Bog Lake Which Has Never Developed a Marginal Mat. Trans. Am. Micr. Soc., **57**: 344–357.

————. 1939. Vertical Distribution of Summer Temperature in the False Bottoms of Certain Michigan Bog Lakes. Ecology, **20**: 38–46.

————. 1945. Some Limnological Features of Water Impounded in a Northern Bog-lake Mat. Trans. Am. Micr. Soc., **64**: 183–195.

WESENBERG-LUND, C. 1930. Contributions to the Biology of the Rotifera. II. The Periodicity and Sexual Periods. Mém. l'Acad. R. Sci. et Let. Danemark, 9me ser., **2**: 3–230.

RUNNING WATERS IN GENERAL

ALLEE, W. C., and M. TORVIK. 1927. Factors Affecting Animal Distribution in a Small Stream of the Panama Rain-forest in the Dry Season. Jour. Ecology, **15**: 66–71.

ALLEN, W. E. 1920. A Quantitative and Statistical Study of the Plankton of the San Joaquin River and Its Tributaries in and near Stockton, California, in 1913. Univ. Calif. Publ. Zool., **22**: 1–292.

ALLEN, W. R., and M. E. CLARK. 1943. Bottom Preferences of Fishes of Northeastern Kentucky Streams. Trans. Ky. Acad. Sci., **11**: 26–30.

BAKER, F. C. 1922. The Molluscan Fauna of the Big Vermillion River, Illinois. Ill. Biol. Monogr., **7**: 5–126.

BEAUCHAMP, R. S. A. 1932. Some Ecological Factors and Their Influence on Competition between Stream and Lake-living Triclads. Jour. Animal Ecology, **1**: 175–190.

BEHNING, A. 1927. Über die Lebensverhältnisse in den Flüssen der U.S.S.R. Deutsch-Russischen Med. Zeit. 6, 4 pp.

————. 1928. Das Leben der Wolga. Zugleich eine Einführung in die Flussbiologie. Die Binnengewässer, Bd. V, 168 pp.

————. 1929. Ueber das Plankton der Wolga. Verh. d. Int. Ver. f. theor. u. angew. Limn., **4**: 192–212.

BERG, K. 1943. Physiographical Studies of the River Susaa. Folia Limnologica Scandinavica, No. 1, 174 pp.

————. 1948. Biological Studies on the River Susaa. Folia Limnologica Scandinavica, No. 4. 318 pp.

BERNER, L. M. 1951. Limnology of the Lower Missouri River. Ecology, **32**: 1–12.

Biological Survey of the Genessee River System. Suppl. to 16th Ann. Rept., State of N.Y. Conserv. Comm., 1927, 100 pp.

Biological Survey of the Oswego River System. Suppl. to 17th Ann. Rept., State of N.Y. Conserv. Comm., 1928, 248 pp.

Biological Survey of the Erie-Niagara System. Suppl. to 18th Ann. Rept., State of N.Y. Conserv. Comm., 1929, 244 pp.

Biological Survey of the Champlain Watershed. Suppl. to 19th Rept., State of N.Y. Conserv. Comm., 1930, 321 pp.

Biological Survey of the Oswegatschie and Black River Systems. Suppl. to 21st Ann. Rept., State of N.Y. Conserv. Comm., 1932, 344 pp.

BROWN, C. J. D. 1944. Michigan Streams—Their Lengths, Distribution and Drainage Areas. Misc. Publ. No. 1, Inst. Fish Res., Mich. Dept. Conserv., 21 pp.

BUTCHER, R. W. 1932. Studies in the Ecology of Rivers. II. The Microflora of Rivers with Special Reference to the Algae on the River Bed. Ann. Botany, **46**: 813–861.

————. 1933. Studies on the Ecology of Rivers. I. On the Distribution of Macrophytic Vegetation in the Rivers of Britain. Jour. Ecology, **21**: 58–89.

————. 1940. Studies in the Ecology of Rivers. IV. Observations on the Growth and Distribution of the Sessile Algae in the River Hull, Yorkshire. Jour. Ecology, **28**: 210–223.

————. 1946. Studies in the Ecology of Rivers. VI. The Algal Growth in Certain Highly Calcareous Streams. Jour. Ecology, **33**: 268–283.

BUTCHER, R. W., F. T. K. PENTELOW, and J. W. A. WOODLEY. 1930. Variations in Composition of River Waters. Int. Rev. d. ges. Hydrobiol. u. Hydrogr., **24**: 47–80.

BURTON, G. W., and E. P. ODUM. 1945. The Distribution of Stream Fish in the Vicinity of Mountain Lake, Virginia. Ecology, **26**: 182–194.

CANFIELD, H. L., and A. H. WIEBE. 1931. A Cursory Survey of the Blue River System of Nebraska. U.S. Bur. Fish., No. 73, 10 pp.

CARPENTER, K. E. 1927. Faunistic Ecology of Some Cardiganshire Streams. Jour. Ecology, **15**: 33–54.

CHANDLER, D. C. 1937. Fate of Typical Lake Plankton in Streams. Ecol. Monogr., **7**: 445–479.

————. 1939. Plankton Entering the Huron River from Portage and Base Line Lakes, Michigan. Trans. Am. Micr. Soc., **58**: 24–41.

CHAPMAN, R. N. 1931. Animal Ecology. New York, 464 pp.

CILLEULS, J. DES. 1928. Revue générale des études sur le plancton des grands fleuves ou rivières. Int. Rev. d. ges. Hydrobiol. u. Hydrogr., **20**: 174–206.

————. 1929. Étude du phytoplancton des affluents de la Loire dans la région saumuroise. Int. Rev. d. ges. Hydrobiol. u. Hydrogr., **22**: 179–231.

CLARKE, F. W. 1924. The Composition of the River and Lake Waters of the United States. U.S. Geol. Surv., Prof. Paper 135, 199 pp.

COWLES, R. P., and A. M. SCHWITALIA. 1923. The Hydrogen-ion Concentration of a Creek, Its Waterfall, Swamp and Ponds. Ecology, **4**: 402–416.

CREASER, C. W., and H. W. BROWN. 1927. The Hydrogen-ion Concentration of Brook Trout Waters of Northern Lower Michigan. Ecology, **8**: 98–105.

DENDY, J. S. 1944. The Fate of Animals in Stream Drift When Carried into Lakes. Ecol. Monogr., **14**: 333–357.

DODDS, G. S., and F. L. HISAW. 1924. Ecological Studies of Aquatic Insects. I. Adaptations of Mayfly Nymphs to Swift Streams. Ecology, **5**: 137–149.

————. 1924. Ecological Studies of Aquatic Insects. II. Size of Respiratory Organs in Relation to Environmental Conditions. Ecology, **5**: 262–271.

————. 1925. Ecological Studies on Aquatic Insects. III. Adaptations of Caddisfly Larvae to Swift Streams. Ecology, **8**: 123–137.

EDDY, S. 1925. Fresh Water Algal Succession. Trans. Am. Micr. Soc., **44**: 138–147.

——. 1932. The Plankton of the Sangamon River in the Summer of 1929. State of Ill. Div. Nat. Hist. Surv., **19**: 469–486.

ELLIS, M. M. 1931. A Survey of Conditions Affecting Fisheries in the Upper Mississippi River. U.S. Bur. Fish., Circ. 5, 18 pp.

——. 1931. Some Factors Affecting the Replacement of the Commercial Freshwater Mussels. U.S. Bur. Fish., Circ. 7, 10 pp.

——. 1936. Erosion Silt as a Factor in Aquatic Environments. Ecology, **17**: 29–42.

——. 1937. Detection and Measurement of Stream Pollution. U.S. Bur. Fish., Bull. 22, pp. 365–437.

FORBES, S. A. 1911. Chemical and Biological Investigations on the Illinois River, Midsummer of 1911. Ill. State Lab. Nat. Hist., 9 pp.

——. 1928. The Biological Survey of a River System—Its Objects, Methods, and Results. State of Ill. Dept. Reg. Ed., Div. Nat. Hist. Surv., **17**: 277–284.

Fox, H. M., and E. J. BALDES. 1935. The Vapour Pressures of the Blood of Arthropods from Swift and Still Fresh Waters. Jour. Exp. Biol., **12**: 174–178.

Fox, J. M., B. G. SIMMONDS, and R. WASHBOURN. 1935. Metabolic Rates of Ephemerid Nymphs from Swiftly Flowing and from Still Waters. Jour. Exp. Biol., **12**: 179–184.

FULLER, H. L., and G. P. COOPER. 1946. A Biological Survey of the Lakes and Ponds of Mount Desert Island, and the Union and Lower Penobscot River Drainage Systems. Fish Surv. Rept. No. 7, Maine Dept. Inland Fisheries and Game, 221 pp.

GALTSOFF, P. S. 1924. Limnological Observations in the Upper Mississippi, 1921. Bull. U.S. Bur. Fish., **39**: 347–438.

HESS, A. D., and A. SWARTZ. 1940. The Forage Ratio and Its Use in Determining the Food Grade of Streams. Trans. 5th N. Am. Wildlife Conf., pp. 162–164.

HIGGINS, E. 1932. Progress in Biological Inquiries, 1931. App. III, Rept. U.S. Comm. Fish. for Fiscal Year 1932, pp. 441–529.

HORA, S. L. 1930. Ecology, Bionomics and Evolution of the Torrential Fauna, with Special Reference to the Organs of Attachment. Phil. Trans. R. Soc. London, **218**: 171–282.

HUBAULT, E. 1927. Contribution à l'étude des invertébrés torrenticoles. Suppl. bull. biol. France et Belg., **9**: 1–390.

HUBBS, C. L., J. R. GREELY, and C. M. TARZWELL. 1932. Methods for the Improvement of Michigan Trout Streams. Bull. Inst. Fish. Res., Univ. Mich., No. 1, 54 pp.

HUTCHINSON, G. E. 1939. Ecological Observations on the Fishes of Kashmir and Indian Tibet. Ecol. Monogr., **9**: 145–182.

IDE, F. P. 1940. Quantitative Determination of the Insect Fauna of Rapid Water. Univ. of Toronto Studies, Biol. ser., Pub. Ont. Res. Lab. 59, 20 pp.

——. 1942. Availability of Aquatic Insects as Food of the Speckled Trout, *Salvelinus fontinalis*. Trans. 7th N. Am. Wildlife Conf., pp. 442–450.

IMANISHI, K. 1941. Mayflies from Japanese Torrents. X. Life Forms and Life Zones of Mayfly Nymphs. Mem. Col. Sci., Kyoto Imp. Univ., ser. B, **16**: 1–35.

JEWELL, M. E. 1922. The Fauna of an Acid Stream. Ecology, **3**: 22–28.

KING, H. W., C. O. WISLER, and J. G. WOODBURN. 1948. Hydraulics. New York, 351 pp.

KLUGH, A. B. 1923. A Common System of Classification in Plant and Animal Ecology. Ecology, **4**: 366–377.

KOFOID, C. A. 1903. The Plankton of the Illinois River, 1894–1899, with Introductory Notes upon the Hydrography of the Illinois River and Its Basin. Part I.

Quantitative Investigations and General Results. Bull. Ill. State Lab. Nat. Hist., **6**: 95–629.

––––––. 1908. The Plankton of the Illinois River, 1894–1899, with Introductory Notes upon the Hydrography of the Illinois River and Its Basin. Part II. Constituent Organisms and Their Seasonal Distribution. Bull. Ill. State Lab. Nat. Hist., **8**: 1–354.

KRIEGER, W. 1927. Zur Biologie des Flussplanktons. Pflanzenforschung, 10, 66 pp.

LIDDELL, W. A. 1927. Stream Gauging. New York, 238 pp.

LINDUSKA, J. P. 1942. Bottom Type as a Factor Influencing the Local Distribution of Mayfly Nymphs. Can. Ent., **74**: 26–30.

LUDWIG, W. B. 1932. The Bottom Invertebrates of the Hocking River. Bull. Ohio Biol. Surv., **5**: 223–249.

McNAMEE, R. L. 1930. The Surface Waters of Michigan. Univ. Mich., Eng. Res. Bull. 16, 321 pp.

MOFFETT, J. W. 1936. A Quantitative Study of the Bottom Fauna in Some Utah Streams Variously Affected by Erosion. Bull. Univ. Utah, vol. 26, No. 9, 32 pp.

MUTTKOWSKI, R. A. 1929. The Ecology of Trout Streams in Yellowstone National Park. Roosevelt Wild Life Annals, **2**: 155–240.

MUTTKOWSKI, R. A., and G. M. SMITH. 1929. The Food of Trout Stream Insects in Yellowstone National Park. Roosevelt Wild Life Annals, **2**: 241–263.

NEEDHAM, P. R. 1930. Ecology of Streams. Biol. Lab., L.I. Biol. Assoc., **2**: 1, 3–6.

––––––. 1932. Bottom Foods in Trout Streams. Field and Stream, February, pp. 40–44.

––––––. 1938. Trout Streams. Ithaca, N.Y., 233 pp.

NEEL, J. K. 1951. Interrelations of Certain Physical and Chemical Features in a Headwater Limestone Stream. Ecology, **32**: 368–391.

PEARSALL, W. H. 1930. Biological Survey of the River Wharfe. Jour. Ecology, **18**: 273–285.

PEARSE, A. S. 1939. Animal Ecology. 2d ed. New York, 642 pp.

PENNAK, R. W. 1943. Limnological Variables in a Colorado Mountain Stream. Am. Midl. Nat., **29**: 186–199.

PENNAK, R. W., and E. D. VAN GERPEN. 1947. Bottom Fauna Production and Physical Nature of the Substrate in a Northern Colorado Trout Stream. Ecology, **28**: 42–48.

PERCIVAL, E. 1930. Biological Survey of the River Wharfe. II. Report on the Invertebrate Fauna. Jour. Ecology, **18**: 286–302.

PERCIVAL, E., and H. WHITEHEAD. 1929. A Quantitative Study of the Fauna of Some Types of Stream-bed. Jour. Ecology, **17**: 282–314.

POWERS, E. B. 1929. Fresh Water Studies. I. The Relative Temperature, Oxygen Content, Alkali Reserve, the Carbon Dioxide Tension and pH of the Waters of Certain Mountain Streams at Different Altitudes in the Smoky Mountain National Park. Ecology, **10**: 97–111.

REINHARD, E. G. 1931. The Plankton Ecology of the Upper Mississippi, Minneapolis to Winona. Ecol. Monogr., **1**: 395–464.

RICHARDSON, R. E. 1921. The Small Bottom and Shore Fauna of the Middle and Lower Illinois River and Its Connecting Lakes, Chillicothe to Grafton: Its Valuation; Its Sources of Food Supply; and Its Relation to the Fishery. State of Ill. Div. Nat. Hist. Surv., **13**: 363–522.

––––––. 1928. The Bottom Fauna of the Middle Illinois River, 1913–1925. Its

Distribution, Abundance, Valuation, and Index Value in the Study of Stream Pollution. State of Ill. Div. Nat. Hist. Surv., **17**: 387–475.

RICKER, W. E. 1934. An Ecological Classification of Certain Ontario Streams. Univ. Toronto Studies, Biol. ser. 37, 114 pp.

ROACH, L. S. 1932. An Ecological Study of the Plankton of the Hocking River. Bull. Ohio Biol. Surv., **5**: 253–279.

SCHROEDER, W. L. 1930. Biological Survey of the River Wharfe. III. Algae Present in the Wharfe Plankton. Jour. Ecology, **18**: 303–305.

SHELFORD, V. E. 1911. Ecological Succession. I. Stream Fishes and the Method of Physiographic Analysis. Biol. Bull., **21**: 9–35.

———. 1913. Animal Communities in Temperate America. Chicago, 362 pp.

———. 1925. The Hydrogen Ion Concentration of Certain Western American Inland Waters. Ecology, **6**: 279–287.

SHELFORD, V. E., and S. EDDY. 1929. Methods for the Study of Stream Communities. Ecology, **10**: 382–391.

SHOUP, C. S. 1944. Geochemical Interpretation of Water Analyses from Tennessee Streams. Trans. Am. Fish. Soc., **74**: 223–229.

———. 1948. Limnological Observations on Some Streams of the New River Watershed in the Vicinity of Mountain Lake, Virginia. Jour. Elisha Mitchell Sci. Soc., **64**: 1–12.

———. 1950. Field Chemical Examination of the Waters in Tennessee Streams. Rep. Reelfoot Lake Biol. Sta., **14**: 4–55.

SMITH, L. L., and J. B. MOYLE. 1944. A Biological Survey and Fishery Management Plan for the Streams of the Lake Superior North Shore Watershed. Tech. Bull. 1, Division of Game and Fish, Minn. Dept. Conserv., 228 pp.

SPRULES, W. M. 1940. The Effect of a Beaver Dam on the Insect Fauna of a Trout Stream. Trans. Am. Fish. Soc., **70**: 236–248.

———. 1947. An Ecological Investigation of Stream Insects in Algonquin Park, Ontario. Univ. of Toronto Studies, Biol. ser., Publ. Ont. Fish. Res. Lab., No. 56, 81 pp.

STEHR, W. C., and J. W. BRANSON. 1938. An Ecological Study of an Intermittent Stream. Ecology, **19**: 294–310.

STEUER, A. 1910. Planktonkunde. Leipzig, 723 pp.

SULLIVAN, K. C. 1929. Notes on the Aquatic Life of the Niangua River, Missouri, with Special Reference to Insects. Ecology, **10**: 322–325.

SURBER, E. W. 1936. Rainbow Trout and Bottom Fauna Production in One Mile of Stream. Trans. Am. Fish. Soc., **66**: 193–202.

THIENEMANN, A. 1931. Neue Beobachtungen an Quellen und Bächen auf Rügen. Arch. f. Hydrobiol., **23**: 663–676.

THOMPSON, D. H., and F. D. HUNT. 1930. The Fishes of Champaign County, a Study of the Distribution and Abundance of Fishes in Small Streams. State of Ill. Div. Nat. Hist. Surv., **19**: 5–101.

TIFFANY, L. H. 1938. Algae. Springfield, Ill., 171 pp.

VAN DER SCHALIE, H. 1938. The Naiad Fauna of the Huron River, in Southeastern Michigan. Univ. Mich. Mus. Zool., Misc. Publ. 40, 83 pp.

VAN OOSTEN, J. 1948. Turbidity as a Factor in the Decline of Great Lakes Fishes with Special Reference to Lake Erie. Trans. Am. Fish. Soc., **75**: 281–322.

VAN OYE, P. 1926. Le potamoplankton du Ruki au Congo-Belge et des pays chauds en général. Int. Rev. d. ges. Hydrobiol. u. Hydrogr., **16**: 1–51.

WARD, H. B. 1938. Placer Mining on the Rogue River, Oregon, in Its Relation to the Fish and Fishing in That Stream. Bull. 10, Dept. Geol. and Min. Ind., State of Oregon, 31 pp.

WASHBOURN, R. 1936. Metabolic Rates of Trout Fry from Swift and Slow-running Waters. Jour. Exp. Biol., **13**: 145–147.

WEBSTER, D. A., and PRISCILLA C. WEBSTER. 1943. Influence of Water Current on Case Weight in Larvae of the Caddisfly, *Goera calcarata* Banks. Can. Ent., **75**: 105–108.

WELCH, P. S. 1948. Limnological Methods. Philadelphia, 381 pp.

WENE, G., and E. L. WICKLIFF. 1940. Modification of a Stream Bottom and Its Effects on the Insect Fauna. Can. Ent., **72**: 131–135.

WIEBE, A. H. 1928. Biological Survey of the Upper Mississippi River with Special Reference to Pollution. Bull. U.S. Bur. Fish., **43**: 137–167.

WRIGHT, H. P. 1932. Aquatic Mollusca of the Tippecanoe River System. Part I. Post-glacial Migration and Present Distribution of Four Species of Snails. Ecol. Monogr., **2**: 234–259.

WU, YI FANG. 1931. A Contribution to the Biology of Simulium (Diptera). Papers Mich. Acad. Sci., Arts, Let., **13**: 543–599.

INDEX

511

Light, diurnal differences in, 77
 effect of, on bacteria, 287
 effect on, of ice cover, 81
 effective, 173
 influence of, on plankton, 170, 240
 intensity of, at surface, 76
 limit of visibility, 73
 methods of measurement, 73
 moonlight, 76
 penetration of, 73, 77
  factors influencing, 76
 in ponds, 367
 quantitative determinations of, 79
 reflection of, 166
 responses to, 171
 seasonal differences in, 77
 in streams, 410
 and suspended materials, 77
 transmission of, 84
  and colors, 81–83
 ultraviolet, 170, 171, 173
Light adaptation, 175
Light relations, 170
 behavior and orientation, 171
 direct influences, 170
 lethal effects, 170
 photosynthesis, 172
Light requirements, 173
Ligumia nasuta, 158
Liljeborg and Sars, 6
Lime-producing organisms, 190
 Algae, 191
 aquatic flowering plants, 195
 bacteria, 191
 Chara, 194
 higher animals, 196
 plankton, 195
Limestone sinks, 17
Limnicythera sancti-patricii, 329
Limnobiology, 10
Limnocalanus, 274, 275
 macruris, 246
Limnodrilus claparedianus, 184
 hoffmeisteri, 184
Limnography, 11
Limnology, 3
 definition, 10
 development, 6
 history, 4
Limnological Commission, 7
Limnoplankton, 226, 420
Lindeman, 350

Linguatula, 220
Lithosphere, 3
Little John, Lake, 285
Littoral fauna, 341
Littorella uniflora, 298
Lloyd, 6, 177, 178, 287, 298, 385
Lobelia Dortmanna, 298
Local variations in plankters, 266
Lochs, Scottish, 8, 26
Locomotion, 144
Logan, 215
Lohman, 291
Lota lota, 313
Lotic series, 13
Low-water marks, 19
Loxodes, 184
 rostrum, 329
Loxophyllum, 184
Lucerne, Lake, 247–249, 251
Luksch, 78
Lundqvist, 26, 316, 354
Lunz Biological Station, 8
Lymnaea reflexa, 376
Lyngbya, 257, 274, 428
 martinsiana calcaria, 194
 nana, 194

M

McCoy, 385
McEwen, 171
Macht, 199
McLaren, 217
McNamee, 413
Macrobiotes, 329
Macromia, 160
Macroplankton, 226
Macrostratification, 126
Magnesium, 99, 110, 191, 196, 204
Maloney, 248
Mammals, 311
 aquatic, 166
 food of, 306
Manganese, 85, 110, 205
Manning, 175, 357
Mare's-tail, 297
Margins of lakes, 19
Marine zoology, influence of, 5
Marl, 25, 26, 100, 190
 Algae, 191, 192
 bacteria, 191
 Chara, 194
 concretions, 192, 193